GARDNER'S
ART
THROUGH THE
AGES
NON-WESTERN
PERSPECTIVES

TWELFTH EDITION

GARDNER'S
ART
THROUGH THE
AGES
NON-WESTERN
PERSPECTIVES

TWELFTH EDITION

FRED S. KLEINER

CHRISTIN J. MAMIYA

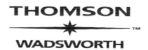

THOMSON

WADSWORTH

AUSTRALIA • CANADA • MEXICO • SINGAPORE • SPAIN
UNITED KINGDOM • UNITED STATES

About the Authors

FRED S. KLEINER received his Ph.D. in art history and archaeology from Columbia University. Author of more than a hundred publications on classical art and architecture, he also served as editor-in-chief of the *American Journal of Archaeology* from 1985–1998. He has taught the art history survey course for more than a quarter century at the University of Virginia and at Boston University, where he is currently professor of art history and archaeology. Long recognized for his inspiring lectures and devotion to students, Professor Kleiner won Boston University's prestigious Metcalf Award for Excellence in Teaching as well as the College Prize for Undergraduate Advising in the Humanities in 2002.

CHRISTIN J. MAMIYA received her Ph.D. in art history from the University of California–Los Angeles, and is professor of art history at the University of Nebraska–Lincoln. A recipient of numerous teaching awards, including the Annis Chaikin Sorensen Award for Distinguished Teaching in the Humanities from the University of Nebraska in 2001, Professor Mamiya specializes in the areas of modern art, postmodern art, and Oceanic art. She has published a book on pop art, as well as many articles, catalog essays, and book reviews. She is an active participant in the wider community as both a curator and lecturer.

About the Cover Art

During the Momoyama period in Japan, the decorations on folding screens, such as *Chinese Lions* (FIG. 6-4), became increasingly bold and lavish. Here, artist KANO EITOKU (1543–1590) created a powerful image of lions that strut across a shimmering field of gold leaf. Chinese lions became an important symbolic motif during the Momoyama period, in part because their association with power and bravery was particularly appropriate during an age of militarism. Indeed, this six-panel screen may have been produced for one of the major warlords of the period.

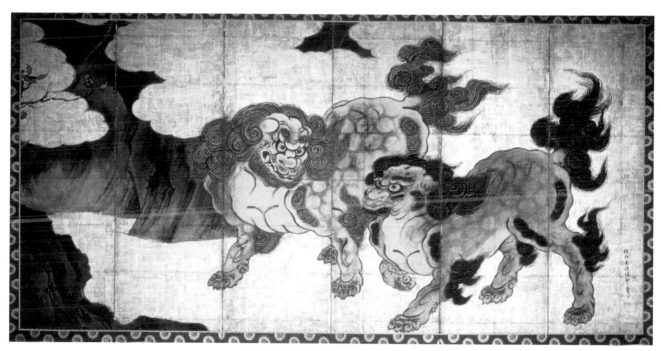

KANO EITOKU, *Chinese Lions*, Momoyama period, late 16th century. Six-panel screen, color, ink, and gold-leaf on paper, 7′ 4″ × 14′ 10″. Imperial Household Agency, Tokyo.

Art Acquisitions Editor
JOHN R. SWANSON

Senior Development Editor
SHARON ADAMS POORE

Assistant Editor
ANNE GITTINGER

Editorial Assistant
BRIANNA BRINKLEY

Technology Project Manager
MELINDA NEWFARMER

Marketing Manager
MARK ORR

Marketing Assistant
ANDREW KEAY

Advertising Project Manager
VICKY WAN

Project Manager, Editorial Production
KIMBERLY ADAMS

Art Director
MARIA EPES

Print/Media Buyer
BARBARA BRITTON

Permissions Editor
JOOHEE LEE

Production Service
JOAN KEYES, DOVETAIL PUBLISHING SERVICES

Text Designer
JOHN WALKER

Photo Researchers
CARRIE WARD, LILI WEINER, ALEX GOLDBERG

Copy Editors
MICHELE JONES, GAIL NELSON-BONEBRAKE

Cover Designer
LINDA BEAUPRÉ

Cover Image
**KANO EITOKU, *CHINESE LIONS*, MOMOYAMA PERIOD,
LATE 16TH CENTURY. SIX-PANEL SCREEN, COLOR,
INK, AND GOLD-LEAF ON PAPER, 7′ 4″ × 14′ 10″.
IMPERIAL HOUSEHOLD AGENCY, TOKYO.
© SAKAMOTO PHOTO RESEARCH LABORATORY/CORBIS**

Cover Printer
PHOENIX COLOR CORP

Compositor
PROGRESSIVE INFORMATION TECHNOLOGIES

Printer
R.R. DONNELLEY/WILLARD

Printed in the United States of America
1 2 3 4 5 6 7 09 08 07 06 05

For more information about our products, contact us at:
Thomson Learning Academic Resource Center
1-800-423-0563

For permission to use material from this text or product, submit a request online at http://www.thomsonrights.com. Any additional questions about permissions can be submitted by e-mail to thomsonrights@thomson.com

Thomson Higher Education
10 Davis Drive,
Belmont, CA 94002-3098
USA

Asia
Thomson Learning
5 Shenton Way #01-01, UIC Building
Singapore 068808

Australia
Nelson Thomson Learning
102 Dodds Street, South Melbourne, Victoria 3205
Australia

Canada
Nelson Thomson Learning
1120 Birchmount Road, Toronto, Ontario M1K 5G4
Canada

Europe/Middle East/Africa
Thomson Learning
High Holborn House, 50/51 Bedford Row, London WC1R 4LR
United Kingdom

Latin America
Thomson Learning
Seneca, 53
Colonia Polanco
11560 Mexico
D.F. Mexico

Spain (including Portugal)
Thomson Paraninfo
Calle Magallanes, 25
28015 Madrid, Spain

Library of Congress Control Number
2004115404

ISBN 0-495-00365-4

CONTENTS IN BRIEF

CONTENTS

Chapter 2

Chapter 3

Chapter 4

Chapter 5

Chapter 6

Chapter 7

Chapter 8

Chapter 9

Chapter 10

Chapter 11

Chapter 12

PREFACE

We take great pleasure in presenting this new version of *Gardner's Art through the Ages*, the most widely read introduction to the history of art in the English language. *Gardner's Art through the Ages: Non-Western Perspectives* includes all the chapters on the art and architecture of South and Southeast Asia, China and Korea, Japan, the Islamic world, Native North and South America, Africa, and Oceania in the 12th edition of *Gardner's Art through the Ages*. We hope that this new survey of non-Western art will earn the same critical acclaim and enthusiastic reception in college classrooms that *Gardner's Art through the Ages* and *Gardner's Art through the Ages: The Western Perspective* have received.

When Helen Gardner wrote the first edition of her classic survey of art and architecture in 1926, she could not have imagined that eight decades later instructors all over the world would still be using her textbook in their classrooms. She would no doubt have been especially proud that the 11th edition of *Gardner's Art through the Ages* was awarded both the 2001 Texty and McGuffey Book Prizes of the Text and Academic Authors Association as the best college textbook in the humanities and social sciences—the only art history book to win either award and the first title ever to win both prizes in the same year.

The fundamental belief that guided Helen Gardner—that the history of art is essential to a liberal education—is one that we also embrace. The study of art history has as its aim the appreciation and understanding of works of high aesthetic quality and historical significance produced throughout the world and across thousands of years of human history. We think, as she did, that the most effective way to tell the story of art through the ages, especially for those who are studying art history for the first time, is to organize the vast array of artistic monuments according to the civilizations that produced them and to consider each work in roughly chronological order. This approach has not only stood the test of time. It is the most appropriate for narrating the *history* of art. We believe that the enormous variation in the form and meaning of paintings, sculptures, buildings, and other artworks is largely the result of the constantly changing historical, social, economic, religious, and cultural context in which artists and architects worked. A historically based narrative is therefore best suited for a history of art through the ages.

Yet, in other ways, Helen Gardner would not recognize the 12th edition of *Gardner's Art through the Ages* as her book. The discipline of art history has changed markedly in recent decades, and so too has *Gardner's Art through the Ages*. In fact, although Gardner was a pioneer in writing a global history of art in the early part of the 20th century, even she would have been surprised that so many college courses now survey *only* the arts of non-Western cultures. This new version of the 12th edition is designed to meet the needs of those instructors. Indeed, its publication was prompted by the many requests we had received for just such a version of the "global Gardner." Like the unabridged version of the 12th edition, *Gardner's Art through the Ages: Non-Western Perspectives* fully reflects the latest art historical research emphases, while maintaining the traditional strengths that have made all the previous editions of *Gardner's Art through the Ages* so successful. While sustaining attention to style, chronology, iconography, and technique, we pay greater attention than ever before to function and context. We consider artworks with a view toward their purpose and meaning in the society that produced them at the time at which they were produced. We also address the very important role of patronage in the production of art and examine the role of the individuals or groups who paid the artists and influenced the shape the monuments took. We devote more space to the role of women and women artists in societies over the course of the millennia. Throughout, we have aimed to integrate the historical, political, religious, and social context of art and architecture with the artistic and intellectual aspects. Consequently, we often treat painting, sculpture, architecture, and the so-called minor arts together, highlighting how they all reflect the conventions and aspirations of a common culture, rather than treating them as separate and distinct media. And we feature many works that until recently art historians would not have considered to be "art" at all. In every chapter, we have tried to reflect in our choice of artworks and buildings the increasingly wide range of interests of scholars today, while not rejecting the traditional list of "great" works or the very notion of a "canon." The selection of works encompasses every artistic medium and almost every era and culture in the history of the non-Western world.

Every edition of *Gardner's Art through the Ages* has gone through a rigorous process of review, and *Non-Western Perspectives* is no exception. Each chapter has been read by experts in the respective fields. And, every chapter has been revised in order to ensure that the text lived up to the Gardner reputation for accuracy as well as readability. All feature superb new color illustrations, including a full-page, chapter-opening image reproducing a characteristic work of each period. In fact, almost 100 percent of the works that we illustrate are in color. The only exceptions are works that were created in black-and-white and a small number of other works of which we were unable to obtain a color view that met our very high standards for reproduction.

The rich illustration program is not, however, confined to the printed page. Every copy of *Gardner's Art through the Ages: Non-Western Perspective* comes with a complimentary copy of

ArtStudy 2.1: Non-Western Perspectives, a CD-ROM that contains over 150 high-quality digital images of the works discussed in the text. To facilitate the coordinated use of the CD-ROM and the book itself, every artwork, building, drawing, and map on the CD-ROM has an identifying icon appended to the caption of the corresponding photograph, drawing, or map in the text.

In response to student requests, every chapter of this edition of *Gardner's Art through the Ages* now ends with a short Conclusion summarizing the major themes discussed. These summaries face a full-page Chronological Overview of the material presented in the chapter, organized as a vertical timeline, with four "thumbnail" illustrations of characteristic works in a variety of media, generally including at least one painting, sculpture, and building. Each thumbnail is numbered. The corresponding number appears on the time rule to the left so that the chronological sequence of production is clear.

The most popular features of previous editions of *Gardner's Art through the Ages* have, of course, been retained. Especially noteworthy are the boxed essays that we introduced in the 11th edition, which were enthusiastically received by students and instructors alike. As before, these essays are presented in six broad categories:

Architectural Basics provide students with a sound foundation for the understanding of architecture. These discussions are concise primers, with drawings and diagrams of the major aspects of design and construction. The information included is essential to an understanding of architectural technology and terminology. The boxes address questions of how and why various forms developed, the problems architects confronted, and the solutions they used to resolve them. Topics discussed include the form and meaning of the stupa, the origin and development of the mosque, and the construction of wooden buildings in China.

Materials and Techniques essays explain the various media artists employed from prehistoric to modern times. Because materials and techniques often influence the character of works of art, these discussions also contain essential information on why many monuments look the way they do. Hollow-casting in bronze in Shang China, Japanese woodblock prints, and Andean weaving are among the many subjects treated.

Written Sources present and discuss key historical documents illuminating important monuments of art and architecture and the careers of leading artists and architects. The passages we quote permit voices from the past to speak directly to the reader, providing vivid and unique insights into the creation of artworks in all media. Examples include Xie He's six canons of Chinese painting and Sinan the Great's commentary on the mosque he built for Selim II.

Religion and Mythology boxes introduce students to the principal elements of the world's great religions, past and present, and to the representation of religious and mythological themes in painting and sculpture of all periods and places. These discussions of belief systems and iconography give readers a richer understanding of some of the greatest artworks ever created. The topics include Buddhism and Buddhist iconography, Muhammad and Islam, and Aztec religion.

Art and Society essays treat the historical, social, political, cultural, and religious context of art and architecture. The subjects addressed include the Japanese tea ceremony, the Mesoamerican ball game, gender roles in African art production, and tattoo in Polynesia.

Art in the News boxes present accounts of the latest archaeological finds and discussions of current controversies in the history of art, for example our discussion of shipwrecks and ceramic chronology in Vietnam.

Full-color maps also remain an important element of every chapter of *Gardner's Art through the Ages*. As in previous editions, we have taken great care to make sure that every site discussed in the text appears on our maps. These maps vary widely in both geographical and chronological scope. Some focus on a single region, while others encompass a vast territory and occasionally bridge two or more continents. Several maps plot the art-producing sites of a given area over hundreds, even thousands, of years. In every instance, our aim has been to provide readers with maps that will easily allow them to locate the places where works of art originated or were found and where buildings were erected. To this end we have regularly placed the names of modern nations on maps of the territories of past civilizations.

In addition, in order to aid our readers in mastering the vocabulary of art history, we have italicized and defined all art historical terms and other unfamiliar words at their first occurrence in the text—and at later occurrences too, whenever the term has not been used again for several chapters. Definitions of all terms introduced in the text appear once more in the Glossary at the back of the book, which includes pronunciations, a feature introduced in the 11th edition. *Gardner's Art through the Ages: Non-Western Perspectives* also has a comprehensive bibliography of books in English, including both general works and a chapter-by-chapter list of more focused studies.

The captions to our more than 250 illustrations contain a wealth of information, including the name of the artist or architect, if known; the formal title (printed in italics), if assigned, description of the work, or name of the building; the findspot or place of production of the object or location of the building; the date; the material or materials used; the size; and the present location if the work is in a museum or private collection. We urge readers to pay attention to the scales provided on all plans and to all dimensions given in the captions. The objects we illustrate vary enormously in size, from colossal stone sculptures and paintings that cover entire walls to figurines and masks that one can hold in the hand. Note too the location of the monuments discussed. Although many buildings and museums may be in cities or countries that a reader may never visit, others are likely to be close to home. Nothing can substitute for standing in the presence of a statue or inspecting the brushwork of a painting close up. Consequently, we have made a special effort to illustrate artworks in geographically wide-ranging public collections.

A host of study resources are available to students on the *ArtStudy CD-ROM 2.1: Non-Western Perspectives*, free with each new copy of this text. Activities and exercises correlate with each of the book's 12 chapters, including over 150 digital images of the works discussed in the text, flashcards, interactive maps and timelines, and links to chapter quizzes and the study guide. Additional resources on the CD-ROM include drag and drop exercises in Architectural Basics, a Museum Guide, Tips on Becoming a Successful Student, The Guide to Researching Art History Online, and Art Links. Students will also find additional resources on the *Companion Web Site* at http://art.wadsworth.com/gardnernonwestern12/. The web site provides chapter outlines; brief chapter overviews; audio glossary flashcards; Internet exercises; InfoTrac College Edition exercises; and a pronunciation guide.

A work as extensive as this one could not be undertaken or completed without the counsel of experts in all areas of non-Western art. We are especially grateful to Herbert Cole, University of California, Santa Barbara, for contributing the chapters on African art; and to Robert L. Brown, University of California, Los Angeles; George Corbin, Lehman College of the City University of New York; Virginia E. Miller, University of Illinois, Chicago; and Quitman Eugene Phillips, University of Wisconsin, Madison for their contributions on non-Western art in the 11th edition of *Gardner's Art through the Ages*. Their chapters laid the foundations for the chapters on South and Southeast Asia, China and Korea, Japan, and the Americas in the 12th edition.

For contributions in the form of extended critiques of the 11th edition or of the penultimate drafts of the 12th edition chapters, as well as other assistance of various sorts, we wish to thank Stanley K. Abe, Duke University; Frederick M. Asher, University of Minnesota; Cynthia Atherton, Middlebury College; Janet Berlo, University of Rochester; Kendall H. Brown, California State University, Long Beach; LouAnn Faris Culley, Kansas State University; Andrew L. Cohen, University of Central Arkansas; Anne D'Allera, University of Connecticut; Cindy Bailey Damschroder, University of Cincinnati; Abraham A. Davidson, Temple University; Carolyn Dean, University of California, Santa Cruz; Daniel Ehnbom, University of Virginia; David Ehrenpreis, James Madison University; Jerome Feldman, Hawaii Pacific University; Barbara Frank, State University of New York, Stony Brook; Eric Garberson, Virginia Commonwealth University; Clive Getty, Miami University; Paula Girshick, Indiana University; Melinda K. Hartwig, Georgia State University; Marsha Haufler, University of Kansas; Mary Beth Heston, College of Charleston; Aldona Jonaitis, University of Alaska Museum; Adrienne Kaeppler, Smithsonian Institution; Padma Kaimal, Colgate University; Stacy L. Kamehiro, University of California, Santa Cruz; Cecilia F. Klein, University of California, Los Angeles; Sandy Kita, University of Maryland, College Park; James Kornwolf, College of William and Mary; Ellen Johnston Laing, University of Michigan; Joseph Lamb, Ohio University; Dana Leibsohn, Smith College; Janice Leoshko, The University of Texas at Austin; Michael Meister, University of Pennsylvania; Samuel C. Morse, Amherst College; Susan E. Nelson, Indiana University; Irene Nero, Southeastern Louisiana University; Esther Pasztory, Columbia University; Jeanette Peterson, University of California, Santa Barbara; Elizabeth Pilliod, Princeton University; Martin Powers, University of Michigan; Jonathan M. Reynolds, University of Southern California; Lisa Rosenthal, University of Illinois, Urbana-Champaign; Ellen Schwartz, Eastern Michigan University; Michael Schwartz, Augusta State University; Ray Silverman, Michigan State University; Rebecca Stone-Miller, Emory University; Peter C. Sturman, University of California, Santa Barbara; Melinda Takeuchi, Stanford University; Woodman Taylor, University of Illinois, Chicago; Jehanne Teilhet-Fisk, Florida State University; Elizabeth ten Grotenhuis, Boston University; Monica Blackmun Visona, Metropolitan State College; Deborah Waite, University of Hawaii; Gerald Waker, Clemson University; Victoria Weston, University of Massachusetts, Boston.

Many other instructors and students have also sent us helpful reactions, comments, and suggestions for ways to improve the non-Western chapters in the global version of *Gardner's Art through the Ages*. We are grateful for their interest and their insights.

Among those at Thomson Wadsworth who worked with us to launch this new version of *Gardner's Art through the Ages* and to make it the best book possible are Sean Wakely, CEO and president, Thomson Wadsworth; Marcus Boggs, vice president and editor-in-chief; Clark Baxter, publisher; David Tatom, executive editor; John R. Swanson, acquisitions editor; Sharon Adams Poore, senior development editor; Anne Gittinger, assistant editor; Brianna Brinkley, editorial assistant; Kathryn M. Stewart, editorial production manager; Kim Adams, senior project manager; and Melinda Newfarmer, senior technology project manager; as well as Susan Badger, CEO of Thomson Higher Education.

In addition, we are deeply indebted to Joan Keyes of Dovetail Publishing Services for her expert work in so many areas; Michele Jones and Gail Nelson-Bonebrake, our eagle-eyed copy editors; and Carrie Ward and Alex Goldberg, our tireless photo researchers. John Walker has designed a beautiful book for us. We also owe thanks to the peerless Thomson Wadsworth marketing staff for their dedication to making the Gardner family of publications a success: Jonathan Hulbert, senior vice president, marketing; Elana Dolberg, director of marketing; Diane Wenckebach, executive marketing manager; Margaret Parks, executive director of advertising and marketing communications; Pat Murphree, senior channel manager, School, Wadsworth Group; Mark Orr, marketing manager; Andrew Keay, marketing assistant; and Vicky Wan, advertising project manager. Finally, we are happy to recognize the important contributions of Pete Shanks and Katherine Hyde, our proofreaders, and Nancy Ball, our indexer.

We also owe a deep debt of gratitude to our colleagues at Boston University and the University of Nebraska–Lincoln, and to the thousands of students and the scores of teaching fellows in our art history courses over many years. They too have contributed to the success of *Gardner's Art through the Ages*.

Fred S. Kleiner
Christin J. Mamiya

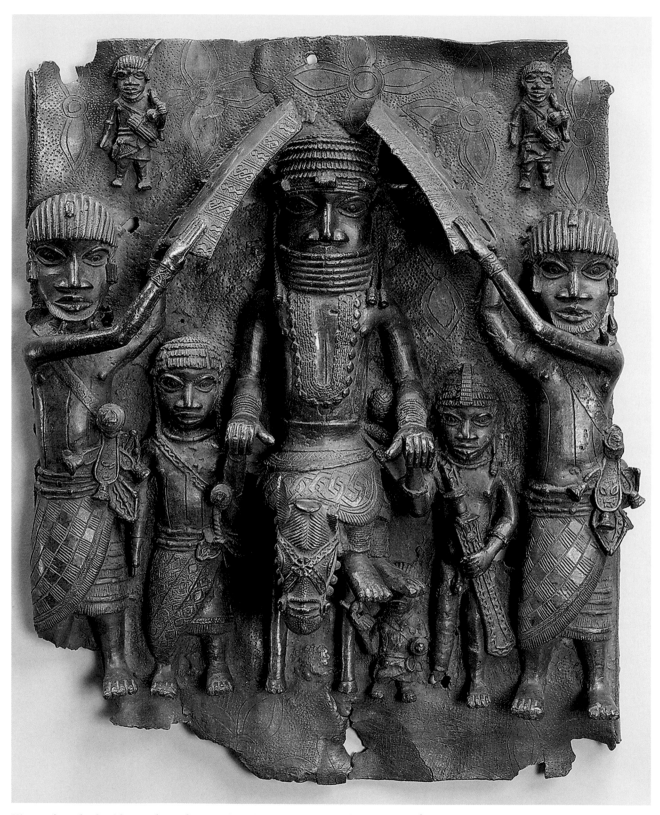

King on horseback with attendants, from Benin, Nigeria, ca. 1550–1680. Bronze, 1′ 7$\frac{1}{2}$″ high. Metropolitan Museum of Art, New York (Michael C. Rockefeller Memorial Collection, gift of Nelson A. Rockefeller).

INTRODUCTION

WHAT IS ART HISTORY?

People do not often juxtapose the terms *art* and *history*. They tend to think of history as the record and interpretation of past human actions, particularly social and political actions. Most think of art, quite correctly, as part of the present—as something people can see and touch. People cannot, of course, see or touch history's vanished human events. But a visible and tangible artwork is a kind of persisting event. One or more artists made it at a certain time and in a specific place, even if no one now knows just who, when, where, or why. Although created in the past, an artwork continues to exist in the present, long surviving its times. The first painters and sculptors died 30,000 years ago, but their works remain, some of them exhibited in glass cases in museums built only a few years ago.

Modern museum visitors can admire these relics of the remote past and the countless other objects humankind has produced over the millennia without any knowledge of the circumstances that led to the creation of those works. An object's beauty or sheer size can impress people, the artist's virtuosity in the handling of ordinary or costly materials can dazzle them, or the subject depicted can move them. Viewers can react to what they see, interpret the work in the light of their own experience, and judge it a success or a failure. These are all valid responses to a work of art. But the enjoyment and appreciation of artworks in museum settings are relatively recent phenomena, as is the creation of artworks solely for museum-going audiences to view.

Today, it is common for artists to work in private studios and to create paintings, sculptures, and other objects commercial art galleries will offer for sale. Usually, someone the artist has never met will purchase the artwork and display it in a setting the artist has never seen. But although this is not a new phenomenon in the history of art—an ancient potter decorating a vase for sale at a village market stall also probably did not know who would buy the pot or where it would be housed—it is not at all typical. In fact, it is exceptional. Throughout history, most artists created the paintings, sculptures, and other objects exhibited in museums today for specific patrons and settings and to fulfill a specific purpose. Often, no one knows the original contexts of those artworks. Although people may appreciate the visual and tactile qualities of these objects, they cannot understand why they were made or why they look the way they do without knowing the circumstances of their creation. *Art appreciation* does not require knowledge of the historical context of an artwork (or a building). *Art history* does.

Thus, a central aim of art history is to determine the original context of artworks. Art historians seek to achieve a full understanding not only of why these "persisting events" of human history look the way they do but also why the artistic "events" happened at all. What unique set of circumstances gave rise to the erection of a particular building or led a specific patron to commission an individual artist to fashion a singular artwork for a certain place? The study of history is therefore vital to art history. And art history is often very important to the study of history. Art objects and buildings are historical documents that can shed light on the peoples who made them and on the times of their creation in a way other historical documents cannot. Furthermore, artists and architects can affect history by reinforcing or challenging cultural values and practices through the objects they create and the structures they build. Thus, the history of art and architecture is inseparable from the study of history, although the two disciplines are not the same.

THE QUESTIONS ART HISTORIANS ASK

Art historians study the visual and tangible objects humans make and the structures humans build. From the earliest Greco-Roman art critics on, scholars have studied works that their makers consciously manufactured as "art" and to which the artists assigned formal titles. But today's art historians also study a vast number of objects that their creators and owners did not consider to be "works of art." That is certainly true for many of the works examined in this book. Art historians, however, generally ask the same kinds of questions about what they study, whether they employ a restrictive or an expansive definition of art.

HOW OLD IS IT? Before art historians can construct a history of art, they must be sure they know the date of each work they study. Thus, an indispensable subject of art historical inquiry is *chronology,* the dating of art objects and buildings. If researchers cannot determine a work's age, they cannot place it in its historical context. Art historians have developed many ways to establish, or at least approximate, the date of an artwork.

Physical evidence often reliably indicates an object's age. The material used for a statue, painting, or vase—bronze, plastic, or porcelain, to name only a few—may not have been invented before a certain time, indicating the earliest possible date someone could have fashioned the work. Or artists may have ceased using certain materials—such as specific kinds of inks and papers for drawings and prints—at a known time, providing the latest possible dates for objects made of such materials. Sometimes the material (or the manufacturing technique) of an object or a building can establish a very precise date of production or construction.

Documentary evidence also can help pinpoint the date of an object or building when a dated written document mentions the work.

Visual evidence, too, can play a significant role in dating an artwork. A painter might have depicted an identifiable person or a kind of hairstyle, clothing, or furniture fashionable only at a certain time. If so, the art historian can assign a more accurate date to that painting.

Stylistic evidence is also very important. The analysis of *style*—an artist's distinctive manner of producing an object, the way a work looks—is the art historian's special sphere. Unfortunately, because it is a subjective assessment, stylistic evidence is by far the most unreliable chronological criterion. Still, art historians sometimes find style a very useful tool for establishing chronology.

WHAT IS ITS STYLE? Defining artistic style is one of the key elements of art historical inquiry, although the analysis of artworks solely in terms of style no longer dominates the field the way it once did. Art historians speak of several different kinds of artistic styles.

Period style refers to the characteristic artistic manner of a specific time, usually within a distinct culture, such as "Classic Maya" in Mesoamerica or "Southern Song" in China.

Regional style is the term art historians use to describe variations in style tied to geography. Like an object's date, its *provenance,* or place of origin, can significantly determine its character. Very often two artworks from the same place made centuries apart are more similar than contemporaneous works from two different regions.

Personal style, the distinctive manner of individual artists or architects, often decisively explains stylistic discrepancies among works of the same time and place.

The different kinds of artistic styles are not mutually exclusive. For example, an artist's personal style may change dramatically during a long career. Art historians then must distinguish among the different period styles of a particular artist.

WHAT IS ITS SUBJECT? Another major concern of art historians is, of course, subject matter, encompassing the story, or *narrative*; the scene presented; the action's time and place; the persons involved; and the environment and its details. Some artworks, such as modern abstract paintings, have no subject, not even a setting. But when artists represent people, places, or actions, the viewer must identify these aspects to achieve complete understanding of the works. Art historians traditionally separate pictorial subjects into various categories, such as religious, historical, *mythological, genre* (daily life), portraiture, *landscape* (a depiction of a place), *still life* (an arrangement of inanimate objects), and their numerous subdivisions and combinations.

Iconography—literally, the "writing of images"—refers both to the *content,* or subject of an artwork, and to the study of content in art. By extension, it also includes the study of *symbols,* images that stand for other images or encapsulate ideas. Artists also may depict figures with unique *attributes,* such as a scepter, headdress, or costume that identifies a figure as a king (FIG. **Intro-1**). Throughout the history of art, artists also used *personifications*—abstract ideas codified in bodily form. Worldwide, people visualize Liberty as a robed woman with a torch because of the fame of the colossal statue set up in New York City's harbor in the 19th century. Even without considering style and without knowing a work's maker, an informed viewer can determine much about the work's period and provenance by iconographical and subject analysis alone.

WHO MADE IT? Although signing (and dating) works is quite common (but by no means universal) today, in the history of art countless works exist whose artists remain unknown. Because personal style can play a large role in determining the character

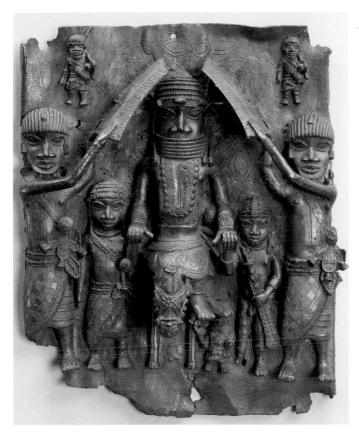

Intro-1 King on horseback with attendants, from Benin, Nigeria, ca. 1550–1680. Bronze, 1' 7½" high. Metropolitan Museum of Art, New York (Michael C. Rockefeller Memorial Collection, gift of Nelson A. Rockefeller).

of an artwork, art historians often try to assign, or *attribute,* anonymous works to known artists. Sometimes they attempt to assemble a group of works all thought to be by the same person, even though none of the objects in the group is the known work of an artist with a recorded name. Scholars base their *attributions* on internal evidence, such as the distinctive way an artist draws or carves drapery folds or earlobes. It requires a keen, highly trained eye and long experience to become a *connoisseur,* an expert in assigning artworks to "the hand" of one artist rather than another.

Sometimes a group of artists works in the same style at the same time and place. Art historians designate such a group as a *school.* "School" does not mean an educational institution. The term only connotes chronological, stylistic, and geographic similarity. Art historians speak, for example, of the Kano School in 17th-century Japan.

WHO PAID FOR IT? The interest many art historians show in attribution reflects their conviction that the identity of an artwork's maker is the major reason the object looks the way that it does. For them, personal style is of paramount importance. But in many times and places artists had little to say about what form their work would take. They toiled in obscurity, doing the bidding of their *patrons,* those who paid them to make individual works or employed them on a continuing basis. The role of patrons in dictating the content and shaping the form of artworks is also an important subject of art historical inquiry.

THE WORDS ART HISTORIANS USE

Like all specialists, art historians have their own specialized vocabulary. That vocabulary consists of hundreds of words, but certain basic terms are indispensable for describing artworks and buildings of any time and place, and we use those terms throughout this book. They make up the essential vocabulary of *formal analysis,* the visual analysis of artistic form. We define the most important of these art historical terms here. For a much longer list, consult the Glossary in this book's end material.

FORM AND COMPOSITION *Form* refers to an object's shape and structure, either in two dimensions (for example, a figure painted on paper) or in three dimensions (such as a statue carved from a stone block). Two forms may take the same shape but may differ in their color, texture, and other qualities. *Composition* refers to how an artist organizes (composes) forms in an artwork, either by placing shapes on a flat surface or by arranging forms in space.

MATERIAL AND TECHNIQUE To create art forms, artists shape materials (pigment, clay, marble, gold, and many more) with tools (pens, brushes, chisels, and so forth). Each of the materials and tools available has its own potentialities and limitations. Part of all artists' creative activity is to select the medium and instrument most suitable to the artists' purpose. The processes artists employ, such as applying paint to silk with a brush, and the distinctive, personal ways they handle materials constitute their *technique.* Form, material, and technique interrelate and are central to analyzing any work of art.

LINE *Line* is one of the most important elements defining an artwork's shape or form. A line can be understood as the path of a point moving in space, an invisible line of sight or a visual *axis.* But, more commonly, artists and architects make a line concrete by drawing (or chiseling) it on a *plane,* a flat two-dimensional surface. A line may be very thin, wirelike, and delicate; it may be thick and heavy; or it may alternate quickly from broad to narrow, the strokes jagged or the outline broken. When a continuous line defines an object's outer shape, art historians call it a *contour* line.

COLOR *Light* reveals all colors. Light in the world of the painter and other artists differs from natural light. Natural light, or sunlight, is whole or *additive light.* As the sum of all the wavelengths composing the visible *spectrum,* it may be disassembled or fragmented into the individual colors of the spectral band. The painter's light in art—the light reflected from pigments and objects—is *subtractive light.* Paint pigments produce their individual colors by reflecting a segment of the spectrum while absorbing all the rest. Green pigment, for example, subtracts or absorbs all the light in the spectrum except that seen as green, which it reflects to the eyes.

TEXTURE *Texture* is the quality of a surface (such as rough or shiny) that light reveals. Art historians distinguish between *actual* textures, or the tactile quality of the surface, and *represented* textures, as when painters depict an object as having a certain texture, even though the pigment is the actual texture. Texture is, of course, a key determinant of any sculpture's character. People's first impulse is usually to handle a piece of sculpture—even though museum signs often warn "Do not touch!" Sculptors plan for this natural human response, using surfaces varying in texture from rugged coarseness to polished smoothness. Textures are often intrinsic to a material, influencing the type of stone, wood, plastic, clay, or metal sculptors select.

SPACE, MASS, AND VOLUME *Space* is the bounded or boundless "container" of objects. For art historians, space can be *actual,* the three-dimensional space occupied by a statue or a vase or contained within a room or courtyard. Or it can be *illusionistic,* as when painters depict an image (or illusion) of the three-dimensional spatial world onto a two-dimensional surface.

Mass and *volume* describe three-dimensional space. In both architecture and sculpture, mass is the bulk, density, and weight of matter in space. Yet the mass need not be solid. It can be the exterior form of enclosed space. "Mass" can apply to a solid stone or wooden statue, to a mosque or Buddhist temple—architectural shells enclosing sometimes vast spaces—and to a hollow metal statue or baked clay pot. Volume is the space that mass organizes, divides, or encloses. It may be a building's interior spaces, the intervals between a structure's masses, or the amount of space occupied by three-dimensional objects such as sculpture, pottery, or furniture. Volume and mass describe both the exterior and interior forms of a work of art—the forms of the matter of which it is composed and the spaces immediately around the work and interacting with it.

CARVING AND CASTING Sculptural technique falls into two basic categories, *subtractive* and *additive. Carving* is a subtractive technique. The final form is a reduction of the original mass of a block of stone, a piece of wood, or another material. Wooden statues were once tree trunks, and stone statues began as blocks pried from mountains. All sculptors of stone or wood cut away (subtract) "excess material." When they finish, they "leave behind" the statue.

In additive sculpture, the artist builds up the forms, usually in clay around a framework, or *armature.* Or a sculptor may fashion a *mold,* a hollow form for shaping, or *casting,* a fluid substance such as bronze.

RELIEF SCULPTURE Statues that exist independent of any architectural frame or setting and that a viewer can walk around are *freestanding sculptures,* or *sculptures in the round,* whether the piece was carved or cast. In *relief sculptures,* the subjects project from the background but remain part of it. In *high relief* sculpture, the images project boldly. In some cases, such as the Benin bronze plaque we illustrate (FIG. Intro-1), the relief is so high that not only do the forms cast shadows on the background, some parts are actually in the round. In *low relief,* or *bas-relief,* the projection is slight. Relief sculpture, like sculpture in the round, can be produced either by carving or casting.

ARCHITECTURAL DRAWINGS Buildings are groupings of enclosed spaces and enclosing masses. People experience architecture both visually and by moving through and around it, so they perceive architectural space and mass together. These spaces and masses can be represented graphically in several ways, including as plans, sections, elevations, and cutaway drawings.

A *plan,* essentially a map of a floor, shows the placement of a structure's masses and, therefore, the spaces they bound and enclose. A *section,* like a vertical plan, depicts the placement of the masses as if the building were cut through along a plane.

Drawings showing a theoretical slice across a structure's width are *lateral sections.* Those cutting through a building's length are *longitudinal sections.* An *elevation* drawing is a head-on view of an external or internal wall. A *cutaway* combines an exterior view with an interior view of part of a building in a single drawing.

This overview of the art historian's vocabulary is not exhaustive, nor have artists used only painting, drawing, sculpture, and architecture as media over the millennia. Ceramics, jewelry, and textiles are just some of the numerous other arts. All of them involve highly specialized techniques described in distinct vocabularies. These are considered and defined where they arise in the text.

DIFFERENT WAYS OF SEEING

Even a cursory look at the works illustrated in this book will quickly reveal that throughout history, artists have created an extraordinary variety of works for a multitude of different purposes. In the Western world, however, certain characteristic ways of representing people, objects, and places have dominated since the ancient Greeks pioneered them half a millennium before the Common Era. Two of the most important are perspective and foreshortening.

PERSPECTIVE *Perspective* is a device to create an illusion of depth or space on a two-dimensional surface. The French painter CLAUDE LORRAIN employed several perspectival devices in *Embarkation of the Queen of Sheba* (FIG. **Intro-2**), a painting of a biblical episode set in a 17th-century European harbor with a Roman ruin in the left foreground. For example, the figures and boats on the shoreline are much larger than those in the distance. Decreasing the size of an object makes it appear farther away from the viewer. Also, the top and bottom of the port building at the painting's right side are not parallel horizontal lines, as they are in an actual building. Instead, the lines converge beyond the structure, leading the eye toward the hazy, indistinct sun on the horizon. These perspectival devices—the reduction of figure size, the convergence of diagonal lines, and the blurring of distant forms—have been familiar features of Western art through the ages. But it is important to note at the outset that all kinds of perspective are only pictorial conventions, even when one or more types of perspective may be so common in a given culture that they are accepted as "natural" or "true" means of representing the natural world.

In *White and Red Plum Blossoms* (FIG. **Intro-3**), a Japanese landscape painting on two folding screens, OGATA KORIN used none of these Western perspective conventions. He showed the two plum trees as seen from a position on the ground, while the viewer looks down on the stream between them from above. Less concerned with locating the trees and stream in space than with composing shapes on a surface, the painter played the water's gently swelling curves against the jagged contours of the branches and trunks. Neither the French nor the Japanese painting can be said to project "correctly" what the viewer "in fact" sees. One painting is not a "better" picture of the world than the other. The European and Asian artists simply approached the problem of picture-making differently.

FORESHORTENING Artists also represent single figures in space in varying ways. When PETER PAUL RUBENS painted *Lion*

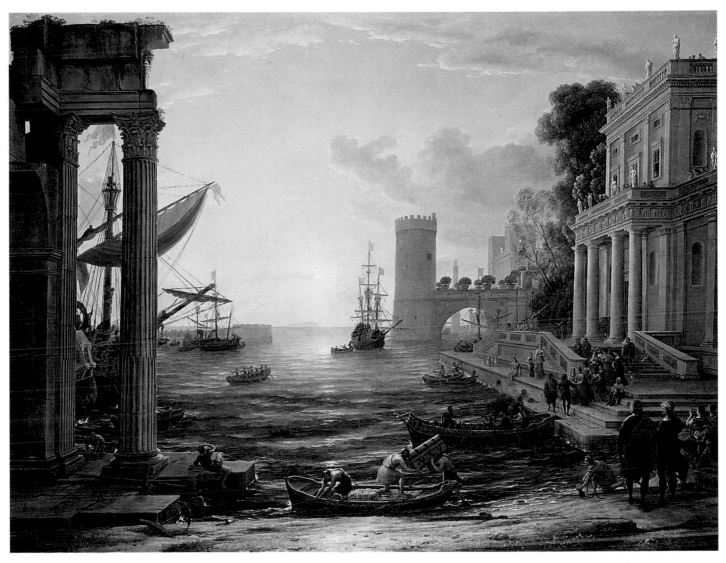

Intro-2 CLAUDE LORRAIN, *Embarkation of the Queen of Sheba*, 1648. Oil on canvas, approx. 4′ 10″ × 6′ 4″. National Gallery, London.

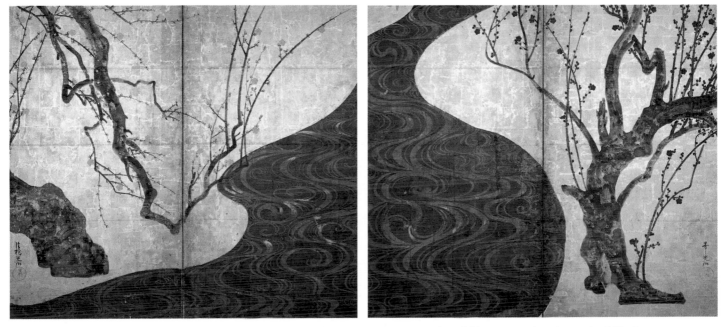

Intro-3 OGATA KORIN, *White and Red Plum Blossoms,* Edo period, ca. 1710–1716. Pair of twofold screens. Ink, color, and gold leaf on paper, each screen 5′ 1$\frac{5}{8}$″ × 5′ 7$\frac{7}{8}$″. MOA Art Museum, Shizuoka-ken.

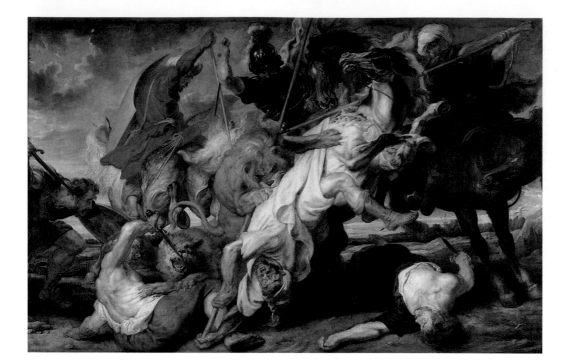

Intro-4 Peter Paul Rubens, *Lion Hunt,* 1617–1618. Oil on canvas, approx. 8′ 2″ × 12′ 5″. Alte Pinakothek, Munich.

Hunt (FIG. **Intro-4**) in the early 17th century, he used *foreshortening* for all the hunters and animals, that is, he represented their bodies at angles to the picture plane. When in life one views a figure at an angle, the body appears to contract as it extends back in space. Foreshortening is a kind of perspective. It produces the illusion that one part of the body is farther away than another, even though all the forms are on the same surface. Especially noteworthy in *Lion Hunt* are the gray horse at the left, seen from behind with the bottom of its left rear hoof facing the viewer and most of its head hidden by its rider's shield, and the fallen hunter at the painting's lower right corner, whose barely visible legs and feet recede into the distance.

Like the Japanese painter (FIG. Intro-3), the African sculptor who depicted a Benin king on horseback with his attendants (FIG. Intro-1) did not employ any of the Western conventions seen in the Rubens painting (FIG. Intro-4). Although the Rubens canvas and the Benin plaque are contemporaneous, the latter's figures are all in the foreground, stand (or sit) in upright positions, and face the viewer directly. Nothing is seen at an angle; even the horse is viewed from the front. Once again, neither approach to pictorial representation is the "correct" manner. The artists' radically different styles reflect the radically different societies of 17th-century Europe and Africa.

PROPORTION AND SCALE The Rubens painting and the Benin relief also differ in the artists' treatment of proportion and scale. *Proportion* concerns the relationships (in terms of size) of the parts of persons, buildings, or objects. "Correct proportions" may be judged intuitively ("that statue's head seems the right size for the body"). Or proportion may be formalized as a mathematical relationship between the size of one part of an artwork or building and the other parts within the work. Proportion in art implies using a *module,* or basic unit of measure. When an artist or architect uses a formal system of proportions, all parts of a building, body, or other entity will be fractions or multiples of the module. A module might be a column's diameter, the height of a human head, or any other component whose dimen-

sions can be multiplied or divided to determine the size of the work's other parts. In certain times and places, artists have formulated *canons,* or systems, of "correct" or "ideal" proportions for representing human figures, constituent parts of buildings, and so forth.

In other cases, artists have used *disproportion* to focus attention on one body part (often the head) or to single out a group member (usually the leader). These intentional "unnatural" discrepancies in proportion constitute what art historians call *hierarchy of scale,* the enlarging of elements considered the most important. On the Benin plaque (FIG. Intro-1), the sculptor enlarged all the heads for emphasis and also varied the size of each figure according to its social status. Central, largest, and therefore most important is the Benin king, mounted on horseback. The horse has been a symbol of power and wealth in many societies from prehistory to the present. That the Benin king is disproportionately larger than his horse, contrary to nature, further aggrandizes him. Two large attendants fan the king. Other figures of smaller size and lower status at the Benin court stand on the king's left and right and in the plaque's upper corners. One tiny figure next to the horse is almost hidden from view beneath the king's feet. In contrast, in the Rubens painting (FIG. Intro-4), no figure is larger than any other.

ART AND CULTURE The history of art can be a history of artists and their works, of styles and stylistic change, of materials and techniques, of images and themes and their meanings, and of contexts and cultures and patrons. The best art historians analyze artworks from many viewpoints. But no art historian (or scholar in any other field), no matter how broad-minded in approach and no matter how experienced, can be truly objective. Like artists, art historians are members of a society, participants in its culture. How can scholars (and museum visitors and travelers to foreign locales) comprehend cultures unlike their own? They can try to reconstruct the original cultural contexts of artworks, but they are bound to be limited by their distance from the thought patterns of the cultures they

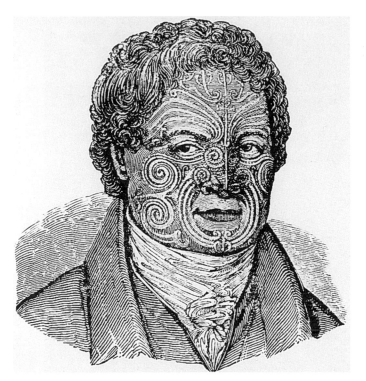 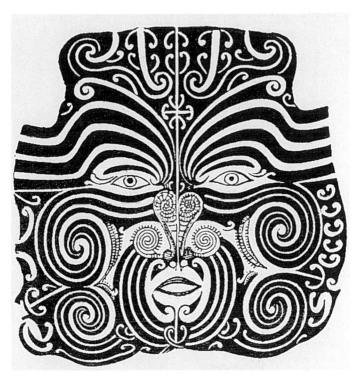

Intro-5 John Sylvester *(left)* and Te Pehi Kupe *(right)*, portraits of Maori chief Te Pehi Kupe, 1826. From *The Childhood of Man,* by Leo Frobenius (New York: J. B. Lippincott, 1909).

study and by the obstructions to understanding—the assumptions, presuppositions, and prejudices peculiar to their own culture—their own thought patterns raise. Art historians may reconstruct a distorted picture of the past because of culture-bound blindness.

One more example can underscore how differently people of diverse cultures view the world and how various ways of seeing can cause sharp differences in how artists depict the world. We illustrate two contemporaneous portraits (FIG. **Intro-5**) of a 19th-century Maori chieftain side by side—one by an Englishman, John Sylvester, and the other by the New Zealand chieftain himself, Te Pehi Kupe. Both reproduce the chieftain's facial tattooing. The European artist included the head and shoulders and underplayed the tattooing. The tattoo pattern is one aspect of the likeness among many, no more or less important than the fact the chieftain is dressed like a European. Sylvester also recorded his subject's momentary glance toward the right and the play of light on his hair, fleeting aspects that have nothing to do with the figure's identity.

In contrast, Te Pehi Kupe's self-portrait—made during a trip to Liverpool, England, to obtain European arms to take back to

New Zealand—is not a picture of a man situated in space and bathed in light. Rather, it is the chieftain's statement of the supreme importance of the design that symbolizes his rank among his people. Remarkably, Te Pehi Kupe created the tattoo patterns from memory, without the aid of a mirror. The splendidly composed insignia, presented as a flat design separated from the body and even from the head, is Te Pehi Kupe's image of himself. Only by understanding the cultural context of each portrait can the viewer hope to understand why either looks the way it does.

As noted at the outset, the study of the context of artworks and buildings is one of the central aims of art history. Our purpose in writing *Art through the Ages: Non-Western Perspectives* is to present a history of art and architecture in Asia, the Islamic world, the Americas, Oceania, and Africa that will help readers understand not only the subjects, styles, and techniques of paintings, sculptures, buildings, and other art forms created in those parts of the world but also their cultural and historical contexts. That story now begins.

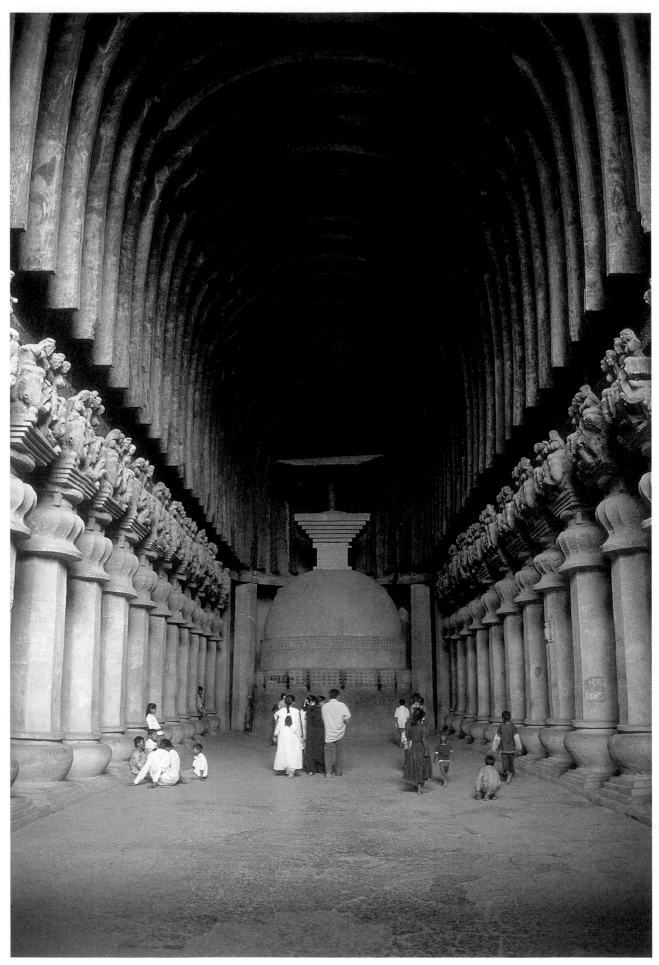

Interior of chaitya hall, Karle, India, ca. 100 CE.

1

PATHS TO ENLIGHTENMENT

THE ART OF SOUTH AND SOUTHEAST ASIA BEFORE 1200

South and Southeast Asia is a vast geographic area comprising, among others, the modern nations of India, Pakistan, Sri Lanka, Thailand, Vietnam, Cambodia, Bangladesh, and Indonesia (MAP 1-1). Not surprisingly, the region's inhabitants display tremendous cultural and religious diversity. The people of India alone speak more than 20 different major languages. Those spoken in the north belong to the Indo-European language family, whereas those in the south form a completely separate linguistic family called Dravidian. The art of South and Southeast Asia is equally diverse — and very ancient. When Alexander the Great, the Greek king whose conquests transformed the ancient Mediterranean and Near East, reached India in 326 BCE, the civilization he and his army encountered was already more than two millennia old. The remains of the first cities in the Indus Valley predate the palaces of the heroes of Homer's *Iliad* by a millennium. This chapter discusses the art and architecture of South and Southeast Asia from their beginnings almost five millennia ago through the 12th century. Chapter 2 treats the later art of the region up to the present day.

INDIA AND PAKISTAN

Indus Civilization

URBAN SOPHISTICATION In the third millennium BCE, a great civilization arose over a wide geographic area along the Indus River in present-day Pakistan and extended into India as far south as Gujarat and east beyond Delhi. Archaeologists have uncovered impressive remains of this Indus Civilization, as it has come to be called, as well as evidence for active trade between the peoples of the ancient Near East and the Indus Valley.

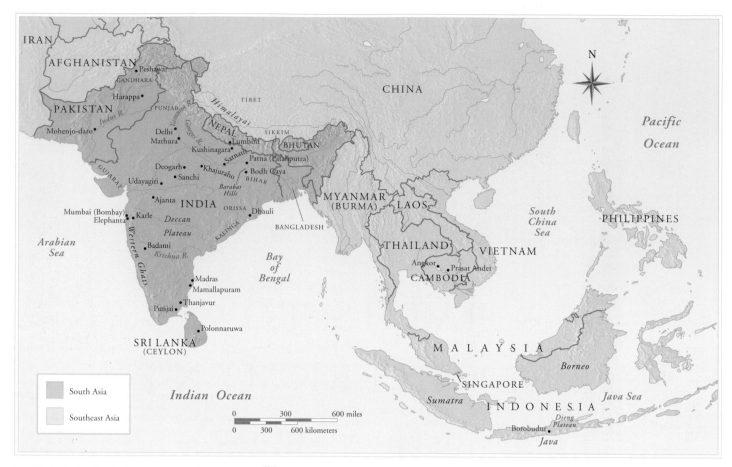

MAP 1-1 Early sites in South and Southeast Asia.

The most important excavated Indus sites are Harappa and Mohenjo-daro. These early fully developed cities featured streets oriented to compass points, and multistoried houses built of carefully formed and precisely laid kiln-baked bricks. The Indus cities also boasted one of the world's first sophisticated systems of water supply and sewage. In Mohenjo-daro, hundreds of wells throughout the city provided fresh water to homes that featured some of the oldest recorded private bathing areas and toilet facilities, with drainage into public sewers. In the heart of the city stood the so-called Great Bath, a complex of rooms centered on a sunken brick pool (FIG. **1-1**) 39 feet long, 23 feet wide, and 8 feet deep. The builders made the pool watertight by sealing the joints between the bricks with bitumen, an asphaltlike material also used in

Mesopotamia. The bath was unlikely to have been a purely recreational facility. Rather, most scholars believe it was designed for ritual bathing of the kind still practiced in the region today.

One intriguing characteristic of the Indus Civilization is that no surviving structures have yet been identified as either temples or palaces. This marks a sharp contrast to the contemporaneous civilizations of Mesopotamia and Egypt.

ELITE SCULPTURE Excavators have discovered surprisingly little art from the long-lived Indus Civilization, and all of the objects found are small. The most impressive is a robed male figure (FIG. **1-2**) found at Mohenjo-daro. This steatite (a soft local soapstone) sculpture depicts a figure with half-closed eyes and a closely trimmed beard with shaved upper lip. He wears a headband with a central circular emblem, matched by a similar armband. Holes on each side of his neck suggest that he also wore a necklace of precious metal. *Trefoils* (cloverlike designs with three stylized leaves) decorate his elegant robe. They, as well as the circles of the head- and armbands, originally held red paste and shell inlays, as did the eyes. The Mohenjo-daro statuette is often compared to the contemporaneous sculptures of the Sumerians in Mesopotamia. There, the trefoil motif appears in sacred contexts, and scholars refer to the person portrayed as a "priest-king," an ambiguous term used for some Sumerian leaders. The identity and rank of the Mohenjo-daro figure are, however, uncertain. Nonetheless, the elaborate costume and precious materials make clear that he too was an elite individual.

INDUS SEALS The most common Indus art objects are steatite seals with incised designs. They are similar in many ways to the seals often found at contemporaneous sites in Mesopotamia. Most

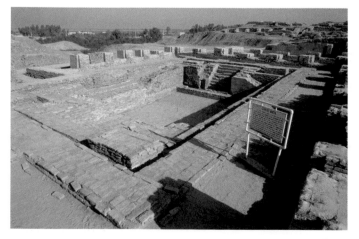

1-1 Great Bath, Mohenjo-daro, Pakistan, ca. 2600–1900 BCE.

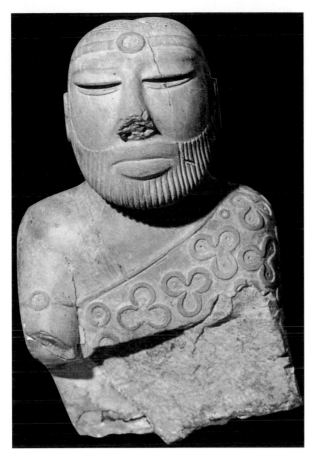

1-2 Robed male figure, from Mohenjo-daro, Pakistan, ca. 2000–1900 BCE. Steatite, $6\frac{7}{8}''$ high. National Museum of Pakistan, Karachi.

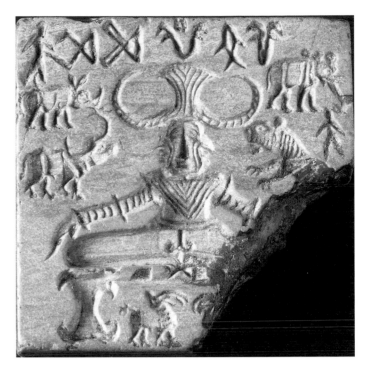

1-3 Seal with seated figure in yogic posture, from Mohenjo-daro, Pakistan, ca. 2600–1900 BCE. Steatite coated with alkali and baked, approx. $1\frac{3}{8}'' \times 1\frac{3}{8}''$. National Museum, New Delhi.

of the Indus examples have an animal or tiny narrative carved on the face, along with an as yet untranslated script. On the back, a *boss* (circular knob) with a hole permitted insertion of a string so that the seal could be worn or hung on a wall. As in the ancient Near East, the Indus peoples sometimes used the seals to make impressions on clay, apparently for securing trade goods wrapped in textiles. The animals most frequently represented include the humped bull, elephant, rhinoceros, and tiger. Each is portrayed in strict profile. Some of the narrative seals appear to show that the Indus peoples considered trees sacred, as both Buddhists and Hindus later did. Many scholars have suggested that religious and ritual continuities existed between the Indus Civilization and later Indian culture.

One of the most elaborate seals (FIG. 1-3) depicts a male figure with a horned headdress and, perhaps, three faces, seated (with erect penis) among the profile animals that regularly appear alone on other seals. The figure's folded legs with heels pressed together and his arms resting on the knees suggest a yogic posture (compare FIG. 1-11). *Yoga* (literally "to yoke") is a method for controlling the body and relaxing the mind used in later Indian religions to yoke, or unite, the practitioner to the divine. Although most scholars reject the identification of this figure as a prototype of the multiheaded Hindu god Shiva (FIG. 1-17) as Lord of Beasts, the yogic posture argues that this important Indian meditative practice began as early as the Indus Civilization.

Vedic and Upanishadic Periods

THE NOBLE ONES By 1700 BCE, the urban phase of the Indus Civilization had ended in most areas. The production of sculptures, seals, and script gradually ceased, and village life replaced urban culture. Very little art survives from the next thousand years, but the religious foundations laid during this period, based on the oral hymns the Aryans brought to India from Central Asia, helped define most later South and Southeast Asian art. The Aryans were a mobile herding people who occupied the Punjab, an area of northwestern India, in the second millennium BCE. They called themselves *Aryas* (Noble Ones) and spoke Sanskrit, the earliest language yet identified in South Asia.

VEDAS AND BRAHMINS Around 1500 BCE, the Aryans composed the first of four *Vedas*. These compilations of religious learning (veda means "knowledge"), written in Sanskrit, included hymns intended for priests (called *Brahmins*) to chant or sing. The Aryan priests headed a social hierarchy that has come to be called the *caste system*, which still forms the basis of Indian society today. Below the priests were the warriors, traders, and manual laborers (including artists and architects), respectively. The Aryan religion centered on sacrifice, the ritual enactment of often highly intricate and lengthy ceremonies in which the Brahmin priests placed materials, such as milk and *soma* (the sacrificial brew), into a fire that took the sacrifices to the gods in the heavens. It was believed that if the priests performed these rituals accurately, the gods would fulfill the prayers of those who sponsored the sacrifices. These gods, primarily male, included Indra, Varuna, Surya, and Agni, gods associated, respectively, with the rains, the ocean, the sun, and fire. It appears that the Aryans did not make images of these deities.

SAMSARA, KARMA, AND MOKSHA The next phase of South Asian urban civilization developed east of the Indus heartland, in the Ganges River Valley. Here, from 800 to 500 BCE, religious thinkers composed a variety of texts called the *Upanishads*. Among the innovative ideas of the Upanishads were *samsara*, *karma*, and *moksha* (or *nirvana*). Samsara is the belief that individuals are born again after death in an almost endless round of rebirths. The type of rebirth can vary. One can be reborn as a human being, an animal, or even a god. An individual's past actions (karma), either good or bad, determine the nature of future rebirths. The ultimate goal of a person's religious life is to escape from the cycle of birth and death by merging the individual self into the vital force of the universe. This escape is called either moksha (liberation, for Hindus) or nirvana (cessation, for Buddhists).

HINDUISM AND BUDDHISM Hinduism and Buddhism, the two major modern religions originating in Asia, developed in the late centuries BCE and the early centuries CE. Hinduism, the dominant religion in India today, discussed in more detail later (see page 12), has its origins in Aryan religion. Buddhism was founded by the Buddha, a historical figure who advocated the path of *asceticism,* or self-discipline and self-denial, as the means to free oneself from attachments to people and possessions, thus ending rebirth (see "Buddhism and Buddhist Iconography," page 5). Unlike their predecessors in South Asia, both Hindus and Buddhists use images of gods and holy persons in religious rituals. Buddhists have the older artistic tradition. Their earliest monuments date to the Maurya period.

Maurya Dynasty

CHANDRAGUPTA AND THE GREEKS When Alexander the Great reached the Indus River in 326 BCE, his troops refused to go further. Reluctantly, Alexander abandoned his dream of conquering India and headed home. After Alexander's death three years later, his generals divided his empire among themselves. One of them, Seleucus Nicator, re-invaded India, but Chandragupta Maurya (r. 323–298 BCE), founder of the Maurya dynasty, defeated him in 305 BCE and eventually consolidated almost all of present-day India under his domain. Chandragupta's capital was Pataliputra (modern Patna) in northeastern India, far from the center of the Indus Civilization. Megasthenes, Seleucus's ambassador to the Maurya court, described Pataliputra in his book on India as a large and wealthy city enclosed within mighty wooden walls so extensive that the circuit had 64 gates and 570 towers.

ASHOKA'S PILLARS The greatest Maurya ruler was Ashoka (r. 272–231 BCE), who left his imprint on history by converting to Buddhism and spreading the Buddha's teaching throughout and beyond India (see "Ashoka's Conversion to Buddhism," page 7). Ashoka formulated a legal code based on the Buddha's dharma and inscribed his laws on enormous *monolithic* (one-piece) stone *columns* erected throughout his kingdom. Ashoka's *pillars* reached 30 to 40 feet high and are the first monumental stone artworks in India. The pillars penetrated deep into the ground, connecting earth and sky, forming an "axis of the universe," a pre-Buddhist concept that became an important motif in Buddhist architecture. The columns stood along pilgrimage routes to sites associated with the Buddha and on the roads leading to Pataliputra. Capping Ashoka's pillars were elaborate *capitals,* also carved from a single block of stone. The finest of these is the seven-foot lion capital (FIG. **1-4**) at Sarnath, where the Buddha gave his first sermon and set the Wheel of the Law into motion (see "Buddhism," page 5). Stylistically, Ashoka's capital owes much to ancient Near Eastern architecture, but its iconography is Buddhist. Two pairs of back-to-back lions stand on a round *abacus* decorated with four wheels and four animals symbolizing the four quarters of the world. The lions once carried a large stone wheel on their backs. The wheel (*chakra*) referred to the Wheel of

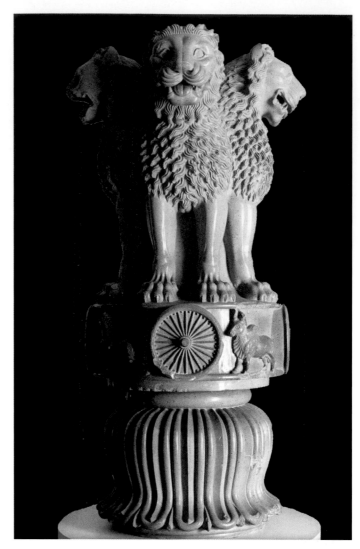

1-4 Lion capital of column erected by Ashoka at Sarnath, India, ca. 250 BCE. Polished sandstone, approx. 7′ high. Archaeological Museum, Sarnath.

the Law but also indicated Ashoka's stature as a *chakravartin* ("holder of the wheel"), a universal king imbued with divine authority.

Shunga, Andhra, and Kushan Dynasties

The Maurya Dynasty came to an abrupt end when its last ruler was assassinated by one of his generals, who founded a new dynasty in his own name. The Shungas, however, never ruled an empire as extensive as that of the Mauryas. Their realm was confined to central India. They were succeeded by the Andhras, who also controlled the Deccan plateau to the south. By the middle of the first century CE, an even greater empire, the Kushan, rose in northern India. Its most celebrated king was Kanishka (r. 78–144 CE), whose capital was at Peshawar in Gandhara, a region largely in Pakistan today, close to the Afghanistan border. The Kushans grew rich on trade between China and the west along one of the main caravan routes bringing the luxuries of the Orient to the Roman Empire (see "Silk and the Silk Road," Chapter 3, page 49). Kanishka even struck coins modeled on the imperial coinage of Rome, some featuring Greco-Roman deities, but Kanishka's coins also carried portraits of himself and images of the Buddha and various Hindu deities.

Buddhism and Buddhist Iconography

THE BUDDHA AND THE EIGHTFOLD PATH

The Buddha (Enlightened One) was born around 563 BCE as Prince Siddhartha Gautama, the eldest son of the king of the Shakya Clan. A prophecy foretold that he would grow up to be either a world conqueror or a great religious leader. His father preferred the secular role for young Siddhartha and groomed him for kingship by shielding the boy from the hardships of the world. When he was 29, however, the prince rode out of the palace, abandoned his wife and family, and encountered firsthand the pain of old age, sickness, and death. Siddhartha responded to the suffering he witnessed by renouncing his opulent life and becoming a wandering ascetic searching for knowledge through meditation. Six years later, he achieved complete enlightenment, or buddhahood, while meditating beneath a pipal tree (the Bodhi tree) at Bodh Gaya ("place of enlightenment") in eastern India. Known from that day on as Shakyamuni (Wise Man of the Shakya Clan), the Buddha preached his first sermon in the Deer Park at Sarnath. There he set in motion the Wheel (chakra) of the Law (dharma) and expounded the Four Noble Truths that are the core insights of Buddhism: (1) life is suffering; (2) the cause of suffering is desire; (3) one can overcome and extinguish desire; (4) the way to conquer desire and end suffering is to follow the Buddha's Eightfold Path of right understanding, right thought, right speech, right action, right livelihood, right effort, right mindfulness, and right concentration. The Buddha's path leads to nirvana, the cessation of the endless cycle of painful life, death, and rebirth. The Buddha continued to preach until his death at 80 at Kushinagara. His disciples carried on his teaching and established monasteries where others could follow the Buddha's path to enlightenment and nirvana.

THE SPREAD OF BUDDHISM

This earliest form of Buddhism is called *Theravada* (the Path of the Elders) Buddhism. The new religion developed and changed over time as the Buddha's teachings spread from India throughout Asia. The second major school of Buddhist thought, *Mahayana* (Great Path) Buddhism, emerged around the beginning of the Common Era. Mahayana Buddhists refer to Theravada Buddhism as *Hinayana* (Lesser Path) Buddhism and believe in a larger goal than nirvana for an individual—namely, buddhahood for all. Mahayana Buddhists also revere *bodhisattvas* ("Buddhas-to-be"), exemplars of compassion who, holding back at the threshold of nirvana, aid others in earning merit and achieving buddhahood (see FIGS. 1-14, 3-12, 5-7, and 5-8). Theravada Buddhism became the dominant sect in southern India, Sri Lanka, and mainland Southeast Asia, whereas Mahayana Buddhism took root in northern India and spread to China, Korea, Japan, and Nepal.

A third important Buddhist sect, especially popular in East Asia, venerates the *Amitabha* Buddha (*Amida* in Japanese), the Buddha of Infinite Light and Life. The devotees of this Buddha hope to be reborn in the Pure Land Paradise of the West (see FIG. 3-13), where the Amitabha resides and can grant them salvation. Pure Land teachings maintain that people have no possibility of attaining enlightenment on their own, but can achieve paradise by faith alone.

THE BUDDHA IN ART

When artists began depicting the Buddha in human form, probably in the first century CE, it was as a robed monk. They distinguished the Enlightened One from monks and bodhisattvas by *lakshanas*, body attributes or characteristics indicating the Buddha's superhuman nature. These distinguishing marks include an *urna*, or curl of hair between the eyebrows, shown as a dot; an *ushnisha*, a cranial bump shown as hair on the earliest images (FIGS. 1-9 to 1-11) but later as an actual part of the head (see FIG. 1-12); and, less frequently, palms of hands and soles of feet imprinted with a wheel (FIG. 1-11). The Buddha is also recognizable by his elongated ears, the result of wearing heavy royal jewelry in his youth, but the enlightened Shakyamuni is rarely bejeweled, as are many bodhisattvas. Sometimes the Buddha appears with a *halo*, or sun disk, behind his head (FIGS. 1-9, 1-11, and 1-12).

Representations of the Buddha also feature a repertory of *mudras*, or hand gestures, conveying fixed meanings. These include the *dhyana* (meditation) mudra, with hands overlapping in the lap, palms upward (FIGS. 1-9 and 2-11); the *bhumisparsha* (earth touching) mudra, right hand down reaching to the ground, calling the earth to witness the Buddha's enlightenment (FIGS. 1-10b, and 3-27); the *dharmachakra* (Wheel of the Law, or teaching) mudra, a two-handed gesture with right thumb and index finger forming a circle (FIGS. 1-12 and 5-8); and the *abhaya* (do not fear) mudra, right hand up, palm outward, a gesture of protection or blessing (FIGS. 1-10c, 1-11, and 5-7).

Episodes from the Buddha's life are among the most popular subjects in all Buddhist artistic traditions. No single text provides the complete or authoritative narrative of his life and death. Thus, numerous versions and variations exist, allowing for a rich artistic repertory. Four of the most important events are his birth at Lumbini from the side of his mother, Queen Maya (FIG. 1-10a) the achievement of buddhahood while meditating beneath the Bodhi tree at Bodh Gaya (FIGS. 1-10b and 3-27); the Buddha's first sermon at Sarnath (FIGS. 1-10c and 1-12); and his attainment of nirvana when he died (parinirvana) at Kushinagara (FIGS. 1-10d and 1-25). Buddhists erected monasteries and monuments at the four sites where these key events occurred. Monks and lay pilgrims from throughout the world continue to visit these places today.

THE GREAT STUPA AT SANCHI In the world of art and architecture, the unifying characteristic of this age of regional dynasties in South Asia was the patronage of Buddhism. One of the most important Buddhist monasteries, founded during Ashoka's reign and in use for more than a thousand years, is at Sanchi in central India. It consists of many buildings constructed over the centuries, including *viharas* (celled structures where monks live), large *stupas* (see "The Stupa," page 6), *chaitya halls* (halls with rounded, or *apsidal*, ends for housing smaller stupas), and temples for sheltering images.

The Great Stupa at Sanchi dates originally to Ashoka's reign, but its present form, with its tall stone fence and four gates, dates

The Stupa

An essential element of Buddhist sanctuaries is the *stupa,* a grand circular mound modeled on earlier South Asian burial mounds of a type familiar in many other ancient cultures. The stupa was not a tomb, however, but a monument housing *relics* of the Buddha. When the Buddha died, his cremated remains were placed in eight *reliquaries,* or containers, similar in function to the later reliquaries housed in medieval churches at pilgrimage sites throughout the Christian world. Unlike their Western equivalents, which were meant to be viewed, the Buddha's relics were buried in solid earthen mounds (stupas) that could not be entered. In the mid-third century BCE, Ashoka opened the original eight stupas and spread the Buddha's relics among thousands of stupas in all corners of his realm.

Buddhists venerated the Buddha's remains by *circumambulation,* walking around the stupa in a clockwise direction, following the path of the sun, bringing the devotee into harmony with the cosmos. Stupas come in many sizes, from tiny handheld objects to huge structures, such as the Great Stupa at Sanchi (FIG. 1-5) that Ashoka constructed in the third century BCE and later kings enlarged.

The monumental stupas are three-dimensional *mandalas,* or sacred diagrams of the universe. The domed stupa itself represents the world mountain, with the cardinal points marked by *toranas,* or gateways (FIGS. 1-5 and 1-6). The *harmika,* positioned atop the stupa dome, is a stone fence or railing that encloses a square area symbolizing the sacred domain of the gods. At the harmika's center, a *yasti,* or pole, corresponds to the axis of the universe, a motif already present in Ashoka's pillars. Three *chatras,* or stone disks, assigned various meanings, crown the yasti. The yasti rises from the mountain-dome and passes through the harmika, thus uniting this world with the heavenly paradise. A stone fence often encloses the entire structure, clearly separating the sacred space containing the Buddha's relics from the profane world outside.

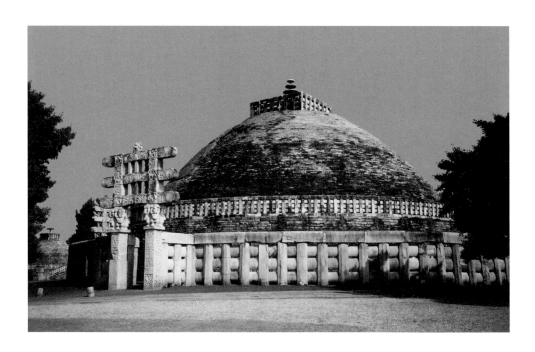

1-5 Great Stupa, Sanchi, India, third century BCE to first century CE (view from the east).

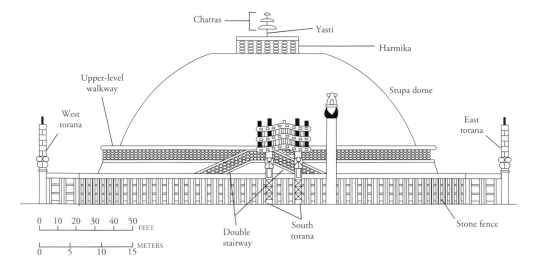

1-6 Exterior diagram of Great Stupa, Sanchi, India, third century BCE to first century CE.

Chatras — Yasti

Harmika

Upper-level walkway

Stupa dome

West torana

East torana

0 10 20 30 40 50 FEET

0   5   10   15 METERS

Double stairway

South torana

Stone fence

Ashoka's Conversion to Buddhism

The reign of the Maurya king Ashoka marks both the beginning of monumental stone art and architecture in India (FIG. 1-4) and the first official sponsorship of Buddhism. The impact of Ashoka's conversion to Buddhism on the later history of art and religion in Asia cannot be overstated. An edict carved into a rock at Dhauli in the ancient region of Kalinga (roughly equivalent to the modern state of Orissa on the Bay of Bengal) records Ashoka's embrace of nonviolence and of the teachings of the Buddha after an especially bloody conquest that claimed more than 100,000 lives. The inscription also captures Ashoka's missionary zeal, which spread Buddhism far beyond the boundaries of his kingdom.

> The Beloved of the Gods [Ashoka], conqueror of the Kalingas, is moved to remorse now. For he has felt profound sorrow and regret because the conquest of a people previously unconquered involves slaughter, death, and deportation. . . . [King Ashoka] now thinks that even a person who wrongs him must be forgiven . . .

[and he] considers moral conquest [conquest by dharma] the most important conquest. He has achieved this moral conquest repeatedly both here and among the peoples living beyond the borders of his kingdom. . . . Even in countries which [King Ashoka's] envoys have not reached, people have heard about dharma and about [the king's] ordinances and instructions in dharma. . . . This edict on dharma has been inscribed so that my sons and great-grandsons who may come after me should not think new conquests worth achieving. . . . Let them consider moral conquest the only true conquest.[1]

The story of Ashoka at Kalinga and his renunciation of violence still resonates today. It inspired one of the most important 20th-century Indian sculptors to take up the theme and imbue it with contemporary meaning (see FIG. 2-14).

[1] Rock Edict XIII. Translated by N. A. Nikam and Richard McKeon, *The Edicts of Asoka* (Chicago: The University of Chicago Press, 1959), 27–30.

from ca. 50 BCE to 50 CE (FIGS. 1-5 and 1-6). The *dome,* solid and filled with earth and rubble, stands 50 feet high. Worshipers enter through one of the gateways, walk on the lower circumambulation path, then climb the stairs on the south side to circumambulate at the second level. Carved onto the different parts of the Great Stupa are more than 600 brief inscriptions showing that the donations of hundreds of individuals

(more than a third of them women) made the monument's construction possible. Veneration of the Buddha was open to all, not just the monks, and most of the dedications are by common laypeople, who hoped to accrue merit for future rebirths with their gifts.

THE BUDDHA'S PAST LIVES The reliefs on the four toranas at Sanchi (FIGS. 1-5 and 1-6) depict not only the Buddha's life story but also the stories of his past lives *(jatakas).* In Buddhist belief, everyone has had innumerable past lives, including Siddhartha. During Siddhartha's former lives, as recorded in the jatakas, he accumulated sufficient merit to achieve enlightenment and become the Buddha. In the life stories recounted in the Great Stupa reliefs, however, the Buddha never appears as a human being. Instead, the artists indicated his presence by using symbols, for example, footprints, a parasol, or an empty seat. Some scholars regard these symbols as markers of where the Buddha once was, so others can follow in his footsteps.

YAKSHI AND FLOWERING TREE Also carved on the eastern gateway is a scantily clad, sensuous woman called a *yakshi* (FIG. 1-7). These goddesses, worshiped throughout India, personified fertility and vegetation. The Sanchi yakshi reaches up to hold on to a mango tree branch while pressing her left foot against the trunk, an action that has brought the tree to flower. Buddhists later adopted this pose, with its rich associations of procreation and abundance, for representing the Buddha's mother, Maya, giving birth (FIG. 1-10*a*). Thus, the Buddhists adopted pan-Indian symbolism, such as the woman under the tree, when creating their own Buddhist iconography.

1-7 Yakshi, detail of eastern gateway, Great Stupa, Sanchi, India, mid-first century BCE to early first century CE.

ROCK-CUT MONASTIC HALLS The best early example of a chaitya hall is the one carved out of the living rock at Karle

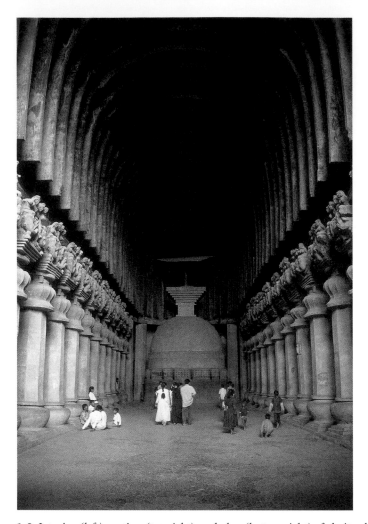
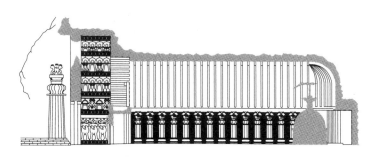
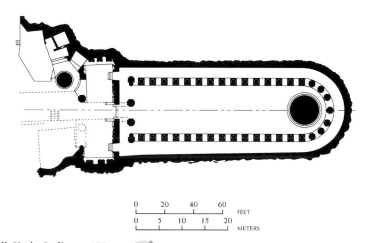

1-8 Interior *(left)*, section *(top right)*, and plan *(bottom right)* of chaitya hall, Karle, India, ca. 100 CE.

(FIG. **1-8**), datable around 100 CE. The Karle hall has pillared *ambulatories* (walking paths) that allow worshipers to circumambulate the stupa placed at the back of the sacred cave. The hall is nearly 45 feet high and 125 feet long. Elaborate capitals atop the rock-cut pillars depict men and women riding on elephants. Outside, amorous couples *(mithunas)* flank the entrance. Like the yakshis at Sanchi, these auspicious figures symbolize the creative life force. The Sanchi and Karle figures are early examples of what will become a long tradition of eroticism in Indian religious art (compare FIG. 1-23).

FIRST BUDDHAS IN HUMAN FORM The first anthropomorphic representations of the Buddha probably appeared in the first century CE. Scholars still debate what brought about this momentous shift in Buddhist iconography, but one factor may be the changing perception of the Buddha himself. Originally revered as an enlightened mortal, the Buddha increasingly became regarded as a divinity. Consequently, the Buddha's followers desired images of him to worship.

Many of the early portrayals of the Buddha in human form come from the Gandhara region and from Mathura, a city about 90 miles south of Delhi. Both were part of the Kushan Empire during the first three centuries CE.

GANDHARA AND GRECO-ROMAN ART In Gandhara, sculptors fashioned representations of the Buddha both in freestanding statuary and narrative reliefs. A second-century CE statue (FIG. **1-9**) carved in gray schist, the local stone, shows the Buddha, with ushnisha and urna, dressed in a monk's robe, seated in a cross-legged yogic posture similar to that of the ancient figure on the Indus seal discussed earlier (FIG. 1-3). His hands overlap, palms upward, in the dhyana mudra, the gesture of meditation (see "Buddhism," page 5). Gandhara was part of a widespread region of Greco-Roman culture and art that stretched across reaches of modern Iran, Russia, Afghanistan, and Pakistan, a legacy of Alexander's incursions in these regions. Gandharan sculpture owes much to Greco-Roman art, both in the treatment of body forms, such as the sharp, arching brows and continuous profile of forehead and nose, and in the draping of the garment, which resembles a Roman toga.

LIFE AND DEATH OF THE BUDDHA One of the earliest pictorial narrative cycles in which the Buddha appears in human form also comes from Gandhara. The schist frieze (FIG. **1-10**) depicts, in chronological order from left to right, the Buddha's birth at Lumbini, the enlightenment at Bodh Gaya, the first sermon at Sarnath, and the Buddha's death at Kushinagara. At the left,

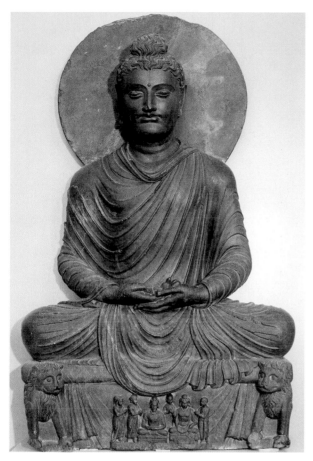

1-9 Meditating Buddha, from Gandhara, Pakistan, second century CE. Gray schist, 3′ 7½″ high. Royal Museum, National Museums of Scotland, Edinburgh.

Queen Maya, in a posture derived from that of earlier South Asian yakshis (FIG. 1-7), gives birth to Prince Siddhartha, who emerges from her right hip, already with his attributes of ushnisha, urna, and halo. Receiving him is the god Indra. Elegantly dressed ladies, one with a fan of peacock feathers, suggest the opulent court life the Buddha left behind. In the next scene, the Buddha sits beneath the Bodhi tree while the soldiers and demons of the evil Mara attempt to distract him from his quest for knowledge. They are unsuccessful, and the Buddha reaches down to touch the earth (bhumisparsha mudra) as witness to his enlightenment. Next, the Buddha preaches the Eightfold Path to nirvana in the Deer Park at Sarnath. The sculptor has set the scene by placing two deer and the Wheel of the Law beneath the figure of the Buddha, who raises his right hand (abhaya mudra) to bless the monks and other devotees who have come to hear his first sermon. In the final section of the frieze, the parinirvana, the Buddha lies dying among his devotees, some of whom wail in grief, while one monk, who realizes that the Buddha has been permanently released from suffering, remains tranquil in meditation.

Although the iconography of the frieze is Buddhist, Roman reliefs must have served as stylistic models for the sculptor. For example, the distribution of standing and equestrian figures over the relief ground, with those behind the first row seemingly suspended in the air, is familiar in Roman art of the second and third centuries CE. The figure of the Buddha on his deathbed finds parallels in the reclining figures on the lids of Roman *sarcophagi*. The type of hierarchical composition placing a large seated central figure between balanced tiers of smaller onlookers is also commonplace in Roman imperial art.

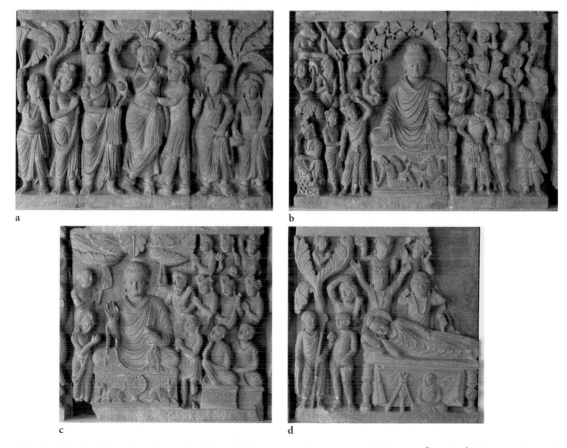

a

b

c

d

1-10 The life and death of the Buddha, frieze from Gandhara, Pakistan, second century CE. Schist, 2′ 2⅜″ × 9′ 6⅛″. Freer Gallery of Art, Washington, D.C. a) birth at Lumbini, b) enlightenment at Badh Gaya, c) first sermon at Sarnath, d) death at Kushinagara.

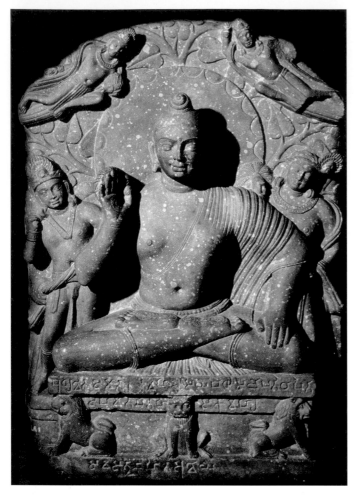

1-11 Buddha seated on lion throne, from Mathura, India, second century CE. Red sandstone, 2′ 3½″ high. Archaeological Museum, Muttra.

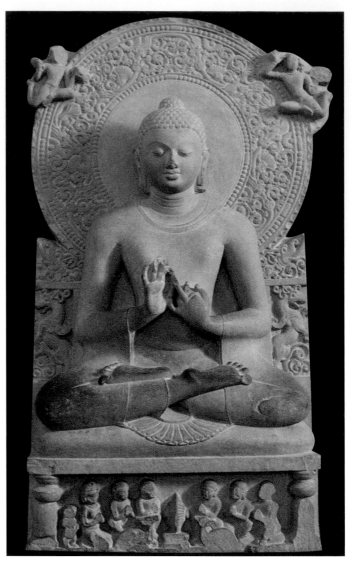

1-12 Seated Buddha preaching first sermon, from Sarnath, India, second half of fifth century. Tan sandstone, 5′ 3″ high. Archaeological Museum, Sarnath.

BUDDHIST IMAGERY IN MATHURA Contemporary to the Gandharan sculptures, but stylistically distinct from them, are the Buddha images of Mathura (FIG. **1-11**). The Mathura statues are more closely linked to the Indian portrayals of *yakshas,* the male equivalents of the yakshis. Indian artists represented yakshas as robust, powerful males with broad shoulders and open, staring eyes. Mathura Buddhas, carved from red sandstone, retain these characteristics but wear a monk's robe (with right shoulder bare) and lack the jewelry and other signs of wealth of the yakshas. The robe appears almost transparent, revealing the full, fleshy body beneath. In our example, the Buddha sits in a yogic posture on a lion throne under the Bodhi tree, attended by fly-whisk bearers. He raises his right hand palm-out in the abhaya gesture, indicating to worshipers that they need have no fear. His hands and feet bear the mark of the dharma Wheel.

The Gupta and Post-Gupta Periods

Around 320* a new empire arose in north central India. The Gupta emperors chose Pataliputra as their capital, deliberately associating themselves with the prestige of the former Maurya Empire. The heyday of this dynasty was under Chandragupta II

----

* From this point on, all dates in this chapter are CE unless otherwise stated.

(r. 375–415), whose very name recalled the first Maurya emperor. The Guptas were great patrons of art and literature.

THE CLASSICAL BUDDHA STATUE Under the Guptas, artists formulated what became the canonical image of the Buddha, combining the Gandharan monastic robe covering both shoulders with the soft, full-bodied Buddha figures with clinging garments of Mathuran sculpture. These disparate styles beautifully merge in a fifth-century Buddha from Sarnath (FIG. **1-12**), whose smooth, unadorned surfaces conform to the Indian notion of perfect body form and emphasize the figure's spirituality. The Buddha's eyes are downcast in meditation, and he holds his hands in front of his body in the Wheel-turning gesture, preaching his first sermon, indicated by the tiny Wheel of the Law seen on its edge below the figure. Flanking the Wheel, two now partially broken deer symbolize the Deer Park at Sarnath. Buddha images such as this one became so popular that temples housing Buddha statues seem largely to have displaced the stupa as the norm in Buddhist sacred architecture.

THE CAVES OF AJANTA The new popularity of Buddha imagery may be seen in the interior of a chaitya hall (FIG. **1-13**) carved out of the mountainside at Ajanta, northeast of Bombay,

The Painted Caves of Ajanta

Art historians assume India had a rich painting tradition in ancient times, but because early Indian artists often used perishable materials, such as palm leaf and wood, and because of the tropical climate in much of India, nearly all early Indian painting has been lost. At Ajanta in the Deccan, however, paintings cover the walls, pillars, and ceilings of several caves datable to the second half of the fifth century. FIG. 1-14 reproduces a detail of one of the Ajanta murals.

To create these paintings, the artists first applied two layers of clay mixed with straw and other materials to the walls. They then added a third layer of fine white lime plaster. Unlike true *fresco* painting, common in the West, in which the painters apply colors

to the wet plaster, the Indian painters waited for the lime to dry. This method produces less durable results, and the Ajanta murals have suffered water damage over the centuries. The painters next outlined the figures in dark red and then painted in the details of faces, costumes, and jewelry. The colors used were water soluble and mostly produced from local minerals, including red and yellow ocher. Blue, used sparingly, came from costly lapis lazuli imported from Afghanistan. The last step was to polish the painted surface with a smooth stone.

The Ajanta caves provide a tantalizing glimpse of early Indian painting. Significant later examples of paintings in India are rare before the 13th century (see Chapter 2).

---

at about the same time a Gupta sculptor created the classic Sarnath seated Buddha. Ajanta had been the site of a small Buddhist monastery for centuries, but royal patrons of the local Vakataka dynasty, allied to the Guptas by marriage, added more than 20 new caves in the second half of the fifth century. The typological similarity of the fifth-century Ajanta chaitya halls to the earlier example at Karle (FIG. 1-8) is immediately evident and consistent with the conservative nature of religious architecture in all cultures. At Ajanta, however, sculptors carved a standing Buddha flanked by columns into the front of the stupa.

PAINTED BODHISATTVAS Ajanta is renowned above all because the caves retain much of their painted wall and ceiling

decoration (see "The Painted Caves of Ajanta," above). We illustrate a detail of one of the restored painted walls in cave 1 depicting the bodhisattva Padmapani (FIG. **1-14**) among a crowd of devotees, both princes and commoners. With long, dark hair hanging down below a jeweled crown, he stands holding his attribute, a blue lotus flower, in his right hand. The bodhisattva's face shows great compassion as he gazes downward at the actual worshipers passing through the shrine entrance on their way to

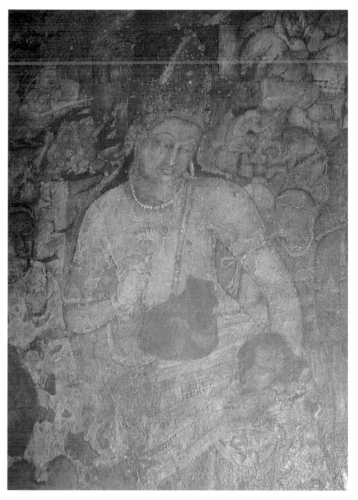

1-13 Interior of cave 19, Ajanta, India, second half of fifth century.

1-14 Bodhisattva Padmapani, wall painting in cave 1, Ajanta, India, second half of fifth century.

Hinduism and Hindu Iconography

Unlike Buddhism (and Christianity, Islam, and other religions), Hinduism recognizes no founder or great prophet. Hinduism also has no simple definition, but means "the religion of the Indians." Both "India" and "Hindu" have a common root in the name of the Indus River. The actual practices and beliefs of Hindus vary tremendously, but the literary origins of Hinduism can be traced to the Vedic period, and some aspects of Hindu practice seem already to have been present in the Indus Civilization of the third millennium BCE. Ritual sacrifice by Brahmin priests is central to Hinduism, as it was to the Aryans. The goal of sacrifice is to please a deity in order to achieve release (*moksha,* liberation) from the endless cycle of birth, death, and rebirth (*samsara*) and become one with the universal spirit.

Not only is Hinduism a religion of many gods, but the Hindu deities have various natures and take many forms. This multiplicity suggests the all-pervasive nature of the Hindu gods. The three most important deities are the gods Shiva and Vishnu and the goddess Devi. Each of the three major sects of Hinduism today considers one of these three to be supreme—Shiva in Shaivism, Vishnu in Vaishnavism, and Devi in Shaktism. (*Shakti* is the female creative force.)

Shiva (FIGS. 1-16, 1-17, and 1-24) is the Destroyer, but, consistent with the multiplicity of Hindu belief, he is also a regenerative force and, in the latter role, can be represented in the form of a *linga* (a phallus or cosmic pillar). When Shiva appears in human form in Hindu art, he frequently has multiple limbs and heads, signs of his superhuman nature. He often has matted locks piled

on top of his head, crowned by a crescent moon. Sometimes he wears a serpent scarf and has a third eye on his forehead (the emblem of his all-seeing nature). Shiva rides the bull *Nandi* (FIG. 1-16) and often carries a *trident,* a three-pronged pitchfork. His son is the elephant-headed *Ganesha* (FIG. 1-16).

Vishnu (FIGS. 1-19 and 1-28) is the Preserver of the Universe. Artists frequently portray him with four arms holding various attributes, including a conch-shell trumpet and discus. He sometimes reclines on a serpent floating on the waters of the cosmic sea. When the evil forces of the universe become too strong, he descends to earth to restore balance and assumes different forms (*avatars,* or incarnations), including a boar (FIG. 1-15), fish, and tortoise, as well as *Krishna,* the divine lover (FIG. 2-6), and even the Buddha himself.

Devi is the Great Goddess who takes many forms and has many names. Hindus worship her alone or as a consort of male gods (*Parvati* or *Uma,* wife of Shiva; *Lakshmi,* wife of Vishnu), as well as *Radha,* lover of Krishna (FIG. 2-6). She has both benign and horrific forms; she both creates and destroys. In one manifestation, she is *Durga,* a multiarmed goddess who rides or is accompanied by a lion.

The stationary images of deities in Hindu temples are often made of stone. Hindus periodically remove portable images of their gods, often of bronze (for example, FIG. 1-24), from the temple, particularly during festivals to enable many worshipers to take *darshan* (seeing the deity and being seen by the deity) at one time. In temples dedicated to Shiva, the stationary form is the linga.

the monumental rock-cut Buddha image housed in a cell at the back of the cave. The painter has rendered with finesse the sensuous form of the richly attired bodhisattva, gently *modeling* the figure with gradations of color and delicate highlights and shadows, especially evident in the face and neck.

BUDDHIST AND HINDU COEXISTENCE Buddhists and Hindus (and adherents of other faiths) practiced their religions side by side in India, often at the same site. The Hindu Vakataka king Harishena (r. 462–481) and members of his court were the sponsors of the new caves at the Buddhist monastery at Ajanta. Buddhism and Hinduism are not monotheistic religions, such as Judaism, Christianity, and Islam. Instead, Buddhists and Hindus approach the spiritual through many gods and varying paths, which permits mutually tolerated differences. In fact, in Hinduism, the Buddha was one of the 10 incarnations of Vishnu, one of the three principal Hindu deities (see "Hinduism and Hindu Iconography," above). More early Buddhist than Hindu art has survived in India, because the Buddhists constructed large monastic institutions with durable materials such as stone and brick. In the Gupta period, Hindu stone sculpture and architecture began to rival the great Buddhist monuments of South Asia.

VISHNU RESCUES THE EARTH The earliest Hindu cave temples are at Udayagiri, near Sanchi. They date to the early fifth century, some 600 years after the first Buddhist examples. Although the Udayagiri temples are architecturally simple and small, the site boasts monumental relief sculptures showing an already fully

developed religious iconography. One of these reliefs (FIG. **1-15**), carved in a shallow niche of rock, shows a 13-foot-tall Vishnu in his incarnation as the boar Varaha (see "Hinduism," above). The avatar has a human body and a boar's head. Vishnu assumed this form when he rescued the earth—personified as the goddess Bhudevi clinging to the boar's tusk—from being carried off to the bottom of the ocean. Vishnu stands with one foot resting on the coils of a snake king (identified by the multiple hoods behind his human head), who represents the conquered demon that attempted to abduct the earth. Rows of gods and sages form lines to witness the event.

The relief served a political as well as a religious purpose. The patron of the relief was a local king who honored the great Gupta king Chandragupta II in a nearby inscription dated to the year 401. Many scholars believe that the local king wanted viewers to see Chandragupta (he is known to have visited the site) as saving his kingdom by ridding it of its enemies in much the same way Varaha saved the earth. Thus, the Udayagiri sculptors, acting on their patron's wishes, clothed contemporary events in mythological guise.

DANCING MANY-ARMED SHIVA During the sixth century, the Huns brought down the Gupta empire, and various regional dynasties rose to power. In the Deccan, a plateau area in central India, the Chalukya kings ruled from their capital at Badami. There, Chalukya sculptors carved a series of reliefs in the walls of halls cut into the cliff above the city. One relief (FIG. **1-16**), datable to the late sixth century, shows Shiva, the second major Hindu

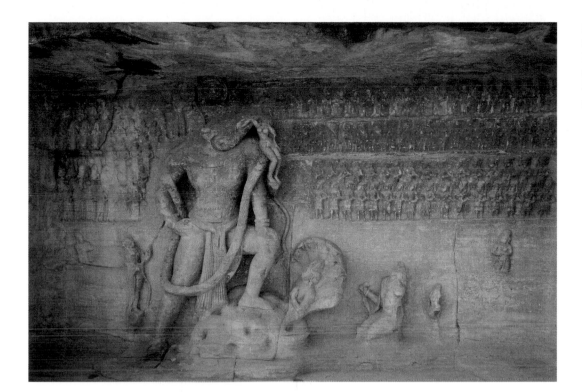

1-15 Boar avatar of Vishnu rescuing the earth, cave 5, Udayagiri, India, early fifth century. Relief approx. 22′ × 13′; Vishnu 12′ 8″ high.

male deity (see "Hinduism," page 12) dancing the cosmic dance, his 18 arms swinging rhythmically in an arc. Some of the hands hold objects, and others form prescribed mudras. At the right, a drummer (not visible in FIG. 1-16) accompanies the dance, while Shiva's son, the elephant-headed Ganesha, tentatively mimics his father. Nandi, Shiva's bull mount, stands at the left.

Artists often represented Hindu deities as part human and part animal (FIG. 1-15) or, as in the Badami relief, as figures with

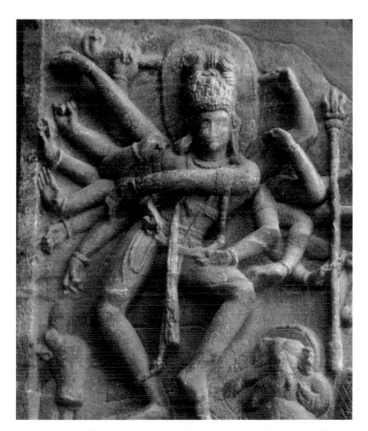

1-16 Dancing Shiva, rock-cut relief in cave temple, Badami, India, late sixth century.

multiple body parts. Such composite and multilimbed forms indicate that the subjects are not human but more-than-human gods with supernatural powers.

SHIVA WITH THREE FACES Another portrayal of Shiva as a superhuman being is found at a third Hindu cave site, on Elephanta, an island in Bombay's harbor named by early Portuguese colonizers who found a life-size stone elephant sculpture there. A king of the Kalachuri dynasty that took control of Elephanta in the sixth century may have commissioned the largest of the island's cave temples. Just inside the cave's west entrance is a shrine housing Shiva's linga, the god's emblem. Deep within the temple, in a niche once closed off with wooden doors, is a nearly 18-foot-high image of Shiva as Mahadeva (FIG. 1-17), the "Great God" or Lord of Lords. Mahadeva appears to emerge out of the depths of the cave as worshipers' eyes become accustomed to the darkness. This image of Shiva has three faces, each showing a different aspect of the deity. (A fourth, unseen at the back, is implied; the god has not emerged fully from the rock.) The central face expresses Shiva's quiet, balanced demeanor. The clean planes of the face contrast with the richness of the piled hair encrusted with jewels. The two side faces differ significantly. That on the right is female, with framing hair curls. The left face is a grimacing male with a curling mustache who wears a cobra as an earring. The female (Uma) indicates the creative aspect of Shiva. The fierce male (Bhairava) represents Shiva's destructive side. Shiva holds these two opposing forces in check, and the central face expresses their balance. The cyclic destruction and creation of the universe, which the side faces also symbolize, are part of Indian notions of time, matched by the cyclic pattern of death and rebirth (samsara).

VISHNU'S TOWER AT DEOGARH The excavated cave shrines just considered are characteristic of early Hindu religious architecture, but temples constructed using quarried stone became more important as Hinduism evolved over the centuries (see "Hindu Temples," page 14). As they did with the cave temples, the Hindus initially built rather small and simple temples but decorated them with narrative reliefs displaying a fully developed

Hindu Temples

The Hindu temple is the home of the gods on earth and the place where they make themselves visible to humans. At the core of all Hindu temples is the *garbha griha,* the "womb chamber," which houses images or symbols of the deity, for example Shiva's linga (see "Hinduism," page 12). Only the Brahmin priests can enter this inner sanctuary to make offerings to the gods. The worshipers can only stand at the threshold and behold the deity as manifest by its image. In the elaborate multiroomed temples of later Hindu architecture, the worshipers and priests progress through a series of ever more sacred spaces, usually on an east-west axis. Hindu priests and architects attached great importance to each temple's plan and sought to make it conform to the sacred geometric diagram *(mandala)* of the universe.

Architectural historians, following ancient Indian texts, divide Hindu temples into two major typological groups tied to geography. The most important distinguishing feature of the *northern,* or *Nagara,* style of temple (FIG. 1-22) is its beehivelike tower or *shikhara* ("mountain peak"), capped by an *amalaka,* a ribbed cushionlike form, derived from the shape of the amala fruit (believed to have medicinal powers). Amalakas appear on the corners of the lower levels of the shikhara too. Northern temples also have smaller towerlike roofs over the halls *(mandapas)* leading to the garbha griha.

Southern, or *Dravida,* temples (FIG. 1-21) can easily be recognized by the flat roofs of their pillared mandapas and by their shorter towered shrines, called *vimanas,* which lack the curved profile of their Nagara counterparts and resemble multilevel pyramids.

iconography. The Vishnu Temple at Deogarh (FIG. **1-18**) in north central India, erected in the early sixth century, is among the first Hindu temples constructed with stone blocks. A simple square building on a stone *plinth* (base), it has an elaborately decorated doorway on the main *facade* and a relief in a niche on each of the

other three sides. Sculpted guardians and mithuna couples protect the doorway at Deogarh, because it is the transition point between the dangerous outside and the sacred interior, the garbha griha. A small shrine once stood at each corner of the plinth. The temple culminates in a tower (poorly preserved).

THE CREATION OF THE UNIVERSE The reliefs in the three niches of the Deogarh temple depict important episodes in the saga of Vishnu. The one we reproduce (FIG. **1-19**) shows Vishnu asleep on the coils of the giant serpent Ananta, whose multiple heads form a kind of umbrella around the god's face. While Lakshmi massages her husband's legs (he has cramps as he gives birth), the four-armed Vishnu dreams the universe into reality. A lotus plant (said

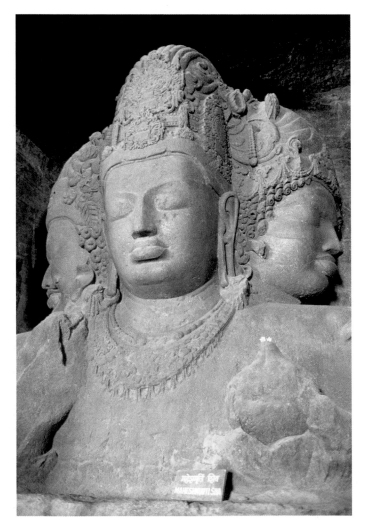

1-17 Shiva as Mahadeva, cave 1, Elephanta, India, ca. 550–575. Basalt, Shiva 17′ 10″ high.

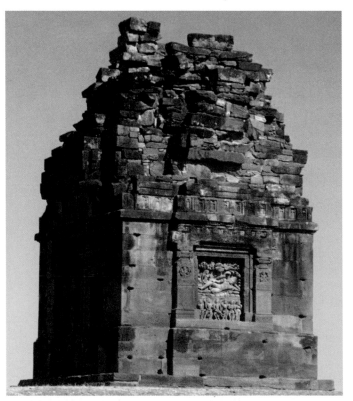

1-18 Vishnu Temple, Deogarh, India, early sixth century.

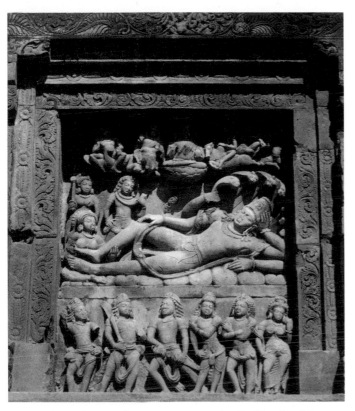

1-19 Vishnu asleep on the serpent Ananta, detail of facade of the Vishnu Temple, Deogarh, India, early sixth century.

to have grown out of Vishnu's navel) supports the four-headed Hindu god of creation, Brahma. Flanking him are other important Hindu divinities, including Shiva on his bull. Below are six figures. The four at the right are personifications of Vishnu's various powers. They will defeat the two armed demons at the left. The sculptor carved all the figures in the classic Gupta style, with smooth bodies and clinging garments (compare FIG. 1-12).

Early Medieval Period

During the several centuries corresponding to the early medieval period in Europe, the early Islamic period in the Near East (see Chapter 7), the Tang and Song dynasties in China (see Chapter 3), and the Hakuho, Nara, and Heian periods in Japan (see Chapter 5), regional dynasties ruled parts of India. Among the most important of these kingdoms were the Palas and Chandellas in northern India and the Pallavas and Cholas in the south. Whereas Buddhism spread rapidly throughout eastern Asia, in medieval India it gradually declined, and the various local kings vied with one another to erect glorious shrines to the Hindu gods.

TEMPLES CARVED FROM BOULDERS In addition to cave temples and masonry temples, Indian architects created a third type of monument: freestanding temples carved out of rocky outcroppings. Such sculpted temples are rare. Some of the earliest and most impressive of these monolithic temples (FIG. 1-20) are

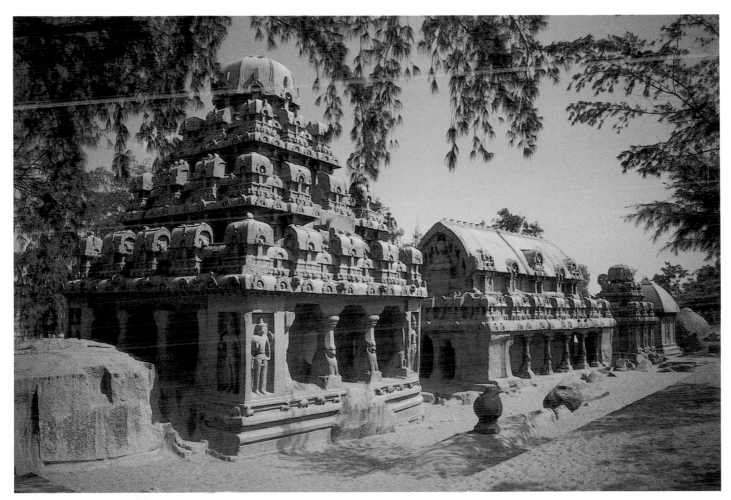

1-20 Rock-cut temples, Mamallapuram, India, second half of seventh century. From *left* to *right*: Dharmaraja, Bhima, Arjuna, and Draupadi rathas.

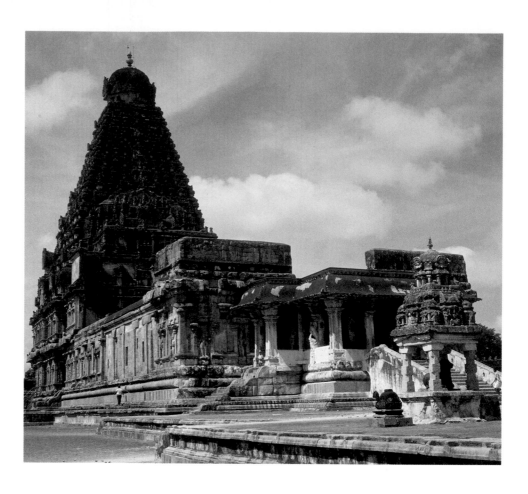

1-21 Rajarajeshvara Temple, Thanjavur, India, ca. 1010.

at Mamallapuram, south of Madras on the Bay of Bengal, where they are called *rathas,* or "chariots" (that is, vehicles of the gods). In the late seventh century, the Pallava dynasty had five rathas carved out of a single huge granite boulder jutting out from the sand. The group is of special interest because it illustrates the variety of temple forms at this period, based on earlier wooden structures, before a standard masonry type of temple became the rule in southern India. The largest Mamallapuram ratha, the Dharmaraja (in the foreground), dedicated to Shiva, is an early example of the typical southern-style temple with stepped-pyramid vimana (see "Hindu Temples," page 14). The tower ascends in pronounced tiers of cornices decorated with miniature shrines. The lower walls include carved columns and figures of deities inside niches. The Bhima ratha to the right, dedicated to Vishnu, has a rectangular plan and a rounded roof; the next ratha, the Arjuna, is a smaller example of the southern Indian type. At the end of the row sits the very small Draupadi ratha, which was modeled on a thatched hut and is dedicated to Durga, a form of the goddess Devi. The two largest temples were never finished.

THE APOGEE OF THE SOUTHERN TEMPLE Under the Cholas, whose territories extended into part of Sri Lanka and even Java, architects constructed temples of unprecedented size and grandeur in the southern Indian tradition. The Rajarajeshvara Temple at Thanjavur (FIG. **1-21**), dedicated in 1010 to Shiva as the lord of Rajaraja, was the largest and tallest temple (210 feet high) in India at its time. The temple stands inside a walled precinct. It consists of a stairway leading to two flat-roofed mandapas, the larger one having 36 pillars, and to the garbha griha in the base of the enormous pyramidal vimana that is as much an emblem of the Cholas' secular power as of their devotion to Shiva. On the exterior walls of the lower stories are numerous reliefs in niches depicting the god in his various forms.

THE HINDU TEMPLE AS MOUNTAIN At the same time the Cholas were building the Rajarajeshvara Temple at Thanjavur in the south, the Chandella dynasty was constructing temples—in northern style—at Khajuraho. The Vishvanatha Temple (FIG. **1-22**) is one of more than 20 large and elaborate temples at that site. Vishvanatha ("Lord of the Universe") is another of the many names for Shiva. Dedicated in 1002, the structure has three towers over the mandapas, each rising higher than the preceding one, leading to the tallest tower at the rear, in much the same way the foothills of the Himalayas, Shiva's home, rise to meet their highest peak. The mountain symbolism applies to the interior of the Vishvanatha Temple as well. Under the tallest of the towers, the shikhara, is the garbha griha, the small and dark inner sanctuary chamber, like a cave, which houses the image of the deity. Thus, temples such as the Vishvanatha symbolize constructed mountains with caves, comparable to the actual cave temples at Elephanta and other Indian sites. In all cases, the deity manifests himself or herself within the cave and takes various forms in sculptures. The temple mountains, however, are not intended to appear natural but rather are perfect mountains designed using ideal mathematical proportions.

THE MITHUNAS OF KHAJURAHO The reliefs of the Rajarajeshvara Temple at Thanjavur (FIG. 1-21) are typical of southern temple decoration, which is generally limited to images of deities. The exterior walls of Khajuraho's Vishvanatha Temple are equally typical of northern temples in the profusion of sculptures depicting not only gods but mortals, especially pairs of men and women (mithunas) embracing or engaged in sexual intercourse in an extraordinary range of positions (FIG. **1-23**). The use of seminude yakshis and amorous couples as motifs on religious buildings in India has a very long history, going back to the earliest architectural traditions, both Hindu and Buddhist (Sanchi, FIG. 1-7, and

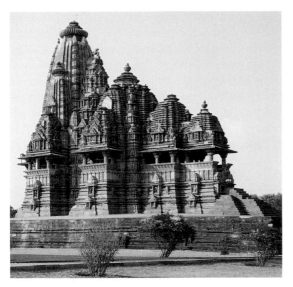

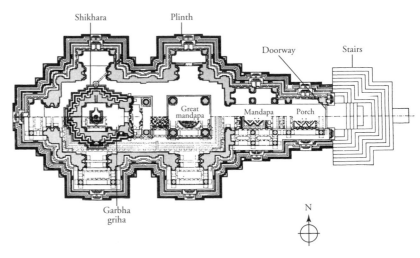

1-22 Vishvanatha Temple, Khajuraho, India, ca. 1000. (View looking northwest and plan).

Karle). As in the earlier examples already discussed, the erotic sculptures of Khajuraho suggest fertility and the propagation of life and serve as auspicious protectors of the sacred precinct.

A PORTABLE BRONZE SHIVA We conclude our survey of early Indian art with an object quite different in function from anything considered thus far. The statuette of Shiva (FIG. **1-24**) in the Naltunai Ishvaram Temple in Punjai, cast in solid bronze around 1000, recalls the sixth-century relief in the Badami cave (FIG. 1-16). It is one of many examples of portable images of deities created under the Chola kings, the builders of the towering Rajarajeshvara Temple at Thanjavur (FIG. 1-21). Here, Shiva dances as Nataraja ("Lord of the Dance") by balancing on one leg atop a dwarf representing ignorance, which the god stamps out as he dances. Shiva extends all four arms, two of them touching the flaming *nimbus* (light of glory) encircling him. These two upper

hands also hold a small drum (at right) and a flame (at left). Shiva creates the universe to the drumbeat's rhythm, while the small fire represents destruction. His lower left hand points to his upraised foot, indicating the foot as the place where devotees can find refuge and enlightenment. Shiva's lower right hand, raised in the fear-not gesture, tells worshipers to come forward without fear. As Shiva spins, his matted hair comes loose and spreads like a fan on both sides of his head.

This Shiva Nataraja is a movable image (the holes on the base held poles for carrying the statuette), but even when stationary, it would not appear as it does in an art history book. Rather, when Hindus worship the Shiva Nataraja, they dress the image, cover it with jewels, and garland it with flowers. The only bronze part visible is the face, marked with colored powders and scented pastes. Considered the embodiment of the deity, the image is not a symbol of the god but the god itself. All must treat the god/image as a

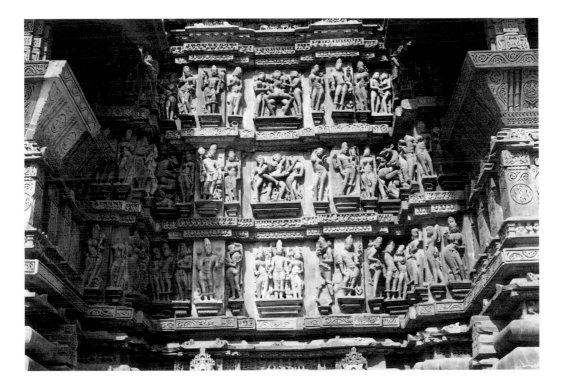

1-23 Sculptures on temple wall, Vishvanatha Temple, Khajuraho, India, ca. 1000.

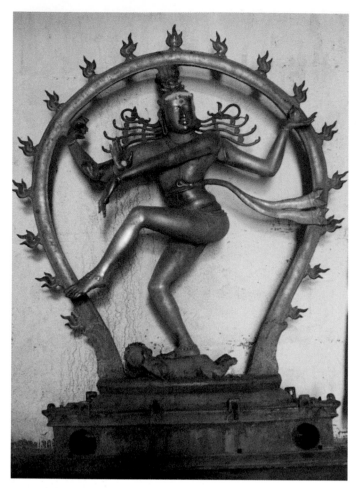

1-24 Shiva as Nataraja, bronze in the Naltunai Ishvaram Temple, Punjai, India, ca. 1000.

living being. Worship of the deity involves taking care of him as if he were an honored person. Bathed, clothed, given foods to eat, and taken for outings, the image also receives such gifts as songs, lights (lit oil lamps), good smells (incense), and flowers—all things he can enjoy through the senses. The food given to the god is particularly important, as he eats the "essence," leaving the remainder for the worshiper. The food is then *prasada* (grace), sacred because it came in contact with the divine. In an especially religious household, the deity resides as an image and receives the food for each meal before the family eats. When the god resides in a temple, it is then the duty of the priests to feed, clothe, and take care of him.

The Chola dynasty ended in the 13th century, a time of political, religious, and cultural change in South Asia. At this point, Buddhism survived in only some areas of India. It soon died out completely there, although the late form of northern Indian Buddhism continued in Tibet and Nepal. At the same time, Islam, which had arrived in India as early as the eighth century, became a potent political force with the establishment of the Delhi Sultanate in 1206. Hindu and Islamic art assumed preeminent roles in India in the 13th century (see Chapter 2).

SOUTHEAST ASIA

For scholars of earlier generations, much of the art of Southeast Asia was merely an extension of Indian civilization. Because the Indian character of many Southeast Asian monuments was readily apparent, some researchers hypothesized that Indian artists

had constructed and decorated them and that Indians had colonized Southeast Asia. Today, historians have concluded that such colonization did not occur. The cultural transfer during the first millennium CE was peaceful and nonimperialistic. It appears to have developed almost as a by-product of trade.

In the early centuries CE, extensive trade took place among Rome, India, and China, their ships passing Southeast Asia on the monsoon winds. The tribal chieftains of Southeast Asia quickly saw an opportunity to participate, mainly with their own forest products, such as aromatic woods, bird feathers, and spices. Accompanying the trade goods from India were Sanskrit, Buddhism, and Hinduism—and Buddhist and Hindu art. The Southeast Asian chiefs initially used the transferred elements as a sort of "cultural vocabulary" to compete with one another and to participate in an Indian world. But the Southeast Asian peoples soon modified the Indian cultural material, including the art, to make it their own. Art historians now recognize Southeast Asian art and architecture as a distinctive and important tradition.

Sri Lanka

Sri Lanka (formerly Ceylon) is an island located at the very tip of the Indian subcontinent. Theravada Buddhism, the oldest form of Buddhism, stressing worship of the historical Buddha, Shakyamuni Buddha (see "Buddhism," page 5), arrived in Sri Lanka as early as the third century BCE. From there it spread to other parts of Southeast Asia. With the demise of Buddhism in India in about the 13th century, Sri Lanka now has the longest-lived Buddhist tradition in the world.

GAL VIHARA'S GIANT BUDDHA One of the largest sculptures in Southeast Asia is the 46-foot-long recumbent Buddha (FIG. **1-25**) carved out of a rocky outcropping at Gal Vihara in the 11th or 12th century. To the left of the Buddha, much smaller in scale, stands his cousin and chief disciple, Ananda, arms crossed, mourning Shakyamuni's death. Although more than half a millennium later in date, the Sri Lankan representation of the Buddha's parinirvana reveals its sculptor's debt to the classic Gupta sculptures of India, with their clinging garments, rounded faces, and distinctive renditions of hair (compare FIG. 1-12). Other Southeast Asian monuments, in contrast, exhibit a marked independence from Indian models.

Java

BOROBUDUR, COSMIC MOUNTAIN On the island of Java, part of the modern nation of Indonesia, the period from the 8th to the 10th centuries witnessed the erection of both Hindu and Buddhist monuments. Borobudur (FIG. **1-26**), a Buddhist monument unique in both form and meaning, is the most impressive. Colossal in size, Borobudur measures about 400 feet per side at the base and about 98 feet tall. Built over a small hill on nine terraces accessed by four stairways aligned with the cardinal points, the structure contains literally millions of blocks of volcanic stone. Visitors ascending the massive monument on their way to the summit encounter more than 500 life-size Buddha images, at least 1,000 relief panels, and some 1,500 stupas of various sizes.

Scholars debate the intended meaning of Borobudur. Most think the structure is a constructed cosmic mountain, a three-dimensional mandala where worshipers pass through various realms on their way to ultimate enlightenment. As they

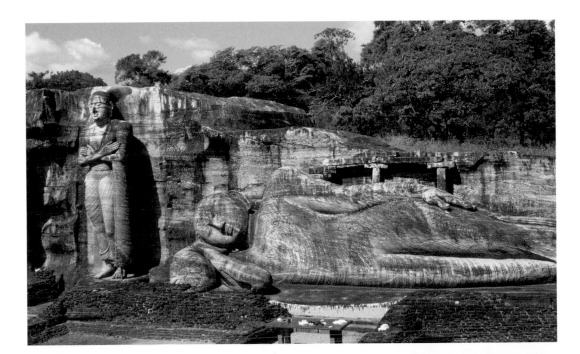

1-25 Death of the Buddha (Parinirvana), Gal Vihara, near Polonnaruwa, Sri Lanka, 11th to 12th century. Granulite, Buddha approx. 46′ long.

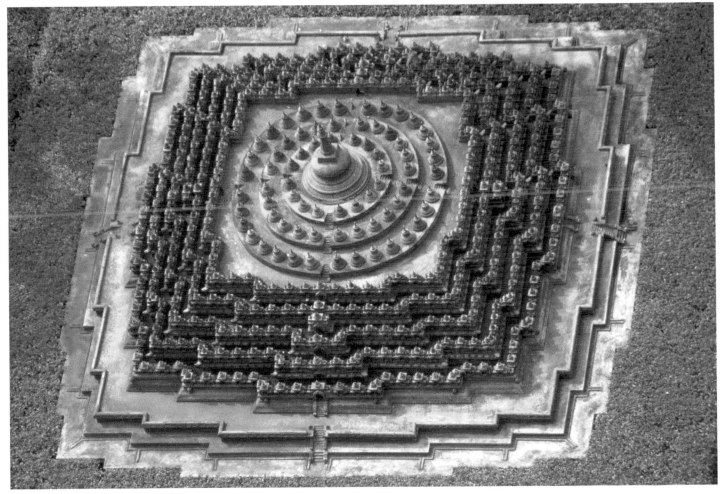

1-26 Borobudur, Java, Indonesia, ca. 800.

circumambulate Borobudur, pilgrims first see reliefs illustrating the karmic effects of various kinds of human behavior, then reliefs depicting jatakas of the Buddha's earlier lives, and, further up, events from the life of Shakyamuni. On the circular terraces near the summit, each stupa is hollow and houses a statue of the seated Buddha, who has achieved spiritual enlightenment and preaches using the wheel-turning mudra. At the very top is the largest, sealed stupa. It may once have contained another Buddha image, but some think it was left empty to symbolize the formlessness of true enlightenment. Although scholars have interpreted the iconographic program in different ways, all agree on two essential points: the dependence of Borobudur on Indian art, literature, and religion, and the fact that nothing comparable exists in India itself. Borobudur's sophistication, complexity, and originality underline how completely Southeast Asians had absorbed, rethought, and reformulated Indian religion and art by 800.

Cambodia

In 802, at about the same time the Javanese built Borobudur, the Khmer King Jayavarman II (r. 802–850) founded the Angkor dynasty, which ruled Cambodia for the next 400 years and sponsored the construction of hundreds of monuments. For at least two centuries before the founding of Angkor, the Khmer (the predominant ethnic group in Cambodia) produced Indian-related sculpture of exceptional quality. Images of Vishnu were particularly important during the pre-Angkorian period.

HARIHARA: SHIVA-VISHNU A statue (FIG. 1-27) from Prasat Andet shows Vishnu in his manifestation as Harihara (Shiva-Vishnu). To represent Harihara, the sculptor divided the statue vertically, with Shiva on the god's right side, Vishnu on his left. The tall headgear reflects the division most clearly. The Shiva half, embellished with the winding locks of an ascetic, contrasts with the kingly Vishnu's plain miter. Attributes (now lost) held in the four hands also helped differentiate the two sides. Stylistically, the Cambodian statue, like the Sri Lankan parinirvana group (FIG. 1-25), derives from Indian sculptures of Gupta style (FIG. 1-12). But unlike almost all stone sculpture in India, carved in relief on *steles* (vertical stone slabs), this Khmer image is in the round. The Harihara's broken arms and ankles vividly attest to the vulnerability of this format. The Khmer sculptors, however, wanted viewers to see their statues from all sides in the center of the garbha grihas of brick temples.

VISHNU ON THE COSMIC OCEAN The Khmer kings were exceedingly powerful and possessed enormous wealth. A now fragmentary statue portraying Vishnu lying on the cosmic ocean (FIG. 1-28) testifies to both the luxurious nature of much Khmer art and to the mastery of Khmer bronze casters. The surviving portion is about 8 feet long. In complete form, at well over 20 feet long, the Vishnu statue was among the largest bronzes of the ancient and medieval worlds, surpassed only by such lost wonders as the gold-and-ivory statue of Athena in the Parthenon in Athens and the 120-foot-tall bronze colossus of Emperor Nero in Rome. Originally, gold and silver inlays and jewels embellished the image, and the god wore a separate miter on his head. The subject of the gigantic statue is the same as that carved in stone on the early Vishnu temple at Deogarh (FIG. 1-19). Vishnu lies asleep on the cosmic ocean at the moment of the creation of the universe. In the myth, a lotus stem grows from Vishnu's navel, its flower supporting Brahma, the creator god. In this statue, Vishnu had a waterspout emerging from his navel, indicating his ability not only to protect the earth and create Brahma but also to create the waters. In fact, the statue was displayed in an island temple in the western *baray* (reservoir) of Angkor.

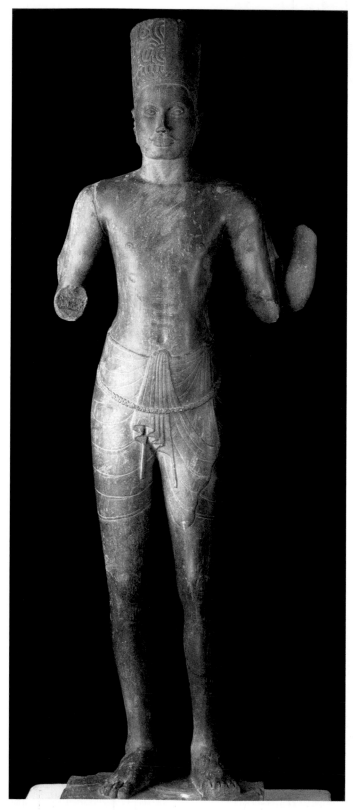

1-27 Harihara, from Prasat Andet, Cambodia, early seventh century. Stone, 6′ 3″ high. National Museum, Phnom Penh.

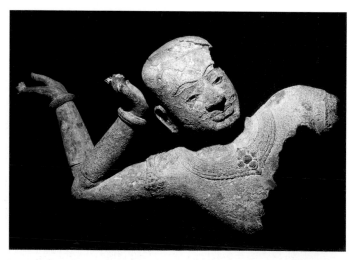

1-28 Vishnu lying on the cosmic ocean, from Mebon temple on island in western baray, Angkor, Cambodia, 11th century. Bronze, approx. 8′ long.

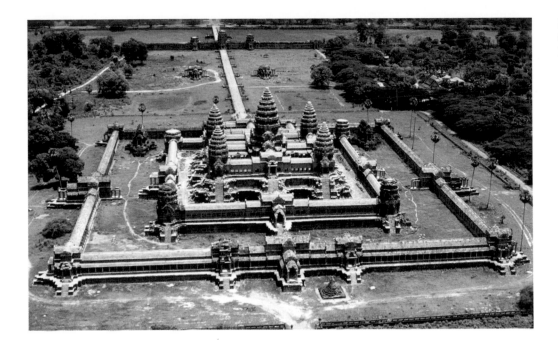

KHMER KINGSHIP For more than four centuries, successive kings worked on the construction of the site of Angkor. Founded by Indravarman (r. 877–889), Angkor is an engineering marvel, a grand complex of temples and palaces within a rectangular grid of canals and reservoirs fed by local rivers. Each of the Khmer kings built a temple mountain at Angkor and installed his personal god—Shiva, Vishnu, or the Buddha—on top. He named the image/god with part of his own royal name, implying that the king was a part or manifestation of the deity. When the king died, the Khmer believed that the god reabsorbed him, because he had been the earthly portion of the deity during his lifetime, so they worshiped the king's image posthumously as the god. This concept of kingship approaches an actual deification of the human ruler, familiar in many other societies.

SURYAVARMAN II AND ANGKOR WAT Of all the monuments the Khmer kings erected, Angkor Wat (FIG. 1-29) is the most spectacular. Built by Suryavarman II (r. 1113–1150), it is the largest of the many Khmer temple complexes. Angkor Wat rises from a huge rectangle of land delineated by a moat measuring about 5,000 × 4,000 feet. Like the other Khmer temples, its purpose was to associate the king with his personal god, in this case Vishnu. The centerpiece of the complex is a tall stepped tower surrounded by four smaller towers connected by covered galleries. The five towers symbolize the five peaks of Mount Meru, the sacred mountain at the center of the universe. Two more circuit walls with galleries, towers, and gates enclose the central block. Thus, as one progresses inward through the complex, the towers rise ever higher, like the towers of the Vishvanatha Temple at Khajuraho (FIG. 1-22), but in a more complex sequence and on a much grander scale.

Throughout Angkor Wat, stone reliefs glorify both Vishnu in his various avatars and Suryavarman II. The example we illustrate (FIG. 1-30), on the inner wall of the lowest gallery, shows the king holding court. Suryavarman II sits on an elaborate wooden throne, its bronze legs rising as cobra heads. Kneeling retainers,

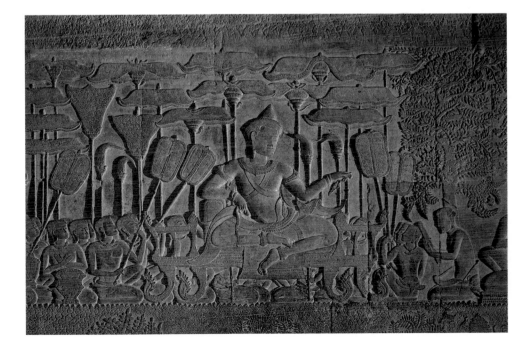

1-30 King Suryavarman II holding court, lowest gallery, south side, Angkor Wat, Angkor, Cambodia, first half of 12th century. Stone.

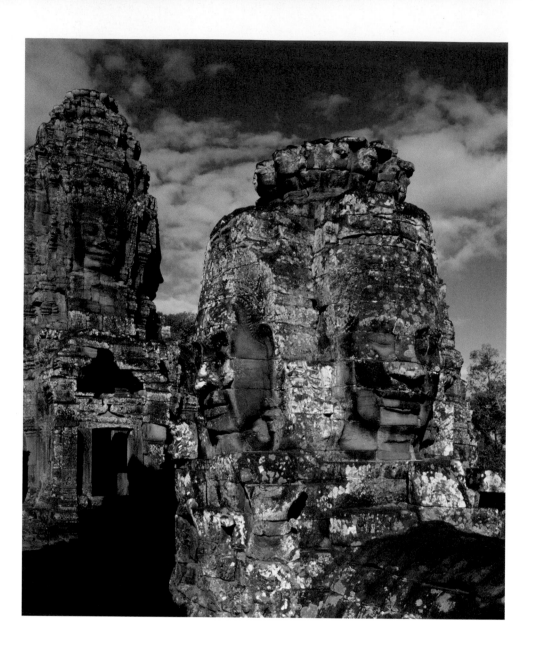

1-31 Bayon, Angkor Thom, Cambodia, ca. 1200.

smaller than the king because they are lesser figures in the Khmer hierarchy, hold a forest of umbrellas and fans, emblems of Suryavarman's exalted rank. In the reliefs of Angkor Wat, religion and politics are united.

JAYAVARMAN VII AND THE BAYON Jayavarman VII (r. 1181–1219), Suryavarman II's son, ruled over much of mainland Southeast Asia and built more during his reign than all the Khmer kings preceding him combined. His most important temple, the Bayon, is a complicated monument constructed with unique circular terraces surmounted by towers carved with giant faces (FIG. **1-31**). Jayavarman turned to Buddhism from the Hinduism embraced by the earlier Khmer rulers, but adapted Buddhism so that the Buddha and the bodhisattva Lokeshvara ("Lord of the World") were seen as divine prototypes of the king, in the Khmer tradition. The faces on the Bayon towers perhaps portray Lokeshvara, intended to indicate the watchful compassion emanating in all directions from the capital. Other researchers have proposed that the faces depict Jayavarman himself. Jayavarman's great experiment in religion and art was short-lived, but it also marked the point of change in Southeast Asia when Theravada Buddhism began to dominate most of the mainland.

CONCLUSION

The Indian subcontinent was the birthplace of Buddhism and Hinduism as well as one of the world's earliest civilizations. Third-millennium BCE sites in the Indus Valley feature monumental architecture and sophisticated water supply and sewage systems. Surviving art objects are few and small, however. The first large-scale sculpture and the first temples in South Asia appeared in connection with the spread of Buddhism at the end of the first millennium BCE. Hindu art and architecture emerged in the mid-first millennium CE. Hindu temples, with their distinctive beehive or pyramidal towers, often covered with elaborate relief sculptures, were built throughout the subcontinent. From India, Buddhist and Hindu art and architecture were exported throughout Southeast Asia.

During the first to fourth centuries, Buddhism also traveled to other parts of Asia—to China, Korea, and Japan. Although the artistic traditions in these countries differ greatly from one another, they share, along with Southeast Asia, a tradition of Buddhist art and an ultimate tie with India. Chapters 3 and 5 trace the changes Buddhist art underwent in East Asia, along with the region's other rich artistic traditions.

	INDIA AND PAKISTAN	SOUTHEAST ASIA		

INDUS CIVILIZATION

2600 BCE

1

1500 BCE

VEDIC AND UPANISHADIC PERIODS

| ARYANS COMPILE FIRST OF FOUR *Vedas*, CA. 1500 BCE
| *Upanishads* COMPOSED, CA. 800–500 BCE
| SIDDHARTHA GAUTAMA, SHAKYAMUNI BUDDHA, CA. 563–483 BCE
| ALEXANDER THE GREAT REACHES INDUS RIVER, 326 BCE

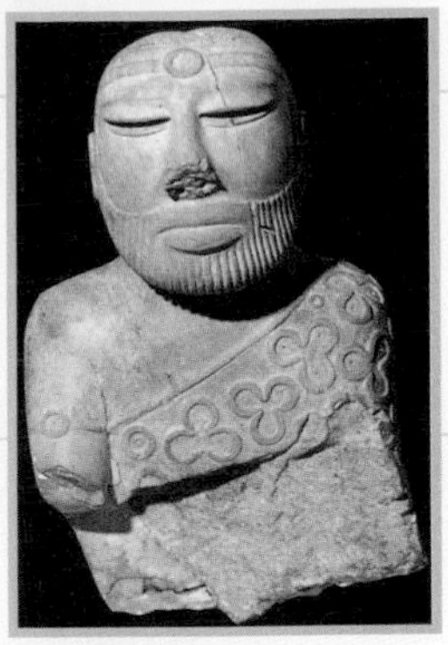

1 Robed male figure, Mohenjo-daro, Pakistan, ca. 2600–1900 BCE

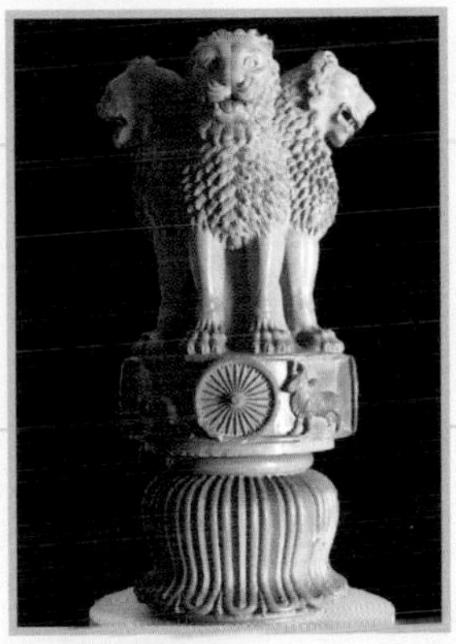

MAURYA DYNASTY

323 BCE

| CHANDRAGUPTA MAURYA, R. 323–298 BCE
2 | ASHOKA, MAURYA KING, R. 272–231 BCE

185 BCE

SHUNGA, ANDHRA, AND KUSHAN DYNASTIES

| SHUNGA DYNASTY, CENTRAL INDIA, 185–72 BCE
| ANDHRA DYNASTY, SOUTHERN INDIA, CA. 50–320 CE
| KUSHAN DYNASTY, NORTHERN INDIA, CA. 50–320 CE
| KANISHKA, KUSHAN KING, R. 78–144 CE

2 Lion capital of Ashoka, Sarnath, India, ca. 250 BCE

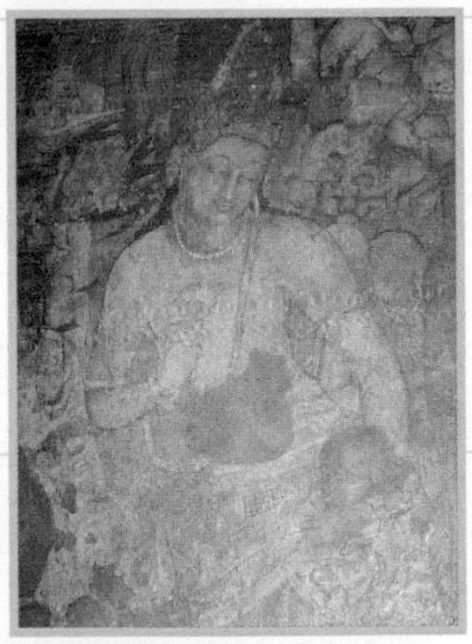

GUPTA AND POST-GUPTA PERIODS

320 CE

| CHANDRAGUPTA II, GUPTA KING, R. 375–415
3 | HARISHENA, VAKATAKA KING, R. 462–481
| CHALUKYA DYNASTY, CENTRAL INDIA, 543–743 AND CA. 975–1189
| PALLAVA DYNASTY, SOUTHERN INDIA, CA. 550–728

647

| PALA AND SENA DYNASTIES, NORTHERN INDIA, CA. 700–1200
| CHANDELLA DYNASTY, NORTHERN INDIA, 800–1308

3 Bodhisattva Padmapani, Ajanta, India, second half of fifth century

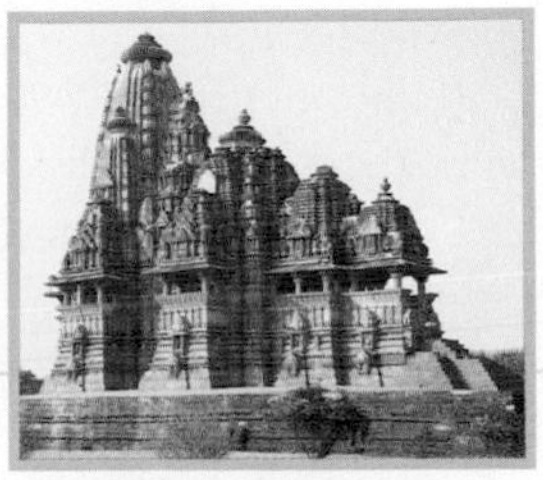

MEDIEVAL PERIOD — ANGKOR DYNASTY, CAMBODIA

802

| JAYAVARMAN II, ANGKOR KING, R. 802–850
| INDRAVARMAN, ANGKOR KING, R. 877–889
4 | CHOLA DYNASTY, SOUTHERN INDIA, CA. 907–1279
| SURYAVARMAN II, ANGKOR KING, R. 1113–1150

1200

| MUSLIM SULTANATE, DELHI, 1206

4 Vishvanatha Temple, Khajuraho, India, ca. 1000

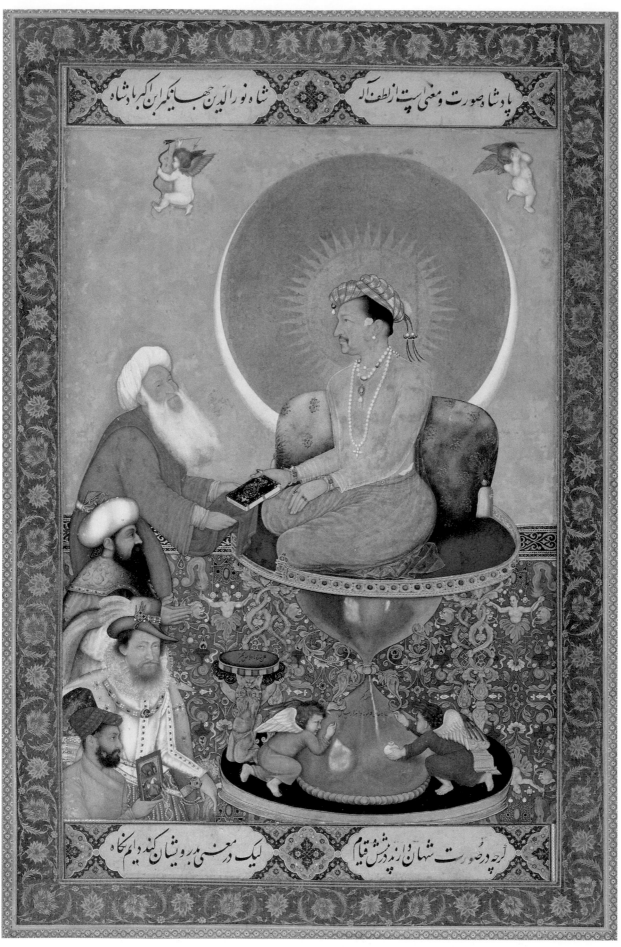

BICHITR, *Jahangir Preferring a Sufi Shaykh to Kings,* ca. 1615–1618. Opaque watercolor on paper, 1′ 6⅞″ × 1′ 1″. Freer Gallery of Art, Washington, D.C.

2

SULTANS, KINGS, EMPERORS, AND COLONISTS

THE ART OF SOUTH AND SOUTHEAST ASIA AFTER 1200

Arab armies first appeared in South Asia—at Sind (Pakistan)—in 712 (MAP **2-1**). With them came Islam, the new religion that had already spread with astonishing speed from the Arabian peninsula to Syria, Iraq, Iran, Egypt, North Africa, and even southern Spain (see Chapter 7). At first, the Muslims established trading settlements but did not press deeper into the subcontinent. At the Battle of Tarain in 1192, however, Muhammad of Ghor (Afghanistan) defeated the armies of a confederation of Indian states. The Ghorids and other Islamic rulers gradually transformed Indian society, religion, and art.

INDIA

Sultanate of Delhi (1206–1526)

Qutb al-Din Aybak, Muhammad of Ghor's general, established the Sultanate of Delhi in 1206 and, on his death in 1211, passed power on to his son. Iltutmish (r. 1211–1236) extended Ghorid rule across northern India.

THE WORLD'S TALLEST MINARET To mark the triumph of Islam, Qutb al-Din Aybak built a great *congregational mosque* (see "The Mosque," Chapter 7, page 119) at Delhi, in part with pillars taken from Hindu and other temples he demolished. He named Delhi's first mosque the Quwwat al-Islam, or Might of Islam, Mosque. During the course of the next century, as the Islamic population of Delhi grew, the sultans enlarged the mosque to more than triple its original size. Construction of the mosque's

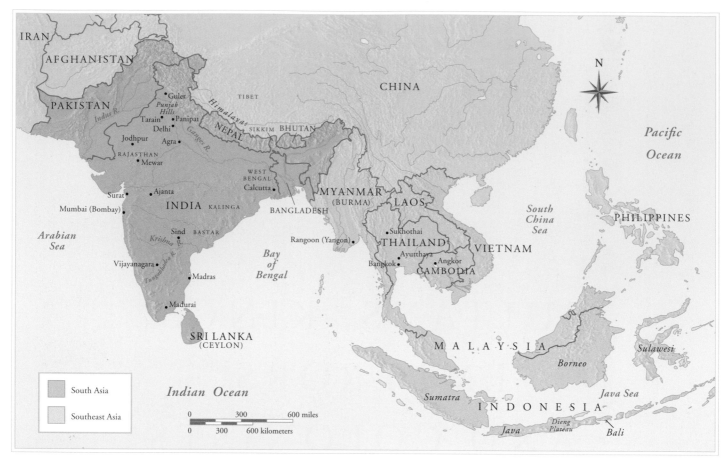

MAP 2-1 Later sites in South and Southeast Asia.

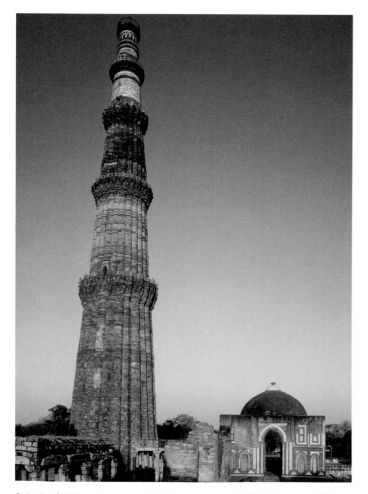

2-1 Qutb Minar, begun early 13th century, and Alai Darvaza, 1311, Delhi, India.

238-foot sandstone *minaret,* the Qutb Minar (FIG. **2-1,** *left*), began under Iltutmish. It is the tallest extant minaret in the world—too tall, in fact, to serve the principal function of a minaret, to provide a platform from which to call the Islamic faithful to prayer. Rather it is a towering monument to the victory of Islam, engraved with inscriptions in Arabic and Persian proclaiming that the minaret casts the shadow of Allah over the conquered Hindu city. Added in 1311, the Alai Darvaza, the entrance pavilion (FIG. 2-1, *right*), is a mix of architectural traditions, combining Islamic pointed *arches,* decorative grills over the windows, and a hemispherical dome, with a crowning *finial* on the dome that recalls Hindu temples of the Dravida type (see "Hindu Temples," Chapter 1, page 14).

Vijayanagar Dynasty (1336–1565)

HINDU KINGS OF THE SOUTH While Muslim sultans from Central Asia ruled much of northern India from Delhi, Hindu dynasts controlled most of the Deccan and the South. The most powerful of the Hindu kingdoms of the era was the Vijayanagar. Established in 1336 by Harihara, a local king, the Vijayanagar Empire takes its name from Vijayanagara ("City of Victory") on the Tungabhadra River. Under the patronage of the royal family, Vijayanagara, located at the junction of several trade routes through Asia, became one of the most magnificent cities in the East. Although the capital lies in ruins today, in its heyday ambassadors and travelers from as far away as Italy and Portugal marveled at Vijayanagara's riches. Under its greatest king, Krishnadevaraya (r. 1509–1520), himself an author of poetry and prose, the Vijayanagar kingdom was a magnet for cultured people from all corners of India.

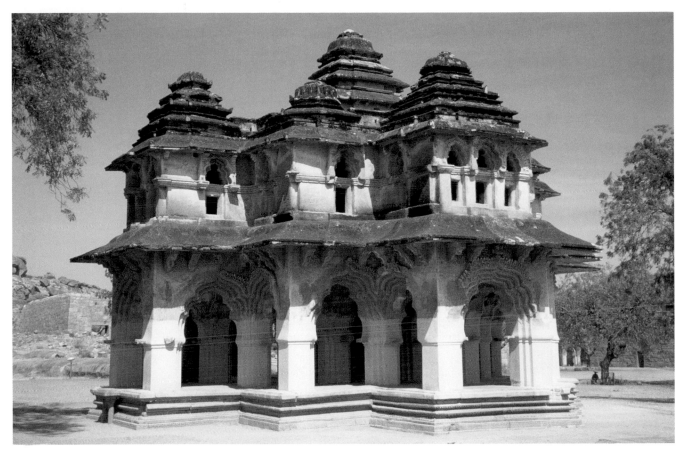

2-2 Lotus Mahal, Vijayanagara, India, 15th or early 16th century.

THE ECLECTIC LOTUS MAHAL Vijayanagara's sacred center, built up over two centuries, boasts imposing temples to the Hindu gods in the Dravida style of southern India with tall pyramidal vimanas (towers) over the inner sanctuary, or garbha griha. The buildings of the so-called Royal Enclave are more eclectic in character. One example in this prosperous royal city is the two-story monument of uncertain function known as the Lotus Mahal (FIG. 2-2). The stepped towers crowning the second-story rooms resemble the pyramidal roofs of Dravida temple mandapas (see FIG. 1-22). But the windows of the upper level as well as the arches of the ground-floor *piers* have the distinctive multilobed contours of Islamic architecture (see FIG. 7-13). The Lotus Mahal, like the entrance pavilion of Delhi's first mosque (FIG. 2-1), exemplifies the stylistic crosscurrents that typify much of Indian art and architecture of the second millennium.

Mughal Empire (1526–1857)

BABUR SEIZES DELHI The 16th century was a time of upheaval in South Asia. In 1565, only a generation after Krishnadevaraya, a confederacy of Deccan sultanates brought the Vijayanagar Empire of southern India to an end. Even before Krishnadevaraya's death in 1526, a Muslim prince named Babur had defeated the last of the Ghorid sultans of northern India at the Battle of Panipat. Declaring himself the ruler of India, he established the Mughal Dynasty at Delhi. (*Mughal* means "descended from the Mongols.") The next year he vanquished the Rajput Hindu kings of Mewar (see page 30). By the time of his death in 1530, Babur headed a vast new empire in India.

IMPERIAL MUGHAL PAINTING The first great flowering of Mughal art and architecture occurred during the long reign of Babur's grandson, Akbar (r. 1556–1605), called the Great, who ascended to the throne at age 14. Like his father Humayun (r. 1530–1556), Akbar was a great admirer of the narrative paintings produced at the court of Shah Tahmasp in Iran (see FIG. 7-27). Just before he died, Humayun had persuaded two Persian masters to move to Delhi and train local artists in the art of painting. When Akbar succeeded his father, he already oversaw an imperial workshop of Indian painters under the direction of the two Iranians. The young ruler enlarged their number to about a hundred and kept them busy working on a series of ambitious projects. One of these was to illustrate the text of the *Hamzanama*—the story of Hamza, Muhammad's uncle—in some 1,400 large paintings on cloth. The assignment took 15 years to complete.

European art, which Akbar knew through illustrated books and engravings, also fascinated him. Such items often arrived with Christian missionaries. Traders, missionaries, and diplomats also brought *prints*. In 1580, Portuguese Jesuits brought one particularly important source, the eight-volume *Royal Polyglot Bible*, as a gift to Akbar. This massive set of books, printed in Antwerp, was illustrated with *engravings* by several Flemish artists. Akbar immediately set his painters to copying the engravings.

AKBAR AND THE ELEPHANT Akbar also commissioned Abul Fazl, a member of his court and close friend, to chronicle his life in a great biography, the *Akbarnama (History of Akbar)*, which the emperor's painters illustrated. One of the full-page *miniatures* (see "Indian Miniature Painting," page 28) in the

Indian Miniature Painting

Although India had a tradition of mural painting going back to ancient times (see "The Painted Caves of Ajanta," Chapter 1, page 11, and FIG. 1-14), the most popular form of painting under the Mughal emperors (FIGS. 2-3 and 2-4) and Rajput kings (FIG. 2-6) was *miniature* painting. Art historians call these paintings "miniatures" because of their small size (about the size of a page in this book) compared to that of paintings on walls, wooden panels, or canvas. Indian miniatures were designed to be held in the hands, either as illustrations in books or as loose-leaf pages in albums. Owners did not place Indian miniatures in frames and only very rarely hung them on walls.

Indian artists used opaque watercolors and paper (occasionally cotton cloth) to produce their miniatures. The manufacturing and painting of miniatures was a complicated process and required years of training as an apprentice in a workshop. The painters' assistants created pigments by grinding natural materials—minerals such as malachite for green and lapis lazuli for blue; earth ochers for red and yellow; and metallic foil for gold, silver, and copper. They fashioned brushes from bird quills and kitten or baby squirrel hairs.

The artist began the painting process by making a full-size sketch of the composition. The artist then transferred the sketch onto paper by *pouncing*, or tracing, using thin, transparent gazelle skin placed on top of the drawing and pricking the contours of the design with a pin. Then, with the skin laid on a fresh sheet of fine paper, the painter forced black pigment through the tiny holes, reproducing the outlines of the composition. Painting proper started with the darkening of the outlines with black or reddish brown ink. Painters of miniatures sat on the ground, resting their painting boards on one raised knee. The paintings usually required several layers of color, with gold always applied last. The final step was to burnish the painted surface. The artists accomplished this by placing the miniature, painted side down, on a hard, smooth surface and stroking the paper with polished agate or crystal.

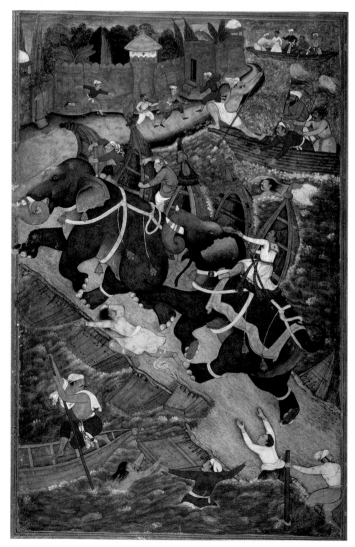

2-3 BASAWAN and CHATAR MUNI, *Akbar and the Elephant Hawai,* folio 22 from the *Akbarnama (History of Akbar)* by Abul Fazl, ca. 1590. Opaque watercolor on paper, 1′ 1⅞″ × 8¾″. Victoria & Albert Museum, London.

emperor's personal copy of the *Akbarnama* was a collaborative effort between the painter BASAWAN, who designed and drew the composition, and CHATAR MUNI, who colored it. The painting depicts the episode of Akbar and Hawai (FIG. **2-3**), a wild elephant that the 19-year-old ruler mounted and pitted against another ferocious elephant. When the second animal fled in defeat, Hawai, still carrying Akbar, chased it to a pontoon bridge. The enormous weight of the elephants capsized the boats, but Akbar managed to bring Hawai under control and dismount safely. The young ruler viewed the episode as an allegory of his ability to govern—that is, to take charge of an unruly state.

For his pictorial record of that frightening day, Basawan chose the moment of maximum chaos and danger—when the elephants crossed the pontoon bridge, sending boatmen flying into the water. The composition is a bold one, with a very high horizon and two strong diagonal lines formed by the bridge and the shore. Together these devices tend to flatten out the vista, yet at the same time Basawan created a sense of depth by diminishing the size of the figures in the background. He was also a master of vivid gestures and anecdotal detail. Note especially the bare-chested figure in the foreground clinging to the end of a boat, the figure near the lower right corner with outstretched arms sliding into the water as the bridge becomes submerged, and the oarsman just beyond the bridge who strains to steady his vessel while his three passengers stand up or lean overboard in reaction to the commotion all around them.

THE EMPEROR ABOVE TIME That the names Basawan and Chatar Muni are known is significant in itself. In contrast to the anonymity of artists in the Hindu and Buddhist traditions, many artists working for the Islamic Mughal emperors signed their work. Another of these was BICHITR, whom Akbar's son and successor, Jahangir (r. 1605–1627), employed in the imperial workshop. The Mughals presided over a cosmopolitan court with refined tastes. After the establishment of the East India Company in 1600 (see page 31), British ambassadors and merchants were frequent visitors to the Mughal capital, and Jahangir, like his father, acquired many luxury goods from Europe, including globes, hourglasses, prints, and portraits.

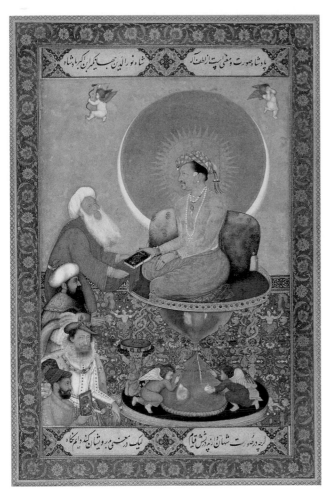

2-4 BICHITR, *Jahangir Preferring a Sufi Shaykh to Kings*, ca. 1615–1618. Opaque watercolor on paper, 1' 6⅞" × 1' 1". Freer Gallery of Art, Washington, D.C.

The impact of European as well as Persian styles on Mughal painting under Jahangir is evident in Bichitr's allegorical portrait of Jahangir seated on an hourglass throne (FIG. 2-4), a miniature from an album made for the emperor around 1615–1618. As the

sands of time run out, two Cupids (clothed, unlike their European models more closely copied at the top of the painting) inscribe the throne with the wish that Jahangir would live a thousand years. Bichitr portrayed his patron as an emperor above time and also placed behind Jahangir's head a radiant halo combining a golden sun and a white crescent moon, indicating that Jahangir is the center of the universe and its light source. One of the inscriptions on the painting gives the emperor's title as "Light of the Faith."

At the left are four figures. The lowest, both spatially and in the social hierarchy, is the Hindu painter Bichitr himself, wearing a red turban. He holds a miniature representing two horses and an elephant, costly gifts from Jahangir, and another self-portrait. In the miniature-within-the-miniature, Bichitr bows deeply before the emperor. In the larger painting, the artist signed his name across the top of the footstool Jahangir uses to step up to his hourglass throne. Thus, the ruler steps on Bichitr's name, further indicating the painter's inferior status.

Above Bichitr is a portrait in full European style of King James I of England (r. 1603–1625), copied from a painting by John de Critz that the English ambassador to the Mughal court had given as a gift to Jahangir. Above the king is a Turkish sultan, a convincing study of physiognomy, but probably not a specific portrait. The highest member of the foursome is an elderly Muslim Sufi *shaykh* (mystic saint). Jahangir's father, Akbar, had gone to the mystic to pray for an heir. The current emperor, the answer to Akbar's prayers, presents the holy man with a sumptuous book as a gift. An inscription explains that "although to all appearances kings stand before him, Jahangir looks inwardly toward the dervishes [Islamic holy men]" for guidance. Bichitr's allegorical painting portrays his emperor in both words and pictures as favoring spiritual over worldly power.

A MAUSOLEUM IN PARADISE Monumental tombs were not part of either the Hindu or Buddhist traditions, but had a long history in Islamic architecture (see Chapter 7). The Delhi sultans had erected tombs in India, but none could compare in grandeur to the fabled Taj Mahal at Agra (FIG. 2-5). Shah Jahan (r. 1628–1658), Jahangir's son, built the immense *mausoleum* as a

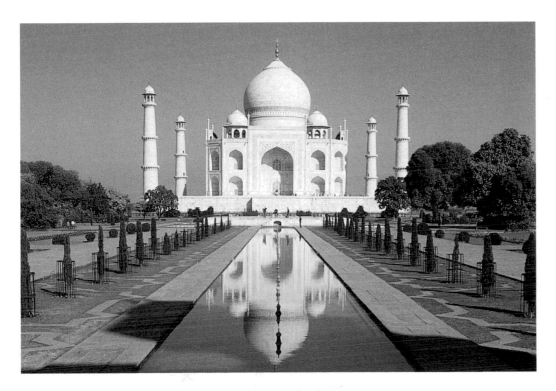

2-5 Taj Mahal, Agra, India, 1632–1647.

memorial to his favorite wife, Mumtaz Mahal, although the ruler himself was eventually buried there as well. The dome-on-cube shape of the central block descends from that of earlier Islamic mausoleums (see FIGS. 7-10 and 7-18) and other Islamic buildings like the Alai Darvaza at Delhi (FIG. 2-1), but modifications and refinements in Agra have converted the earlier massive structures into an almost weightless vision of glistening white marble. The Agra mausoleum seems to float magically above the tree-lined reflecting pools that punctuate the garden leading to it. The illusion that the marble tomb is suspended above the water is reinforced by the absence of any visible means of ascent to the upper platform. A stairway in fact exists, but the architect intentionally hid it from the view of anyone who approaches the memorial.

The Taj Mahal follows the plan of Iranian garden pavilions, except that the building is placed at one end rather than in the center of the formal garden. The tomb is octagonal in plan and has typically Iranian *arcuated* (arch-shaped) niches (see FIG. 7-25) on each side. The interplay of shadowy voids with light-reflecting marble walls that seem paper thin creates an impression of translucency. The pointed arches lead the eye in a sweeping upward movement toward the climactic dome, shaped like a crown *(taj)*. Carefully related minarets and corner pavilions enhance and stabilize this soaring central theme. The architect achieved this delicate balance between verticality and horizontality by strictly applying an all-encompassing system of proportions. The Taj Mahal (excluding the minarets) is exactly as wide as it is tall, and the height of its dome is equal to the height of the facade.

Abd al-Hamid Lahori, a court historian who witnessed the construction of the Taj Mahal, compared its minarets to ladders reaching toward Heaven and the surrounding gardens to Paradise. In fact, the gateway to the gardens and the walls of the mausoleum are inscribed with carefully selected excerpts from the Koran that confirm the historian's interpretation of the tomb's symbolism. The Taj Mahal may have been conceived as the Throne of God perched above the gardens of Paradise on Judgment Day. The minarets hold up the canopy of that throne. In Islam, the most revered place of burial is beneath the Throne of God.

Hindu Rajput Kingdoms (ca. 1500–1850)

RAJPUTS AND MUGHALS The Mughal emperors ruled vast territories, but much of northwestern India (present-day Rajasthan) remained under the control of Hindu Rajput (literally "sons of kings") dynasties. These small kingdoms had stubbornly resisted Mughal expansion, but even the strongest of them, Mewar, eventually submitted to the Mughal emperors. When Jahangir defeated the Mewar forces in 1615, the Mewar *maharana* (great king), like the other Rajput rulers, maintained a degree of independence but had to pay tribute to the Mughal treasury.

Rajput painting resembles Mughal (and Persian) painting in format and material, but it differs sharply in other respects. Most Rajput artists, for example, worked in anonymity, never inserting self-portraits into their paintings as the Mughal painter Bichitr did in his miniature of Jahangir on an hourglass throne (FIG. 2-4).

VISHNU THE LOVER One of the most popular subjects for Rajput paintings was the amorous adventures of Krishna, the "Blue God," the most popular of the *avatars,* or incarnations, of the Hindu god Vishnu, who descends to earth to aid mortals (see "Hinduism," Chapter 1, page 12). Krishna was a herdsman who spent an idyllic existence tending his cows, fluting, and sporting

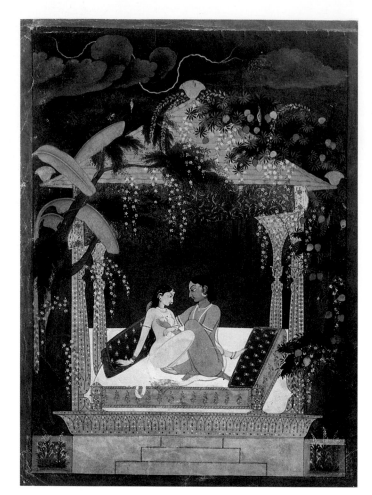

2-6 *Krishna and Radha in a Pavilion,* ca. 1760. Opaque watercolor on paper, $11\frac{1}{8}'' \times 7\frac{3}{4}''$. National Museum, New Delhi.

with beautiful herdswomen. His favorite lover was Radha. The 12th-century poet Jayadeva related the story of Krishna and Radha in the *Gita Govinda (Song of the Cowherd).* Their love was a model of the devotion, or *bhakti,* paid to Vishnu. Jayadeva's poem was the source for hundreds of later paintings, including *Krishna and Radha in a Pavilion* (FIG. 2-6), a miniature painted in the Punjab Hills, probably for Raja Govardhan Chand of Guler (r. 1741–1773). The rulers of the Punjab Hills states were related to the Rajputs, but their painters, referred to collectively as the Pahari School, had a distinctive style. Although Pahari painting owed much to Mughal drawing style, its coloration, lyricism, and sensuality are readily recognizable.

In *Krishna and Radha in a Pavilion,* the lovers sit naked on a bed beneath a jeweled pavilion in a lush garden of ripe mangoes and flowering shrubs. Krishna gently touches Radha's breast while looking directly into her face. Radha shyly averts her gaze. It is night, the time of illicit trysts, and the dark monsoon sky momentarily lights up with a lightning flash indicating the moment's electric passion. Lightning is one of the standard symbols used in Rajput and Pahari miniatures for sexual excitement.

Nayak Dynasty (1529–1736)

THE TOWERS OF MADURAI The Nayakas, governors under the Vijayanagar kings, declared their independence in 1529, and after their former overlords' defeat in 1565 at the hands of the Deccan sultanates, they continued Hindu rule in the far south of India for

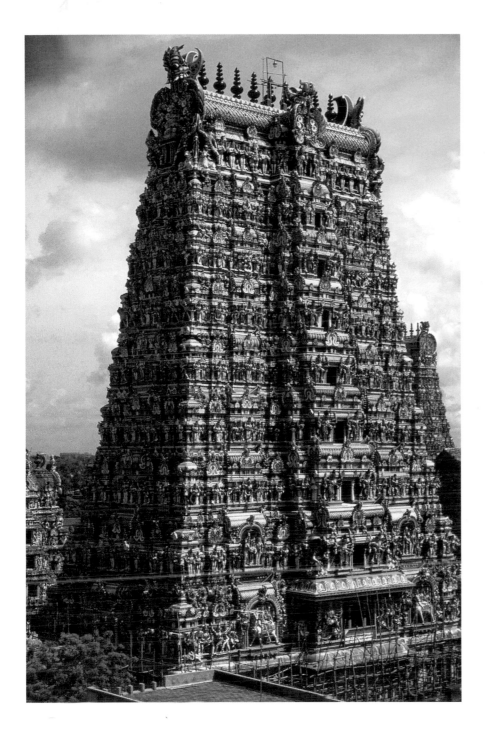

two centuries. Construction of some of the largest temple complexes in India occurred under Nayak patronage. The builders of these huge complexes expanded them outward from the center by erecting ever larger enclosure walls, punctuated at the cardinal points by gateway towers called *gopuras*. Positioned like boxes within boxes, each set of walls had taller gopuras than those of the previous circuit, the towers reaching colossal size and dwarfing the actual central temples. The outer gopuras of the Great Temple (FIG. 2-7) at Madurai, dedicated to Shiva (under his local name, Sundareshvara, the Handsome One) and his consort Minakshi (the Fish-eyed One), stand about 150 feet tall. Rising in a series of tiers of diminishing size, they culminate in a *barrel-vaulted* roof with finials. The ornamentation is extremely rich, consisting of row after row of brightly painted stucco sculptures representing the vast pantheon of Hindu deities and a host of attendant figures. At 12-year intervals, the temple is reconsecrated and the gopura sculptures are repainted, accounting for the vibrancy of their colors today. The Madurai Nayak temple complex also contains large and numerous mandapas, as well as great water tanks the worshipers use for ritual bathing. Such temples were, and continue to be, almost independent cities, with thousands of pilgrims, merchants, and priests flocking from far and near to the many yearly festivals the temples host.

The British in India (1600–1947)

FROM TRADERS TO RULERS English merchants first arrived in India toward the end of the 16th century, attracted by the land's spices, gems, and other riches. In 1600, Queen Elizabeth I (r. 1558–1603) granted a charter to the East India Company, which sought to compete with the Portuguese and Dutch in the lucrative trade with South Asia. The Company established a "factory" (trading post) at the port of Surat, approximately 150 miles from Mumbai (Bombay) in western India in 1613. After securing trade privileges with the Mughal emperor Jahangir, the British expanded their factories to Chennai (Madras), Kolkata (Calcutta),

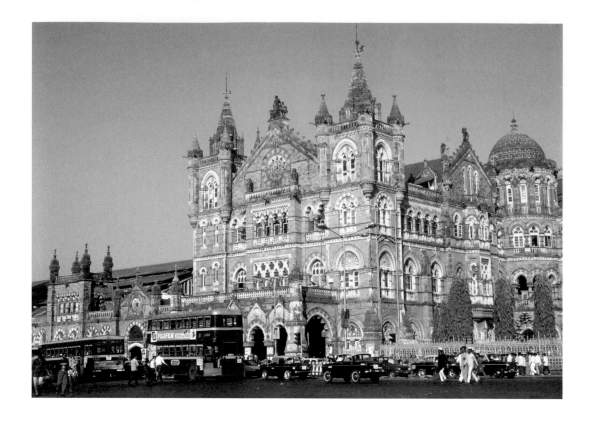

2-8 FREDERICK W. STEVENS, Victoria Terminus (Chhatrapati Shivaji Terminus), Mumbai (Bombay), India, 1878–1887.

and Bombay by 1661. British outposts gradually spread throughout India, especially after the defeat at their hands of the ruler of Bengal in 1757. By the opening of the 19th century, the East India Company effectively ruled large portions of the subcontinent, and in 1835, the British declared English India's official language. A great rebellion in 1857 persuaded the British Parliament that the East India Company could no longer be the agent of British rule. The next year Parliament abolished the Company and replaced its governor-general with a viceroy of the Crown. Two decades later, in 1877, Queen Victoria (r. 1837–1901) was proclaimed Empress of India with sovereignty over all the former Indian states.

BOMBAY'S RAILROAD CATHEDRAL The British brought the Industrial Revolution and railways to India. One of the most enduring monuments of British rule, still used today by millions of travelers, is the Victoria Terminus in Bombay (FIG. **2-8**), named for the new Empress of India (but now called Chhatrapati Shivaji Terminus). Designed by FREDERICK W. STEVENS (1847–1900), a British architect, the railway station was begun in 1878 and completed a decade later. Although built of the same local sandstone used for temples and statues throughout India's long history, the giant terminal is a European transplant to the subcontinent, the architectural counterpart of colonial rule. Conceived as a cathedral to modernization, the terminus fittingly has an allegorical statue of Progress crowning its tallest dome (not visible in FIG. 2-8). Nonetheless, the building's design looks backward, not forward. Inside, passengers gaze up at *groin-vaulted* ceilings and *stained-glass* windows, and the exterior of the station resembles a Western church with a gabled facade and flanking towers. Stevens modeled Victoria Terminus, with its tiers of screened windows, on the architecture of late medieval Venice.

JODHPUR'S BRITISH GENTLEMAN With British rulers and modern railways also came British or, more generally, European

ideas, but Western culture and religion never supplanted India's own rich traditions. Many Indians, however, readily took on the trappings of European society. When Jaswant Singh, the ruler of Jodhpur in Rajasthan (r. 1873–1895), sat for his portrait (FIG. **2-9**), he chose to sit alone in an ordinary chair, rather than on a throne, with his arm resting on a simple table with a bouquet and a book on it. In other words, he posed like an ordinary British gentleman in his sitting room. Nevertheless, the painter, an anonymous local artist who had embraced Western style, left no question about Jaswant Singh's regal presence and pride. The ruler's powerful chest and arms, along with the sword and his leather riding boots, indicate his abilities as a warrior and hunter. The curled beard was regarded at the time as indicative of fierceness. The unflinching gaze records the ruler's confidence. Perhaps the two necklaces Jaswant Singh wears best exemplify the combination of his two worlds. One necklace is a bib of huge emeralds and diamonds, the heritage of the wealth and splendor of his family's rule. The other, a wide gold band with a cameo, is the Order of the Star of India, a high honor his British overlords bestowed on him.

The painter of this portrait worked on the same scale and employed the same materials—opaque watercolor on paper—that Indian miniature painters had used for centuries (see "Indian Miniature Painting," page 28), but the artist copied the ruler's likeness from a photograph. This accounts in large part for the realism of the portrait. Indian artists sometimes even painted directly on top of photographs. Photography arrived in India in 1840, just one year after its invention in Paris. Indian artists readily adopted the new medium, not just to produce portraits but also to record landscapes and monuments.

In 19th-century India, however, admiration of Western art and culture was by no means universal. During the half-century after Jaswant Singh's death, calls for Indian self-government grew ever louder. Under the leadership of Mahatma Gandhi (1869–1948) and others, India achieved independence in 1947,

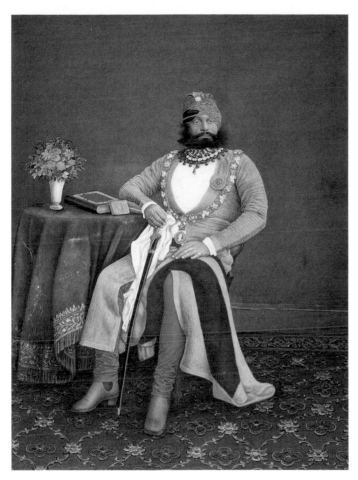

2-9 *Maharaja Jaswant Singh of Marwar*, ca. 1880. Opaque watercolor on paper, 1′ 3½″ × 11⅝″. The Brooklyn Museum, Brooklyn (gift of Mr. and Mrs. Robert L. Poster).

but was partitioned into the two present-day nations of India and Pakistan. The contemporary art of South and Southeast Asia is the subject of the last section of this chapter.

SOUTHEAST ASIA

India was not alone in experiencing major shifts in political power and religious preferences during the last 800 years. The Khmer of Angkor (see Chapter 1), after reaching the height of their power at the beginning of the 13th century, lost one of their outposts in northern Thailand to their Thai vassals at midcentury. The newly founded Thai kingdoms quickly replaced Angkor as the region's major powers, while Theravada Buddhism (see "Buddhism and Buddhist Iconography," Chapter 1, page 5) became the religion of the entire mainland except Vietnam. The Vietnamese, restricted to the northern region of today's Vietnam, gained independence in the 10th century after a thousand years of Chinese political and cultural domination. They pushed to the south, ultimately destroying the indigenous Cham culture, which had dominated there for more than a millennium. A similar Burmese drive southward in Myanmar matched the Thai and Vietnamese expansions. All these movements resulted in demographic changes during the second millennium that led to the cultural, political, and artistic transformation of mainland Southeast Asia. A religious shift also occurred in Indonesia. With Islam growing in importance, all of Indonesia but the island of Bali became predominantly Muslim by the 16th century.

Thailand

Southeast Asians practiced both Buddhism and Hinduism, but by the 13th century, in contrast to developments in India, Hinduism was dying out and Buddhism was dominating much of the mainland. Two prominent Buddhist kingdoms came to power in Thailand during the 13th and early 14th centuries. Historians date the beginning of the Sukhothai kingdom to 1292, the year King Ramkhamhaeng (r. 1279–1299) erected a four-sided stele bearing the first inscription written in the Thai language. Sukhothai's political dominance was, however, short-lived. Ayuthaya, a city founded in central Thailand in 1350, quickly became the more powerful kingdom and warred sporadically with other states in Southeast Asia until the mid-18th century. Scholars nonetheless regard the Sukhothai period as the golden age of Thai art. In the inscription on his stele, Ramkhamhaeng ("Rama the Strong") describes Sukhothai as a city of monasteries and many images of the Buddha.

THE WALKING BUDDHA Theravada Buddhism came to Sukhothai from Sri Lanka (see Chapter 1). At the center of the city stood Wat Mahathat, Sukhothai's most important Buddhist monastery. Its stupa (see "The Stupa," Chapter 1, page 6) housed a relic of the Buddha (Wat Mahathat means "Monastery of the Great Relic") and attracted crowds of pilgrims. Sukhothai's crowning artistic achievement was the development of a type of walking Buddha statue (FIG. **2-10**) displaying a distinctively Thai approach

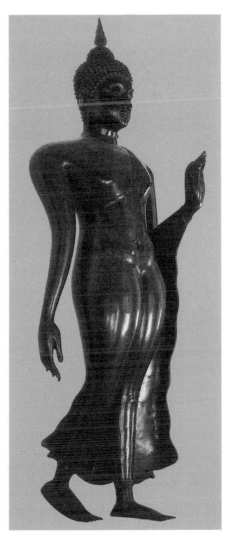

2-10 *Walking Buddha*, from Sukhothai, Thailand, 14th century. Bronze, 7′ 2½″ high. Wat Bechamabopit, Bangkok.

to body form. The Buddha, wearing a clinging monk's robe, strides forward, his right heel off the ground and his left arm raised with the hand held in the fear-not gesture, encouraging worshipers to come forward in reverence. A flame leaps from the top of the Buddha's head, and a sharp nose projects from his rounded face. The right arm hangs loosely, seemingly without muscles or joints, like an elephant's trunk. The Sukhothai artists intended the body type to suggest a supernatural being and to express the Buddha's beauty and perfection. Although images in stone exist, the Sukhothai artists handled bronze best, a material well suited to their conception of the Buddha's body as elastic. The Sukhothai walking-Buddha statuary type does not occur elsewhere in Buddhist art.

BANGKOK'S *EMERALD BUDDHA* A second distinctive Buddha image from northern Thailand is the *Emerald Buddha* (FIG. 2-11), housed in Bangkok in the Emerald Temple on the Royal Palace grounds. The sculpture is small, only about 30 inches tall, and conforms to the ancient type of the Buddha seated in meditation in a yogic posture with his legs crossed and his hands in his lap, palms upward (see FIG. 1-9). It first appears in historical records in 1434 in northern Thailand, where Buddhist chronicles record its story. The chronicles state that the Buddha image was covered in plaster, and thus no one knew it was made of green stone. A lightning bolt caused some of the plaster to flake off, disclosing its gemlike nature. Taken by various rulers to a series of cities in northern Thailand and in Laos for more than 300 years, the small image finally reached Bangkok in 1778 in the possession of the founder of the present Thai royal dynasty.

The *Emerald Buddha* is not carved from an actual emerald. It is probably green jade, but its nature as a gemstone gives it a special aura. It is said that the gem enables the universal king, or *chakravartin,* possessing the statue to bring the rains. The historical Buddha renounced his secular destiny for the spiritual life, yet his likeness carved from the gem of a universal king allows fulfillment of the Buddha's royal destiny as well. The Buddha can also be regarded as the universal king. Thus, the combination of the sacred and the secular in the small image explains its symbolic power. The Thai king dresses the *Emerald Buddha* at different times of the year in a monk's robe and a king's robe (in FIG. 2-11 the Buddha wears the royal garment), reflecting the image's dual nature and accentuating its symbolic role as both Buddha and king. The Thai king possessing the image therefore has both religious and secular authority.

Myanmar

RANGOON'S GOLDEN STUPA Myanmar, like Thailand, is overwhelmingly a Theravada Buddhist country today. Important Buddhist monasteries and monuments dot the countryside. In fact, one of the largest stupas in the world is the Shwedagon Pagoda (FIG. 2-12) in Rangoon. (*Pagoda* derives from the Portuguese version of a word for stupa.) It houses two of the Buddha's hairs, traditionally said to have been brought to Myanmar by merchants who received them from the Buddha himself. This highly

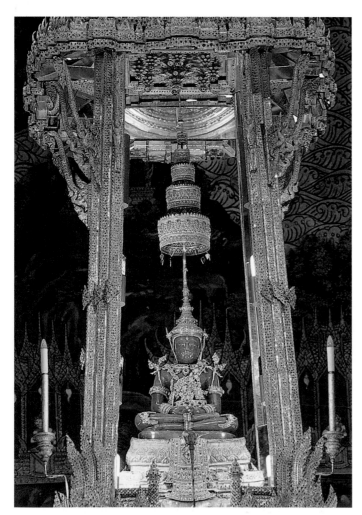

2-11 *Emerald Buddha,* Emerald Temple, Bangkok, Thailand, 15th century. Jade or jasper, 2′ 6″ high.

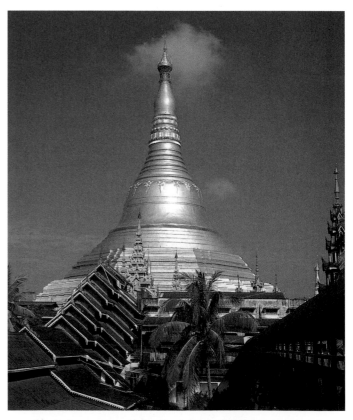

2-12 Schwedagon Pagoda, Rangoon (Yangon), Myanmar (Burma), 14th century or earlier (rebuilt several times). Stupa, gold, silver, and jewel encrusted, approx. 344′ high. Top of stupa, gold ball inlaid with 4,351 diamonds.

Shipwrecks and Ceramic Chronology

The vast majority of early Vietnamese ceramics (FIG. 2-13) have not been found in Vietnam but in Indonesia, particularly on the islands of Java and Sulawesi, and in the Philippines, where they served as grave goods to bury with the dead. The Vietnamese exported their ceramic wares to the Southeast Asian islands as early as the 14th century but primarily during the 15th through 17th centuries, when Vietnamese ceramics reached markets even more distant—the Middle East, Egypt, Turkey, and Persia.

Chinese and European—primarily English, Dutch, and Portuguese—merchants traded the Vietnamese wares, along with ceramics from China and Thailand. According to the inventory of a Dutch ship that arrived in Java in 1669, the ship's cargo included 381,200 Vietnamese ceramic bowls. Recent finds of shipwrecks with their cargoes of ceramic wares intact, discovered in the waters along the mainland coasts and around the islands in the South China Sea, are helping to clarify the dating and interrelationships among the various ceramic traditions. Before investigation of the shipwrecks began, art historians had to rely on buried Vietnamese ceramics, which rarely could be dated. It was usually impossible to know dates of the individual pieces gathered together in the burial. Researchers thus could not ascertain whether the buried ceramics dated from different centuries or were contemporaneous.

The recent shipwreck finds have shown that many of the assumptions based on art historians' stylistic analysis of Southeast Asian ceramics were incorrect. Researchers often can date shipwrecks rather precisely, especially if any wood remains that they can analyze using radiocarbon dating techniques. The ceramics in shipwrecks, then, can be placed together at a precise moment. Wrecks have revealed groupings of ceramics that, until now, were considered separated in time. The technology of underwater archaeology is leading to a new understanding of the entire Vietnamese ceramic tradition.

revered stupa was rebuilt several times. Renowned for the gold, silver, and jewels encrusting its surface, the Shwedagon Pagoda stands 344 feet high. Its upper part is covered with 13,153 plates of gold, each about a foot square. At the very top is a seven-tiered umbrella crowned with a gold ball inlaid with 4,351 diamonds, one of which weighs 76 carats. This great wealth was a gift to the Buddha from the laypeople of Myanmar to produce merit. The stupa is at the center of an enormous complex of buildings, including wooden shrines filled with Buddha images.

Vietnam

VIETNAMESE CERAMICS AND CHINA Vietnam's art history is particularly complex, as it reveals both an Indian-related art and culture, broadly similar to those of the rest of Southeast Asia, and a unique and intense relationship with China's art and culture. Vietnam's tradition of fine ceramics is of special interest. Vietnamese ceramics go back to the Han period (206 BCE–220 CE) in China, when the Chinese began to govern the northern area of Vietnam. China directly controlled Vietnam for a thousand years, and early Vietnamese ceramics closely reflected Chinese wares. But during the Ly (1009–1225) and Tran (1225–1400) dynasties, when Vietnam had regained its independence, Vietnamese potters developed an array of ceramic shapes, designs, and glazes that brought their wares to the highest levels of quality and creativity.

In the 14th century, the Vietnamese began exporting underglaze wares modeled on the blue-and-white ceramics first produced in China (see "Chinese Porcelain," Chapter 4, page 69). During the 15th and 16th centuries, the ceramic industry in Vietnam had become the supplier of pottery of varied shapes to an international market extending throughout Southeast Asia and to the Middle East (see "Shipwrecks and Ceramic Chronology," above). A 16th-century Vietnamese dish (FIG. **2-13**) with two mynah birds on a flowering branch reveals both the potter's debt to China and how the spontaneity, power, and playfulness of Vietnamese painting contrast with the formality of Chinese wares (see FIG. 4-4). The artist suggested the foliage with curving and looped lines executed in almost one continuous movement of the brush over the surface. This technique—very different from the more deliberate Chinese habit of lifting the brush after painting a single motif in order to separate the shapes more sharply—facilitated rapid production. Combined with the painter's control, it allowed a fresh and unique design that made Vietnamese pottery attractive to a wide export market.

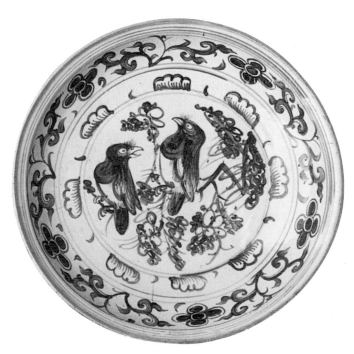

2-13 Dish with two mynah birds on flowering branch, from Vietnam, 16th century. Stoneware painted with underglaze-cobalt, 1' 2½" in diameter. Pacific Asia Museum, Pasadena.

Contemporary South and Southeast Asian Art

LOCAL AND INTERNATIONAL ART Contemporary art in India and Southeast Asia is as multifaceted a phenomenon as contemporary art elsewhere in the world. In India, for example, many traditional artists work at the village level, making images of deities out of inexpensive materials, such as clay, plaster, and papier-mâché, for local use. Some artists in the cities use these same materials to produce elaborate religious tableaux, such as depictions of the goddess Durga killing the buffalo demon, during the annual 10-day Durga Festival in Calcutta. Participants in the festival often ornament the tableaux with thousands of colored electric lights. The most popular art form for religious imagery, however, is the brightly colored print, sold for only a few rupees each. In the Buddhist countries of Southeast Asia (Thailand, Cambodia, Myanmar, and Laos), some artists continue to produce traditional images of the Buddha, primarily in bronze, for worship in homes, businesses, and temples.

Many contemporary artists, in contrast, create works for the international market. Although many of them were trained in South or Southeast Asia or Japan, others received their training in schools in Europe or the United States, and some now work outside their home countries. They face one of the fundamental quandaries of many contemporary Asian artists—how to identify themselves and situate their work between local and international, traditional and modern, and non-Western and Western cultures.

MEERA MUKHERJEE AND ASHOKA One Indian artist who successfully bridged these two poles of modern Asian art was MEERA MUKHERJEE (1923–1998). Mukherjee studied with European masters in Germany, but when she returned to India, she rejected much of what she had learned in favor of the techniques that traditional sculptors of the Bastar tribe in central India had long employed. Mukherjee went to live with the Bastar bronze casters, who had perfected a variation on the ancient *lost-wax* (*cire perdue*) process. Beginning with a rough core of clay, the Bastar sculptors build up what will be the final shape of the statue by placing long threads of beeswax over the core. Then they apply a coat of clay paste to the beeswax and tie up the mold with metal wire. After heating the mold over a charcoal fire, which melts the wax away, they pour liquid bronze into the space once occupied by the wax threads. Large sculptures require many separate molds. The Bastar artists complete their statues by welding together the separately cast sections, usually leaving the seams visible.

Many scholars regard *Ashoka at Kalinga* (FIG. **2-14**) as Mukherjee's greatest work. Twice life size and assembled from 26 cast bronze sections, the towering statue combines the intricate surface textures of traditional Bastar work with the expressive swelling abstract forms of some 20th-century European sculpture. Mukherjee's subject is the third-century BCE Maurya emperor Ashoka standing on the battlefield at Kalinga. There, Ashoka witnessed more than 100,000 deaths and, shocked by the horrors of the war he had unleashed, rejected violence and adopted Buddhism as the official religion of his empire (see "Ashoka's Conversion to Buddhism," Chapter 1, page 7). Mukherjee conceived her statue as a pacifist protest against political violence in late 20th-century India. By reaching into India's remote history to make a contemporary political statement and by em-

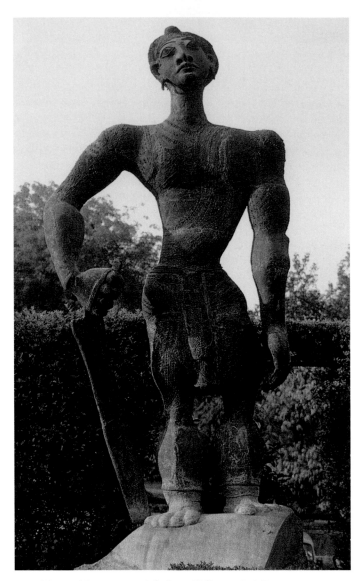

2-14 MEERA MUKHERJEE, *Ashoka at Kalinga,* 1972. Bronze, 11′ 6¾″ high. Maurya Sheraton Hotel, New Delhi.

ploying the bronze casting methods of tribal sculptors while molding her forms in a modern idiom, she united her native land's past and present in a single work of great emotive power.

CONCLUSION

Islam arrived in the Indian subcontinent in the eighth century. With the establishment of the Sultanate of Delhi in 1206, Islamic art and architecture began to spread throughout South Asia. The Muslim Mughal emperors of India were especially lavish art patrons. In fact, one of the most famous Islamic buildings in the world, the Taj Mahal, was a Mughal commission. But elsewhere in South Asia, Hindu art continued to flourish, especially under the Vijayanagar and Nayak dynasties and the Rajput kingdoms. Buddhism and Buddhist art dominated much of Southeast Asia.

The Mughal Empire came to an end in 1857, and for nearly a century thereafter India was ruled by the British. Under the leadership of Mahatma Gandhi (1869–1948), India and Pakistan attained independence in 1947. Throughout the period of British sovereignty, local traditions mixed with imported European styles in both art and architecture. The rich and varied contemporary art of South and Southeast Asia continues to draw upon these diverse traditions.

DELHI SULTANATE, 1206–1526

HINDU KINGDOM OF VIJAYANAGARA, 1336–1565

MUGHAL EMPIRE, 1526–1857

HINDU NAYAK DYNASTY, 1529–1736

HINDU RAJPUT DYNASTIES, CA. 1500–1850

BRITISH RULE IN INDIA, 1858–1947

INDEPENDENT INDIA AND PAKISTAN, 1947–

| MUHAMMAD OF GHOR INVADES INDIA, 1192

1200

| QUTB AL-DIN AYBAK FOUNDS DELHI SULTANATE, 1206

| ILTUTMISH, DELHI SULTAN, R. 1211–1236

| TRAN DYNASTY IN VIETNAM, 1225–1400

| RAMKHAMHAENG, SUKHOTHAI KING, R. 1279–1299

1300

| HARIHARA FOUNDS VIJAYANAGAR KINGDOM, 1336

| AYUTHAYA KINGDOM FOUNDED IN THAILAND, 1350

1400

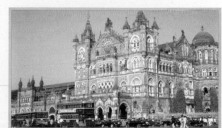

1 Qutb Minar, Delhi, India, begun early 13th century

| KRISHNADEVARAYA, VIJAYANAGAR KING, R. 1509–1520

| BABUR FOUNDS MUGHAL DYNASTY, 1526

| NAYAKAS DECLARE INDEPENDENCE FROM VIJAYANAGARA, 1529

| AKBAR, MUGHAL EMPEROR, R. 1556–1605

1500

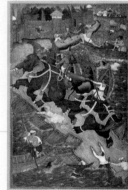

2 Emerald Buddha, Bangkok, Thailand, 15th century

1600

| QUEEN ELIZABETH I CHARTERS EAST INDIA COMPANY, 1600

| JAHANGIR, MUGHAL EMPEROR, R. 1605–1627

| BRITISH ESTABLISH TRADING POST AT SURAT, 1613

| JAHANGIR DEFEATS THE MEWAR MAHARANA, 1615

| SHAH JAHAN, MUGHAL EMPEROR, R. 1627–1658

1700

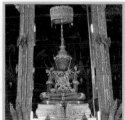

3 Basawan and Chatar Muni, *Akbar and the Elephant Hawai*, ca. 1590

1800

| GREAT REBELLION AGAINST THE BRITISH, 1857

| BRITISH CROWN RULE IN INDIA, 1858–1947

| MAHATMA GANDHI, 1869–1948

| QUEEN VICTORIA BECOMES EMPRESS OF INDIA, 1877

1900

| INDEPENDENCE OF INDIA AND PAKISTAN, 1947

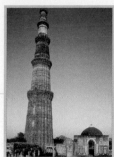

4 Frederick W. Stevens, Victoria Terminus, Bombay, India, 1878–1887

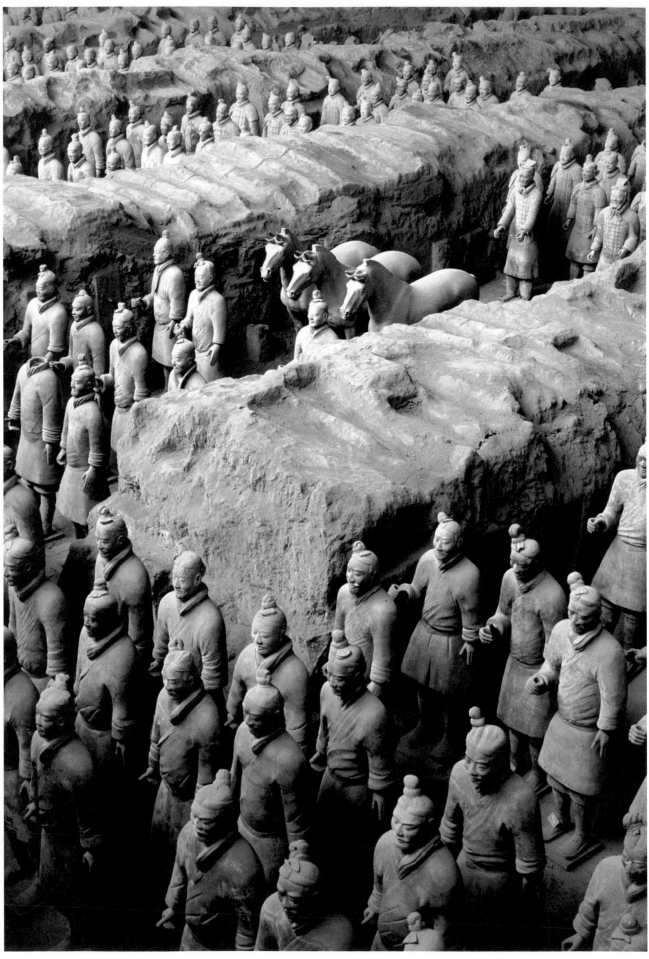

Army of the First Emperor of Qin in pits next to his burial mound, Lintong, China, Qin dynasty, ca. 210 BCE. Painted terracotta, average figure 5′ 10$\frac{7}{8}$″ high.

3

THE SILK ROAD
AND BEYOND

THE ART OF EARLY CHINA AND KOREA

East Asia is a vast area, varied both topographically and climatically. Dominated by the huge land mass of China, the region also encompasses the peninsula of Korea and the islands of Japan. In this chapter and Chapter 4, we examine the art and architecture of China and Korea. Japanese art and architecture are treated in Chapters 5 and 6.

CHINA

China's landscape includes sandy plains, mighty rivers, towering mountains, and fertile farmlands (MAP **3-1**). Its political and cultural boundaries have varied over the millennia and at times have grown to about twice the area of the United States, encompassing Tibet, Chinese Turkestan (Xinjiang), Mongolia, Manchuria, and parts of Korea. China boasts the world's largest population and is ethnically diverse. The spoken language varies so much that speakers of different dialects do not understand one another. However, the written language, which employs *characters* (signs that record meaning rather than sounds), has permitted different peoples living thousands of miles apart to share literary, philosophic, and religious traditions.

Neolithic China

China is the only continuing civilization that originated in the ancient world. The Chinese archaeological record, extraordinarily rich, goes back to Neolithic times. Discoveries in recent years have expanded the early record enormously. They have provided evidence of settled village life as far back as the seventh or early sixth millennium BCE. Excavators have uncovered sites with large multifamily houses constructed of wood, bamboo, wattle, daub, and mud plaster, and equipped with hearths. These early villages also had pens for domesticated animals, kilns for pottery production, pits

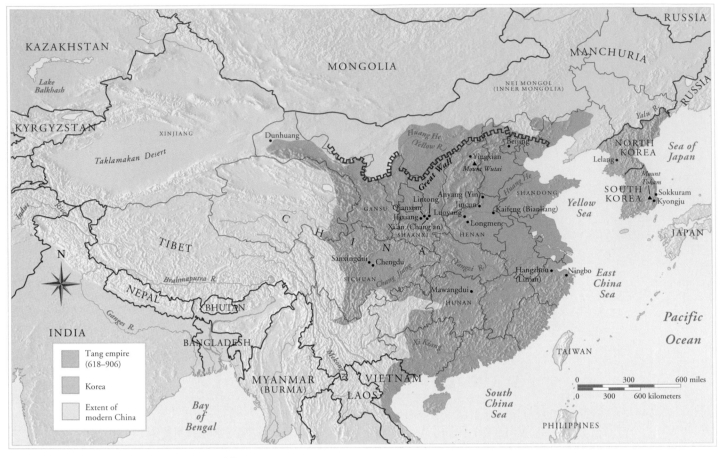

MAP 3-1 Early sites in China and Korea.

for storage and refuse, and cemeteries for the dead. Chinese Neolithic artisans produced impressive artworks, especially from jade and clay.

YANGSHAO POTTERY Mastery of the art of pottery occurred at a very early date in China. The potters of the Yangshao Culture, which arose along the Yellow River in northeastern China, produced fine decorated *earthenware* bowls (see "Chinese Earthenwares and Stonewares," page 41) even before the invention of the potter's wheel in the fourth millennium BCE. In the third millennium, the Yangshao potters of Gansu Province manufactured painted vessels (FIG. **3-1**) of astonishing sophistication. The multiplicity of shapes suggests that the vessels served a wide variety of functions in daily life, but most of the finds come from graves. Decoration is in red and brownish black on a cream-colored ground. Some pots and bowls have stylized animal motifs, but most feature abstract designs. The painters reveal a highly refined aesthetic sensibility, effectively integrating a variety of angular and curvilinear geometric motifs, including stripes, zigzags, lozenges, circles, spirals, and waves.

Shang Dynasty

During the past century, China's earliest royal dynasties, long thought to have been mythical, have begun to be confirmed archaeologically. Most recently, excavators have found what they believe to be traces of the Xia (ca. 2000–1600 BCE), China's oldest dynasty. Much better documented, however, is the Shang dynasty (ca. 1600–1050 BCE), the first great Chinese dynasty of the

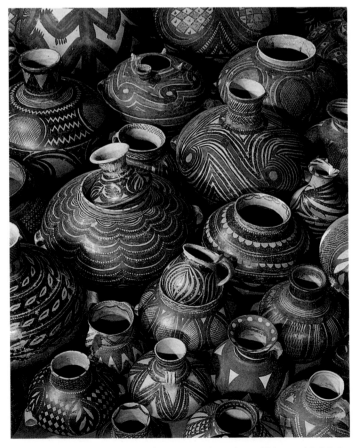

3-1 Yangshao Culture vases, from Gansu Province, China, mid-third millennium BCE. Earthenware.

Chinese Earthenwares and Stonewares

China has no rival in the combined length and richness of its ceramic history. Beginning with the makers of the earliest pots in prehistoric villages, ancient Chinese potters showed a flair for shaping carefully prepared and kneaded clay into diverse, often dramatic and elegant vessel forms.

Until Chinese potters developed true *porcelains* (extremely fine, hard white ceramics; see "Chinese Porcelain," Chapter 4, page 69) in about 1300 CE, they produced only two types of clay vessels or objects—earthenwares and stonewares. For both types, potters used clays colored by mineral impurities, especially iron compounds ranging from yellow to brownish black.

The clay bodies of *earthenwares* (FIG. 3-1), fired at low temperatures in open pits or simple kilns, remain soft and porous, thus allowing liquids to seep through. Chinese artists also used the low-fire technique to produce *terracotta* (baked clay) sculptures, even life-size figures of humans and animals (FIG. 3-5). Over time, Chinese potters developed kilns allowing them to fire their clay vessels at much higher temperatures—more than 2000° Fahrenheit. Such temperatures produce *stonewares,* named for their stonelike hardness and density.

Potters in China excelled at the various techniques commonly used to decorate earthenwares and stonewares. Most of these decorative methods depend on changes occurring in the kiln to chemical compounds found in clay as natural impurities. When fired, many compounds change color dramatically, de-pending on the conditions in the kiln. For example, if little oxygen remains in a hot kiln, iron oxide (rust) turns either gray or brownish black, whereas an abundance of oxygen produces a reddish hue.

Chinese potters also decorated vessels simply by painting their surfaces. In one of the oldest decorative techniques, the potters applied *slip* (a mixture of clay and water like a fine, thin mud)—by painting, pouring, or dipping—to a clay body not yet fully dry. The natural variety of clay colors produced a broad, if not bright, *palette,* as seen in Neolithic vessels (FIG. 3-1). But Chinese potters often also added compounds such as iron oxide to the slip to change or intensify the colors. After the vessels had partially dried, the potters could *incise* (cut into with a sharp instrument) lines through the slip down to the clay body to produce designs such as those often seen in later Chinese stonewares (FIG. 3-20).

Chinese artists sometimes *inlaid* designs, too, carving them into plain vessel surfaces and then filling them with slip or soft clay of a contrasting color. Such techniques spread throughout East Asia (FIG. 3-28).

To produce a hard, glassy surface after firing, potters coated plain or decorated vessels with a *glaze,* a finely ground mixture of minerals. Clear or highly translucent glazes best reveal decorated surfaces. More opaque, richly colored glazes (FIG. 3-17) serve as primary decoration.

Bronze Age. The Shang kings ruled from a series of royal capitals in the Yellow River valley and vied for power and territory with the rulers of neighboring states.

ROYAL BURIALS AT ANYANG In 1928, excavations at Anyang (ancient Yin) brought to light the last Shang capital. There, archaeologists found a large number of objects—turtle shells, animal bones, and bronze containers—inscribed in the earliest form of the Chinese language. These fragmentary records and the other finds at Anyang provide important information about the Shang kings and their affairs. They reveal a warlike, highly stratified society. Walls of pounded earth protected Shang cities. Servants, captives, and even teams of charioteers with chariots and horses accompanied Shang kings to their tombs. The excavated tomb furnishings include weapons and a great wealth of objects in jade, ivory, lacquer, and bronze. Not only the kings received lavish burials. The tomb of Fu Hao, the wife of Wu Ding (r. ca. 1215–1190 BCE), for example, contained more than a thousand bronze and jade objects, as well as an ivory beaker inlaid with turquoise.

SHANG BRONZES Shang artists perfected the casting of elaborate bronze vessels in piece molds (see "Shang Bronze-Casting," page 42). Many of these vessels were used in sacrifices to ancestors and in funerary ceremonies. Shang bronzes held wine, water, grain, or meat for sacrificial rites. Each vessel's shape matched its intended purpose. One of the most dramatic Shang vessel forms is the *guang* (FIG. **3-2**), a libation vessel shaped like a covered gravy boat. Preserved examples display the characteristic Shang decorative vocabulary of abstract and animal motifs. These range from

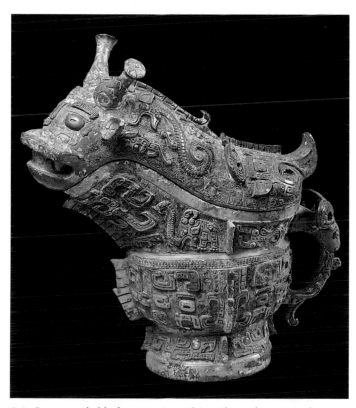

3-2 Guang, probably from Anyang, China, Shang dynasty, 12th or 11th century BCE. Bronze, $6\frac{1}{2}''$ high. Asian Art Museum of San Francisco, San Francisco (Avery Brundage Collection).

Shang Bronze-Casting

Among the finest bronzes of the second millennium BCE are those that Shang artists created using piece molds (FIG. 3-2). The Shang bronzeworkers began the process by producing a solid clay model of the desired object and allowing it to dry to durable hardness. Then they pressed damp clay around it to form a *mold* that hardened but remained somewhat flexible. At that point, they carefully cut the mold in pieces, removed the pieces from the model, and baked the pieces in a kiln to form hard earthenware sections. Sculptors then carved the intricate details of the relief decoration into the inner surfaces of the piece molds. Next, the artists shaved the model to reduce its size to form a core for the piece mold. They then reassembled the mold around the model using bronze spacers to preserve a void between the model and

the mold. The Shang bronze casters then added a final clay layer on the outside to hold everything together, leaving open ducts for pouring molten bronze into the space between the model and the mold and to permit gases to escape. Once the mold cooled, they broke it apart, removed the new bronze vessel, and cleaned and polished it.

Shang bronzes show a skill in *casting* rivaling that of any other ancient civilization and indicating a long developmental period for achieving such mastery. The great numbers of cast-bronze vessels strongly suggest well-organized workshops, but no records provide a clear picture of such matters or of the place the artists held in their society. Bronze-casting may have been a hereditary occupation.

mere suggestions of animal forms emerging out of linear patterns to identifiable representations of specific creatures. Often, distinct motifs stand out against a background of round or squared spirals ending in hooks. Sometimes the same motifs also cover the figures.

In the Shang guang we illustrate (FIG. 3-2), the multiple designs and their fields of background spirals integrate so closely with the form of the vessel that they are not merely an external embellishment but an integral part of the sculptural whole. Some motifs on the vessel's side may represent the eyes of a tiger and the horns of a ram. A horned animal forms the front of the lid, and at the rear is a horned head with a bird's beak. Another horned head appears on the handle. Fish, birds, elephants, rabbits, and more abstract composite creatures swarm over the surface against a background of spirals. The fabulous animal forms, real and imaginary, are unlikely to have been purely decorative. They are probably connected with the world of spirits addressed in the rituals.

SURPRISING SANXINGDUI Recent excavations in other regions of China have greatly expanded historical understanding of the Bronze Age. They suggest that at the same time Anyang flourished under its Shang rulers in northern China, so did other major centers with distinct aesthetic traditions. For example, in 1986, pits at Sanxingdui, near Chengdu in southwestern China, yielded a treasure of elephant tusks and objects in gold, bronze, jade, and clay of types never before discovered. They attest to an independent kingdom of enormous wealth contemporary with the better-known Shang dynasty.

The most dramatic find, a bronze statue (FIG. **3-3**) more than eight feet tall, matches anything from Anyang in masterful casting technique. Very different in subject and style from the Shang bronzes, it initially shocked art historians who had formed their ideas about Bronze Age Chinese aesthetics based on Shang material. This figure—of unknown identity—is highly stylized, with elongated proportions and large, staring eyes. It stands on a thin platform supported by four legs formed of fantastic animal heads with horns and trunklike snouts. These, in turn, rest on a thick, heavy square base. The statue as a whole tapers gently as it rises, and the figure gradually becomes rounder. Just below the neck, great arms branch dramatically outward, ending in oversized hands that once held an object, perhaps an attribute revealing its

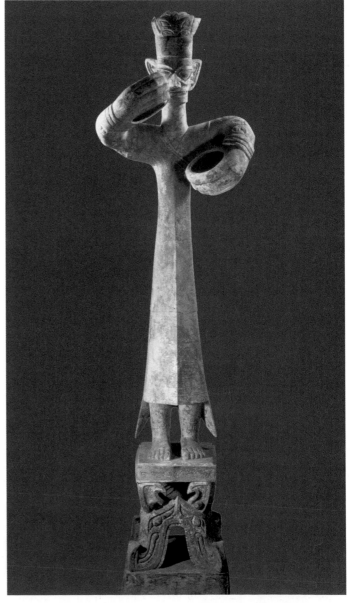

3-3 Standing figure, from Sanxingdui, China, ca. 1200-1050 BCE. Bronze, 8′ 5″ high, including base. Museum, Sanxingdui.

Chinese Jade

The Chinese first used jade, or more precisely, nephrite, for artworks and ritual objects in the Neolithic period. Nephrite polishes to a more lustrous, slightly buttery finish than jadeite (the stone Chinese sculptors preferred from the 18th century on), which is quite glassy. Both stones come in colors other than the well-known green and are tough, hard, and heavy, as well as beautiful. In China, such qualities became metaphors for the fortitude and moral perfection of superior persons. Jade was also believed to have magical qualities that could protect the dead. Archaeologists have found the tomb of a prince and princess of the Han dynasty (206 BCE–220 CE), each of whom was laid to rest in a suit composed of more than 2,000 jade tablets sewn together with gold wire.

Because of its extreme hardness, jade could not be carved with the Neolithic sculptor's stone tools. Researchers can only speculate on how these early artists were able to cut, shape, and incise the nephrite objects discovered at many Neolithic Chinese sites. The sculptors probably used cords embedded with sand to incise lines into the surfaces. Sand placed in a bamboo tube drill could perforate the hard stone, but the process would have been long and arduous, requiring great patience as well as superior skill. Even after the invention of bronze tools, Chinese sculptors still had to rely on grinding and *abrasion* rather than simple drilling and chiseling to produce the intricately shaped, pierced, and engraved works such as the *bi* illustrated in FIG. 3-4.

identity. Representations of the human figure on this scale in this period are otherwise unknown. Surface decoration of squared spirals and hook-pointed curves is all that links this gigantic statue with the intricate piece-mold bronze vessels of the Shang (FIG. 3-2). Archaeology will probably continue to produce such surprises and cause art historians to revise once again their picture of Chinese art in the second half of the second millennium BCE.

Zhou Dynasty

Around 1050 BCE, the Zhou, former vassals of the Shang, captured Anyang and overthrew their Shang overlords. The Zhou dynasty proved to be the longest lasting in China's history — so long that historians divide the Zhou era into two great periods: Western Zhou (ca. 1050–771 BCE) and Eastern Zhou (770–256 BCE). The dividing event is the transfer of the Zhou capital from Chang'an (modern Xi'an) in the west to Luoyang in the east. The closing centuries of Zhou rule include a long period of warfare among competing states (Warring States Period, ca. 475–221 BCE). The Zhou fell to one of these states, the Qin, in 256 BCE. By 221 BCE the Qin had defeated all their other rivals.

Under the Zhou, the decline of old ceremonial rules and the development of markets, together with bronze coinage and the rise of freelance artists, supported a taste for lavish products, such as bronzes inlaid with gold and silver. Late Zhou bronzes featured scenes of hunting, religious rites, and magic practices. These may relate to the subjects and compositions of lost paintings mentioned in Zhou literature. Other materials favored in the late Zhou period were jade (see "Chinese Jade," above) and *lacquer*, a varnishlike substance made from the sap of the Asiatic sumac, used to decorate wood furniture and other objects (see "Lacquered Wood," Chapter 4, page 71).

JADE DRAGONS The carving of jade objects for burial with the dead, beginning in Neolithic times, reached a peak of technical perfection during the Zhou dynasty. Among the most common finds in tombs of the period are *bi* disks — thin, flat circular pieces of jade with a hole in the center, which may have symbolized the circle of Heaven. Our example (FIG. 3-4) probably came

from a royal Eastern Zhou tomb at Jincun, near Luoyang in north central China. Rows of raised spirals, created by laborious grinding and polishing, decorate the disk itself. Within the inner circle and around the outer edge of the bi are elegant dragons, which required long hours of work to pierce through the hard jade. The bi testifies to the Zhou sculptor's mastery of this difficult material. The Chinese thought dragons inhabited the water and flew between Heaven and Earth, bringing rain, so these animals long have been symbols of good fortune in East Asia. They also symbolized the rulers' power to mediate between Heaven and Earth.

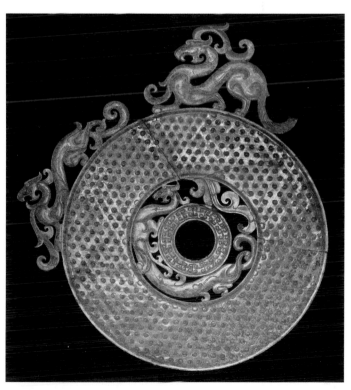

3-4 *Bi* disk with dragons, from Jincun(?), China, Eastern Zhou dynasty, fourth to third century BCE. Nephrite, $6\frac{1}{2}$" in diameter. Nelson-Atkins Museum of Art, Kansas City.

Daoism and Confucianism

Daoism and Confucianism are both philosophies and religions native to China. Both schools of thought attracted wide followings during the Warring States Period (ca. 475–221 BCE), when political turbulence led to social unrest.

Daoism emerged out of the metaphysical teachings attributed to Laozi (604?–531? BCE) and Zhuangzi (370?–301? BCE). It takes its name from Laozi's treatise *Daodejing* (*The Way and Its Power*). Daoist philosophy stresses an intuitive awareness, nurtured by harmonious contact with nature, and eschews everything artificial. Daoists seek to follow the universal path, or principle, called the Dao, whose features cannot be described but only suggested through analogies. For example, the Dao is said to be like water, always yielding but eventually wearing away the hard stone that does not yield. For Daoists, strength comes from flexibility and inaction. Historically, Daoist principles encouraged retreat from society in favor of personal cultivation.

Confucius (551–479 BCE) was born in the state of Lu (roughly modern Shandong Province) to an aristocratic family that had fallen on hard times. From an early age, he showed a strong interest in the rites and ceremonies that helped unite people into an orderly society. As he grew older, he developed a deep concern for the suffering caused by the civil conflict of his day. Thus, he adopted a philosophy he hoped would lead to order and stability.

The ideal social order Confucius sought is personified by the *junzi* ("superior person" or "gentleman"), who possesses *ren* ("human-heartedness"). Although the term junzi originally assumed noble birth, in Confucian thought anyone can become a junzi by cultivating the virtues Confucius espoused, especially empathy for suffering, pursuit of morality and justice, respect for ancient ceremonies, and adherence to traditional social relationships, such as those between parent and child, elder and younger sibling, husband and wife, and ruler and subject.

Confucius's disciple Mencius (or Mengzi, 371?–289? BCE), developed the master's ideas further, stressing that the deference to age and rank that is at the heart of the Confucian social order brings a reciprocal responsibility. For example, a king's legitimacy depends on the good will of his people. A ruler should share his joys with his subjects, and will know his laws are unjust if they bring suffering to the people.

Confucius spent much of his adult life trying to find rulers willing to apply his teachings, but he died in disappointment. However, he and Mencius had a profound impact on Chinese thought and social practice. Chinese traditions of venerating deceased ancestors and outstanding leaders encouraged the development of Confucianism as a religion as well as a philosophic tradition. Eventually, Emperor Wu Di (r. 140–87 BCE) of the Han dynasty established Confucianism as the state's official doctrine. Thereafter, it became the primary subject of the civil service exams required for admission into and advancement within government service.

"Confucian" and "Daoist" are broad, imprecise terms scholars often use to distinguish aspects of Chinese culture stressing social responsibility and order (Confucian) from those emphasizing cultivation of individuals, often in reclusion (Daoist). But both philosophies share the idea that anyone can cultivate wisdom or ability, regardless of birth.

Qin Dynasty

THE FIRST EMPEROR During the Warring States Period, China endured more than two centuries of political and social turmoil. This was also a time of intellectual and artistic upheaval, when conflicting schools of philosophy, including Legalism, Daoism, and Confucianism, emerged (see "Daoism and Confucianism," above). Order was finally restored when the powerful armies of the ruler of the state of Qin (from which the modern name "China" derives) conquered all rival states. Qin's ruler took the name Zheng, but he is known to history by his title, Qin Shi Huangdi, the First Emperor of Qin. Between 221 and 210 BCE he controlled an area equal to about half of modern China, much larger than the territories of any of the dynasties before him. During his reign, he ordered the linkage of active fortifications along the northern border of his realm to form the famous Great Wall. The wall defended China against the fierce nomadic peoples of the north, especially the Huns, who eventually made their way to eastern Europe. By sometimes brutal methods, Shi Huangdi consolidated rule through a centralized bureaucracy and adopted standardized written language, weights and measures, and coinage. He also repressed schools of thought other than Legalism, which espoused absolute obedience to the state's authority and advocated strict laws and punishments. Chinese historians long have condemned China's First Emperor, but the bureaucratic system he put in place had a long-lasting impact. Its success was due in large part to Shi Huangdi's decision to replace the feudal lords with talented salaried administrators and to reward merit rather than favor high birth.

THE EMPEROR'S ARMY In 1974, excavations started at the site of the immense burial mound of the First Emperor of Qin at Lintong. For its construction, the ruler conscripted many thousands of laborers and had the tomb filled with treasure—a task that continued after his death. The mound itself remains unexcavated, but researchers believe it contains a vast underground funerary palace designed to match the fabulous palace the emperor occupied in life. The historian Sima Qian (136–85 BCE) described both palaces, but scholars did not take his account seriously until the discovery of pits around the tomb filled with more than 6,000 life-size painted terracotta figures of soldiers and horses (FIG. **3-5**), as well as bronze horses and chariots. Replicating the emperor's invincible hosts, they served as the immortal imperial bodyguard deployed in trenches outside the First Emperor's tomb.

The terracotta army, comprised of cavalry, chariots, archers, lancers, and hand-to-hand fighters, was one of the 20th century's greatest archaeological discoveries. Lesser versions of Shi Huangdi's army have since been uncovered at other Chinese sites, suggesting that the First Emperor's tomb became the model for many others. The huge assemblage at Lintong testifies to a very high degree of

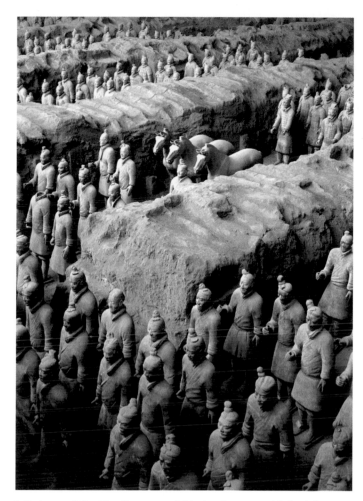

3-5 Army of the First Emperor of Qin in pits next to his burial mound, Lintong, China, Qin dynasty, ca. 210 BCE. Painted terracotta, average figure 5' 10⅞" high.

organization in the Qin imperial workshop. Manufacturing this army of statues required a veritable army of sculptors and painters as well as a large number of huge kilns. The First Emperor's artisans could have opted to use the same molds over and over again to produce thousands of identical soldiers standing in strict formation. In fact, they did employ the same molds repeatedly for different parts of the statues, but assembled the parts in many different combinations. Consequently, the stances, arm positions, garment folds, equipment, coiffures, and facial features vary, sometimes slightly, sometimes markedly, from statue to statue. Additional hand modeling of the cast body parts before firing permitted the sculptors to differentiate the figures even more. The Qin painters undoubtedly added further variations to the appearance of the terracotta army. The result of these efforts was a brilliant balance of uniformity and individuality.

Han Dynasty

Soon after Qin Shi Huangdi's death, the people who had suffered under his reign revolted, assassinated his son, and founded the Han dynasty in 206 BCE. The Han ruled China for four centuries and extended its southern and western boundaries. Chinese armies penetrated far into Central Asia (modern Xinjiang) and even began to trade indirectly with distant Rome via the fabled Silk Road (see "Silk and the Silk Road," page 49).

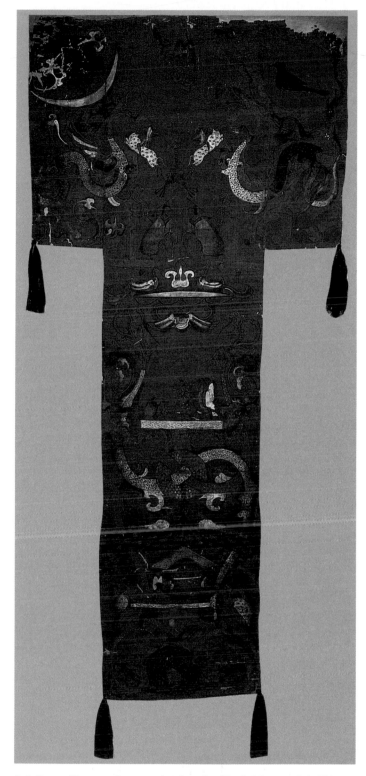

3-6 Funeral banner, from tomb 1 (tomb of Dai), Mawangdui, China, Han dynasty, ca. 168 BCE. Painted silk, 6' 8¾" × 3' ¼". Hunan Provincial Museum, Changsha.

PAINTING ON SILK In 1972, archaeologists excavated the tomb of the wife of the Marquis of Dai at Mawangdui in Hunan Province. The tomb contained a rich array of burial goods used during the funerary ceremonies and to accompany the deceased into the afterlife. Among the many finds were decorated lacquer utensils, various textiles, and an astonishingly well-preserved corpse in the innermost of four nested sarcophagi. Most remarkable of all, however, was the discovery of a painted T-shaped silk banner (FIG. **3-6**) draped over the woman's coffin. Scholars generally agree that

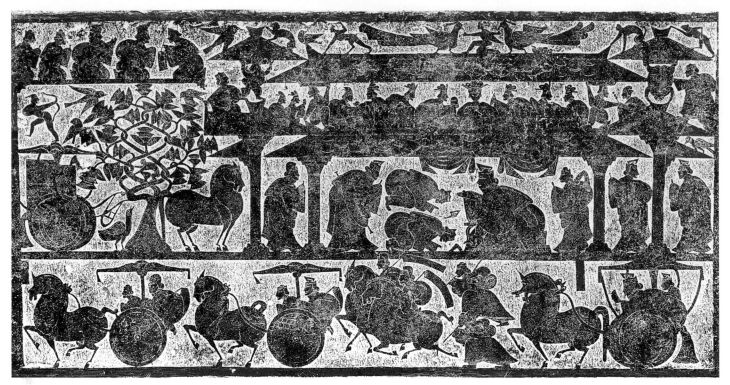

3-7 The archer Yi(?) and a reception in a mansion, Wu family shrine, Jiaxiang, China, Han dynasty, 147–168 CE. Rubbing of a stone relief, approx. 3′ × 5′.

the area within the cross at the top of the **T** represents Heaven. Most of the vertical section below is the human realm. At the very bottom is the Underworld. In the heavenly realm, dragons and immortal beings appear between and below two orbs—the red sun and its symbol, the raven, on the right, and the silvery moon and its symbol, the toad, on the left. Below, the standing figure on the first white platform near the center of the vertical section is probably the Marquise of Dai herself—one of the first portraits in Chinese art. The Marquise awaits her ascent to Heaven, where she can attain immortality. Nearer the bottom, the artist depicted the wealthy woman's funeral. Between these two sections is a form resembling a bi disk with two intertwining dragons (compare FIG. 3-4). Their tails reach down to the Underworld and their heads point to Heaven, unifying the whole composition.

HAN ANCESTRAL SHRINES Even more extensive Han pictorial narratives were carved into the stone walls of the Wu family shrines at Jiaxiang in Shandong Province between 147 and 168 CE. The shrines document the emergence of private, nonaristocratic families as patrons of religious and mythological art with political overtones. Dedicated to deceased male family members, the Wu shrines consist of three low walls covered by a pitched roof. On the interior surfaces, images of flat polished stone stand out against an equally flat, though roughly textured, ground. The historical scenes include a representation of the attempt to assassinate the tyrannical First Emperor of Qin by the celebrated third-century BCE hero Jing Ke. On the slab shown here (FIG. **3-7**, a rubbing taken from the stone relief) the archer at the upper left is probably the hero Yi, saving the Earth from scorching by shooting down the nine extra suns, represented as crows in the Fusang tree. (The small orbs below the sun on the Mawangdui banner probably allude to the same story.) The lowest zone shows a procession of umbrella-carriages moving to the left. Above, underneath the overhanging eaves of a two-story mansion, robed men bearing

gifts pay homage to a central figure of uncertain identity, who is represented as larger and therefore more important. Two men kneel before the larger figure. Women occupy the upper story. Again, one figure is singled out as the most important; she faces forward. Whatever the identities of the individual figures (interpretations vary widely), these scenes of homage and loyalty are consistent with the Confucian ideals of Han society (see "Daoism and Confucianism," page 44).

HAN HOUSES AND PALACES No actual remains of Han buildings survive, but ceramic models of houses deposited in Han tombs, together with representations such as those in the Wu family shrines, provide a good idea of Chinese architecture during the early centuries CE. An especially large painted earthenware model (FIG. **3-8**) reproduces a Han house with sharply projecting tiled roofs resting on a framework of timber posts, lintels, and brackets. This construction method, in which the walls do not bear the weight of the roof but serve only as screens separating inside from outside and room from room, typifies much Chinese architecture even today (see "Chinese Wooden Construction Methods and Principles," page 48). Descriptions of Han palaces suggest that they were grandiose versions of the type of house reproduced in this model, but with more luxurious decoration, including walls of lacquered wood and mural paintings.

Period of Disunity

BUDDHISM REACHES CHINA For three and a half centuries, from 220 to 589,* civil strife divided China into competing states. Scholars variously refer to this era as the Period of Disunity or the

---

* From this point on, all dates in this chapter are CE unless otherwise stated.

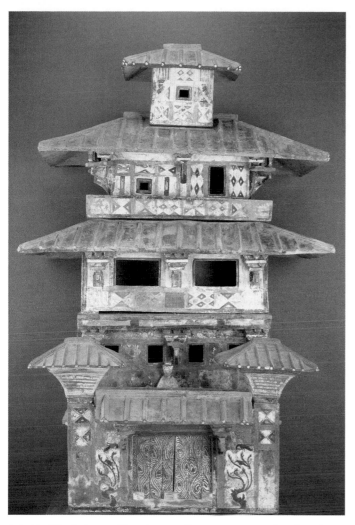

els in the flat, relief-like handling of the robe's heavy concentric folds, the ushnisha (cranial bump) on the head, and the cross-legged position. So new were the icon and its meaning, however, that the Chinese sculptor misrepresented the canonical dhyana mudra, or meditation gesture. Here, the Buddha clasps his hands across his stomach. In South Asian art, they are turned palms upward, with thumbs barely touching in front of the torso.

PAINTING MATERIALS AND FORMATS Secular arts also flourished in the Period of Disunity. Rulers sought calligraphers and painters to lend prestige to their courts. Several distinctive materials and formats characterize early Chinese painting. The basic requirements for paintings not on walls are the same as for writing— a round tapered brush, soot-based ink, and either silk or paper. The Chinese were masters of the brush. Sometimes they employed modulated lines that elastically thicken and thin to convey not only outline but depth and mass as well. In other works, they used *iron-wire lines* (thin, unmodulated lines with a suggestion of tensile strength) to define the figures. Chinese painters also used richly colored minerals as pigments, finely ground and suspended in a gluey medium, and watery washes of mineral and vegetable dyes.

The formats of Chinese paintings (other than mural paintings) tend to be personal and intimate. Some pictures were mounted on scrolls for vertical display (unrolled) on appropriate occasions. Others were attached to long, narrow scrolls that the viewer unrolled horizontally, section by section. Stiff round or arched folding fans were also popular painting formats. Artists also painted small panels on paper leaves, which were collected in albums. Although some Chinese paintings are monumental in size, most are intimate in scale and best viewed by only one or two people at a time.

3-8 Model of a house, Han dynasty, first century CE. Painted earthenware, 4′ 4″ high. Nelson-Atkins Museum of Art, Kansas City.

period of the Six Dynasties or of the Northern and Southern Dynasties. The history of this era is extremely complex, but one development deserves special mention—the occupation of the north by peoples who were not ethnically Han Chinese and who spoke non-Chinese languages. It was in the northern states, connected to India by the desert caravan routes of the Silk Road (see "Silk and the Silk Road," page 49), that Buddhism first took root in China during the Han dynasty (see "Buddhism," Chapter 1, page 5). Certain practices shared with Daoism, such as withdrawal from ordinary society, helped Buddhism gain an initial foothold in the north. But Buddhism's promise of hope beyond the troubles of this world earned it an ever broader audience during the upheavals of the Period of Disunity. In addition, the fully developed Buddhist system of thought attracted intellectuals. Buddhism never fully displaced Confucianism and Daoism, but it did prosper throughout China for centuries and had a profound effect on the further development of the religious forms of those two native traditions.

The earliest extant precisely datable Chinese Buddhist image is a gilded bronze statuette (FIG. 3-9) of Shakyamuni Buddha, the historical Buddha, dated by inscription to the year 338. The oldest Chinese Buddhist texts describe the Buddha as golden and radiating light. This no doubt accounts for the choice of gilded bronze as the sculptor's medium. In both style and iconography, this early Buddha resembles the prototype conceived and developed at Gandhara (see FIG. 1-9). The Chinese figure recalls its presumed South Asian mod-

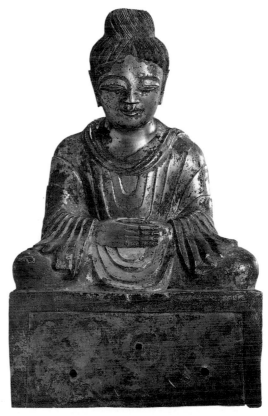

3-9 Shakyamuni Buddha, Zhao dynasty, Period of Disunity, 338. Gilded bronze, 1′ 3½″ high. Asian Art Museum of San Francisco, San Francisco (Avery Brundage Collection).

Chinese Wooden Construction Methods and Principles

Although the basic unit of Chinese architecture, the rectangular hall with columns supporting a roof, was common in many ancient civilizations, Chinese buildings are distinguished by the curving silhouettes of their roofs and by their method of construction.

The Chinese, like other ancient peoples, used wood to construct their earliest buildings. Although those structures do not survive, scholars believe that many of the features giving East Asian architecture its specific character may go back to Zhou times. Even the simple buildings reproduced on Han stone carvings (FIG. 3-7) or in clay models (FIG. 3-8) reveal a style and a method of construction long basic to China.

The typical Chinese hall has a pitched roof with projecting *eaves*. Wooden columns, *lintels*, and brackets provide the support. The walls serve no weight-bearing function but act only as screens. The colors of Chinese buildings, predominantly red, black, yellow, and white, are also distinctive. Chinese timber architecture is customarily multicolored throughout, save for certain parts left in natural color, such as railings made of white marble. The builders usually painted the screen walls and the columns red. Chinese designers often chose dazzling combinations of colors and elaborate patterns for the *beams*, brackets, eaves, *rafters*, and ceilings. The builders painted or lacquered the surfaces to protect the timber from rot and wood parasites, as well as to produce an arresting aesthetic effect.

Our diagram shows the basic construction method of Chinese architecture, with the major components of a Chinese building labeled. The builders laid beams (no. 1) between columns, decreasing the length of the beams as the structure rose. The beams supported vertical *struts* (no. 2), which in turn supported higher beams and eventually the *purlins* (no. 3) running the length of the building and carrying the roof's sloping rafters (no. 4). Unlike the rigid elements of the triangular trussed timber roof common in the West, which produce flat sloping rooflines, the varying lengths of the Chinese structure's cross beams and the variously placed purlins can create curved profiles. Early Chinese roofs have flat profiles (FIGS. 3-7 and 3-8), but curving rafters later became the norm, not only in China but throughout East Asia (FIGS. 3-14, 3-21, 3-22, 5-6, 5-10, and 5-12). In addition, the interlocking clusters of brackets could cantilever (support with brackets) the roof to allow for broad overhang of the eaves (no. 5), another typical feature of Chinese architecture. Multiplication of the *bays* (spaces between the columns) could extend the building's length to any dimension desired, although each bay could be no wider or longer than the length of a single tree trunk. The proportions of the structural elements could be fixed into modules, allowing for standardization of parts. This enabled rapid construction of a building. The workers fit the parts together without using any adhesive substance, such as mortar or glue. Delicately joined as the parts were, they still could easily carry the heavy tiled roofs of Chinese buildings (FIGS. 3-8, 3-14, 3-21, and 4-5).

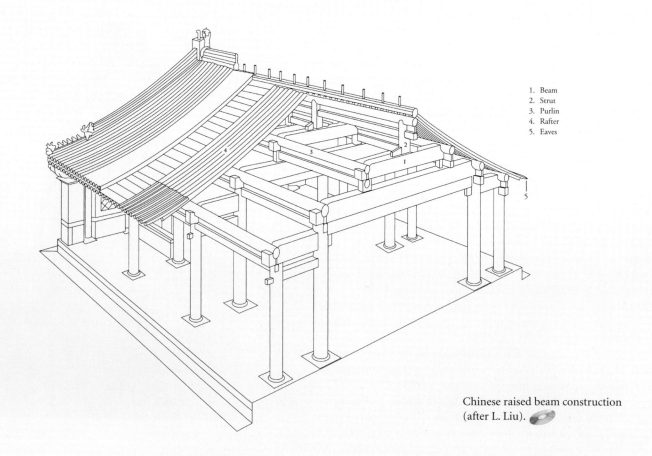

1. Beam
2. Strut
3. Purlin
4. Rafter
5. Eaves

Chinese raised beam construction (after L. Liu).

Silk and the Silk Road

Silk is the finest natural fabric ever produced. It comes from the cocoons of caterpillars called silkworms. The manufacture of silk was a well-established industry in China by the second millennium BCE. The basic procedures probably have not changed much since then. Farmers today still raise silkworms from eggs, which they place in trays. The farmers also must grow mulberry trees or purchase mulberry leaves, the silkworms' only food source. Eventually, the silkworms form cocoons out of very fine filaments they extrude as liquid from their bodies. The filaments soon solidify with exposure to air. Before the transformed caterpillars emerge as moths and badly damage the silk, the farmers kill them with steam or high heat. They soften the cocoons in hot water and unwind the filaments onto a reel. The filaments are so fine that workers generally unwind those from 5 to 10 cocoons together to bond into a single strand while the filaments are still soft and sticky. Later, the silkworkers twist several strands together to form a thicker yarn and then weave the yarn on a loom to produce silk cloth. Both the yarn and the cloth can be dyed, and the silk fabric can be decorated by weaving threads of different colors together in special patterns (*brocades*) or by stitching in threads of different colors (*embroidery*). Many Chinese artists painted directly on plain silk (FIGS. 3-6, 3-10, 3-15, 3-18, 3-19, 3-23, 3-24, 4-9, and 4-14).

Greatly admired throughout most of Asia, Chinese silk and the secrets of its production gradually spread throughout the ancient world. The Romans knew of silk as early as the second century BCE and treasured it for garments and hangings. Silk came to the Romans along the ancient fabled Silk Road, actually a network of caravan tracts across Central Asia linking China and the Mediterranean world. The western part, between the Mediterranean region and India, developed first, due largely to the difficult geographic conditions to India's northeast. In Central Asia, the caravans had to skirt the Taklamakan Desert, one of the most inhospitable environments on earth, as well as climb high, dangerous mountain passes.

Very few traders actually traveled the entire route. Along the way, goods usually passed through the hands of people from many lands, who often only dimly understood the ultimate origins and destinations of what they traded. The Roman passion for silk ultimately led to the modern name for the caravan tracts, but silk was far from the only product traded along the way. Gold, ivory, gems, glass, lacquer, incense, furs, spices, cotton, linens, exotic animals, and other merchandise precious enough to warrant the risks passed along the Silk Road.

Ideas moved along these trade routes as well. Most important perhaps, travelers on the Silk Road brought Buddhism to China from India in the first century CE, opening up a significant new chapter in both the history of religion and the history of art in China.

LADY FENG'S HEROISM The most famous early Chinese painter with whom extant works can be associated was GU KAIZHI (ca. 344–406). Gu was a friend of important members of the Eastern Jin dynasty (317–420) and was renowned as a calligrapher, a painter of court portraits, and a pioneer of landscape painting. A horizontal scroll now in the British Museum, although attributed to Gu Kaizhi in the 11th century, is not actually by his hand, but it provides a good idea of the key elements of his art. Called *Admonitions of the Instructress to the Court Ladies*, the scroll contains painted scenes and accompanying explanatory text. Like all Chinese *handscrolls*, this one was unrolled and read from right to left, with only a small section exposed for viewing at one time. The section we illustrate (FIG. 3-10) records a well-known act of heroism, the Lady Feng saving her emperor's life by

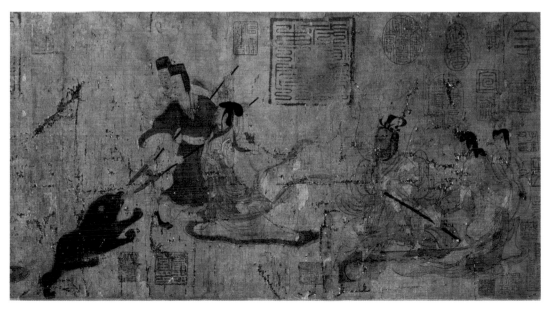

3-10 GU KAIZHI, Lady Feng and the Bear, detail of *Admonitions of the Instructress to the Court Ladies*, Period of Disunity, late fourth century. Handscroll, ink and colors on silk, $9\frac{3}{4}''$ × 11' $4\frac{1}{2}''$. British Museum, London.

Xie He's Six Canons

China has a long and rich history of scholarship on painting, preserved today in copies of texts from as far back as the fourth century and in citations to even earlier sources. Few of the first texts on painting survive, but later authors often quoted them, preserving the texts for posterity. Thus, educated Chinese painters and their clients could steep themselves in a rich art historical tradition. Perhaps the most famous subject of later commentary is a set of six "canons" or "laws" of painting formulated in the early sixth century by Xie He. The canons, as translated by James Cahill,[1] are as follows:

1. Engender a sense of movement through spirit consonance.
2. Use the brush with the bone method.
3. Responding to things, depict their forms.
4. According to kind, describe appearances [with color].
5. Dividing and planning, positioning and arranging.
6. Transmitting and conveying earlier models through copying and transcribing.

Several variant translations have also been proposed, and scholars actively debate the precise meaning of these succinct (Xie He employed only four characters for each) and cryptic laws. Interpreting the canons in connection with actual paintings is often difficult, but nonetheless offers valuable insights into what the Chinese valued in painting.

The simplest canons to understand are the third, fourth, and fifth, because they show painters' concern for accuracy in rendering forms and colors and for care in composition, concerns common in many cultures. However, separating form and color into different laws gives written expression to a distinctive feature of early Chinese painting. Painters such as Gu Kaizhi (FIG. 3-10) and Yan Liben (FIG. 3-15) used an outline-and-color technique. Their brushed-ink outline drawings employ flat applications of color. To suggest volume, they used ink shading along edges, such as drapery folds.

Also noteworthy is the order of the laws, suggesting Chinese painters' primary concern: to convey the vital spirit of their subjects and their own sensitivity to that spirit. Next in importance was the handling of the brush and the careful placement of strokes, especially of ink. The sixth canon also speaks to a standard Chinese painting practice: copying. Chinese painters, like painters in other cultures throughout history, trained by copying the works of their teachers and other painters. In addition, artists often copied famous paintings as sources of forms and ideas for their own works and to preserve great works created using fragile materials (FIG. 3-10). In China, as elsewhere, change and individual development occurred in constant reference to the past, the artists always preserving some elements of it.

[1] James Cahill, "The Six Laws and How to Read Them," *Ars Orientalis* 4 (1961), 372–81.

placing herself between him and an attacking bear—a perfect model of Confucian behavior. As in many early Chinese paintings, the figures are set against a blank background with only a minimal setting for the scene, although in other works Gu provided landscape settings for his narratives. The figures' poses and fluttering drapery ribbons, in concert with individualized facial expressions, convey a clear quality of animation. This style accords well with painting ideals expressed in texts of the time, when representing inner vitality and spirit took precedence over reproducing surface appearances (see "Xie He's Six Canons," above).

THE MEETING OF TWO BUDDHAS A gilded bronze statuette (FIG. 3-11) shows how the sculptors of the Northern Wei dynasty (386–534) had transformed the Gandhara-derived style of earlier Buddhist art in China (FIG. 3-9). Dated 518, the piece was probably made for private devotion in a domestic setting or as a votive offering in a temple. It represents the meeting of Shakyamuni Buddha (at the viewer's right) and Prabhutaratna, the Buddha who had achieved nirvana in the remote past, as recounted in the *Lotus Sutra,* an encyclopedic collection of Buddhist thought and poetry. When Shakyamuni was preaching on Vulture Peak, Prabhutaratna's stupa miraculously appeared in the sky. Shakyamuni opened it and revealed Prabhutaratna himself, who had promised to be present whenever the Lotus Law was preached. Shakyamuni sat beside him and continued to expound the Law. The meeting of the two Buddhas symbolized the continuity of Buddhist thought across the ages.

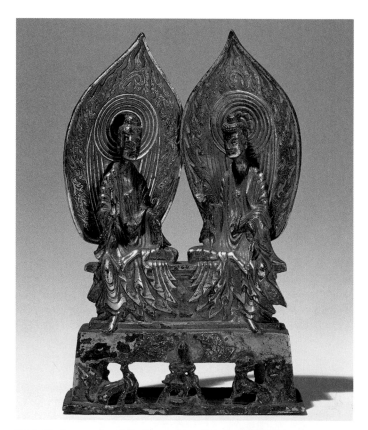

3-11 Shakyamuni and Prabhutaratna, Northern Wei dynasty, 518. Gilded bronze, 10¼″ high. Musée Guimet, Paris.

Behind each Buddha is a flamelike nimbus *(mandorla)*. Both figures sit in the *lalitasana* pose—one leg folded and the other hanging down. This standard pose, which indicates relaxation, underscores the ease of communication between the two Buddhas. Their bodies have elongated proportions, and their smiling faces have sharp noses and almond eyes. The folds of the garments drop like a waterfall from their shoulders to their knees and spill over onto the pedestal, where they form sharp ridges resembling the teeth of a saw. The rhythmic sweep and linear elegance of the folds recall the brushwork of contemporary painting.

Tang Dynasty

The emperors of the short-lived Sui dynasty (581–618) succeeded in reuniting China and prepared the way for the brilliant Tang dynasty (618–906). Under the Tang emperors, China entered a period of unequaled magnificence (MAP 3-1). Chinese armies marched across Central Asia, prompting an influx of foreign peoples, wealth, and ideas into China. Traders, missionaries, and other travelers journeyed to the cosmopolitan Tang capital at Chang'an, and the Chinese, in turn, ventured westward.

WU ZETIAN'S COSMIC BUDDHA In its first century, the new dynasty continued to support Buddhism and to sponsor great monuments for Buddhist worshipers. Cave complexes decorated with reliefs and paintings, modeled on those of India (see Chapter 1), were especially popular. One of the most spectacular Tang Buddhist sculptures is carved into the face of a cliff in the great Longmen Cave complex near Luoyang in north central China. Work at Longmen had begun almost two centuries earlier, during the Period of Disunity, under the Northern Wei dynasty (386–534). The site's 1,352 caves, 97,000 statues, 3,600 inscriptions, and 785 carved niches attest to its importance as a Buddhist center.

The colossal relief (FIG. 3-12) that dominates the Longmen complex features a central figure of the Buddha that is 44 feet tall—seated. An inscription records that the project was completed in 675 when Gaozong (r. 649–683) was the Tang emperor and that in 672 the empress Wu Zetian underwrote a substantial portion of the considerable cost with her private funds. Wu Zetian was an exceptional woman by any standard, and when Gaozong died in 683, she declared herself emperor and ruled until 705, when she was forced to abdicate at age 82.

Wu Zetian's Buddha is the Vairocana Buddha, not the historical Buddha of FIGS. 3-9 and 3-11 but the Mahayana Cosmic Buddha, the Buddha of Boundless Space and Time (see "Buddhism," Chapter 1, page 5). Flanking him are two of his monks, attendant bodhisattvas, and guardian figures—all smaller than the Buddha but still of colossal size. (FIG. 3-12, which includes two visitors to the site, underscores the scale of the work.) The sculptors represented the Buddha in serene majesty. An almost geometric regularity of contour and smoothness of planes emphasize the volume of the massive figure. The folds of his robes fall in a few concentric arcs. The artists suppressed surface detail in the interest of monumental simplicity and dignity.

THE DUNHUANG GROTTOES The westward expansion of the Tang Empire increased the importance of Dunhuang, the westernmost gateway to China on the Silk Road. Dunhuang long had been a wealthy, cosmopolitan trade center, a Buddhist pilgrimage destination, and home to thriving communities of Buddhist monks and nuns of varied ethnicity, as well as to adherents of other religions. In the course of several centuries, hundreds of sanctuaries with painted murals were cut into the soft rock of the cliffs near Dunhuang. Known today as the Mogao Grottoes and in antiquity as the Caves of a Thousand Buddhas, the caves also contain images of painted unfired clay and stucco. The earliest recorded cave at Dunhuang was dedicated in 366, but the oldest extant caves date to the late fifth century.

The Dunhuang caves are especially important because in 845 the emperor Wuzong instituted a major persecution, destroying 4,600 Buddhist temples and 40,000 shrines and forcing the return of 260,500 monks and nuns to lay life. Wuzong's policies did not affect Dunhuang, then under Tibetan rule, so the site preserves much of the type of art lost elsewhere.

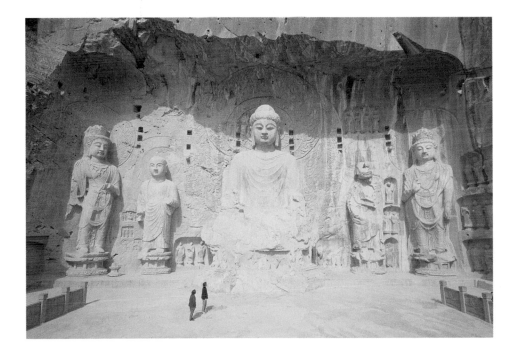

3-12 Vairocana Buddha, disciples, and bodhisattvas, Longmen Caves, Luoyang, China, Tang dynasty, completed 675. Buddha, approx. 44′ high.

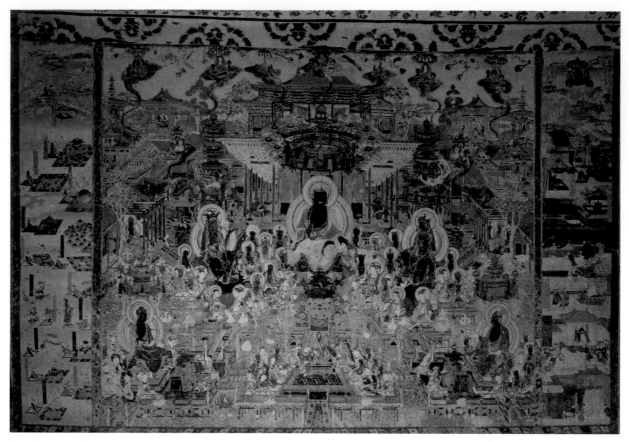

3-13 Paradise of Amitabha, cave 172, Dunhuang, China, Tang dynasty, mid-eighth century. Wall painting, approx. 10′ high. 💿

Paradise of Amitabha (FIG. **3-13**), on the wall of one of the Dunhuang caves, shows how the splendor of the Tang era and religious teachings could come together in a powerful image. Buddhist Pure Land sects, especially those centered on Amitabha, Buddha of the West, had captured the popular imagination in the Period of Disunity under the Six Dynasties and continued to flourish during the Tang dynasty. Pure Land teachings asserted that individuals had no hope of attaining enlightenment through their own power because of the waning of the Buddha's Law. Instead, they could obtain rebirth in a realm free from spiritual corruption simply through faith in Amitabha's promise of salvation. Richly detailed, brilliantly colored pictures steeped in the opulence of the Tang dynasty, such as this one, greatly aided worshipers in gaining faith by visualizing the wonders of such a paradise. Amitabha sits in the center of a raised platform, his principal bodhisattvas and lesser divine attendants surrounding him. Before them a celestial dance takes place. Bodhisattvas had strong appeal in East Asia as compassionate beings ready to achieve buddhahood but dedicated to humanity's salvation. Some received direct worship and became the main subjects of sculpture and painting.

TANG TEMPLES In the Dunhuang mural, Amitabha appears against a backdrop of ornate buildings characteristic of the Tang era. The Tang rulers embellished their empire with extravagant wooden structures, colorfully painted and of colossal size, possessing furnishings of great luxury and elaborate gold, silver, and bronze ornaments. Unfortunately, few Tang buildings survive. Among them is the Foguang Si (Buddha Radiance Temple), one of the oldest surviving Buddhist temples in China. It lacks the costly embellishment of imperial structures in the capital, but its east main hall (FIG. **3-14**) displays the distinctive curved roofline

of later Chinese architecture, which was not present in the Han examples (FIGS. 3-7 and 3-8) discussed earlier. A complex grid of beams and purlins, and a thicket of interlocking brackets, support the overhang of the eaves—some 14 feet out from the column faces—as well as the timbered and tiled roof.

COURT PAINTING Chang'an, the Tang capital captured from the Sui, was laid out on a grid scheme and occupied more than 30 square miles. It was the greatest city in the world during the seventh and eighth centuries. The Tang emperors also fostered a brilliant tradition of painting. Although few examples are preserved, many art historians regard the early Tang dynasty as the golden age of Chinese figure painting.

In perfect accord with the glowing descriptions of Tang painting style by Chinese poets and critics are the unrestored portions

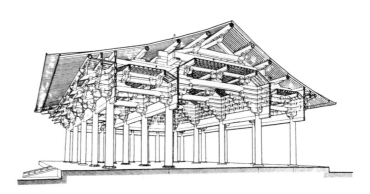

3-14 Schematic cross-section and perspective drawing of east main hall, Foguang Si (Buddha Radiance Temple), Mount Wutai, China, Tang dynasty, ca. 857 (after L. Liu). 💿

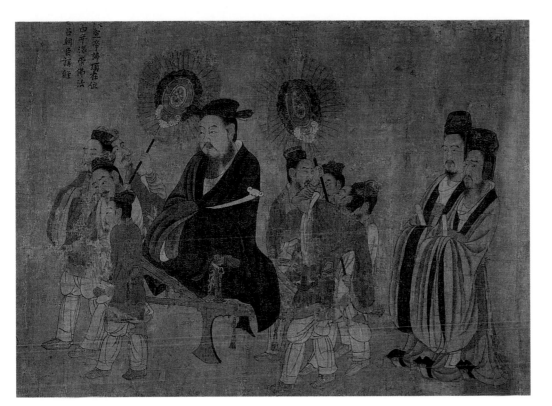

3-15 Attributed to YAN LIBEN, Emperor Xuan and attendants, detail of *The Thirteen Emperors*, Tang dynasty, ca. 650. Handscroll, ink and colors on silk, detail: $1' 8\frac{1}{4}'' \times 1' 5\frac{1}{2}''$; entire scroll: 17' 5" long. Museum of Fine Arts, Boston.

of *The Thirteen Emperors* (FIG. **3-15**), a masterpiece of line drawing and colored washes. The painting has long been attributed to YAN LIBEN (d. 673). Born into an aristocratic family and the son of a famous artist, Yan Liben was prime minister under the emperor Gaozong as well as a celebrated painter. This handscroll depicts 13 Chinese rulers from the Han to the Sui dynasties. Its purpose was to portray these historical figures as exemplars of moral and political virtue, in keeping with the Confucian ideal of learning from the past. Each emperor stands or sits in an undefined space, his eminence clearly indicated by his great size relative to his attendants. Simple shading in the faces and the robes gives the figures an added semblance of volume and presence. Our detail represents the emperor Xuan of the Chen dynasty (557–589) seated among his attendants, two of whom carry the ceremonial fans that signify his imperial status. The poses of the attendants vary sharply from figure to figure, lending vitality to the composition. Xuan stands out easily from the others not only because of his size and central position but also because of his dark robes and majestic serenity.

A PRINCESS'S PAINTED TOMB Wall paintings in the tomb of the Tang princess Yongtai (684–701) at Qianxian, near Chang'an, permit an analysis of court painting styles unobscured by problems of authenticity and reconstruction. When she was 17 years old, Yongtai was either murdered or forced to commit suicide by Wu Zetian. Her underground tomb dates to 706, however, because her formal burial had to await Wu Zetian's own death. The detail illustrated here (FIG. **3-16**) depicts palace ladies and their attendants, images of pleasant court life to accompany the princess into her afterlife. The figures appear as if on a shallow stage. The artist did not provide any indications of background or setting, but intervals between the two rows and the figures' grouping in an oval suggest a consistent ground plane. The women assume a variety of poses, seen in full-face and in three-quarter views, from the front or the back. The device of paired figures facing into and out of the space of the picture appears often in paintings of this period and effectively creates depth. Thick, even contour lines describe full-volumed faces

and suggest solid forms beneath the drapery, all with the utmost economy. This simplicity of form and line, along with the measured cadence of the poses, results in an air of monumental dignity.

By the eighth century, China had become an international cultural center, integrating concepts and artistic forms from farther west and affecting developments to the south and east. In particular, Tang artists and craftspeople taught visitors from Korea and Japan, and some even traveled abroad. Thus, fair approximations of the Tang artists' elegant approach to figurative painting, dominated by sweeping brush lines, began to appear elsewhere in East Asia (see FIG. 5-9). They cannot, however, make up for the loss of famous works, including those by the greatest Tang figure painter, Wu Daozi (active ca. 710–760).

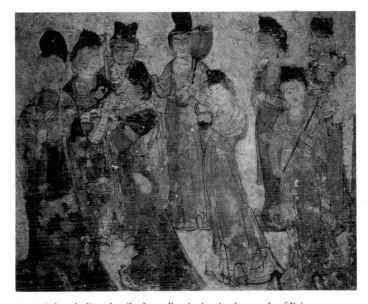

3-16 Palace ladies, detail of a wall painting in the tomb of Princess Yongtai, Qianxian, China, Tang dynasty, 706. Approx. 5' 10" × 6' 6".

GLAZED EARTHENWARE SCULPTURE Tang ceramists also achieved renown. They produced thousands of earthenware figures of people, domesticated animals, and fantastic creatures for burial in tombs. These statuettes attest to a demand for such objects by a much wider group of patrons than ever before, but terracotta funerary sculpture has a long history in China. The most spectacular example is the ceramic army of the First Emperor of Qin (FIG. 3-5). The subjects of the Tang figurines are also much more diverse than in earlier periods. The depiction of a broad range of foreigners, including Semitic traders and Central Asian musicians on camels, accurately reflects the cosmopolitanism of Tang China.

The artists painted some figurines with colored slips and decorated others, such as the spirited, handsomely adorned neighing horse in FIG. 3-17, with colorful lead glazes that ran in dramatic streams down the objects' sides when fired. The popularity of the horse as a subject of Chinese art reflects the importance the emperors placed on the quality of their stables. The breed represented here is powerful in build. Its beautifully arched neck terminates in a small, elegant head. Richly harnessed and saddled, the horse testifies to its rider's nobility. During the period of Tang power, representing horses in painting and ceramics was a special genre, on equal footing with figural composition and landscape.

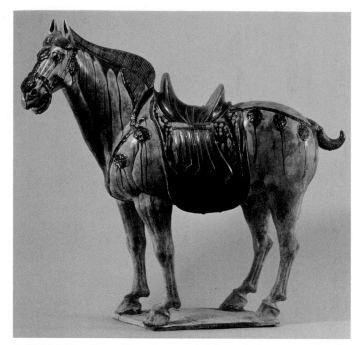

3-17 Neighing Horse, Tang dynasty, eighth to ninth century. Glazed earthenware, 1′ 8″ high. Victoria & Albert Museum, London.

Song Dynasty

The last century of Tang rule witnessed many popular uprisings and the empire's gradual disintegration. After an interim of internal strife known as the Five Dynasties period (906–960), General Zhao Kuangyin succeeded in consolidating the country once again. He established himself as the first emperor (r. 960–976) of the Song dynasty (960–1279), which ruled China from a capital in the north at Bianliang (modern Kaifeng) during the Northern Song period (960–1127). Under the Song emperors, many of the hereditary privileges of the elite class were curtailed. Political appointments were made on the basis of scores on civil service examinations, and education came to be a more important prerequisite for Song officials than high birth.

The three centuries of Song rule, including the Southern Song period (1127–1279) when the capital was at Lin'an (modern Hangzhou) in southern China, were also a time of extraordinary technological innovation. Under the Song emperors, the Chinese invented the magnetic compass for sea navigation, printing with movable clay type, paper money, and gunpowder. Song China was the most technologically advanced society in the world in the early second millennium.

FAN KUAN'S LANDSCAPES For many observers, the Song dynasty also marks the apogee of Chinese landscape painting, which first emerged as a major subject during the Period of Disunity. Although many of the great Northern Song masters worked for the imperial court, FAN KUAN (ca. 960–1030) was a Daoist recluse (see "Daoism and Confucianism," page 44) who shunned the cosmopolitan life of Bianliang. He believed that nature was a better teacher than other artists, and he spent long days in the mountains studying not only configurations of rocks and trees but also the effect of sunlight and moonlight on natural forms. Song critics lauded Fan Kuan and other leading painters of the day as the first masters of the recording of light, shade, distance, and texture.

In *Travelers among Mountains and Streams* (FIG. 3-18), painted in the early 11th century, Fan Kuan presents a vertical landscape of massive mountains rising from the distance. The overwhelming natural forms dwarf the few human and animal figures (for example, the mule train in the lower right corner), which the artist reduced to minute proportions. The nearly seven-foot-long silk hanging scroll cannot contain nature's grandeur, and the landscape continues in all directions beyond its borders. The painter depicted some elements from level ground (for example, the great boulder in the foreground), and others obliquely from the top (the shrubbery on the highest cliff). The shifting perspectives lead viewers on a journey through the mountains. To appreciate such landscapes fully, viewers must focus not only on the larger composition but also on intricate details and on the character of each brush stroke. Numerous "texture strokes" help model massive forms and convey a sense of tactile surfaces. For the face of the mountain, for example, Fan Kuan employed small, pale brush marks, the kind of texture stroke the Chinese call "raindrop strokes."

HUIZONG, EMPEROR AND PAINTER A century after Fan Kuan painted in the mountains of Shanxi, the emperor HUIZONG (1082–1135; r. 1101–1125) assumed the Song throne at Bianliang. Less interested in governing than in the arts, he brought the country to near bankruptcy and lost much of China's territory to the armies of the Tartar Jin dynasty (1115–1234), who captured the Song capital in 1126 and took Huizong as a prisoner. He died in their hands several years later. Himself an accomplished poet, calligrapher, and painter, Huizong reorganized the imperial painting academy and required the study of poetry and calligraphy as part of the official training of court painters. *Calligraphy*, or the art of writing, was highly esteemed in China throughout its history, and prominent inscriptions are frequent elements of Chinese paintings (see "Calligraphy and Inscriptions on Chinese Paintings," Chapter 4, page 68). Huizong also promoted the careful study both of

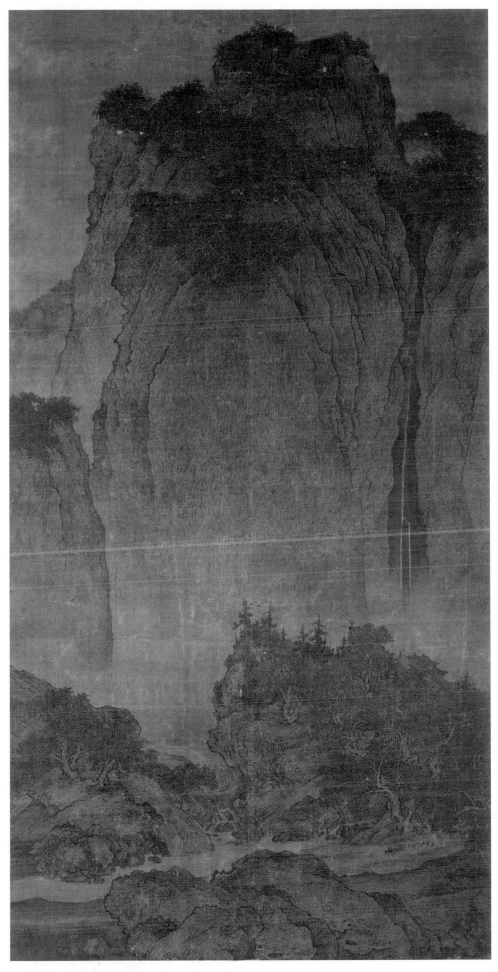

3-18 FAN KUAN, *Travelers among Mountains and Streams,* Northern Song period, early 11th century. Hanging scroll, ink and colors on silk, 6′ 7¼″ × 3′ 4¼″. National Palace Museum, Taibei.

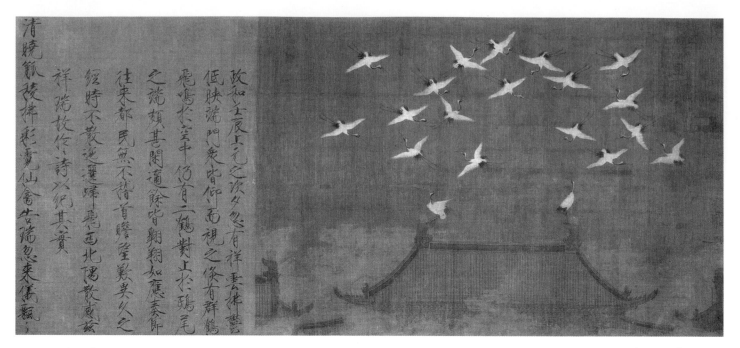

3-19 Attributed to HUIZONG, *Auspicious Cranes*, Northern Song period, 1112. Section of a handscroll, ink and colors on silk, 1′ 8⅛″ × 4′ 6⅜″. Liaoning Provincial Museum, Shenyang.

nature and of the classical art of earlier periods, and was an avid art collector as well as the sponsor of a comprehensive catalogue of the vast imperial art holdings.

A short handscroll (FIG. 3-19) usually attributed to Huizong is more likely the work of court painters under his direction, but it displays the emperor's style as both calligrapher and painter. Huizong's characters represent one of many styles of Chinese calligraphy. They are made up of thin strokes, and each character is meticulously aligned with its neighbors to form neat vertical rows. The painting depicts cranes flying over the roofs of Bian-liang. It is a masterful combination of elegant composition and realistic observation. The black and red feathers of the white cranes are carefully recorded, and the birds are depicted from a variety of viewpoints to suggest that they were circling around the roof. Huizong did not, however, choose this subject because of his interest in the anatomy and flight patterns of birds. The painting was a propaganda piece commemorating the appearance of 20 white cranes at the palace gates during a festival in 1112. The cranes were regarded as an auspicious sign, proof that Heaven had blessed Huizong's rule. Although few would ever have viewed the handscroll, the cranes were also displayed on painted banners on special occasions, where they could be seen by a larger public.

CIZHOU POTTERY Song artists also produced superb ceramics. Some reflect their patrons' interests in antiquities and imitate the powerful forms of the Shang and Zhou bronzes. However, Song ceramics more commonly had elegant shapes with fluid silhouettes. Many featured monochrome glazes, such as the famous celadon wares, also produced in Korea (FIG. 3-28), but a quite different kind of pottery, loosely classed as Cizhou, emerged in northern China. The example shown (FIG. 3-20) is a vase of the high-shouldered shape known as *meiping*. Chinese potters developed the subtle techniques of *sgraffitto* (incising the design through a colored slip) during the Northern Song period. They achieved the intricate black-and-white design here by cutting through a black slip (see "Chinese Earthenwares and Stonewares,"

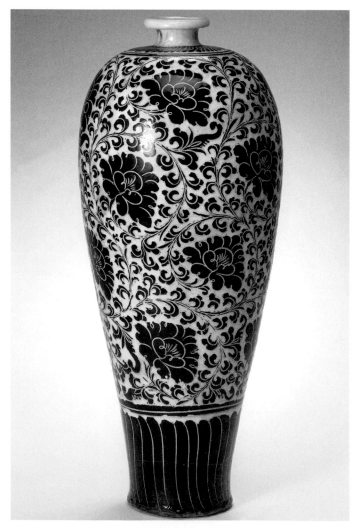

3-20 Meiping vase, from Xiuwi, China, Northern Song period, 12th century. Stoneware, Cizhou type, with sgraffito decoration, 1′ 7½″ high. Asian Art Museum of San Francisco, San Francisco (Avery Brundage Collection).

page 41). The tightly twining vine and flower petal motifs on this vase closely embrace the vessel in a perfect accommodation of surface design to vase shape.

CHINESE PAGODAS For two centuries during the Northern Song period, the Liao dynasty (907–1125) ruled part of northern China. In 1056, the Liao rulers built the Foguang Si Pagoda (FIGS. **3-21** and **3-22**), the tallest wooden building in the world, at Yingxian in Shanxi Province. The *pagoda*, or tower, the building type most often associated with Buddhism in China and other parts of East Asia, is the most eye-catching feature of a Buddhist temple complex. It somewhat resembles the tall towers of Indian temples (see "Hindu Temples," Chapter 1, page 14) and their distant ancestor, the Indian stupa (see "The Stupa," Chapter 1, page 6). Like stupas, many early pagodas housed relics and provided a focus for devotion to the Buddha. Later pagodas served other functions, such as housing sacred images and texts. The Chinese and Koreans built both stone and brick pagodas, but wooden pagodas were also common and became the standard in Japan.

The nine-story octagonal pagoda at Yingxian is 216 feet tall and made entirely of wood (see "Chinese Wooden Construction," page 48). Sixty giant four-tiered bracket clusters carry the floor beams and projecting eaves of the five main stories. They rest on two concentric rings of columns at each level. Alternating main stories and windowless mezzanines with cantilevered balconies, set back further on each story as the tower rises, form an elevation of nine stories altogether. Along with the open veranda on the ground level and the soaring pinnacle, the balconies visually lighten the building's mass. Our cross-section (FIG. 3-22) shows the symmetrical placement of statues of the Buddha inside, the colossal scale of the ground-floor statue, and the intricacy of the beam-and-bracket system at its most ingenious.

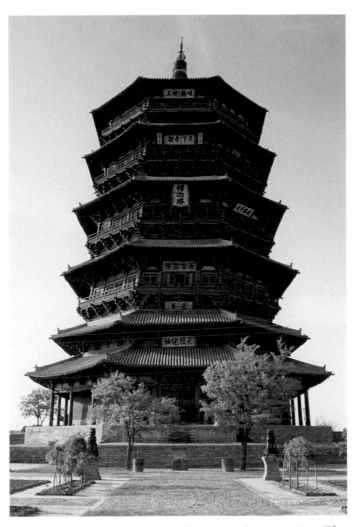

3-21 Foguang Si Pagoda, Yingxian, China, Liao dynasty, 1056.

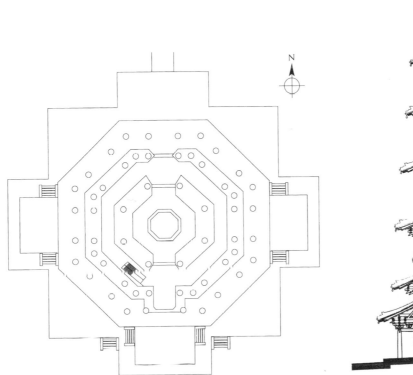

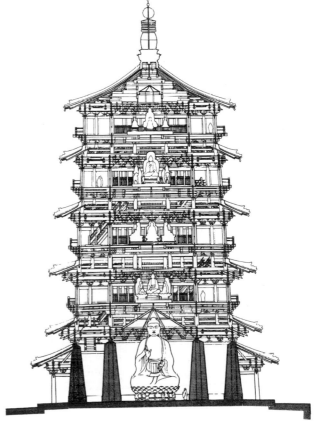

3-22 Plan and cross-section of Foguang Si Pagoda, Yingxian, China, Liao dynasty, 1056 (after L. Liu).

Southern Song Period

When the Jin captured Bianliang and the emperor Huizong in 1126 and took control of northern China, Gaozong (r. 1127–1162), Huizong's sixth son, escaped and eventually established a new Song capital in the south at Lin'an (present-day Hangzhou). From there, he and his successors during the Southern Song period ruled their reduced empire until 1279.

EMPERORS, POETS, AND PAINTERS Court sponsorship of painting continued in the new capital and, as in the Northern Song period, some of the emperors were directly involved with the painters of the imperial painting academy. During the reign of Ningzong (r. 1194–1224), members of the court, including Ning-zong himself and the empress Yang, frequently added brief poems to the paintings created under their direction. Some of the painters belonged to families that had worked for the Song emperors for several generations. The most famous of these was the Ma family, which began working for the Song dynasty during the Northern Song period.

MA YUAN (ca. 1160–1225) painted *On a Mountain Path in Spring* (FIG. **3-23**), a small silk album leaf, for Ningzong in the early 13th century. In his composition, in striking contrast to Fan Kuan's much larger *Travelers among Mountains and Streams* (FIG. 3-18), the landscape is reduced to a few elements and confined to the foreground and left side of the page. A large, solitary figure gazes out into the infinite distance. Framing him are the carefully placed diagonals of willow branches. Near the upper right corner a bird flies toward the couplet that Ningzong added in ink, demonstrating his mastery of both poetry and calligraphy (see "Calligraphy and Inscriptions," Chapter 4, page 68):

> *Brushed by his sleeves, wild flowers dance in the wind;*
> *Fleeing from him, hidden birds cut short their songs.*

Some scholars have suggested that the author of the two-line poem is actually the empress Yang, but the inscription is in the emperor's hand. In any case, landscape paintings such as this one are perfect embodiments of the Chinese ideals of peace and unity with nature.

TWO SPHERES OF BEING Religious painting also flourished under the Southern Song emperors. Neo-Confucianism, a blend of traditional Chinese thought and selected Buddhist concepts, became the leading philosophy, but Buddhist themes were still the subject of many painters. ZHOU JICHANG (ca. 1130–1190) painted *Arhats Giving Alms to Beggars* (FIG. **3-24**) in 1184 as part of a series of 100 scrolls produced at the southern coastal city of Ningbo for an abbot who invited individual donors to pay for the paintings as offerings in the nearby Buddhist temple. *Arhats* are enlightened disciples of the Buddha who have achieved freedom from rebirth (nirvana) by suppression of all desire for earthly things. They were charged with protecting the Buddhist Law until the arrival of the Buddha of the Future.

In the scroll we illustrate (FIG. 3-24), Zhou Jichang arranged the foreground, middle ground, and background vertically to clarify the arhats' positions relative to one another and to the

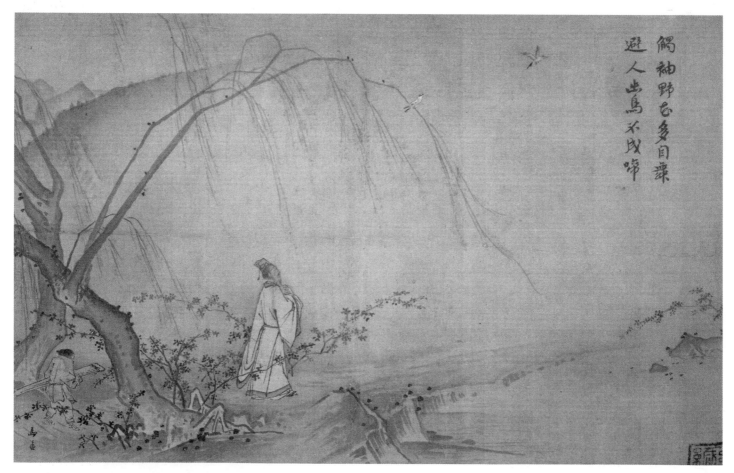

3-23 MA YUAN, *On a Mountain Path in Spring*, Southern Song period, early 13th century. Album leaf, ink and colors on silk, 10¾″ × 17″. National Palace Museum, Taibei.

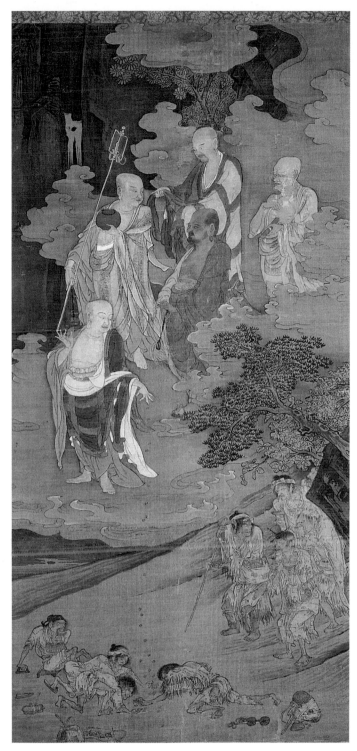

3-24 ZHOU JICHANG, *Arhats Giving Alms to Beggars*, Southern Song period, 1184. Ink and colors on silk, 3′ 8″ × 1′ 9″. Museum of Fine Arts, Boston. 💿

beggars. The arhats move with slow dignity in a plane above the ragged wretches who scramble miserably for the alms their serene benefactors throw down. The extreme difference in deportment between the two groups distinguishes their status, as do their contrasting features. The arhats' vividly colored attire, flowing draperies, and quiet gestures set them off from the dirt-colored and jagged shapes of the people physically and spiritually beneath them. The composition of the landscape—the cloudy platform and lofty peaks of the arhats and the desertlike setting of the beggars—also sharply distinguishes the two spheres of being.

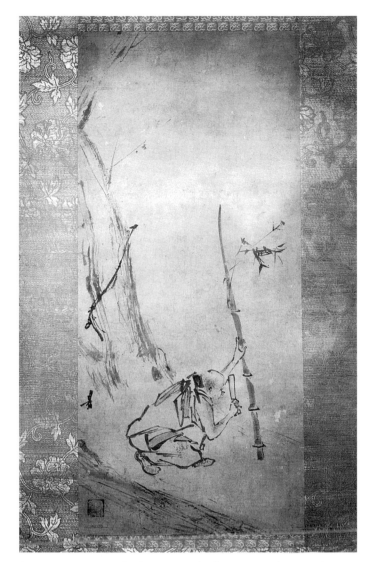

3-25 LIANG KAI, *Sixth Chan Patriarch Chopping Bamboo*, Southern Song period, early 13th century. Hanging scroll, ink on paper, 2′ 5¼″ high. Tokyo National Museum, Tokyo.

LIANG KAI AND CHAN Chan Buddhism (see "Chan Buddhism," page 60), which stressed the quest for personal enlightenment through meditation, flourished under the Song dynasty. LIANG KAI (active early 13th century) was a master of an abbreviated, expressive style of ink painting that found great favor among Chan monks in China, Korea, and Japan. He served in the painting academy of the imperial court in Hangzhou, and his early works include poetic landscapes typical of the Southern Song. Later in life, he left the court and concentrated on figure painting, including Chan subjects.

Surviving works attributed to him include an ink painting (FIG. 3-25) of the Sixth Chan Patriarch, Huineng, crouching as he chops bamboo. In Chan thought, the performance of even such mundane tasks had the potential to become a spiritual exercise. More specifically, this scene represents the patriarch's "Chan moment," when the sound of the blade striking the bamboo resonates within his spiritually attuned mind to propel him through the final doorway to enlightenment. The scruffy, caricature-like representation of the revered figure suggests that Huineng's mind is not burdened by worldly matters, such as physical appearance or signs of social status. Liang Kai utilized a variety of brushstrokes in the execution of this deceptively

Chan Buddhism

Under the Song emperors (960–1279), the new school of *Chan* Buddhism gradually gained importance, until it was second only to Neo-Confucianism. The Chan school traced its origins through a series of patriarchs (the founder and early leaders, joined in a master–pupil lineage). The First Chan Patriarch was Bodhidharma, a semilegendary sixth-century Indian missionary. By the time of the Sixth Chan Patriarch, Huineng (638–713; FIG. 3-25) in the early Tang period, the religious forms and practices of the school were already well established.

Although Chan monks adapted many of the rituals and ceremonies of other schools over the course of time, they focused on the cultivation of the mind or spirit of the individual in order to break through the illusions of ordinary reality, especially by means of meditation. In Chan thought, the means of enlightenment lie within the individual, and direct personal experience with some ultimate reality is the necessary step to its achievement. Meditation is a critical practice. In fact, the word "Chan" is a translation of the Sanskrit word for meditation. Bodhidharma is said to have meditated so long in a cave that his arms and legs withered away. The "Northern School" of Chan holds that enlightenment comes only gradually after long meditation, but the "Southern School" believes that the breakthrough to enlightenment can be sudden and spontaneous.

These beliefs influenced art and aesthetics as they developed in China and spread to Korea and Japan. In Japan, Chan (Japanese *Zen*) had an especially extensive, long-term impact on the arts and remains an important school of Buddhism there today (see "Zen and Zen-Inspired Art," Chapter 6, page 99).

simple picture. Most are pale and wet, ranging from the fine lines of Huineng's beard to the broad texture strokes of the tree. A few darker strokes, which define the vine growing around the tree and the patriarch's clothing, offer visual accents in the painting. This kind of quick and seemingly casual execution of paintings has traditionally been interpreted as a sign of a painter's ability to produce compelling pictures spontaneously as a result of superior training and character, or, in the Chan setting, progress toward enlightenment.

KOREA

Korea is a northeast Asian peninsula that shares borders with China and Russia, and faces the islands of Japan (MAP 3-1). Korea's pivotal location is a key factor in understanding the relationship of its art to that of China and the influence of its art on that of Japan. Ethnically, the Koreans are related to the peoples of eastern Siberia and Mongolia, as well as to the Japanese. In the early centuries, the Koreans used Chinese characters to write Korean words, but later they invented their own phonetic alphabet. Korean art, although frequently based on Chinese models, is not merely derivative but has, like Korean civilization, a distinct identity.

Three Kingdoms Period

CHINA AND THE THREE KINGDOMS Pottery-producing cultures appeared on the Korean peninsula in the Neolithic period no later than 6000 BCE, and the Korean Bronze Age dates from ca. 1000 BCE. Bronze technology was introduced from the area that is today northeastern China (formerly known as Manchuria). About 100 BCE, during the Han dynasty, the Chinese established outposts in Korea. The most important was Lelang, which became a prosperous commercial center. By the middle of the century, however, three native kingdoms—Koguryo, Paekche, and Silla—controlled most of the Korean peninsula and reigned for more than seven centuries until Silla completed its conquest of its neighbors in 668. During this era, known as the Three Kingdoms period (ca. 57 BCE–688 CE), Korea remained in continuous contact with both China and Japan. Buddhism was introduced into Korea from China in the fourth century CE. The Koreans in turn transmitted it from the peninsula to Japan in the sixth century.

GOLD CROWNS IN SILLA TOMBS Tombs of the Silla kingdom have yielded spectacular artifacts representative of the wealth and power of its rulers. Finds in the region of Kyongju justify the city's ancient name—Kumsong ("City of Gold"). The gold-and-jade crown (FIG. 3-26) from a tomb at Hwangnam-dong, near Kyongju, dated to the fifth or sixth century, also attests to the high quality of artisanship among Silla artists. The crown's major elements, the band and the uprights, as well as the myriad spangles adorning them, were cut from sheet gold and embossed along the edges. Gold rivets and wires secure the whole, as do the comma-shaped pieces of jade further embellishing the crown. Archaeologists interpret the uprights as stylized tree and antler forms believed to symbolize life and supernatural power. The Hwangnamdong crown has no counterpart in China, although the technique of working sheet gold may have come to Korea from northeast China.

Unified Silla Kingdom

Aided by China's emperor, the Silla Kingdom conquered the Koguryo and Paekche kingdoms and unified Korea in 668. The era of the Unified Silla Kingdom (688–935) is roughly contemporary with the Tang dynasty's brilliant culture in China, and many consider it to be Korea's golden age.

BUDDHIST SOKKURAM The Silla rulers embraced Buddhism both as a source of religious enlightenment and as a protective force. They considered the magnificent Buddhist temples they constructed in and around their capital of Kyongju to be not only places of worship but also a supernatural defense against external

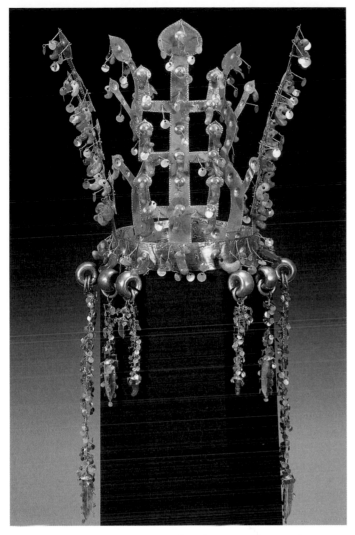

3-26 Crown, from north mound of tomb 98 at Hwangnamdong, near Kyongju, Korea, Silla kingdom, fifth to sixth century. Gold, 10$\frac{3}{4}$" high. Kyongju National Museum, Kyongju.

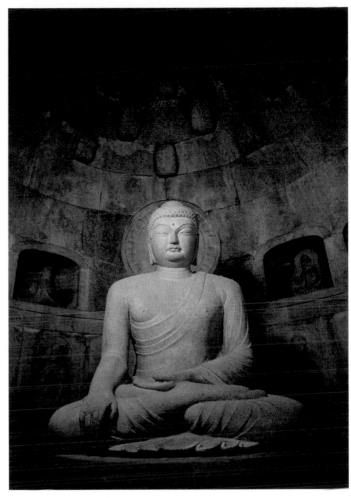

3-27 Shakyamuni Buddha, at entrance to cave temple, Sokkuram, Korea, Great Silla, 751–774. Granite, approx. 11' high.

threats. Unfortunately, none of these temples survived Korea's turbulent history. However, at Sokkuram, near the summit of Mount Toham, northeast of the city, a splendid granite Buddhist monument is preserved. Scant surviving records suggest that it was built under the supervision of Kim Tae-song, a member of the royal family who served as prime minister. He initiated construction in 742 to honor his parents in his previous life. Certainly the intimate scale of Sokkuram and the quality of its reliefs and freestanding figures support the idea that it was a private chapel for royalty.

The main *rotunda* (circular area under a dome; FIG. **3-27**) measures about 21 feet in diameter. Despite its modest size, the Sokkuram project required substantial resources. Unlike the Chinese Buddhist caves at Longmen (FIG. 3-12), the interior wall surfaces and sculpture were not cut from the rock in the process of excavation. Instead, workers assembled hundreds of granite pieces of various shapes and sizes, attaching them with stone rivets instead of mortar. Sculpted images of bodhisattvas, arhats, and guardians line the lower zone of the wall. Above, 10 niches contain miniature statues of seated bodhisattvas and believers.

All these figures face inward toward the 11-foot-tall statue of Shakyamuni, the historical Buddha, which dominates the cham-

ber as it sits slightly back from center and faces the entrance. Carved from a single block of granite, the image represents the Buddha as he touched the earth to call it to witness the realization of his enlightenment at Bodh Gaya (see FIG. 1-10*b*). Although remote in time and place from the Sarnath Buddha in India (see FIG. 1-12), this majestic image remains faithful to its iconographic prototype. More immediately, the Korean statue draws on the robust, round-faced figures of Tang China (FIG. 3-12), and its drapery is a more schematic version of the fluid type found in Tang sculpture. However, the figure has a distinctly broad-shouldered dignity combined with harmonious proportions that are without close precedents. It is regarded as one of the finest images of the Buddha in East Asia.

Koryo Dynasty

Although Buddhism was the established religion of Korea, Confucianism, introduced from China during the Silla era, increasingly shaped social and political conventions. In the ninth century, the three old kingdoms began to reemerge as distinct political entities, but by 935 the Koryo (from Koguryo) had taken control, and they dominated for the next three centuries. The Unified Silla and Koryo kingdoms overlap slightly (the period

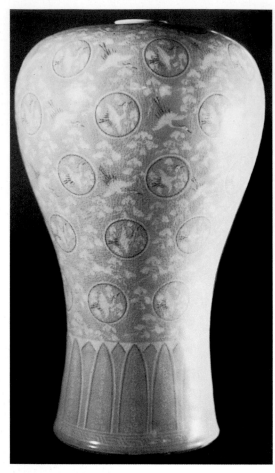

3-28 Maebyong vase, Koryo period, ca. 918–1000. Celadon with inlaid decoration, 1′ 4½″ tall. Kansong Art Museum, Seoul.

glazes, fired in an oxygen-deprived kiln to become gray, pale blue, pale green, or brownish olive. Incised or engraved designs in the vessel alter the thickness of the glaze to produce elegant tonal variations.

A vase in the shape known as *maebyong* in Korean (FIG. **3-28;** *meiping* in Chinese, FIG. 3-20) probably dates to early in the Koryo period (ca. 918–1000). It is decorated using the inlay technique for which Koryo potters were famous. On our vase, the artist incised delicate motifs of flying cranes—some flying down and others, in *roundels* (circular frames), flying up—into the clay's surface and then filled the grooves with white and colored slip. Next, the potter covered the incised areas with the celadon green glaze. Variation in the spacing of the motifs shows the potter's sure sense of the dynamic relationship between ornamentation and ceramic volume.

CONCLUSION

Chinese culture has its roots long before recorded history, and China has often been in the vanguard of technological innovation. The Chinese invented, for example, the magnetic compass, movable type, paper money, and gunpowder, and Chinese silk was treasured in the West.

The Chinese also excelled in the fields of art and architecture. The bronzes of the Shang dynasty are among the finest produced anywhere during the Bronze Age, and Chinese artists were masters in working jade, ivory, and lacquer. Although Chinese artworks of monumental scale, such as the Qin terracotta army, are world renowned, many of the most famous Chinese artists worked on a much more intimate scale, painting landscapes and other subjects in handscrolls and displaying their expertise in recording light, shade, distance, and texture. The Chinese method of bracketed wooden construction, in which walls do not bear weight but serve as screens, was emulated throughout Asia.

China's achievements in virtually every field spread beyond even the boundaries of the vast empires it sometimes controlled. Although Buddhism began in India, the Chinese adaptations and transformations of its teachings, religious practice, and artistic forms were those that spread farther east. The cultural debt of China's neighbors to China is immense. But it was Korea that was the crucial artistic, cultural, and religious link between the mainland and the islands of Japan (see Chapter 5).

ca. 918–935) because both kingdoms existed as these shifts in power occurred. In 1231, the Mongols, who had invaded China, pushed into Korea, beginning a war lasting 30 years. In the end, the Koryo had to submit to forming an alliance with the Mongols, who eventually conquered all of China (see Chapter 4).

CELADON WARE Koryo potters in the 12th century produced the famous Korean *celadon* wares, admired worldwide. Celadon wares are characterized by highly translucent iron-pigmented

CHINA	KOREA		
LATE NEOLITHIC		5000 BCE	
		2000 BCE	
XIA		1600 BCE	
SHANG		1050 BCE	

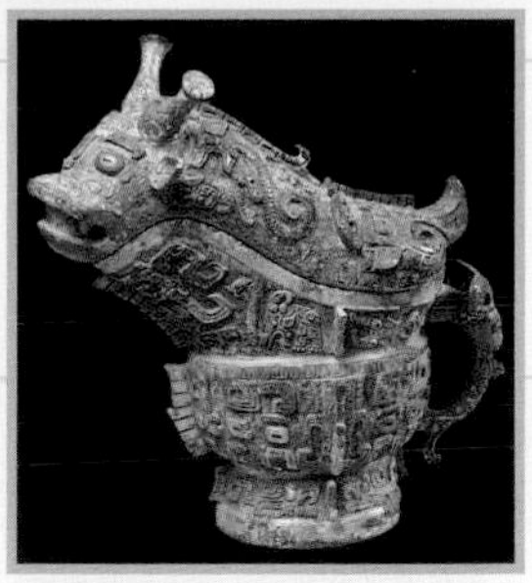

1 Guang, from Anyang, 12th or 11th century BCE

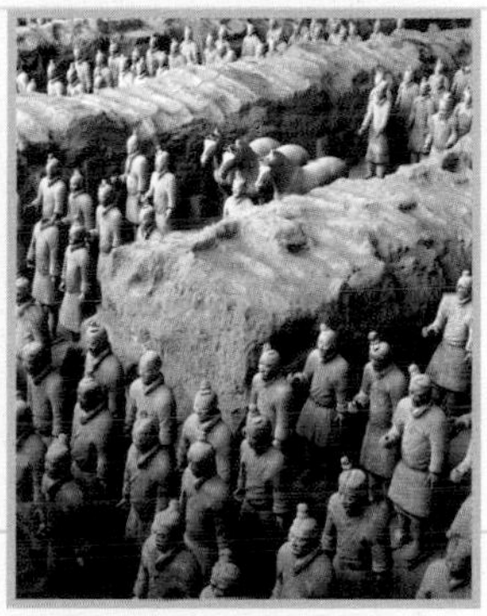

ZHOU (WARRING STATES, 475–221 BCE)

| LAOZI, DAOIST PHILOSOPHER, CA. 604–531 BCE |
| XIE HE, *Six Laws of Painting*, EARLY SIXTH CENTURY BCE |
| SHAKYAMUNI BUDDHA, CA. 563–483 BCE |
| CONFUCIUS, 551–479 BCE |
| MENCIUS, CONFUCIAN PHILOSOPHER, CA. 371–289 BCE |
| ZHUANGZI, DAOIST PHILOSOPHER, CA. 370–301 BCE |

221 BCE

QIN

2 THE FIRST EMPEROR OF QIN, R. 221–210 BCE

206 BCE

2 Army of the First Emperor of Qin, Lintong, ca. 210 BCE

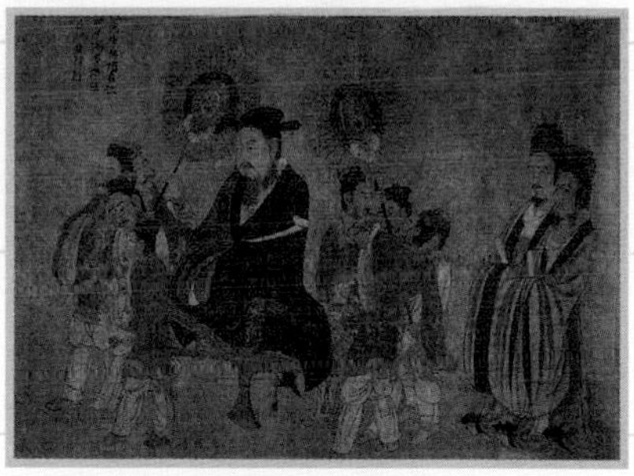

HAN

220 CE

PERIOD OF DISUNITY

THREE KINGDOMS PERIOD (57 BCE–668 CE)

BUDDHISM INTRODUCED TO KOREA, 372

589

SUI

BODHIDHARMA, FIRST CHAN BUDDHIST PATRIARCH, SIXTH CENTURY

618

TANG

3 BUDDHIST PERSECUTION BY WUZONG, 845

3 Yan Liben, *The Thirteen Emperors*, ca. 650

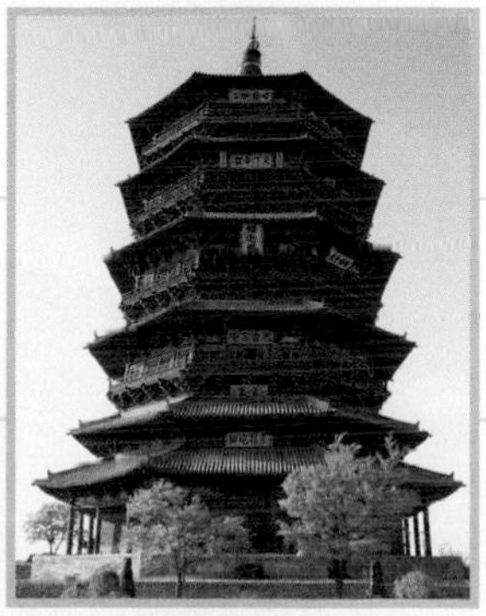

UNIFIED SILLA KINGDOM (TO 935)

906

FIVE DYNASTIES

960

NORTHERN SONG

4 JIN CAPTURE BIANLIANG FROM SONG, 1126

1127

SOUTHERN SONG

KORYO (TO 1392)

MONGOLS INVADE KOREA, 1231

1279

4 Foguang Si Pagoda, Yingxian, China, Liao Dynasty, 1056

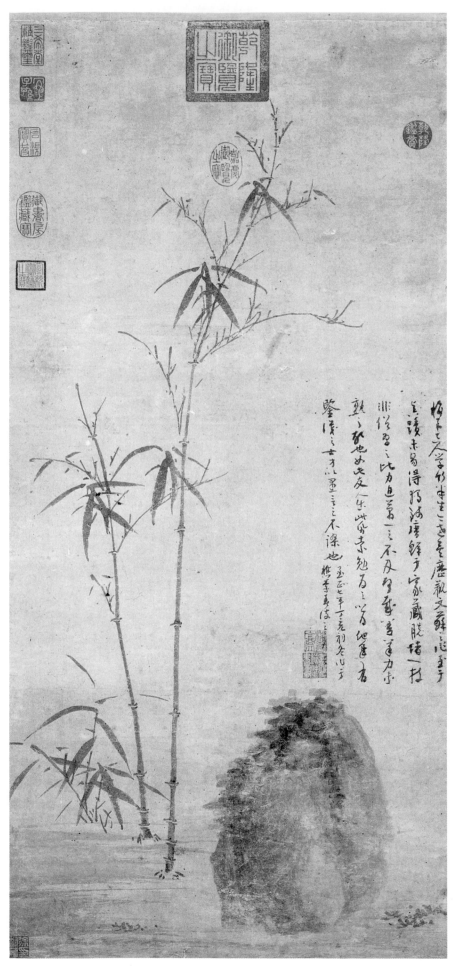

Wu Zhen, *Stalks of Bamboo by a Rock,* Yuan dynasty, 1347. Hanging scroll, ink on paper, 2′ 11$\frac{1}{2}$″ × 1′ 4$\frac{5}{8}$″. National Palace Museum, Taibei.

4

FROM THE MONGOLS TO THE MODERN

THE ART OF LATER CHINA AND KOREA

The 13th century was a time of profound political upheaval in Asia. The opening decade saw the Islamic armies of Muhammad of Ghor wrest power from India's Hindu kings and the establishment of a Muslim Sultanate at Delhi (see Chapter 2). Then, in 1210, Genghis Khan (1167–1230) and the Mongols invaded northern China from Central Asia (MAP 4-1). By 1215 they had destroyed the Jin dynasty's capital at Beijing. In 1235, the Mongols attacked the Song dynasty in southern China, but it was not until 1279 that the last Song emperor fell at the hands of Genghis Khan's grandson, Kublai Khan (1215–1294). Kublai proclaimed himself the new emperor of China (r. 1279–1294) and founded the Yuan dynasty.

CHINA

Yuan Dynasty (1279–1368)

During the relatively brief tenure of the Yuan, trade between Europe and Asia increased dramatically. It is no coincidence that the most famous early European visitor to China, Marco Polo (1254–1324), arrived during the reign of Kublai Khan. Part fact and part fable, Marco Polo's chronicle of his travels to and within China was the only eyewitness description of East Asia available in Europe for several centuries. What emerges from his account is a profound admiration for Yuan China. The Venetian marveled not only at Kublai Khan's opulent lifestyle and palaces, but also at the volume of commercial traffic on the Yangtze River, the splendors of Hangzhou, the use of paper currency, porcelain, and coal, the efficiency of the Chinese postal system, and the hygiene of the Chinese people. In the early second millennium, China was richer and technologically more advanced than late medieval Europe.

GUAN DAOSHENG AND BAMBOO The Mongols were great admirers of Chinese art and culture, but they were very selective in admitting former Southern Song

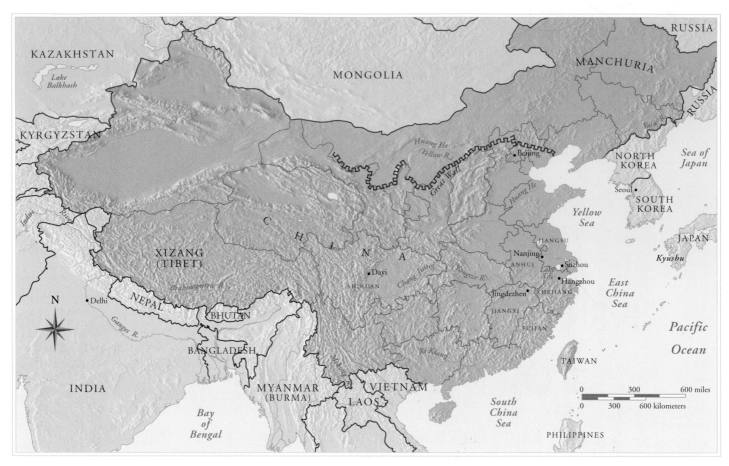

MAP 4-1 Later sites in China and Korea.

subjects into their administration. In addition, many Chinese loyal to the former emperors refused to collaborate with their new foreign overlords, whom they considered barbarian usurpers. One who did accept an official post under Kublai Khan was Zhao Mengfu (1254–1322), a descendant of the first Song emperor, who continued to serve the Yuan under four subsequent rulers (and was condemned by history for doing so). A learned man, skilled in both calligraphy and poetry, he was renowned as a painter of horses and of landscapes. His wife, GUAN DAOSHENG (1262–1319), was also a successful painter, calligrapher, and poet. Although she painted a variety of subjects,

including Buddhist murals in Yuan temples, Guan achieved renown as a painter of bamboo.

Bamboo was a favorite subject of Chinese painters because the plant was a symbol of the ideal Chinese gentleman, who bends in adversity but does not break. Artists were also attracted to bamboo because depicting its branches and leaves approximated the cherished art of calligraphy. *Bamboo Groves in Mist and Rain* (FIG. 4-1) is a handscroll with an inscribed dedication by Guan Daosheng to another noblewoman and a second inscription stating that she painted the handscroll "in a boat on the green waves of the lake" (see "Calligraphy and Inscriptions

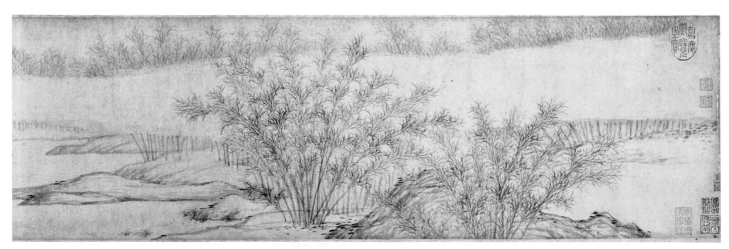

4-1 GUAN DAOSHENG, *Bamboo Groves in Mist and Rain* (detail), Yuan dynasty, 1308. Section of a handscroll, ink on paper, $9\frac{1}{8}''\times 3'\ 8\frac{7}{8}''$. National Palace Museum, Taibei.

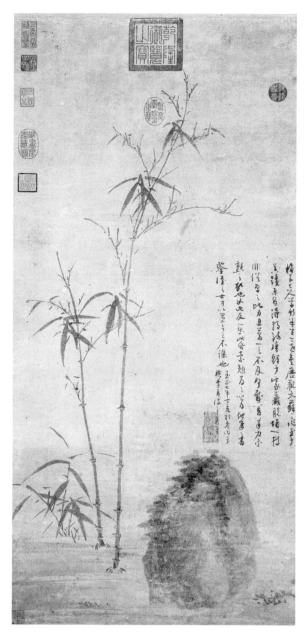

on Chinese Paintings," page 68). Guan achieved the misty atmosphere by restricting the ink tones to a narrow range and by blurring the bamboo thickets in the distance, suggesting not only recession but fog.

WU ZHEN AND THE LITERATI The Yuan painter WU ZHEN (1280–1354), in stark contrast to Zhao Mengfu and Guan Daosheng, shunned the Mongol court and lived as a hermit, far from the luxurious milieu of the Yuan emperors. He was one of the *literati,* or scholar-artists, who emerged during the Song dynasty. The literati painted primarily for a small audience of their educational and social peers. These men and women came from prominent families and were highly educated and steeped in traditional Chinese culture. They cultivated painting, calligraphy, poetry, and other arts as a sign of social status and refined taste. Literati art is usually personal in nature and often shows a nostalgia for the past.

Wu Zhen's treatment of the bamboo theme, *Stalks of Bamboo by a Rock* (FIG. **4-2**), differs sharply from Guan's. In his hanging scroll, the individual bamboo plants are clearly differentiated and the artist revels in the abstract patterns the stalks and leaves form. The bamboo plants are perfect complements to the calligraphic beauty of the Chinese black characters and red seals so prominently featured on the scroll. Both the bamboo and the inscriptions gave Wu Zhen the opportunity to display his proficiency with the brush.

TEXTURED MOUNTAINS One of the great works of Yuan literati painting is *Dwelling in the Fuchun Mountains* (FIG. **4-3**) by HUANG GONGWANG (1269–1354), a former civil servant and a teacher of Daoist philosophy. According to the artist's explanatory inscription at the end of the long handscroll, he sketched the full composition in one burst of inspiration, but then added to and modified his painting whenever he felt moved to do so over a period of years. In the detail we reproduce, the painter built up the textured mountains with richly layered brush strokes, at times interweaving dry brush strokes and at other times placing dry strokes over wet ones, darker strokes over lighter ones, often with ink-wash accents. The rhythmic play of brush and ink renders the landscape's inner structure and momentum.

4-2 WU ZHEN, *Stalks of Bamboo by a Rock,* Yuan dynasty, 1347. Hanging scroll, ink on paper, 2′ 11½″ × 1′ 4⅝″. National Palace Museum, Taibei.

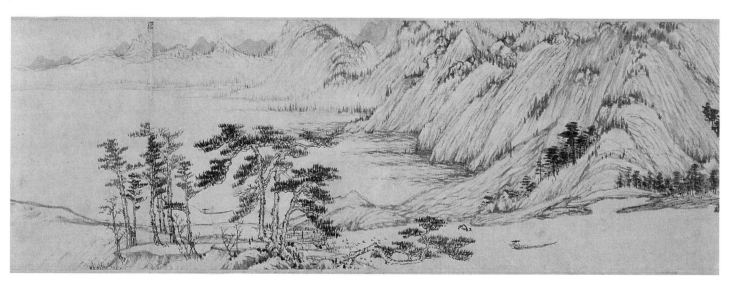

4-3 HUANG GONGWANG, *Dwelling in the Fuchun Mountains,* Yuan dynasty, 1347–1350. Section of a handscroll, ink on paper, 1′ ⅞″ × 20′ 9″. National Palace Museum, Taibei.

Calligraphy and Inscriptions on Chinese Paintings

Many Chinese paintings (FIGS. 3-19, 3-23, 4-2, and 4-10 to 4-12) bear *inscriptions,* texts written on the same surface as the picture, or *colophons,* texts written on attached pieces of paper or silk. Throughout Chinese history, calligraphy and painting have been closely connected and equally esteemed. Even the primary implements and materials for writing and drawing are the same—a round tapered brush, soot-based ink, and paper or silk. Calligraphy depends for its effects on the controlled vitality of individual brush strokes and on the dynamic relationships of strokes within a character and among the characters themselves. Training in calligraphy was a fundamental part of the education and self-cultivation of Chinese scholars and officials, and inscriptions are especially common on literati paintings.

Chinese characters are best described as *logograms,* each character corresponding to one meaningful language unit. Many stylistic variations exist in Chinese calligraphy. At the most formal extreme, each character is separated from the next and comprised of distinct straight and angular strokes. At the other extreme, the characters flow together as cursive abbreviations with many rounded forms. The inscriptions on the paintings we illustrate show the wide range of styles.

A long tradition in China links pictures and texts. Famous poems frequently provided subjects for paintings, and poets composed poems inspired by paintings. Either practice might prompt inscriptions on art, some addressing painted subjects, some praising the painting's quality or the painter's character. Other inscriptions explain the circumstances of the work—for example, Guan Daosheng's statement that she painted *Bamboo Groves in Mist and Rain* (FIG. 4-1) in a boat. Later admirers and owners of paintings often inscribed their own appreciative words.

Painters, inscribers, and even owners usually also added seal impressions in red ink (FIGS. 4-1 to 4-3 and 4-10 to 4-14) to identify themselves. With all these textual additions, some paintings that have passed through many collections may seem cluttered to Western eyes. However, the historical importance given to such inscriptions and ownership history has been and remains a critical aspect of painting appreciation in China.

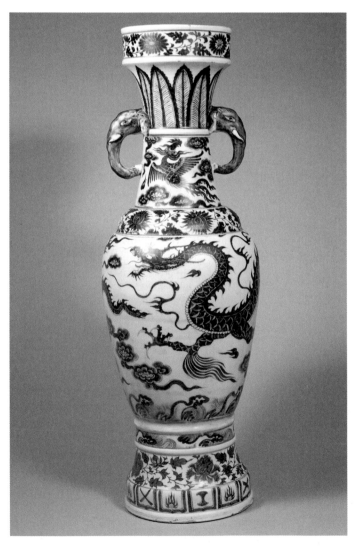

4-4 Temple vase, Yuan dynasty, 1351. White porcelain with cobalt blue underglaze, 2′ 1″ × 8⅛″. Percival David Foundation of Chinese Art, London.

DRAGON AND PHOENIX By the Yuan period, Chinese potters had extended their mastery to fully developed porcelains, a very technically demanding medium (see "Chinese Porcelain," page 69). A tall temple vase from the Jingdezhen kilns (FIG. 4-4), which during the Ming dynasty became the official source of porcelains for the court, is one of a nearly identical pair dated by inscription to 1351. The inscription also says the vases, together with an incense burner, made up an altar set donated to a Buddhist temple as a prayer for peace, protection, and prosperity for the donor's family. The vase is one of the earliest dated examples of fine porcelain with cobalt blue underglaze decoration. The painted decoration consists of bands of floral motifs between broader zones containing auspicious symbols, including phoenixes in the lower part of the neck and dragons (compare FIG. 3-4) on the main body of the vessel, both among clouds. These motifs may suggest the donor's high status or invoke prosperity blessings. Because of their vast power and associations with nobility and prosperity, the dragon and the phoenix also symbolize the emperor and empress, respectively, and often appear on objects made for the imperial household. The dragon also may represent *yang,* the Chinese principle of active masculine energy, while the phoenix may represent *yin,* the principle of passive feminine energy.

Ming Dynasty (1368–1644)

THE FORBIDDEN CITY In 1368, Zhu Yuanzhong led a popular uprising that drove the last Mongol emperor from Beijing. After expelling the foreigners from China, he founded the native Chinese Ming dynasty, proclaiming himself its first emperor under the official name of Hongwu (r. 1368–1398). The new emperor built his capital at Nanjing, but the third Ming emperor, Yongle (r. 1403–1424), moved the capital back to Beijing. Although Beijing had been home to the Yuan dynasty, Ming architects designed much of the city as well as the imperial palace at its core.

Chinese Porcelain

No other Chinese art form has been so admired by the rest of the world, inspired such imitation, or penetrated so deeply into everyday life as porcelain (FIGS. 4-4 and 4-15). Long imported by neighboring countries as luxury goods and treasures, Chinese porcelains later captured great attention in the West, where potters did not succeed in mastering the production process until the early 18th century.

In China, primitive porcelains emerged during the Tang dynasty (618–906) and mature forms developed in the Song (960–1279). Like stoneware (see "Chinese Earthenwares and Stonewares," Chapter 3, page 41), porcelain is fired at an extremely high temperature (well over 2,000° F) in a kiln until its clay body is fully fused into a dense, hard substance resembling stone or glass. Unlike stoneware, however, porcelain is made from a fine white clay called kaolin mixed with ground petuntse (a type of feldspar). True porcelain is translucent and rings when struck.

Porcelains are often decorated with colored designs or pictures. The decorators work with finely ground minerals suspended in water and a binding agent (such as glue). The minerals change color dramatically in the kiln. The painters apply some mineral colors to the clay surface before the main firing and then apply a clear glaze over them. Such *underglaze* decoration fully bonds to the piece in the kiln, but only a few colors are possible, because the raw materials must withstand intense heat. The most stable and widely used coloring agents for porcelains are cobalt compounds, which fire to an intense blue (FIG. 4-4). Rarely, potters use copper compounds to produce stunning reds by carefully manipulating the kiln's temperature and oxygen content. To obtain a wider palette, ceramic decorators must paint on top of the glaze after the work has been fired (FIG. 4-15). The *overglaze* colors, or *enamels,* then fuse to the glazed surface in an additional firing at a much lower temperature. Enamels also offer glaze decorators a much brighter palette, with colors ranging from deep browns to brilliant reds and greens, but they do not have the durability of underglaze decoration.

Ming Beijing was planned as three nested walled cities. The outer perimeter wall was 15 miles long and enclosed the walled Imperial City, with a perimeter of $6\frac{1}{2}$ miles, and the vast imperial palace compound, the moated Forbidden City (FIG. 4-5), so named because access to it was very restricted. There resided the Ming emperor, the Son of Heaven. The layout of the Forbidden City provided the perfect setting for the elaborate ritual of the imperial court. For example, the entrance gateway, the Noon Gate (in the foreground in the aerial view) has five portals. Only the emperor could walk through the central doorway. The two entrances to its left and right were reserved for the imperial family and high officials. Others had to use the outermost passageways.

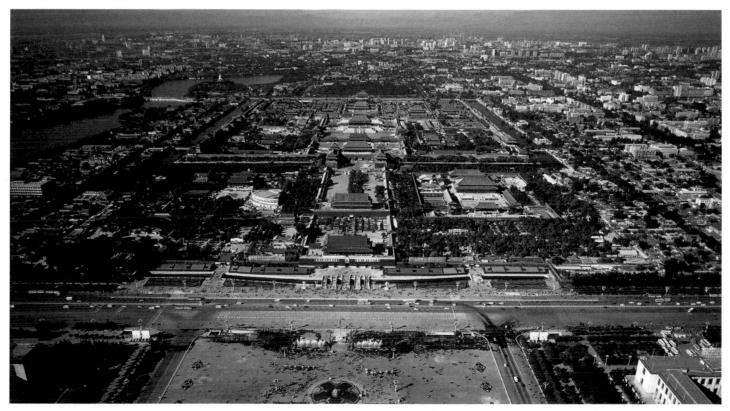

4-5 Aerial view of the Forbidden City, Beijing, China, Ming dynasty, 15th century and later.

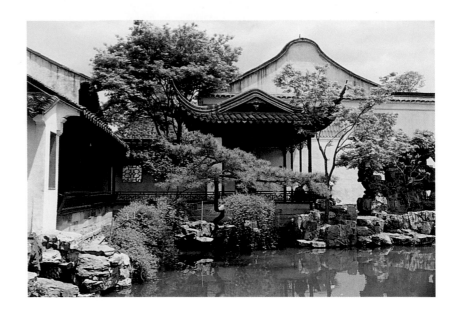

4-6 Wangshi Yuan (Garden of the Master of the Fishing Nets), Suzhou, China, Ming dynasty, 16th century and later.

4-7 Liu Yuan (Lingering Garden), Suzhou, China, Ming dynasty, 16th century and later.

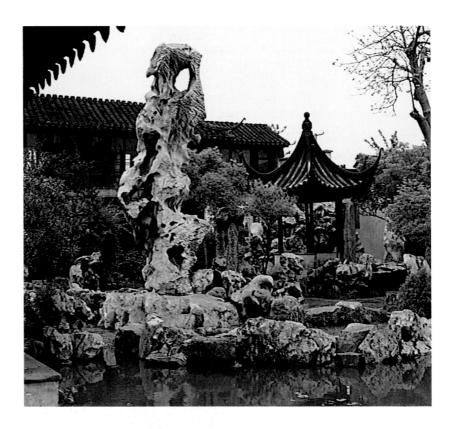

More gates and a series of courtyards and imposing buildings, all erected using the traditional Chinese bracketing system (see "Chinese Wooden Construction," Chapter 3, page 48), led eventually to the Hall of Supreme Harmony, perched on an immense platform above marble staircases, the climax of a long north-south axis. Within the hall, the emperor sat on his throne on another high stepped platform.

THE GARDENS OF SUZHOU At the opposite architectural pole from the formality and rigid axiality of palace architecture is the Chinese pleasure garden. Several Ming gardens at Suzhou have been meticulously restored, including the huge (almost 54,000 square feet) Wangshi Yuan (Garden of the Master of the Fishing Nets; FIG. 4-6). Designing a Ming garden was not a mat-

ter of cultivating plants in rows or of laying out terraces, flower beds, and avenues in geometric fashion, as was the case in many other cultures. Instead, the gardens are often scenic arrangements of natural and artificial elements intended to reproduce the irregularities of uncultivated nature. Verandas and pavilions rise on pillars above the water, and stone bridges, paths, and causeways encourage wandering through ever-changing vistas of trees, flowers, rocks, and their reflections in the ponds. The typical design is a sequence of carefully contrived visual surprises.

A favorite garden element, fantastic rockwork, may be seen at Liu Yuan (Lingering Garden; FIG. 4-7) in Suzhou. The stones were dredged from nearby Lake Tai and then shaped by sculptors to create an even more natural look. The Ming gardens of Suzhou were the pleasure retreats of high officials and the landed gentry,

Lacquered Wood

*L*acquer is produced from the sap of the Asiatic sumac tree, native to central and southern China. From ancient times it was used to cover wood, because when it dries, it cures to great hardness and prevents the wood from decaying. Often colored with mineral pigments, lacquered objects have a lustrous surface that transforms the appearance of natural wood. The earliest examples of lacquered wood to survive in quantity date to the Eastern Zhou period (770–256 BCE).

The first step in producing a lacquered object is to heat and purify the sap. Then the lacquer worker mixes the minerals—

carbon black and cinnabar red are the most common—into the sap. To apply the lacquer, the artisan uses a hair brush similar to a calligrapher's or painter's brush. The lacquer goes on one layer at a time. Then it must dry and be sanded before another coat can be applied. If a sufficient number of layers is built up, the lacquer can be carved as if it were the wood itself (FIG. 4-8).

Other techniques for decorating lacquer include inlaying metals and lustrous materials, such as mother-of-pearl, and sprinkling gold powder into the still-wet lacquer. Such techniques also flourished in both Korea and Japan (see FIG. 6-9).

---

sanctuaries where the wealthy could commune with nature in all its representative forms and as an ever-changing and boundless presence. Chinese poets never cease to sing of the restorative effect of gardens on mind and spirit.

THE ART OF LACQUER The Ming court's lavish appetite for luxury goods gave new impetus to brilliant technical achievement in the decorative arts. Like the Yuan rulers, the Ming emperors turned to the Jingdezhen kilns for fine porcelains. For objects in lacquered wood (see "Lacquered Wood," above), their patronage went to a large workshop known today as the Orchard Factory. One of its masterpieces is a table with drawers (FIG. 4-8)

made between 1426 and 1435. The artist carved floral motifs, along with the dragon and phoenix imperial emblems, into the thick cinnabar-colored lacquer, which had to be built up in numerous layers.

MING COURT PAINTING At the Ming court, the official painters were housed in the Forbidden City itself, and portraiture of the imperial family was their major subject. The court artists also depicted historical figures as exemplars of virtue, wisdom, or heroism. An exceptionally large example of Ming history painting is a hanging scroll that SHANG XI (active in the second quarter of the 15th century) painted around 1430. *Guan Yu Captures*

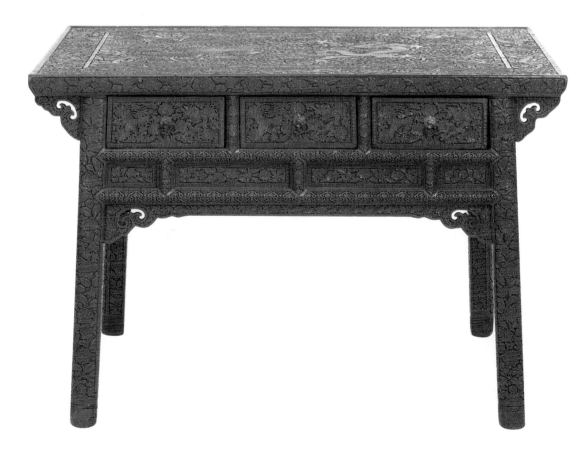

4-8 Table with drawers, Ming dynasty, ca. 1426–1435. Carved red lacquer on a wood core, 3′ 11″ long. Victoria & Albert Museum, London.

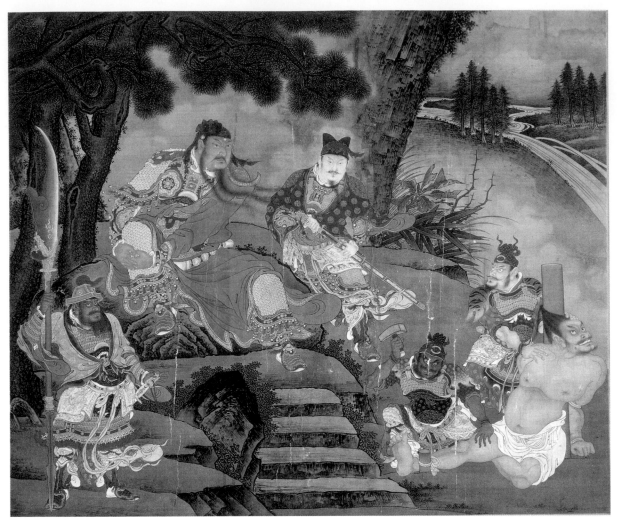

4-9 SHANG XI, *Guan Yu Captures General Pang De,* Ming dynasty, ca. 1430. Hanging scroll, ink and colors on silk, 6′ 5″ × 7′ 7″. Palace Museum, Beijing.

General Pang De (FIG. **4-9**) represents an episode from the tumultuous third century (Period of Disunity; see Chapter 3), whose wars inspired one of the first great Chinese novels, *The Romance of the Three Kingdoms.* Guan Yu was a famed general of the Wei dynasty (220–280) and a fictional hero in the novel. The painting depicts the historical Guan Yu, renowned for his loyalty to his emperor and his military valor, being presented with the captured enemy general Pang De. In his painting, Shang Xi uses color to focus attention on Guan Yu and his attendants, who stand out sharply from the ink landscape. He also contrasts the victors' armor and bright garments with the vulnerability of the captive, who has been stripped almost naked, further heightening his humiliation.

MING LITERATI The work of Shang Xi and other professional court painters, designed to promote the official Ming ideology, is far removed from the venerable tradition of literati painting, which also flourished during the Ming dynasty, but, as under the Yuan emperors, was largely independent of court patronage. One of the leading figures was SHEN ZHOU (1427–1509), a master of the Wu School of painting, so called because of the ancient name (Wu) of the city of Suzhou. Shen Zhou came from a family of scholars and painters and turned down an offer to serve in the Ming bureaucracy in order to devote himself to poetry and painting. His hanging scroll, *Lofty Mount Lu* (FIG. **4-10**), a birthday gift to one of his teachers, bears a long poem he wrote in the teacher's honor. Shen Zhou had never seen Mount Lu, but he chose the subject because he wished the lofty mountain peaks to express the grandeur of his teacher's virtue and character. The artist suggested the immense scale of Mount Lu by placing a tiny figure at the bottom center of the painting, sketched in lightly and partly obscured by a rocky outcropping. The composition owes a great deal to early masters like Fan Kuan (see FIG. 3-18). But, characteristic of literati painting in general, the scroll is in the end a very personal conversation—in pictures and words—between the painter and the teacher for whom it was created.

DONG QICHANG One of the most intriguing and influential literati of the late Ming dynasty was DONG QICHANG (1555–1636), a wealthy landowner and high official who was a poet, calligrapher, and painter. He also amassed a vast collection of Chinese art and achieved great fame as an art critic. In Dong Qichang's view, most Chinese landscape painters could be classified as belonging to either the Northern School of precise, academic painting or the Southern School of more subjective, freer painting. "Northern" and "Southern" were therefore not geographic but stylistic labels. Dong Qichang chose these names for the two schools because he determined that their characteristic styles had parallels in the northern and southern schools of Chan Buddhism (see "Chan Buddhism," Chapter 3, page 60). Northern Chan Buddhists were "gradualists" and believed that enlightenment could be achieved only after long training. The Southern Chan Buddhists believed that enlightenment could come suddenly. The professional, highly trained court painters belonged to the Northern School. The leading painters of the Southern School

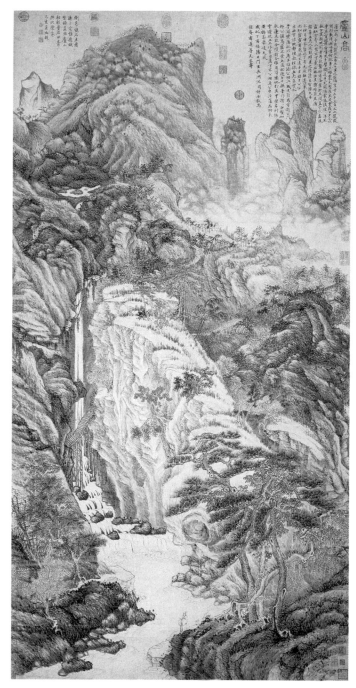

4-10 SHEN ZHOU, *Lofty Mount Lu*, Ming dynasty, 1467. Hanging scroll, ink and color on paper, 6' 4¼" × 3' 2⅝". National Palace Museum, Taibei.

were the literati, whose freer and more expressive style Dong Qichang judged to be far superior.

Dong Qichang's own work—for example, *Dwelling in the Qingbian Mountains* (FIG. **4-11**), painted in 1617—belongs to the Southern School he admired so much. His debt to earlier literati painters can readily be seen in both subject and style as well as in the incorporation of a long inscription at the top. But Dong Qichang was also an innovator, especially in his treatment of the towering mountains, where shaded masses of rocks alternate with flat, blank bands, flattening the composition and creating highly expressive and abstract patterns. Some critics have even called Dong Qichang the first modernist painter, foreshadowing developments in 19th-century European landscape painting.

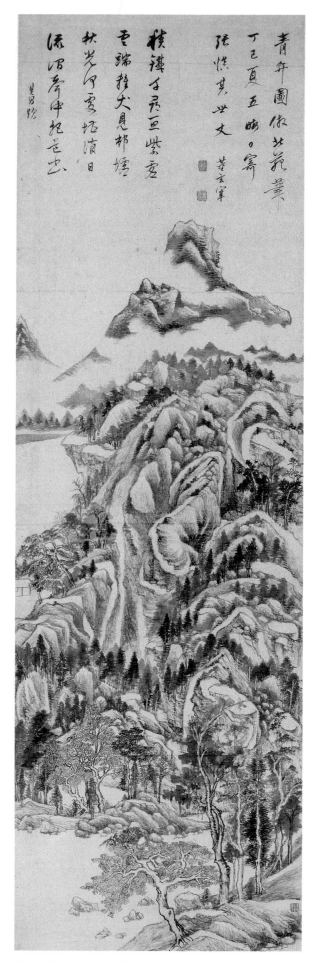

4-11 DONG QICHANG, *Dwelling in the Qingbian Mountains*, Ming dynasty, 1617. Hanging scroll, ink on paper, 7' 3½" × 2' 2½". Cleveland Museum of Art, Cleveland (Leonard C. Hanna, Jr. bequest).

CHINA **73**

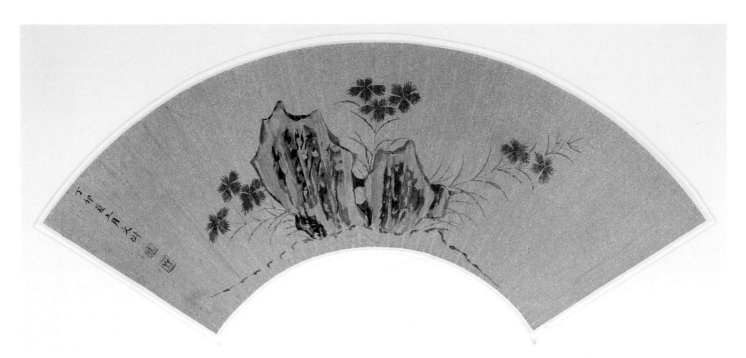

4-12 WEN SHU, *Carnations and Garden Rock,* Ming dynasty, 1627. Fan, ink and colors on gold paper, $6\frac{3}{8}''$ × 1' $9\frac{1}{4}''$. Honolulu Academy of Arts, Honolulu (gift of Mr. Robert Allerton).

WEN SHU AND FAN PAINTING Landscape painting was considered the most prestigious artistic subject in Ming China, and was the preferred theme of male literati. Ming women artists usually painted other subjects, especially flowers. WEN SHU (1595–1634), the daughter of an aristocratic Suzhou family and the wife of Zhao Jun, descended from Zhao Mengfu and the Song imperial house, was probably the finest flower painter of the Ming era. Her *Carnations and Garden Rock* (FIG. **4-12**) is also an example of Chinese arc-shaped fan painting, a format imported from Japan. In this genre, the artist paints on flat paper, but when the painting is completed, it is mounted on sticks and folded. The best fan paintings were probably never actually used as fans, but were purchased by collectors and stored in albums. As in her other flower paintings, Wen Shu focused on a few essential elements, in this instance a central rock formation and three sprays of flowers, and presented them against a plain background. Using delicate brush strokes and a restricted palette, she brilliantly communicated the fragility of the red flowers, contrasting them with the solidity of the brown rock. The spare composition creates a quiet mood of contemplation.

Qing Dynasty (1644–1911)

The Ming bureaucracy's internal decay permitted another group of invaders, the Manchus of Manchuria, to overrun China in the 17th century. Established in 1644 as the Qing, these northerners quickly restored effective imperial rule, although southern China remained rebellious. But during his long reign, the second Qing emperor, Kangxi (r. 1662–1722), succeeded in pacifying all of China. The Manchus adapted themselves to Chinese life and cultivated knowledge of China's arts.

PRIMORDIAL LINE Traditional literati painting continued to be fashionable among conservative Qing artists, but other painters experimented with extreme effects of massed ink or individualized brushwork patterns. Bold and freely manipulated compositions with a new, expressive force began to appear. A prominent painter in this mode was SHITAO (DAOJI, 1642–1707). Shitao was a descendant of the Ming imperial family who became a Chan Buddhist monk at age 20. His theoretical writings, most notably his *Sayings on Painting from Monk Bitter Gourd* (the name he gave himself), called for use of the "single brush stroke" or "primordial line" as the root of all phenomena and representation. Although he carefully studied classical paintings, Shitao opposed mimicking earlier works and believed that he could not learn anything from them unless he changed them. The figure in a hut in Shitao's album leaf *Man in a House beneath a Cliff*

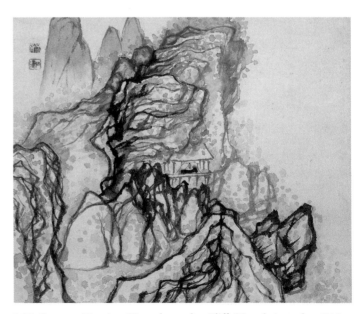

4-13 SHITAO, *Man in a House beneath a Cliff,* Qing dynasty, late 17th century. Album leaf, ink and colors on paper, $9\frac{1}{2}''$ × 11". C. C. Wang Collection, New York.

(FIG. **4-13**) is surrounded by the surging energy of free-floating colored dots and multiple sinuous contour lines. Unlike traditional literati painters, Shitao did not so much depict the landscape's appearance as animate it, molding the forces running through it.

JESUITS AT THE QING COURT During the Qing dynasty, European Jesuit missionaries were familiar figures at the imperial court. Many of the missionaries were also artists, and they were instrumental in introducing European Renaissance and Baroque painting styles to China. The Chinese, while admiring the Europeans' technical virtuosity, found Western style unsatisfactory. Those Jesuit painters who were successful in China adapted their styles to Chinese tastes.

The most prominent European artist at the Qing court was GIUSEPPE CASTIGLIONE (1688–1768), who went by the name LANG SHINING in China. His hybrid Italian-Chinese painting style is on display in *Auspicious Objects* (FIG. **4-14**), which he painted in 1724 in honor of the Yongzheng (r. 1723–1735) emperor's birthday. Castiglione's emphasis on a single source of light that creates consistent shadows, and his interest in three-dimensional volume, are unmistakably European (see Introduction). But the impact on the Italian artist of Chinese literati painting is equally clear, especially in the composition of the branches and leaves of the overhanging pine tree and in the incorporation of the red seal at the upper left. Above all, the subject is purely Chinese. The white eagle, the pine tree, the rocks, and the red mushroomlike plants (*lingzhi*) are traditional Chinese symbols. The eagle connotes imperial status, courage, and military achievement. The evergreen pines and the rocks connote longevity. Eating lingzhi was thought to promote long life. All are fitting motifs with which to celebrate the birthday of an emperor.

QING PORCELAIN Qing potters at the imperial kilns at Jingdezhen continued to expand on the Yuan and Ming achievements in developing fine porcelain pieces with underglaze and overglaze decoration, gaining wide admiration in Europe. A dish with a lobed rim (FIG. **4-15**) exemplifies the overglaze technique. All of its colors— black, green, brown, yellow, and even blue — come from applying enamels (see "Chinese Porcelain," page 69). The decoration reflects important social changes in China. Economic prosperity and the possibility of advancement through success on civil service examinations made it realistic for many more families to hope that their sons could achieve both wealth and higher social standing. In the center of the dish are Fu, Lu, and Shou, the three star gods of happiness, success, and longevity. The cranes and spotted deer, believed to live to advanced ages, and the pine trees around the rim are all symbols of long life. Similar themes appear in the cheap woodblock prints produced in great quantities during the Qing era. They were the commoners' equivalent of Castiglione's imperial painting of auspicious symbols (FIG. 4-14).

4-14 GIUSEPPE CASTIGLIONE (LANG SHINING), *Auspicious Objects*, Qing dynasty, 1724. Hanging scroll, ink and colors on silk, 7' 11$\frac{3}{8}$" × 5' 1$\frac{7}{8}$". Palace Museum, Beijing.

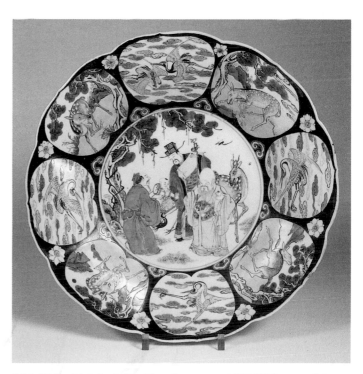

4-15 Dish with lobed rim, Qing dynasty, ca. 1700. White porcelain with overglaze, 1' 1$\frac{5}{8}$" diameter. The Percival David Foundation of Chinese Art, London.

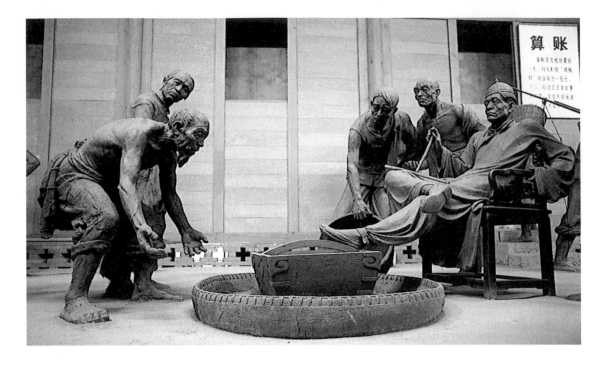

4-16 Ye Yushan and others, *Rent Collection Courtyard* (detail of larger tableau), Dayi, China, 1965. Clay, approx. 100 yards long with life-size figures.

Modern China (1912–Present)

MARXIST ART The overthrow of the Qing dynasty and the establishment of the Republic of China under the Nationalist Party in 1912 did not bring an end to the traditional themes and modes of Chinese art. But the Marxism that triumphed in 1949, when the Communists took control of China and founded the People's Republic, inspired a social realism that broke drastically with the past. The intended purpose of such art was to serve the people in the struggle to liberate and elevate the masses. In *Rent Collection Courtyard* (FIG. **4-16**), a 1965 tableau about 100 yards long and incorporating 114 life-size figures, YE YUSHAN (b. 1935) and a team of sculptors grimly depicted the old times before the People's Republic. Peasants, worn and bent by toil, bring their taxes (in produce) to the courtyard of their merciless, plundering landlord. The message is clear—this kind of thing must not happen again. When the work was first exhibited, the artists' names were not revealed. The anonymity of those who depicted the event was significant in itself. The secondary message was that only collective action could effect the transformations the People's Republic sought.

A HEAVENLY BOOK In the late 1980s and 1990s, Chinese artists began to make a mark on the international art scene. One of them was XU BING (b. 1955), who created a large installation called *A Book from Heaven* (FIG. **4-17**) in 1988. First exhibited in China and then in Japan, the United States, and Hong Kong, the work presents an enormous number of *woodblock*-printed texts in characters that look like Chinese writing but that the artist invented. Producing them required both an intimate knowledge of actual characters and extensive training in block carving. Xu's work is, however, no hymn to tradition. It has been interpreted both as a stinging critique of the meaninglessness of contemporary political language and as a commentary on the illegibility of the past. Like many works of art, past and present, Eastern and Western, it can be read on many levels.

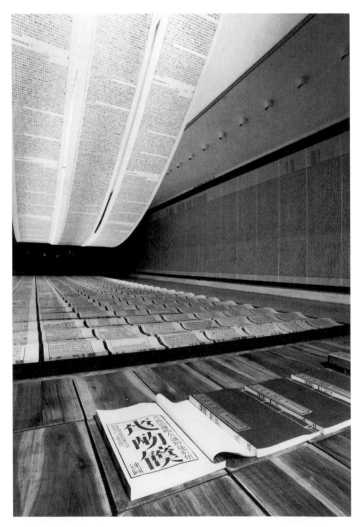

4-17 XU BING, *A Book from Heaven*, 1988. Installation at Elvehjem Museum of Art, University of Wisconsin, Madison, 1991. Movable-type prints and books.

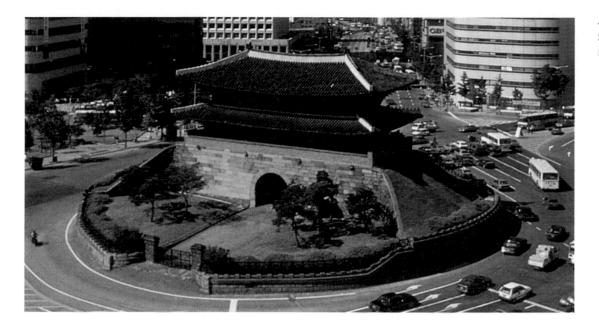

KOREA

The great political, social, religious, and artistic changes that took place in China from the Mongols to the People's Republic find parallels elsewhere in East Asia. At the time that the Yuan overthrew the Song dynasty, the Koryo dynasty (918–1392), which had ruled Korea since the downfall of China's Tang dynasty, was still in power (see Chapter 3). The Koryo kings outlasted the Yuan as well. Toward the end of the Koryo dynasty, however, the Ming emperors of China attempted to take control of northeastern Korea. They were repelled by General Yi Song-gye, who founded the last Korean dynasty, the Choson (1392–1910), with its capital at Seoul. The long rule of the Choson kings ended only in 1910, when Japan annexed Korea.

Choson Dynasty (1392–1910)

THE GATEWAY TO SEOUL Public building projects helped give the new Korean state an image of dignity and power. One impressive early monument, built for the new capital, is Seoul's south gate, or Nandaemun (FIG. 4-18). It combines the imposing strength of its impressive stone foundations with the sophistication of its intricately bracketed wooden superstructure. In East Asia, elaborate gateways, often in a processional series, are a standard element in city designs, as well as royal and sacred compounds, all usually surrounded by walls, like Beijing's Forbidden City (FIG. 4-5). Such gateways served as magnificent symbols of the ruler's authority. Passage into the city through such an impressive monument reminded the populace of the power of the Choson state.

THE DIAMOND MOUNTAINS Over the long course of the Choson dynasty, Korean painters worked in many different modes and treated the same wide range of subjects seen in Ming and Qing China. One of Korea's most renowned painters was CHONG SON (1676–1759), a great admirer of Chinese Southern School painting who brought his own unique vision to the traditional theme of the mountainous landscape. In his *Kumgang (Diamond)*

Mountains (FIG. 4-19), Chong Son evoked an actual scene, an approach known in Korea as "true view" painting. He used sharper, darker versions of the fibrous brush strokes favored by most Chinese literati in order to represent the bright crystalline appearance of the mountains and to emphasize their spiky forms.

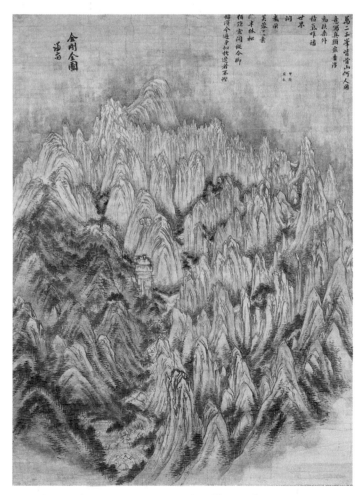

4-19 CHONG SON, *Kumgang Mountains,* Choson dynasty, 1734. Hanging scroll, ink and colors on paper, 4′ 3½″ × 1′ 11¼″. Hoam Art Museum, Kyunggi-Do.

4-20 SONG SU-NAM, *Summer Trees*, 1983. Ink on paper, 2′ 1⅝″ high. British Museum, London.

Modern Korea (1910–Present)

After its annexation by Japan in 1910, Korea remained part of Japan until 1945, when the Western Allies and the Soviet Union took control of the peninsula nation at the end of World War II. Korea was divided into the Democratic People's Republic of Korea (North Korea) and the Republic of Korea (South Korea) in 1948. South Korea at least has emerged as a fully industrialized nation, and its artists have had a wide exposure to art styles from around the globe. While some Korean artists continue to work in a traditional East Asian manner, others have embraced developments in contemporary Europe and America.

ORIENTAL INK MOVEMENT One painter who has very successfully combined native and international traditions is SONG SU-NAM (b. 1938), a professor at Hongik University in Seoul and one of the founders of the Oriental Ink Movement of the 1980s. His *Summer Trees* (FIG. **4-20**), painted in 1983, owes a great deal to the Abstract Expressionist movement of the 20th century and to the work of American painters like Morris Louis. But in place of Louis's acrylic resin on canvas, Song used ink on paper, the preferred medium of East Asian literati. He forsook, however, the traditional emphasis on brush strokes to explore the subtle tonal variations made possible by broad stretches of ink wash. The landscapes of earlier Korean and Chinese masters are, nonetheless, recalled in the painting's name. Such simultaneous respect for tradition and innovation is a hallmark of both Chinese and Korean art through their long histories.

CONCLUSION

From 1279 until the founding of the Republic of China in 1912, three great dynasties ruled China. Under the Yuan and Ming emperors, China was the richest and most technologically advanced civilization in the world. Beijing became China's capital, and its Forbidden City was developed as a vast imperial compound. This period also saw the rise of the literati movement in art, when scholar-artists retreated from court life and practiced painting, calligraphy, and poetry. Landscape continued to be a favorite theme for painters, and Chinese intellectuals also cultivated gardens designed to reproduce the irregularities of nature. With the establishment of Communist rule in 1949, art began to serve Marxist ideology, but the contemporary art of China and Korea has made a mark on the international art scene.

CHINA
KOREA

YUAN DYNASTY

MING DYNASTY

QING DYNASTY

REPUBLIC OF CHINA

PEOPLE'S REPUBLIC OF CHINA

KORYO DYNASTY

CHOSON DYNASTY

JAPANESE RULE

POSTWAR PARTITION

1279

1300

1368

1392

1450

1500

1644

1700

1800

1911

1945

1949

Last Song emperor falls to Kublai Khan, 1279

Zhu Yuanzhong drives last Mongol emperor from Beijing, 1369

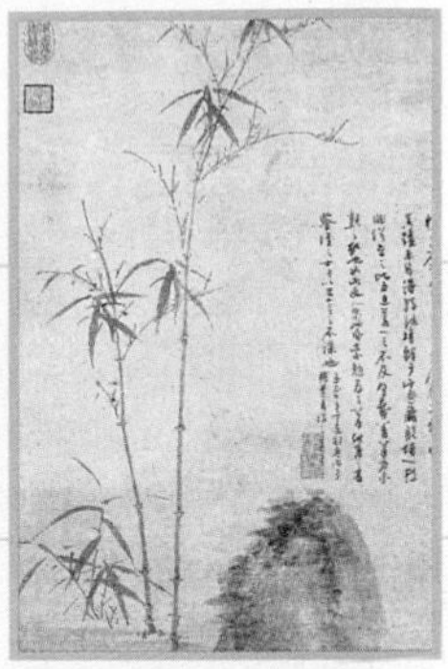

Yi Song-gye repels Chinese from Korea, 1392

Manchus seize power in China, 1644

Giuseppe Castiglione (1688–1766), Jesuit missionary at Qing court

Japan annexes Korea, 1910

Republic of China founded, 1912

Korea given independence from Japan, 1945

Division of North and South Korea, 1948

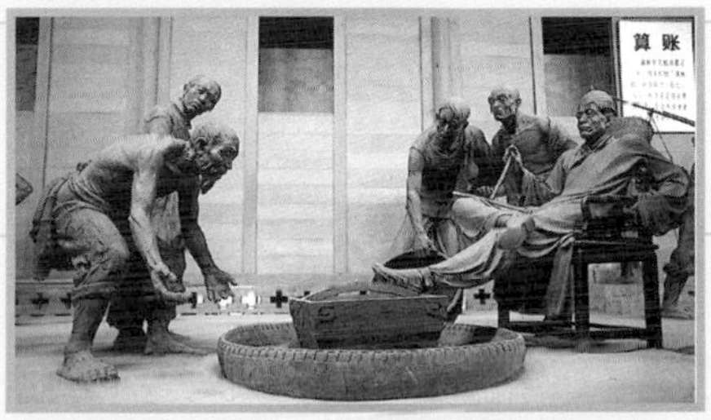

People's Republic of China established, 1949

1. Wu Zhen, *Stalks of Bamboo by a Rock*, 1347

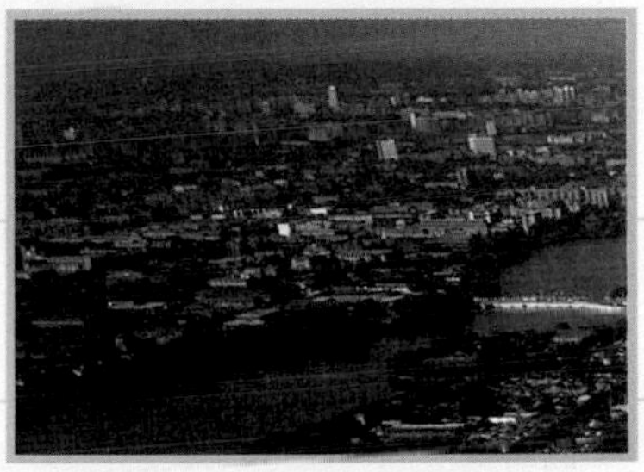

2. Forbidden City, Beijing, begun 15th century

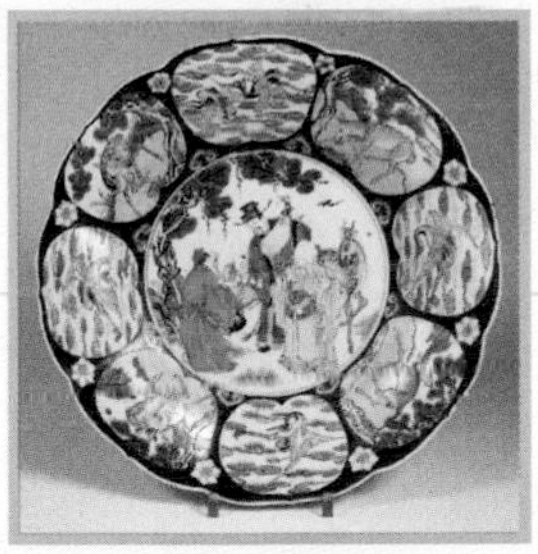

3. Dish with lobed rim, ca. 1700

4. Ye Yushan, *Rent Collection Courtyard*, 1965

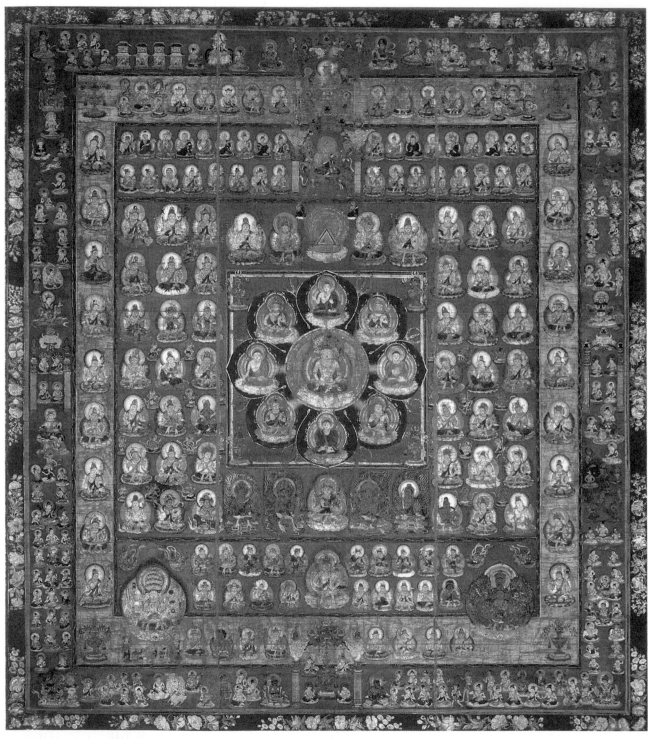

Taizokai (Womb World) of Ryokai Mandara, Kyoogokokuji (Toji), Kyoto, Japan, Early Heian period, second half of ninth century. Hanging scroll, color on silk, $6' \times 5' \frac{5}{8}''$.

5

SHRINES, STATUES, AND SCROLLS

THE ART OF EARLY JAPAN

The Japanese archipelago (MAP 5-1) consists of four main islands—Hokkaido, Honshu, Shikoku, and Kyushu—and hundreds of smaller ones, a surprising number of them inhabited. Two distinct population groups lived on the islands by earliest historical times, and the great majority of Japan's inhabitants trace their ancestry to one of these two early groups. The history of Japanese art and culture is a history of change and adaptation. Over the centuries, the Japanese have demonstrated a remarkable ability to surmount challenges, such as a mountainous island terrain that made travel and communication difficult. Japanese culture also reveals a responsiveness to imported ideas, such as Buddhism and Chinese writing systems, filtering in from continental eastern Asia. To acknowledge this responsiveness to mainland influences is not to suggest that Japan simply absorbed these imported ideas and practices. Indeed, over the centuries, Japan has developed a truly distinct culture, characterized by wide variety. There are strong regional variations, not just in art but in dialect, cuisine, and local customs—differences that persist to some degree even today. Ultimately, Japan's close proximity to the continent has promoted extensive exchange with mainland cultures, while the sea has helped protect it from outright invasions and allowed it to develop an individual and unique character.

JAPAN BEFORE BUDDHISM

Jomon Period (ca. 10,500–300 BCE)

CORD-MARKED POTTERY Japan's earliest distinct culture is the Jomon. The term *jomon*, meaning "cord markings," refers to the technique that this culture used to decorate earthenware vessels. The Jomon people were hunter-gatherers, but in contrast to most hunter-gatherer societies, which were nomadic, the Jomon enjoyed surprisingly

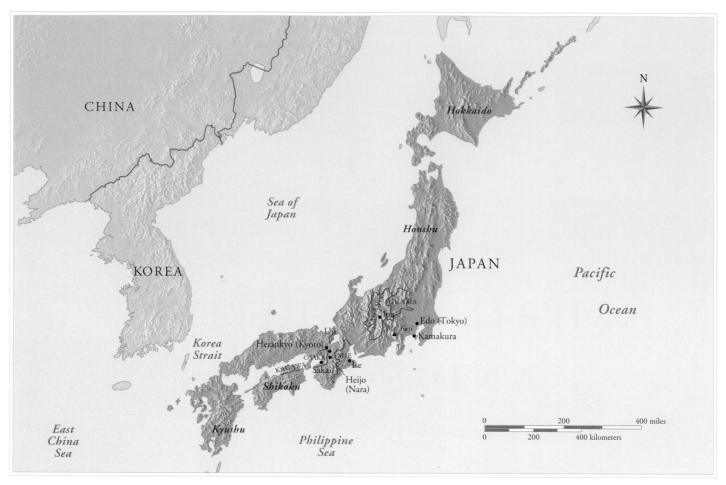

MAP 5-1 Early Japan.

settled lives. Their villages consisted of pit dwellings—shallow round excavations with raised earthen rims and thatched roofs. Their settled existence permitted the Jomon people to develop distinctive ceramic technology, even before their development of agriculture. In fact, archaeologists have dated some ceramic sherds found in Japan to before 10,000 BCE—older than the sherds from any other area of the world.

In addition to rope markings, incised lines and applied coils of clay adorned Jomon pottery surfaces. The most impressive examples come from the Middle Jomon period (2500–1500 BCE). Much of the population then lived in the mountainous inland region, where local variations in ceramic form and surface treatment flourished. However, all Jomon potters shared a highly developed feeling for modeled, rather than painted, ceramic ornament. Jomon pottery displays such a wealth of applied clay coils, striped incisions, and sometimes quasi-figural motifs that the sculptural treatment in certain instances even jeopardizes the basic functionality of the vessel. Jomon vessels served a wide variety of purposes, from storage to cooking to bone burial. Some of the most elaborate pots may have served ceremonial functions.

A dramatic example (FIG. **5-1**) from Miyanomae in Nagano Prefecture (a prefecture is a district with a governor) shows a characteristic, intricately modeled surface and a partially sculpted rim. Jomon pottery contrasts strikingly with China's most celebrated Neolithic earthenwares (see FIG. 3-1) in that the Japanese vessels are extremely thick and heavy. The harder, thinner, and lighter Neolithic Chinese earthenware emphasizes basic ceramic form and painted decoration.

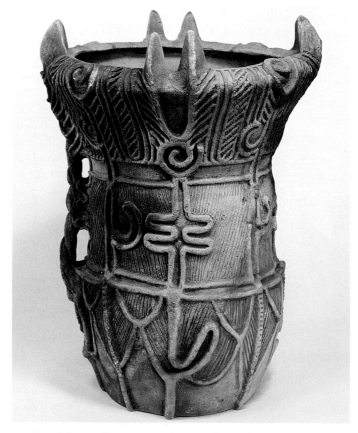

5-1 Vessel, from Miyanomae, Nagano Prefecture, Japan, Middle Jomon period, 2500–1500 BCE. Earthenware, 1′ 11$\frac{2}{3}$″ × 1′ 1$\frac{1}{4}$″. Tokyo National Museum, Tokyo.

Yayoi (ca. 300 BCE – 300 CE) and Kofun (ca. 330 – 552 CE) Periods

Jomon culture gradually gave way to Yayoi beginning around 300 BCE in Kyushu, the southernmost of the main Japanese islands. Increased interaction with both China and Korea and immigration from Korea brought dramatic social and technological transformations. People continued to live in pit dwellings, but their villages grew in size, and they developed fortifications, indicating a perceived need for defense. Toward the end of this period, near 300 CE,* Chinese visitors noted that Japan had walled towns, many small kingdoms, and a highly stratified social structure. Wet-rice agriculture provided the social and economic foundations for such development.

BANDED BRONZE BELLS The Yayoi period was a time of tremendous change in Japanese material culture as well. The Yayoi produced pottery that was less sculptural and sometimes polychrome, a departure from the modeled Jomon ceramic vessels. In addition, they developed bronze casting and loom weaving. Among the most intriguing objects Yayoi artisans produced are the *dotaku*, or bells, based on Han Chinese bell forms. However, the Yayoi eventually abandoned the Chinese use of dotaku as musical instruments, and the bells evolved into treasured ceremonial bronzes. Cast in clay molds, these bronzes generally featured raised geometric decoration presented in bands or blocks. On a few, including one from Kagawa Prefecture (FIG. **5-2**), the ornament consists of simple line drawings of people and animals. Scholars have reached no consensus on the meaning of these images. Whatever their meaning, the dotaku engravings are the earliest surviving examples of pictorial art in Japan.

TREASURE-FILLED BURIAL MOUNDS Historians named the succeeding Kofun period (*ko* means "old"; *fun* means "tomb") after the great *tumuli* (pit graves covered by sometimes enormous mounds) that had begun to appear in the third century. These burial mounds were most likely initially built by a horse-riding people

---

* From this point on, all dates in this chapter are CE unless otherwise stated.

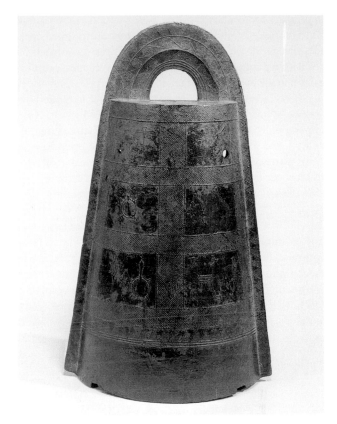

5-2 *Dotaku* (bell) with incised figural motifs, from Kagawa Prefecture, Japan, late Yayoi period, 100 – 300. Bronze, 1′ 4$\frac{7}{8}$″ high. Tokyo National Museum, Tokyo.

from the Korean peninsula. The tumuli recall earlier Jomon practices of placing the dead on sacred mountains. The mounds grew dramatically in number and scale in the fourth century. The largest tumulus in Japan (FIG. **5-3**) is believed by scholars to be the tomb of Emperor Nintoku. The central mound, which takes the "keyhole"

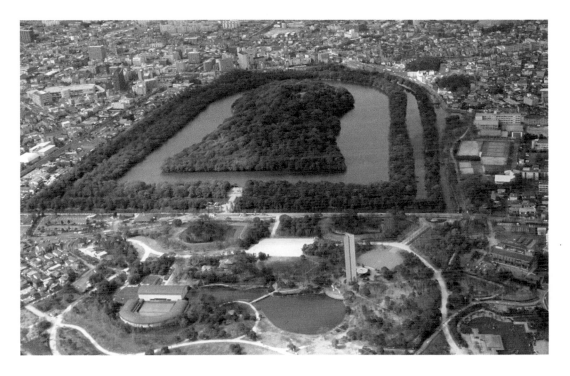

5-3 Tomb of Emperor Nintoku. Sakai, Osaka Prefecture, Japan, Kofun period, late fourth to early fifth century.

form standard for tumuli during the Kofun period, is approximately 1,600 feet long and rises to a height of 90 feet. Surrounded by three moats, the entire site covers 458 acres. Numerous objects were placed with the coffin in the pit-shaft burial chamber to assist in the transition to the next life. For exalted individuals like Emperor Nintoku, objects buried included important symbolic items and imperial regalia—mirrors, swords, and comma-shaped jewels. Numerous bronze mirrors came from China, but the form of the tombs themselves and many of the buried goods suggest even closer connections with Korea. For example, the comma-shaped jewels closely resemble those found on Korean Silla crowns (see FIG. 3-26), whose simpler gilt bronze counterparts lay in the Japanese tombs.

CYLINDER-STATUES FOR THE DEAD Burial practices at Japanese tumuli also included the placement of unglazed ceramic sculptures called *haniwa* on and around the pit grave mounds. These sculptures, such as one from Gunma Prefecture (FIG. **5-4**), are distinctly Japanese. Compared to the terracotta soldiers and horses buried with the Qin emperor at Lintong, China (see FIG. 3-5), these statues appear deceptively whimsical as variations on a cylindrical theme (*hani* means "clay," *wa* means "circle"). Yet

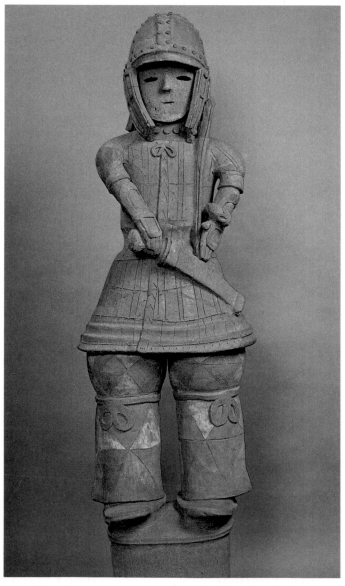

5-4 *Haniwa* (cylindrical) warrior figure, from Gunma Prefecture, Japan, late Kofun period, fifth to mid-sixth century. Low-fired clay, 4′ 1¼″ high. Aikawa Archaeological Museum, Aikawa.

haniwa sculptors skillfully adapted the basic clay cylinder into a host of forms, from abstract shapes to objects, animals (for example, deer, bears, horses, and monkeys), and human figures, such as warriors and female shamans. These artists altered the shapes of the cylinders, emblazoned them with applied ornaments, excised or built up forms, and then painted the haniwa. The variety of figure types suggests that haniwa functioned not as military guards but as a spiritual barrier protecting both the living and the dead from contamination. The Japanese of the Kofun period set these sculptures, usually several feet in height, both in curving rows and in tableaux, or scenes, around a haniwa house placed directly over the deceased buried in the mound. Presumably, the number of sculptures reflected the status of the deceased; scholars estimate that Emperor Nintoku's tumulus included 20,000 haniwa placed around the mound.

AMATERASU'S ANCIENT SHRINE The shrine of the sun goddess, Amaterasu (FIG. **5-5**), at Ise in Mie Prefecture, is the greatest of all monuments associated with the religious system that came to be known as Shinto (see "Pre-Buddhist Beliefs and Rituals in Japan," page 85). The location, use, and ritual reconstruction of this shrine every 20 years (with occasional interruptions) reflect the primary characteristics of Shinto—sacred space, ritual renewal, and purification. The Ise shrine is traditionally dated to the Kofun period. Recent scholarship, however, suggests a later date, but the shrine still serves as a representative example of sacred architecture in ancient Japan. The imperial clan traced its origins to Amaterasu, which reinforced her position as the dominant *kami*, or spiritual being. Although shrine architecture varies tremendously in Japan, scholars believe that the Ise shrine preserves some of the very earliest design elements. Yet the Ise shrine is unique; because of its connection to the Japanese imperial family, no other shrines may be constructed with this same design. The original source of the main sanctuary's form appears to be early granaries, sometimes represented on bronze mirrors or as clay haniwa. This is certainly appropriate, given that granaries were among the most important buildings in Japan's early agrarian society. Although not every aspect of the Ise shrine is equally ancient, the three main structures of the inner shrine convey some sense of Japanese architecture before the introduction of Buddhism and before the development of more elaborately constructed and adorned buildings.

Aside from the thatched roofs and some metallic decorations, the sole construction material at Ise is wood, fitted together in a *mortise-and-tenon* system, in which the wallboards were slipped into slots in the pillars. Two massive freestanding posts (once great cypress trunks), one at each end of the main sanctuary, support most of the weight of the *ridgepole,* the beam at the crest of the roof. The golden-hued cypress columns and planks contrast in color and texture with the white gravel covering the sacred grounds. The roof was originally constructed of thatch, which was smoked, sewn into bundles, and then laid in layers. The smooth shearing of the entire surface produced a gently changing contour. Today, cypress bark covers the roof. Decorative elements enhance the roofline, and include *chigi*, or ridge billets, which were originally extensions of the gable rafters at each end of the roof, and cylindrical wooden weights placed at right angles across the ridgepole. These decorative touches originally had a structural function. This shrine highlights the connection, central to Shinto, between nature and spirit. Not only are the materials derived from the natural world, but the shrine is sited in a specific location at which a kami is believed to have taken up residence.

Pre-Buddhist Beliefs and Rituals in Japan

The early beliefs and practices of pre-Buddhist Japan, which form a part of the belief system later called *Shinto* ("Way of the Gods"), did not derive from the teachings of any individual founding figure or distinct leader. Formal scriptures, in the strict sense, do not exist for these beliefs and practices either. Shinto developed in Japan in conjunction with the advent of agriculture during the Yayoi period. Shinto thus originally focused on the needs of this agrarian society, and included agricultural rites surrounding planting and harvesting. Villagers venerated and prayed to a multitude of local, sometimes specialized, deities or spirits called *kami*. The early Japanese believed kami existed in mountains, waterfalls, trees, and other features of nature, as well as in charismatic people, and they venerated not only the kami themselves but also the places the kami occupy, which are considered sacred.

Each clan (a local group claiming a common ancestor, and the basic societal unit during the Kofun period) had its own protector kami, to whom members offered prayers in the spring for successful planting and in the fall for good harvests. Clan members built shrines made up of several buildings, such as the one at Ise (FIG. 5-5), for kami. Priests made offerings of grains and fruits at these shrines and prayed on behalf of the clans. Rituals of divination, water purification, and ceremonial purification at the shrines proliferated. Visitors to the shrine area had to wash before entering in a ritual of spiritual and physical cleansing.

Purity was such a critical aspect of Japanese religious beliefs that people would abandon buildings and even settlements if negative events, such as poor harvests, suggested spiritual defilement. Even the early imperial court moved several times to newly built towns to escape impurity and the trouble it caused. Such purification concepts are also the basis for the cyclical rebuilding of the sanctuaries at grand shrines. The actual buildings of the inner shrine at Ise, for example, have been rebuilt every 20 years—at least 60 times—with few interruptions. Such rebuilding rids the sacred site of physical and spiritual impurities that otherwise might accumulate. During rebuilding, the old structure remains standing until the carpenters erect an exact duplicate next to it. In this way, the Japanese have preserved ancient forms with great precision.

When Buddhism arrived in Japan from the mainland in the sixth century, Shinto practices changed under its influence. For example, until the introduction of Buddhism, painted or carved images of Shinto deities did not exist. Yet despite the eventual predominance of Buddhism in Japan, Shinto continues to exist as a vital religion for many Japanese.

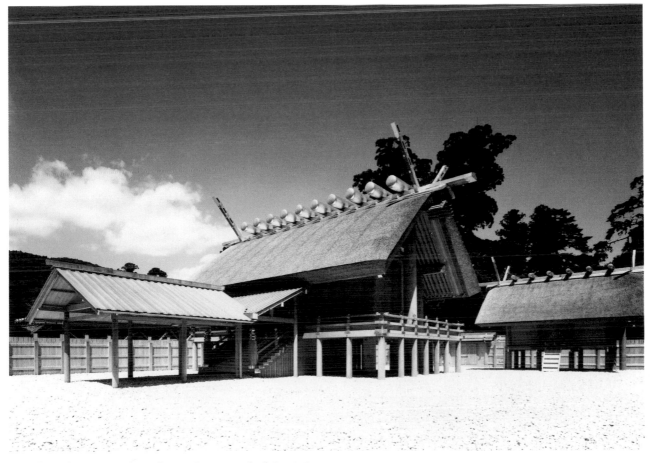

5-5 Main hall, Ise shrine, Ise, Mie Prefecture, Japan, as rebuilt in 1993.

BUDDHIST JAPAN

Asuka (552–645), Early Nara (Hakuho; 645–710), and Nara (710–784) Periods

ESTABLISHING BUDDHISM IN JAPAN In 552, according to traditional interpretation, the ruler of Paekche, one of Korea's Three Kingdoms (see Chapter 3), sent Japan's ruler a gilded bronze statue of the Buddha along with *sutras* (Buddhist scriptures) translated into Chinese, at the time the written language of eastern Asia. This event marked the beginning of the Asuka period, when Japan's ruling elite embraced major elements of continental culture that had been gradually filtering into Japan. These cultural components became firmly established in Japan and included Chinese writing, Confucianism (see "Daoism and Confucianism," Chapter 3, page 44), and Buddhism (see "Buddhism and Buddhist Iconography," Chapter 1, page 5). The Japanese court, ruling from a series of capitals south of modern Kyoto, increasingly adopted the forms and rites of the Chinese court. In 710, the Japanese finally established what they intended as a permanent capital at Heijo (present-day Nara). City planners laid out the new capital on a symmetrical grid closely modeled on the plan of the Chinese capital of Chang'an. However, Nara remained the capital only until 784; after a transitional period, Heiankyo became the capital in 794.

For half a century after 552, Buddhism met with opposition, but by the end of that time, the new religion was established firmly in Japan. Older beliefs and practices (those that came to be known as Shinto) continued to have significance (and do to the present day), especially as agricultural rituals and imperial court rites. As time passed, Shinto deities even gained new identities as local manifestations of Buddhist deities.

In the arts associated with Buddhist practices, Japan followed Korean and Chinese prototypes very closely, especially during the Asuka, Early Nara (Hakuho), and Nara periods. In fact, early Buddhist architecture in Japan adhered so closely to mainland standards (although generally with a considerable time lag) that surviving Japanese temples have helped greatly in the reconstruction of what was almost completely lost on the continent. Buddhist temples served as monasteries as well and were actually building complexes rather than individual structures.

A GOLDEN HALL FOR WORSHIP The main building in a Japanese Buddhist temple complex, the image hall, housed the major sculptural icons and provided a site of worship and prayer. At Horyuji, an important surviving early temple complex located outside Nara, the image hall (FIG. 5-6) is known as the *kondo* (Golden Hall) and dates from around 680. Although periodically repaired and somewhat altered (the covered porch is an eighth-century addition; the upper railing dates to the 17th century), the structure retains its graceful but sturdy forms beneath the modifications. The main pillars (not visible in our illustration due to the porch addition) decrease in diameter from bottom to top, as in classical architecture. The tapering provides an effective transition between the more delicate brackets above and the columns' stout forms. Also somewhat masked by the added porch is the harmonious reduction in scale from the first to the second story. Following Chinese models, the builders used ceramic tiles as roofing material. Other buildings at the site include a five-story pagoda that serves as a reliquary.

A BRONZE BUDDHA TRIAD Although wood later became the primary material of Buddhist sculpture through much of Japanese history, bronze was not uncommon. Among the earliest extant examples of Japanese Buddhist sculpture is a bronze *Buddha triad* (Buddha flanked by two bodhisattvas; FIG. 5-7). Rescued from Horyuji's predecessor, which was destroyed by fire in the seventh century, it became one of the main images in the Horyuji kondo. The central figure in the triad is Shaka (the Indian/Chinese Sakyamuni), the historical Buddha. Despite this identification, this depiction is not, properly speaking, a portrait (in the Western sense of the term). Rather, Shaka is presented in a transhistorical guise, having achieved a higher state of being. Behind the main

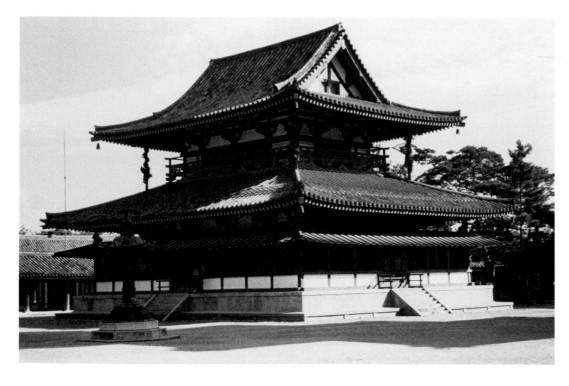

5-6 Horyuji *kondo* (Golden Hall), Nara, Japan, Early Nara (Hakuho) period, ca. 680.

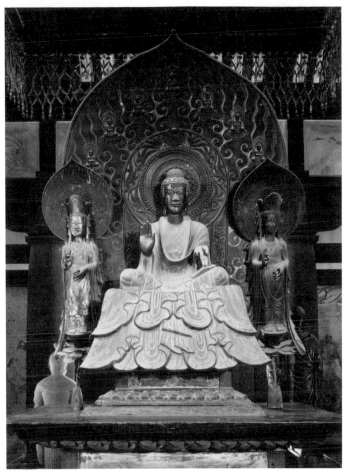

image, a flaming *mandorla* (a lotus-petal-shaped *nimbus*) bears small figures of other Buddhas. The sculptor, TORI BUSSHI (*busshi* means "maker of Buddhist images"), was a descendant of a Chinese immigrant. Tori's Buddha triad dates to 623 but reflects the style of the early to mid-sixth century in China and Korea. He elongated the heads and gave greater attention to the drapery's elegantly stylized folds than to a naturalistic modeling of the physical substance of the bodies or their garments.

MANDORLA-FRAMED STATUES Within little more than half a century, however, Japan began to move beyond the style of the Asuka period in favor of new ideas and forms coming out of Tang China and Korea. More direct relations with China also narrowed the time lag between developments there and their transfer to Japan. In the triad of Yakushi (Bhaisajyaguru, the Buddha of Healing who presides over the Eastern Pure Land; FIG. **5-8**) in the kondo at the Yakushiji temple of the late seventh century in Nara, the sculptor favored greater anatomical definition and shape-revealing drapery over the dramatic stylizations of the Horyuji statues. The attendant bodhisattvas, especially, reveal the long stylistic trail back through China (see FIG. 3-12) to the sensuous fleshiness of Indian sculpture (see FIG. 1-12). The sculpture's original gilding was destroyed by fire.

THE PAINTED WALLS OF HORIYUJI Until a disastrous fire in 1949, the interior walls of the Golden Hall at Horyuji preserved some of the finest examples of Buddhist wall painting in eastern Asia, executed around 710, the beginning of the Nara period. Now the only record of them consists of color photographs. The most important paintings depicted the Buddhas of the four directions. Like the other three, Amida (Amitabha), the Buddha of immeasurable light and infinite life, ruler of the Western Pure

5-7 TORI BUSSHI, Shaka triad, Horyuji kondo, Nara, Japan, Asuka period, 623. Bronze, 5′ 9½″ high.

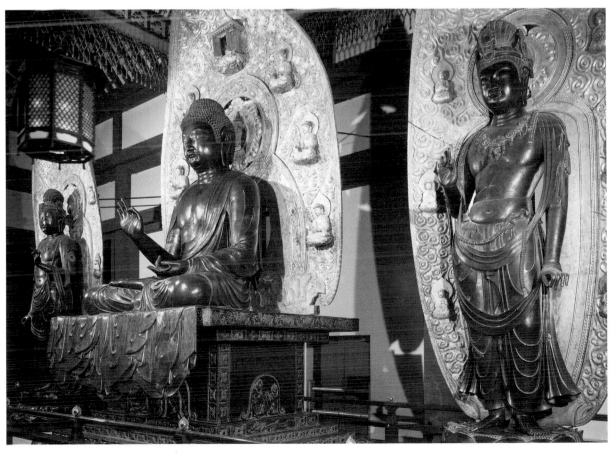

5-8 Yakushi triad, Yakushiji kondo, Nara, Japan, Early Nara (Hakuho) period, late seventh or early eighth century. Bronze, central figure 8′ 4″ high.

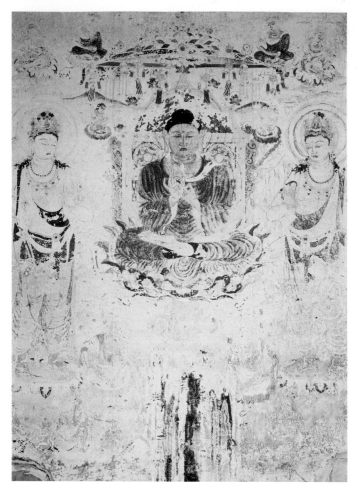

5-9 Amida triad, wall painting (damaged), from Horyuji kondo, Nara, Japan, Early Nara (Hakuho) period, ca. 710. Ink and colors, 10′ 3″ × 8′ 6″. Horyuji Treasure House, Nara.

743 was historically important as part of an imperial attempt to unify and strengthen the country by utilizing religious authority to reinforce imperial power. The temple served as the administrative center of a network of branch temples built in every province. Thus, the consolidation of imperial authority and thorough penetration of Buddhism throughout the country went hand in hand. The dissemination of a common religion contributed to the eventual disruption of the clan system and the unification of disparate political groups. So important was the construction of both the building and the Daibutsu that court and government officials as well as Buddhist dignitaries from China and India were present at the opening ceremonies in 752. Sadly, the current building does not match the original—it is significantly smaller (the current building has 7 bays; the original had 11). Yet it still radiates enormous presence. Even in its diminished size, the Daibutsuden is still the largest wooden building in the world. The treasures that Todaiji houses serve today as almost a museum of eighth-century pan-Asian culture. Many of the temple's sculptures were inspired by the finest Tang Chinese art forms.

Heian Period (794–1185)

In 784, possibly to escape the power of the Buddhist priests in Nara, the imperial house moved its capital north, eventually relocating in 794 in what became its home until modern times. Originally called Heiankyo ("capital of peace and tranquility"), it is known today as Kyoto. In the early Heian period, Japan maintained fairly close ties with China, but from the middle of the ninth century on, relations between Japan and China deteriorated so rapidly that, by that century's end, court-sponsored contacts had ceased. Japanese culture, especially at court, became much more self-directed than it had been in the preceding few centuries.

ESOTERIC BUDDHISM Among the major developments during the early Heian period was the introduction of Esoteric Buddhism to Japan from China. Esoteric, or secret, Buddhism is so named because of the secret transmission of its teachings. Two Esoteric sects made their appearance in Japan during the early Heian period: Tendai in 805 and Shingon in 806. The teachings of Tendai were based on the *Myohorenge kyo,* the *Lotus Sutra,* one of the Buddhist scriptural narratives. Tendai was brought to Japan by a Buddhist priest who traveled to China specifically to study Tendai Buddhism. He believed that all individuals possessed buddha nature and could become enlightened to this reality through such acts as meditation and careful living.

The introduction of Shingon (True Word) Buddhism had a wider impact. Conveyed by a Japanese student-priest, after a trip to the Chinese capital of Chang'an, Shingon is based on the various sutras. Shingon followers believe that anyone can achieve enlightenment through contemplation and rituals. To aid focus during meditation, Shingon disciples use special hand gestures (mudras; see "Buddhism," Chapter 1, page 5) and recite particular words or syllables (mantras in Sanskrit, shingon in Japanese). Shingon became the primary form of Buddhism in Japan through the mid-10th century.

Because of the emphasis on ritual and meditation in Shingon, the arts flourished during the early Heian period. Both paintings and sculptures provided followers with visualizations of specific Buddhist deities and allowed them to contemplate the transcendental concepts central to the religion. Of particular importance in Shingon meditation was the *mandala* (*mandara* in Japanese), a diagram of the cosmic universe. Among the most famous mandalas is the Womb World (Taizokai), which was usually hung on

Land (FIG. 5-9), sits enthroned in his paradisical land, attended by bodhisattvas. The exclusive worship of Amida later became a major trend in Japanese Buddhism, and much grander depictions of his paradise appeared, resembling those at Dunhuang in China (see FIG. 3-13). Here, however, the representation is simple and iconic. Although executed on a dry wall, the painting process involved techniques similar to fresco, such as transferring designs from paper to wall by piercing holes in the paper and pushing colored powder through the perforations. As with the Buddha triad at Yakushiji, the mature Tang style, with its echoes of Indian sensuality, surfaces in this work. The smooth brush lines, thoroughly East Asian, give the figures their substance and life. Such lines belong to a particular type, often seen in Buddhist painting, called iron-wire lines because they are thin and even with a suggestion of tensile strength. Also, as in many other Buddhist paintings, the lines are red instead of black. The identity of the painters of these pictures is unknown, but some scholars have suggested they were Chinese or Korean rather than Japanese.

THE GREAT BUDDHA During the Nara period, the imperial court sponsored the construction in Nara of a temple complex, the Golden Hall (FIG. 5-10) at the Todaiji temple. Later destroyed, it was rebuilt in the early 18th century. Also known as the Great Buddha Hall (Daibutsuden), it housed a 53-foot bronze image of the Cosmic Buddha, Roshana (Vairocana), inspired by colossal stone statues of this type in China (see FIG. 3-12). The commissioning of Todaiji and its Great Buddha (Daibutsu) by Emperor Shomu in

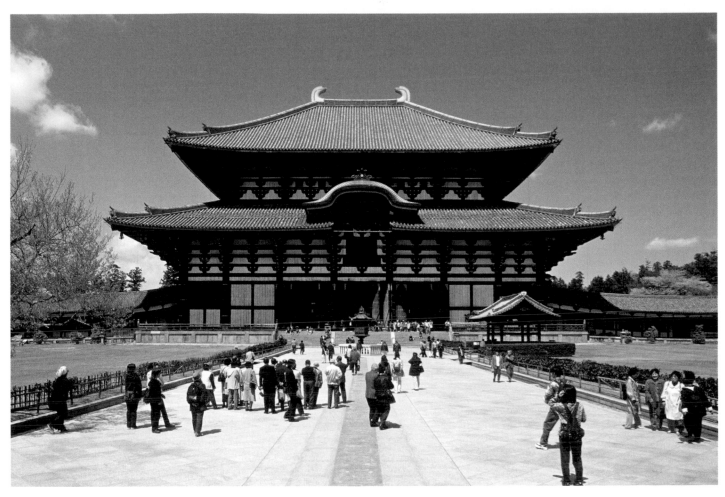

5-10 Daibutsuden, Todaiji, Japan, Nara period, eighth century, rebuilt ca. 1700.

the wall of a Shingon kondo. The Womb World is composed of 12 zones, each representing one of the various dimensions of buddha nature (for example, universal knowledge, wisdom, achievement, and purity). The mandala we illustrate here (FIG. **5-11**) is among the best preserved in Japan, and is located at Kyoogokokuji (Toji), the Shingon teaching center established in 823.

SUGGESTING CELESTIAL ARCHITECTURE During the middle and later Heian period, belief in the vow of Amida, the Buddha of the Western Pure Land, to save believers through rebirth in his realm gained great prominence among the Japanese aristocracy. Eventually, the simple message of Pure Land Buddhism—universal salvation—facilitated the spread of Buddhism to all classes of Japanese. The most important surviving monument in Japan related to Pure Land beliefs is the so-called Phoenix Hall (FIG. **5-12**) of the Byodoin, a temple built by Fujiwara Yorimichi (r. 990–1074) in memory of his father Michinaga on the grounds of Michinaga's summer villa at Uji. Dedicated in 1053, the Phoenix Hall houses a wooden statue of Amida carved from multiple joined blocks, the predominant wooden sculpture technique by this time. The building's elaborate winged form evokes images of the Buddha's palace in his Pure Land, as depicted in East Asian paintings (see FIG. 3-13) based on the design of great Chinese palaces. By placing only light pillars on the exterior, elevating the wings, and situating the whole on a reflective pond, the Phoenix Hall builders suggested the floating weightlessness of a celestial architecture. The building's name derives

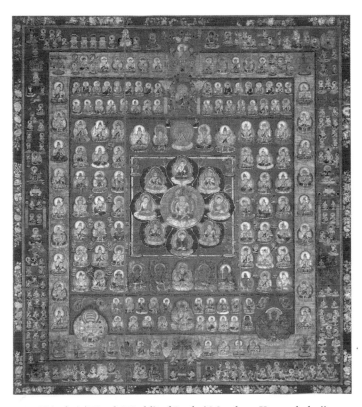

5-11 Taizokai (Womb World) of Ryokai Mandara, Kyoogokokuji (Toji), Kyoto, Japan, Early Heian period, second half of ninth century. Hanging scroll, color on silk, $6' \times 5' \frac{5}{8}''$.

Japanese Literature and Court Culture

During the Nara and Heian periods (710–1185), the Japanese imperial court developed as the center of an elite culture. Both men and women produced literature, paintings, calligraphy, and decorative arts that critics generally consider "classical" today. Heian court members, especially those from the great Fujiwara clan that dominated the court for a century and a half, compiled the first great anthologies of Japanese poetry and wrote Japan's most influential secular prose.

Japanese poetry and related painting and decorative art emphasize human sentiments intertwined with responses to nature, seasonality, and a body of standard metaphors and symbols. For example, the full moon, flying geese, crying deer, and certain plants symbolize autumn, which in turn evokes somber emotions, fading love, and dying. Such concrete but evocative images frequently appear in paintings. Exchanging poems was a common Japanese social practice and a frequent preoccupation of lovers.

A lady-in-waiting to an empress of the early 11th century wrote the best-known and longest-admired work of literature in Japan, *Tale of Genji*. Known as Lady Murasaki, the author is one of many important Heian women writers, including especially diarists and poets. Generally considered the world's first lengthy novel, *Tale of Genji* tells of the life and loves of Prince Genji and, after his death, of his heirs. The novel and much of Japanese literature consistently display a sensitivity to the sadness in the world caused by the transience of love and life. Illustrated scrolls (FIG. 5-13) of *Tale of Genji* rely on key poetic motifs and careful compositions to convey such feelings.

---

from its overall birdlike shape and from two bronze phoenixes decorating the ridgepole ends. In eastern Asia, these birds were believed to alight on lands properly ruled. Here, they represented imperial might, sometimes associated especially with the empress. The authority of the Fujiwara family derived primarily from the marriage of daughters to the imperial line.

A TALE OF LOVE AND INTRIGUE Japan's most admired literary classic is *Tale of Genji* (see "Japanese Literature and Court Culture," above), written around 1000 by Murasaki Shikubu (usually referred to as Lady Murasaki), a lady-in-waiting at the court. Recounting the lives and loves of Prince Genji and his descendants, *Tale of Genji* provides readers with a view of Heian court culture. The oldest extant examples of illustrated copies are fragments from a deluxe set of early-12th-century handscrolls. From textual and physical evidence, scholars have suggested that the set originally consisted of about 10 handscrolls produced by about five teams of artisans. Each team consisted of a nobleman talented in calligraphy, a chief painter, and assistants. The script is primarily *hiragana*, a sound-based writing system developed in Japan from Chinese characters. Hiragana originally served the needs of women (who were not taught Chinese) and became the primary script for Japanese court poetry. In these handscrolls, pictures alternate with text, as in Gu Kaizhi's *Admonitions* scrolls (see FIG. 3-10). However, the Japanese work focuses on emotionally charged moments in personal relationships, rather than on lessons in exemplary behavior. In the scene illustrated here (FIG. 5-13), for example, Genji meets with his greatest love near the time of her death. The bush-clover in the garden identifies the season as autumn, the season associated with the fading of life and love.

Here, a radically upturned ground plane and strong diagonal lines suggest three-dimensional space rather than depict it illusionistically. Further, these features convey an elevated viewpoint. The painter omitted roofs and ceilings to allow a privileged view of the emotionally charged moments typically represented in the interiors. Flat fields of unshaded color emphasize the painting's two-

5-12 Phoenix Hall, Byodoin, Uji, Japan, Heian period, 1053.

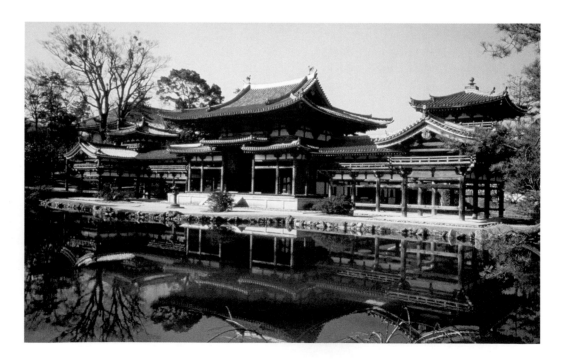

dimensional character, but rich patterns in the textiles and architectural ornament give a feeling of sumptuousness. The human figures appear constructed of stiff layers of contrasting fabrics, and the artist simplified and generalized the aristocratic faces, using a technique called "line for eye and hook for nose." This lack of individualization may reflect societal restrictions on looking directly at exalted persons, or it may have served to ease viewers' identification with a character in the story. Several formal features of the *Genji* illustrations—native subjects, bright mineral pigments, lack of emphasis on strong brushwork, and general flatness—were later considered typical of *yamato-e* (native-style painting; the term *yamato* means "Japan" and is used to describe anything that is characteristically Japanese). In the early Heian period before this example was made, however, yamato-e probably referred only to Japanese subject matter.

PAINTINGS OF BUDDHIST TALES Painted during the late 12th century, at the end of the Heian period, *The Legends of Mount Shigi* (FIG. 5-14) represents a different facet of narrative

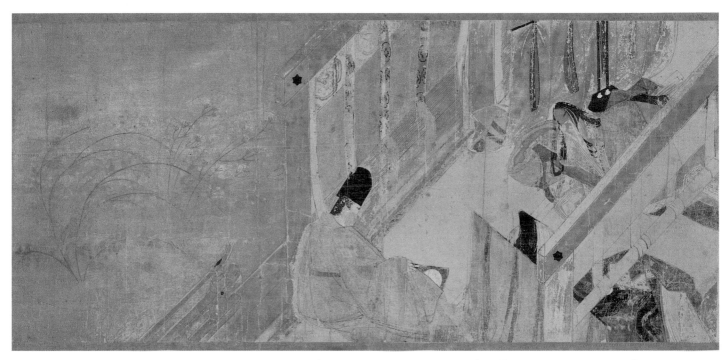

5-13 Scene from Minori chapter, *Tale of Genji*, Late Heian period, first half of 12th century. Handscroll, ink and color on paper, $8\frac{5}{8}''$ high. Goto Art Museum, Tokyo.

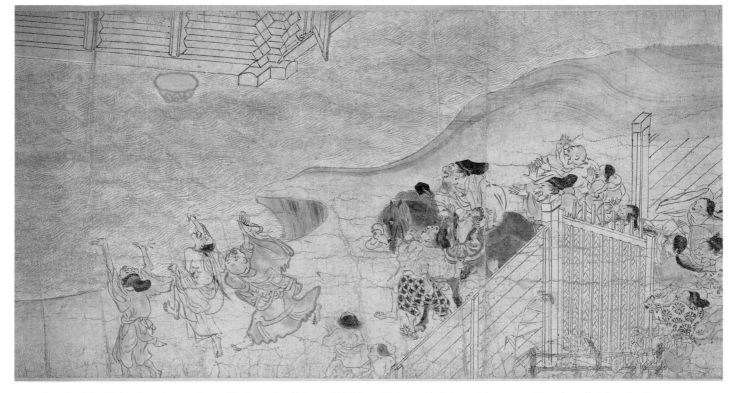

5-14 Detail of the Flying Storehouse, from *The Legends of Mount Shigi*, Late Heian period, late 12th century. Handscroll, ink and colors on paper, $1'\frac{1}{2}''$ high. Chogosonshiji, Nara.

handscroll painting. The stories belong to a genre of pious Buddhist tales devoted to miraculous events involving virtuous individuals. Unlike the *Genji* scrolls, short segments of text and pictures do not alternate. Instead, the painters took advantage of the scroll format to present several scenes in a long, unbroken stretch. For example, the first scroll shows the same travelers at several stages of their journey through a continuous landscape.

The *Mount Shigi* scrolls illustrate three miracles associated with a Buddhist monk named Myoren and his mountaintop temple. The first relates the story of the flying storehouse and depicts Myoren's begging bowl lifting the rice-filled storehouse of a wealthy landowner and carrying it off to the monk's hut in the mountains (FIG. 5-14). The painter depicted the astonished landowner, his attendants, and several onlookers in various poses—some grimacing, others gesticulating wildly and scurrying about in frantic amazement. The artist exaggerated each feature of the painted figures, in striking contrast to the *Genji* scroll figures.

Kamakura Period (1185–1332)

In the late 12th century, a series of civil wars between rival warrior families led to the end of the Japanese imperial court as a major political and social force. The victors, headed by the Minamoto family, established their *shogunate* (military government) at Kamakura in eastern Japan. The imperial court remained in Kyoto as the theoretical source of political authority but without actual power. During the Kamakura period, more frequent and positive contact with China brought with it an appreciation for more recent cultural developments there, ranging from new architectural styles to Zen Buddhism.

A PRIESTLY PORTRAIT Rebuilding in Nara presented an early opportunity for architectural experimentation. A leading figure in planning and directing the reconstruction efforts was the priest Shunjobo Chogen (1121–1206), who is reputed to have made three trips to China between 1166 and 1176. After learning about contemporary Chinese architecture, he oversaw the rebuilding of Todaiji, among other projects. His portrait statue (FIG. 5-15) is one of the most striking examples of the high level of naturalism prevalent in the early Kamakura period. Characterized by finely painted details, a powerful rendering of the signs of aging, and the inclusion of such personal attributes as prayer beads, the statue of Chogen exhibits the carving skill and style of the Kei school of sculptors (see "Japanese Artists, Workshops, and Patrons," page 93). The Kei school traced its lineage to Jocho, a famous sculptor of the mid-11th century. Its works display fine Heian carving

5-15 Detail of the priest Shunjobo Chogen, Todaiji, Nara, Japan, Kamakura period, early 13th century. Painted cypress wood, 2′ 8⅜″ high. 💿

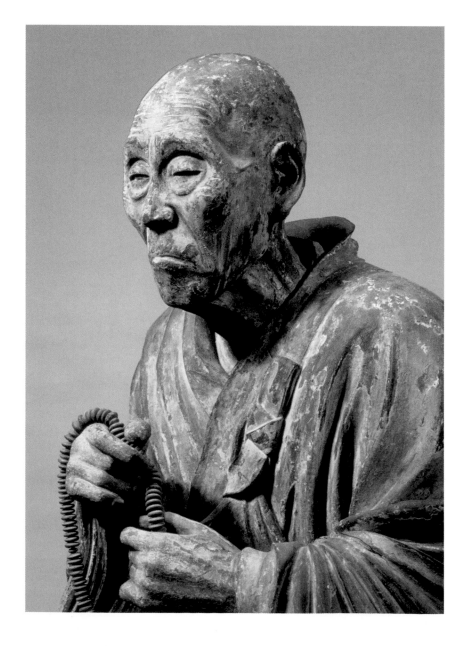

Japanese Artists, Workshops, and Patrons

For much of early Japanese history, art production was largely dependent on commissions. Until the Late Heian period (1086–1185), major commissions came almost exclusively from the imperial court or the great temples. As warrior families gained wealth and power, they too extended great commissions—in many cases closely following the aristocrats' precedents in subject and style.

Artists, for the most part, did not work independently, but rather were affiliated with workshops. Indeed, until recently, hierarchically organized male workshops produced most Japanese art. Membership in these workshops was often based on familial relationships. Each workshop was dominated by a master, and many of his main assistants and apprentices were relatives. Outsiders of considerable skill sometimes joined workshops, often through marriage or adoption. The eldest son usually inherited the master's position, after rigorous training in the necessary skills from a very young age. Therefore, one meaning of the term "school of art" in Japan is a network of workshops tracing their origins back to the same master, a kind of artistic clan. Inside the workshops, the master and senior assistants handled the most important production stages, but artists of lower rank helped with the more routine work. The portrait statue of Chogen (FIG. 5-15), for example, was created by a workshop based on familial ties.

Artistic cooperation also surfaced in court bureaus, an alternative to family workshops. These official bureaus, located at the imperial palace, had emerged by the Heian period. The painting bureau accrued particular fame. Teams of court painters, led by the bureau director, produced pictures such as the scenes in the *Tale of Genji* handscrolls (FIG. 5-13). This system remained vital into the Kamakura period and well beyond. Under the direction of a patron or the patron's representative, the master painter laid out the composition by brushing in the initial outlines and contours. Under his supervision, junior painters applied the colors. The master then completed the work by brushing in fresh contours and details such as facial features. Very junior assistants and apprentices assisted in the process by preparing paper, ink, and pigments. Unlike mastership in hereditarily run workshops, competition among several families determined control of the Court Painting Bureau during the Heian and Kamakura periods.

Not all art was controlled by the bureaus or family workshops. Priest-artists were trained in temple workshops. These artists produced Buddhist art objects for public viewing as well as images for private priestly meditation. Amateur painting was common among aristocrats of all ranks. As they did for poetry composition and calligraphy, aristocrats frequently held elegant competitions in painting. Both women and men participated in such activities. In fact, court ladies probably played a significant role in developing the painting style seen in the *Genji* scrolls, and a few participated in public projects.

techniques combined with an increased concern for natural volume and detail learned from studying, among other sources, surviving Nara period works and works imported from Song China. Enhancing the natural quality of Japanese portrait statues is the use of inlaid rock crystal for the eyes, a technique found only in Japan.

MOUNTED WARRIORS ON A HANDSCROLL All the painting types flourishing in the Heian period continued to prosper in the Kamakura period. A striking example of narrative handscroll painting is *The Burning of the Sanjo Palace* (FIG. 5-16), a fragment of a work illustrating some of the battles in the civil wars at the end of the Heian period. Here, the viewer sees the drama unfold in swift and violent staccato brushwork and vivid flashes of color. At the beginning of the scroll (read from right to left), the eye focuses first on a mass of figures rushing toward a blazing building (not shown here)—the painting's crescendo—and then moves at a slowed pace through swarms of soldiers, horses, and bullock

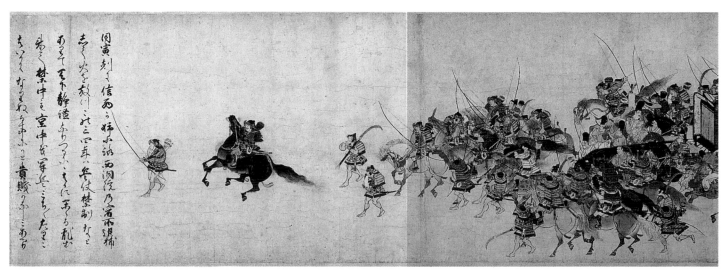

5-16 Detail of *The Burning of the Sanjo Palace*, Kamakura period, 13th century. Handscroll, ink and colors on paper, 1′ 4¼″ high; complete scroll, 22′ 10″ long. Museum of Fine Arts, Boston (Fenollosa-Weld Collection).

5-17 *Amida Descending over the Mountains,* Kamakura period, 13th century. Hanging scroll, ink and colors on silk, 4′ 3$\frac{1}{8}$″ × 3′ 10$\frac{1}{2}$″. Zenrinji, Kyoto.

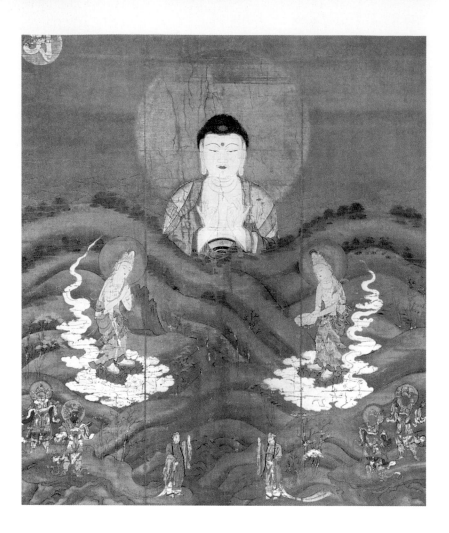

carts. Finally, a warrior on a rearing horse arrests the viewer's gaze. The horse and rider, however, serve as a *deceptive cadence* (false ending). They are merely a prelude to the single figure of an archer, who picks up and completes the soldiers' mass movement, drawing the turbulent narrative to a quiet close.

THE SAVING POWER OF AMIDA Buddhism and Buddhist painting remained vital in the Kamakura period. Evangelical monks spread Pure Land beliefs throughout Japan to people from all levels of society, and new Pure Land sects emerged that the lower ranks of society, including peasants, found especially appealing. But elite patrons continued to commission major Pure Land artworks. Pure Land Buddhism in Japan stressed the saving power of Amida, who, if called on, hastened to believers at the moment of death and conveyed them to his Pure Land. Pictures of this scene often hung in the presence of a dying person, who recited Amida's name to ensure salvation.

In *Amida Descending over the Mountains* (FIG. **5-17**), a gigantic Amida appears to move directly toward the viewer. His two main attendant bodhisattvas have already made the passage. The grand frontal presentation of Amida gives the painting an iconic quality even as the bodhisattvas' movement continues his descent. Particularly striking in this painting is the way in which Amida's halo resembles a rising moon, an image long admired in Japan for its spiritual beauty.

CONCLUSION

Striking transformations mark the long history of Japanese art as the country's population received, responded to, and developed new forms and ideas from continental eastern Asia. Early metalwork, Buddhist architecture, and the basic painting formats and media, to name only a few examples, readily reveal Japan's close ties to the continent. However, from earliest times, Japan maintained distinctive aesthetic ideals and preferences. For instance, the dynamic forms of Jomon pottery and haniwa figures suggest that the early Japanese derived a deep pleasure from allowing the colors and textures of their raw materials to remain prominent in the final objects. This tendency may not have been exclusive to Japanese art and certainly did not dominate in later centuries, but it did remain a vital part of Japan's aesthetic heritage, helping determine what people accepted from the continent and how they adapted it. In the end, however, the most distinctive feature of Japanese art is its great variety. This reflects the people's capacity to embrace radically different aesthetics simultaneously, appreciating their separate contributions to a richly diverse material culture. Chapter 6 shows how this cultural flexibility continued after several decades of upheaval, the Kamakura rulers' downfall in the early 14th century (1332), and the establishment of a new shogunate by the end of the century.

JOMON	10,500 BCE	▌ HUNTING AND FISHING
MIDDLE JOMON	2500 BCE	
	▣1	
	1500 BCE	
	300 BCE	
		▌ RICE GROWING AND METALWORKING
YAYOI	100 CE	
	▣2	
	300	
KOFUN		▌ EMERGENCE OF IMPERIAL FAMILY
	552	
ASUKA	▣3	▌ BUDDHISM OFFICIALLY INTRODUCED, 552
	645	
EARLY NARA (HAKUHO)		
	710	
NARA		▌ TRANSFER OF CAPITAL TO NARA, 710
	794	
HEIAN		▌ TRANSFER OF CAPITAL TO HEIANKYO (KYOTO), 794
		▌ NEW SECTS OF ESOTERIC BUDDHISM INTRODUCED, CA. 805
		▌ SUSPENSION OF DIPLOMATIC RELATIONS WITH CHINA, 894
		▌ PURE LAND BUDDHISM TEACHINGS GAIN IMPORTANCE, FROM 10TH CENTURY
		▌ WARRIOR CLANS RISE IN POWER, 12TH CENTURY
	1185	
		▌ KAMAKURA SHOGUNATE ESTABLISHED, 1185
		▌ POPULAR PURE LAND SECTS EMERGE, 13TH CENTURY
KAMAKURA		
	▣4	
	1332	

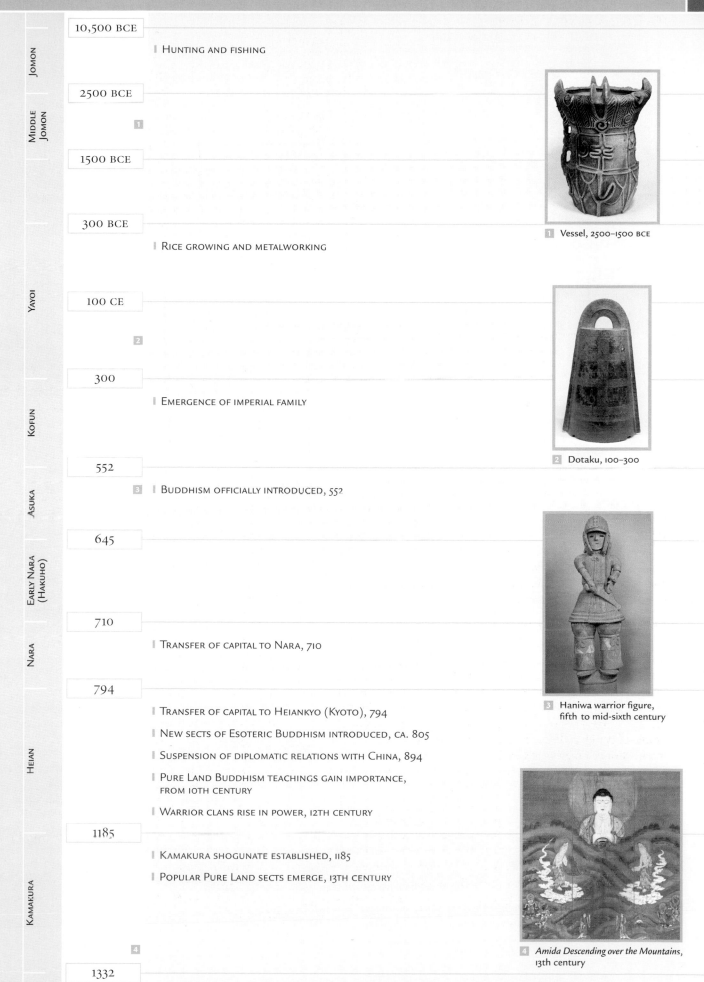

1 Vessel, 2500–1500 BCE

2 Dotaku, 100–300

3 Haniwa warrior figure, fifth to mid-sixth century

4 *Amida Descending over the Mountains,* 13th century

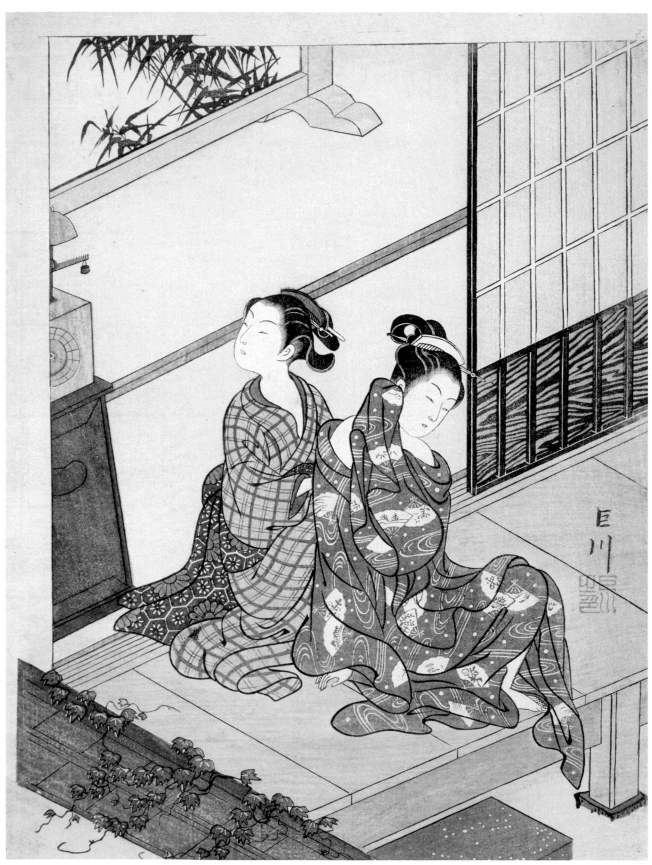

Suzuki Harunobu, *Evening Bell at the Clock,* from *Eight Views of the Parlor* series, Edo period, ca. 1765. Woodblock print, $11\frac{1}{4}'' \times 8\frac{1}{2}''$. The Art Institute of Chicago, Chicago (Clarence Buckingham Collection).

6

FROM THE SHOGUNS
TO THE PRESENT

THE ART OF LATER JAPAN

Early Japanese cultural history (as recounted in Chapter 5) reveals the dialogue that took place between the Japanese islands (MAP 6-1) and continental eastern Asia. Still, the Japanese developed a rich variety and unique identity in their art. This ability to incorporate foreign elements while maintaining a consciousness of their own heritage and traditions became more apparent as time progressed, even as Japan experienced turmoil and political instability.

AN AGE OF UPHEAVAL AND WAR

Muromachi Period (1336–1573)

SHOGUNS AND SAMURAI In 1336, after years of upheaval and conflict within the imperial family, a *shogun* (the head of the most powerful military family), Ashikaga Takauji (1305–1358), managed to accrue sufficient power to establish the domination of his clan over the country. This marked the beginning of the Muromachi period, named after the district in Kyoto in which the Ashikaga maintained their headquarters. The reign of the imperial family continued to be recognized. In theory, the shogun managed the country and maintained unity on the ruling emperor's behalf. However, in reality, the emperor's political power had waned over time until he lost all governing authority. Thus, although the imperial family maintained the illusion of power, control ultimately rested predominantly in the *shogunate*, or military government. Shogunates were largely political and economic arrangements, with local lords, the leaders of powerful warrior bands composed of *samurai* (warriors), paying obeisance to the shogun. These local lords had considerable power over affairs in their own domains. To manage their territories, both the shogun and the local lords also needed strong administrative skills. These skills included handling judicial matters and land-holding issues, and cultivating both culture and scholarship.

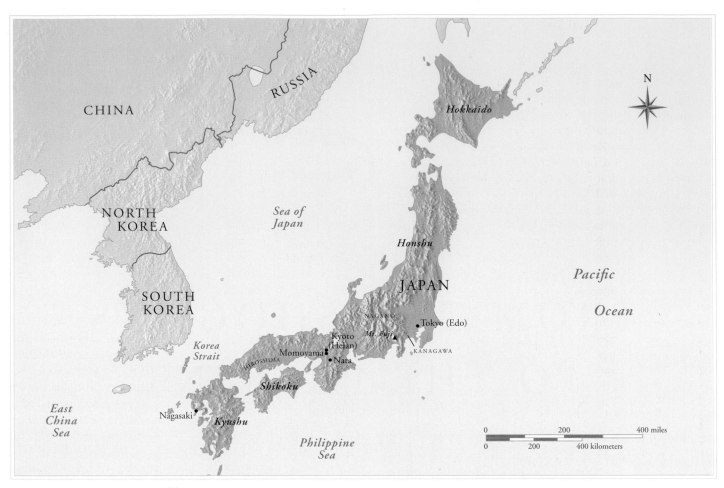

MAP 6-1 Later sites in Japan.

Despite the hierarchical nature of this societal organization, the control that shoguns exerted during this period was, in fact, tenuous and precarious. Ambitious lords often seized opportunities to expand their power (perhaps aspiring to become shogun themselves). As a result, Japan experienced violent confrontations over territory and control.

Appropriately, recent scholars have referred to the late 15th through the late 16th century in Japan as the Age of Wars (or the Era of Warring States). The significance of this label is that it highlights the instability of Japanese political and social institutions at this time. This instability contributed to widespread cultural change. For example, Japanese society became more egalitarian, especially in the cities, where commoners mingled with the aristocracy and warriors. Indeed, many wealthy merchants were able to rise to positions of considerable power. In addition, these changes and the resulting liberation from governmental strictures and societal tradition allowed the arts to flourish.

In sum, the Muromachi period was one of upheaval. By 1573, the Ashikaga shogunate had been overthrown, and much of Japan was ravaged by provincial wars—battles between lords, conflicts between militant religious groups, and peasant uprisings.

THE DISCIPLINE OF ZEN During the Muromachi period, *Zen* (*Chan* in Chinese) Buddhism (see "Zen and Zen-Inspired Art: Ideals and Realities," page 99) flourished alongside the older traditions, such as Pure Land and Esoteric Buddhism. Unlike the Pure Land faith, which stressed reliance on the saving power of Amida, the Buddha of the West, Zen emphasized rigorous discipline and personal responsibility. For this reason, Zen held a special attraction for upper echelons of the warrior class, whose behavioral codes placed high values on loyalty, courage, and

self-control. Further, familiarity with Chinese Zen culture carried implications of superior knowledge and refinement, thereby legitimizing the elevated status of the warrior elite.

Zen, however, was not simply the religion of Zen monks and highly placed warriors. Aristocrats, merchants, and others studied at and supported Zen temples, reflecting the increasing egalitarianism of Japanese society. Furthermore, those who embraced Zen, including samurai, also generally accepted other Buddhist teachings, especially the ideas of the Pure Land sects. These sects gave much greater attention to the problems of death and salvation. Zen temples stood out not only as religious institutions but also as centers of secular culture, where people could study Chinese Song and Yuan art, literature, and learning (see Chapter 4), which the Japanese imported along with Zen Buddhism.

MEDITATIVE ZEN GARDENS The Saihoji temple gardens in Kyoto bear witness to both the continuities and changes that marked religious art in the Muromachi period. In the 14th century, this Pure Land temple with its extensive gardens was transformed into a Zen institution. However, Zen leaders did not attempt to erase other religious traditions, and the Saihoji gardens in their totality originally included some Pure Land elements even as they served the Zen faith's more meditative needs. In this way, they perfectly echo the complementary roles of these two Buddhist traditions in the Muromachi period, Pure Land providing a promise of salvation and Zen promoting study and meditation.

Saihoji's lower gardens owe their renown today to their iridescently green mosses, whose beauty almost seems to belong to another world. In contrast, arrangements of rocks and sand on the hillsides of the upper garden, especially the dry cascade and pools (FIG. 6-1), are treasured early examples of Muromachi dry

Zen and Zen-Inspired Art
Ideals and Realities

Zen, as a fully developed Buddhist tradition, began filtering into Japan in the 12th century and had its most pervasive impact on Japanese culture starting in the 14th century. As in other forms of Buddhism, Zen followers hope for the experience of enlightenment. Zen teachings assert that everyone has the potential for enlightenment, but worldly knowledge and mundane thought patterns suppress it. Thus, to achieve enlightenment, followers must break through the boundaries of everyday perception and logic. This is most often achieved through meditation; indeed, the word *zen* means "meditation." Some Zen schools stress meditation as a long-term practice eventually leading to enlightenment, whereas others stress the benefits of sudden shocks to the worldly mind, as through the posing of abstruse questions. One such shock is depicted in Kano Motonobu's *Zen Patriarch Xiangyen Zhixian Sweeping with a Broom* (FIG. 6-3), in which the shattering of a fallen roof tile opens the monk's mind. Beyond personal commitment, the guidance of an enlightened teacher is essential to arriving at enlightenment. Long and strict training that includes manual labor under the tutelage of this master, coupled with years of meditation, provide the foundation for a receptive mind. According to Zen beliefs, by cultivating discipline and intense concentration, one can transcend one's ego and release oneself from the shackles of the mundane world. Although Zen is not primarily devotional, followers do pray to specific deities. In general, Zen teachings view mental calm, lack of fear, and spontaneity as signs of a person's advancement on the path to enlightenment.

Zen training for monks takes place at temples. In addition, early Japanese Zen temples provided other services. For example, they sometimes served as centers of Chinese learning and handled funeral rites. Zen temples even embraced many traditional Buddhist observances, such as devotional rituals before images, that had little to do with meditation per se.

Over the years, Zen monks have produced an extensive body of art, which aids meditation and serves as a form of teaching. Zen paintings often depict Zen masters, whereas calligraphers usually produce works featuring poems or conundrums. In their quest to distill the Zen experience into strokes of the brush, Zen works are visually bold and convey a spontaneity and energy, although there is no identifiable Zen style.

Zen ideals of discipline and rejection of worldliness reverberated throughout Japanese culture as the teachings spread. Lay followers painted pictures and produced other artworks that appear to reach toward Zen ideals through their subjects and their direct expression. Other cultural practices reflected the widespread appeal of Zen. For example, the tea ceremony (see "The Japanese Tea Ceremony," page 103), or ritual drinking of tea, as it developed in the 15th and 16th centuries, offered a temporary respite from everyday concerns, a brief visit to a quiet retreat with a meditative atmosphere, such as the Taian teahouse (FIG. 6-7). All of these activities attest to the power of Zen as a cultural force in Japan—not just historically, but to the present day.

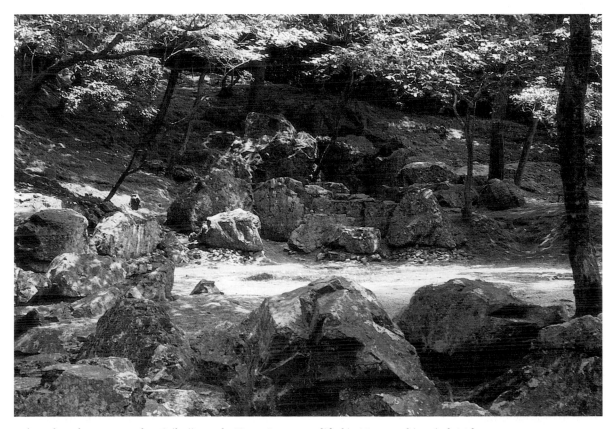

6-1 Dry cascade and pools, upper garden, Saihoji temple, Kyoto, Japan, modified in Muromachi period, 14th century.

landscape gardening. The designers stacked the rocks to suggest a swift mountain stream rushing over the stones to form pools below. In eastern Asia, people long considered gazing at dramatic natural scenery highly beneficial to the human spirit. Such activities refreshed people after too much contact with daily affairs and helped them reach beyond mundane reality. The dry landscape, or rock garden, became very popular in Japan in the Muromachi period and afterward, especially at Zen temples. Excluding actual water and arranging stones to suggest far more expansive landscapes, as seen in Chinese paintings (see FIG. 3-18), encouraged deep mental, aesthetic, and spiritual engagement with the scene, which could be fully visualized only in the mind.

BROKEN-INK PAINTING During the Muromachi period, many artists produced pictures primarily in India ink. As was common in the long history of Japanese art, styles and subjects usually closely followed Chinese precedents (often arriving by way of Korea), and painters filled their pictures with Chinese scenes and figures. Most of the ink painting masters were at least ostensibly Zen monks. The most celebrated priest-painter was TOYO SESSHU (1420–1506). One of the very few painters who actually traveled to China, he learned much from viewing contemporaneous Ming paintings (see FIGS. 4-9 and 4-10). Sesshu (individuals who lived before 1868 are often referred to by their adopted "pen names," which follow their family names) worked in a great variety of styles, ranging from tight compositions in precise brushwork to dramatic works in the *broken-* or *flung-ink style* (sometimes called "splashed-ink style"), a technique Zen monks in eastern Asia often, but not exclusively, adopted. Despite the Zen monks' interest in this style, the origins of broken ink in China were in fact secular.

The painter of a broken-ink picture paused to visualize the image, loaded the brush with ink, and then applied primarily broad, rapid strokes, sometimes even dripping the ink onto the paper. The result often hovers at the edge of legibility, without dissolving into sheer abstraction. This balance between spontaneity and a thorough knowledge of the painting tradition gives the pictures their artistic strength. In one of Sesshu's broken-ink landscape paintings (FIG. **6-2**), images of mountains, trees, and buildings emerge from the ink-washed surface. Two figures appear in a boat (to the lower right), and the two swift strokes nearby represent the pole and banner of a wine shop.

Ink painting was far from the only type of painting that flourished in the Muromachi period. Artists at court, in temples, and in the service of various powerful families painted portraits, icons, narrative handscrolls, folding screens, and other types of pictures in rich colors. Sesshu, for example, did not limit his work to monochrome.

THE TOSA AND KANO SCHOOLS Two major painting schools—the Tosa School and the Kano School—emerged in Japan during the 15th and 16th centuries. Tosa Mitsunobu (1434–1525), director of the Painting Bureau (see "Japanese Artists, Workshops, and Patrons," Chapter 5, page 93) and chief painter at the imperial court in the late Muromachi, was the pivotal figure in the history of the Tosa School. The Tosa style featured bright, contrasting color, detailed textile patterns, and thickly applied paint. Contemporary with the Tosa School, the Kano School became a virtual national academy in the 17th century, ending only in the late 19th century. KANO MOTONOBU (1476–1559), very likely the son-in-law of Tosa Mitsunobu, was

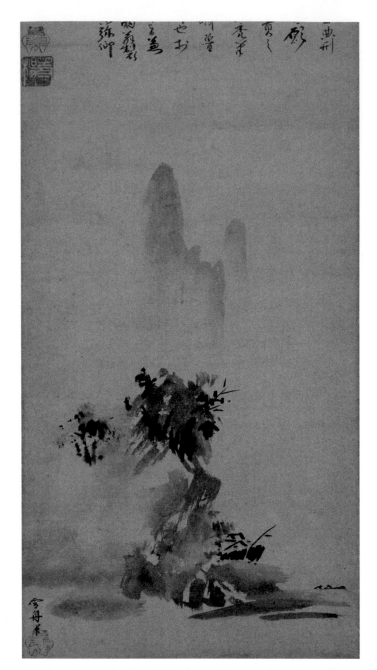

6-2 TOYO SESSHU, broken-ink landscape, Muromachi period, 1495. Hanging scroll, ink on paper, $4' 10\frac{1}{4}'' \times 1' \frac{7}{8}''$. Tokyo National Museum, Tokyo.

largely responsible for establishing the Kano style. Characterized by bold outlines and the presentation of objects along the vertical plane of the painting surface (rather than utilization of *atmospheric perspective*), the Kano style is revealed in Motonobu's *Zen Patriarch Xiangyen Zhixian Sweeping with a Broom* (FIG. **6-3**). This work depicts a scene from the spiritual life of a Zen patriarch. In this painting, the monk experiences the moment of enlightenment. As he sweeps the ground near his rustic retreat, a roof tile falls at his feet and shatters. The patriarch's Zen training is so deep that the resonant sound propels him into an awakening. This work reveals Motonobu's exacting precision in ink and light color. It incorporates stylistic features of Chinese academic models of ink painting, such as the sharp, angular rock forms Japanese painters, including Sesshu, long had adopted and modified. Motonobu's picture of the patriarch is one of a set of sliding doors he and his assistants painted at a Zen temple. During the

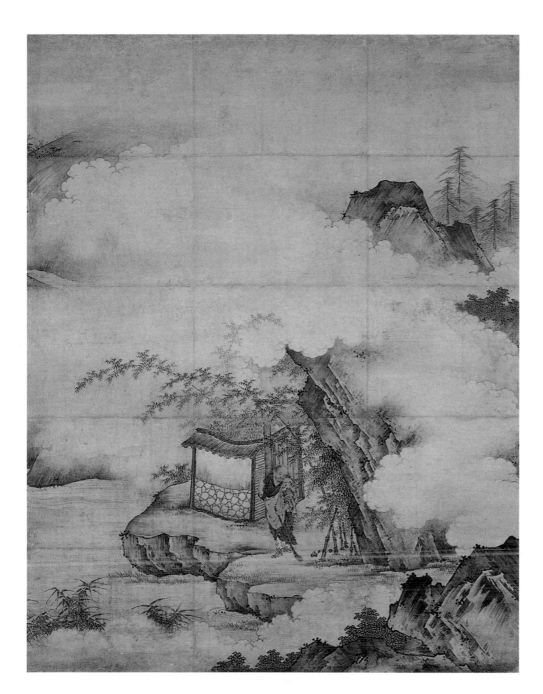

16th century, architectural decoration such as painted sliding doors formed a growing component of the repertoires of the Kano School.

Momoyama Period (1573–1615)

THE UNIFICATION OF JAPAN During the Momoyama period, the government was centralized, laying the foundation for the establishment of a Japanese nation. After the fractious Muromachi era, the successive efforts of three powerful warlords—Oda Nobunaga (1534–1582), Toyotomi Hideyoshi (1536–1598), and Tokugawa Ieyasu (1542–1616)—resulted in the ouster of the last Ashikaga shogun and the consolidation of political authority. The era's designation, Momoyama (Peach Blossom Hill), is derived from the scenic foliage at the castle of one of these warlords.

PAINTED CHINESE LIONS To reinforce their power, these warlords constructed huge castles with palatial residences—partly as symbols of their authority and partly as fortresses. Each warlord commissioned lavish decorations for the interior of his castle, including paintings, sliding doors, and folding screens in ink, color, and gold leaf. Gold screens had been known since Muromachi times, but Momoyama painters made them even bolder, reducing the number of motifs and often greatly enlarging them against flat, shimmering fields of gold leaf.

The grandson of Motonobu, Kano Eitoku (1543–1590), was the leading painter of such murals and screens and received numerous commissions from the powerful warlords. So extensive were these commissions (in both scale and number) that Eitoku utilized a system of painting developed by his grandfather that relied on a team of specialized painters to assist him. Unfortunately, little of Eitoku's elaborate work remains. The ostentatious castles

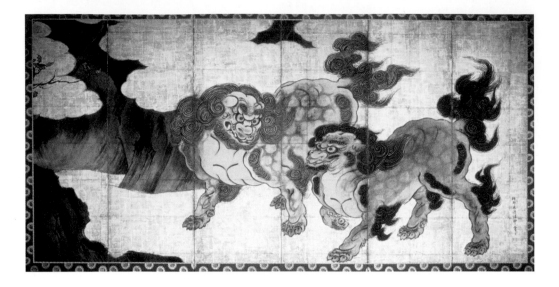

6-4 KANO EITOKU, *Chinese Lions,* Momoyama period, late 16th century. Six-panel screen, color, ink, and goldleaf on paper, 7′ 4″ × 14′ 10″. Imperial Household Agency, Tokyo.

he helped decorate were subsequently destroyed (not surprising in an era marked by power struggles). However, a painting of Chinese lions on a single six-panel screen (FIG. **6-4**) offers a glimpse of his work's grandeur. Possibly created for Hideyoshi, the second of the three warlords of the period, this screen appropriately speaks to the emphasis on militarism so prevalent at the time. These Chinese lions depicted by Eitoku refer to mythological beasts that have their origin in ancient Chinese legends. Appearing in both religious and secular contexts, the lions came to be associated with power and bravery, and are thus fitting imagery for a military leader. Indeed, Chinese lions became an important

symbolic motif during the Momoyama period. In Eitoku's painting, the colorful beasts' powerfully muscled bodies, defined and flattened by broad contour lines, stride forward within a gold field and minimal setting elements. The dramatic impact of this work derives in part from its scale—it is more than 7 feet tall and close to 15 feet long. Because of the expansive scope of Eitoku's decoration projects, he often worked in the monumental style this painting typifies. Momoyama painting was not limited to such bold displays of isolated forms, however. It also included native and Chinese figural subjects rich in cultural, religious, and philosophical meanings.

6-5 HASEGAWA TOHAKU, *Pine Forest,* Momoyama period, late 16th century. One of a pair of six-panel screens, ink on paper, 5′ 1$\frac{3}{8}$″ × 11′ 4″. Tokyo National Museum, Tokyo.

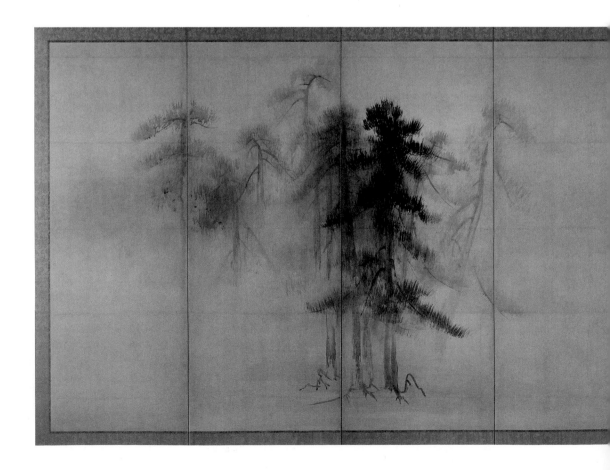

The Japanese Tea Ceremony

The Japanese tea ceremony involves the ritual preparation, serving, and drinking of green tea. The fundamental practices began in China, but they developed in Japan to a much higher degree of sophistication, peaking in the Momoyama period. Simple forms of the tea ceremony started in Japan in Zen temples as a symbolic withdrawal from the ordinary world to cultivate the mind and spirit. The practices spread to other social groups, especially warriors and, by the late 16th century, wealthy merchants. Until the late Muromachi period, grand tea ceremonies in warrior residences served primarily as an excuse to display treasured collections of Chinese objects, such as porcelains, lacquers, and paintings.

Initially, tea ceremonies were held in a room or section of a house. As the popularity of tea ceremonies increased, freestanding teahouses (FIG. 6-7) were constructed. Many scholars credit the revered tea master Sen no Rikyu with the design of the first independent teahouse.

The ceremony involves a sequence of rituals in which both host and guests participate. The host's responsibilities include serving the guests; selecting special utensils, such as water jars (FIG. 6-6) and tea bowls; and determining the tea room's decoration, which changes according to occasion and season. Acknowledged as having superior aesthetic sensibilities, individuals recognized as master tea ceremony practitioners (tea masters) advise patrons on the ceremony and acquire students. Tea masters even direct or influence the design of teahouses and tea rooms within larger structures (including interiors and gardens), as well as the design of tea utensils. They often make simple bamboo implements and occasionally even ceramic vessels.

A FOREST IN THE MIST Momoyama painters did not work exclusively in the colorful style exemplified by Eitoku's *Chinese Lions*. HASEGAWA TOHAKU (1539–1610) was a protégé of Sen no Rikyu, a renowned tea master with close connections to Zen temples. Tohaku became familiar with the aesthetics and techniques of Chinese Chan (Zen) painters and sometimes painted in ink monochrome using loose brushwork with brilliant success, as seen in *Pine Forest* (FIG. **6-5**). His wet brush strokes— long and slow, short and quick, dark and pale—present a grove of great pines shrouded in mist. His trees emerge from and recede into the heavy atmosphere, as if the landscape hovers at the edge of formlessness. In Zen terms, the picture suggests the illusory nature of mundane reality while evoking a calm, meditative mood.

THE ROLE OF THE TEA CEREMONY A favorite exercise of cultivation and refinement in the Momoyama period was the tea ceremony (see "The Japanese Tea Ceremony," above). In Japan, this important practice eventually came to carry various political and ideological implications. For example, it provided a means for those relatively new to political or economic power to assert authority in the cultural realm. For instance, upon returning from a major military campaign, warlord Hideyoshi held an immense tea ceremony that was scheduled to last 10 days and was open to everyone in Kyoto. So serious did the tea ceremony's political implications become that warlords granted or refused their vassals the right to practice it. Despite these demonstrations of authoritative control, the tea ceremony also contributed to the democratization of Japanese society. Venerated tea master Sen no Rikyu insisted that there was no rank in a teahouse, and indeed, the manner of entry into a teahouse—crawling on one's hands and knees—is intended to foster humility and egalitarianism.

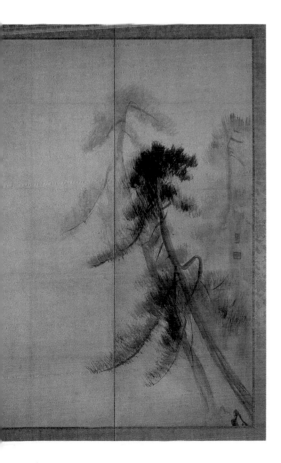

A NEW REFINED RUSTICITY This democratic ideal also influenced the aesthetics of teahouses and tea ceremony utensils. In keeping with the egalitarian principle that value and refinement lay in character and ability and not in bloodline or rank, Rikyu encouraged the use of tea items that were valued for their inherent beauty rather than their monetary worth. Accordingly, starting around the late 15th century, admiration of the technical brilliance of Chinese objects slowly gave way to ever greater appreciation of the virtues of rustic Korean and Japanese wares. This new aesthetic of refined rusticity, or *wabi*, included the design of very simple tea rooms and houses that evoked the hut of a recluse in the mountains. Wabi suggests austerity and simplicity. (Zen concepts also played a significant role in this shift.) Related to wabi and also important as a philosophical and aesthetic principle was *sabi*—

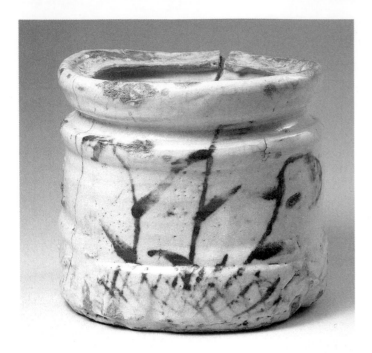

6-6 *Kogan* (ancient stream bank), tea ceremony water jar, Momoyama period, late 16th century. Shino ware with underglaze design, 7″ high. Hatakeyama Memorial Museum, Tokyo.

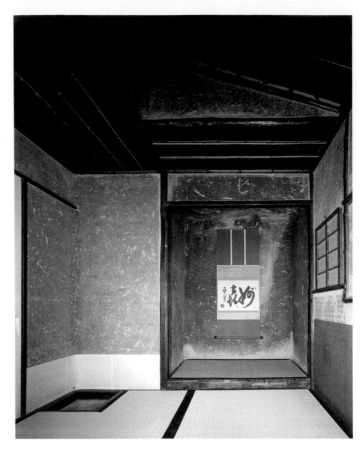

6-7 Sen no Rikyu, Taian teahouse (interior view), Myokian Temple, Kyoto, Japan, Momoyama period, ca. 1582.

the value found in the old and weathered, suggesting the tranquility reached in old age.

Wabi and sabi aesthetics are visible in the ceramic vessels produced for the tea ceremony, such as the well-known Shino water jar named *Kogan* (FIG. **6-6**). The jar's name, which means "ancient stream bank," comes from the painted design on its surface, as well as from its coarse texture and rough form, both reminiscent of earth cut by water. The term *Shino* generally refers to bowls produced during the late 16th and early 17th centuries in kilns in Mino Province. Shino wares, typically simple forms with rough surfaces, feature heavy glazes containing feldspar. These glazes are predominantly white when fired, but can include pinkish red or gray hues. Their coarse stoneware body, simple form, and seemingly casual decoration offer the same sorts of aesthetic and interpretive challenges and opportunities as the dry landscape gardens (FIG. 6-1).

CEREMONIAL TEA SPACES The ultimate representation of the new wabi aesthetic in the Momoyama period was the Taian (FIG. **6-7**), a teahouse designed under the direction of SEN NO RIKYU (1522–1591). The interior displays two standard features of Japanese residential architecture that developed in the late Muromachi period—very thick, rigid straw mats called *tatami* and an alcove called a *tokonoma*. The tatami accommodate the traditional Japanese customs of not wearing shoes indoors and of sitting on the floor and can still be found in Japanese homes today. Less common in contemporary houses are tokonoma, which developed as places to hang scrolls of painting or calligraphy and to display other prized objects.

The Taian tokonoma and the tea room as a whole have unusually dark walls, with earthen plaster covering even some of the square corner posts. The room's dimness and tiny size (about six feet square) produce a cavelike feel and encourage intimacy among the tea host and guests. The guests enter from the garden outside through a small sliding door that forces them to crawl inside. Such conditions foster humility and emphasize a guest's passage into a ceremonial space—set apart from the ordinary world—where, in theory, all are equal.

Edo Period (1615–1868)

In 1615, shogun Tokugawa Ieyasu consolidated power and established a new shogunate that lasted until 1868. (The shogun title had been abandoned after the deposition of the Ashikaga shogunate in 1573. Ieyasu revived the title for himself in 1603.) Rather than remain in Kyoto, the official capital, Ieyasu set up his seat of power in Edo (modern Tokyo). The new regime instituted many policies designed to limit severely the pace of social and cultural change in Japan. Faced with the threat of conquest, the Tokugawa rulers banned Christianity and expelled all Western foreigners except the Dutch. Those in power transformed Confucian ideas of social stratification and civic responsibility into public policy, and they tried to control the social influence of urban merchants, some of whose wealth far outstripped that of most warrior leaders. However, the population's great expansion in urban centers, the spread of literacy in the cities and beyond, and a growing thirst for knowledge and diversion made for a very lively popular culture not easily subject to tight control.

A PRINCELY VILLA AT KYOTO The imperial court's power remained as it had been for centuries, symbolic and ceremonial,

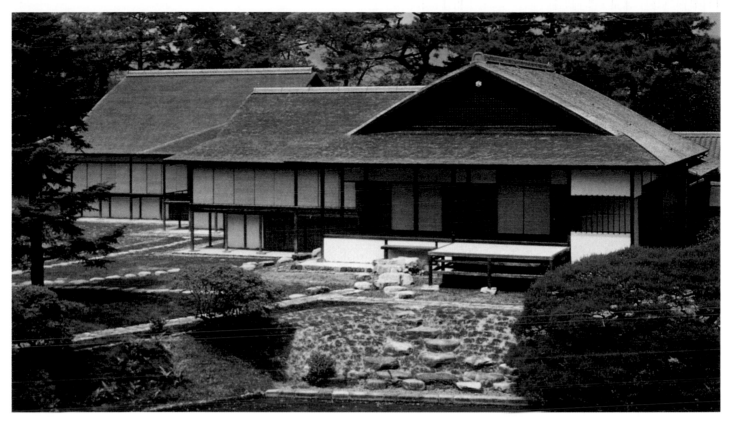

6-8 Eastern façade of Katsura Imperial Villa, Kyoto, Japan, Edo period, 1620–1663.

but the court continued to wield influence in matters of taste and culture. For example, for a period of some 50 years in the 17th century, a princely family developed a modest country retreat into a villa that became the admired, but rarely equaled, standard for domestic Japanese architecture. Since the early 20th century, it has inspired architects worldwide, even as ordinary living environments in Japan became increasingly Westernized in structure and decor. The Katsura Imperial Villa (FIG. **6-8**), built between 1620 and 1663, dates to the time of the tea ceremony's greatest popularity. Therefore, many of the villa's design features and tasteful subtleties derive from earlier teahouses, such as Rikyu's Taian (FIG. 6-7). However, more recent tea ceremony aesthetics had moved away from Rikyu's wabi extremes, and the Katsura Villa's designers and carpenters incorporated elements of courtly gracefulness as well.

Ornament that disguises structural forms has little place in this architecture's appeal, which relies instead on subtleties of proportion, color, and texture. A variety of textures (stone, wood, tile, and plaster) and subdued colors and tonal values enrich the villa's lines, planes, and volumes. Subtlety and finesse in the treatment of the building components were important. Artisans painstakingly rubbed and burnished all surfaces to bring out the natural beauty of their grains and textures. The rooms are not large, but parting or removing the sliding doors between them can create broad rectangular spaces. Perhaps most important, the residents can open the doors to the outside to achieve a harmonious integration of building and garden—one of the primary ideals of Japanese residential architecture.

THE RIMPA SCHOOL EMERGES In painting, the Kano School enjoyed official governmental sponsorship during the Edo period, and its workshops provided paintings to the Tokugawa and their major vassals. By the mid-18th century, Kano masters also served as the primary painting teachers for nearly everyone aspiring to a career in the field. Even so, individualist painters and other schools emerged and flourished, working in quite distinct styles.

The earliest major alternative school to emerge in the Edo period, Rimpa, was quite different in nature from the Kano and Tosa Schools. It did not have a similar continuity of lineage and training through father and son, master and pupil. Instead, over time, Rimpa aesthetics and principles attracted a variety of individuals as practitioners and champions. Many Rimpa works focused on literary themes favored by the nobility, and many of the Rimpa artists affiliated themselves with court culture. Stylistically, Rimpa works are characterized by vivid color and extensive use of gold and silver, and often incorporated decorative patterns. Rimpa takes its first syllable from the last syllable in the name of its ostensible founder, Ogata Korin. However, two closely linked artists, HONAMI KOETSU (1558–1637) and Tawaraya Sotatsu (1576–1643), laid its foundations a few generations earlier.

COMBINING PAINTING AND CRAFT Koetsu was the heir to an important family in the ancient capital of Kyoto and a greatly admired calligrapher. He also participated in and produced ceramics for the tea ceremony. Many scholars credit him with overseeing the design of lacquers (primarily wooden objects with lacquer decoration), perhaps with the aid of Sotatsu, the proprietor of a fan-painting shop. Scholars do know that together they drew on ancient traditions of painting and craft decoration to develop a style that collapsed boundaries between the two arts.

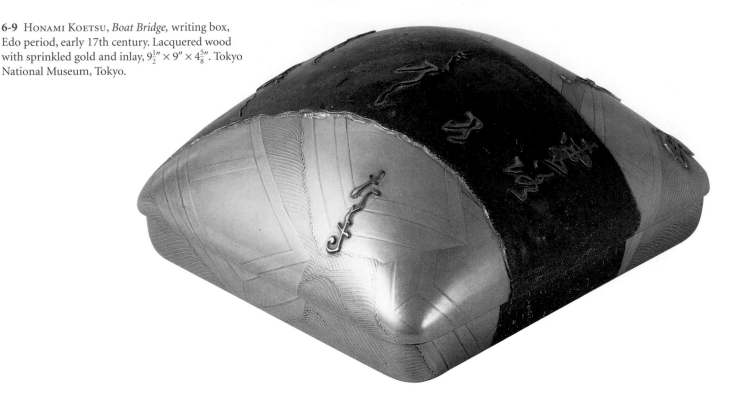

Paintings, the lacquered surfaces of writing boxes, and ceramics shared motifs and compositions.

In typical Rimpa fashion, Koetsu's *Boat Bridge* writing box (FIG. 6-9) exhibits motifs drawn from a 10th-century poem about the boat bridge at Sano, in the Eastern provinces. The lid presents a subtle, gold-on-gold scene of small boats lined up side by side in the water to support the planks of a temporary bridge. The bridge itself, a dull metal inlay, forms a band across the lid's convex surface. The raised, dull linear forms on the water, boats, and bridge are a few Japanese characters from the poem, which describes the experience of crossing such a bridge as evoking reflection on life's insecurities. The box also shows the dramatic contrasts of form, texture, and color that mark Rimpa aesthetics, especially the juxtaposition of the bridge's dull metal inlay and the brilliant gold surface. The gold decoration comes from careful sprinkling of actual gold dust in wet lacquer. Whatever Koetsu's contribution to the design process, specialists well versed in the demanding techniques of inlaying and sprinkling gold actually applied the lacquer decoration.

PLUM BLOSSOMS AND TARASHIKOMI Ogata Korin (1658–1716) developed the principles that Koetsu and Sotatsu established. The son of an important textile merchant, Korin was primarily a painter but also designed lacquers in Koetsu's manner. One of Korin's painted masterpieces is a pair of twofold screens depicting red and white blossoming plum trees separated by a stream (see FIG. Intro-3). As Koetsu did with his writing box, Korin reduced the motifs to a minimum to offer a dramatic contrast of forms and visual textures. Beneath delicate, slender branches, the gnarled, aged tree trunks flank the stream's smooth, precise curves of oxidized silver leaf. The contrast extends even to the painting techniques. The mottling of the trees comes from a signature Rimpa technique called *tarashikomi*, the dropping of ink and pigments onto surfaces still wet with previously applied ink and pigments. In striking contrast, the pattern in the stream has the precision and elegant stylization of a textile design, produced by applying pigment through the forms cut in a paper stencil.

THE LITERATI STYLE In the 17th and 18th centuries, Japan's increasingly urban, educated population spurred a cultural and social restlessness among commoners and samurai of lesser rank that the policies of the restrictive Tokugawa could not suppress. People eagerly sought new ideas and images, directing their attention primarily to China, as had happened throughout Japanese history, but also to the West. From each direction dramatically new ideas (for the isolated Japanese) about painting emerged.

Starting in the late 17th century, illustrations in printed books and actual paintings of lesser quality brought limited knowledge of the Chinese literati style into Japan. As a result, several individual Japanese painters and their followers embraced elements of the Chinese literati style (see Chapter 4). Although these artists derived their inspiration from Chinese models, the difference in context resulted in variations. In China, literati were scholars whose education and upbringing as landed gentry afforded them positions in the bureaucracy that governed the country. Chinese literati artists were predominantly amateurs and pursued painting as one of the proper functions of an educated and cultivated man. Chinese literati were cultured intellectuals. In contrast, although Japanese literati artists acquired a familiarity with and appreciation for Chinese literature, they were mostly professionals, painting to earn a living. Because the infiltration of Chinese literati painting into Japan was diffused, the resulting character of Japanese literati painting was less stylistically defined than that found in China. Despite the inevitable changes as Chinese ideas were disseminated throughout Japan, the newly seen Chinese models were valuable in supporting emerging ideals of self-expression in painting by offering a worthy alternative to the Kano School's standardized repertoire.

One of the outstanding early representatives of Japanese literati painting was Yosa Buson (1716–1783). A master writer of *haiku* (the 17-syllable Japanese poetic form that became very popular from the 17th century on), Buson had a command of literati painting that extended beyond a knowledge of Chinese models. His poetic abilities gave rise to a lyricism that pervaded both his haiku and his painting. *Cuckoo Flying over New Verdure* (FIG. 6-10) reveals his

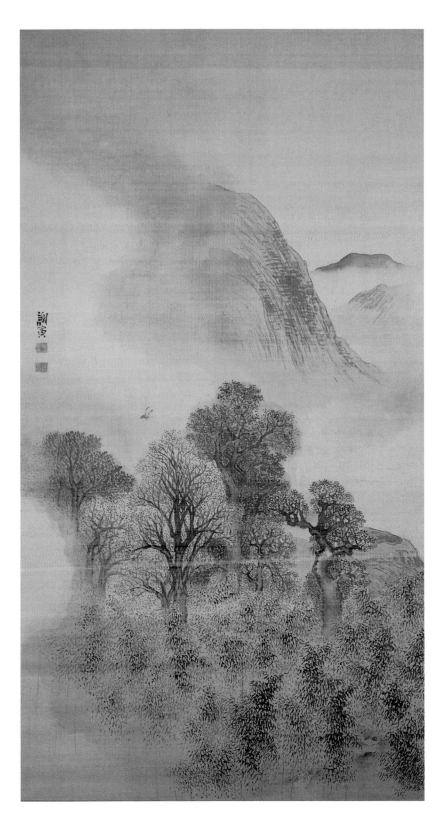

fully mature style. He incorporated in this work basic elements of Chinese and Japanese literati style by rounding the landscape forms and rendering their soft texture in fine fibrous brush strokes, and by including dense foliage patterns. Although Buson imitated the vocabulary of brush strokes associated with the Chinese literati, his touch was bolder and more abstract, and the gentle palette of pale colors was very much his own.

EDO'S FLOATING WORLD The growing urbanization in cities such as Osaka, Kyoto, and Edo led to an increase in the pursuit of sensual pleasure and entertainment in the brash popular theaters and the pleasure houses found in such locales as Edo's Yoshiwara brothel district. The Tokugawa tried to hold such activities in check, but their efforts were largely in vain. Their failure in this regard was due in part to demographics; the significant samurai population (whose families remained in their home territories) in Edo during this period was eager to enjoy city life. Those of lesser means could partake in these pleasures and amusements vicariously. Rapid developments in the printing industry led to the availability of numerous books and printed images (see "Japanese

Japanese Woodblock Prints

During the Edo period, *ukiyo-e* (pictures of the floating world) woodblock prints became enormously popular. Sold in small shops and on the street, an ordinary print went for the price of a bowl of noodles. People of very modest income could therefore collect prints in albums or paste them on their walls. A highly efficient production system made this wide distribution of Japanese graphic art possible.

Ukiyo-e artists were generally painters who did not participate in the actual making of the prints that made them so famous both in their own day and today. As the designers, they sold drawings to publishers, who in turn oversaw their printing. The publishers also played a role in creating ukiyo-e prints by commissioning specific designs or adapting them before printing. Certainly, the names of both designer and publisher appeared on the final prints.

Unacknowledged in nearly all cases are the individuals who actually made the prints, the block-carvers and printers. Using skills honed since childhood, they worked with both speed and precision for relatively low wages and thus made ukiyo-e prints affordable. The master ukiyo-e printmakers seem to have all been men. Women, especially wives and daughters, often assisted painters and other artists, but few gained separate recognition. Among the exceptions, the daughter of Katsushika Hokusai (FIG. 6-12), Katsushika Oi, became well known as a painter and probably helped her father with his print designs.

Stylistically, Japanese prints during the Edo period tend to have black outlines separating distinct color areas (FIG. 6-11). This format is a result of the printing process. A master carver pasted painted designs face down on a wooden block. Wetting and gently scraping the thin paper revealed the reversed image to guide the cutting of the block. After the carving, only the outlines of the forms and other elements that would be black in the final print remained raised in relief. The master printer then coated the block with black ink and printed several initial outline prints.

These master prints became the guides for carving the other blocks, one for each color used. On each color block, the carver left in relief only the areas to be printed in that color. Even ordinary prints sometimes required up to 20 colors and thus 20 blocks. To print a color, a printer applied the appropriate pigment to a block's raised surface, laid a sheet of paper on it, and rubbed the back of the paper with a smooth flat object. Then another printer would print a different color on the same sheet of paper. Perfect alignment of the paper in each step was critical to prevent overlapping of colors, so the block-carvers included printing guides—an L-shaped ridge in one corner and a straight ridge on one side—in their blocks. The printers could cover small alignment errors with a final printing of the black outlines from the last block.

The materials used in printing varied over time but by the mid-18th century had reached a level of standardization. The blocks were planks of fine-grained hardwood, usually cherry. The best paper came from the white layer beneath the bark of mulberry trees, because its long fibers helped the paper stand up to repeated rubbing on the blocks. The printers used a few mineral pigments but tended to favor inexpensive dyes made from plants for most colors. As a result, the colors of ukiyo-e prints were and are highly susceptible to fading, especially when exposed to strong light. In the early 19th century, more permanent European synthetic dyes began to enter Japan. The first, Prussian Blue, can be seen in Hokusai's *The Great Wave off Kanagawa* (FIG. 6-12).

The popularity of ukiyo-e prints extended to the Western world as well. Their affordability and the ease with which they could be transported facilitated the dissemination of such prints, especially throughout Europe. Ukiyo-e prints appear in the backgrounds of a number of Impressionist and Post-Impressionist paintings, attesting to the appeal these works held for Westerners.

Woodblock Prints," above), and these could convey the city's delights for a fraction of the cost of actual participation. Taking part in the emerging urban culture involved more than simple physical satisfactions and rowdy entertainments. Many who participated were highly educated in literature, music, and the other arts.

The best-known products of this sophisticated counterculture are known as *ukiyo-e*—"pictures of the floating world." The main subjects of these paintings and especially prints come from the realms of pleasure, such as the Yoshiwara brothels and the popular theater. The term *ukiyo* (floating world) originated in relation to Buddhism and reinforced the notion of the transience of human life and the ephemerality of the material world. It was during the Edo period that the floating world came to be associated with the constantly changing nature of the temporal world of sensual pleasures and entertainment—hence the emergence of ukiyo-e.

VIEWS OF AN UKIYO PARLOR The urban appetite for ukiyo pleasures and for their depiction in ukiyo-e provided fertile

ground for many print designers to flourish. Consequently, competition among publishing houses led to ever greater refinement and experimentation in printmaking. One of the most admired and emulated 18th-century designers, SUZUKI HARUNOBU (ca. 1725–1770), played a key role in developing multicolored prints. Called *nishiki-e* (brocade pictures) because of their sumptuous and brilliant color, these pictures were printed on the best-quality paper using costly pigments and were highly valued. Harunobu gained a tremendous advantage over his fellow designers when he received commissions from members of a poetry club to design limited-edition nishiki-e prints. Harunobu transferred much of the knowledge he derived from nishiki-e to his design of more commercial prints. He even issued some of the private designs later under his own name for popular consumption.

The sophistication of Harunobu's work is evident in *Evening Bell at the Clock* (FIG. **6-11**), from a series called *Eight Views of the Parlor*. This series draws upon a Chinese series usually titled *Eight Views of the Xiao and Xiang Rivers,* each image of which

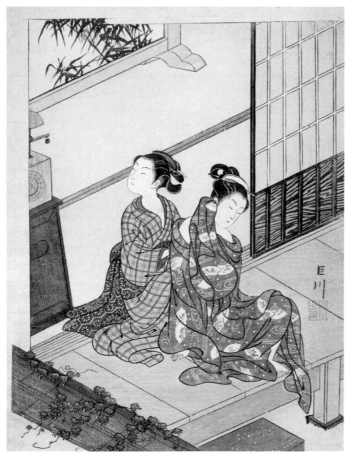

focuses on a particular time of day or year. In Harunobu's adaptation, beautiful young women and the activities that occupy their daily lives become the subject. In *Evening Bell at the Clock,* two young women sit on a veranda. One appears to be drying herself after a bath, while the other turns to face the chiming clock. Here, the artist has playfully transformed the great temple bell that rings over the waters in the Chinese series into a modern Japanese clock. This image incorporates the refined techniques characteristic of nishiki-e. Further, the flatness of the depicted objects and the rich color recall the traditions of court painting, a comparison many nishiki-e artists openly sought.

WESTERN PERSPECTIVE IN PRINTS Woodblock prints afforded artists great opportunity for experimentation, and many printmakers used this medium to set up a dialogue between the traditional and the modern. For example, in producing landscapes (another printmaking subject that emerged in the late 18th century), artists often incorporated Western perspective techniques. One of the most famous designers in this genre was KATSUSHIKA HOKUSAI (1760–1849), whose famous print, *The Great Wave off Kanagawa* (FIG. **6-12**), belongs to a woodblock series called *Thirty-Six Views of Mount Fuji.* In this view, the huge foreground wave dwarfs the artist's representation of a distant Fuji. This contrast and the whitecaps' ominous fingers magnify the wave's threatening aspect. The men in the trading boats bend low to dig their oars against the rough sea and drive their long low vessels past the danger. This print, although it draws somewhat on Western techniques, also engages the Japanese pictorial tradition. Against a background with the low horizon typical of Western painting, Hokusai placed the wave's more traditionally flat and powerfully graphic forms in the foreground.

6-11 SUZUKI HARUNOBU, *Evening Bell at the Clock,* from *Eight Views of the Parlor* series, Edo period, ca. 1765. Woodblock print, $11\frac{1}{4}'' \times 8\frac{1}{2}''$. The Art Institute of Chicago, Chicago (Clarence Buckingham Collection).

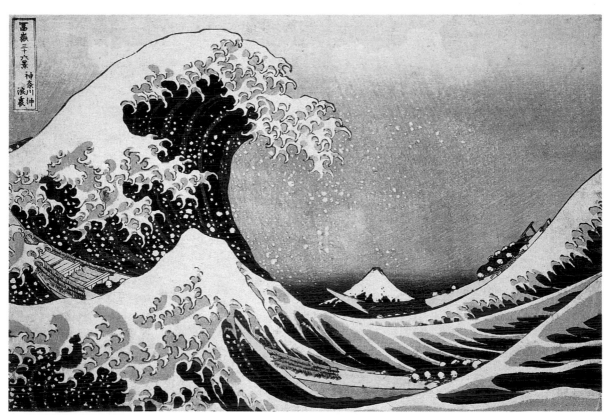

6-12 KATSUSHIKA HOKUSAI, *The Great Wave off Kanagawa,* from *Thirty-Six Views of Mount Fuji* series, Edo period, ca. 1826–1833. Woodblock print oban, ink and colors on paper, $9\frac{7}{8}'' \times 1' \ 2\frac{3}{4}''$. Museum of Fine Arts, Boston (Bigelow Collection).

Modern Japan

The Meiji and Taisho Periods (1868–1926)

THE END OF SHOGUN RULE The Edo period and the rule of the shogun ended in 1868, when rebellious samurai from provinces far removed from Edo toppled the Tokugawa shogunate. This overthrow was facilitated by the Tokugawa's inability to handle increasing pressure from Western nations for Japan to throw open its doors to the outside world. Although the rebellion restored direct sovereignty to the imperial throne, real power rested with the emperor's cabinet. As a symbol of imperial authority, however, this new period was officially called the Meiji ("Enlightened Rule"), after the emperor's chosen reign name. This practice continues today.

WESTERN OIL PAINTING *Oil painting,* the preferred painting medium in Europe from the 15th century on, became a major genre in Japan in the late 19th century. Ambitious students studied with Westerners at government schools and during trips abroad. One oil painting highlighting the cultural ferment of the early Meiji period is *Oiran* (*Grand Courtesan;* FIG. **6-13**), painted by TAKAHASHI YUICHI (1828–1894). The artist created it for a client nostalgic for vanishing elements of Japanese culture. Ukiyo-e printmakers frequently represented such grand

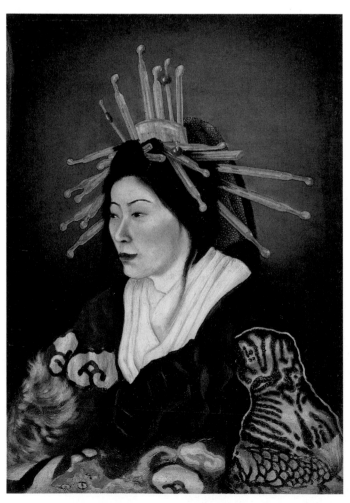

6-13 TAKAHASHI YUICHI, *Oiran (Grand Courtesan),* Meiji period, 1872. Oil on canvas, 2′ 6½″ × 1′ 9⅝″. Tokyo National University of Fine Arts and Music, Tokyo.

courtesans of the pleasure quarters. In this painting, however, Takahashi (historical figures from the Meiji period onward are usually referred to by their family names, which come first) did not portray the courtesan's features in the idealizing manner of ukiyo-e artists but in the more analytical manner of Western portraiture. Yet the painter's more abstract rendering of the garments reflects a very old practice in East Asian portraiture.

RESISTING WESTERNIZATION Unbridled enthusiasm for Westernization in some quarters led to resistance and concern over a loss of distinctive Japanese identity in other quarters. Ironically, one of those most eager to preserve "Japaneseness" in the arts was Ernest Fenollosa (1853–1908), an American professor of philosophy and political economy at Tokyo Imperial University. He and a former student named Okakura Kakuzo (1862–1913) joined with others in a movement that eventually led to the founding of an arts university dedicated to Japanese arts under Okakura's direction. Their goal for Japanese painting was to make it viable in the modern age rather than preserve it as a relic, so they encouraged incorporating some Western techniques such as *chiaroscuro* (*modeling* in light and dark), perspective, and bright hues in basically Japanese-style paintings. The resulting style was called *nihonga* (Japanese painting), as opposed to *yoga* (Western painting).

Kutsugen (FIG. **6-14**), a silk scroll by YOKOYAMA TAIKAN (1868–1958), is an example of the former. It combines a low horizon line and subtle shading effects taken from Western painting with East Asian techniques, such as anchoring a composition in one corner (see FIGS. 3-23 and 4-13), employing strong ink brushwork to define its contours, applying washes of water-and-glue-based pigments, and using applications of heavy mineral pigments. The painting's subject, a Chinese poet who fell out of the emperor's favor and subsequently committed suicide, no doubt resonated with Taikan and his associates. It provided a nice analogy to a real-life situation. At the time, Okakura was locked in a battle over his artistic principles with the Ministry of Education. Whether intended or not, this painting, in which the poet stands his ground, staunchly defying the strong winds that agitate the foliage behind him, was perceived as a comment on the friction between Okakura and authorities.

The Showa and Heisei Periods (1926–Present)

During the 20th century, Japan became increasingly prominent on the world stage in economics, politics, and culture. Among the events that propelled Japan into the spotlight was its participation in World War II. Among the most tragic consequences of that participation were widespread devastation, loss of life, and, more specifically, the atomic bombings of Hiroshima and Nagasaki in 1945. During the succeeding occupation period, the United States imposed new democratic institutions on Japan, with the emperor serving as a ceremonial head of state. Japan rebounded with remarkable speed. From the second half of that century to the present, Japan has also assumed a positive and productive place in the international art world. As they had done in earlier times with the art and culture of China and Korea, Japanese artists have internalized Western lessons and transformed them into a part of Japan's own vital culture.

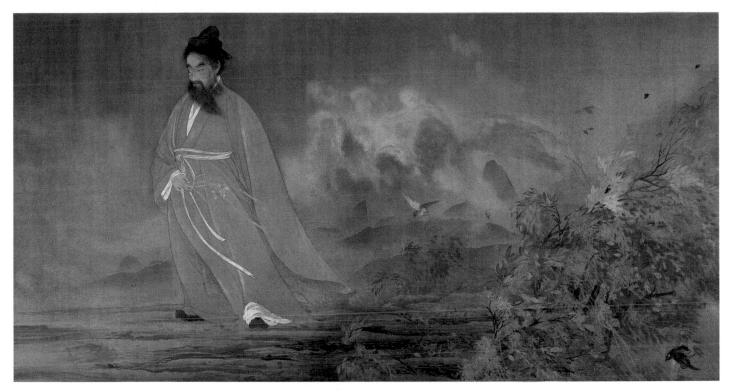

6-14 YOKOYAMA TAIKAN, *Kutsugen,* Itsukushima Shrine, Hiroshima Prefecture, Japan, Meiji period, 1898. Hanging scroll, color on silk, 4′ 4″ × 9′ 6″.

A HOME FOR THE OLYMPICS Japanese architecture, especially public and commercial building, was rapidly transformed along Western lines. In fact, architecture may be the art form that provided Japanese practitioners the most substantial presence on the world scene during the latter half of the 20th century. They made major contributions to both modern and postmodern developments. One of the most daringly experimental architects of the post–World War II period is TANGE KENZO (b. 1913). When designing the stadiums for the 1964 Olympics (FIG. **6-15**), he employed a cable suspension system that allowed him to shape steel and concrete into remarkably graceful structures. His attention to both the sculptural qualities of each building's raw concrete form and the fluidity of its spaces allies him with architects worldwide who carried on the legacy of the late style of Le

Corbusier (1887–1965) in France. His stadiums thus bear comparison with Joern Utzon's contemporaneous Sydney Opera House in Australia.

MODERN FOLK POTTERY Another Japanese art form of the 20th century attracting great attention worldwide is ceramics. Like other international folk art, traditional Japanese ceramics and other so-called crafts are highly valued today. A formative figure in Japan's folk art movement, the philosopher Yanagi Soetsu (1889–1961), promoted an ideal of beauty that was inspired by the tea ceremony and could only be achieved in functional objects made of natural materials by anonymous craftspeople. Among the ceramists who produced this type of folk pottery, known as *mingei,* was HAMADA SHOJI (1894–1978). Although Hamada did

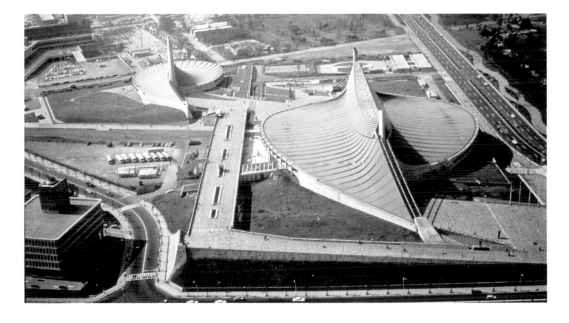

6-15 TANGE KENZO, national indoor Olympic stadiums, Tokyo, Japan, Showa period, 1961–1964.

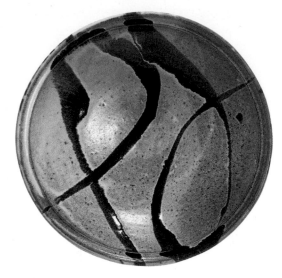

6-16 HAMADA SHOJI, large bowl, 1962. Black trails on translucent glaze, $5\frac{7}{8}'' \times 1'\ 10\frac{1}{2}''$. National Museum of Modern Art, Kyoto.

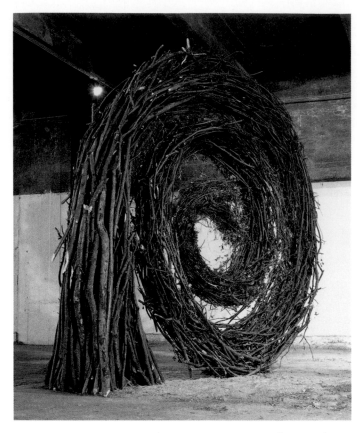

6-17 TSUCHIYA KIMIO, *Symptom,* 1987. Branches, $13'\ 1\frac{1}{2}'' \times 14'\ 9\frac{1}{8}'' \times 3'\ 11\frac{1}{4}''$. Installation view, *Jeune Sculpture '87,* Paris 1987.

espouse Yanagi's selfless ideals, he still gained international fame and received official recognition in Japan as an "Intangible Important Cultural Property," more commonly called a "Living National Treasure." Works such as his dish with casual slip designs (FIG. **6-16**) are unsigned, but connoisseurs easily recognize them as his. Such stoneware is coarser, darker, and heavier than porcelain and lacks the latter's fine decoration. To those who appreciate simpler, earthier beauty, however, this dish holds great attraction. Hamada's artistic influence extended beyond the production of pots. He traveled to England in 1920 and, along with English potter Bernard Leach (1887–1978), established a community of ceramists committed to the mingei aesthetic. Together, Hamada and Leach expanded international knowledge of Japanese ceramics, and even now, the Hamada-Leach aesthetic (as it is known) is part of potters' education worldwide.

NATURAL SCULPTURE Although no one style, medium, or subject dominates contemporary Japanese art, much of it does spring from ideas or beliefs that have been integral to Japanese culture over the years. For example, the Shinto belief in the generative forces in nature and in humankind's position as part of the totality of nature hold great appeal for contemporary artists, including TSUCHIYA KIMIO (b. 1955), who produces large-scale sculptures constructed of branches (FIG. **6-17**) or driftwood. Despite their relatively abstract nature, his works assert the life forces found in natural materials, thereby engaging viewers in a consideration of their own relationship to nature. Tsuchiya does not specifically invoke Shinto (see "Pre-Buddhist Beliefs and Rituals in Japan," Chapter 5, page 85) when speaking about his art, but it is clear that he has internalized Shinto principles. He identifies as his goal "to bring out and present the life of nature emanating from this energy of trees. . . . It is as though the wood is part of myself, as though the wood has the same kind of life force."[1]

CONCLUSION

Over the past seven centuries, Japanese history has been one of dramatic change. The emergence of shogun rule in the early 14th century ushered in an era of persistent war and conflict. Not until the restoration of the emperor in 1868 was relative stability established. Also emerging as a major presence in 14th-century Japan was Zen. Its influence extended far beyond the realm of religion, and it suffused Japanese culture with its ideals of discipline and meditative focus. Despite the centuries of turmoil, Japanese art flourished. Among the great strengths of Japanese art has been innovation through adaptation. Contact with the rest of eastern Asia and later the world's other areas, as well as knowledge of Japan's own past, provided artists and patrons a wealth of aesthetic and ideological options. As they integrated the new, they found cultural spaces where less radical adaptations of the old could survive. Even today, as Japan embraces a vision of its postindustrial future, very traditional artists, as well as thoroughly contemporary ones, flourish side by side.

[1] Quoted in Junichi Shiota, *Kimio Tsuchiya, Sculpture 1984–1988* (Tokyo: Morris Gallery, 1988), 3.

1334

| Restoration of imperial power, 1334–1336

| Ashikaga Shogunate established, 1336

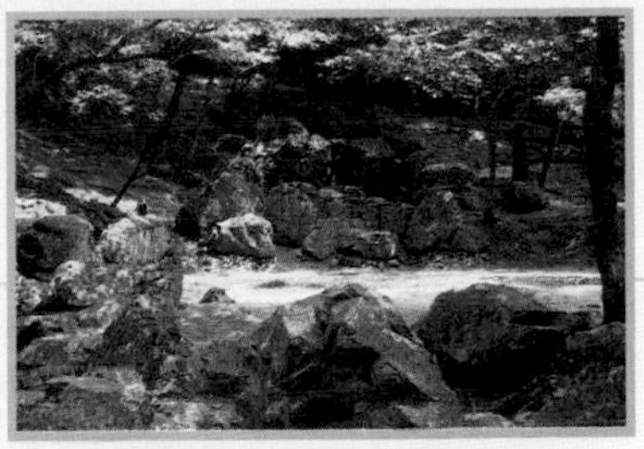

1

1400

| Official relations established with China's Ming government, 1401

| Emergence of Tosa and Kano Schools, 15th and 16th centuries

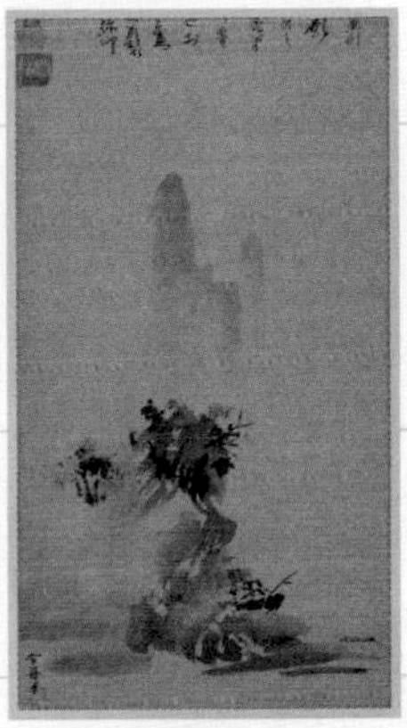

1 Dry cascade and pools, Saihoji temple, 14th century

2

1500

| Reunification of Japan begins, ca. 1560s

| Tea ceremony emerges as exercise of cultivation and refinement, 16th and 17th centuries

1573

1615

3

| Tokugawa Ieyasu consolidation of power, 1615

| Closing of Japan to foreigners, 1639

| Rapid developments in printing industry, late 17th century

2 Toyo Sesshu, splashed-ink landscape, 1495

1700

| Arrival of American warships to force open Japan, 1853

| Enthronement of Emperor Mutsuhito (Meiji), 1867

1868

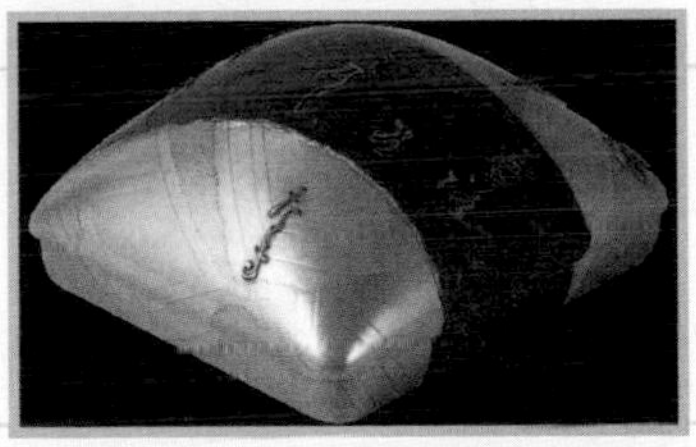

3 Honami Koetsu, *Boat Bridge*, early 17th century

| Beginning of cabinet system, 1885

| Sino-Japanese War, 1894–1895

| Russo-Japanese War, 1904–1905

1926

| Japan invades China, 1937

| World War II, 1939–1945

| Surrender of Japan to United States, 1945

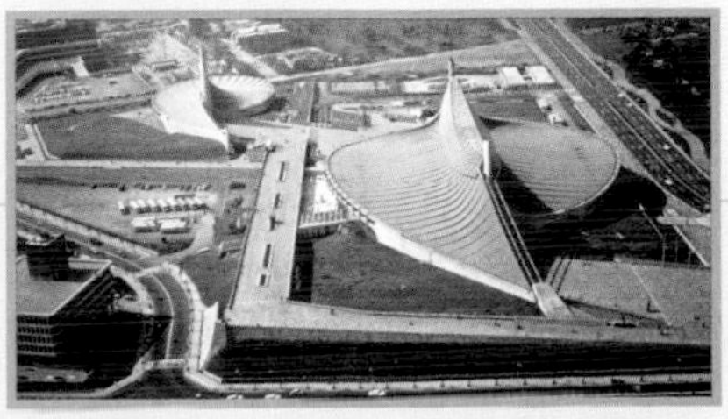

4 Tange Kenzo, national indoor Olympic stadiums, 1961–1964

4 | American occupation ends, 1952

1964

| Tokyo hosts Olympic Games, 1964

MUROMACHI

MOMOYAMA

EDO

MEIJI AND TAISHO

SHOWA AND HEISEI

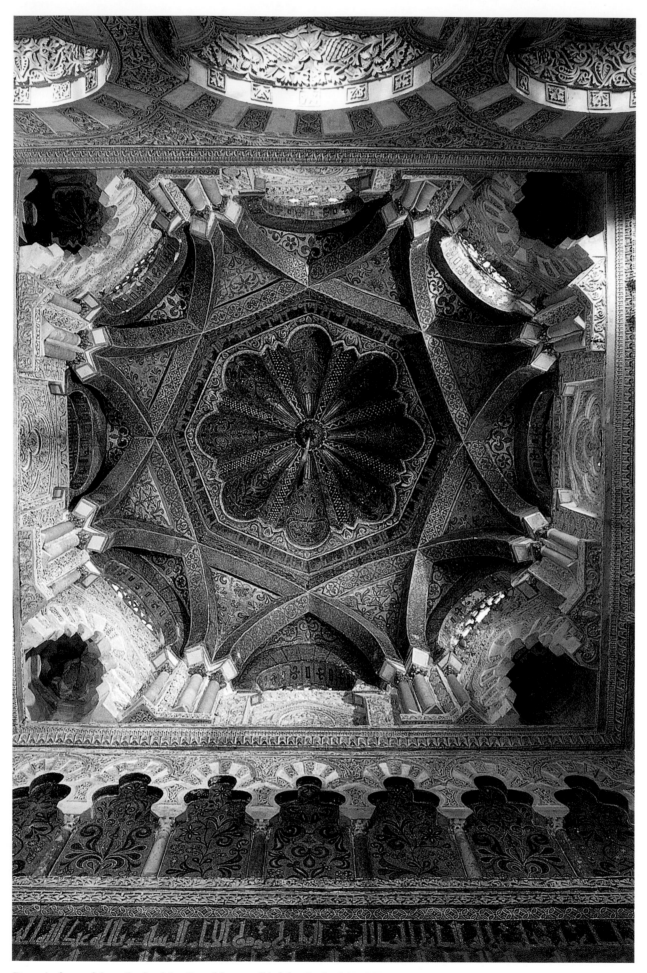

Dome in front of the mihrab of the Great Mosque, Córdoba, Spain, 961–965.

7

IN PRAISE OF ALLAH

THE ART OF THE ISLAMIC WORLD

The religion of *Islam* (an Arabic word meaning "submission to God") arose among the peoples of the Arabian peninsula early in the seventh century (see "Muhammad and Islam," page 117). The Arabs were nomadic herders and caravan merchants traversing, from ancient times, the wastes and oases of the vast Arabian desert and settling and controlling its coasts. When Islam arose, the Arabs were peripheral to the Byzantine and Persian empires. Yet within little more than a century, the Mediterranean, once ringed and ruled by Byzantium, had become an Islamic lake, and the armies of Islam had subdued the Middle East, long the seat of Persian dominance and influence.

The swiftness of the Islamic advance is among the wonders of world history. By 640, Muslims ruled Syria, Palestine, and Iraq in the name of Allah. In 642, the Byzantine army abandoned Alexandria, marking the Muslim conquest of Lower (northern) Egypt. In 651, the successors of Muhammad brought more than 400 years of Sasanian rule in Iran to an end. By 710, all of North Africa was under Muslim control. A victory at Jerez de la Frontera in southern Spain in 711 seemed to open all of western Europe to the Muslims. By 732, they had advanced north to Poitiers in France. There, however, an army of Franks under Charles Martel, the grandfather of Charlemagne, opposed them successfully. Although Islamic forces continued to conduct raids in France, they could not extend their control beyond the Pyrenees along the French-Spanish border. But in Spain, the Muslim rulers of Córdoba flourished until 1031, and not until 1492 did Islamic influence and power in the Iberian Peninsula end. That year the caliphs of Granada fell to King Ferdinand and Queen Isabella, the sponsors of Columbus's voyage to the New World. In the East, the Muslims reached the Indus River by 751, and only in Anatolia could stubborn Byzantine resistance slow their advance. Relentless Muslim pressure against the shrinking Byzantine Empire eventually caused its collapse in 1453, when the Ottoman Turks entered Constantinople.

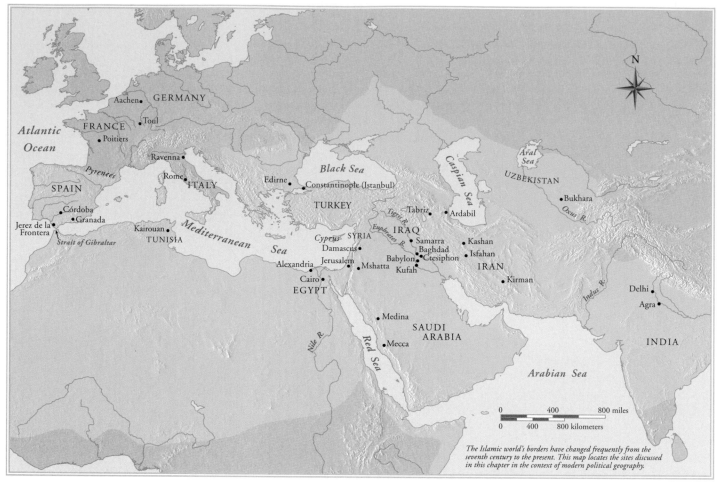

MAP 7-1 The Islamic world.

THE IMPACT OF ISLAM The irresistible and far-ranging sweep of Islam from Arabia to India to North Africa and Spain (MAP **7-1**) was not due to military might alone. That the initial victories had effects that endured for centuries can be explained only by the nature of Islamic faith and its appeal to millions of converts. Islam remains today one of the world's great religions, with adherents on all continents. And the sophistication of its culture has had a profound impact around the globe. Christian scholars in the West during the 12th and 13th centuries eagerly studied Arabic translations of Aristotle and other Greek writers of antiquity. Arabic love lyrics and poetic descriptions of nature inspired the early French troubadours. Arab scholars laid the foundations of arithmetic and algebra, and their contributions to astronomy, medicine, and the natural sciences have made a lasting impression in the Western world.

The triumph of Islam also brought a new and compelling tradition to the history of world art and architecture. Like Islam itself, Islamic art spread quickly both eastward and westward from the land once inhabited by the peoples of the ancient Near East and their Sasanian successors. In the Middle East and North Africa, Islamic art largely replaced Mediterranean Late Antique art. And from a foothold in the Iberian peninsula, Islamic art made an impact on Western medieval art, although Islamic art stands in sharp contrast both to the figural art of Europe and the Mediterranean and to the Western architectural vocabulary. Islamic artists and architects also brought their distinctive style to South Asia, where a Muslim sultanate was established at Delhi in India in the early 13th century (see Chapter 2). In fact, perhaps the most famous building in Asia, the Taj Mahal (see FIG. 2-5) at Agra, is an Islamic mausoleum.

EARLY ISLAMIC ART

During the early centuries of Islamic history, the Muslim world's political and cultural center was the Fertile Crescent of ancient Mesopotamia. This crescent-shaped area of cultivable land was strewn with impressive ruins of earlier cultures, from the Sumerians to the Sasanians. The caliphs of Damascus (capital of modern Syria) and Baghdad (capital of Iraq) appointed provincial governors to rule the vast territories they controlled. These governors eventually gained relative independence by setting up dynasties in various territories and provinces: the Umayyads in Syria (661–749) and in Spain (756–1031), the Abbasids in Iraq (750–1258, largely nominal after 945), the Fatimids in Egypt (909–1171), and so on. Like other potentates before and after, the Islamic rulers were builders on a grand scale.

Architecture

TRIUMPH IN JERUSALEM The first great achievement of Islamic architecture is the Dome of the Rock (FIG. **7-1**) in Jerusalem. The Muslims had taken the city from the Byzantines in 638, and the Umayyad caliph Abd al-Malik (r. 685–705) erected the monumental sanctuary between 687 and 692 as an architectural tribute to the triumph of Islam. The Dome of the Rock marked the coming of the new religion to the city that had been, and still is, sacred to both Jews and Christians. The structure rises from a huge platform known as the Noble Enclosure. Even today it dominates the skyline of the holy city. The sanctuary was erected

Muhammad and Islam

Muhammad, founder of Islam and revered as its Final Prophet, was a native of Mecca on the west coast of Arabia. Born around 570 into a family of merchants in the great Arabian caravan trade, Muhammad was inspired to prophecy. Critical of the polytheistic religion of his fellow Arabs, he preached a religion of the one and only God (*Allah* in Arabic), whose revelations Muhammad received beginning in 610 and for the rest of his life. Opposition to Muhammad's message among the Arabs was strong enough to prompt the Prophet and his growing number of followers to flee from Mecca to a desert oasis eventually called Medina ("City of the Prophet"). Islam dates its beginnings from this flight in 622, known as the *Hijra* (emigration).[1] Barely eight years later, in 630, Muhammad returned to Mecca with 10,000 soldiers. He took control of the city, converted the population to Islam, and destroyed all the idols. But he preserved as the Islamic world's symbolic center the small cubical building that had housed the idols, the *Kaaba* (from the Arabic for "cube"). The Arabs associated the Kaaba with the era of Abraham and Ishmael, the common ancestors of Jews and Arabs. Muhammad died in Medina in 632.

The essential meaning of Islam is acceptance of and submission to Allah's will. Believers in Islam are called *Muslims* ("those who submit"). Islam requires living according to the rules laid down in the collected revelations communicated through Muhammad during his lifetime. These are recorded in the *Koran,* Islam's sacred book, codified by the Muslim ruler Uthman (r. 644–656). The word "Koran" means "recitations"—a reference to the archangel Gabriel's instructions to Muhammad in 610 to "recite in the name of Allah." The Koran is composed of 114 *surahs* (chapters) divided into verses.

The profession of faith in the one God, Allah, is the first of five obligations binding all Muslims. In addition, the faithful must worship five times daily, facing in Mecca's direction; give alms to the poor; fast during the month of Ramadan; and once in a lifetime—if possible—make a pilgrimage to Mecca. Muslims are guided not only by the revelations in the Koran but also by Muhammad's life. The Prophet's exemplary ways and customs, collected in the *Sunnah,* are supplemental to the Koran, offering guidance to the faithful on ethical problems of everyday life. The reward for the Muslim faithful is Paradise.

Islam has much in common with Judaism and Christianity. Its adherents think of it as a continuation, completion, and in some sense a reformation of those other great monotheisms. Islam incorporates many of the Old Testament teachings, with their sober ethical standards and hatred of idol worship, and those of the New Testament Gospels. Adam, Abraham, Moses, and Jesus are acknowledged as the prophetic predecessors of Muhammad, the final and greatest of the prophets. Muhammad did not claim to be divine, as did Jesus, and he did not perform miracles. Rather, he was God's messenger, the purifier and perfecter of the common faith of Jews, Christians, and Muslims in one God. Islam also differs from Judaism and Christianity in its simpler organization. Muslims worship God directly, without a hierarchy of rabbis, priests, or saints acting as intermediaries.

In Islam, as Muhammad defined it, religious and secular authority were united even more completely than in Byzantium. Muhammad established a new social order, replacing the Arabs' old decentralized tribal one. In this he was influenced, no doubt, by the examples of the emperors and kings reigning in the lands his people would occupy. He took complete charge of his community's temporal, as well as spiritual, affairs. After Muhammad's death, the *caliphs* (from the Arabic for "successor") continued this practice of uniting religious and political leadership in one ruler.

[1] Muslims date events beginning with the Hijra in the same way Christians reckon events from Christ's birth and the Romans before them began their calendar with Rome's founding by Romulus in 753 BCE. The Muslim year is, however, a 354-day year of 12 lunar months, and dates cannot be converted by simply adding 622 to Christian-era dates.

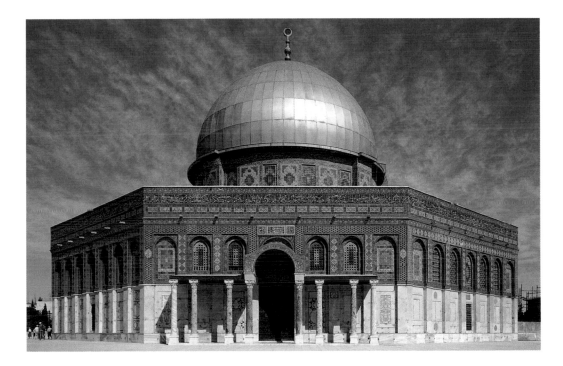

7-1 Dome of the Rock, Jerusalem, 687–692.

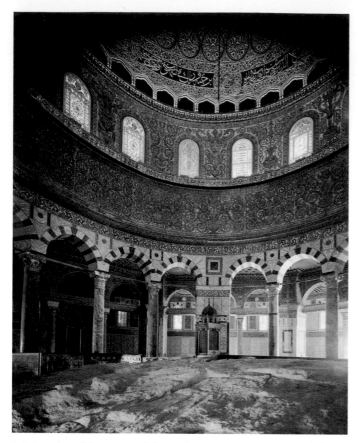

7-2 Interior of the Dome of the Rock, Jerusalem, 687–692.

design, construction, and ornamentation principles that had long been applied in, and were still current in, Byzantium and the Middle East. The Dome of the Rock is a domed octagon resembling San Vitale, a Byzantine church in Ravenna, Italy, in its basic design. In all likelihood, a neighboring Christian monument, Constantine the Great's Rotunda of the Holy Sepulchre, inspired the Dome of the Rock's designers. That fourth-century rotunda bore a family resemblance to the roughly contemporary Constantinian mausoleum (later rededicated as Santa Costanza) in Rome. The Dome of the Rock is a member of the same extended family. Its double-shelled wooden dome, however, some 60 feet across and 75 feet high, so dominates the elevation as to reduce the octagon to function merely as its base. This soaring, majestic unit creates a decidedly more commanding effect than that of Late Roman and Byzantine domical structures, such as the Pantheon in Rome and Hagia Sophia in Constantinople (Istanbul). The silhouettes of those domes are comparatively insignificant when seen from the outside.

The building's exterior has been much restored. Tiling from the 16th century and later has replaced the original *mosaic*. Yet the vivid, colorful patterning that wraps the walls like a textile is typical of Islamic ornamentation. It contrasts markedly with Byzantine brickwork and Greco-Roman sculptured profiling and carved decoration. The interior's rich mosaic ornament (FIG. 7-2) has been preserved. From it one can imagine how the exterior walls originally appeared. Islamic practice does not significantly distinguish interior and exterior decor. The splendor of infinitely various surfaces is given to public gaze both within and outside buildings.

NEW CAPITAL, NEW MOSQUE The Umayyads transferred their capital from Mecca to Damascus in 661. There, Abd al-Malik's son, the caliph al-Walid (r. 705–715), purchased a Byzantine church (formerly a Roman temple) and built an imposing new mosque for the expanding Muslim population (see "The Mosque," page 119). The Umayyads demolished the church, but they used the Roman precinct walls as a foundation for their own construction. Like the Dome of the Rock, the Great Mosque of Damascus (FIG. 7-3) owes much to the architecture of the Greco-

on the traditional site of Adam's burial, of Abraham's preparation for Isaac's sacrifice, and of the Temple of Solomon the Romans destroyed in 70. It houses the rock (FIG. 7-2) from which Muslims later came to believe Muhammad ascended to Heaven.

As Islam took much of its teaching from Judaism and Christianity, so its architects and artists borrowed and transformed

7-3 Aerial view of the Great Mosque, Damascus, Syria, 706–715.

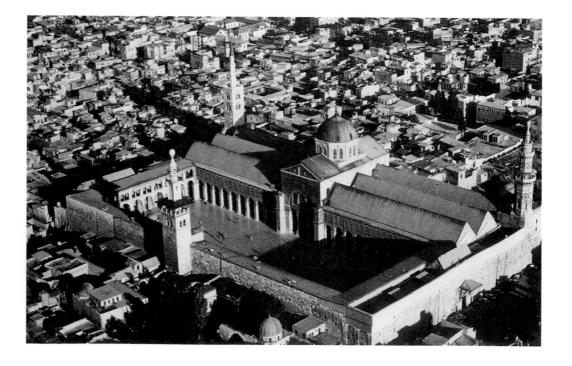

The Mosque

Islamic religious architecture is closely related to Muslim prayer, an obligation laid down in the Koran for all Muslims. In Islam, worshiping can be a private act. It requires neither prescribed ceremony nor a special locale. Only the *qibla*—the direction (toward Mecca) Muslims face while praying—is important. But worship also became a communal act when the first Muslim community established a simple ritual for it. To celebrate the Muslim sabbath, which occurs on Friday, the community convened each Friday at noon, probably in the Prophet's house in Medina. The main feature of Muhammad's house was a large square court with rows of palm trunks supporting thatched roofs along the north and south sides. The southern side was wider and had a double row of trunks. It faced Mecca. During these communal gatherings, the *imam,* or leader of collective worship, stood on a stepped pulpit, or *minbar,* set up in front of the southern (qibla) wall.

These features became standard in the Islamic house of worship, the *mosque* (from Arabic *masjid,* a place of prostration), where the faithful gathered for the five daily prayers. The *congregational mosque* (also called the *Friday mosque* or *great mosque*), was ideally large enough to accommodate a community's entire population for the Friday noonday prayer. A very important feature both of ordinary mosques and of congregational mosques is the *mihrab,* a semicircular niche usually set into the qibla wall (FIG. 7-8). Often a dome over the bay in front of it marked its position (FIGS. 7-3, 7-8, and 7-13). The niche was a familiar Greco-Roman architectural feature, generally enclosing a statue. But for Islamic architecture, its origin, purpose, and meaning are still debated. Some scholars believe the mihrab originally may have honored the place where the Prophet stood in his house at Medina

when he led communal worship. It thus would have been a revered religious memorial.

In some mosques, a *maqsura* precedes the mihrab. The maqsura is the area generally reserved for the ruler or his representative and can be quite elaborate in form (FIG. 7-12). Many mosques also have one or more *minarets* (FIGS. 7-3, 7-9, and 7-20), towers from which the faithful are called to worship. When buildings of other faiths were converted into mosques, the change was clearly signaled on the exterior by the erection of minarets. Early mosques are generally characterized by *hypostyle halls,* communal worship halls with roofs held up by a multitude of columns (FIGS. 7-8 and 7-11). Later variations of the early mosque formulation include mosques with four *iwans* (vaulted rectangular recesses), one on each side of the courtyard (FIG. 7-23), and *central-plan* mosques with a single large dome-covered interior space (FIGS. 7-20 to 7-22).

The mosque's origin is still in dispute, although one prototype may well have been the Prophet's house in Medina. Once the Muslims had firmly established themselves in their acquired territories, they began to build on a large scale, impelled, perhaps, by a desire to create such visible evidence of their power as would surpass in size and splendor that of their non-Islamic predecessors. Today, mosques continue to be erected throughout the world. Despite many variations in design and detail and the employment of modern building techniques and materials unknown in Muhammad's day, the mosque's essential features are unchanged. All mosques, wherever they are built and whatever their plan, are oriented toward Mecca, and the faithful worship facing the qibla wall.

Roman and Early Christian East. It is constructed of masonry blocks, columns, and capitals salvaged from the Roman and Early Christian structures on the land al-Walid acquired for his mosque. The courtyard is bounded by pier *arcades* reminiscent of Roman aqueducts. The minarets, two at the southern corners and one at the northern side of the enclosure—the earliest in the Islamic world—are modifications of the preexisting Roman square towers. The grand prayer hall, taller than the rest of the complex, is on the south side of the courtyard (facing Mecca). Its main entrance is distinguished by a facade with a triangular *pediment* and arches, recalling classical and Byzantine models, respectively. The facade faces into the courtyard, like a Roman forum temple, a plan maintained throughout the long history of mosque architecture. The Damascus mosque synthesizes elements received from other cultures into a novel architectural unity, which includes the distinctive Islamic elements of mihrab, mihrab dome, minbar, and minaret.

An extensive cycle of mosaics once covered the walls of the Great Mosque. In one of the surviving sections (FIG. **7-4**), a conch shell niche "supports" an arcaded pavilion with a flowering rooftop flanked by structures shown in classical perspective. Like the architectural design, the mosaics owe much to Roman, Early Christian, and Byzantine art. Indeed, some evidence indicates that the Great Mosque mosaics were the work of Byzantine mosaicists. Characteristically, temples, clusters of houses, trees,

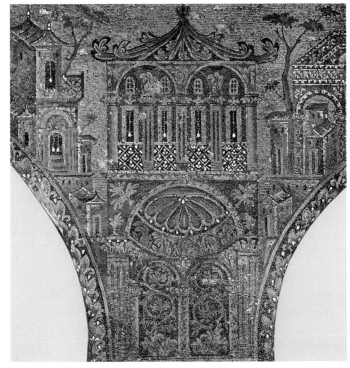

7-4 Detail of a mosaic in the courtyard arcade of the Great Mosque, Damascus, Syria, 706–715.

and rivers compose the pictorial fields, bounded by stylized vegetal design, familiar in Roman, Early Christian, and Byzantine ornament. No zoomorphic forms, human or animal, appear either in the pictorial or ornamental spaces. This is true of all the mosaics in the Great Mosque as well as the mosaics in the earlier Dome of the Rock (FIG. 7-2). Islamic tradition shuns the representation of fauna of any kind in sacred places. The world shown in the Damascus mosaics, suspended miragelike in a featureless field of gold, was explained in accompanying (but now lost) inscriptions as an image of Paradise. Many passages from the Koran describe the gorgeous places of Paradise awaiting the faithful—gardens, groves of trees, flowing streams, and "lofty chambers." Indeed, the abundant luxurious images and ornament, floating free of all human reference, create a vision of Paradise appealing to the spiritually oriented imagination, whatever its religion.

AN UMAYYAD DESERT PALACE The Umayyad rulers of Damascus constructed numerous palatial residences throughout the vast territories they governed. The urban palaces are lost, but some rural palaces survive. The latter were not merely idyllic residences removed from the congestion, noise, and disease of the cities. They seem to have served as nuclei for the agricultural development of acquired territories and possibly as hunting lodges. In addition, the Islamic palaces were symbols of authority over new lands, as well as expressions of their owners' wealth.

One of the most impressive Umayyad palaces, despite the fact that it was never completed, is at Mshatta in the Jordanian desert. Its plan (FIG. **7-5**) resembles that of a Roman fortified camp. The high walls of the Mshatta palace incorporate 25 towers but lack parapet walkways for patrolling guards. The walls, nonetheless, offered safety from marauding nomadic tribes and provided privacy for the caliph and his entourage. Visitors entered the palace through a large portal on the south side. To the right was a mosque (the plan shows the mihrab niche in the qibla wall), in which the rulers and their guests could fulfill their obligation to pray five times a day. The mosque was separated from the palace's residential wing and official audience hall by a small ceremonial area and an immense open courtyard. Most Umayyad palaces also were provided with fairly elaborate bathing facilities that displayed technical features, such as heating systems, adopted from Roman baths. Just as under the Roman Empire, these baths probably served more than merely hygienic purposes. Indeed, in several Umayyad palaces, excavators have uncovered in the baths paintings and sculptures of hunting and other secular themes, including depictions of dancing women—themes traditionally associated with royalty in the Near East. Large halls frequently attached to many of these baths seem to have been used as places of entertainment, as was the case in Roman times. Thus, the bath-spa-social center, a characteristic amenity of Roman urban culture that died out in the Christian world, survived in Islamic culture.

The architectural ornamentation of many of the early Islamic palaces was confined to simply molded stucco and decorative brickwork, but at Mshatta the facade is enlivened by a richly carved stone *frieze* (FIG. **7-6**). The long band is more than 16 feet high and consists of a series of triangles framed by elaborately carved *moldings*. Each triangle contains a large rosette that

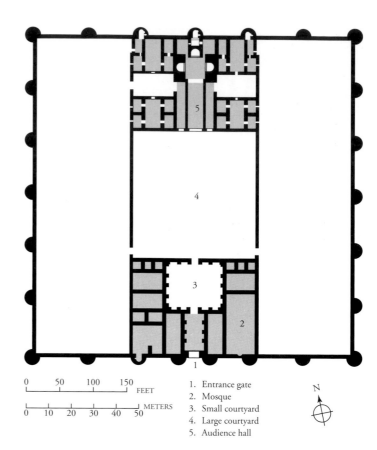

7-5 Plan of the Umayyad palace, Mshatta, Jordan, ca. 740–750 (after Alberto Berengo Gardin).

0   50   100   150 FEET
0 10 20 30 40 50 METERS

1. Entrance gate
2. Mosque
3. Small courtyard
4. Large courtyard
5. Audience hall

N

projects from a field densely covered with curvilinear, vegetal designs. No two triangles were treated the same way, and animal figures appear in some of them. Similar compositions of birds, felines, and vegetal scrolls can be found in Roman, Byzantine, and Sasanian art. The Mshatta frieze, however, has no animal figures to the right of the entrance portal—that is, on the part of the facade corresponding to the mosque's qibla wall.

THE ABBASID CITY OF PEACE In 750, after years of civil war, the Abbasids, who claimed descent from Abbas, an uncle of Muhammad, overthrew the Umayyad caliphs. The new rulers moved the capital from Damascus to a site in Iraq near the old Sasanian capital of Ctesiphon. There the caliph al-Mansur (r. 754–775) established a new capital, Baghdad, which he called Madina al-salam, the City of Peace. The city was laid out in 762 at a time astrologers determined as favorable. It was round in plan, about a mile and a half in diameter. The shape signified that the new capital was the center of the universe. At the city's center was the caliph's palace, oriented to the four compass points.

For almost 300 years Baghdad was the hub of Arab power and of a brilliant Islamic culture. The Abbasid caliphs were renowned throughout the world and even established diplomatic relations with the medieval Roman emperor Charlemagne at Aachen in Germany. The Abbasids lavished their wealth on art, literature, and science and were responsible for

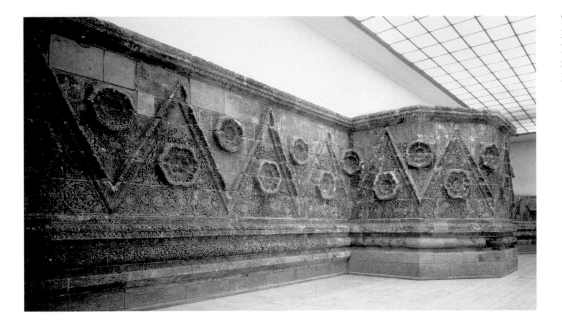

7-6 Frieze of the Umayyad palace, Mshatta, Jordan, ca. 740–750. Limestone, 16' 7" high. Museum für Islamische Kunst, Staatliche Museen, Berlin.

the translation of numerous Greek texts that otherwise would have been lost. Many of these works were introduced to the medieval West through their Arabic versions.

KAIROUAN'S HYPOSTYLE MOSQUE Of all the variations in mosque plans, the hypostyle mosque most closely reflects the mosque's supposed origin, Muhammad's house in Medina (see "The Mosque," page 119). One of the finest hypostyle mosques, still in use today, is the mid-eighth-century Great Mosque at Kairouan (FIGS. 7-7 and 7-8) in Abbasid Tunisia. It still houses its carved wooden minbar of 862, the oldest known. The precinct takes the form of a slightly askew parallelogram of huge scale, some 450 × 260 feet. Built of stone, its walls have sturdy

buttresses, square in profile. A series of lateral entrances on the east and west lead to an arcaded forecourt (no. 7 on the plan), oriented north-south on axis with the mosque's impressive minaret (no. 8) and the two domes (nos. 3 and 6) of the hypostyle prayer hall (no. 4). The first dome (no. 6) is over the entrance bay, the second (no. 3) over the bay that fronts the mihrab (no. 2) set into the qibla wall (no. 1). A raised *nave* connects the domed spaces and prolongs the north-south axis of the minaret and courtyard. Eight columned *aisles* flank the nave on either side, providing space for a large congregation.

SAMARRA'S SPIRAL MINARET The three-story minaret of the Kairouan mosque is square in plan and believed to be a near

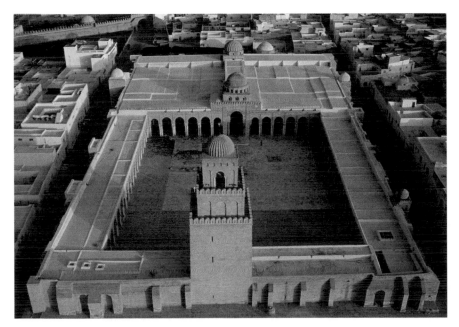

7-7 Aerial view of the Great Mosque, Kairouan, Tunisia, ca. 836–875.

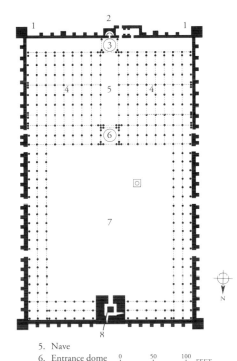

1. Qibla wall   5. Nave
2. Mihrab   6. Entrance dome
3. Mihrab dome   7. Forecourt
4. Hypostyle prayer hall   8. Minaret

7-8 Plan of the Great Mosque, Kairouan, Tunisia, ca. 836–875.

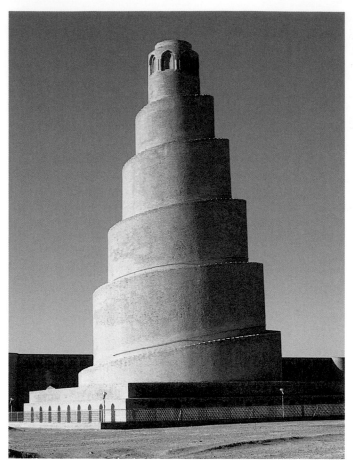

7-9 *Malwiya* minaret of the Great Mosque, Samarra, Iraq, 848–852.

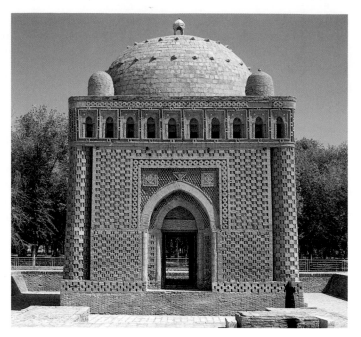

7-10 Mausoleum of the Samanids, Bukhara, Uzbekistan, early 10th century.

copy of a Roman lighthouse, but minarets can take a variety of forms. Perhaps the most striking and novel is that of the immense (more than 45,000 square yards) Great Mosque at Samarra, Iraq, the largest mosque in the world. The Abbasid caliph al-Mutawakkil (r. 847–861) erected it between 848 and 852. Known as the *Malwiya* ("snail shell" in Arabic) minaret (FIG. **7-9**) and more than 165 feet tall (note how it dwarfs the modern fence), it now stands alone, but originally a bridge linked it to the mosque. The brick tower is distinguished by its stepped spiral ramp, which increases in slope from bottom to top. Too tall to have been used to call Muslims to prayer, the *Malwiya* minaret, visible from a considerable distance in the flat plain around Samarra, was probably intended to announce the presence of Islam in the Tigris Valley.

MEMORIALIZING THE DEAD The eastern realms of the Abbasid empire were overseen by dynasties of governors who exercised considerable independence while recognizing the ultimate authority of the Baghdad caliphs. One of these dynasties, the Samanids (r. 819–1005), presided over the eastern frontier beyond the Oxus River (Transoxiana) on the border with India. In the early 10th century, they erected an impressive domed brick mausoleum (FIG. **7-10**) at Bukhara in modern Uzbekistan. Monumental tombs were virtually unknown in the early Islamic period. Muhammad had been opposed to elaborate burials and instructed his followers to bury him in a simple unmarked grave. In time, however, the Prophet's resting place in Medina was enclosed by a wooden screen and covered by a dome. By the ninth century, Abbasid caliphs were laid to rest in dynastic mausoleums.

The Samanid mausoleum at Bukhara is one of the earliest preserved tombs in the Islamic world. It is constructed of baked bricks and takes the form of a cube with slightly sloping sides capped by a dome. With exceptional skill, the builders painstakingly shaped the bricks to create a vivid and varied surface pattern. Some of the bricks form *engaged* (attached) columns at the corners. A brick *blind arcade* (a series of arches in relief, with blocked openings) runs around all four sides. Inside, the walls are as elaborate as the exterior. The brick dome rests on arcuated brick *squinches* framed by engaged *colonnettes*. The dome-on-cube form had a long and distinguished future in Islamic funerary architecture.

UMAYYAD CÓRDOBA At the opposite end of the Muslim world, Abd-al-Rahman I, the only Umayyad notable to escape the Abbasid massacre of his clan in Syria, fled to Spain in 750. There, the Arabs had overthrown the Christian kingdom of the Visigoths in 711. The Arab military governors of the peninsula accepted the fugitive as their overlord, and he founded the Spanish Umayyad dynasty, which lasted for almost three centuries. The capital of the Spanish Umayyads was Córdoba, which became the center of a brilliant culture rivaling that of the Abbasids at Baghdad and exerting major influence on the civilization of the Christian West.

The jewel of the capital at Córdoba was its Great Mosque, begun in 784 and enlarged several times during the 9th and 10th centuries. It eventually became one of the largest mosques in the Islamic West. The additions followed the original style and arrangement of columns and arches, and the builders maintained a striking stylistic unity for the entire building. The hypostyle prayer hall (FIG. **7-11**) has 36 piers and 514 columns topped by a unique system of double-tiered arches that carried a wooden roof (now replaced by vaults). The two-story system was the builders' response to the need to raise the roof to an acceptable height using short columns that had been employed earlier in other structures. The lower arches are horseshoe-shaped, a form perhaps adapted from earlier Near Eastern architecture or of medieval Spanish origin. In the West, the horseshoe arch quickly became closely associated with Muslim architecture. Visually, these arches seem to

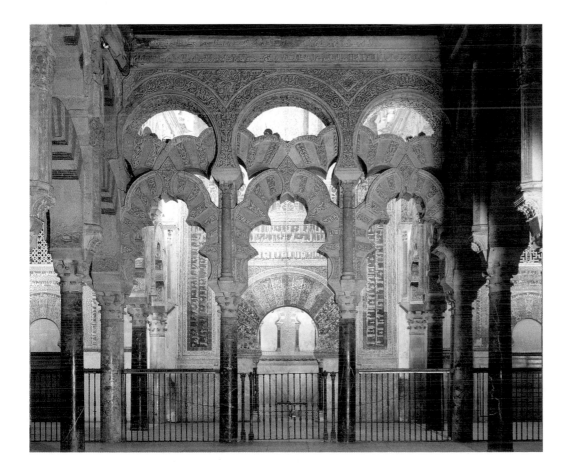

billow out like sails blown by the wind, and they contribute greatly to the light and airy effect of the Córdoba mosque's interior.

The caliph al-Hakam II (r. 961–976) undertook major renovations to the mosque. His builders expanded the prayer hall and added a series of domes. They also erected the elaborate maqsura (FIG. **7-12**), the area reserved for the caliph and connected to his palace by a corridor in the qibla wall. The Córdoba maqsura is a prime example of Islamic experimentation with highly decorative multilobed arches. The builders created rich and varied abstract patterns and further enhanced the magnificent effect of the complex arches by sheathing the walls with marbles and mosaics. The mosaicists and even the tesserae were brought to Spain from

7-12 Maqsura of the Great Mosque, Córdoba, Spain, 961–965.

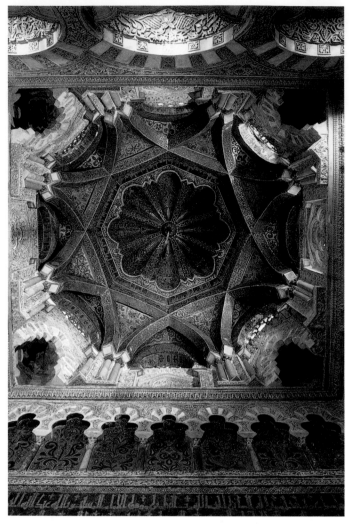

7-13 Dome in front of the mihrab of the Great Mosque, Córdoba, Spain, 961–965. 💿

Constantinople by al-Hakam II, who wished to emulate the great mosaic-clad monuments his Umayyad predecessors had erected in Jerusalem (FIG. 7-2) and Damascus (FIG. 7-4).

The same desire for decorative effect also inspired the design of the dome (FIG. 7-13) that covers the area in front of the mihrab, one of the four domes built during the 10th century to emphasize the axis leading to the mihrab. The dome rests on an octagonal base of arcuated squinches and is crisscrossed by *ribs* that form an intricate pattern centered on two squares set at 45-degree angles to each other. The mosaics are the work of the same Byzantine artists responsible for the maqsura's decoration.

Luxury Arts

ARABESQUES In the mosaics at Córdoba, as elsewhere in the Islamic world, most of the design elements are based on plant motifs, which are sometimes intermingled with abstract geometric shapes and, in secular settings, with animal figures. Often the natural forms are so stylized that they are lost in the purely decorative tracery of the tendrils, leaves, and stalks. These *arabesques*—so called because they are one of the most distinctive features of Islamic ("Arab") art—form abstract patterns of extraordinary beauty and complexity, usually covering an entire surface, whether that of a small utensil or the wall of a building. This ornamental system offers a potential for unlimited growth, as it

permits extension of the designs in any desired direction. Most characteristic, perhaps, is the arabesque's independence of its carrier. Neither its size (within limits) nor its forms are dictated by anything but the design itself.

ISLAMIC SILK Both arabesques and figural patterns appear frequently on movable furnishings, such as rugs and hangings. Wood is scarce in most of the Islamic world, and the kind of furniture used in the West—beds, tables, and chairs—is rarely found in Muslim structures. Architectural spaces, therefore, are not defined by the type of furniture placed in them. A room's function (eating or sleeping, for example) can change simply by rearranging the carpets and cushions.

Silk textiles and wool carpets are among the glories of Islamic art. Unfortunately, because of their fragile nature and the heavy wear carpets endure, early Islamic textiles are rare today and often fragmentary. Silk thread was also very expensive. Silk is produced by silkworms, which can flourish only in certain temperate regions. Silk textiles were manufactured first in China in the third millennium BCE. They were shipped over what came to be called the Silk Road through Asia to the Middle East and Europe (see "Silk and the Silk Road," Chapter 3, page 49).

One of the earliest Islamic silks (FIG. 7-14) is found today in Nancy, France. Unfortunately, it is fragmentary, and its colors, once rich blues, greens, and oranges, faded long ago. The silk survives because it was associated with the relics of Saint Amon housed in Toul Cathedral. The precious fabric may have been used to wrap the treasures when they were transported to France in 820. It probably dates to the eighth century and is said to come from Zandana near Bukhara. The design consists of repeated medallions with confronting lions flanking a palm tree. Other animals scamper across the silk between the *roundels*. Such zoomorphic

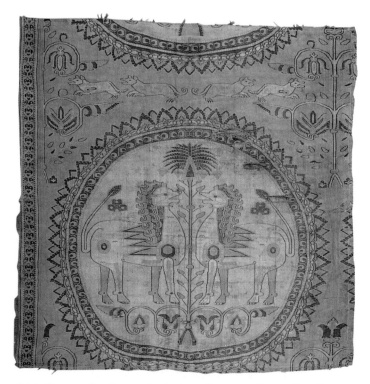

7-14 Confronting lions and palm tree, fragment of a textile said to be from Zandana, near Bukhara, Uzbekistan, eighth century. Silk compound twill, 2′ 11″ × 2′ 9½″. Musée Historique de Lorraine, Nancy. 💿

motifs are foreign to the decorative vocabulary of mosque architecture, but they could be found in Muslim households—even in Muhammad's in Medina. The Prophet, however, was said to have objected to curtains decorated with figures and permitted only cushions adorned with animals or birds.

A SIGNED ZOOMORPHIC EWER The furnishings of Islamic palaces and mosques reflected a love of sumptuous materials and rich decorative patterns. Metal, wood, glass, and ivory were artfully worked into a great variety of objects for the mosque or home. Colored glass was used with striking effect in mosque lamps. Ornate ceramics of high quality were produced in large numbers. Basins, ewers, jewel cases, writing boxes, and other decorative items were made of bronze or brass, engraved, and inlaid with silver.

One of the most striking examples of the metalworker's art is the cast brass ewer in the form of a bird (FIG. **7-15**) signed by SULAYMAN and dated 796. (The place of origin also was inscribed but is illegible today.) Some 15 inches tall, the ewer is nothing less than a freestanding statuette, although the holes between the eyes and beak function as a spout and betray its utilitarian purpose. The decoration on the body, which bears traces of silver and copper inlay, takes a variety of forms. In places, the incised lines seem

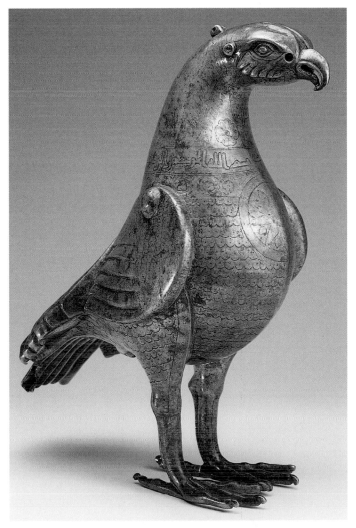

7-15 SULAYMAN, Ewer in the form of a bird, 796. Brass with silver and copper inlay, 1′ 3″ high. Hermitage, Saint Petersburg.

to suggest natural feathers, but the rosettes on the neck, the large medallions on the breast, and the inscribed collar have no basis in anatomy. Similar motifs can be found in Islamic textiles, pottery, and architectural tiles. The ready adaptability of motifs to various scales and to various techniques again illustrates both the flexibility of Islamic design and its relative independence from its carrier.

THE ART OF THE KORAN In the Islamic world, the art of calligraphy, ornamental writing, was more revered even than the art of textiles. The faithful wanted to reproduce the Koran's sacred words in as beautiful a script as human hands could contrive. And these words were displayed not only on the fragile pages of books but also on the walls of buildings. Quotations from the Koran appear, for example, in a mosaic band above the outer ring of columns inside the Dome of the Rock (FIG. 7-2). The practice of calligraphy was itself a holy task and required long and arduous training. The scribe had to possess exceptional spiritual refinement. An ancient Arabic proverb proclaims, "Purity of writing is purity of soul." Only in China does calligraphy hold so supreme a position among the arts (see "Calligraphy and Inscriptions on Chinese Paintings," Chapter 4, page 68).

Arabic script predates Islam. It is written from right to left with certain characters connected by a baseline. Although the chief Islamic book, the sacred Koran, was codified in the midseventh century, the earliest preserved Korans are datable to the ninth century. Koran pages were either bound into books or stored as loose sheets in boxes. Most of the early examples are written in the script form called *Kufic*, after the city of Kufah, one of the renowned centers of Arabic calligraphy. Kufic script is quite angular, with the uprights forming almost right angles with the baseline. As with Hebrew and other Semitic languages, the usual practice was to write in consonants only. But to facilitate recitation of the Koran, scribes often indicated vowels by red or yellow symbols above or below the line.

All of these features can be seen on a 9th- or early 10th-century page (FIG. **7-16**) in Dublin that carries the heading and opening lines of surah 18 of the Koran. Five text lines in black ink with red vowels appear below a decorative band incorporating the chapter title in gold and ending in a palm-tree *finial* (a crowning ornament). This approach to page design has parallels at the extreme northwestern corner of the then-known world—in the early medieval manuscripts of the British Isles, where text and ornament are similarly united. But the stylized human and animal forms that populate those Christian books never appear in Korans.

LATER ISLAMIC ART

Architecture

THE NASRIDS' RED FORTRESS In the early years of the 11th century, the Umayyad caliphs' power in Spain unraveled, and their palaces fell prey to Berber soldiers from North Africa. The Berbers ruled southern Spain for several generations but could not resist the pressure of Christian forces from the north. Córdoba fell to the Christians in 1236. From then until the final Christian triumph in 1492, the Nasrids, an Arab dynasty that had established its capital at Granada in 1230, ruled the remaining Muslim territories in Spain.

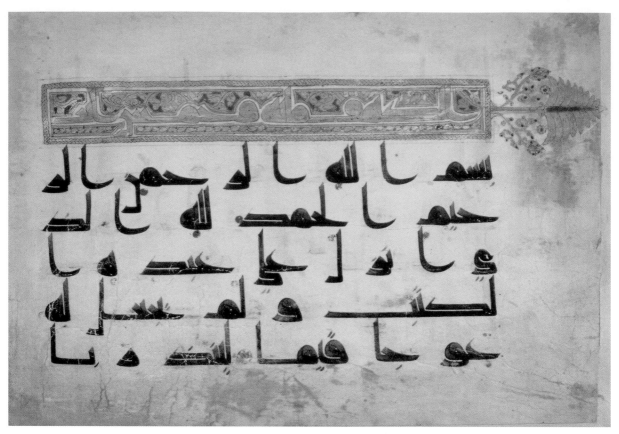

7-16 Koran page with beginning of surah 18, *al-Kahf (The Cave)*, 9th or early 10th century. Ink and gold on vellum, $7\frac{1}{4}'' \times 10\frac{1}{4}''$. Chester Beatty Library and Oriental Art Gallery, Dublin.

On a rocky spur at Granada, the Nasrids constructed a huge palace-fortress called the Alhambra ("the Red" in Arabic) because of the rose color of the stone used for its walls and 23 towers. By the end of the 14th century, the complex, a veritable city with a population of 40,000, included at least a half dozen royal residences. Only two of these fared well over the centuries. They present a vivid picture of court life in Islamic Spain before the Christian reconquest. Paradoxically, the two palaces owe their preservation to the Christian victors, who maintained a few of the buildings as trophies commemorating the expulsion of the Nasrids.

PARADISE AND HEAVEN One of those palaces is the Palace of the Lions, named for the courtyard fountain with marble lions carrying its water basin on their backs. It is an unusual instance of freestanding stone sculpture in the Islamic world. The palace was the residence of Muhammad V (r. 1354–1391), and its courtyards, lush gardens, and luxurious carpets and other furnishings were designed to conjure the image of Paradise. The complex is noteworthy also for its elaborate stucco ceilings and walls, which never fail to impress visitors.

We reproduce a view of the ceiling of the so-called Hall of the Two Sisters (FIG. **7-17**) in the Palace of the Lions. The dome of the square room rests on an octagonal drum supported by squinches and pierced by eight pairs of windows, but its structure is difficult to discern because of the intricately carved stucco decoration. The ceiling is covered with some 5,000 *muqarnas*—tier after tier of stalactite-like prismatic forms that seem aimed at denying the structure's solidity. The muqarnas ceiling was intended to catch and reflect sunlight as well as form beautiful abstract patterns. The lofty vault in this hall and others in the palace were meant to symbolize the dome of Heaven. The flickering light

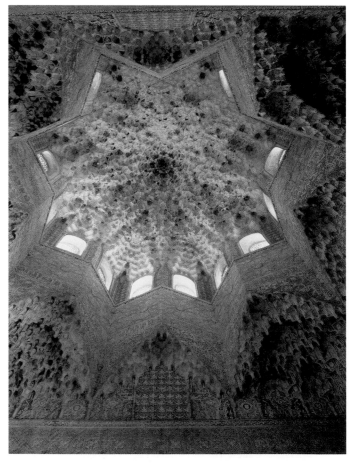

7-17 Muqarnas dome, Hall of the Two Sisters, Alhambra palace, Granada, Spain, 1354–1391.

and shadows create the effect of a starry sky as the sun's rays move from window to window during the day. To underscore the symbolism, the palace walls were inscribed with verses by the court poet Ibn Zamrak, who compared the Alhambra's lacelike muqarnas ceilings to "the heavenly spheres whose orbits revolve."

THE SLAVE SULTANS OF EGYPT In the mid-13th century, the Mongols from east-central Asia (see Chapter 4) conquered much of the eastern Islamic world. The center of Islamic power moved from Baghdad to Egypt. The lords of Egypt at the time were former Turkish slaves (*mamluks* in Arabic) who converted to Islam. The capital of the Mamluk *sultans* (rulers) was Cairo, which became the largest Muslim city of the late Middle Ages. The Mamluks were prolific builders, and Sultan Hasan, although not an important figure in Islamic history, was the most ambitious of all. He ruled briefly as a child and was deposed, but regained the sultanate from 1354 until 1361, when he was assassinated.

MADRASA AND MAUSOLEUM Hasan's major building project in Cairo was a huge madrasa complex (FIGS. **7-18** and **7-19**) on a plot of land about 8,000 square yards in area. A *madrasa* ("place of study" in Arabic) is a theological college devoted to the teaching of Islamic law. Hasan's complex was so large that it housed not only four such colleges for the study of the four major schools of Islamic law but also a mosque, mausoleum, orphanage, and hospital, as well as shops and baths. Like all Islamic building complexes incorporating religious, educational, and charitable functions, this one was supported by an endowment funded by rental properties. The income from these paid the salaries of attendants and faculty, provided furnishings and supplies such as oil for the lamps or free food for the poor, and supported scholarships for needy students.

The grandiose structure has a large central courtyard with a monumental fountain in the center and four iwans (rectangular vaulted recesses) opening onto it, a design used earlier for Iranian mosques (FIG. 7-23). In each corner of the main courtyard (FIG. 7-19), between the iwans, is a madrasa with its own courtyard and four or five stories of rooms for the students. The largest iwan in the complex, on the southern side, served as a mosque. Contemporaries believed the soaring vault that covered this iwan was taller than the arch of the Sasanian palace at Ctesiphon, which was then one of the most admired engineering feats in the world. Behind the qibla wall stands the sultan's mausoleum, a gigantic version of the type of tomb the Samanids erected at Bukhara (FIG. 7-10). The siting of the dome-covered cube south of the mosque was carefully calculated. The prayers of the faithful facing Mecca, therefore, were directed toward Hasan's tomb. (Only the sultan's two sons are actually buried there. Hasan's body was not returned when he was killed.)

A muqarnas *cornice* crowns the exterior walls of the complex, and marble plaques of several colors cover the mihrab in the mosque and the walls of Hasan's mausoleum. But the complex as a whole is relatively austere, characterized by its massiveness and geometric clarity. It presents a striking contrast to the filigreed elegance of the contemporary Alhambra, and testifies to the diversity of regional styles within the Islamic world, especially after the end of the Umayyad and Abbasid dynasties.

THE OTTOMANS COME TO POWER During the course of the 9th to 11th centuries, the Turkic people, of central Asian origin, largely converted to Islam. They moved into Iran and the Near East in the 11th century, and by 1055 the Seljuk Turkish dynasty had built an extensive, although short-lived, empire that stretched from India to western Anatolia. By the end of the 12th

7-18 Madrasa-mosque-mausoleum complex of Sultan Hasan (view from the south with the mausoleum in the foreground), Cairo, Egypt, begun 1356.

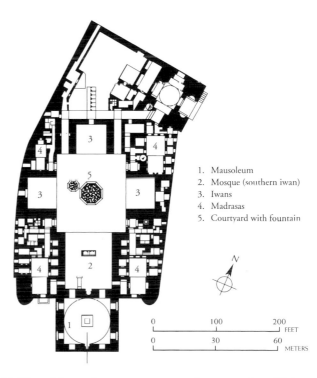

1. Mausoleum
2. Mosque (southern iwan)
3. Iwans
4. Madrasas
5. Courtyard with fountain

7-19 Plan of the madrasa mosque-mausoleum complex of Sultan Hasan, Cairo, Egypt, begun 1356.

century, this empire had broken up into regional states, and in the early 13th century it came under the sway of the Mongols, led by Genghis Khan (see Chapter 4). After the Seljuks fell, several local dynasties established themselves in Anatolia, among them the Ottomans, founded by Osman I (r. 1281–1326). Under Osman's successors, the Ottoman state expanded for a period of two and a half centuries throughout vast areas of Asia, Europe, and North Africa to become, by the middle of the 15th century, one of the great world powers.

The Ottoman emperors were lavish patrons of architecture. Ottoman builders developed a new type of mosque with a square prayer hall covered by a dome as its core. In fact, the dome-covered square, which had been a dominant form in Iran and was employed for the 10th-century mausoleum at Bukhara (FIG. 7-10), became the nucleus of all Ottoman architecture. The combination had an appealing geometric clarity. At first used singly, the domed units came to be used in multiples, a turning point in Ottoman architecture.

After the Ottoman Turks conquered Constantinople (Istanbul) in 1453, they firmly established their architectural code. The new lords of Constantinople were impressed by the sixth-century Byzantine church of Hagia Sophia, which, in some respects, conformed to their own ideals. They converted the church into a mosque with minarets. But the longitudinal orientation of Hagia Sophia's interior never satisfied Ottoman builders, and Anatolian development moved instead toward the central-plan mosque.

SINAN THE GREAT The first examples of the central-plan mosque were built in the 1520s, eclipsed later only by the works of the most famous Ottoman architect, SINAN (ca. 1491–1588). Sinan perfected the Ottoman architectural style. By his time, the basic domed unit was universally used. It could be multiplied, enlarged, or contracted as needed, and almost any number of units could be used together. Thus, the typical Ottoman building of Sinan's time was a creative assemblage of domical units and artfully juxtaposed geometric spaces. Builders usually erected domes with an extravagant margin of structural safety that has since served them well in earthquake-prone Istanbul and other Ottoman cities. (The sound construction of the Ottoman mosques was vividly demonstrated in August 1999 when a powerful earthquake centered 65 miles east of Istanbul toppled hundreds of modern buildings and killed thousands of people but caused no damage to the centuries-old mosques.) Working within this architectural tradition, Sinan searched for solutions to the problems of unifying the additive elements and of creating a monumental centralized space with harmonious proportions.

THE CENTRAL PLAN AT EDIRNE Sinan's efforts to overcome the limitations of a segmented interior found their ultimate expression in the Mosque of Selim II (FIGS. **7-20** to **7-22**) at Edirne, which had been the capital of the Ottoman Empire from 1367 to 1472 and where Selim II (r. 1566–1574) maintained a palace. There, Sinan created a structure that made it possible to see the mihrab from almost any spot in the mosque. The massive dome, effectively set off by four slender pencil-shaped minarets (each more than 200 feet high, among the tallest ever constructed), dominates the city's skyline (FIG. 7-20). Various dependent structures were placed around the mosque. Most important Ottoman mosques had numerous annexes, including libraries and schools, hospices, baths, soup kitchens for the poor, markets,

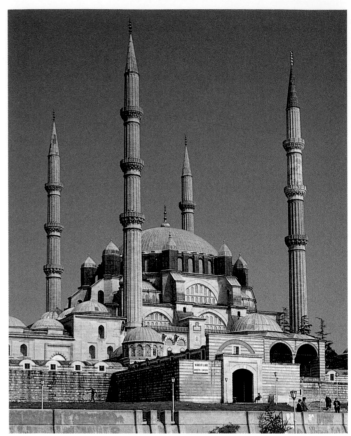

7-20 SINAN, Mosque of Selim II, Edirne, Turkey, 1568–1575.

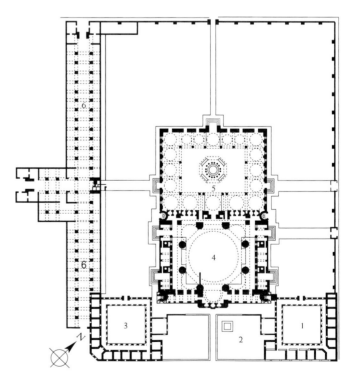

1. Madrasa
2. Cemetery
3. Darül-Kurra (house for the readers of the Quran)
4. Mosque
5. Avlu (courtyard forming summer extension of mosque)
6. Arasta (covered market)

| 0 | 250 | 500 FEET |
| 0 | 75 | 150 METERS |

7-21 SINAN, plan of the Mosque of Selim II, Edirne, Turkey, 1568–1575.

Sinan the Great, the Mosque of Selim II, and Hagia Sophia

Sinan (ca. 1491–1588), called Sinan the Great, was in fact the greatest Ottoman architect. Born a Christian, he was recruited for service in the Ottoman government, converted to Islam, and was trained in engineering and the art of building while in the Ottoman army. His talent was quickly recognized, and he was entrusted with increasing responsibility until, in 1538, he was appointed the chief court architect for Suleyman the Magnificent (r. 1520–1566), a generous patron of art and architecture. Hundreds of building projects, both sacred and secular, have been attributed to Sinan, although he could not have been involved with all that bear his name.

The capstone of Sinan's distinguished career was the Edirne mosque (FIGS. 7-20 to 7-22) of Suleyman's son, Selim II, which Sinan designed when he was almost 80 years old. There, he sought to surpass the greatest achievements of Byzantine architects just as Sultan Hasan's builders in Cairo attempted to rival and exceed the Sasanian architects of antiquity. Sa'i Mustafa Çelebi, Sinan's biographer, recorded the architect's accomplishment in his own words:

Sultan Selim Khan ordered the erection of a mosque in Edirne. . . . His humble servant [I, Sinan] prepared for him a drawing depicting, on a dominating site in the city, four minarets on the four corners of a dome. . . . Those who consider themselves architects among Christians say that in the realm of Islam no dome can equal that of the Hagia Sophia; they claim that no Muslim architect would be able to build such a large dome. In this mosque, with the help of God and the support of Sultan Selim Khan, I erected a dome six cubits higher and four cubits wider than the dome of the Hagia Sophia.[1]

The Edirne dome is, in fact, higher than Hagia Sophia's when measured from its base, but its crown is not as far above the pavement as that of the dome of the Byzantine church. Nonetheless, Sinan's feat was universally acclaimed as a triumph, and the Mosque of Selim II was considered proof that the Ottomans finally had outshone the Christian emperors of Byzantium in the realm of architecture.

[1] Aptullah Kuran, *Sinan: The Grand Old Master of Ottoman Architecture* (Washington, D.C.: Institute of Turkish Studies, 1987), 168–69.

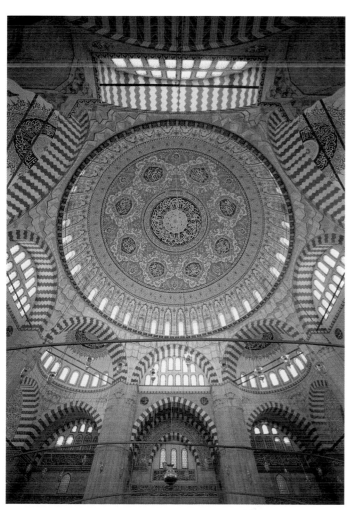

7-22 SINAN, interior of the Mosque of Selim II, Edirne, Turkey, 1568–1575.

and hospitals, as well as a cemetery containing the mausoleum of the sultan responsible for building the mosque (compare Hasan's complex in Cairo, FIG. 7-19). These utilitarian buildings were grouped around the mosque and axially aligned with it if possible. More generally, they were adjusted to their natural site and linked with the central building by planted shrubs and trees.

The Edirne mosque is preceded by a rectangular court covering an area equal to that of the building (FIG. 7-21). *Porticos* formed by domed squares surround the courtyard. Behind it, the building rises majestically to its climactic dome, whose height surpasses that of Hagia Sophia (see "Sinan the Great, the Mosque of Selim II, and Hagia Sophia," above). But it is the organization of this mosque's interior space (FIG. 7-22) that reveals the genius of its builder. The mihrab is recessed into an apselike alcove deep enough to permit window illumination from three sides, making the brilliantly colored tile panels of its lower walls sparkle as if with their own glowing light. The plan of the main hall is an ingenious fusion of an octagon with the dome-covered square (FIG. 7-21). The octagon, formed by the eight massive dome supports, is pierced by the four half-dome-covered corners of the square. The result is a fluid interpenetration of several geometric volumes that represents the culminating solution to Sinan's lifelong search for a monumental unified interior space. Sinan's forms are clear and legible, like mathematical equations. Height, width, and masses are related to one another in a simple but effective ratio of 1:2. The building is generally regarded as the climax of Ottoman architecture. Sinan proudly proclaimed it his masterpiece.

ISFAHAN'S GREAT MOSQUE The Mosque of Selim II at Edirne was erected during a single building campaign under the direction of a single master architect, but many other major

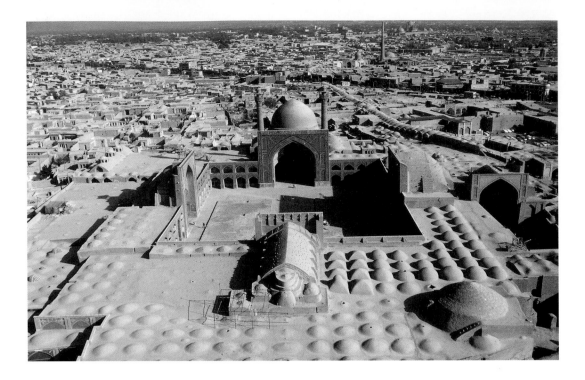

7-23 Aerial view of the Great Mosque (looking southwest), Isfahan, Iran, 11th to 17th centuries.

Islamic architectural projects were built or remodeled over several centuries. A case in point is the Great Mosque at Isfahan (FIG. **7-23**) in Iran. The earliest mosque on the site, of the hypostyle type, was constructed in the eighth century during the caliphate of the Abbasids. But Sultan Malik Shah I (r. 1072–1092), whose capital was at Isfahan, transformed the structure in the 11th century. Later remodeling further altered the mosque's appearance. The present mosque, which retains its basic 11th-century plan, consists of a large courtyard bordered by a two-story arcade on each side. As in the 14th-century complex of Sultan Hasan (FIG. 7-19) in Cairo, four iwans open onto the courtyard, one at the center of each side. The southwestern iwan leads into a dome-covered room in front of the mihrab. It func-

tioned as a maqsura reserved for the sultan and his attendants. It is uncertain whether this plan, with four iwans and a dome before the mihrab, was employed for the first time in the Great Mosque at Isfahan, but it became standard in Iranian mosque design. In four-iwan mosques the qibla iwan is always the largest. Its size (and the dome that often accompanied it) immediately indicated to worshipers the proper direction for prayer.

IRANIAN TILEWORK The iwans of the Isfahan mosque feature soaring pointed arches framing tile-sheathed muqarnas vaults. The muqarnas ceilings probably were installed in the 14th century, and the ceramic-tile *revetment* on the walls and vaults is the work of the 17th-century Safavid rulers of Iran. The use of glazed

7-24 Winter prayer hall of the Shahi (Imam) Mosque, Isfahan, Iran, 1611–1638.

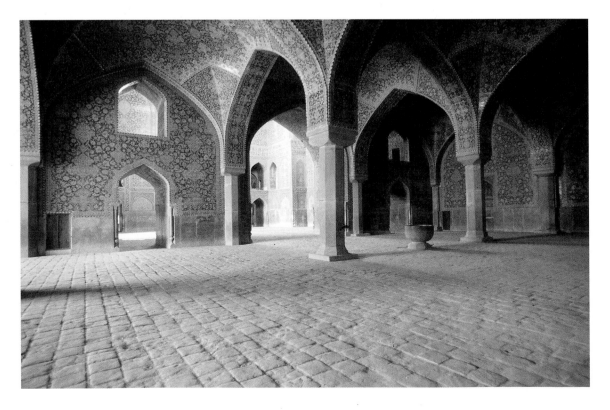

Islamic Tilework

From the Dome of the Rock (FIGS. 7-1 and 7-2), the earliest major Islamic building, to the present day, mosaics or ceramic tiles have been used to decorate the walls and vaults of mosques, madrasas, palaces, and tombs. The golden age of Islamic tilework was the 16th and 17th centuries. At that time, Islamic artists used two basic techniques to enliven building interiors with brightly colored tiled walls and to sheathe their exteriors with gleaming tiles that reflected the sun's rays.

In *mosaic tilework* (for example, FIG. 7-25), large ceramic panels of single colors are fired in the potter's kiln and then cut into smaller pieces and set in plaster in a manner similar to the laying of mosaic *tesserae* of stone or glass.

Cuerda seca (dry cord) tilework was introduced in Umayyad Spain during the 10th century—hence its Spanish name even in Middle Eastern and Central Asian contexts. Cuerda seca tiles (for example, FIG. 7-24) are polychrome and can more easily bear complex arabesque patterns as well as Arabic script. They are more economical to use because vast surfaces can be covered with large tiles much more quickly than they can with thousands of smaller mosaic tiles. But when such tiles are used to sheathe curved surfaces, the ceramists must fire the tiles in the exact shape required.

Polychrome tiles have other drawbacks. Because all the glazes are fired at the same temperature, cuerda seca tiles are not as brilliant in color as mosaic tiles and do not reflect light the way the more irregular surfaces of tile mosaics do. The preparation of the multicolored tiles also requires greater care. To prevent the colors from running together during firing, the potters outline the motifs on cuerda seca tiles with greased cords containing manganese, which leaves a matte black line between the colors after firing.

---

tiles has a long history in the Middle East. Even in ancient Mesopotamia, gates and walls were sometimes covered with colorful baked bricks. In the Islamic world, the art of ceramic tilework reached its peak in the 16th and 17th centuries in Iran and Turkey (see "Islamic Tilework," above). Employed as a veneer over a brick core, tiles could sheathe entire buildings, including domes and minarets.

The Shahi (or Royal) Mosque in Isfahan, recently renamed the Imam Mosque, which dates from the early 17th century, is widely recognized as one of the masterpieces of Islamic tilework. Its dome is a prime example of tile mosaic, and its winter prayer hall (FIG. 7-24) houses one of the finest ensembles of cuerda seca tiles in the world. Covering the walls, arches, and vaults of the prayer hall presented a special challenge to the Isfahan ceramists. They had to manufacture a wide variety of shapes with curved surfaces to sheathe the complex forms of the hall. The result was a technological triumph as well as a dazzling display of abstract ornament.

CERAMIC CALLIGRAPHY We noted earlier the Koran's central importance to the Islamic world and how its verses appeared in the mosaics of the earliest great Islamic building, the Dome of the Rock in Jerusalem (FIG. 7-2). Excerpts from the Koran appear on the walls of numerous other Islamic structures in a variety of media. Indeed, some of the masterworks of Arabic calligraphy are found not in manuscripts but on walls. A 14th-century mihrab (FIG. 7-25) from the Madrasa Imami in Isfahan exemplifies the perfect aesthetic union between the calligrapher's art and arabesque ornament. The pointed arch that immediately enframes the mihrab niche bears an inscription from the Koran in Kufic, the stately rectilinear script employed for the early Koran page illustrated (FIG. 7-16). Many supple cursive styles also make up the repertoire of Islamic calligraphy. One of these styles, known as *Muhaqqaq,* fills the mihrab's outer rectangular frame. The mosaic tile ornament on the curving surface of the niche and the area above the pointed arch are composed of tighter and looser networks of geometric and abstract floral motifs. The mosaic technique is masterful. Every piece

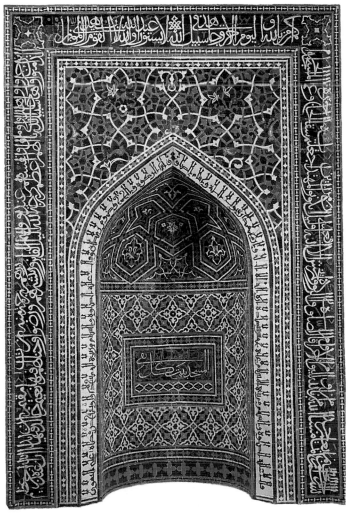

7-25 Mihrab from the Madrasa Imami, Isfahan, Iran, ca. 1354. Glazed mosaic tilework, 11′ 3″ × 7′ 6″. Metropolitan Museum of Art, New York.

had to be chiseled and cut to fit its specific place in the mihrab—even the tile inscriptions. The framed inscription in the center of the niche—proclaiming that the mosque is the domicile of the pious believer—is smoothly integrated with the subtly varied patterns. The mihrab's outermost inscription—detailing the five pillars of Islamic faith—serves as a fringelike extension, as well as a boundary, for the entire design. The calligraphic and geometric elements are so completely unified that only the practiced eye can distinguish them. The artist transformed the architectural surface into a textile surface, the three-dimensional wall into a two-dimensional hanging, weaving the calligraphy into it as another cluster of motifs within the total pattern.

Luxury Arts

The tile-covered mosques of Isfahan, Sultan Hasan's madrasa complex in Cairo, and the architecture of Sinan the Great in Edirne are enduring testaments to the brilliant artistic culture of the Safavid, Mamluk, and Ottoman rulers of the Muslim world. But these are just some of the most conspicuous public manifestations of the greatness of later Islamic art and architecture (see Chapter 2 for the achievements of the Muslim rulers of India). In the smaller-scale, and often private, realm of the luxury arts, Muslim artists also excelled. From the vast array of manuscript paintings, ceramics, textiles, and metalwork, five masterpieces may serve to suggest both the range and the quality of the inappropriately dubbed Islamic "minor arts" of the 13th to 16th centuries.

MILLIONS OF KNOTS The first of these artworks (FIG. **7-26**) is by far the largest, one of a pair of carpets from Ardabil in Iran. They come from the funerary mosque of Shaykh Safi al-Din (1252–1334), the founder of the Safavid line, but were made in 1540, two centuries after the erection of the mosque, during the reign of Shah Tahmasp (r. 1524–1576). Tahmasp elevated carpet weaving to a national industry and set up royal factories at Isfahan, Kashan, Kirman, and Tabriz. The name of MAQSUD OF KASHAN is woven into the design of the carpet we illustrate. He must have been the designer who supplied the master pattern to two teams of royal weavers (one for each of the two carpets). The carpet, almost 35 × 18 feet, consists of roughly 25 million knots, some 340 to the square inch. (Its twin has even more knots.)

The design consists of a central sunburst medallion, representing the inside of a dome, surrounded by 16 pendants. Mosque lamps (appropriate motifs for the Ardabil funerary mosque) are suspended from two pendants on the long axis of the carpet. The lamps are of different sizes, and some scholars have suggested that this is an optical device to make the two appear equal in size when viewed from the end of the carpet at the room's threshold (the bottom end in our illustration). The rich blue background is covered with leaves and flowers attached to delicate stems that spread over the whole field. The entire composition presents the illusion of a heavenly dome with lamps reflected in a pool of water full of floating lotus blossoms. No human or animal figures appear, as befits a carpet intended for a mosque, although they can be found on other Islamic textiles used in secular contexts, both earlier (FIG. 7-14) and later.

THE BOOK OF KINGS Shah Tahmasp was also a great patron of books. Around 1525 he commissioned an ambitious decade-long project to produce an illustrated 742-page copy of the *Shahnama (Book of Kings)*. The *Shahnama* is the Persian national epic poem by Firdawsi (940–1025). It recounts the history of Iran from the Creation until the Muslim conquest. Tahmasp's *Shahnama*

contains 258 illustrations by many artists, including some of the most renowned painters of the day. It was eventually presented as a gift to Selim II, the Ottoman sultan who was the patron of Sinan's mosque at Edirne (FIGS. 7-20 to 7-22). The manuscript later entered a private collection in the West and ultimately was auctioned off as a series of individual pages, destroying its integrity—an unfortunate consequence of the esteem in which Islamic art is held throughout the world.

The page we reproduce (FIG. 7-27) is the work of SULTAN-MUHAMMAD and depicts Gayumars, the legendary first king of Iran, and his court. Gayumars was said to have ruled from a mountaintop when humans first learned to cook food and clothe themselves in leopard skins. In Sultan-Muhammad's representation of the story, Gayumars presides over his court (all the figures

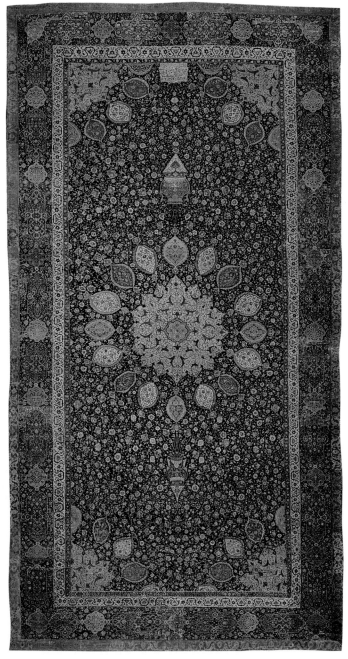

7-26 MAQSUD OF KASHAN, carpet from the funerary mosque of Shaykh Safi al-Din, Ardabil, Iran, 1540. Knotted pile of wool and silk, 34′ 6″ × 17′ 7″. Victoria & Albert Museum, London.

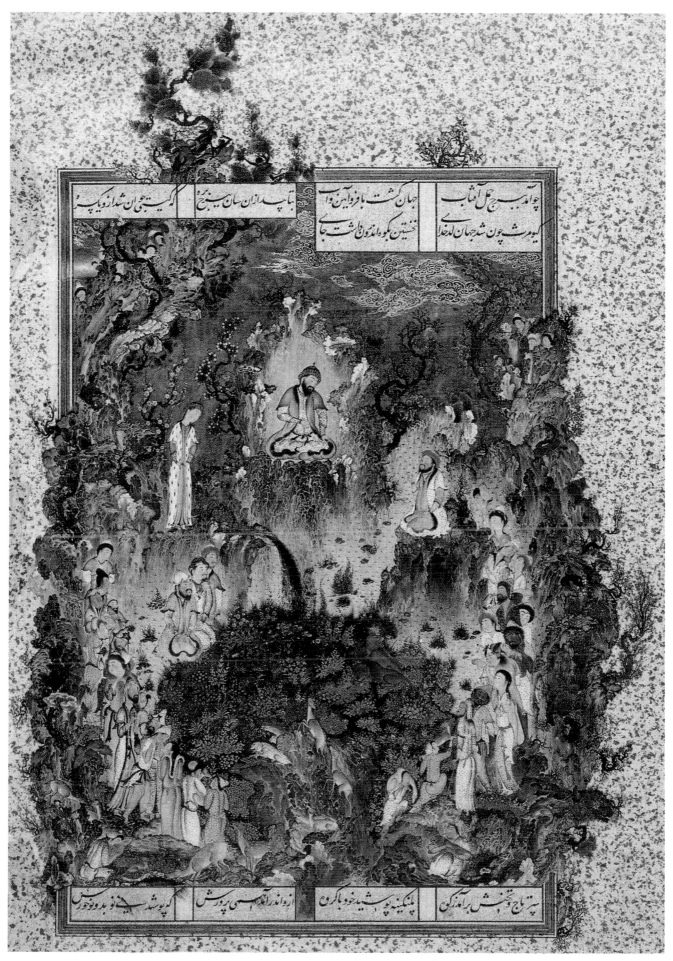

7-27 Sultan-Muhammad, the court of Gayumars, detail of folio 20 verso of the *Shahnama* of Shah Tahmasp, from Tabriz, Iran, ca. 1525–1535. Ink, watercolor, and gold on paper, full page approx. 1′ 1″ × 9″. Prince Sadruddin Aga Khan Collection, Geneva.

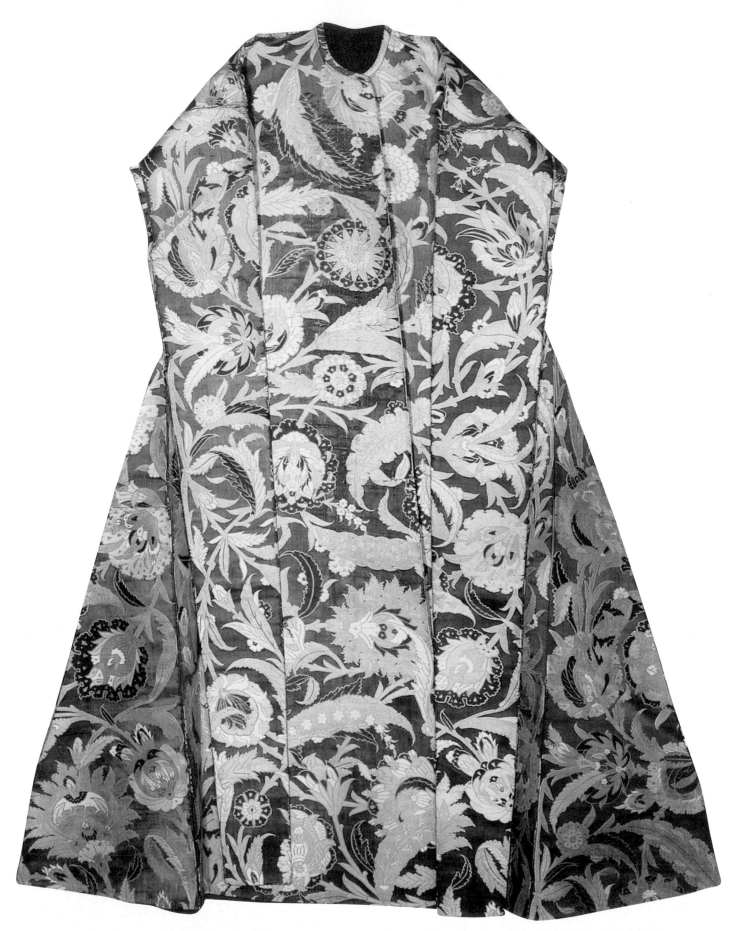

7-28 Ottoman royal ceremonial caftan, from Istanbul, Turkey, ca. 1550. Polychrome silk and gilt-metal thread, 4′ 9″ high. Topkapi Palace Museum, Istanbul.

wear leopard skins) from his mountain throne. The king is surrounded by light amid a golden sky. His son and grandson are perched on multicolored rocky outcroppings to the viewer's left and right, respectively. The court encircles the ruler and his heirs. Dozens of human faces are portrayed within the rocks themselves. Many species of animals populate the lush landscape. According to the *Shahnama,* wild beasts became instantly tame in the presence of Gayumars. Sultan-Muhammad rendered the figures, animals, trees, rocks, and sky with an extraordinarily delicate touch. The sense of lightness and airiness that permeates the painting is enhanced by its placement on the page—floating, off center, on a speckled background of gold leaf. The painter gave his royal patron a singular vision of Iran's fabled past.

A ROYAL OTTOMAN CAFTAN When Tahmasp's *Shahnama* was presented to Selim II, the Ottoman sultan would have received the precious gift with due pomp and circumstance, perhaps wearing a majestic ceremonial caftan like the one illustrated here (FIG. **7-28**). It was woven of silk thread around 1550, perhaps for Suleyman the Magnificent's son Bayezid. More than a thousand such caftans are preserved in the Ottoman Topkapi Palace, now a museum. But this caftan was one of the most difficult to create on a loom because of its large number of colors and because of the complexity of its floral designs. This kind of distinctive Ottoman design of sinuous curved leaves and complex blossoms is known as *saz,* a Turkish term recalling an enchanted

forest. The saz design is never repeated on this garment, a remarkable feat. The designer, nonetheless, made sure the pattern matched across the front opening. Court protocol dictated that Ottoman rulers stood absolutely motionless in the presence of visitors. This explains why the caftan has no fastenings to prevent it from opening. The wearer's arms protruded through slits at the shoulders. The sleeves are ankle length; they served only for decoration and were draped over the back.

ISLAMIC ART FOR CHRISTIANS Like most Islamic artworks, the Ottoman caftan has no figural ornament, but figures and animals adorn a brass basin (FIG. **7-29**) from Egypt inlaid with gold and silver and signed—six times—by the Mamluk artist MUHAMMAD IBN AL-ZAYN. The basin, used for washing hands at official ceremonies, must have been fashioned for a specific Mamluk patron. Some scholars think a court official named Salar ordered the piece as a gift for his sultan, but no inscription identifies him. The central band depicts Mamluk hunters and Mongol enemies. Running animals fill the friezes above and below. Arabesques of inlaid silver fill the background of all the bands and roundels. Figures and animals also decorate the inside and underside of the basin.

The basin has long been known as the *Baptistère de Saint Louis,* but the association with the famous 13th-century French king who became a saint is a myth, for he died before the piece was made. Nonetheless, the *Baptistère,* brought to France long ago, was used in the baptismal rites of newborns of the French

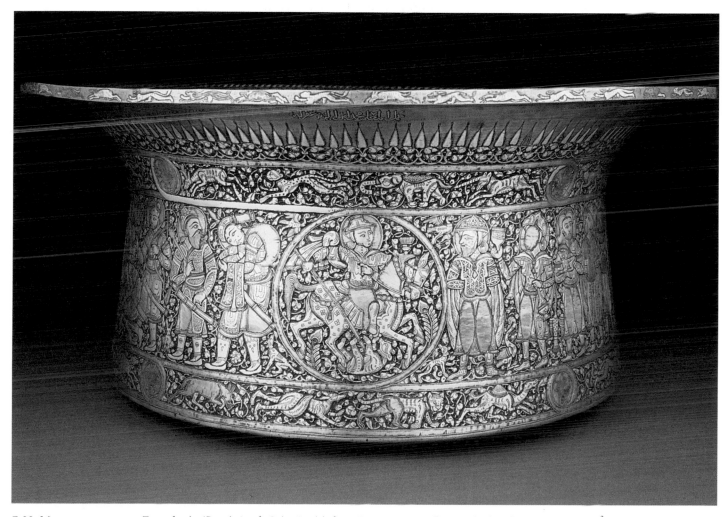

7-29 MUHAMMAD IBN AL-ZAYN, basin (*Baptistère de Saint Louis*), from Egypt, ca. 1300. Brass, inlaid with gold and silver, $8\frac{3}{4}''$ high. Louvre, Paris.

Christian Patronage of Islamic Art

During the 11th, 12th, and 13th centuries, large numbers of Christians traveled to Islamic lands, especially to the Christian holy sites in Jerusalem and Bethlehem, either as pilgrims or as Crusaders. Many returned with mementos of their journey, usually in the form of inexpensive mass-produced souvenirs. But some wealthy individuals commissioned local Islamic artists to produce custom-made pieces using costly materials.

A unique brass canteen (FIG. 7-30) inlaid with silver and decorated with scenes of the life of Christ appears to be the work of a 13th-century Ayyubid metalsmith in the employ of a Christian patron. The canteen is a luxurious version of the "pilgrim flasks" Christian visitors to the Holy Land often brought back to Europe. Four inscriptions in Arabic promise eternal glory, secure life, perfect prosperity, and increasing good luck to the canteen's owner, who is unfortunately not named. That the owner was a Christian is suggested not only by the type of object but by the choice of scenes

engraved into the canteen. The Madonna and Christ Child appear enthroned in the central medallion, and three panels depicting New Testament events fill most of the band around the medallion. The narrative unfolds in a counterclockwise sequence (Arabic is read from right to left), beginning with the Nativity (at 2 o'clock) and continuing with the Presentation in the Temple (10 o'clock) and the Entry into Jerusalem (6 o'clock). The scenes may have been chosen because the patron had visited their locales (Bethlehem and Jerusalem).

Most scholars believe that the artist used Syrian Christian manuscripts as the source for the canteen's Christian iconography. Many of the decorative details, however, are common in contemporary Islamic metalwork inscribed with the names of Muslim patrons. Whoever the owner was, the canteen testifies to the fruitful artistic interaction between Christians and Muslims in 13th-century Syria.

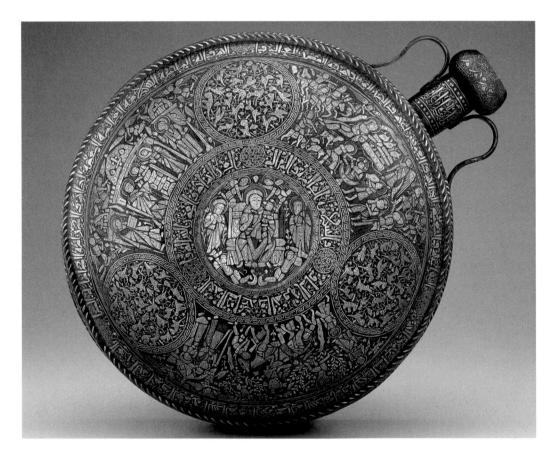

7-30 Canteen with episodes from the life of Christ, from Syria, ca. 1240–1250. Brass, inlaid with silver, 1′ 2½″ diameter. Freer Gallery of Art, Washington, D.C.

royal family as early as the 17th century. Like the Zandana silk in Toul Cathedral (FIG. 7-14) and a canteen (FIG. **7-30**) with scenes of the life of Christ (see "Christian Patronage of Islamic Art," above), Muhammad ibn al-Zayn's basin testifies to the prestige of Islamic art in western Europe.

CONCLUSION

The irresistible and far-ranging sweep of Islam from Arabia to India to North Africa and Spain brought a new and compelling

tradition to the history of world art and architecture. Like Islam itself, Islamic art spread quickly. In the Middle East and North Africa, Islamic art largely replaced Roman Late Antique art. And from a foothold in the Iberian peninsula, it made an impact on Western medieval art, although Islamic art stands in sharp contrast both to the figural art of Europe and the Mediterranean and to the Western architectural vocabulary. Islamic artists and architects also brought their distinctive style to South Asia, where a Muslim sultanate was established at Delhi in India in the early 13th century (see Chapter 2).

SYRIA AND IRAQ	SPAIN	IRAN AND CENTRAL ASIA	EGYPT	TURKEY	INDIA	

600

| BIRTH OF MUHAMMAD IN MECCA, CA. 570 |

UMAYYAD CALIPHATE

| MUHAMMAD'S FIRST REVELATION, 610 |
| MUHAMMAD'S FLIGHT TO MEDINA (HIJRA), 622 |
| DEATH OF MUHAMMAD IN MEDINA, 632 |
| MUSLIMS CAPTURE JERUSALEM, 638 |
| MUSLIM CONQUEST OF LOWER EGYPT, 642 |
| **1** UMAYYAD CALIPHATE ESTABLISHED, 661 |

700

| MUSLIM ARMIES ENTER SPAIN, 711 |
| CHARLES MARTEL DEFEATS MUSLIMS AT POITIERS, 732 |
| ABBASID CALIPHATE ESTABLISHED, 750 |
| UMAYYAD CALIPHATE ESTABLISHED IN SPAIN, 756 |
| ABBASIDS FOUND BAGHDAD, 762 |

1 Dome of the Rock, Jerusalem, 687–692

ABBASID CALIPHATE

UMAYYAD CALIPHATE

SAMANID DYNASTY

800

| SAMANID DYNASTY ESTABLISHED IN TRANSOXIANA, 819 |

900

FATIMID DYNASTY

| **2** FATIMID DYNASTY ESTABLISHED IN EGYPT, 909 |
| FATIMIDS FOUND CAIRO, 969 |

2 Koran page, Dublin, ca. 900

1000

SELJUK DYNASTY

| FALL OF UMAYYAD CALIPHATE IN SPAIN, 1031 |
| SELJUK DYNASTY ESTABLISHED IN IRAN, 1038 |
| **3** FIRST CRUSADE CAPTURES JERUSALEM, 1099 |

1100

AYYUBID DYNASTY

| SALADIN FOUNDS AYYUBID DYNASTY IN EGYPT, 1171 |
| SALADIN CAPTURES JERUSALEM FROM CRUSADERS, 1187 |

1200

NASRID DYNASTY

MAMLUK DYNASTY

OTTOMAN EMPIRE

DELHI SULTANATE

| SULTANATE OF DELHI ESTABLISHED, 1206 |
| NASRID DYNASTY ESTABLISHED AT GRANADA, 1230 |
| MAMLUK DYNASTY ESTABLISHED IN EGYPT, 1250 |
| MONGOLS SACK BAGHDAD, 1258 |
| OTTOMAN EMPIRE FOUNDED, 1281 |

3 Great Mosque, Isfahan, begun late 11th century

1300

TIMURID DYNASTY

1400

| OTTOMANS CAPTURE CONSTANTINOPLE, 1453 |
| FALL OF GRANADA TO THE CHRISTIANS, 1492 |

SAFAVID DYNASTY

MUGHAL DYNASTY

1500

| SAFAVID DYNASTY ESTABLISHED IN IRAN, 1501 |
| **4** MUGHAL DYNASTY ESTABLISHED IN INDIA, 1526 |
| OTTOMANS CAPTURE BAGHDAD, 1534 |

4 Maqsud of Kashan, Ardabil carpet, 1540

1600

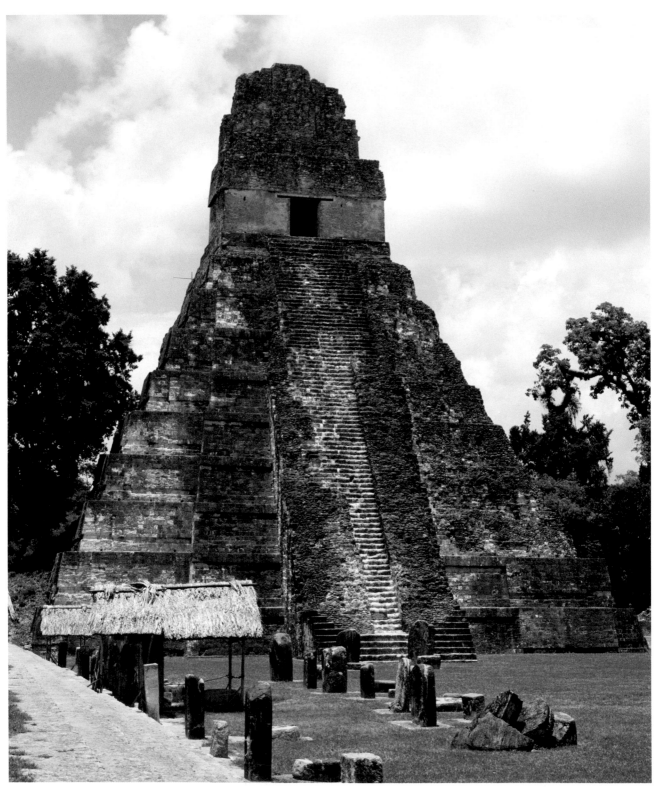

Temple I (Temple of the Giant Jaguar), Maya, Tikal, Petén, Guatemala, ca. 732 CE.

8

FROM ALASKA
TO THE ANDES

NATIVE ARTS OF THE AMERICAS BEFORE 1300

The origins of the indigenous peoples of the Americas are still disputed. Sometime no later than 30,000 to 10,000 BCE these first Americans probably crossed the now submerged land bridge called Beringia, which connected the shores of the Bering Strait between Asia and North America (MAP **8-1**). Some scholars also have proposed that at least some migrants reached the Western Hemisphere via boats traveling along the Pacific coast of North America.

These Stone Age nomads were hunter-gatherers. They made tools only of bone, pressure-flaked stone, and wood. They had no knowledge of agriculture but possibly some of basketry. They could control fire and probably built simple shelters. For many centuries, they spread out until they occupied the two American continents. But they were always few in number. When the first Europeans arrived at the end of the 15th century (see Chapter 9), the total population of the Western Hemisphere may not have exceeded 40 million.

Between 8000 and 2000 BCE, a number of the migrants learned to fish, farm cotton, and domesticate such plants as squash and maize (corn). The nomads settled down in villages and learned to make clay pottery utensils and lively figurines. Metal technology, although extremely sophisticated when it existed, developed only in the Andean region of South America (eventually spreading north into modern-day Mexico) and generally met only the need for ornament, not for tools. With these skills as a base, many cultures rose and fell over long periods.

Several of the peoples of North, Central, and South America had already reached a high level of social complexity and technological achievement by the early centuries CE. Although most relied on stone tools, did not use the wheel (except for toys), and had no pack animals but the llama (in South America), the early Americans developed complex agricultural techniques and excelled in the engineering arts associated with the planning and construction of cities, civic and domestic buildings, roads and bridges, and irrigation and drainage systems. They carved monumental stone statues and reliefs, painted extensive murals, and mastered the arts of weaving, pottery, and metalwork. The Maya of Mesoamerica even had a highly developed writing system and knowledge of mathematical calculation that allowed them to keep precise

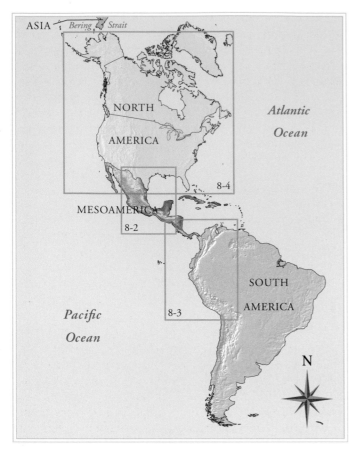

MAP 8-1 The Americas.

records and create a sophisticated calendar and a highly accurate astronomy.

DESTRUCTION AND RECONSTRUCTION These advanced civilizations abruptly collapsed, however, in the 16th century when Hernan Cortés, Francisco Pizarro, and their armies conquered the Aztec and Inka empires. Most of the once-glorious American cities were destroyed in the Spaniards' zeal to obliterate all traces of pagan beliefs. Other sites were abandoned to the forces of nature—erosion and the encroachment of tropical forests. But despite the ruined state of the pre-Hispanic cities today, archaeologists and art historians have been able to reconstruct much of the art and architectural history of ancient America. This chapter examines in turn the artistic achievements of the native peoples of Mesoamerica, South America, and North America before 1300. Chapter 9 treats the art and architecture of the Americas from 1300 to the present.

MESOAMERICA

GEOGRAPHY AND CLIMATE The term *Mesoamerica* names the region that comprises part of present-day Mexico, Guatemala, Belize, Honduras, and the Pacific coast of El Salvador (MAP **8-2**). Mesoamerica was the homeland of several of the great civilizations that flourished before the arrival of Christopher Columbus and the subsequent European invasion. The principal regions of *pre-Columbian* Mesoamerica are the Gulf Coast region (Olmec culture); the states of Jalisco, Colima, and Nayarit, collectively known as West Mexico; Chiapas, Yucatán, Quintana Roo, and Campeche states in Mexico and the Petén area of Guatemala (Maya culture); southwestern Mexico and the state of Oaxaca (Zapotec and Mixtec cultures); and the central plateau surrounding

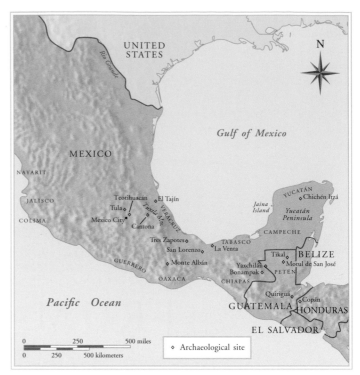

MAP 8-2 Early sites in Mesoamerica.

modern-day Mexico City (Teotihuacán, Toltec, and Aztec cultures). These cultures were often influential over extensive areas.

The Mexican highlands are a volcanic and seismic region. In highland Mexico, great reaches of arid plateau land, fertile for maize and other crops wherever water is available, lie between heavily forested mountain slopes, which at some places rise to a perpetual snow level. The moist tropical rain forests of the coastal plains yield rich crops, when the land can be cleared. In Yucatán, a subsoil of limestone furnishes abundant material for both building and carving. This limestone tableland merges with the vast Petén region of Guatemala, which separates Mexico from Honduras. Yucatán and the Petén, where dense rain forest alternates with broad stretches of grassland, host some of the most spectacular Maya ruins. The great mountain chains of Mexico and Guatemala extend into Honduras and slope sharply down to tropical coasts. Highlands and mountain valleys, with their chill and temperate climates, alternate dramatically with the humid climate of tropical rain forest and coastlines.

LANGUAGE AND CHRONOLOGY The variegated landscape of Mesoamerica may have much to do with the diversity of languages its native populations speak. Numerous languages are distributed among no fewer than 14 linguistic families. Many of the languages spoken in the preconquest periods survive to this day. Various Mayan languages linger in Guatemala and southern Mexico. The Náhuatl of the Aztecs endures in the Mexican highlands. The Zapotec and Mixtec languages persist in Oaxaca and its environs. Diverse as the languages of these peoples were, their cultures otherwise had much in common. The Mesoamerican peoples shared maize cultivation, religious beliefs and rites, myths, social structures, customs, and arts.

Archaeologists, with ever-increasing refinement of technique, have been uncovering, describing, and classifying Mesoamerican monuments for more than a century. Since the 1950s, when linguists made important breakthroughs in deciphering the Maya hieroglyphic script, evidence for a detailed account of Maya history and art has emerged. Many Maya rulers now can be listed by name and the dates of their reigns fixed with precision. Other writing systems, such as that of the Zapotec, who began to record dates at a very early time, are less well understood, but researchers are making rapid progress in their interpretation. The general Mesoamerican chronology is now well established and widely accepted. The standard chronology, divided into three epochs, involves some overlapping of subperiods—the Preclassic (Formative) extends from 2000 BCE to about 300 CE; the Classic period runs from about 300 to 900; and the Postclassic begins ca. 900 and ends with the Spanish conquest of 1521.

Preclassic (ca. 2000 BCE–300 CE)

THE OLMEC The Olmec culture of the present-day states of Veracruz and Tabasco is often called the "mother culture" of Mesoamerica, because many distinctive Mesoamerican religious, social, and artistic traditions can be traced to it. Although little is known of Olmec origins, history, or language, the wide diffusion of Olmec institutional forms, monuments, arts, and artifacts reflects the culture's broad influence. Excavations in and around not only the principal Gulf Coast sites of Olmec culture—Tres Zapotes, San Lorenzo, and La Venta—but also in central Mexico and along the Pacific coast from the Mexican state of Guerrero to El Salvador indicate that Olmec influence was far more widespread than scholars once supposed.

Settling in the tropical lowlands of the Gulf of Mexico, the Olmec peoples cultivated a terrain of rain forest and alluvial lowland washed by numerous rivers flowing into the gulf. Here, between approximately 1500 and 400 BCE, social organization assumed the form that later Mesoamerican cultures adapted and developed. The mass of the population—food-producing farmers scattered in hinterland villages—provided the sustenance and labor

that maintained a hereditary caste of rulers, hierarchies of priests, functionaries, and artisans. The nonfarming population presumably lived, arranged by rank, within precincts that served ceremonial, administrative, and residential functions, and perhaps also as marketplaces. At regular intervals, the whole community convened for ritual observances at the religious-civic centers of towns such as San Lorenzo and La Venta. These centers were the formative architectural expressions of the structure and ideals of Olmec society.

COLOSSAL RULER PORTRAITS At La Venta, low clay-and-earthen platforms and stone fences enclosed two great courtyards. At one end of the larger area was a mound almost 100 feet high. Although now very eroded, this early pyramid, built of earth and adorned with colored clays, may have been intended to mimic a mountain, held sacred by Mesoamerican peoples as both a life-giving source of water and a feared destructive force. (Volcanic eruptions and earthquakes still wreak havoc in this region.) The La Venta layout is an early form of the temple-pyramid and plaza complex aligned on a north-south axis that characterized later Mesoamerican ceremonial center design.

Four colossal basalt heads (FIG. 8-1), weighing about 10 tons each and standing between 6 and 10 feet high, face out from the plaza. More than a dozen similar heads have been found at San Lorenzo and Tres Zapotes. Almost as much of an achievement as the carving of these huge stones with stone tools was their transportation across the 60 miles of swampland from the nearest known basalt source, the Tuxtla Mountains. Although the identities of the colossi are uncertain, their individualized features and distinctive headgear and ear ornaments, as well as the later Maya practice of carving monumental ruler portraits, suggest that the Olmec heads portray rulers rather than deities. The sheer size of the heads and their intensity of expression evoke great power, whether mortal or divine.

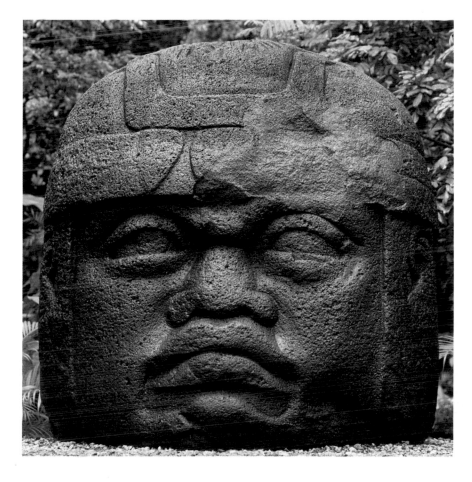

8-1 Colossal head, Olmec, La Venta, Mexico, 900–400 BCE. Basalt, 9′4″ high. Museo-Parque La Venta, Villahermosa.

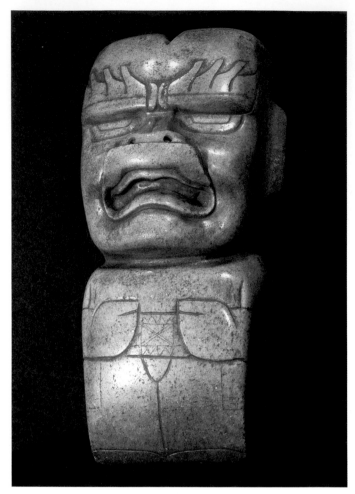

8-2 Ceremonial ax in the form of a jaguar-human, Olmec, from La Venta, Mexico, 900–400 BCE. Jadeite, 11½″ high. British Museum, London.

JADE CELTS The Olmec also carved sculptures in jade, an extremely hard dark green stone they acquired from unknown sources far from their homeland. All Mesoamerican peoples prized jade, as did the ancient Chinese (see "Chinese Jade," Chapter 3, page 43). Sometimes the Olmec carved it into ax-shaped polished forms called *celts,* which they then buried as *votive offerings* to the gods under their ceremonial courtyards or platforms. The celt shape could be modified into a figural form, combining relief carving with incising. Stone-tipped drills and abrasive materials, such as sand, were used to carve jade. Subjects represented include crying babies (of unknown significance) and figures combining human and animal features and postures (FIG. **8-2**). Although Olmec religious beliefs and practices are little known, such human-animal representations may refer to the belief that religious practitioners underwent dangerous transformations to wrest power from supernatural forces and harness it for the good of the community.

WEST MEXICAN SCULPTURE Far to the west of the tropical heartland of the Olmec are the Preclassic sites along Mexico's Pacific coast. The ancient peoples of the modern West Mexican states of Nayarit, Jalisco, and Colima were long thought to have existed at Mesoamerica's geographic and cultural fringes. Recent archaeological discoveries, however, have revealed that although the West Mexicans did not produce large-scale stone sculpture, they did build permanent structures. These included tiered platforms and ball courts (see "The Mesoamerican Ball Game," page 147), architectural features found in nearly all Mesoamerican

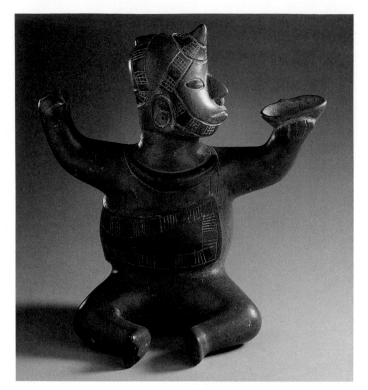

8-3 *Drinker* (seated figure with raised arms), from Colima, Mexico, ca. 200 BCE–500 CE. Clay with orange and red slip, 1′ 1″ high. Los Angeles County Museum of Art (The Proctor Stafford Collection, purchased with funds provided by Mr. and Mrs. Allan C. Balch).

cultures. Yet West Mexico is best known for its rich tradition of clay sculpture.

The sculptures come from tombs consisting of shafts as deep as 50 feet with chambers at their base. Because scientific excavations began only recently, much of what is known about West Mexican tomb contents derives primarily from the artifacts found and sold by grave robbers. Researchers believe, however, that most of these tombs were built and filled with elaborate offerings during the late Preclassic period, the half millennium before 300 CE.

The large ceramic figures found in the Colima tombs are consistently a highly burnished red orange, in contrast with the distinctive polychrome surfaces of the majority of other West Mexican ceramics. The area also is noted for small-scale clay narrative scenes that include modeled houses and temples and numerous solid figurines shown in a variety of lively activities. These sculptures, which may provide informal glimpses of daily life, are not found in any other ancient Mesoamerican culture. Although their subjects are often described as anecdotal and secular rather than religious, the Mesoamerican belief system did not recognize such a division. Consequently, scholars are unsure whether the figure we illustrate (FIG. **8-3**) is a religious practitioner with a horn on his forehead (a common indigenous symbol of special powers) or a political leader wearing a shell ornament (often a Mesoamerican emblem of rulership)—or a person serving both roles.

Teotihuacán (ca. 100 BCE–750 CE)

THE PLACE OF THE GODS At Olmec sites, the characteristic later Mesoamerican temple-pyramid-plaza layout appeared in embryonic form. At Teotihuacán (FIG. **8-4**), northeast of modern Mexico City, the Preclassic scheme underwent a monumental

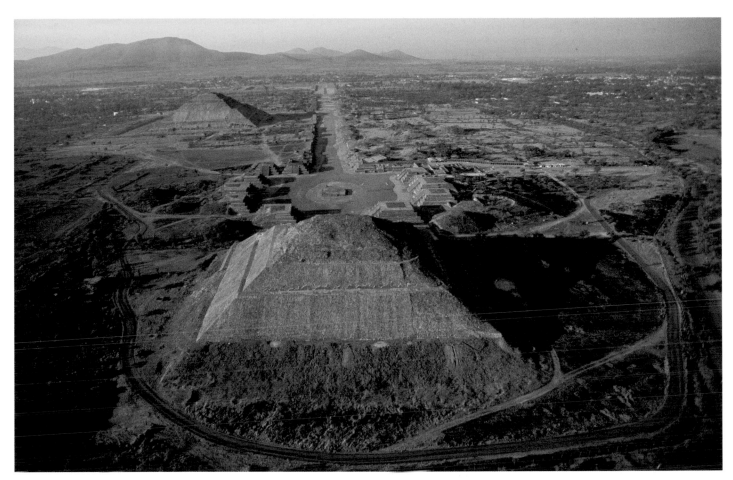

8-4 Aerial view of Teotihuacán (from the north), Valley of Mexico, Mexico. Pyramid of the Moon *(foreground)*, Pyramid of the Sun *(top left)*, and the Citadel *(background)*, all connected by the Avenue of the Dead; main structures ca. 50–200 CE; site ca. 100 BCE–750 CE.

expansion into a genuine city. Teotihuacán was a large, densely populated metropolis that fulfilled a central civic, economic, and religious role for the region and indeed for much of Mesoamerica. Built up during nearly a millennium, ca. 100 BCE to 750 CE, the site's major monuments were constructed between 50 and 250 CE, during the late Preclassic period. Teotihuacán covers nine square miles, laid out in a grid pattern with the axes oriented by sophisticated surveying. The city's orientation, as well as the placement of some of its key pyramids, also appear to have been related to astronomical phenomena.

At its peak, around 600 CE, Teotihuacán may have had as many as 125,000–200,000 residents, which would have made it the sixth largest city in the world at that time. Divided into numerous wardlike sectors, this metropolis must have had a uniquely cosmopolitan character, with Zapotec peoples located in the city's western wards, and merchants from Veracruz living in the eastern wards, importing their own pottery and building their houses and tombs in the style of their homelands. The city's urbanization did nothing to detract from its sacred nature. In fact, it vastly augmented Teotihuacán's importance as a religious center. The Aztecs, who visited Teotihuacán regularly and reverently long after it had been abandoned, gave it its current name, which means "the place of the gods." Because the city's inhabitants left only a handful of undeciphered hieroglyphs and linguists do not yet even know what language they spoke, the names of many major features of the site are unknown. The Avenue of the Dead and the Pyramids of the Sun and Moon are later Aztec designations that do not necessarily relate to the original names of these entities.

The grid plan is quartered by a north-south and an east-west axis, each four miles in length. The rational scheme is very unusual in Mesoamerica before the Aztecs. The main north-south axis, the Avenue of the Dead (FIG. 8-4), is 130 feet wide and connects the Pyramid of the Moon complex with the Citadel and its Temple of Quetzalcoatl. This two-mile stretch is not a continuously flat street but is broken by sets of stairs, giving pedestrians a constantly changing view of the surrounding buildings and landscape.

TEOTIHUACÁN'S PYRAMIDS The Pyramid of the Sun (FIG. 8-4, *top left*), facing west on the east side of the Avenue of the Dead, was erected in the first century CE during the late Preclassic period. It is the city's centerpiece and its largest structure, rising to a height of more than 200 feet. The Pyramid of the Moon (FIG. 8-4, *foreground*) was built a century or more later, ca. 150–250 CE. The shapes of the monumental structures at Teotihuacán echo the surrounding mountains. Their imposing mass and scale surpass those of all other Mesoamerican sites. Rubble-filled and faced with the local volcanic stone, the pyramids consist of stacked squared platforms diminishing in perimeter from the base to the top. Ramped stairways led to crowning temples constructed of perishable materials such as wood and thatch, no longer preserved.

The Teotihuacanos built the Pyramid of the Sun over a cave, which they reshaped and filled with ceramic offerings. The pyramid may have been constructed to honor a sacred spring within the now-dry cave. The excavators found children buried at the four corners of each of the pyramid's tiers. The later Aztec

8-5 Detail of Temple of Quetzal-coatl, the Citadel, Teotihuacán, Valley of Mexico, Mexico, third century CE.

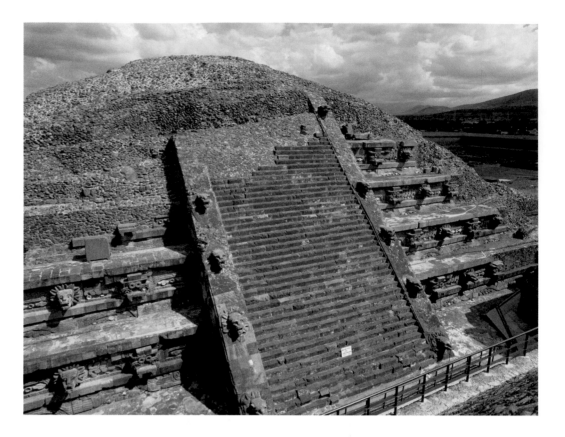

sacrificed children to bring rainfall, and Teotihuacán art abounds with references to water, so the Teotihuacanos may have shared the Aztec preoccupation with rain and agricultural fertility. The city's inhabitants rebuilt the Pyramid of the Moon (currently being excavated) at least five times in Teotihuacán's early history. It may have been positioned to mimic the shape of Cerro Gordo, the volcanic mountain behind it, undoubtedly an important source of life-sustaining streams.

THE FEATHERED SERPENT At the south end of the Avenue of the Dead is the great quadrangle of the Citadel (FIG. 8-4, *background*). It encloses a smaller pyramidal shrine datable to the third century CE, the Temple of Quetzalcoatl (FIG. **8-5**). Quetzalcoatl, the "feathered serpent," was a major god in the Mesoamerican pantheon at the time of the Spanish conquest, hundreds of years after the fall of Teotihuacán. The later Aztecs associated him with wind, rain clouds, and life. Beneath the temple, archaeologists found a tomb looted in antiquity, perhaps that of a Teotihuacán ruler. The discovery has led them to speculate that like the Maya, the Teotihuacanos also buried their elite in or under pyramids. Surrounding the tomb both beneath and around the pyramid were the remains of at least a hundred sacrificial victims. Some were adorned with necklaces made of strings of human jaws, both real and sculpted from shell. Like most other Mesoamerican groups, the Teotihuacanos invoked and appeased their gods through human sacrifice. The presence of such a large number of victims also may reflect Teotihuacán's militaristic expansion—throughout Mesoamerica, the victors often sacrificed captured warriors.

The temple's sculptured panels, which feature projecting stone heads of Quetzalcoatl alternating with heads of a long-snouted scaly creature with rings on its forehead, decorate each of the temple's six terraces. This is the first unambiguous representation of the feathered serpent in Mesoamerica. The scaly

creature's identity is unclear. Linking these alternating heads are low-relief carvings of feathered-serpent bodies and seashells. The latter reflect Teotihuacán contact with the peoples of the Mexican coasts and also symbolize water, an essential ingredient for the sustenance of an agricultural economy.

MURAL PAINTING Like those of most ancient Mesoamerican cities, Teotihuacán's buildings and streets were once stuccoed over and brightly painted. In a treatment unique to Teotihuacán during the Classic period, however, elaborate murals covered the walls of the rooms of its elite residential compounds. The paintings chiefly depict deities, ritual activities, and processions of priests, warriors, and even animals. Experimenting with a variety of surfaces, materials, and techniques over the centuries, Teotihuacán muralists finally settled on applying pigments to a smooth lime-plaster surface coated with clay. They then polished the surface to a high sheen. Although some Teotihuacán paintings have a restricted palette of varying tones of red (largely derived from the mineral hematite), creating subtle contrasts between figure and ground, most employ vivid hues arranged in flat, carefully outlined patterns. One mural (FIG. 8-6) depicts an earth or nature goddess who some scholars think was the city's principal deity. Always shown frontally with her face covered by a jade mask, she is dwarfed by her large feathered headdress and reduced to a bust placed upon a stylized pyramid. She stretches her hands out to provide liquid streams filled with bounty, but the stylized human hearts that flank the frontal bird mask in her headdress reflect her dual nature. They remind viewers that the ancient Mesoamericans saw human sacrifice as essential to agricultural renewal.

The influence of Teotihuacán was all-pervasive in Mesoamerica. Colonies were established as far away as the southern borders of Maya civilization, in the highlands of Guatemala, some 800 miles from Teotihuacán.

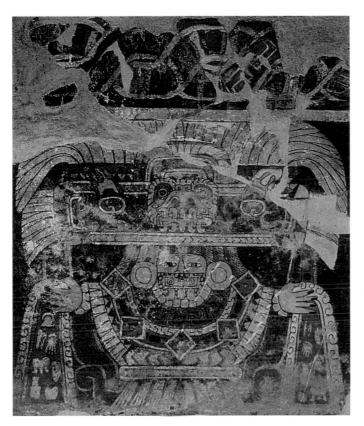

8-6 Goddess, mural painting from Tetitla apartment complex at Teotihuacán, Valley of Mexico, Mexico, 650–750 CE. Pigments over clay and plaster.

Classic (ca. 300–900 CE)

THE MAYA Strong cultural influences stemming from the Olmec tradition and from Teotihuacán contributed to the development of Classic Maya culture. As was true of Teotihuacán, the foundations of Maya civilization were laid in the Preclassic period, perhaps by 600 BCE or even earlier. At that time, the Maya, who occupied the moist lowland areas of Belize, southern Mexico, Guatemala, and Honduras, seem to have abandoned their early somewhat egalitarian pattern of village life and adopted a hierarchical autocratic society. This system evolved into the typical Maya city-state governed by hereditary rulers and ranked nobility. How and why this happened is still uncertain.

Stupendous building projects signaled the change. Vast complexes of terraced temple-pyramids, palaces, plazas, ball courts (see "The Mesoamerican Ball Game," page 147), and residences of the governing elite dotted the Maya area. Unlike the Teotihuacán civilization, no one site ever achieved complete dominance as the single center of power. The new architecture, and the art embellishing it, advertised the power of the rulers, who appropriated cosmic symbolism and stressed their descent from gods to reinforce their claims to legitimate rulership. The unified institutions of religion and kingship were established so firmly, their hold on life and custom was so tenacious, and their meaning was so fixed in the symbolism and imagery of art that the rigidly conservative system of the Classic Maya lasted almost a thousand years. Maya civilization began to decline in the eighth century. By 900, it had vanished.

Although the causes of the beginning and end of Classic Maya civilization are obscure, researchers are gradually revealing its history, beliefs, ceremonies, conventions, and patterns of daily life. Long romanticized, the Maya now enter the world history stage as believably as the peoples of other great civilizations. No longer viewed as a peaceful, benign society under theocratic rule, the Maya are now seen as flesh-and-blood peoples who glorified their rulers and oppressed the lower classes, undertook (and broke) strategic political alliances, waged war, and practiced human sacrifice. This more accurate picture is the consequence of modern interdisciplinary scholarship. Archaeologists, epigraphers (scholars who decipher writing systems), art historians, and ethnographers (those who study contemporary societies) all have contributed to a clearer understanding of ancient Maya culture.

DECODING MAYAN SCRIPT Like the decipherment of Egyptian *hieroglyphic* writing early in the 19th century, the decoding of the Mayan script has been an exciting intellectual adventure. By the end of the 19th century, numbers, dates, and some astronomical information could be read, but little else, leading scholars to conclude that the Maya were obsessed with time and religion and uninterested in recording the mundane events of human lives. Two important breakthroughs beginning in the 1950s radically altered the understanding of both Mayan writing and the Maya worldview. The first was the realization that the Maya depicted their rulers (rather than gods or anonymous priests) in their art and noted their rulers' achievements in their texts. The second was that Mayan writing is largely phonetic; that is, the hieroglyphs are made up of signs representing sounds in the Mayan language. Fortunately, the various Mayan languages were recorded in colonial texts and dictionaries, and most are still spoken today. Although perhaps only half of the ancient Mayan script can be translated accurately into spoken Mayan, today scholars can at least grasp the general meaning of many more hieroglyphs.

ASTRONOMY AND CALENDARS The Maya possessed a highly developed knowledge of arithmetic calculation and the ability to observe and record the movements of the sun, the moon, and numerous planets. They contrived an intricate but astonishingly accurate calendar, and although their calendric structuring of time was radically different in form from the Western calendar used today, it was just as precise and efficient. With their calendar, the Maya established the all-important genealogical lines of their rulers, which certified their claim to rule, and created the only true written history in ancient America. Although other ancient Mesoamerican societies, even in the Preclassic period, also possessed calendars, only the Maya calendar can be translated directly into today's calendrical system.

ARCHITECTURE AND RITUAL The most sacred and majestic buildings of Maya cities were raised in enclosed, centrally located precincts. The religious-civic transactions that guaranteed the order of the state and the cosmos occurred in these settings. The Maya held dramatic rituals within a sculptured and painted environment, where huge symbols and images proclaimed the nature and necessity of that order. Maya builders designed spacious plazas for vast audiences who were exposed to overwhelming propaganda. The programmers of that propaganda, the ruling families and troops of priests, nobles, and retainers, wore its symbolism in their costumes. In Maya paintings and sculptures, the Maya elite wear extravagant profusions of vividly colorful cotton textiles, feathers, jaguar skins, and jade, all emblematic of their rank and wealth. On the different levels of the painted and polished temple platforms, the ruling classes performed the offices of their rites in clouds of incense to the music of maracas, flutes, and drums. The Maya transformed the architectural complex at each city's center into a theater of religion and statecraft. In the stagelike layout of a characteristic Maya city

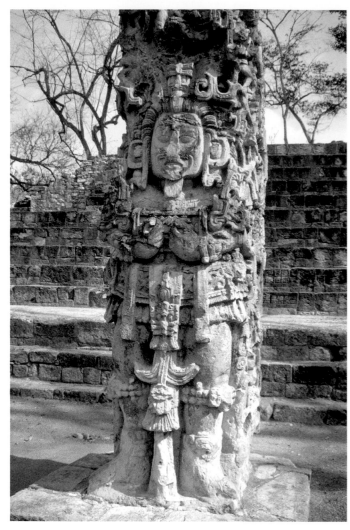

8-7 Stele D portraying the ruler 18-Rabbit, Maya, Great Plaza at Copán, Honduras, 736 CE. Stone, 11′ 9″ high.

well-preserved carved monuments than any other site in the Americas, it was one of the first Maya sites excavated. It also has proved one of the richest in the trove of architecture, sculpture, and artifacts recovered. Conspicuous plazas dominated the heart of the city. In Copán's Great Plaza, the Maya set up tall, sculpted stone *stelae*. Carved with the portraits of the rulers who erected them, these stelae also recorded their names, dates of reign, and notable achievements in glyphs on the front, sides, or back.

Stele D (FIG. 8-7), erected in 736 CE, represents one of the city's foremost rulers, Waxaklahun-Ubah-K'awil, known as 18-Rabbit (r. 695–738). In a dynastic succession of 16 rulers, 18-Rabbit was the 13th. During his long reign, Copán may have reached its greatest physical extent and range of political influence. On Stele D, 18-Rabbit wears an elaborate headdress and ornamented kilt and sandals. He holds across his chest a double-headed serpent bar, symbol of the sky and of his absolute power. His features have the quality of a portrait likeness, although highly idealized. The Maya elite tended to have themselves portrayed in a conventionalized manner and as eternally youthful. The dense, deeply carved ornamental details that frame the face and figure in florid profusion stand almost clear of the block and wrap around the sides of the stele. The high relief, originally painted, gives the impression of a freestanding statue, although a hieroglyphic text is carved on the flat back side of the stele. Although a powerful ruler who erected many stelae and buildings at Copán, including one of Mesoamerica's best-preserved (and carefully restored) ball courts (FIG. 8-8; see "The Mesoamerican Ball Game," page 147), 18-Rabbit eventually was captured and beheaded by the king of neighboring Quiriguá.

CLASSIC TIKAL Another great Maya site of the Classic period is Tikal in Guatemala, some 150 miles north of Copán. Tikal is one of the oldest and largest of the Maya cities. Together with its suburbs, Tikal originally covered some 75 square miles and served as the ceremonial center of a population of perhaps 75,000. The Maya did not lay out central Tikal on a grid plan as did the designers of contemporary Teotihuacán. Instead, causeways connected irregular groupings. Modern surveys have uncovered the remains of as many as 3,000 separate structures in an area of about six square miles. The site's nucleus, the Great Plaza, is studded with stelae and defined by numerous architectural complexes. The most prominent monuments are the two soaring

center, its principal group, or "site core," was the religious and administrative nucleus for a population of dispersed farmers settled throughout a suburban area of many square miles.

COPÁN'S PORTRAIT STELAE Because Copán, on the western border of Honduras, has more hieroglyphic inscriptions and

8-8 Ball court (view looking north), Middle Plaza, Copán, Maya, Copán Valley, Honduras, 738 CE.

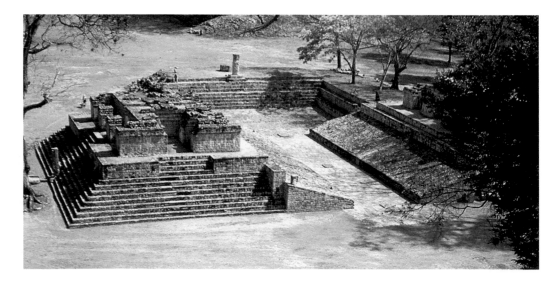

The Mesoamerican Ball Game

After witnessing the native ball game of Mexico soon after their arrival in the 16th century, the Spanish conquerors took Aztec ball players back to Europe to demonstrate the novel sport. Their chronicles remark on the athletes' great skill, the heavy wagering that accompanied the competition, and the ball itself, made of rubber, a substance the Spaniards had never seen before.

The game was played throughout Mesoamerica and into the southwestern United States, beginning at least 3,400 years ago, the date of the earliest known ball court. The Olmec were apparently avid players. Their very name—a modern invention in Nahuatl, the Aztec language—means "rubber people," after the latex-growing region they inhabited. Not only are ball players represented in Olmec art, but remnants of sunken earthen ball courts and even rubber balls have been found at Olmec sites.

The Olmec earthen playing field evolved in other Mesoamerican cultures into a plastered masonry surface, I- or T-shaped in plan, flanked by two parallel sloping or straight walls. Sometimes the walls were wide enough to support small structures on top, as at Copán (FIG. 8-8). At other sites, temples stood at either end of the ball court. These structures were common features of Mesoamerican cities. At Cantona, for example, archaeologists have uncovered 22 ball courts even though only a small portion of the site has been excavated. Teotihuacán (FIG. 8-4) is an exception. The excavators have not yet found a ball court there, but mural paintings at the site illustrate people playing the game with portable markers and sticks. Most ball courts were adjacent to the important civic structures of Mesoamerican cities, such as palaces and temple-pyramids, as at Copán.

Surprisingly little is known about the rules of the ball game itself—how many players were on the field, how goals were scored and tallied, and how competitions were arranged. Unlike a modern soccer field with its standard dimensions, Mesoamerican ball courts vary widely in size. The largest known—at Chichén Itzá—is nearly 500 feet long. Copán's is about 93 feet long. Some have stone rings, which a ball conceivably could have been tossed through, set high up on their walls at right angles to the ground, but many courts lack this feature. Alternatively, the ball may have been bounced against the walls and into the end zones. As in soccer, players could not touch the ball with their hands but used their heads, elbows, hips, and legs. They wore thick leather belts, and sometimes even helmets, and padded their knees and arms against the blows of the fast-moving solid rubber ball. Typically, the Maya portrayed ball players wearing heavy protective clothing and kneeling, poised to deflect the ball (FIG. 8-10).

Although widely enjoyed as a competitive spectator sport, the ball game did not serve solely for entertainment. The ball, for example, may have represented a celestial body such as the sun, its movements over the court imitating the sun's daily passage through the sky. Reliefs on the walls of ball courts at certain sites make clear that the game sometimes culminated in human sacrifice, probably of captives taken in battle and then forced to participate in a game they were predestined to lose.

Ball playing also had a role in Mesoamerican mythology. In the ancient Maya epic known as the *Popol Vuh (Council Book)*, first written down in Spanish in the colonial period, a legendary pair of twins is forced to play ball with the evil lords of the Underworld. The brothers lose and are sacrificed. The sons of one twin eventually travel to the Underworld and, after a series of trials including a ball game, outwit the lords and kill them. They revive their father, buried in the ball court after his earlier defeat at the hands of the Underworld gods. The younger twins rise to the heavens to become the sun and the moon, and the father becomes the god of maize, principal sustenance of all Mesoamerican peoples. The ball game and its aftermath, then, were a metaphor for the cycle of life, death, and regeneration that permeated Mesoamerican religion.

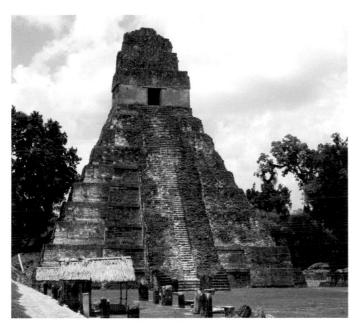

8-9 Temple I (Temple of the Giant Jaguar), Maya, Tikal, Petén, Guatemala, ca. 732 CE. 💿

pyramids, taller than the surrounding rain forest, that face each other across an open square. The larger pyramid (FIG. **8-9**), Temple I (also called the Temple of the Giant Jaguar after a motif on one of its carved wooden lintels), reaches a height of about 150 feet. It is the temple-mausoleum of a great Tikal ruler, Hasaw Chan K'awil, who died in 732 CE. His body was placed in a vaulted chamber under the pyramid's base. The towering structure is made up of nine sharply inclining platforms, probably a reference to the nine levels of the Underworld. A narrow stairway leads up to a three-chambered temple. The temple is surmounted by an elaborately sculpted *roof comb,* a vertical architectural projection that once bore the ruler's giant portrait modeled in stucco. The entire structure exhibits most concisely the ancient Mesoamerican formula for the stepped temple-pyramid and the compelling aesthetic and psychological power of Maya architecture.

JAINA CLAY SCULPTURE The almost unlimited variety of figural attitude and gesture permitted in the modeling of clay explains the profusion of Maya ceramic figurines that, like their West Mexican predecessors (FIG. 8-3), may illustrate aspects of everyday life. Small-scale sculptured figures in the round, they are remarkably lifelike, carefully descriptive, and even comic at times.

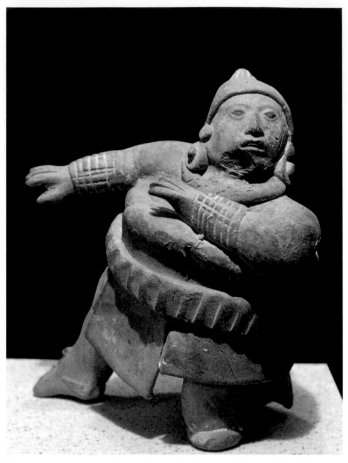

8-10 Ball player, Maya, from Jaina Island, Mexico, 700–900 CE. Painted clay, 6¼" high. National Museum of Anthropology, Mexico City. 💿

They represent a wider range of human types and activities than is commonly depicted on Maya stelae. Ball players (FIG. 8-10), women weaving, older men, dwarves, supernatural beings, and amorous couples, as well as elaborately attired rulers and warriors, make up the figurine repertory. Many of the hollow figurines are also whistles. They were made in ceramic workshops on the mainland, often with molds, but burials on the island cemetery of Jaina, off the western coast of Yucatán, yielded hundreds of such figures, including the ball player we illustrate. Traces of blue remain on the figure's belt, remnants of the vivid pigments that once covered many of these figurines. The Maya used "Maya blue," a combination of a particular kind of clay and indigo, a vegetable dye, to paint both ceramics and murals. This pigment has proven virtually indestructible, unlike the other colors that largely have disappeared over time. Like the larger terracotta figures of West Mexico, these figurines were made to accompany the dead on their inevitable voyage to the Underworld. The excavations at Jaina, however, have revealed nothing more that might clarify the meaning and function of the figures. Male figurines were not found exclusively in the burials of male individuals, for example.

HISTORY PAINTING AT BONAMPAK The vivacity of the Jaina figurines and their variety of pose, costume, and occupation were reinterpreted in two dimensions at Bonampak (Mayan for "painted walls") in southeastern Mexico. Three chambers in one Bonampak structure contain mural paintings that record important aspects of Maya court life. The example we reproduce (FIG. 8-11) shows warriors surrounding captives on a terraced platform. The figures represented have naturalistic proportions and overlap, twist, turn, and gesture. The artists used fluid and calligraphic line to outline the figures, working with color to indicate both texture and

8-11 Presentation of captives to Lord Chan Muwan, Maya, room 2, structure 1, Bonampak, Mexico, ca. 790 CE. Mural, approx. 17′ × 15′; watercolor copy by Antonio Tejeda. Peabody Museum, Harvard University, Cambridge. 💿

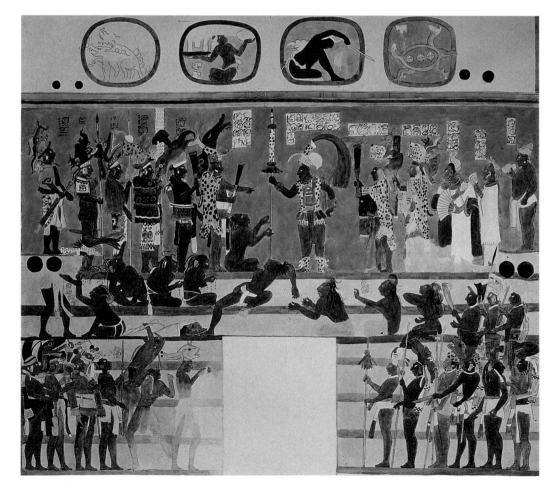

volume. The Bonampak painters combined their pigments—both mineral and organic—with a mixture of water, crushed limestone, and vegetable gums and applied them to their stucco walls in a technique best described as a cross between fresco and tempera.

The Bonampak murals are filled with circumstantial detail. The information given is comprehensive, explicit, and presented with the fidelity of an eyewitness report. The royal personages are identifiable by both their physical features and their costumes, and accompanying inscriptions provide the precise day, month, and year for the events recorded. All the scenes at Bonampak relate the events and ceremonies that welcome a new royal heir (shown as a toddler in some scenes). They include presentations, preparations for a royal fete, dancing, battle, and the taking and sacrificing of prisoners. On all occasions of state, public bloodletting was an integral part of Maya ritual. The ruler, his consort, and certain members of the nobility drew blood from their own bodies and sought union with the supernatural world. The slaughter of captives taken in war regularly accompanied this ceremony. Indeed, Mesoamerican cultures undertook warfare largely to provide victims for sacrifice. The torture and eventual execution of prisoners served both to nourish the gods and to strike fear into enemies and the general populace.

The scene in structure 1, room 2, depicts the presentation of prisoners to Lord Chan Muwan (FIG. 8-11). The painter arranged the figures in registers that may represent a pyramid's steps. On the uppermost step, against a blue background, is a file of gorgeously appareled nobles wearing animal headgear. Conspicuous among them on the right are retainers clad in jaguar pelts and jaguar headdresses. Also present is Chan Muwan's wife (third from right). The ruler himself, in jaguar jerkin and high-backed sandals, stands at the center, facing a crouching victim who appears to beg for mercy. Naked captives, anticipating death, crowd the middle level. One of them, already dead, sprawls at the ruler's feet. Others dumbly contemplate the blood dripping from their mutilated hands. The lower zone, cut through by a doorway into the structure housing the murals, shows clusters of attendants who are doubtless of inferior rank to the lords of the upper zone. The stiff formality of the victors contrasts graphically with the supple imploring attitudes and gestures of the hapless victims. The Bonampak victory was short-lived. The murals were never finished, and shortly after the dates written on the walls the site seems to have been abandoned.

SHIELD JAGUAR AND LADY XOC A rare representation in monumental art of a woman playing an important role in Maya ritual appears on the painted lintels of a temple (structure 23) at Yaxchilán. Lintel 24 (FIG. **8-12**) depicts the ruler Itzamna Balam II (r. 681–742 CE), known as Shield Jaguar, and his principal wife, Lady Xoc. Lady Xoc is magnificently outfitted in an elaborate woven garment, headdress, and jewels. She pierces her tongue with a barbed cord in a bloodletting ceremony that, according to accompanying inscriptions, celebrated the birth of a son to one of

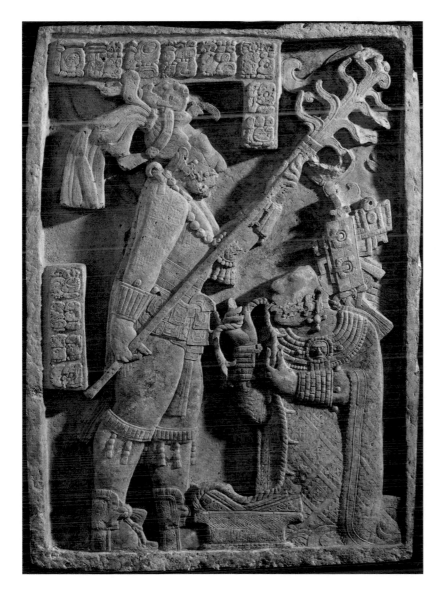

8-12 Shield Jaguar and Lady Xoc, Maya, lintel 24, temple 23, Yaxchilán, Mexico, ca. 725 CE. Limestone, 3′ 7″ × 2′ 6½″. British Museum, London.

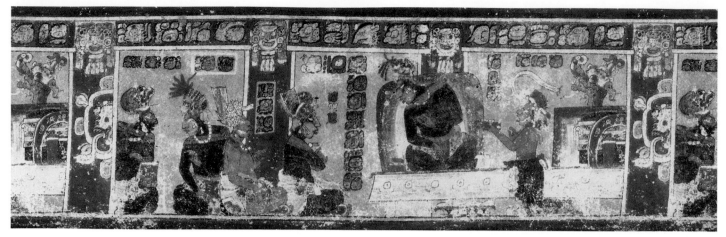

8-13 Enthroned Maya lord and courtiers, cylinder vase (rollout view), Maya, from Motul de San José region, Guatemala, 672–830 CE. Ceramic with red, rose, orange, white, and black on cream slip, approx. 8″ high. Dumbarton Oaks Research Library and Collections, Washington, D.C.

the ruler's other wives as well as an alignment between the planets Saturn and Jupiter. The celebration must have taken place in a dark chamber or at night because Shield Jaguar provides illumination with a blazing torch. These ceremonies were intended to produce hallucinations. (Lintel 25 depicts Lady Xoc and her vision of an ancestor emerging from the mouth of a serpent.)

MAYA VASE PAINTING Vivid narratives also appear on the much smaller surfaces of painted cylinder vases. A rollout view of a typical vase design (FIG. **8-13**) shows a palace scene where an enthroned lord sits surrounded by courtiers and attendants. In this scene, at once regal and intimate, the participants gesture and talk. The elaborate costumes of the Copán stele, the Bonampak paintings, and the Yaxchilán lintel are absent. Instead, the figures wear simple loincloths, turbans of wrapped cloth and feathers, and black body paint. The red frame that surrounds the scene suggests an architectural setting. The painter provided a glimpse of the event through the open doorways of a palace.

The horizontal band of hieroglyphs at the top describes the vessel and names the artist. Although this particular name has not been completely deciphered, the names of a handful of Maya vase painters, all male, are now known. Some texts even list the contents of the vessel. One pot marked with the glyph for cacao, or chocolate, still contained remnants of the prestigious drink when it was discovered. In our example, the artist may have portrayed himself among the participants. He repeats his name in one of the vertical texts, which refer to both the figures and ritual events. Some artists even recorded their parentage, clearly stating they were of noble birth and high status. Vases such as this one may have been used as drinking and food vessels for noble Maya, but their final destination was the tomb, where they accompanied the deceased to the Underworld. They likely were commissioned by the deceased before his death or by his survivors and occasionally were sent from distant sites as funerary offerings. (The Maya intermarried with other powerful families to consolidate power between important cities, and both trade and gift exchanges were common.)

Terminal Classic and Early Postclassic (ca. 800–1250 CE)

Throughout Mesoamerica, the Classic period ended at different times with the disintegration of the great civilizations. Teotihuacán's political and cultural empire, for example, was disrupted

around 600, and its influence waned. About 650 the center of the great city was destroyed by fire, but the cause is still unknown. Within a century, however, Teotihuacán was deserted. Around 900, many of the great Maya sites were abandoned to the jungle, leaving a few northern Maya cities to flourish for another century or two before they, too, became depopulated. The Classic culture of the Zapotecs, centered at Monte Albán in the state of Oaxaca, came to an end around 700, and the neighboring Mixtec peoples assumed supremacy in this area during the Postclassic period. Classic El Tajín, later heir to the Olmec in the Veracruz plain, survived the general crisis that afflicted the others but was burned sometime in the 12th century. The war and confusion that followed the collapse of the Classic civilizations broke the great states up into small, local political entities isolated in fortified sites. The collapse encouraged even more warlike regimes and chronic aggression. The militant city-state of Chichén Itzá dominated Yucatán, while in central Mexico the Toltec and the later Aztec peoples, both ambitious migrants from the north, forged empires by force of arms.

CHICHÉN ITZÁ AND THE NORTH Yucatán, a flat, low limestone peninsula covered with scrub vegetation, lies north of the rolling and densely forested region of the Guatemalan Petén. During the Classic period, Mayan-speaking peoples sparsely inhabited this northern region. For reasons that are still the subject of debate, when the southern Classic Maya sites were abandoned after 900, the northern Maya continued to build many new temples in this area. They also experimented with building construction and materials to a much greater extent than their cousins farther south. Piers and columns appeared in doorways, and stone mosaics enlivened outer facades. The northern groups also invented a new type of construction, a solid core of coarse rubble faced inside and out with a veneer of square limestone plates.

CARACOL AND CASTILLO The design of the structure known as the Caracol ("snail" in Spanish) at Chichén Itzá (FIG. **8-14**, *foreground*) suggests that the northern Maya were as inventive of architectural form as they were experimental with construction and materials. A cylindrical tower rests on a broad terrace that is in turn supported by a larger rectangular platform measuring 169 × 232 feet. The tower, composed of two concentric walls, encloses a circular staircase that leads to a small chamber near the top of the structure. In plan, the building recalls the cross-section of a conch shell. The conch shell was an attribute of the feathered serpent, and round temples were dedicated to him in central Mexico.

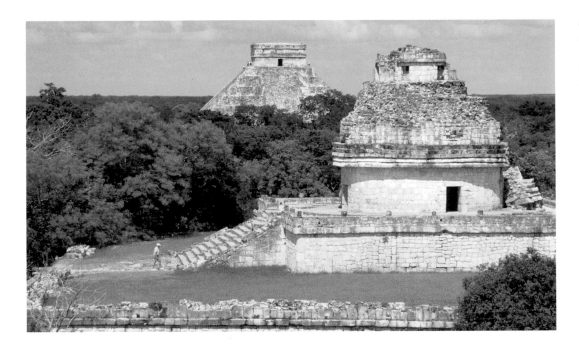

8-14 The Caracol (*foreground*) and the Castillo (*background*), Maya, Chichén Itzá, Yucatán, Mexico, ca. 800–900 CE.

This building may therefore have been a temple to Kukulkan, the Maya equivalent of Quetzalcoatl. Windows along the Caracol's staircase and an opening at the summit probably were used for astronomical observation, which has given the building another nickname—the Observatory. Noted astronomers, the Maya tracked celestial events closely, both for practical reasons, such as determining when to plant and the date of the next eclipse, and to foretell and attempt to manipulate the future.

Behind the Caracol in our photograph (FIG. 8-14) is the Castillo ("Castle"), 98 feet high and 182 feet wide at the base. The monument is a temple dedicated to Kukulkan atop a great pyramid, the signature form of sacred architecture throughout Mesoamerica. Steps on four sides of the nine-tiered pyramid converge on the temple level. Painted reliefs throughout the structure relating to the cult of Quetzalcoatl are signatures of Central Mexican influence on the northern Maya of Yucatán.

TOLTEC GUARDIANS The name *Toltec*, which signifies "makers of things," generally refers to a powerful tribe of invaders from the north, whose arrival in central Mexico coincided with the great disturbances that must have contributed to the fall of the Classic civilizations. The Toltec capital at Tula flourished from about 900 to 1200. The Toltecs were great political organizers and military strategists, dominating large parts of north and central Mexico. They also were respected both as master artisans and farmers, and later peoples such as the Aztec looked back on them admiringly, proud to claim descent from them.

At Tula, four colossal *atlantids* (male statue-columns; FIG. 8-15) portraying armed warriors reflect the grim, warlike regime of the Toltecs. These images of brutal authority stand eternally at attention, warding off all hostile threats. Built up of four stone *drums* each, the sculptures stand atop Pyramid B. They wear feathered headdresses and, as breastplates, stylized butterflies, heraldic symbols of the

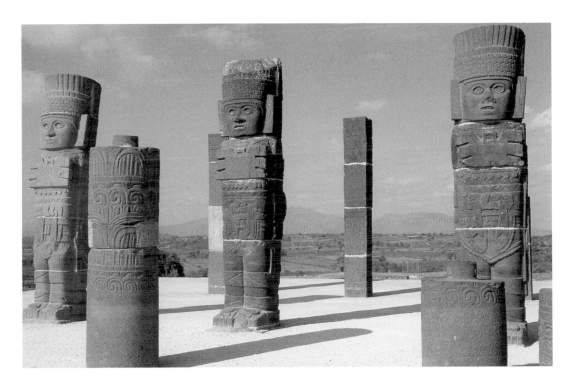

8-15 Colossal atlantids, Pyramid B, Toltec, Tula, Hidalgo, Mexico, ca. 900–1180 CE. Stone, each approx. 16′ high.

Toltec. In one hand they clutch a bundle of darts and in the other an *atlatl* (spear-thrower), typical weapons of highland Mexico. The figures originally supported a temple roof, now missing. Such an architectural function requires rigidity of pose, compactness, and strict simplicity of contour. The unity and regularity of architectural mass and silhouette here combine perfectly with abstraction of form.

By 1180, the last Toltec ruler abandoned Tula, followed by most of his people. Some years later, the city was catastrophically destroyed, its ceremonial buildings burned to their foundations, its walls thrown down, and the straggling remainder of its population scattered. The exact reasons for the Toltecs' departure and for their city's destruction are unknown. Although the stage was set for the rise of the last great civilization of Mesoamerica, the Aztecs (see Chapter 9), they did not reach the height of their power for another 300 years.

INTERMEDIATE AREA

Between the highly developed civilizations of Mesoamerica and the South American Andes (MAPS 8-2 and 8-3) lies a region archaeologists have dubbed the "Intermediate Area." Comprising parts of El Salvador, Honduras, Ecuador, and Venezuela, and all of Panama, Costa Rica, Nicaragua, and Colombia, at the time of the European invasion it was by no means a unified political territory but rather was occupied by many small rival chiefdoms. Although the people of the Intermediate Area did not produce monumental architecture on the scale of their neighbors to the north and south and, unlike the Mesoamericans, left no written records, they too were consummate artists. Potters in the Intermediate Area made some of the earliest ceramics of the Americas, and they continued to create an astonishing variety of terracotta vessels and figures until the time of the Spanish conquest. Among the other arts practiced in the Intermediate Area was stone sculpture, including large-scale figures and elaborately carved *metates* (ceremonial grinding stones, possibly used as thrones). The ancient Costa Ricans excelled at carving jade as well, particularly anthropomorphic and zoomorphic celts. Throughout the area, goldworking was prized, and the first Europeans to make contact here were astonished to see the inhabitants nearly naked but covered in gold jewelry. The legend of El Dorado, a Colombian chief who coated himself in gold as part of his accession rites, was largely responsible for the Spanish invaders' ruthless plunder of the region.

TAIRONA GOLD In northern Colombia, the Sierra Nevada de Santa Marta rises above the Caribbean. The topography of lofty mountains and river valleys allowed for considerable isolation and the independent development of various groups. Late inhabitants of this region (from about 1000 to contact with the Spanish conquerors, in the poorly documented chronology of the area) included a group known as the Tairona, whose metalwork is among the finest of all the ancient American goldworking styles.

Goldsmiths in Peru, Ecuador, and southern Colombia produced technologically advanced and aesthetically sophisticated work in gold mostly by cutting and hammering thin gold sheets. The Tairona smiths, however, who had to obtain gold by trade, used the lost-wax process in part to preserve the scarce amount of the precious metal available to them. They cast small works of the highest quality in both fabrication and design.

Tairona pendants were not meant to be worn simply as rich accessories to costume but as *amulets* or talismans representing

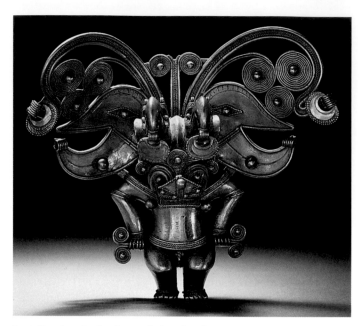

8-16 Pendant in the form of a bat-faced man, Tairona, from northeastern Colombia, after 1000 CE. Gold, $5\frac{1}{4}''$ high. Metropolitan Museum of Art, New York (Jan Mitchell and Sons Collection).

powerful beings who gave the wearer protection and status. Our example (FIG. 8-16) shows a bat-faced man—perhaps a masked man rather than a composite being, or a man in the process of spiritual transformation. In local mythology, the bat was the first animal to be created. This bat-man wears an immense headdress made up of two birds in the round, two great beaked heads, and a series of spirals crowned by two overarching stalks. The harmony of repeated curvilinear motifs, the rhythmic play of their contours, and the precise delineation of minute detail bespeak the anonymous artist's technical control and aesthetic sensitivity.

SOUTH AMERICA

As in Mesoamerica, the indigenous civilizations of Andean South America (MAP 8-3) jarred against and stimulated one another, produced towering monuments and sophisticated paintings, sculptures, ceramics, and textiles, and were exterminated in violent confrontations with the Spanish conquistadors. Although less well studied than the ancient Mesoamerican cultures, those of South America are actually older, and in some ways they surpassed the accomplishments of their northern contemporaries. Andean peoples, for example, mastered metalworking much earlier, and their monumental architecture predates that of the earliest Mesoamerican culture, the Olmec, by more than a millennium. The peoples of northern Chile even began to mummify their dead at least 500 years before the Egyptians.

GEOGRAPHY The Central Andean region of South America lies between Ecuador and northern Chile, its western border the Pacific Ocean. It consists of three well-defined geographic zones, running north and south and roughly parallel to one another. The narrow western coastal plain is a hot desert crossed by rivers, creating habitable fertile valleys. Next, the high peaks of the great Cordillera of the Andes hem in plateaus of a temperate climate. The region's inland border, the eastern slopes of the Andes, is a hot and humid jungle.

CHRONOLOGY Andean civilizations flourished both in the highlands and on the coast. Highland cave dwellers fashioned the

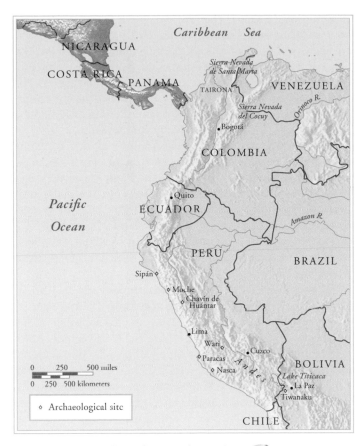

MAP 8-3 Early sites in Andean South America.

first rudimentary art objects by 8800 BCE. Sophisticated textiles started to be produced as early as 2500 BCE during the Preceramic period. The firing of clay began around 1800 BCE during the so-called Initial period. Beginning about 800 BCE, Andean chronology alternates between periods known as "horizons," when a single culture appears to have dominated a broad geographic area for a relatively long period, and "intermediate periods" characterized by more independent regional development. The first period, Early Horizon, is represented by the Chavín culture (ca. 800–200 BCE); the Middle Horizon by the Tiwanaku and Wari cultures (ca. 600–1000 CE); and the Late Horizon by the Inka Empire (see Chapter 9). Among the many regional styles that flourished between these horizons, the most important are the Early Intermediate period (ca. 200 BCE–700 CE) Paracas and Nasca cultures of the south coast of Peru, and the Moche in the north.

Early Cultures (ca. 3000–800 BCE)

The discovery of complex ancient communities documented by radiocarbon dating is changing the picture of early South American cultures. Planned communities boasting organized labor systems and monumental architecture dot the narrow river valleys that drop from the Andes to the Pacific Ocean. In the Central Andes, these early sites began to develop around 3000 BCE, about a millennium before the invention of pottery there. Carved gourds and some fragmentary cotton textiles survive from this early period. They depict composite creatures, such as crabs turning into snakes, as well as doubled and then reversed images, both hallmarks of later Andean art.

CEREMONIAL ARCHITECTURE The architecture of the early coastal sites typically consists of large U-shaped flat-topped plat-

forms—some as high as a 10-story building—around sunken courtyards. Many had numerous small chambers on top. Construction materials included both uncut fieldstones and handmade *adobes* (sun-dried mud bricks) in the shape of cones, laid point to point in coarse mud plaster to form walls and platforms. These complexes almost always faced toward the Andes mountains, source of the life giving rivers on which these communities depended for survival. Mountain worship, which continues in the Andean region to this day, was probably the focus of early religious practices as well. In the highlands, archaeologists also have discovered large ceremonial complexes. In place of the numerous interconnecting rooms found on top of many coastal mounds, the highland examples have a single small chamber at the top, often with a stone-lined firepit in the center. These pits probably played a role in ancient fire rituals. Burnt offerings, often of exotic objects such as marine shells and tropical bird feathers, have been found in the pits.

Chavín (ca. 800–200 BCE)

CHAVÍN DE HUÁNTAR Named after the ceremonial center of Chavín de Huántar, located in the northern highlands of Peru, the Chavín culture developed and spread throughout much of the coastal region and the highlands during the first millennium BCE. Once thought to be the "mother culture" of the Andean region, the Chavín horizon style is now seen as the culmination of developments that began some 2,000 years earlier elsewhere.

The main temple of Chavín de Huántar (FIG. 8-17) resembles some sacred complexes of the Preceramic and Initial periods. It is a U-shaped, stone-faced structure facing east between two rivers. Although at first glance its three stories appear to be a solid stepped platform, in fact a labyrinth of narrow passageways, small chambers, and stairways penetrate the temple. No windows, however, light the interior spaces. The few members of Chavín society with access to these rooms must have witnessed secret and sacred torch-lit ceremonies. The temple is fronted by sunken courts, an arrangement also adopted from earlier coastal sites. Modifications to the structure during the centuries have resulted in the asymmetrical shape seen today.

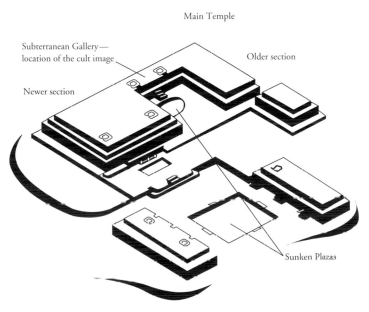

8-17 Reconstructed drawing of sacred center showing temple and associated sunken courtyards, Chavín de Huántar, Peru, first millennium BCE.

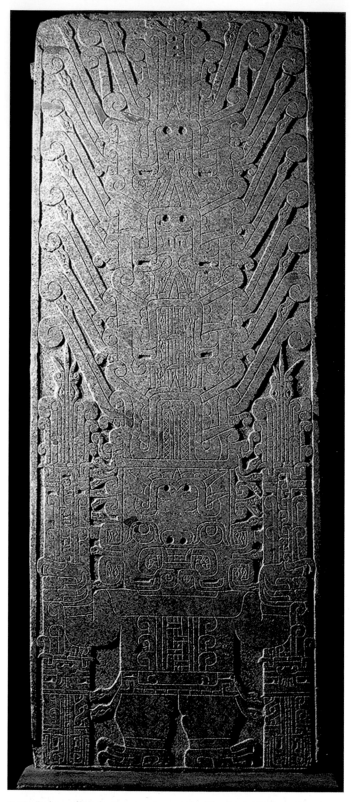

8-18 *Raimondi Stele,* from main temple, Chavín de Huántar, Peru, first millennium BCE. Incised green diorite, 6′ high. Instituto Nacional de Cultura, Lima.

The temple complex at Chavín de Huántar is famous for its extensive stone carvings. The most common subjects are composite creatures that combine feline, avian, reptilian, and human features. Consisting largely of low relief on panels, cornices, and columns, and some rarer instances of freestanding sculpture, Chavín carving is essentially shallow, linear incision. An immense oracular cult image stood in the center of the temple's oldest part. Other examples of sculpture in the round include heads of mythological creatures *tenoned* (attached by stone pegs) into the exterior walls.

A REVERSIBLE GOD The *Raimondi Stele* (FIG. **8-18**), named after its discoverer, represents a figure called the "staff god." He appears in various versions from Colombia to northern Bolivia but always holds staffs. Seldom, however, do the representations have the degree of elaboration found at Chavín. The Chavín god bares his teeth and gazes upward. His elaborate headdress dominates the upper two-thirds of the slab. Inverting the image reveals that the headdress is composed of a series of fanged jawless faces, each emerging from the mouth of the one above it. Snakes abound. They extend from the deity's belt, make up part of the staffs, serve as whiskers and hair for the deity and the headdress creatures, and form a braid at the apex of the composition. The *Raimondi Stele* clearly illustrates the Andean artistic tendency toward both multiplicity and dual readings. Upside down, the god's face turns into not one but two faces. The ability of gods to transform before the viewer's eyes is a core aspect of Andean religion.

Chavín iconography spread widely throughout the Andean region through portable media such as goldwork, textiles, and ceramics. For example, more than 300 miles from Chavín on the south coast of Peru, archaeologists have discovered cotton textiles with imagery recalling Chavín sculpture. Painted staff-bearing female deities, apparently local manifestations or consorts of the highland staff god, decorate these large cloths, which may have served as wall hangings in temples. Ceramic vessels found on the north coast of Peru also carry motifs much like those found on Chavín stone carvings.

Paracas (ca. 400 BCE–200 CE)

Several coastal traditions developed during the period between about 500 BCE and 600 CE. Together they exemplify the great variations within Peruvian art styles. The Paracas culture, which lasted about six centuries (ca. 400 BCE–200 CE), occupied a desert peninsula and a nearby river valley on the south coast of Peru.

FUNERARY MANTLES Outstanding among the Paracas arts are the funerary textiles used to wrap the bodies of the dead in multiple layers. The dry desert climate preserved the textiles, buried in shaft tombs beneath the sands. These textiles are among the enduring masterpieces of Andean art (see "Andean Weaving," page 155). Most are of woven cotton with designs embroidered onto the fabric in alpaca or vicuña wool imported from the highlands. The weavers used more than 150 vivid colors, the majority derived from plants.

Feline, bird, and serpent motifs appear on many of the textiles, but the human figure, real or mythological, predominates. A common theme on the grave mantles is humans dressed up as or changing into animals—consistent with the Andean transformation theme noted on the *Raimondi Stele* (FIG. **8-18**). On the example we illustrate (FIG. **8-19**) is a figure with prominent eyes, who appears scores of times over the surface. The flowing hair and the slow kicking motion of the legs suggest airy, hovering movement. The flying or floating being carries what some have identified as batons and fans and others as knives and hallucinogenic mushrooms. On other mantles the figures carry the skulls or severed heads of enemies. Some scholars have interpreted the flying figures as Paracas religious practitioners dancing or flying during an ecstatic trance. Others believe they are images of the deceased. Despite endless repetitions of the figure, variations of detail occur throughout each textile, notably in the figures' positions and in subtle color changes.

Andean Weaving

When the Inka first encountered the Spanish conquistadors, they were puzzled by the Europeans' fixation on gold and silver. The Americans valued finely woven cloth just as highly as precious metal. Textiles and clothing dominated every aspect of their existence. Storing textiles in great warehouses, their leaders demanded cloth as tribute, gave it as gifts, exchanged it during diplomatic negotiations, and even burned it as a sacrificial offering. Although both men and women participated in cloth production, the Inka rulers selected the best women weavers from around the empire and sequestered them for life to produce textiles exclusively for the rulers.

The Andean weavers manufactured their textiles by spinning into yarn the cotton grown in five different shades on the warm coast and the fur sheared from highland llamas, alpacas, vicuñas, or guanacos, and then weaving the yarn into cloth. Rare tropical bird feathers and small plaques of gold and silver were sometimes sewn onto cloth destined for the nobility. Andean weavers mastered nearly every textile technique known today, many executed with a simple device known as a *backstrap loom*. Such looms are still in use in the Andes. The weavers stretch the long *warp* (vertical) threads between two wooden bars. The top one is tied to an upright. A belt or backstrap, attached to the bottom bar, encircles the waist of the seated weaver, who maintains the tension of the warp threads by leaning back. The weaver passes the *weft* (horizontal) threads over and under the warps and pushes them tightly against each other to produce the finished cloth. In ancient textiles, the sturdy cotton often formed the warp, and the wool, which can be dyed brighter colors, served to create complex designs in the weft. *Embroidery,* the sewing of threads onto a finished ground cloth to form contrasting designs, was the specialty of the Paracas culture (FIG. 8-19).

The dry deserts of coastal Peru have preserved not only numerous textiles from different periods but also hundreds of finely worked baskets containing spinning and weaving implements. These tools are invaluable sources of information about Andean textile production processes. The baskets found in documented contexts came from women's graves, attesting to the close identity between weaving and women, the reverence for the cloth-making process, and the Andean belief that textiles were necessary in the afterlife.

A special problem all weavers confront is that they must visualize the entire design in advance and cannot easily change it during the weaving process. No records exist of how Andean weavers learned, retained, and passed on the elaborate patterns they wove into cloth, but some painted ceramics depict weavers at work, apparently copying designs from finished models. However, the inventiveness of individual weavers is evident in the endless variety of colors and patterns in surviving Andean textiles. This creativity often led Andean artists to design textiles that are highly abstract and geometric. Paracas embroideries (FIG. 8-19), for example, may depict humans, down to the patterns on the tunics they wear, yet the figures are reduced to their essentials in order to focus on their otherworldly role. The culmination of this tendency toward abstraction may be seen in the Wari compositions (FIG. 8-25) in which figural motifs become stunning blocks of color that overwhelm the subject matter itself.

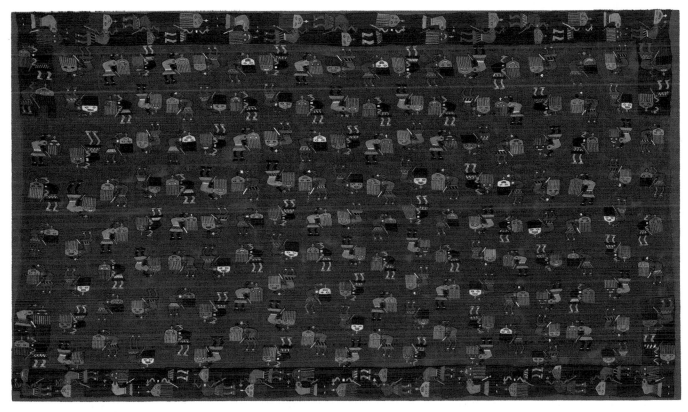

8-19 Embroidered funerary mantle, Paracas, from southern coast of Peru, first century CE. Plain weave camelid fiber with stem-stitch embroidery of camelid wool, 4′ 7$\frac{7}{8}$″ × 7′ 10$\frac{7}{8}$″. Museum of Fine Arts, Boston (William A. Paine Fund).

Nasca (ca. 200 BCE–600 CE)

NASCA PAINTED POTTERY The Nasca culture takes its name from the Nasca River Valley south of Paracas. The early centuries of the Nasca civilization are contemporary with the closing centuries of the Paracas culture, and Nasca style followed closely the Paracas flowing line and strong emphasis on color. The Nasca were renowned for their pottery. Thousands of their ceramic vessels survive. The vases usually have round bottoms, double spouts connected by bridges, and smoothly burnished polychrome surfaces. The subjects vary greatly, but plants, animals, and composite mythological creatures, partly human and partly animal, are most common. Nasca painters often represented ritual impersonators, some of whom, like the Paracas flying figures, hold trophy heads and weapons. In the example we illustrate (FIG. **8-20**), two such costumed figures fly around the vessel. The painter reduced their bodies and limbs to abstract appendages and focused on the heads. The figures wear a multicolored necklace, a whiskered gold mouthpiece, circular disks hanging from the ears, and a rayed crown on the forehead. Masks or heads with streaming hair, possibly more trophy heads, flow over the impersonators' backs, increasing the sense of motion.

EARTH DRAWINGS Nasca artists also depicted figures on a gigantic scale. Some 800 miles of lines drawn in complex networks on the dry surface of the Nasca Plain have long attracted world attention because of their colossal size, which defies human perception from the ground. Preserved today on the Nasca Plain are about three dozen images of birds, fish, and plants. Our illustration (FIG. **8-21**) shows a hummingbird several hundred feet long. The Nasca artists also drew geometric forms, such as trapezoids, spirals, and straight lines running for miles.

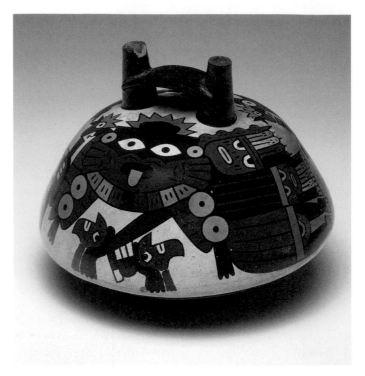

8-20 Bridge-spouted vessel with flying figures, Nasca, from Nasca River valley, Peru, ca. 50–200 CE. Painted ceramic, approx. $5\frac{1}{2}''$ high. Art Institute of Chicago, Chicago (Kate S. Buckingham Endowment).

These Nasca Lines, as the immense earth drawings are called, were produced when the artists selectively removed the dark top layer of stones to expose the light clay and calcite below. The lines were constructed quite easily from available materials and with

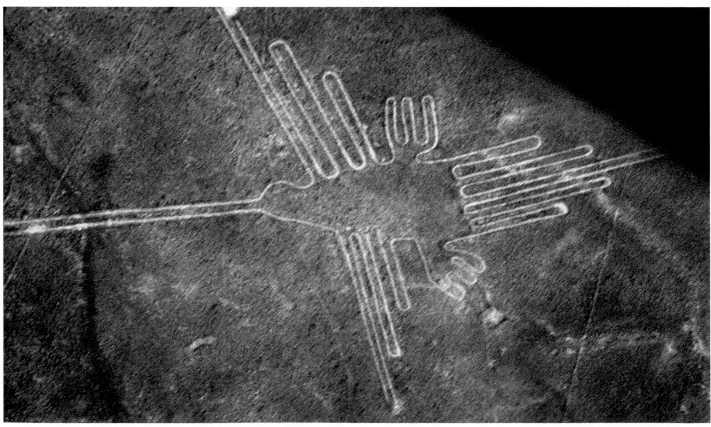

8-21 Hummingbird, Nasca Plain, Nasca, Peru, ca. 500 CE. Dark layer of pebbles scraped aside to reveal lighter clay and calcite beneath.

some rudimentary geometry. Small groups of workers have made modern reproductions of them with relative ease. The lines seem to be paths laid out using simple stone-and-string methods. Some lead in traceable directions across the deserts of the Nasca River drainage. Others are punctuated by many shrinelike nodes, like the knots on a cord. Some lines converge at central places usually situated close to water sources and seem to be associated with water supply and irrigation. They may have marked pilgrimage routes for those who journeyed to local or regional shrines on foot. Altogether, the vast arrangement of the Nasca Lines is a system—not a meaningless maze but a traversable map that plotted out the whole terrain of Nasca material and spiritual concerns. Remarkably, until quite recently similar ritual pathways were made and used in association with shrines in highland Bolivia, demonstrating the tenacity of the Andean indigenous belief systems.

Moche (ca. 1–700 CE)

MOCHE CERAMICS Among the most famous art objects the ancient Peruvians produced are the painted clay vessels of the Moche, who occupied a series of river valleys on the north coast of Peru around the same time the Nasca flourished to the south. Among ancient civilizations, only the Greeks and the Maya surpassed the Moche in the information recorded on their ceramics.

Moche pots illustrate architecture, metallurgy, weaving, the brewing of *chicha* (fermented maize beer), human deformities and diseases, and even sexual acts. Moche vessels are predominantly flat-bottomed stirrup-spouted jars derived from Chavín prototypes. They are generally decorated with a bichrome (two-color) slip. Although the Moche made early vessels by hand without the aid of a potter's wheel, they fashioned later ones in two-piece molds. Thus, numerous near-duplicates survive. Moche potters continued to refine the stirrup spout, making it an elegant slender tube, much narrower than the Chavín examples. This refinement may be seen in the portrait vessel illustrated here (FIG. **8-22**), an elaborate example of a common Moche type. It may depict the face of a warrior, a ruler, or even a royal retainer whose image may have been buried with many other pots to accompany his dead master. The realistic rendering of the physiognomy is particularly striking.

THE LORD OF SIPÁN Elite men, along with retinues of sacrificial victims, appear to be the occupants of several rich Moche tombs excavated near the village of Sipán on the arid northwest coast of Peru. The Sipán burials have yielded a treasure of golden artifacts and more than a thousand ceramic vessels. The discovery of the tombs in the late 1980s made a great stir in the archaeological world, contributing significantly to the knowledge of Moche culture. Beneath a large adobe platform adjacent to two high but greatly eroded pyramids, excavators found several lavish burials, including the tomb of a man known today as the Lord of Sipán or the Warrior Priest. The splendor of the funeral trappings that adorned his body, the quantity and quality of the sumptuous accessories, and the bodies of the retainers buried with him indicate that he was a personage of the highest rank. Indeed, he may have been one of the warrior priests so often pictured on Moche ceramic wares and murals (and in this tomb on a golden pyramid-shaped rattle) assaulting his enemies and participating in sacrificial ceremonies.

An ear ornament (FIG. **8-23**) of turquoise and gold found in one Sipán tomb shows a warrior priest clad much like the Lord of Sipán. Two retainers appear in profile to the left and right of the

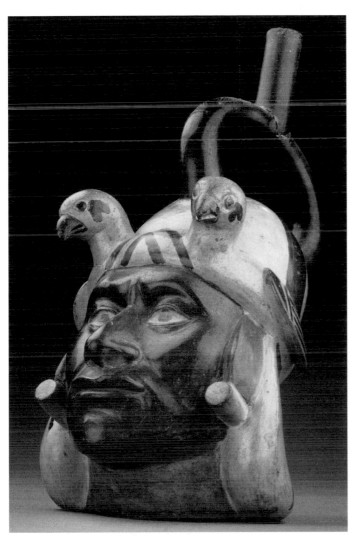

8-22 Vessel in the shape of a portrait head, Moche, from north coast Peru, fifth to sixth century CE. Painted clay, $1'\frac{1}{2}''$ high. Museu Arqueológico Rafael Larco Herrera, Lima.

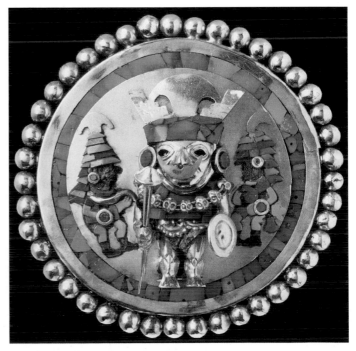

8-23 Ear ornament, from a tomb at Sipán, Moche, Peru, ca. 300 CE. Gold and turquoise, approx. $4\frac{4}{5}''$ diameter. Bruning Archaeological Museum, Lambayeque.

central figure. Represented frontally, he carries a war club and shield and wears a necklace of owl-head beads. The figure's blade-like crescent-shaped helmet is a replica of the large golden one buried with the Sipán lord. The war club and shield also match finds in the Warrior Priest's tomb. The ear ornament of the jewelry image is a simplified version of the piece itself. Other details also correspond to actual finds—for example, the removable nose ring that hangs down over the mouth. The value of the Sipán find is incalculable for what it reveals about elite Moche culture and for its confirmation of the accuracy of the iconography of Moche artworks.

Tiwanaku (ca. 100–1000 CE)

The bleak highland country of southeastern Peru and southwestern Bolivia contrasts markedly with the warm valleys of the coast. In the mountains, another culture developed beginning in the second century CE. Named Tiwanaku after its principal archaeological site on the southern shore of Lake Titicaca, the culture flourished for nearly a millennium, spreading to the adjacent coastal area as well as to other highland areas, eventually extending from southern Peru to northern Chile.

THE GATEWAY OF THE SUN Tiwanaku was an important ceremonial center. Its inhabitants constructed grand buildings using the region's fine sandstone, andesite, and diorite. Tiwanaku's imposing Gateway of the Sun (FIG. **8-24**) is a huge monolithic block of andesite pierced by a single doorway. Moved in ancient times from its original location within the site, the gateway now forms part of an enormous walled platform. The gate is crowned with relief sculpture. The central figure is a Tiwanaku version of the Chavín staff god (FIG. 8-18). Larger than all the other figures and presented frontally, he dominates the composition and presides over the passageway. Rays project from his head. Many terminate in puma heads, representing the power of the highlands' fiercest predator. The staff god—possibly a sky and weather deity rather than the sun deity the rayed head suggests—appears in art throughout the Tiwanaku horizon, associated with smaller attendant figures. Those of the Gateway of the Sun are winged and have human or condor heads. Like the puma, the condor is an impressive carnivore, the largest raptor in the world. Sky and earth beings thus converge on the gate, which probably served as the doorway to a sacred area, a place of transformation. The reliefs were once colorfully painted. The figures' eyes were apparently also inlaid with turquoise, and the surfaces covered with gold, producing a dazzling effect.

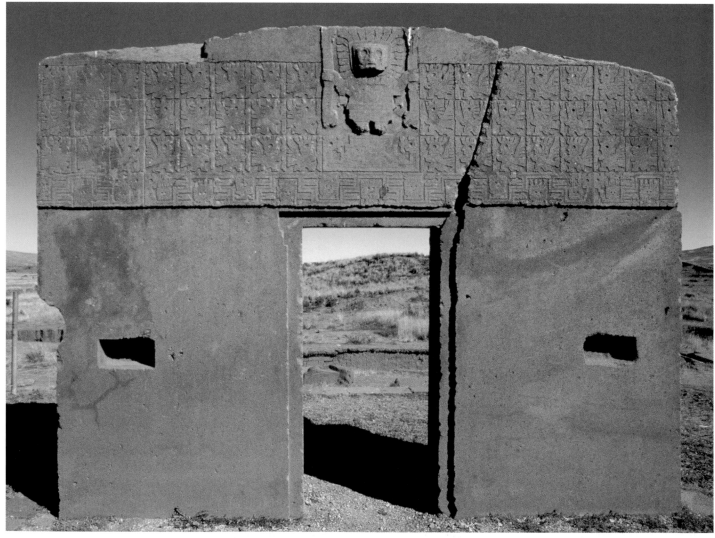

8-24 Gateway of the Sun, Tiwanaku, Bolivia, ca. 375–700 CE. Stone, 9′ 10″ high.

Wari (ca. 500–800 CE)

The flat, abstract, and repetitive figures surrounding the central figure on the Gateway of the Sun recall woven textile designs. Indeed, the people of the Tiwanaku culture, like those of Paracas, were consummate weavers, although many fewer textiles survive from the damp highlands. However, from a contemporaneous Peruvian culture known as Wari, which dominated parts of the dry coast, many examples of weaving, especially tunics, have been recovered.

ABSTRACTION IN TAPESTRY Although Wari weavers fashioned cloth, like the earlier Paracas textiles (FIG. 8-19), from both wool and cotton fibers, the resemblance between the two textile styles ends there. Whereas Paracas motifs were embroidered onto the plain woven surface, Wari designs were woven directly into the fabric, the weft threads packed densely over the warp threads in a technique known as *tapestry*. Some particularly fine pieces have more than 200 weft threads per inch. Furthermore, unlike the relatively naturalistic individual figures depicted on Paracas mantles, those appearing on Wari textiles are so closely connected and so abstract as to be nearly unrecognizable. In the tunic shown here, the so-called *Lima*

Tapestry (FIG. **8-25**), the Wari designer expanded or compressed each figure in a different way and placed them in vertical rows pressed between narrow red bands of plain cloth. Elegant tunics such as this must have been prestige garments made for the elite.

NORTH AMERICA

REGIONS AND PEOPLES In many parts of the United States and Canada, indigenous cultures have been discovered that reach back as far as 12,000 years ago. Most of the surviving art objects, however, come from the past 2,000 years. Scholars divide the vast and varied territory of North America (MAP **8-4**) into cultural regions based on the relative homogeneity of language and social and artistic patterns. Native lifestyles varied widely over the continent, ranging from small bands of migratory hunters to settled—at times even urban—agriculturalists. Among the art-producing peoples who inhabited the continent before the arrival of Europeans are the Eskimos of Alaska and the Inuits of Canada, who hunted and fished across the Arctic from Greenland to Siberia, and the maize farmers of the American Southwest, who wrested water from their arid

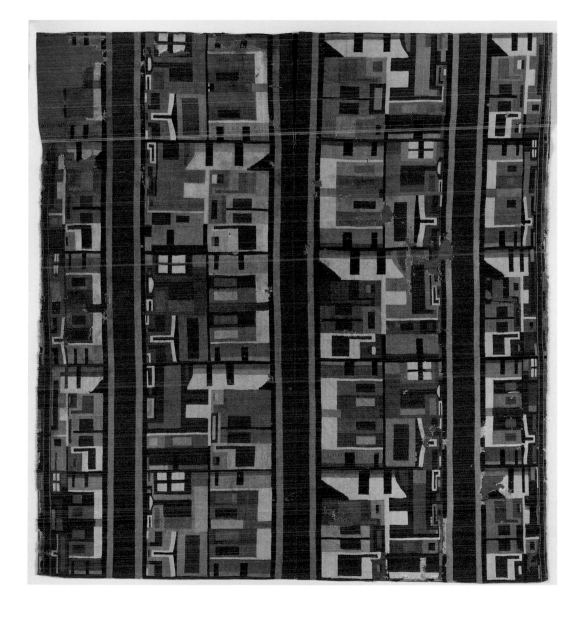

8-25 *Lima Tapestry* (tunic), Wari, from Peru, ca. 500–800 CE. 3′ 3⅜″ × 2′ 11⅜″. National Museum of Archaeology, Anthropology, and History of Peru, Lima.

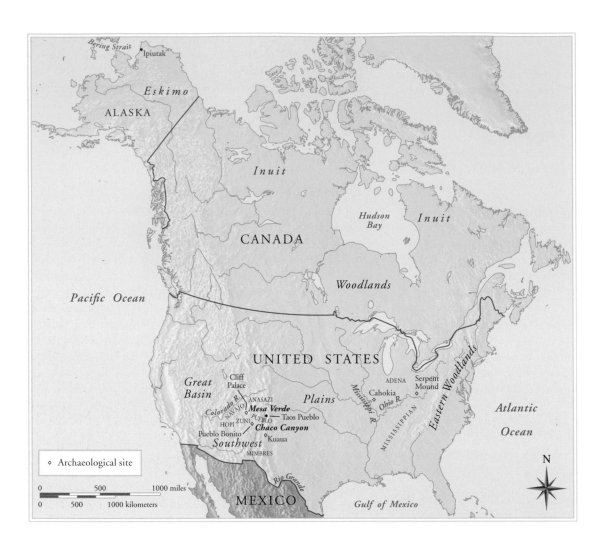

MAP 8-4 Early Native American sites in North America.

environment and built effective irrigation systems as well as roads and spectacular cliff dwellings. The vast, temperate Eastern Woodlands—ranging from eastern Canada to Florida and from the Atlantic to the Great Plains west of the Mississippi—also were home to farmers. Some of them left behind great earthen mounds that once functioned as their elite residences or burial places.

Eskimo

A MASK OF SEVERAL FACES The Eskimoan peoples originally migrated to North America across the Bering Strait. During the early first millennium CE, a community of Eskimo sea mammal hunters and tool makers occupied the Ipiutak site at Point Hope in Alaska during the Norton, or Old Bering Sea, culture that began around 500 BCE. Finds from the site include a variety of burial goods as well as tools. Of special interest is a burial mask (FIG. **8-26**) datable to ca. 100 CE, fashioned, like most Arctic artworks, out of walrus ivory because of the scarcity of wood in the region. The mask is composed of nine carefully shaped parts that are interrelated to produce several faces, both human and animal, echoing the transformation theme noted in other ancient American cultures. The confident, subtle composition in shallow relief is a tribute to the artist's imaginative control over the material. The mask's abstract circles and curved lines are common motifs on the decorated tools discovered at Point Hope. For centuries, the Eskimo also carved human and animal figures, always at small scale, reflecting a nomadic lifestyle that required the creation of portable objects.

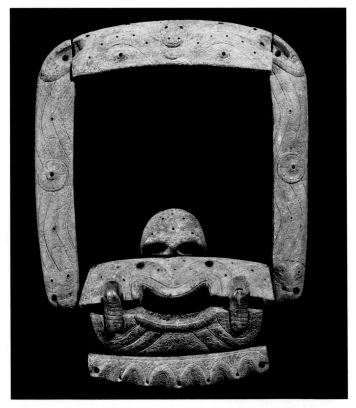

8-26 Burial mask, Ipiutak, from Point Hope, Alaska, ca. 100 CE. Ivory, greatest width $9\frac{1}{2}''$. American Museum of Natural History, New York.

Woodlands

ADENA PIPES Early Native American artists also excelled in working stone into a variety of utilitarian and ceremonial objects. A pipe in the shape of a man (FIG. **8-27**) is a product of the Adena culture of Ohio, documented at about 500 sites in the Central Woodlands. Carved between 500 BCE and the end of the millennium, the pipe is related in form and costume (note the prominent ear spools) to some Mesoamerican sculptures. The Adena buried their elite in great earthen mounds and often placed ceremonial pipes such as this one in the graves. Smoking was an important social and religious ritual in many Native American cultures, and pipes were treasured status symbols that men wanted to take with them into the afterlife. The standing figure on the illustrated pipe has naturalistic joint articulations and musculature, a lively flexed-leg pose, and an alert facial expression—all combining to suggest movement.

MISSISSIPPIAN MOUNDS The Adena were the first great mound builders of North America, but the Mississippian culture, which emerged around 800 CE and eventually encompassed much of the eastern United States, surpassed all earlier Woodlands peoples in the size and complexity of their communities. One Mississippian mound site, Cahokia in southern Illinois, was the largest city in North America in the early second millennium CE, with a population of at least 20,000 and an area of more than six square miles. There were approximately 120 mounds at Cahokia. The grandest, 100 feet tall and built in stages between ca. 900 and 1200 CE, was Monk's Mound. It is aligned with the position of the sun at the equinoxes and may have served as an astronomical observatory as well as the site of agricultural ceremonies. Each stage was topped by wooden structures that then were destroyed in preparation for the building of a new layer.

The Mississippians also constructed *effigy mounds* (mounds built in the form of animals or birds). One of the best preserved is Serpent Mound (FIG. **8-28**), a twisting earthwork on a bluff overlooking a creek in Ohio. It measures nearly a quarter mile

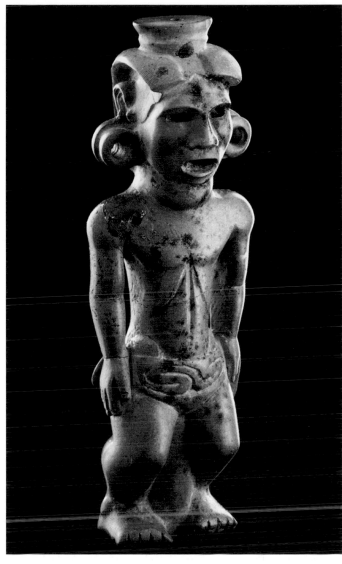

8-27 Pipe, Adena, from a mound in Ohio, ca. 500–1 BCE. Stone, 8″ high. Ohio Historical Society, Columbus.

8-28 Serpent Mound, Mississippian, Ohio, ca. 1070 CE. 1200′ long, 20′ wide, 5′ high.

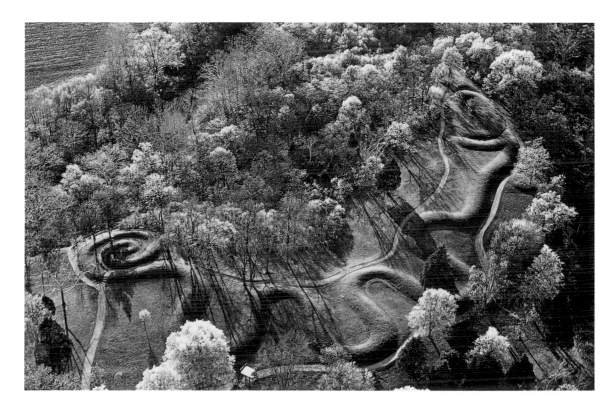

Serpent Mound

Serpent Mound (FIG. 8-28) is one of the largest and best known of the Woodlands effigy mounds, but it is the subject of considerable controversy. The mound was first excavated in the 1880s and represents one of the first efforts at preserving a Native American site from destruction at the hands of pot hunters and farmers. For a long time after its exploration, archaeologists attributed its construction to the Adena culture, which flourished in the Ohio area during the last several centuries BCE. New radiocarbon dates taken from the mound, however, indicate that it was built much later by the people known as Mississippians. Unlike most other ancient mounds, Serpent Mound contained no evidence of burials or temples. Serpents, however, were important in Mississippian iconography, appearing, for example, etched on shell gorgets similar to the one illustrated in FIG. 8-29. Snakes were strongly associated with the earth and the fertility of crops.

A stone figurine found at one site, for example, depicts a woman digging her hoe into the back of a large serpentine creature whose tail turns into a vine of gourds.

Another possible meaning for the construction of Serpent Mound, however, has been proposed recently. The new date suggested for it is 1070, not long after the brightest appearance in recorded history of Halley's Comet in 1066. Could Serpent Mound have been built in response to this important astronomical event? It even has been suggested that the serpentine form of the mound replicates the comet itself streaking across the night sky. Whatever its meaning, such a large and elaborate earthwork only could have been built by a large labor force under the firm direction of a powerful elite eager to leave its mark on the landscape forever.

from its open jaw (at the top right in our photograph), which seems to clasp an oval-shaped mound in its mouth, to its tightly coiled tail (at the far left). Both its date and meaning are controversial (see "Serpent Mound," above).

MISSISSIPPIAN GORGETS The Mississippian peoples, like their predecessors in North America, also manufactured small portable art objects. The shell *gorget*, or neck pendant, was a favorite item. Our example (FIG. **8-29**) was found at a site in Tennessee and dates from ca. 1250 to 1300 CE. The incised

gorget depicts a running warrior, shown in the same kind of bent-arms-and-legs configuration used to suggest motion in other ancient cultures (compare, for example, FIG. 10-1). The Tennessee warrior wears an elaborate headdress incorporating an arrow. He carries a mace in his left hand and a severed human head in his right. On his face is the painted forked eye of a falcon. Most Mississippian gorgets come from burial and temple mounds and are thought to have been gifts to the dead to ensure their safe arrival and prosperity in the land of the spirits. Other art objects found in such contexts include fine mica cutouts and

8-29 Incised shell gorget, Mississippian, from Sumner County, Tennessee, ca. 1250–1300 CE. 4″ wide. National Museum of the American Indian, Smithsonian Institution, Washington, D.C.

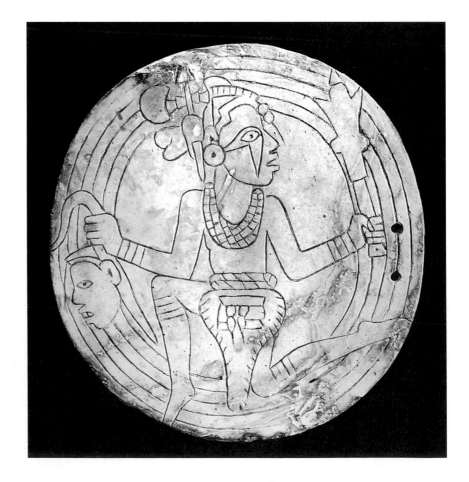

embossed copper cutouts of hands, bodies, snakes, birds, and other presumably symbolic forms.

Southwest

MIMBRES POTTERY In the Southwest, Native Americans have been producing pottery since before the beginning of the Common Era. The most impressive examples of decorated pottery, however, date after 1000 CE. The Mimbres culture of southwestern New Mexico, which flourished between ca. 1000 and 1250 CE, is renowned for its black-on-white painted bowls. The one we illustrate (FIG. **8-30**) dates to ca. 1250 and features an animated graphic rendering of two black cranes on a white ground. The contrast between the bowl's abstract border designs and the birds creates a dynamic tension. Thousands of different compositions are known from Mimbres pottery. They range from lively and complex geometric patterns to abstract pictures of humans, animals, and composite mythological beings. Almost all are imaginative creations by artists who seem to have been bent on not repeating themselves. Their designs emphasize linear rhythms balanced and controlled within a clearly defined border. Because the potter's wheel was unknown in the Americas, the artists used the coiling method to build countless sophisticated shapes of varied size, always characterized by technical excellence. Although historians have no direct knowledge about the potters' identities, the fact that pottery making was usually women's work in the Southwest during the historic period (see "Gender Roles in Native American Art," Chapter 9, page 177) suggests that the Mimbres potters also may have been women.

Mimbres bowls have been found in burials under house floors, inverted over the head of the deceased and ritually "killed" by puncturing a small hole at the base, perhaps to allow the spirits of the deceased to join their ancestors in the sky (viewed as a dome by contemporary Southwestern peoples).

ANASAZI PUEBLOS The Anasazi (Navajo for "enemy ancestors"), northern neighbors of the Mimbres, emerged as an identifiable culture around 200 CE, but the culture did not reach its peak until about 1000. The Anasazi constructed architectural complexes that reflect masterful building skills. Many ruined Anasazi *pueblos* (urban settlements) are scattered throughout the Southwest. In Chaco Canyon, New Mexico, the Anasazi built a great semicircle of 800 rooms reaching to five stepped-back stories, the largest of several such sites in and around the canyon. Chaco Canyon was the center of a wide trade network extending as far as Mexico.

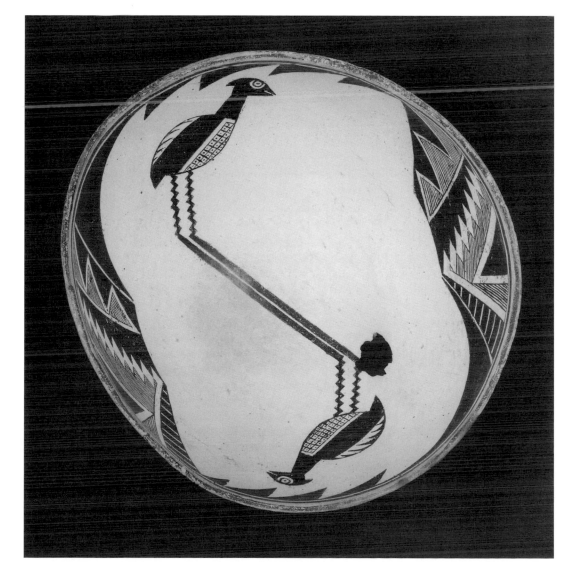

8-30 Bowl with two cranes and geometric forms, Mimbres, from New Mexico, ca. 1250 CE. Ceramic, black-on-white, approx. 1′ $\frac{1}{2}$″ diameter. Art Institute of Chicago, Chicago (Hugh L. and Mary T. Adams Fund).

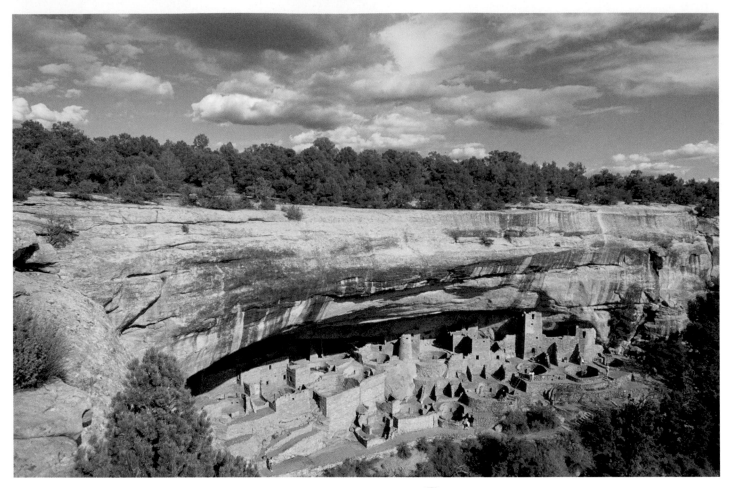

8-31 Cliff Palace, Anasazi, Mesa Verde National Park, Colorado, ca. 1150–1300 CE.

Sometime in the late 12th century, a drought occurred, and the Anasazi largely abandoned their open canyon-floor dwelling sites to move farther north to the steep-sided canyons and lusher environment of Mesa Verde in southwestern Colorado. Cliff Palace (FIG. **8-31**) is wedged into a sheltered ledge above a valley floor. It contains about 200 rectangular rooms (mostly communal dwellings) of carefully laid stone and timber, once plastered inside and out with adobe. The location for Cliff Palace was not accidental. The Anasazi designed it to take advantage of the sun to heat the pueblo in winter and shade it during the hot summer months.

Scattered in the foreground of our Cliff Palace photograph are two dozen large circular semisubterranean structures, called *kivas,* which once were roofed over and entered with a ladder through a hole in the flat roof. These chambers were (and remain) the spiritual centers of native Southwest life, male council houses where ritual regalia are stored and private rituals and preparations for public ceremonies take place.

The Anasazi did not disappear but gradually evolved into the various Pueblo peoples who still live in Arizona, New Mexico, Colorado, and Utah. They continue to speak their native languages, practice deeply rooted rituals, and make pottery in the traditional manner. Their art is discussed in Chapter 9.

CONCLUSION

When Europeans first arrived in the Americas in the late 15th and early 16th centuries, they encountered native peoples whose artistic traditions were at least as ancient as those of classical Greece and Rome. In Mesoamerica, the Olmec erected great earthen pyramids and colossal stone portraits between ca. 900 and 400 BCE. At Teotihuacán, a great city featuring a grid plan and towering stone pyramids arose between 100 BCE and 750 CE. The Classic Maya (ca. 300–900 CE) built vast complexes of temple-pyramids, palaces, plazas, and ball courts, and decorated them with monumental sculptures and mural paintings. In Andean South America, the Chavín culture erected monumental ceremonial complexes with extensive stone carvings between 800 and 200 BCE. The Paracas, Nasca, Moche, and Wari cultures (ca. 400 BCE–800 CE) have left behind fabulous ceramics and textiles. In North America, the Mississippian culture constructed huge earthen mounds beginning around 900 CE. From an early date, the native peoples of the American Southwest lived in sophisticated urban communities and excelled in the art of pottery. The extraordinary diversity of American art and architecture before contact with Europeans reflects the enormous variety and vitality of the native cultures of the Western Hemisphere.

MESOAMERICA	SOUTH AMERICA	NORTH AMERICA		
	PRECERAMIC		3000 BCE	
			2000 BCE	
	INITIAL PERIOD		1200 BCE	
				1 ■ OLMEC CULTURE, CA. 1200–400 BCE (M)
PRECLASSIC (FORMATIVE)	EARLY HORIZON		800 BCE	

1 Olmec colossal head, La Venta, ca. 900–400 BCE

		VARIOUS OVERLAPPING INDIGENOUS CULTURES (SEE LIST)		■ CHAVÍN CULTURE, CA. 800–200 BCE (S)
				■ BEGINNINGS OF MAYA CIVILIZATION, CA. 600 BCE (M)
				■ EARLIEST MESOAMERICAN WRITING, CA. 500 BCE (M)
				■ ADENA CULTURE, CA. 500–1 BCE (N)
				■ NORTON (OLD BERING SEA) CULTURE, 500 BCE–1000 CE (N)
				■ PARACAS CULTURE, CA. 400 BCE–200 CE (S)
				■ SHAFT-TOMB CULTURES OF WEST MEXICO, CA. 200 BCE–250 CE (M)
				■ NASCA CULTURE, CA. 200 BCE–600 CE (S)
				■ FOUNDATION OF TEOTIHUACÁN, CA. 100 BCE (M)

CLASSIC	EARLY INTERMEDIATE PERIOD		1 CE	
				2 ■ MOCHE CULTURE, CA. 1–700 (S)
				■ TIWANAKU CULTURE, CA. 100–1000 (S)
				■ ANASAZI CULTURE, CA. 200–1400 (N)

2 Embroidered funerary mantle, Paracas, first century CE

			300	
			400	
	MIDDLE HORIZON			■ WARI CULTURE, CA. 500–800 (S)
				■ ITZAMNA BALAM II, YAXCHILÁN, R. 681–742 (M)
				■ HASAW CHAN K'AWIL, TIKAL, R. 682–732 (M)
				■ WAXAKLAHUN-UBAH-K'AWIL, COPÁN, R. 695–738 (M)
				3 ■ ABANDONMENT OF TEOTIHUACÁN, CA. 750 (M)

3 Temple I, Tikal, ca. 732

EARLY POSTCLASSIC	LATE INTERMEDIATE PERIOD		800	
				■ ASCENDANCE OF CHICHÉN ITZÁ, CA. 800 (M)
				■ MISSISSIPPIAN CULTURE, CA. 800–1500 (N)
			900	
				■ ABANDONMENT OF SOUTHERN MAYA SITES, CA. 900 (M)
				■ TOLTEC DOMINATION AT TULA, CA. 900–1200 (M)
			1000	
				4 ■ MIMBRES CULTURE, CA. 1000–1250 (N)

4 Serpent Mound, Ohio, ca. 1070

			1300	

KEY: M = MESOAMERICA / N = NORTH AMERICA / S = SOUTH AMERICA

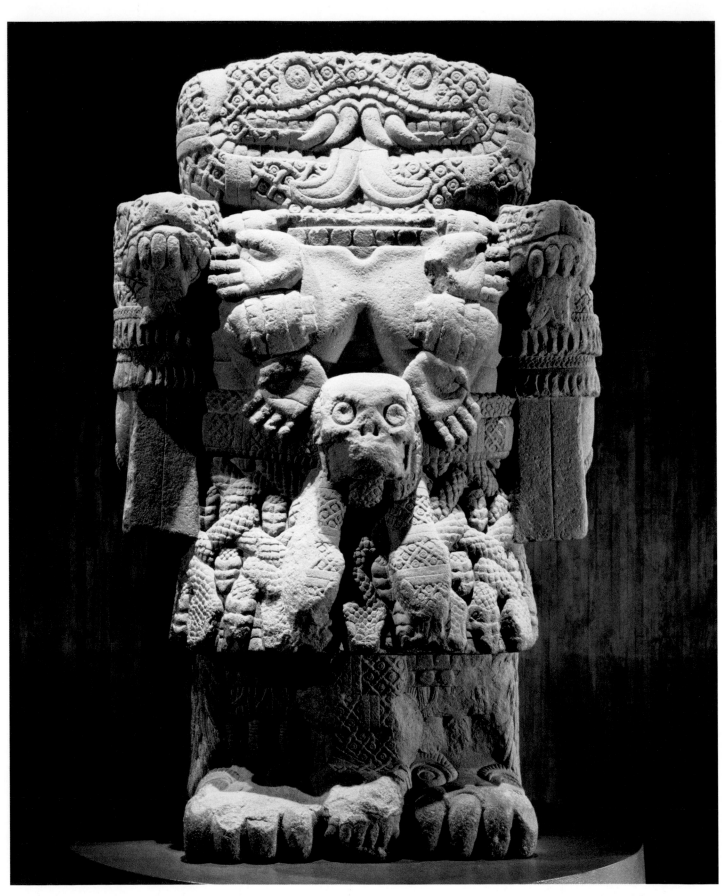

Coatlicue (She of the Serpent Skirt), Aztec, from Tenochtitlán, Mexico City, ca. 1487–1520. Andesite, 11′ 6″ high. Museo Nacional de Antropología, Mexico City.

9

BEFORE AND AFTER THE CONQUISTADORS

NATIVE ARTS OF THE AMERICAS AFTER 1300

In the years following Christopher Columbus's arrival in the "New World" in 1492, the Spanish monarchs poured money into expeditions that probed the coasts of North and South America (MAP **9-1**), but had little luck in finding the wealth they sought. When brief stops on the coast of Yucatán, Mexico, yielded a small but still impressive amount of gold and other precious artifacts, the Spanish governor of Cuba outfitted yet another expedition. Headed by Hernán Cortés, this contingent of Spanish explorers was the first to make contact with the great Aztec emperor Moctezuma (r. 1502–1521). In only two years, with the help of guns, horses, and native allies revolting against their Aztec overlords, Cortés managed to overthrow the vast and rich Aztec Empire. His victory in 1521 opened the door to hordes of Spanish conquistadors seeking their fortunes, to missionaries eager for new converts to Christianity, and to a host of new diseases for which the native Americans had no immunity. The ensuing clash of cultures led to a century of turmoil and an enormous population decline throughout the Spanish king's new domains.

The Aztec Empire that the Spanish encountered and defeated was but the latest of a series of highly sophisticated indigenous art-producing cultures in the Americas. Their predecessors have been treated in Chapter 8. This chapter examines in turn the artistic achievements of the native peoples of Mesoamerica, South America, and North America after 1300.

MESOAMERICA

After the fall and destruction of the great central Mexican city of Teotihuacán in the eighth century and the abandonment of the southern Maya sites around 900, new cities arose to take their places (MAP **9-2**). Notable were the Maya city of Chichén Itzá in Yucatán and Tula, the Toltec capital not far from modern Mexico City (see Chapter 8). Their dominance was relatively short-lived, however, and neither city left extensive

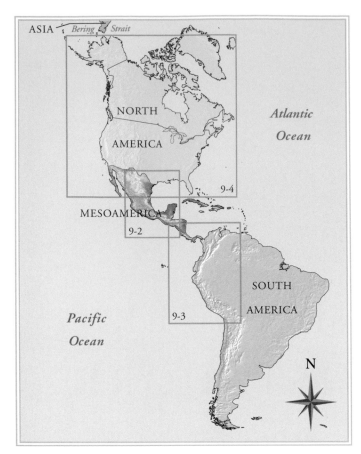

MAP 9-1 The Americas.

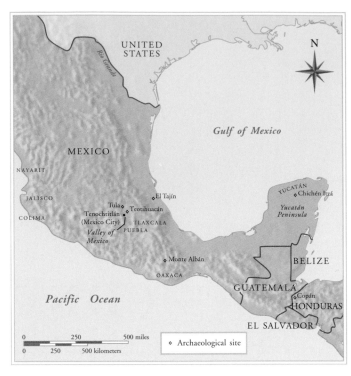

MAP 9-2 Later sites in Mesoamerica.

written records. Thus, Mesoamerican history in the early Post-classic period (ca. 900–1250) is less well documented than that of Classic Mesoamerica. For the cultures of the late Postclassic period (ca. 1250–1521), however, some illustrated manuscripts miraculously survived the depredations of the Spanish invasion, and their history is better known.

Mixteca-Puebla

The Mixtecs, who succeeded the Zapotecs at Monte Albán in southern Mexico after 700, extended their political sway in Oaxaca by dynastic intermarriage, as well as by war. The treasures found in the tombs at Monte Albán bear witness to Mixtec wealth, and the quality of these works demonstrates the high level of Mixtec artistic achievement. Metallurgy was introduced into Mexico in Late Classic times, and the Mixtec became the skilled goldsmiths of Mesoamerica. Also renowned for their work in mosaic, they used turquoise obtained from far-off regions such as present-day New Mexico.

THE ART OF THE BOOK Illustrated books were highly prized in Mesoamerica. The Postclassic Maya were preeminent in the art of writing. Their books were precious vehicles for recording not only history but also rituals, astronomical tables, calendrical calculations, maps, and trade and tribute accounts. The texts consisted of hieroglyphic columns read from left to right and top to bottom. Unfortunately, only four Maya books survive. Bishop Diego de Landa, the 16th-century Spanish chronicler of the Maya of Yucatán, explains why: "We found a large number of books in these [Indian] characters and, as they contained nothing in which

there were not to be seen superstition and lies of the devil, we burned them all, which they regretted to an amazing degree, and which caused them much affliction."[1]

In contrast, 14 non-Maya books are preserved, all but 3 from Mixtec Oaxaca or from the Puebla region. Art historians have named the style they represent Mixteca-Puebla. The Mixteca-Puebla artists painted on long sheets of bark paper or deerskin, which they first coated with fine white lime plaster and folded into accordion-like pleats. Wooden covers protected the manuscripts, called *codices* (singular, *codex*). Seven Mixtec codices, largely genealogical and historical in content, survived the Spanish destruction.

THE *BORGIA CODEX* The extensively illuminated *Borgia Codex,* from somewhere in central highland Mexico (possibly the states of Puebla or Tlaxcala), is one of a group of codices treating primarily ritual subjects. The page we illustrate (FIG. **9-1**) shows two vividly gesticulating gods rendered predominantly in reds and yellows with black outlines. The god of life, the black Quetzalcoatl (depicted here as a masked human rather than in the usual form of a feathered serpent), sits back-to-back with the god of death, the white Mictlantecuhtli. Below them is an inverted skull with a double keyboard of teeth, a symbol of the Underworld (Mictlan), which could be entered through the mouth of a great earth monster. Both figures hold scepters in one hand and gesticulate with the other. The image conveys the inevitable relationship of life and death, an important theme in much

---

[1]Alfred M. Tozzer, ed., *Landa's Relacíon de las cosas de Yucatán: A Translation* (Cambridge, Mass.: Peabody Museum Papers, 1941), 18.

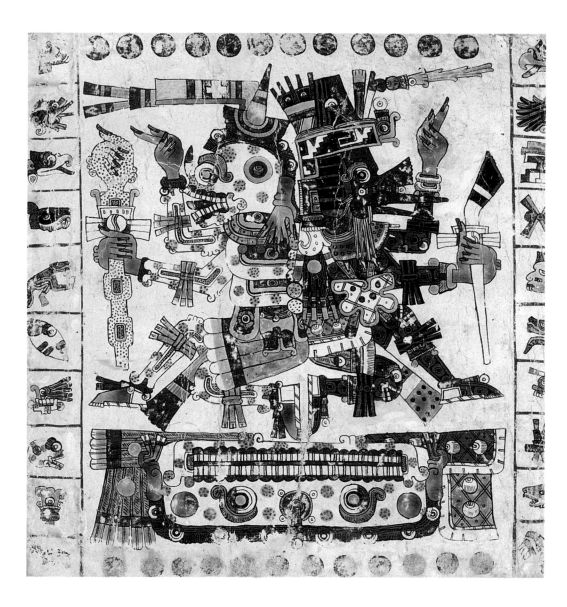

9-1 Mictlantecuhtli and Quetzalcoatl, illuminated page from the *Borgia Codex,* from Puebla/Tlaxcala(?), Mexico, ca. 1400–1500. Mineral and vegetable pigments on deerskin, approx. $10\frac{5}{8}'' \times 10\frac{3}{8}''$. Biblioteca Apostolica Vaticana, Rome.

Mesoamerican art. Symbols of the thirteen 20-day divisions of the 260-day Mesoamerican ritual calendar appear in panels in the margins. The origins of this calendar, used even today in remote parts of Mexico and Central America, are lost in time. Except for the Mixtec genealogical codices, most books painted before and immediately after the Spanish conquest deal with astronomy, calendrics, divination, and ritual, and are still poorly understood.

Aztec

THE RISE OF THE AZTECS The destruction of Tula in about 1200 and the disintegration of the Toltec Empire in central Mexico made for a century of anarchy in the Valley of Mexico, the vast highland valley 7,000 feet above sea level that now contains sprawling Mexico City. Waves of northern invaders established warring city-states and wrought destruction in the valley. The last and greatest of these conquerors were the Aztecs. With astonishing rapidity, they transformed themselves within a few generations from migratory outcasts and serfs to mercenaries for local rulers and then to masters in their own right of the Valley of Mexico's small kingdoms. In the process, they acquired, like their neighbors, the Toltec culture. They began to call themselves *Mexica,* and, following a legendary prophecy that they would build a city where they saw an eagle perched on a cactus with a serpent in its mouth, they settled on an island in Lake Texcoco (Lake of the Moon). Their settlement grew into the magnificent city of Tenochtitlán, which in 1519 amazed Cortés and his small band of adventurers.

Recognized by those they subdued as fierce in war and cruel in peace, the Aztecs indeed seemed to glory in warfare and in military prowess. They radically changed the social and political situation in Mexico. Subservient groups not only had to submit to Aztec military power but also had to provide victims to be sacrificed to Huitzilopochtli, the hummingbird god of war, and to other Aztec deities (see "Aztec Religion," page 170). Bloodletting and human sacrifice were intended to please the gods and sustain the great cycles of the universe and had a long history in Mesoamerica (see Chapter 8). The Aztecs, however, seem to have practiced human sacrifice on a greater scale than any of their predecessors, even waging special battles, called the "flowery wars," expressly to obtain captives for future sacrifice. It is one of the reasons why Cortés found ready allies among the peoples the Aztecs had subjugated.

TENOCHTITLÁN The ruins of the Aztec capital, Tenochtitlán, lie directly beneath the center of modern-day Mexico City. In the late 1970s, Mexican archaeologists identified the exact location of many of the most important structures within the Aztec sacred precinct, and extensive excavations near the cathedral in Mexico

Aztec Religion

The Aztecs saw their world as a flat disk resting on the back of a monstrous earth deity. Tenochtitlán, their capital, was at its center, with the Great Temple (FIG. 9-2) representing a sacred mountain and forming the axis passing up to the heavens and down through the Underworld—a concept with parallels in other cultures (see, for example, "The Stupa," Chapter 1, page 6). Each of the four cardinal points had its own god, color, tree, and calendrical symbol. The sky consisted of 13 layers, whereas the Underworld had 9. The Aztec Underworld was an unpleasant place where the dead gradually ceased to exist.

The Aztecs often adopted the gods of conquered peoples, and their pantheon was complex and varied. When the Aztecs arrived in the Valley of Mexico, their own patron, Huitzilopochtli, a war and sun deity, joined such well-established Mesoamerican gods as Tlaloc and Quetzalcoatl, the feathered serpent who was a benevolent god of life, wind, and learning and culture, as well as the patron of priests. As the Aztecs went on to conquer much of Mesoamerica, they appropriated the gods of their subjects, such as Xipe Totec, a god of early spring and patron of gold workers imported from the Gulf Coast and Oaxaca. Images of the various gods made of stone (FIG. 9-4), terracotta, wood, and even dough (eaten at the end of rituals) stood in and around their temples. Reliefs (FIG. 9-3) depicting Aztec deities, often with political overtones, also adorned the temple complexes.

The Aztec ritual cycle was very full, given that they celebrated events in two calendars—the sacred calendar (260 days) and the solar one (360 days plus 5 unlucky and nameless days). The Spanish friars of the 16th century noted that the solar calendar dealt largely with agricultural matters. The two Mesoamerican calendars functioned simultaneously, requiring 52 years for the same date to recur in both. A ritual called the New Fire Ceremony commemorated this rare event. Pots were broken and new ones made for the next period, pregnant women were hidden away, and all fires were extinguished. At midnight on a mountaintop, fire priests took out the heart of a sacrificial victim and with a fire drill renewed the flame in the exposed cavity. Bundles of sticks representing the 52 years that had just passed were then set ablaze,

ensuring that the sun would rise in the morning and that another cycle would begin.

Most Aztec ceremonies involved the burning of incense (made from copal, resin from conifer trees), colorfully attired dancers and actors, and music provided by conch shell trumpets, drums, rattles, rasps, bells, whistles, and, of course, the human voice. Almost every Aztec festival also included human sacrifice. For Tlaloc, the rain god, small children were especially desirable, because their tears brought the rains.

Rituals also marked the completion of important religious structures. The dedication of the last major rebuilding of the Great Temple at Tenochtitlán in 1487, for example, reportedly involved the sacrifice of thousands of captives from recent wars in the Gulf Coast region. Varied offerings have been found within earlier layers of the temple, many representing tribute from subjugated peoples. These include blue-painted stone and ceramic vessels representing the rain deity Tlaloc, conch shells, a jaguar skeleton, flint and obsidian knives, and even Mesoamerican "antiques"—carved stone Olmec and Teotihuacán masks made hundreds of years before the Aztec ascendancy.

Thousands of priests served in Aztec temples. Distinctive hairstyles, clothing, and black body paint identified the priests. Women served as priestesses, particularly in temples dedicated to various earth-mother cults. Bernal Díaz del Castillo, a soldier who accompanied Cortés when the Spanish first entered Tenochtitlán, was shocked to witness a group of foul-smelling priests with uncut fingernails, long hair matted with blood, and ears covered in cuts, not realizing they were performing rites in honor of the deities they served, including autosacrifice by piercing their skin with cactus spines to draw blood. These priests were the opposite of the "barbarians" the European conquerors considered them to be. They were, in fact, the most educated of all Aztecs. The Spanish reaction to the customs they encountered in the New World has colored popular opinion about Aztec culture ever since. The Aztec religious practices that horrified their European conquerors were, however, not unique to them, but deeply rooted in earlier Mesoamerican society (see Chapter 8).

City continue. The principal building is the Great Temple (FIG. 9-2), a temple-pyramid honoring the Aztec god Huitzilopochtli and the local rain god Tlaloc. Two great staircases originally swept upward from the plaza level to the double sanctuaries at the summit. The Great Temple is a remarkable example of *superimposition,* a common trait in Mesoamerican architecture. The excavated structure, composed of seven shells, indicates how the earlier walls nested within the later. (Today, only two of the inner structures are visible. The later ones were destroyed at the time of the Spanish conquest.) The sacred precinct also contained the temples of other deities, a ball court (see "The Mesoamerican Ball Game," Chapter 8, page 147), a skull rack for the exhibition of the heads of victims killed in sacrificial rites, and a school for children of the nobility.

Tenochtitlán was a city laid out on a grid plan in quarters and wards, reminiscent of Teotihuacán (see FIG. 8-4), which, long abandoned, had become a pilgrimage site for the Aztecs. Tenochtitlán's island location required conducting communication

and transport via canals and other waterways. Many of the Spaniards thought of Venice in Italy when they saw the city rising from the waters like a radiant vision. Crowded with buildings, plazas, and courtyards, the city also boasted a vast and ever-busy marketplace. In the words of Díaz del Castillo, "Some of the soldiers among us who had been in many parts of the world, in Constantinople, and all over Italy, and in Rome, said that so large a marketplace and so full of people, and so well regulated and arranged, they had never beheld before."[2] The city proper had a population of more than 100,000. (The total population of the area of Mexico the Aztecs dominated at the time of the conquest was approximately 11 million.)

COYOLXAUHQUI DISMEMBERED The Temple of Huitzilopochtli at Tenochtitlán commemorated the god's victory over

---

[2]Bernal Díaz del Castillo, *The Discovery and Conquest of Mexico,* translated by A. P. Maudslay (New York: Farrar, Straus, Giroux, 1956), 218–19.

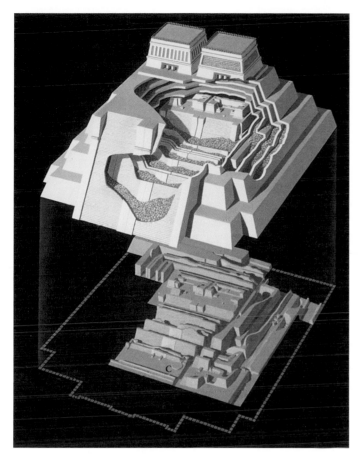

9-2 Reconstruction drawing with cutaway view of various rebuildings of the Great Temple, Aztec, Tenochtitlán, Mexico City, Mexico, ca. 1400–1500. C = Coyolxauhqui stone (FIG. 9-3).

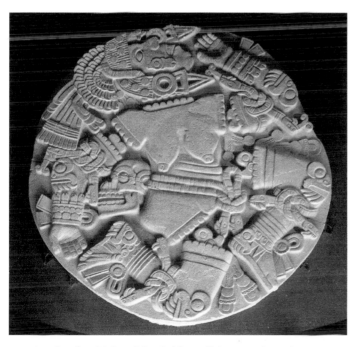

9-3 Coyolxauhqui (She of the Golden Bells), Aztec, from the Great Temple of Tenochtitlán, Mexico City, ca. 1469. Stone, diameter approx. 10′ 10″. Museo del Templo Mayor, Mexico City.

his sister and 400 brothers, who had plotted to kill their mother, Coatlicue (She of the Serpent Skirt). The myth signifies the birth of the sun at dawn, a role sometimes assumed by Huitzilopochtli, and the sun's battle with the forces of darkness, the stars and moon. Huitzilopochtli chased away his brothers and dismem-

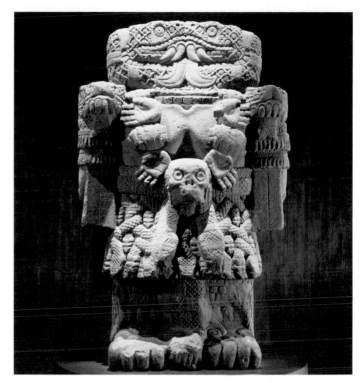

9-4 Coatlicue (She of the Serpent Skirt), Aztec, from Tenochtitlán, Mexico City, ca. 1487–1520. Andesite, 11′ 6″ high. Museo Nacional de Antropología, Mexico City.

bered the body of his sister, the moon goddess Coyolxauhqui (She of the Golden Bells, referring to the bells on her cheeks), at a hill near Tula (represented by the pyramid itself). The mythical event is depicted on a huge stone disk (FIG. 9-3), whose discovery in 1971 set off the ongoing archaeological investigations near the main plaza in Mexico City. The relief had been placed at the foot of the staircase leading up to one of Huitzilopochtli's earlier temples on the site. (Cortés and his army never saw it because it was concealed within the outermost shell of the Great Temple.) Carved on the disk is an image of the murdered and segmented body of Coyolxauhqui. The mythological theme also carried a contemporary political message. The bodies of conquered enemies were sacrificed and then hurled down the Great Temple's stairs to land on this stone. The Aztecs likened their foes to the female deity that Huitzilopochtli dismembered.

The disk is an unforgettable expression of Aztec temperament and taste. The image proclaimed the power of the Mexica and their gods over their enemies and the inevitable fate that must befall them when defeated. Marvelously composed, the relief has a kind of dreadful, yet formal, beauty. Within the circular space, the design's carefully balanced, richly detailed components are so adroitly placed that they seem to have a slow turning rhythm, like a revolving galaxy. The carving is confined to a single level, a smoothly even, flat surface raised from a flat ground. It is the sculptural equivalent of the line and flat tone, the figure and neutral ground, characteristic of Mesoamerican painting.

COATLICUE BEHEADED In addition to relief carving, the Aztecs produced freestanding statuary. A colossal image of Coatlicue (FIG. 9-4) was discovered in 1790 near Mexico City's cathedral. The sculpture's original setting is unknown, but some scholars believe that it was one of a group set up at the Great Temple. The main forms are carved in high relief, the details executed either in low relief or by incising. The overall aspect is of an enormous blocky mass, its ponderous weight looming over awed viewers.

From the beheaded goddess's neck writhe two serpents whose heads meet to form a tusked mask. Coatlicue wears a necklace of severed human hands and excised human hearts. The pendant of the necklace is a skull. Entwined snakes form her skirt. From between her legs emerges another serpent, symbolic perhaps of both menses and the male member. Like most Aztec deities, Coatlicue has both masculine and feminine traits. Her hands and feet have great claws, which she used to tear the human flesh she consumed. All her attributes symbolize sacrificial death. Yet, in Aztec thought, this mother of the gods combined savagery and tenderness, for out of destruction arose new life, a theme seen earlier at Teotihuacán (see FIG. 8-6).

THE AZTEC ACHIEVEMENT Given the Aztecs' almost meteoric rise from obscurity to their role as the dominant culture of Mesoamerica, the quality of the art they sponsored is astonishing. Granted, they swiftly appropriated the best artworks and most talented artists of conquered territories, bringing both back to Tenochtitlán. Thus, craftspeople from other areas, such as the Mixtecs of Oaxaca, may have created much of the exquisite pottery, goldwork, and turquoise mosaics the Aztec elite used. Gulf Coast artists probably made the life-size terracotta sculptures of eagle warriors found at the Great Temple.

Nonetheless, the Aztecs' own sculptural style, developed at the height of their power in the later 15th century, is unsurpassed. Unfortunately, much of Aztec and Aztec-sponsored art did not survive the Spanish conquest and the subsequent period of evangelization. The conquerors took Aztec gold artifacts back to Spain and melted them down, zealous friars destroyed "idols" and codices, and perishable materials such as textiles and wood largely disappeared. Aztec artisans also fashioned beautifully worked feathered objects and even created mosaic-like images with feathers, an art they put to service for the Catholic Church for a brief time after the Spanish conquest, creating religious pictures and decorating ecclesiastical clothing with the bright feathers of tropical birds.

CORTÉS AND MOCTEZUMA The Spanish conquerors found it impossible to reconcile the beauty of the great city of Tenochtitlán with what they regarded as its hideous cults. They admired its splendid buildings ablaze with color, its luxuriant and spacious gardens, its sparkling waterways, its teeming markets, and its grandees resplendent in exotic bird feathers. But when the emperor Moctezuma brought Cortés and his entourage into the shrine of Huitzilopochtli's temple, the newcomers started back in horror and disgust from the huge statues clotted with dried blood. Cortés was furious. Denouncing Huitzilopochtli as a devil, he proposed to put a high cross above the pyramid and a statue of the Virgin in the sanctuary to exorcise its evil.

This proposal came to symbolize the avowed purpose and the historic result of the Spanish conquest of Mesoamerica. The conquerors venerated the cross and the Virgin, triumphant, in new shrines raised on the ruins of the plundered temples of the ancient American gods, and the banner of the Most Catholic King of Spain waved over new atrocities of a European kind.

SOUTH AMERICA

Inka

THE INKA EMPIRE The Inka were a small highland group who established themselves in the Cuzco Valley of Andean South America (MAP 9-3) around 1000. In the 15th century, however,

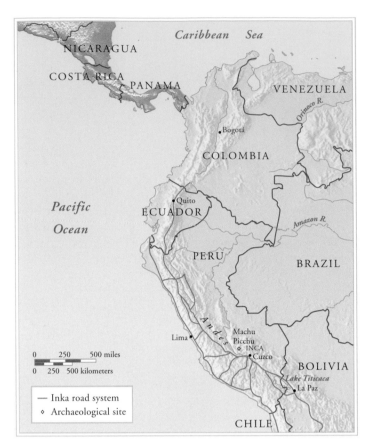

MAP 9-3 Later sites in Andean South America.

they rapidly extended their power until their empire stretched from modern Quito, Ecuador, to central Chile, a distance of more than 3,000 miles. Perhaps 12 million subjects inhabited the area the Inka ruled. The Inka Empire was the largest in the world at the time of the Spanish conquest. Expertise in mining and metalwork enabled the Inka to accumulate enormous wealth and to amass the fabled troves of gold and silver that the Spanish so coveted. Such a vast and rich empire required skillful organizational and administrative control, and the Inka had rare talent for both. In this respect, they resembled the ancient Romans. They divided their Andean empire, which they called Tawantinsuyu, the Land of the Four Quarters, into sections and subsections, provinces and communities, whose boundaries all converged on, or radiated from, the capital city of Cuzco.

ENGINEERING The Inka's engineering prowess matched their organizational talent. They mastered the difficult problems of Andean agriculture with expert terracing and irrigation, and knitted together the fabric of their empire with networks of roads and bridges. Eschewing wheeled vehicles and horses, they used their highway system to move goods by llama back and armies by foot throughout their territories. The Inka upgraded or built more than 14,000 miles of roads, one main highway running through the highlands and another along the coast, with connecting roads linking the two regions. They also established a highly efficient, swift communication system of relay runners who carried messages the length of the empire. It was said the Inka emperor in Cuzco could get fresh fish from the coast in only three days. Where the terrain was too steep for a paved flat surface, the Inka built stone steps, and their rope bridges crossed canyons high over impassable rivers. They placed small settlements along the roads no more than a day apart where travelers could rest and obtain supplies for the journey.

RECORD-KEEPING The Inka never, however, developed a writing system. Nevertheless, they maintained strict control over their vast empire by developing a remarkably sophisticated record-keeping system using a device known as the *quipu*. The Inka used the quipu to record calendrical and astronomical information, census and tribute totals, and inventories. For example, the Spaniards noted that Inka officials always knew exactly how much maize or cloth was in any storeroom in their empire. Not a book or a tablet, the quipu was made of fiber with a main cord and other knotted threads hanging perpendicularly off it. The color and position of each thread, as well as the kind of knot and its location, recorded numbers and categories of things, whether people, llamas, or crops. Studies of quipus have demonstrated that the Inka used the decimal system, were familiar with the zero concept, and could record numbers up to five digits. The Inka census taker or tax collector could easily roll up and carry the quipu, one of the most lightweight and portable "computers" ever invented.

CLOTHING AND STATUS The Inka aimed at imposing not only political and economic control but also their art style throughout their realm, subjugating local traditions to those of the empire. Control even extended to clothing, which communicated the social status of the person wearing the garment. The Inka wove bands of small squares of various repeated abstract designs into their fabrics. Scholars believe the patterns had political meaning,

connoting membership in particular social groups. Such motifs completely covered the Inka ruler's tunics, perhaps to indicate his control over all such groups. Those the Inka conquered, however, had to wear their characteristic local dress at all times, a practice reflected in the distinctive and varied clothing of today's indigenous Andean peoples.

MACHU PICCHU The imperial Inka were also great architects. Although they worked with adobe, the Inka were supreme masters of shaping and fitting stone. As a militant conquering people, they selected breathtaking, naturally fortified sites and further strengthened them by building various defensive structures. Inka city planning reveals an almost instinctive grasp of the proper relation of architecture to site.

One of the world's most awe-inspiring sights, the Inka city of Machu Picchu (FIG. 9-5), perches on a ridge between two jagged peaks 9,000 feet above sea level. Completely invisible from the Urubamba River Valley some 1,600 feet below, the site remained unknown to the outside world until Hiram Bingham, an American explorer, discovered it in 1911. In the very heart of the Andes, Machu Picchu is about 50 miles north of Cuzco and, like some of the region's other cities, was the private estate of a powerful mid-15th-century Inka ruler. Though relatively small and insignificant compared to its neighbors (with a resident population of little more than a thousand), the city is of great archaeological importance as a rare site left undisturbed since Inka times. The accommodation of its architecture to the landscape is so complete that Machu Picchu seems a natural part of the mountain ranges that surround it on all sides. The Inka even cut large stones to echo the shapes of the

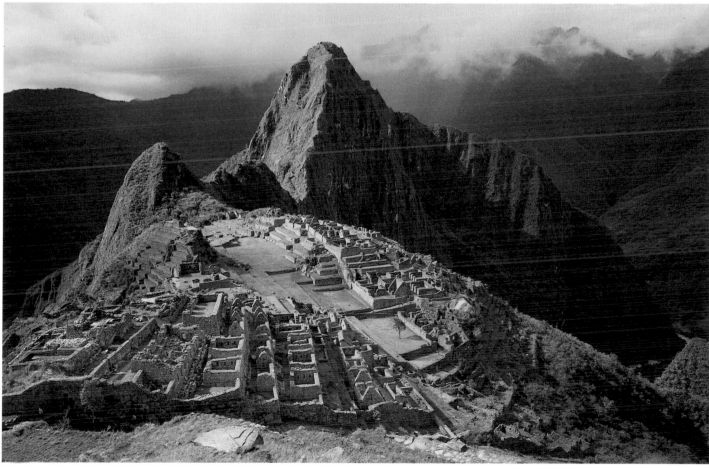

9-5 Machu Picchu (view from adjacent peak), Inka, Peru, 15th century.

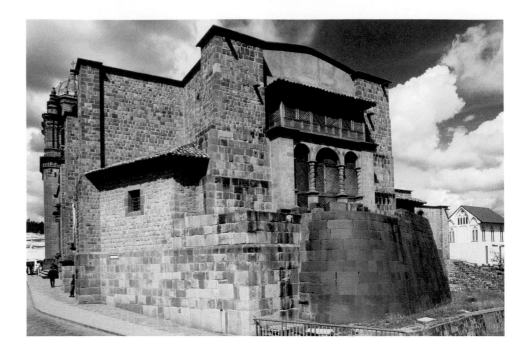

9-6 Wall of the Golden Enclosure (surmounted by the church of Santo Domingo), Inka, Cuzco, Peru, 15th century.

mountain beyond. Terraces spill down the mountainsides and are built even up to the very peak of Huayna Picchu, the great hill just beyond the city's main plaza. The Inka carefully sited buildings so that windows and doors framed spectacular views of sacred peaks and facilitated the recording of important astronomical events.

THE PUMA CITY The Inka capital, Cuzco, was largely destroyed during the Spanish conquest and subsequent colonial period. Thus, most of what is known about the city has been gleaned from often-contradictory Spanish sources rather than from archaeology. Some descriptions state that Cuzco's plan was in the shape of a puma, with a great shrine-fortress on a hill above the city representing its head and the southeastern convergence of two rivers forming its tail. Cuzco residents still refer to the river area as "the puma's tail." A great plaza, still the hub of the modern city, was nestled below the animal's stomach. The puma referred to Inka royal power.

THE GOLDEN ENCLOSURE The Inka, like the ancient Greeks, were masters of *ashlar masonry* (fitting stone blocks together without mortar). The joints could be beveled to show their tightness or laid in courses with perfectly joined faces so that the lines of separation were hardly visible. The Inka produced the close joints of their masonry by abrasion alone, grinding the surfaces to a perfect fit. For the walls of more important buildings, such as temples or administrative palaces, the workers usually laid the stones in regular horizontal courses. For lesser structures, they set the blocks in polygonal (mostly trapezoidal) patterns. Inka builders were so skilled that they could fashion walls with curved surfaces, their planes as level and continuous as if they were a single form poured in concrete.

One example of this single-form effect is a surviving wall from the Temple of the Sun in Cuzco (FIG. **9-6**). Originally known as Coricancha (Golden Enclosure), this structure was the most magnificent of all Inka shrines and was built on the site of the home of Manco Capac, son of the sun god and founder of the Inka dynasty. Mummies of some of the early rulers were said to be housed there. The temple was dedicated to the worship of several Inka deities, including the creator god Viracocha and the gods of the sun, moon, stars, and the elements. The 16th-century Spanish chroniclers wrote in awe of Coricancha's splendor, its interior veneered with sheets of gold, silver, and emeralds. The remaining hewn stones, precisely fitted and polished, form a curving semi-parabola (sickle shape) and were set for flexibility in earthquakes, allowing for a temporary dislocation of the courses, which then return to their original position.

THE END OF THE INKA The Temple of the Sun was badly burned at the time of the Spanish conquest. Soon afterward, small-pox spreading south from Spanish-occupied Mesoamerica killed the last Inka emperor and his heir before they ever laid eyes on a Spaniard. The Inka empire quickly plunged into a civil war that only aided the Europeans in their conquest. In 1532, Francisco Pizarro, the Spanish explorer of the Andes, ambushed the would-be emperor Atawalpa on his way to be crowned at Cuzco after vanquishing his rival half-brother. Although Atawalpa paid a huge ransom of gold and silver, the Spaniards killed him and took control of his vast domain, only a decade after Cortés had defeated the Aztecs in Mexico.

After the murder of Atawalpa, the Spanish erected the church of Santo Domingo, in an imported European style, on what remained of the Golden Enclosure. A curved section of Inka wall serves to this day as the foundation for the church's apse. A violent earthquake in 1950 seriously damaged the colonial building, but Santo Domingo has been rebuilt. The two contrasting structures remain standing one atop the other (FIG. 9-6). The Coricancha is therefore of more than architectural and archaeological interest. It is a symbol of the Spanish conquest of the Americas and serves as a composite monument to it.

NORTH AMERICA

Southwest

BEFORE THE SPANISH The dominant culture of the American Southwest during the centuries preceding the arrival of Europeans was the Anasazi, the builders of great architectural complexes like Chaco Canyon and Cliff Palace (see FIG. 8-31). The spiritual center of Anasazi life was the kiva, or male council house. Between 1300 and 1500, the Anasazi decorated their

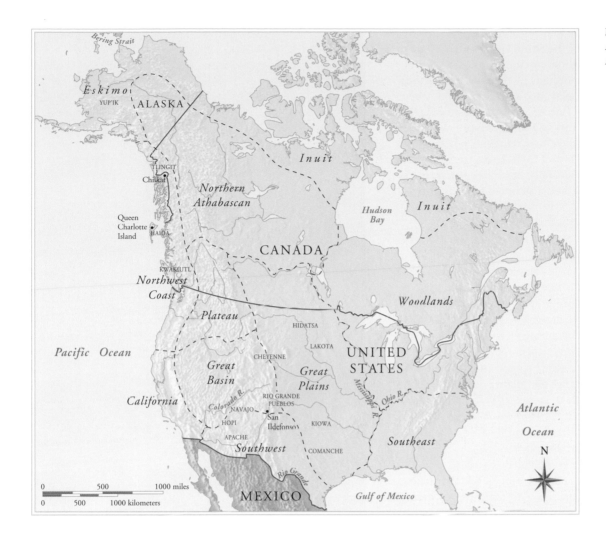

MAP 9-4 Later Native American sites in North America.

kivas with elaborate mural paintings representing deities associated with agricultural fertility. According to their descendants, the present-day Hopi and Zuni, the detail of the Kuaua Pueblo mural shown here (FIG. 9-7) depicts a "lightning man" on the left side. Fish and eagle images (associated with rain) appear on the right side. Seeds, a lightning bolt, and a rainbow stream from the eagle's mouth. All these figures are associated with the fertility of the earth and the life-giving properties of the seasonal rains, a constant preoccupation of Southwest farmers. The Anasazi painter depicted the figures with great economy, using thick black lines, dots, and a restricted palette of black, brown, yellow, and white. The frontal figure of the lightning man seen against a neutral ground makes an immediate visual impact.

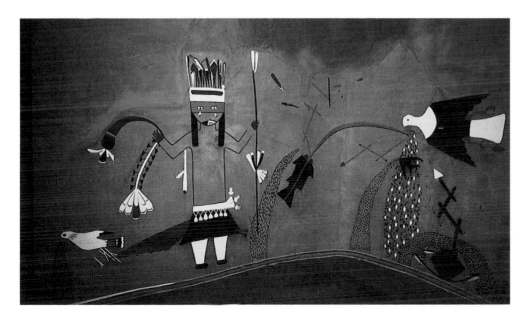

9-7 Detail of a kiva mural from Kuaua Pueblo (Coronado State Monument), Anasazi, New Mexico, late 15th to early 16th century. Museum of New Mexico, Santa Fe.

PUEBLO INDIANS When the first Europeans came into contact with the ancient peoples of the Southwest, they called them "Pueblo Indians." The successors of the Anasazi and other Southwest groups, the Pueblo Indians include linguistically diverse but culturally similar peoples such as the Hopi of northern Arizona and the Rio Grande Pueblos of New Mexico. Living among them are the descendants of nomadic hunters who arrived in the Southwest from their homelands in northwestern Canada sometime between 1200 and 1500. These are the Apache and Navajo, who, although culturally quite distinct from the original inhabitants of the Southwest, adopted many features of Pueblo life.

NAVAJO SAND PAINTINGS Among these borrowed elements is sand painting, which the Navajo learned from the Pueblos but transformed into an extraordinarily complex ritual art form. The temporary sand paintings (also known as dry paintings), constructed to the accompaniment of prayers and chants, are an essential part of ceremonies for curing disease. (In the healing ceremony, the patient sits in the painting's center to absorb the life-giving powers of the gods and their representations.) The Navajo perform similar rites to assure success in hunting and to promote fertility in human beings and nature alike. The artists who supervise the making of these complex images are religious leaders or "medicine men" (rarely women), thought to have direct contact with the powers of the supernatural world, which they use to help both individuals and the community.

The natural materials used—corn pollen, charcoal, sand, and varicolored powdered stones—play a symbolic role that reflects the Native Americans' preoccupation with the forces of nature. The paintings, which depict the gods and mythological heroes whose help is sought, are destroyed in the process of the ritual, so no models exist. However, the traditional prototypes, passed on from artist to artist, must be adhered to as closely as possible. Mistakes can render the ceremony ineffective. Navajo dry painting is therefore highly stylized. Simple curves, straight lines, right angles, and serial repetition characterize most sand paintings. Because of their sacred nature, the Navajo do not permit the photographing of sand paintings.

NAVAJO WEAVING By the mid-17th century, the Navajo had also learned how to weave from their Hopi and other Pueblo neighbors, quickly adapting to new materials such as sheep's wool and synthetic dyes introduced by Spanish settlers and, later, by Anglo-Americans. They rapidly transformed their wearing blankets into handsome rugs in response to the new market created by the arrival of the railroad and early tourists in the 1880s. Other tribes, including those of the Great Plains, also purchased Navajo textiles. The Navajo mastered an incredible variety of designs, including vivid abstract designs known as "eye dazzlers" and copies of sand paintings (altered slightly to preserve the sacred quality of the impermanent ritual images).

HOPI KATSINAS Another art form from the Southwest, the *katsina* figurine, also has deep roots in the area. Katsinas are benevolent supernatural spirits personifying natural elements and living in mountains and water sources. Humans, too, join their world after death. Among contemporary Pueblo groups, masked dancers ritually impersonate katsinas during yearly festivals dedicated to rain, fertility, and good hunting. To educate young girls in ritual lore, the Hopi traditionally give them miniature representations of the masked dancers. We illustrate a Hopi katsina (FIG. **9-8**) carved

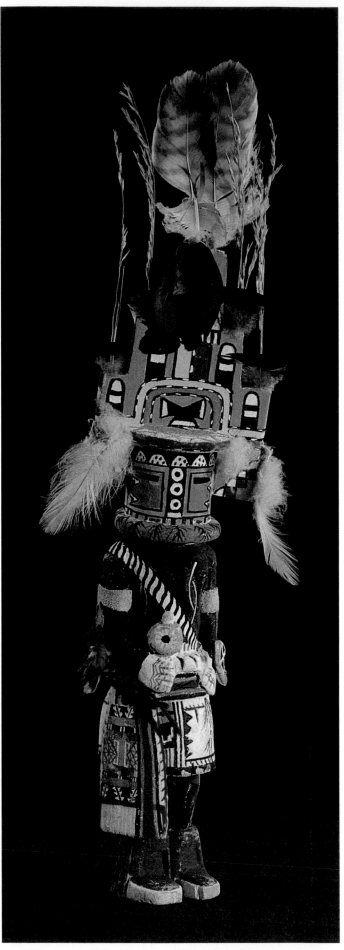

9-8 OTTO PENTEWA, Katsina figurine, Hopi, New Oraibi, Arizona, carved before 1959. Cottonwood root and feathers, about 1′ high. Arizona State Museum, University of Arizona, Tucson.

Gender Roles in Native American Art

Although both Native American women and men have created art objects for centuries, they have traditionally worked in different media or at different tasks. Among the Navajo, for example, weavers tend to be women, whereas among the neighboring Hopi the men weave. According to Navajo myth, long ago Spider Woman's husband built her a loom for weaving. In turn, she taught Navajo women how to spin and weave so that they might have clothing to wear. Today, young girls learn from their mothers how to work the loom, just as Spider Woman instructed their ancestors, passing along the techniques and designs from one generation to the next.

Among the Pueblos, pottery making normally has been the domain of women. But in response to heavy demand for her wares, María Martínez, of San Ildefonso Pueblo in New Mexico, coiled, slipped, and burnished her pots, and her husband Julian painted the designs. Although they worked in many styles, some based on prehistoric ceramics, around 1918 they invented the black-on-black ware (FIG. 9-9) that made María, and indeed the whole pueblo, famous. The elegant shapes of the pots, as well as the traditional but abstract designs, were particularly compatible with the contemporary Art Deco style in architecture and interior design, and collectors avidly sought (and continue to seek) them. When nonnative buyers suggested she sign her pots to increase their value, María obliged, but, in the communal spirit typical of the Pueblos, she also signed her neighbors' names so that they might share in her good fortune. Though María died in 1980, her descendants continue to garner awards as outstanding potters.

Women also produced the elaborately decorated skin and, later, the trade-cloth clothing of the Woodlands and Plains using moose hair, dyed porcupine quills, and imported beads. Among the Cheyenne, quillworking was a sacred art, and young women worked at learning both proper ritual and correct techniques to obtain membership in the prestigious quillworkers' guild. Women gained the same honor and dignity from creating finely worked utilitarian objects that men earned from warfare. Both women and men painted on tipis and clothing (FIGS. 9-15 and 9-16), with women creating abstract designs (FIG. 9-15) and men working in a more realistic narrative style, often celebrating their exploits in war or recording the cultural changes the transfer to reservations brought about.

In the far north, women tended to work with soft materials such as animal skins, whereas men were sculptors of wood masks among the Alaskan Eskimos and of walrus ivory pieces (see FIG. 8-26) throughout the Arctic. The introduction of printmaking, a foreign medium with no established gender associations, to some Canadian Inuit communities in the 1950s provided both native women and men with a new creative outlet. Printmaking became an important source of economic independence vital to these isolated and once-impoverished settlements. Today, both Inuit women and men make prints, but men still dominate in carving stone sculpture, another new medium also produced for and sold to outsiders.

Throughout North America, indigenous artists continue to work in traditional media, such as ceramics, beadwork, and basketry, marketing their wares through museum shops, galleries, regional art fairs, and, most recently, the Internet. Many also obtain degrees in art and express themselves in European media such as oil painting and mixed-media sculpture.

---

by OTTO PENTEWA (d. 1963) before 1959. It represents a rain-bringing deity who wears a mask painted in geometric patterns symbolic of water and agricultural fertility. Topping the mask is a stepped shape signifying thunderclouds and feathers to carry the Hopis' airborne prayers. The origins of the katsina figurines have been lost in time (they even may have developed from carved saints the Spanish introduced during the colonial period). However, the cult is probably very ancient.

PUEBLO POTTERY The Southwest has also provided the finest examples of North American pottery. Originally producing utilitarian forms, Southwest potters worked without the potter's wheel and instead coiled shapes that they then slipped, polished, and fired. Decorative motifs, often abstract and conventionalized, dealt largely with forces of nature—clouds, wind, and rain. The efforts of San Ildefonso Pueblo potter MARÍA MONTOYA MARTÍNEZ (1887–1980) and her husband Julian Martínez (see "Gender Roles in Native American Art," above) in the early decades of the 20th century revived old techniques to produce forms of striking shape, proportion, and texture. Her black-on-black pieces (FIG. 9-9) feature matte designs on highly polished surfaces achieved by extensive polishing and special firing in an oxygen-poor atmosphere.

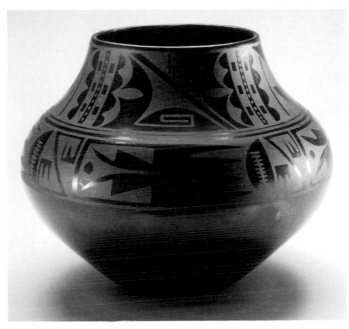

9-9 MARÍA MONTOYA MARTÍNEZ, jar, San Ildefonso Pueblo, New Mexico, ca. 1939. Blackware, $11\frac{1}{8}'' \times 1' \ 1''$. National Museum of Women in the Arts, Washington, D.C. (gift of Wallace and Wilhelmina Hollachy).

Northwest Coast

The Native Americans of the coasts and islands of northern Washington state, the province of British Columbia in Canada, and southern Alaska were blessed with a rich and reliable environment. They fished, hunted sea mammals and game, gathered edible plants, and made their homes, utensils, ritual objects, and even clothing from the region's great cedar forests. Among the numerous groups who make up the Northwest Coast area are the Kwakiutl of southern British Columbia; the Haida, who live on the Queen Charlotte Islands off the coast of the province; and the Tlingit of southern Alaska. In the Northwest, a class of professional artists developed, in contrast to the more typical Native American pattern of part-time artists.

MASKS AND WAR HELMETS Working in a highly formalized, subtle style, these Northwest Coast artists have produced a wide variety of art objects for centuries: totem poles, masks, rattles, chests, bowls, clothing, charms, and decorated houses and canoes. Some artistic traditions originated as early as 500 BCE, although others developed only after the arrival of Europeans in North America.

The Northwest Coast masks were used by religious specialists in their healing rituals and by other male participants in dramatic public performances during the winter ceremonial season. The animals and mythological creatures represented in masks and a host of other carvings derive from the Northwest Coast's rich oral tradition and celebrate the mythological origins and inherited privileges of high-ranking families. Meant to be seen in flickering firelight, the Kwakiutl mask we illustrate (FIG. **9-10**) was ingeniously constructed to open and close rapidly when the wearer manipulated hidden strings. He could thus magically transform himself from human to eagle and back again as he danced. The transformation theme, in myriad forms, is a central aspect of the art and religion of the Americas. Our Kwakiutl mask's human aspect also owes its dramatic character to the exaggeration and distortion of facial parts—such as the hooked beaklike nose and flat flaring nostrils—and to the

9-10 Eagle transformation mask, closed and open views, Kwakiutl, Alert Bay, late 19th century. Wood, feathers, and string, approx. 1′ 10″ × 11″. American Museum of Natural History, New York.

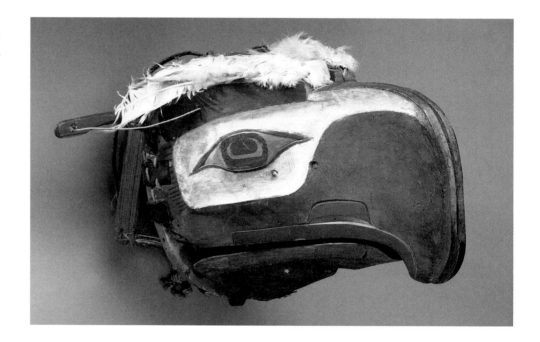

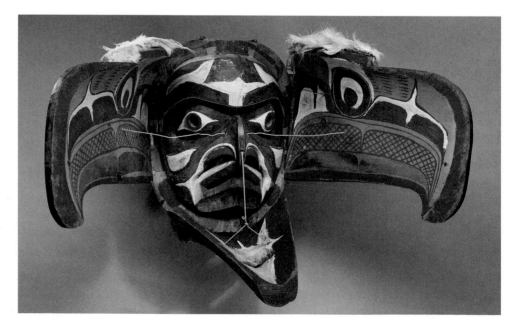

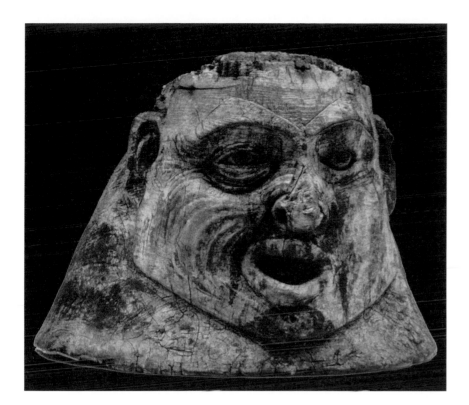

9-11 War helmet, Tlingit, collected 1888–1893. Wood, 1′ high. American Museum of Natural History, New York.

deeply undercut curvilinear depressions, which form strong shadows. In contrast to the carved human face, but painted in the same colors, is the two-dimensional abstract image of the eagle painted on the inside of the outer mask.

The Kwakiutl mask is a refined, yet forceful, carving typical of the area's more dramatic styles. Others are more subdued, and some, such as a wooden Tlingit war helmet (FIG. 9-11), are exceedingly naturalistic. Although the helmet mask may be an actual portrait, it might also represent a supernatural being whose powers enhance the wearer's strength. In either case, the artist surely created its grimacing expression to intimidate the enemy.

HAIDA TOTEM POLES Although Northwest Coast arts have a spiritual dimension, they are often more important as expressions of social status. Haida house frontal poles, displaying totemic emblems of clan groups, strikingly express this interest in prestige and family history. Totem poles emerged as a major art form about 300 years ago. Our examples (FIG. 9-12) date to the 19th century and are shown as part of a reconstructed Haida village that BILL REID (1920–1998, Haida) and his assistant DOUG KRANMER (b. 1917, Kwakiutl) completed in 1962. Each of the superimposed figures carved on these poles represents a crest, an animal, or a supernatural being who figures in the clan's origin story.

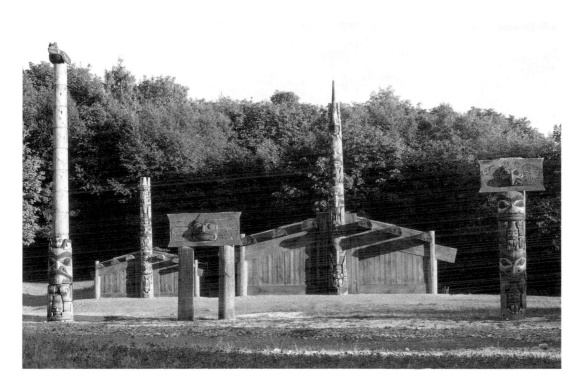

9-12 BILL REID (Haida), assisted by DOUG KRANMER (Kwakiutl), reconstruction of a 19th-century Haida village with totem poles, Queen Charlotte Island, 1962. Museum of Anthropology, University of British Columbia, Vancouver.

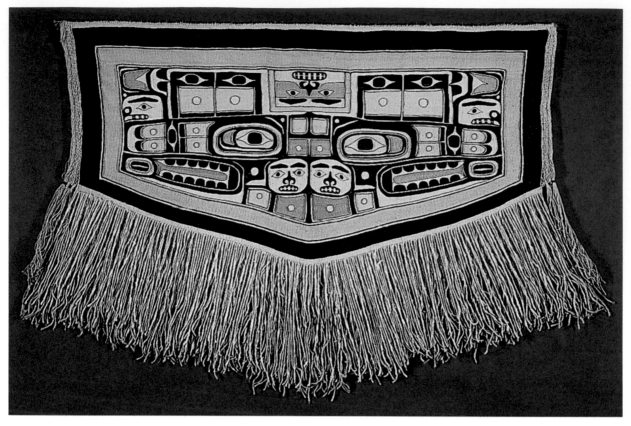

9-13 Chilkat blanket with stylized animal motifs, Tlingit, early 20th century. Mountain goat's wool and cedar bark, 6' × 2' 11". Southwest Museum, Los Angeles.

Additional crests could also be obtained through marriage and trade. The right to own and display such crests was so jealously guarded that even warfare could break out over the disputed ownership of a valued crest. In the poles shown, the crests represented include an upside-down dogfish (a small shark), an eagle with a downturned beak, and a killer whale with a crouching human between its snout and its upturned tail flukes. During the 19th century, the Haida erected more poles and made them larger in response to greater competitiveness and the availability of metal tools. The artists carved poles up to 60 feet tall from the trunks of single cedar trees. Because of the damp coastal climate, however, most of the poles decayed in a century or less. Nonetheless, many well-preserved 19th-century poles exist in museum collections. The Haida continue to carve totem poles in large numbers today.

ALASKAN CEREMONIAL BLANKETS Another characteristic Northwest Coast art form is the Chilkat blanket (FIG. **9-13**), named for an Alaskan Tlingit village where the blankets were woven. Male designers provided the templates for these blankets in the form of wooden pattern boards for the female weavers. Woven of shredded cedar bark and mountain goat wool on an upright loom, the Tlingit blankets took at least six months to complete. Actually robes worn over the shoulders, these became widespread prestige items of ceremonial dress during the 19th century. They display several characteristics of the Northwest Coast style recurrent in all media: symmetry and rhythmic repetition, schematic abstraction of animal motifs (in the robe illustrated, a bear), eye designs, a regularly swelling and thinning line, and a tendency to round off corners.

The devastating effects of 19th-century epidemics, coupled with government and missionary repression of Northwest Coast

ritual and social activities, threatened to wipe out the traditional arts entirely. Nevertheless, outstanding Northwest Coast artists continue to produce art objects today, some for the nonnative trade. The last half century has seen an impressive revival of traditional art forms, as well as the development of new ones, such as printmaking.

Eskimo

THE NORTH WIND The 19th-century Yupik Eskimos living around the Bering Strait of Alaska also had a highly developed ceremonial life focused on game animals, particularly seal. Their religious specialists wore highly imaginative masks with moving parts. The Yupik generally made these masks for single occasions and then abandoned them. Consequently, many masks have ended up in museums and private collections. Our example (FIG. **9-14**) represents the spirit of the north wind, its face surrounded by a hoop representing the universe, its voice re-created by the rattling appendages. The paired human hands commonly found on such masks refer to the wearer's power to attract animals for hunting. The painted white spots represent snowflakes.

In more recent years, Canadian Eskimos, known as the Inuit, have set up cooperatives to produce and market stone carvings and prints. With these new media, artists generally depict themes from the rapidly vanishing traditional Inuit way of life.

Great Plains

After colonial governments disrupted settled indigenous communities on the East Coast and the Europeans introduced the horse to North America, a new mobile Native American culture may be called his biography—a composite artistic statement in several media that neighboring Native Americans could have "read" easily. The concentric circle design over his left shoulder, for example, is an abstract rendering of an eagle-feather warbonnet.

Plains peoples also made shields and shield covers that were both artworks and "power images." Shield paintings often derived from personal religious visions. The owners believed that the symbolism, the pigments themselves, and added materials, such as feathers, provided them with magical protection and supernatural power.

Plains warriors battled incursions into their territory throughout the 19th century, but they were finally defeated by a combination of broken treaties, the rapid depletion of the buffalo, and military defeats at the hands of the U.S. Army. The pursuit of Plains natives culminated in the 1890 slaughter of Lakota participants who had gathered for a ritual known as the Ghost Dance at Wounded Knee Creek, South Dakota. Indeed, from the 1830s on, U.S. troops forcibly removed Native Americans from their homelands and resettled them in other parts of the country. Toward the end of the century, governments confined them to reservations in both the United States and Canada.

LEDGER PAINTINGS During the reservation period, some Plains arts continued to flourish, notably beadwork for the women and painting in ledger books for the men. Traders, the army, and Indian agents had for years provided Plains peoples with pencils

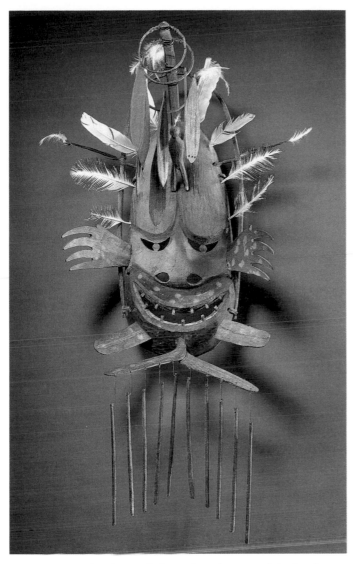

9-14 Mask, Yupik Eskimo, Alaska, early 20th century. Wood and feathers, approx. 3′ 9″ high. Metropolitan Museum of Art, New York (The Michael C. Rockefeller Memorial Collection, gift of Nelson Rockefeller).

flourished for a short time on the Great Plains. Artists of the Great Plains worked in materials and styles quite different from those of the Northwest Coast and Eskimo peoples. Much artistic energy went into the decoration of leather garments, pouches, and horse trappings, first with compactly sewn quill designs and later with beadwork patterns. Artists painted tipis, tipi linings, and buffalo-skin robes with geometric and stiff figural designs prior to about 1830. After that, they gradually introduced naturalistic scenes, often of war exploits, in styles adapted from those of visiting European artists.

HIDATSA REGALIA Because, at least in later periods, most Plains peoples were nomadic, they focused their aesthetic attention largely on their clothing and bodies and on other portable objects, such as shields, clubs, pipes, tomahawks, and various containers. Transient but important Plains art forms can sometimes be found in the paintings and drawings of visiting American and European artists. The Swiss KARL BODMER (1809–1893), for example, portrayed the personal decoration of Two Ravens, a Hidatsa warrior, in an 1833 watercolor (FIG. **9-15**). The painting depicts his pipe, painted buffalo robe, bear-claw necklace, and feather decorations, all symbolic of his affiliations and military accomplishments. They

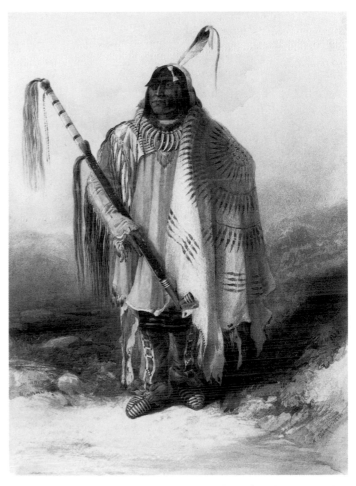

9-15 KARL BODMER, *Hidatsa Warrior Pehriska-Ruhpa (Two Ravens)*, 1833. Watercolor, 1′ 3⁷⁄₈″ × 11½″. Joslyn Art Museum, Omaha (gift of the Enron Art Foundation).

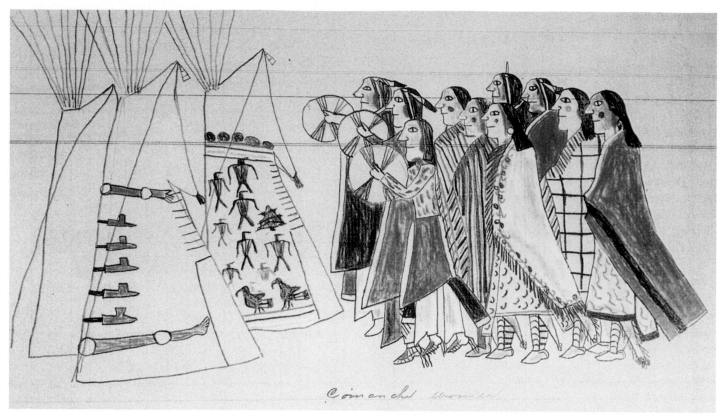

9-16 Honoring song at painted tipi, in Julian Scott Ledger, Kiowa, 1880. Pencil, ink, and colored pencil, $7\frac{1}{2}'' \times 1'$. Mr. and Mrs. Charles Diker Collection.

and new or discarded ledger books. They, in turn, used them to draw their personal exploits for themselves or for interested Anglo buyers. Sometimes warriors carried them into battle, where U.S. Army opponents retook the ledgers. After confinement to reservations, Plains artists began to record not only their heroic past and vanished lifestyle but also their reactions to their new surroundings, frequently in a state far from home. These images, often poignant and sometimes humorous, are important native documents of a time of great turmoil and change. In our example (FIG. **9-16**) by an unknown Kiowa artist, a group of men and women, possibly Comanches (allies of the Kiowa), appear to dance an honoring song before three tipis, the left forward one painted with red stone pipes and a dismembered leg and arm. The women (at the center and right) wear the mixture of clothing typical of the late 19th century among the Plains Indians—traditional high leather moccasins, dresses made from calico trade cloth, and (on the right) a red Hudson's Bay blanket with a black stripe.

Although ledger-book paintings are no longer made, beadwork has never completely died out. The ancient art of creating quilled, beaded, and painted clothing has evolved into the elaborate costumes displayed today at competitive dances called *powwows*.

CONCLUSION

The discovery of the "New World" at the end of the 15th century led quickly to confrontation, conquest, and the wholesale destruction of buildings and artworks. The loss is irreparable, but fortunately not total. The monuments that survive attest to the greatness of the art and architecture of the native peoples of the Americas.

In Mesoamerica, the Aztecs produced colossal stone sculptures and towering pyramids, and also excelled in the design and manufacture of textiles, metalwork, and books. In Andean South America, the Inka Empire was the largest in the world in the 16th century and boasted a sophisticated system of record-keeping and administration, as well as monumental art and architecture. In North America, power was much more widely dispersed and the native art and architecture more varied. Whether secular and decorative or spiritual and highly symbolic, the diverse styles and forms of Native American art in the United States and Canada reflect the indigenous peoples' reliance on and reverence toward the environment they considered it their privilege to inhabit.

MESOAMERICA
SOUTH AMERICA
NORTH AMERICA

LATE POSTCLASSIC

LATE INTERMEDIATE PERIOD

LATE HORIZON

VARIOUS OVERLAPPING INDIGENOUS CULTURES

1300

| Founding of Tenochtitlán, 1325 (M)

1400

| Aztecs become an imperial power, 1427 (M)
| Inka Empire begins to expand, 1438 (S)
1
| Columbus arrives in the Americas, 1492

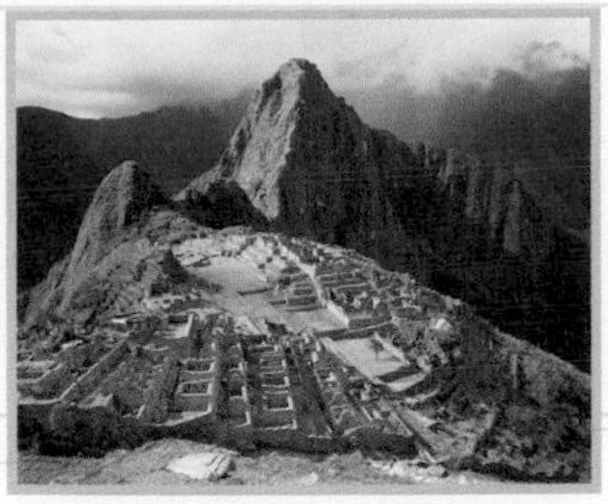

1 Machu Picchu, Peru, 15th century

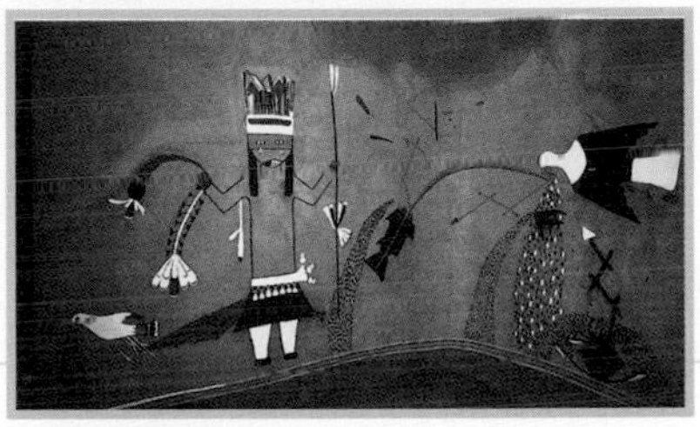

1500

2 | Moctezuma, Aztec emperor, r. 1502–1521 (M)
| Cortés arrives in Mexico, 1519 (M)
| Cortés topples Aztec Empire, 1521 (M)
| Pizarro conquers Inka Empire, 1532 (S)

1600

2 Kiva painting, Kuaua Pueblo, late 15th or early 16th century

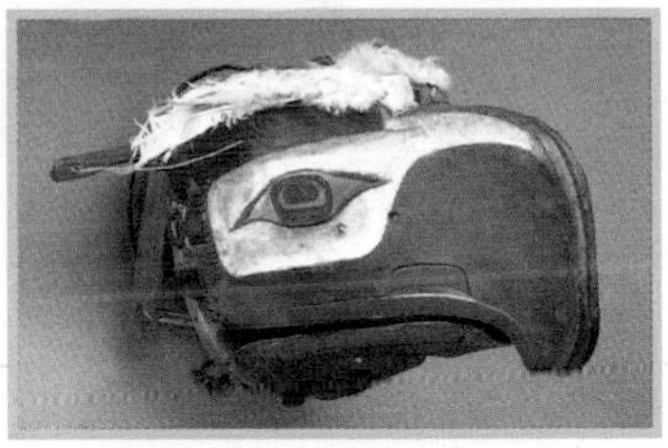

1700

| Europeans explore Northwest Coast, 1778 (N)

1800

| U.S. Government begins to resettle Native Americans on reservations, 1830s (N)
| Lakota massacre at Wounded Knee, 1890 (N)

3 Eagle transformation mask, Kwakiutl, late 19th century

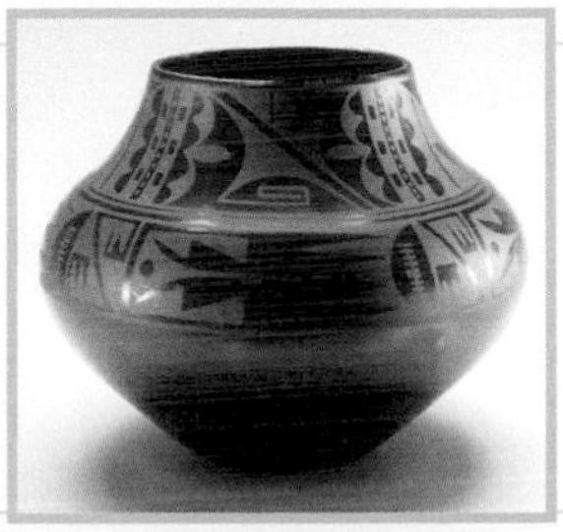

3

1900

| Native Americans receive U.S. citizenship, 1924 (N)
| U.S. Congress authorizes national Museum
4 of the American Indian, 1989 (N)

2000

4 María Montoya Martínez, jar, San Ildefonso Pueblo, ca. 1939

KEY: M = Mesoamerica / N = North America / S = South America

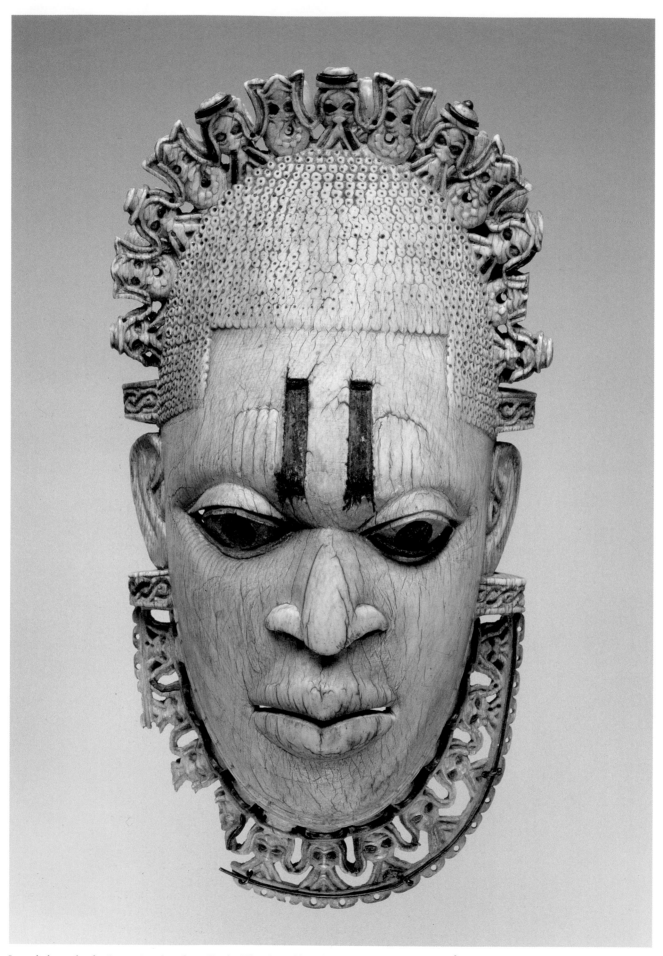

Ivory belt mask of a Queen Mother, from Benin, Nigeria, mid-16th century. Ivory and iron, 9⅜″ high. Metropolitan Museum of Art, New York (The Michael C. Rockefeller Memorial Collection, gift of Nelson A. Rockefeller, 1972).

10

SOUTH FROM
THE SAHARA

EARLY AFRICAN ART

Africa (MAP **10-1**) is a vast continent comprising more than one-fifth of the world's land mass and many distinct topographical and ecological zones. Parched deserts occupy northern and southern regions, high mountains rise in the east, and three great rivers—the Niger, the Congo, and the Nile—and their lush valleys support agriculture and large settled populations. It is not yet possible to present a coherent, continent-wide history of early African art. A few areas have been fairly well surveyed archaeologically, but most of the continent remains little known in periods prior to European contact, which began along the seacoasts in the late 15th century. Many inland areas were virtually unknown to outsiders before 1850 or 1900.

Hundreds of distinct ethnic, cultural, and linguistic groups, often but inaccurately called "tribes," long have inhabited this enormous continent. Currently comprising more than 52 nations, such population groups historically have ranged in size from a few hundred, in hunting and gathering bands, to several million, in kingdoms and empires. Councils of elders often governed smaller groups, whereas larger populations sometimes have joined with other ethnic groups within a centralized state under a king. Kingdoms and empires headed by sacred rulers are known from several parts of Africa from about 1000 CE onward.

Within this great variety of African peoples are many shared core beliefs and practices. These include honoring ancestors and worshiping nature deities, often with blood sacrifice, and a tendency to elevate rulers to sacred status. Most peoples also consult diviners or fortune tellers. These beliefs have given rise to many richly expressive art traditions: rock engraving and painting, personal decoration, masquerades and other lavish festivals, the display of court arts and regalia, figural sculpture (often in shrines), elaborate architecture, and domestic arts, among other forms.

All the hundreds of ethnic groups in Africa, speaking as many mutually unintelligible languages, made visual arts that differ according to economy, lifestyle, ideology, and the materials available to them. Rock engravings and paintings in the Sahara and southern Africa, for example, depict thousands of animals as well as rituals held by the hunting and gathering or herding peoples who created most of the art. These nomadic and semi-nomadic peoples also excelled in the arts of personal adornment. Among farmers, in

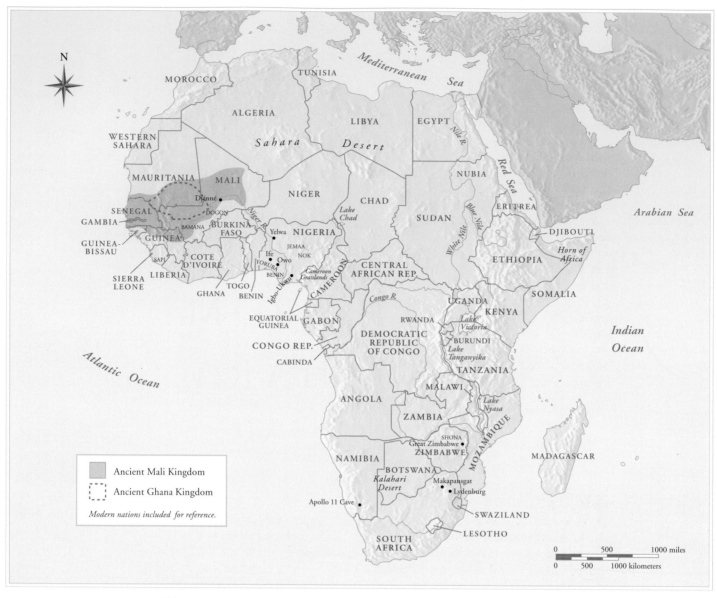

MAP 10-1 Africa before 1800.

contrast, figural sculpture in terracotta, wood, and metal was often housed in shrines to legendary ancestors or nature deities held responsible for the health of crops and the well-being of the people. The regalia, art, and architecture of kings and their courts project ideas of wealth and power. Nearly all African peoples lavished artistic energy on the decoration of their own bodies to express their identity and status, and many communities mounted richly layered festivals, including masquerades, to celebrate harvests, the New Year, and the deaths of great people. In Africa, art helps define and create culture. It is integrated within African life and thought, and was not created solely for display until the final decades of the 20th century.

This chapter provides a chronological survey of sub-Saharan African art through the 18th century (see "Dating African Art and Identifying African Artists," page 187). Chapter 11 treats the past two centuries. The art and architecture of Islamic North Africa were examined in Chapter 7.

PREHISTORIC AFRICAN ART

AFRICA'S EARLIEST ART Thousands of rock engravings and paintings found in hundreds of sites across the continent constitute the earliest known African art. Some painted animals from the Apollo 11 Cave in Namibia date to perhaps as long ago as 25,000 years, earlier than all but the oldest Paleolithic art of Europe. As humankind apparently originated in Africa, the world's earliest art may yet be discovered there as well. The greatest concentrations of rock art are in what are now dry desert regions—the Sahara to the north, the Horn in the east, and the Kalahari to the south—as well as in caves and on rock outcroppings in southern Africa. Probably because rock artists were more often hunter-gatherers or herders than farmers, these are precisely *not* the areas where most African sculpture is found. Accurately naturalistic renderings as well as stylized images on rock surfaces show animals and humans in many different positions and activities, singly or in groups, stationary or in motion. Most of these works date to within the past 4,000 to 6,000 years or slightly more, and they provide a rich record of the environment, human activities, and animal species.

The central Saharan painting shown here (FIG. **10-1**), for example, depicts a running woman with convincing animation and significant detail. The dotted marks on her shoulders, legs, and torso probably show body painting applied for a ritual. The white parallel patterns attached to her arms and waist appear to

Dating African Art and Identifying African Artists

Most African objects are unlabeled and unsigned and, consequently, insecurely dated. Early collectors did not bother to ask the names of artists or when the works were made. Organizing the vast array of African artworks into a firm chronology is therefore extremely difficult. Broad historical trends are reasonably clear, but more extensive archaeological work is needed in numerous parts of the continent before many artworks and even cultures can be firmly dated.

Some African peoples have left written documents that help date their artworks, even when their methods of measuring time differ from those used today. Other cultures, such as the Benin kingdom, preserve complex oral records of past events. Historians can check these against the accounts of Portuguese, German, and Dutch travelers and traders who visited the kingdom and recorded their observations.

The work of individual artists is now also being recognized, even if their names are often lost. Biographies have been compiled for some famous sculptors who worked in the late 19th or early 20th centuries. When artists are members of craft or occupational guilds—such as blacksmiths and brass casters in the Western Sudan—commissions go to the group chief, and the specific artist who worked on the commission may never be known. Nevertheless, individual hands can be identified if their work is distinctive. Documentation now exists for several hundred individual artists.

Where documentation on authorship or dating is fragmentary or unavailable, art historians sometimes try to establish chronology from an object's style, determining what sorts of changes occurred over time to forms of a similar type. Scientific techniques such as *radiocarbon dating* (measuring the decay rate of carbon isotopes in organic matter to provide dates for wood, fiber, and ivory) and *thermoluminescence* (dating the amounts of radiation found in fired clay objects) have also proved useful. The history of African art is slowly being written, but there are still large gaps that need to be filled in. One of the major problems impeding compilation of an accurate African art history is illegal and uncontrolled excavation. By removing artworks from the ground, treasure hunters disturb or ruin their original contexts, and the possibility of establishing accurate chronologies is compromised or wholly lost.

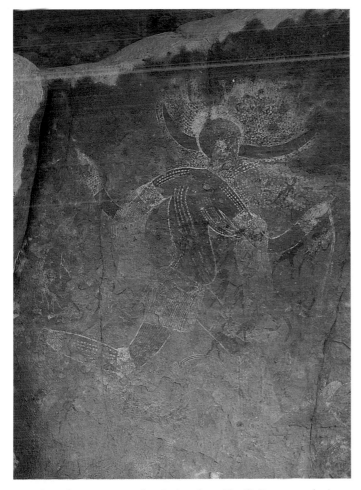

10-1 Running woman, rock painting, from Tassili (Inauouanrhat), Algeria, ca. 6000–4000 BCE.

represent flowing raffia decorations and her skirt, also probably raffia. Horns are part of her ceremonial attire. Notably, this detailed image was painted over a field of much smaller painted human beings, an indication of why it is often so difficult to date and interpret art on rock surfaces, as superimpositions are frequent.

Although both the precise dating and meaning are problematic for much rock art, a considerable literature exists that describes, analyzes, and interprets the varied human and animal activities shown, as well as the evidently symbolic, more abstract patterns. Overall meanings and uses probably coincide with those of the later arts—references to ideas and rituals about the origin, survival, health, and continuity of human populations. The human and humanlike renderings depict people and a host of spirits and other supernatural beings and gods.

AFRICAN ART, CA. 500 BCE—1000 CE

Nok Art (Central Sudan)

NOK TERRACOTTA HEADS Outside Egypt and neighboring Nubia, the earliest African sculptures in the round have been found at several sites in the Central Sudan, part of a broad band of grassland that spans the continent south of the Sahara. These dispersed sites are collectively designated the Nok culture, but there is no reason to believe that they were unified politically or socially. Named after the site where such sculptures were first discovered in 1928, Nok art dates between 500 BCE and 200 CE. Hundreds of Nok-style human and animal heads, body parts, and figures have been found accidentally during tin mining operations, as well as in archaeological excavations.

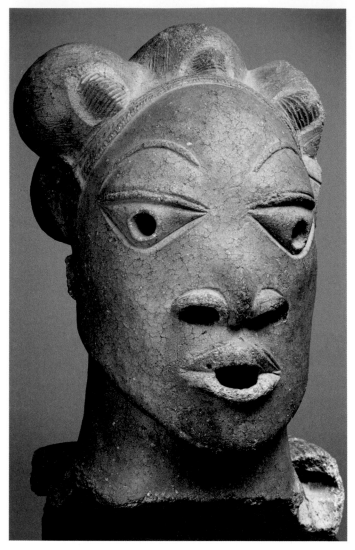

10-2 Nok head, from Rafin Kura, Nigeria, ca. 500 BCE–200 CE. Terracotta, 1′ 2 3/16″ high. National Museum, Lagos.

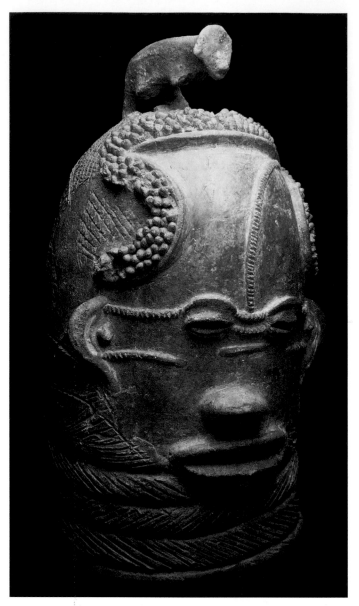

10-3 Head, from Lydenburg, South Africa, sixth to eighth century CE. Terracotta, 1′ 2 15/16″ high. IZIKO Museums of Cape Town, Cape Town.

A representative Nok terracotta head (FIG. 10-2), a fragment of a full figure, depicts an expressive face with large alert eyes, flaring nostrils, and parted lips. The sculptor probably pierced the eyes, mouth, and ear holes—a characteristic of Nok style—to help equalize the heating of the hollow clay head during the firing process. The coiffure with incised grooves, the raised eyebrows, the deeply cut triangular eyes, and the sharp jaw line suggest that the sculptor carved some details of the head while modeling the rest. A probable earlier artistic tradition of woodcarving that has not survived may explain the lack of any known art tradition leading to the highly sophisticated Nok sculptures. The gender of Nok artists is unknown. Because the primary ceramists and clay sculptors across the continent are women, Nok sculptors may have been as well (see "Gender Roles in African Art Production," Chapter 11, page 211). Researchers are unclear about the function of these objects, but a ritual context is more likely than a simply decorative one.

Lydenburg Art (Southern Africa)

SCULPTURE IN SOUTH AFRICA Later in date than the Nok examples are the seven life-size (or nearly life-size) terracotta heads discovered outside the town of Lydenburg in present-day South Africa. They date to the later centuries of the first millennium of our era, although dating is controversial and still imprecise. The head shown here (FIG. 10-3), reconstructed from fragments, has a humanlike form, although its inverted pot shape differs markedly from the sculptural Nok heads. The artist created the eyes, ears, nose, and mouth, as well as the hairline, by applying thin clay fillets onto the head. The same method produced what are probably *scarification* marks (scars intentionally created to form patterns on the flesh) on the forehead, temples, and between the eyes. The horizontal neck bands, with their incised surfaces, resemble the ringed or banded necks that are considered signs of beauty in many parts of the continent. A small, unidentifiable animal sits atop the head. One can only guess at the uses and meanings of these heads, but a ritual function is again more likely than a purely secular one.

Igbo-Ukwu Art (Lower Niger Region)

EARLY BRONZE CASTING By the 9th or 10th century, a West African bronze-casting tradition of great sophistication had developed in the lower Niger area, just east of that great river. Dozens of refined, varied objects in an extremely intricate style were excavated in a family compound near the community of Igbo-Ukwu.

Art and Leadership in Africa

The relationships between leaders and art forms are strong, complex, and universal in Africa. Political, spiritual, and social leaders—kings, chiefs, titled people, and religious specialists—have the power and wealth to command the best artists and to require the richest, most durable materials to adorn themselves, furnish their homes, and make visible the cultural and religious organizations they lead. Leaders dispense art or the prerogative to use it. They use it instrumentally both to maintain existing patterns and to cause change. Thus the uses and meanings of leaders' arts are varied, whether overt or subtle, active or passive.

A number of formal or structural principles or trends characterize leaders' arts and thus set them off from the popular arts owned and used by ordinary people. Leaders' arts—for example, the sumptuous and layered regalia of chiefs and kings—tend to be durable and are often made of expensive materials, such as ivory, beads, copper alloys, and other rich metals. The art and architecture commissioned by African leaders also tend to be larger and more complex than those of other patrons. A palace, for example, is more extensive, with more rooms and finer decoration, than an ordinary dwelling. The arts often elevate leaders and draw attention to their superior status: stools or chairs, ornate clothing, and special weaponry serve these purposes. A leader's reach is often extended by handheld objects: staff, spear, or knife; pipe, fly whisk (FIG. 10-4), or scepter. Such forms also serve to magnify gestures. These and other objects, such as fans (see FIG. Intro-1), shields, umbrellas, and architectural forms, protect leaders physically or spiritually. Many of these forms have the effect of magnifying the apparent size and grandeur of the leader, further setting him or her off from the people at large. Sometimes a person is overloaded with regalia and implements to the point of virtual immobility, suggesting that the temporary holder of an office is less significant than the eternal office itself. Still, these arts render both the office and its holder visibly prominent and grand, thus contributing to the person's place at the center and top of the hierarchy.

Although it is easier to see leaders' arts in centralized, hierarchical societies (such as Benin, FIG. 10-11), leaders among less centralized peoples are no less conversant with the power of art to move people and effect change. Masquerades and religious cults, for example, are usually established and run by leaders who themselves may be less visible than the forms they commission and manipulate: shrines, altars, festivals, and rites of passage such as funerals, the last being especially elaborate and festive in many parts of Africa. Arts controlled by leaders thus help create pageantry, mystery, and spectacle, enriching and changing the lives of the people.

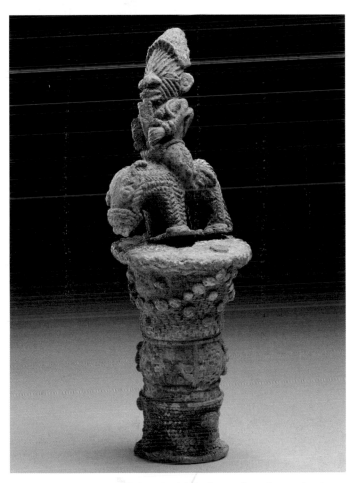

10-4 Equestrian figure on fly-whisk hilt, from Igbo-Ukwu, Nigeria, 9th to 10th century CE. Copper-alloy bronze, figure $6\frac{3}{16}''$ high. National Museum, Lagos.

The ceramic, copper, cast bronze, and iron artifacts included basins, bowls, altar stands, staffs, swords, scabbards, knives, and pendants. In one burial, the grave goods consisted of numerous prestige objects—copper anklets, armlets, spiral ornaments, a fan handle, and thousands of beads. The tomb also contained three elephant tusks, a beaded armlet, a crown, and a bronze leopard's skull. These items, doubtless the regalia of a leader (see "Art and Leadership in Africa, above), are the earliest metal castings known from regions south of the Sahara.

A lost-wax cast bronze (FIG. **10-4**), the earliest found in Africa, depicts an equestrian figure on a fly-whisk handle. The sculpture's upper section comprises a figure seated on a horselike animal, and the lower is an elaborately embellished handle with beaded and threadlike patterns. The facial stripes on the human figure probably represent marks of titled status, as can still be found among contemporary Igbo-speaking peoples in the same region today.

AFRICAN ART, CA. 1000–1800*

Inland Niger Delta Art (Western Sudan)

The inland floodplain of the Niger River in the Western Sudan was for the African continent a kind of "fertile crescent," analogous to that of ancient Mesopotamia, home of the world's oldest civilizations. The metal-casting techniques used in Igbo-Ukwu, for example, may have come from this region. Although firm evidence for bronze casting in the Inland Delta has yet to

---

* From this point on, all dates in this chapter are CE unless otherwise stated.

Idealized Naturalism at Ile-Ife

When the German anthropologist Leo Frobenius first "discovered" the refined and naturalistic sculpture of Ile-Ife just after the turn of the 19th century in the Lower Niger River region, he could not believe that such works were locally made. Rather, he ascribed authorship to ancient Greece, where similarly lifelike art was well known. Other scholars traced such works to ancient Egypt, along with patterns of sacred kingship that were also believed to have been diffused several thousand miles from the Nile Valley to Yorubaland. Kings are known in numerous Yoruba city-states, all of which trace their origin to Ile-Ife, where Yoruba legends recount the world, its peoples, and sacred kingship began. Many careful archaeological excavations in and around the contemporary city of Ile-Ife, especially near the king's palace, moreover, confirm that the Yoruba ancestors of present-day residents were indeed the artists who made the extraordinary sculptures in stone, terracotta, and copper alloys ascribed to Ile-Ife. A number of these works were employed in the service of kingship, in ceremonies of installation, in funerals, and probably in annual festivals that reaffirmed the sacred power of the ruler and the allegiance of his people. Radiocarbon dates associated with several excavated Ife sites and with works of idealized naturalism place most of this art between the 11th or 12th and the 15th centuries.

Like the king figure we illustrate (FIG. 10-6), most Ife heads and figures are modeled with focused attention on naturalistic detail, apart from blemishes or signs of age, which are absent. Thus Ife style is lifelike but at the same time idealized, as if most of the people were portrayed as young adults in the prime of life and without any disfiguring warts or wrinkles. Some life-size heads,

although still idealized, take naturalism to the point of descriptive, imitative portraiture. This is especially true of a group of about 30 heads cast in copper alloys. Many of these are sufficiently individualized that scholars are quite certain specific persons were being portrayed, although nearly all their names are lost. Among the most convincing portraits, however, is a mask of almost pure copper that has long carried the name of a famous early king, Obalufon. Until it became a holding of the Ife museum, the mask was apparently kept in the palace of the *oni* (king) from the time that it was made. Several very naturalistic heads have small holes above the forehead and around the lips and jaw, where black beads were found. These suggest that some heads were fitted with beaded veils, such as those known among Yoruba kings today, and perhaps human hair as well. Elaborate beadwork, a Yoruba royal prerogative, is also seen on the Ife king's image we illustrate (FIG. 10-6).

The hundreds of terracotta and copper-alloy heads, body parts and fragments, animals, and ritual vessels from Ile-Ife attest to a remarkable period in African art history, a period during which sensitive, meticulously rendered idealized naturalism prevailed. To this day, works in this style stand in contrast to the vast majority of African objects, which show the human figure in many different quite strongly conventionalized styles. Also clear is the distinction between the "perceptual naturalism" of most Ife works and the "conceptual naturalism" of most other African art. The latter suggests that for the most part, the representation of human forms conformed to local conventions passed down from one artist to another, whereas Ife style came about when artists actually perceived the human faces and bodies they portrayed.

---

be discovered, a copper industry is known to have flourished there from around 500, and sophisticated sculpture dates from around 1000.

JENNE TERRACOTTAS By about 800, a walled town, called Jenne-Jeno by archaeologists, had been built on high ground left dry during the flooding season. The archaeological evidence suggests the presence of several ethnic groups and many specialist workshops of blacksmiths, sculptors, potters, and others. Hundreds of accomplished, confidently modeled terracotta sculptures dating to between 1000 and 1500 have been found at numerous unmapped sites in the Jenne region. Unfortunately, as is true of the Nok terracottas, the vast majority of these sculptures were excavated illegally, and contextual information about them has been destroyed. The subject matter includes equestrians, male and female couples, emaciated and diseased people with lesions and swellings, and snake-entwined figures. There are seated, reclining, kneeling, and standing human figures. Some wear elaborate jewelry, but many are without adornment. The group we illustrate (FIG. **10-5**) appears at first to be a mother and her children, but the "children" clambering up their "mother's" torso are in fact adults, easily discerned as such by their proportions. In some similar groups the "children" have beards. The woman therefore seems to be a metaphorical or legendary mother and the group is not a common family, although everyday genre scenes also occur among the preserved ceramic sculptures from the Inland Niger Delta.

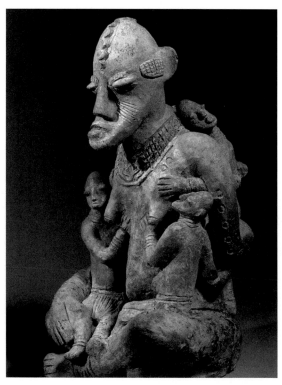

10-5 Mother with children(?), from the Inland Niger Delta, Mali, ca. 1000–1500. Terracotta, 1' 1¾" high. Private collection.

Ile-Ife Art (West of the Lower Niger)

By the 11th and 12th centuries, a very naturalistic style had appeared at Ile-Ife, about 200 miles west of Igbo Ukwu. Ile-Ife has long been considered the cradle of Yoruba civilization, the place where the gods created the universe. Origin stories also account for a line of divine Yoruba rulers extending from the legendary past until today.

SACRED KINGS An early work (FIG. 10-6), cast in a zinc-brass alloy, undoubtedly represents a ruler. This finely rendered figure, unlike most later African wood sculpture, shows fleshlike modeling in the torso and the kind of idealized naturalism in facial features that approaches portraiture (see "Idealized Naturalism at Ile-Ife," page 190). Its proportions are less lifelike, however, than they are ideological. For modern Yoruba, the head is the locus of wisdom, destiny, and the essence of being. Such ideas probably developed at least 800 years ago. The sculptor accurately recorded the precise details of the heavily beaded costume, crown, and jewelry worn by both ancient and contemporary kings in Ile-Ife and other Yoruba city-states. The Ile-Ife figures and related works from the Yoruba kingdom of Owo to the southeast served mainly in rituals focused on sacred kingship. Many of these rituals have survived into the 21st century.

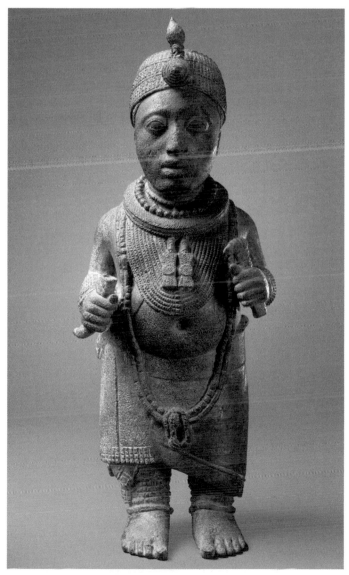

10-6 King, from Ife, Nigeria, 11th to 12th century. Zinc brass, 1' 6½" high. Ife Museum, Ife.

Great Zimbabwe Art (Southern Africa)

RUINS OF A LOST EMPIRE The most famous southern African site is a complex of stone ruins at the large southeastern political center called Great Zimbabwe. First occupied in the 11th century, the site features walled enclosures and towers that date from about the late 13th to the middle of the 15th century, when the Great Zimbabwe empire had a wide trade network. Finds of beads and pottery from Persia, the Near East, and China, along with copper and gold objects, underscore that Great Zimbabwe was a prosperous trade center well before Europeans began their coastal voyaging in the late 15th century. Most archaeologists and historians agree that the rulers at Great Zimbabwe and other nearby royal towns were ancestors of the area's present Shona-speaking peoples.

Using ethnographic information gathered from Portuguese accounts of the 16th to early 19th centuries and more recent studies of Shona culture, scholars have tried to interpret the meanings of the buildings and artifacts found at Great Zimbabwe. Most agree that the complex was a royal residence with special areas for the ruler (the royal hill complex), his wives, and nobles, including an open court for ceremonial gatherings. At the zenith of the empire's power, as many as 18,000 people may have lived in the surrounding area, with most of the commoners living outside the enclosed structures reserved for royalty. Although the actual habitations are gone, the remaining enclosures are unusual for their size and the excellence of their stonework. Some perimeter walls reach heights of 30 feet. One of these, known as the Great Enclosure (FIG. 10-7), houses one large

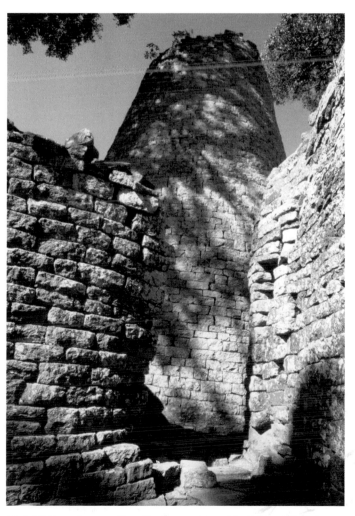

10-7 Walls and tower, Great Enclosure, Great Zimbabwe, Zimbabwe, 14th century.

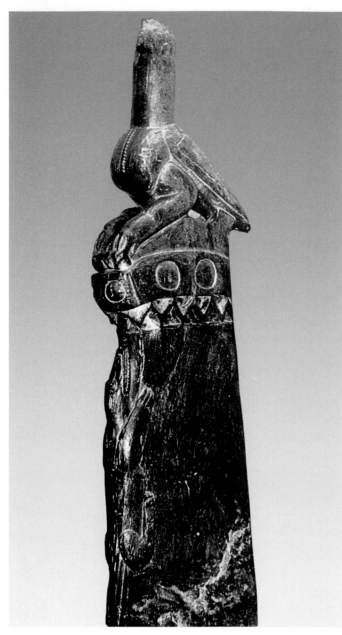

10-8 Bird with crocodile image on top of stone monolith, from Great Zimbabwe, Zimbabwe, 15th century. Soapstone, bird image 1′ 2½″ high. Great Zimbabwe Site Museum, Great Zimbabwe.

10-9 Beta Medhane Alem church, Lalibela, Ethiopia, 14th century.

and several small conical towerlike stone structures. Scholars have interpreted these symbolically as masculine (large) and feminine (small) forms, but their precise significance is unknown. The form of the largest tower suggests a granary. Such grain bins were symbols of royal power and generosity, as the ruler received tribute in grain and dispensed it to the people in times of need.

SOAPSTONE BIRDS Explorations at Great Zimbabwe have yielded eight soapstone monoliths. Seven came from the royal hill complex and probably were set up as part of shrines to ancestors. The eighth bird monolith (FIG. **10-8**), found in an area now considered the ancestral shrine of the ruler's first wife, stands several feet tall. Some have interpreted the bird as symbolizing the first wife's ancestors. (Ancestral spirits among the present-day Shona take the form of birds, especially eagles, believed to communicate between the sky and the earth.) The crocodile on the front of the monolith may represent the wife's elder male ancestors. The circles beneath the bird are called the "eyes of the crocodile" in Shona and may symbolically represent elder female ancestors. The double- and single-chevron motifs may represent young male and young female ancestors, respectively. The bird perhaps represents some form of bird of prey, such as an eagle, although this and other bird sculptures from the site have feet with five humanlike toes, rather than an eagle's three-toed talons. In fact, the species of the birds cannot be identified. Some researchers have speculated that the bird and crocodile symbolize previous rulers who would have acted as messengers between the living and the dead, as well as between the sky and the earth.

Lalibela Art and Architecture (Ethiopia)

CHRISTIAN ETHIOPIA The rugged highlands of present-day Ethiopia, where land travel is difficult, nevertheless played host to a Christian kingdom in the 13th to 15th centuries. Christianity had arrived in Ethiopia in the early fourth century, when the region was part of the indigenous Aksum Empire, where some fine stone monoliths were made. In the early 13th century, a ruler of the Zagwe dynasty, named Lalibela, commissioned a series of churches to be cut from living bedrock at his capital, today also called Lalibela. The largest of these rock-cut churches (FIG. **10-9**), Beta Medhane Alem ("House of the Savior of the World"), has a *nave* and

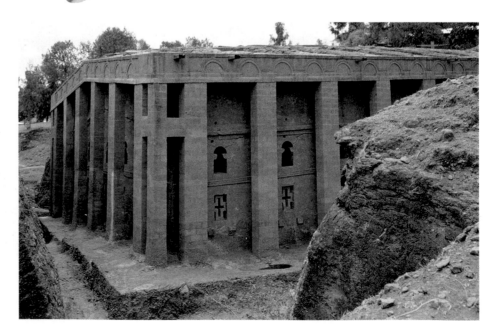

four flanking *aisles*, as is standard in churches in the West. The exterior takes the form of a *colonnade* of closely set square pillars, with a crowning pitched roof decorated with semicircular motifs in relief, one each above and between every column, reinforcing the rhythm of the pillars. The planning and skilled labor needed to carve from the bedrock a complex building such as this, with all its details, is truly astonishing. The bedrock tufa is soft and easily worked. Nonetheless, the entire design had to be visualized before the work began because there was no possibility of revision or correction. More amazing still is the fact that more than 1,500 such sculpted churches exist in Ethiopia. Churches are being "constructed" in this manner as acts of devotion even today.

Benin Art (Lower Niger)

The Benin kingdom was established just west of the lower reaches of the Niger River before 1400, most likely in the 13th century. It reached its greatest power and geographical extent in the 15th and 16th centuries. The kingdom's vicissitudes and slow decline thereafter culminated in the burning and sacking of the Benin palace and city by the British in 1897. Benin City thrives today, however, and the palace, where the Benin king continues to live, has been partially rebuilt. By observing current rituals and regalia and talking with elderly specialists who understand the significance of these cultural features, researchers continue to learn about earlier royal Benin art.

Benin artists have produced many complex, finely cast copper-alloy sculptures, as well as artworks in ivory, wood, ceramic, and wrought iron. Royalty commissioned (and sometimes still do) cast-metal pieces and ivory carvings from guilds of highly trained professional men. The hereditary *oba*, or sacred king, and his court still use and dispense art objects as royal favors to title holders and other chiefs (see "Art and Leadership," page 189). Benin kings to this day maintain ritual relationships with their Yoruba counterparts at Ile-Ife, and Benin oral tradition says that the first king of the new dynasty in the 14th century was the grandson of a Yoruba king. Other traditions, although contested, credit the Yoruba with the introduction of copper-alloy casting to Benin.

IVORY FOR A KING The ivory masquette we illustrate (FIG. **10-10**) was almost certainly worn by a Benin king at his waist. Probably this and the few other known naturalistic ivory carvings of human "masks" were commissioned by Oba Esigie (r. ca. 1504–1550), under whom, with the help of the Portuguese, the Benin kingdom flourished and expanded. Esigie's mother, Idia, helped him in warfare, and in return he created for her the title of Queen Mother, Iy'oba, and built her a separate palace and court. The mask probably represents Idia. Its sensitive naturalism places it in the 16th century. On its crown are alternating Portuguese heads and mudfish, respectively symbolic references to Benin's trade and diplomatic relationships with the Portuguese and to Olokun, god of the sea, wealth, and creativity. Another series of Portuguese heads also adorns the lower part of the carving. In the late 15th and 16th centuries, Benin people probably associated the Portuguese, with their large ships from across the sea, their powerful weapons, and their wealth in metals, cloth, and other goods, with Olokun, the deity they deem responsible for abundance and prosperity.

THE HAND AND ARM The centrality of the sacred oba in Benin culture is well demonstrated by his depiction twice on a cast-brass royal shrine called an *ikegobo* (FIG. **10-11**). It features symmetrical hierarchical compositions centered on the dominant

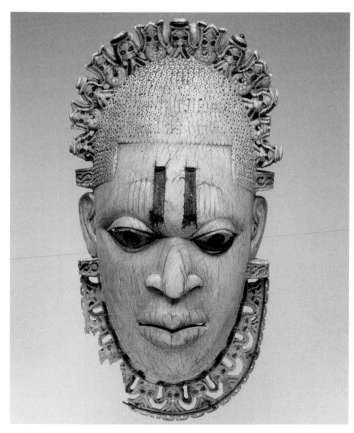

10-10 Ivory belt mask of a Queen Mother, from Benin, Nigeria, mid-16th century. Ivory and iron, $9\frac{3}{8}$" high. Metropolitan Museum of Art, New York (The Michael C. Rockefeller Memorial Collection, gift of Nelson A. Rockefeller, 1972).

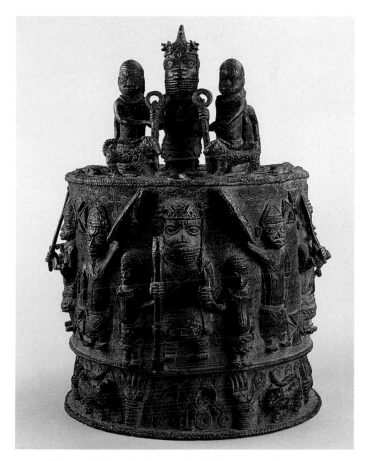

10-11 Altar to the Hand and Arm (*ikegobo*), from Benin, Nigeria, 17th to 18th century(?). Bronze, 1' $5\frac{1}{2}$" high. British Museum, London.

king. Flanking and supporting him are smaller, lesser members of the court, and in front, a pair of leopards, animals sacrificed by the sacred king and symbolic of his power over all creatures. Similar compositions are common in Benin arts, as exemplified by the royal plaque from Benin discussed in the Introduction (see FIG. Intro-1). Notably, too, the proportions of the king are distorted to emphasize his head, the seat of his will and power. One of the king's praise names is "great head." The treatment of human faces on this altar is more conventionalized than on the ivory, attesting to its later manufacture (17th or 18th century).

At such personal altars, the king and other high-ranking officials made sacrifices to their own powers of success and accomplishment—symbolized by the hand and arm. The altar invokes power, both in the ritual's anticipated outcome and in the shrine's iconography. The inclusion of leopards on the top and around the base, along with ram and elephant heads and crocodiles (not all visible in FIG. 10-11), reiterates this power.

Sapi Art (West Atlantic Coast)

During the 15th and 16th centuries, the Sapi people on the Atlantic coast of Africa carved stone, wood, and ivory images for their own use. Between 1490 and 1540, however, Portuguese explorers and traders commissioned Sapi artists to create objects exclusively for export to Europe: delicate spoons, forks, and elaborate containers usually referred to as saltcellars, as well as boxes, hunting horns, and knife handles. All were meticulously carved from elephant tusk ivory with refined and even elegant detail and careful finish. Ivory was plentiful in those early days and was one of the coveted exports in early West and Central Africa trade with Europe. The Sapi export ivories are a fascinating hybrid art form. They are the earliest examples of African tourist art.

The saltcellar shown here (FIG. **10-12**), almost 17 inches high, has been attributed to the MASTER OF THE SYMBOLIC EXECUTION, one of the three major Sapi ivory carvers during the period 1500–1540. It is his name piece and depicts an extraordinary execution scene. A kneeling figure with a shield in one hand holds an axe in the other hand over another sitting figure about to lose his head. On the ground before the executioner, six severed heads (five visible here) grimly testify to the executioner's power. A double zigzag line separates the lid of the globular container from the rest of the vessel. This vessel rests in turn on a circular platform held up by slender rods adorned with crocodile images. Two male and two female figures sit between these rods, grasping them. The men wear European-style pants, and the women wear skirts, but the women have elaborate raised patterns, surely decorative scars, on their upper chests. The European components of this saltcellar are the overall design of a spherical container on a pedestal and some of the geometric patterning on the base and the sphere, as well as certain elements of dress such as the shirts and hats. What is distinctly African is the style of the human heads and figures and their proportions, the latter skewed here to emphasize the head, as so often seen in African art. Identical large noses with flaring nostrils, as well as the conventions for rendering eyes and lips, can be seen on Sapi stone figures from the same region and period. Scholars cannot be sure whether it was the African carver or the European patron who specified the subject matter and the configurations of various parts.

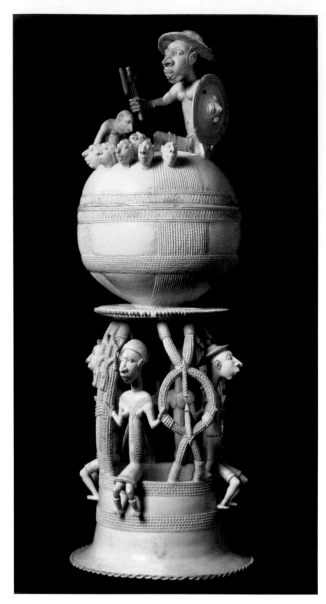

10-12 MASTER OF THE SYMBOLIC EXECUTION, saltcellar, Sapi-Portuguese, from Sierra Leone, 15th to 16th century. Ivory, 1' 4$\frac{7}{8}$" high. Museo Nazionale Preistorico e Etnografico Luigi Pigorini, Rome.

CONCLUSION

The art forms discussed in this chapter have survived for many centuries in large measure because they are made of durable materials such as terracotta, ivory, and cast metal (bronze or one of several copper alloys). It is clear that many of these art forms were used in elite contexts and were associated with kings and chieftains. Some of these traditions still continue in altered form. In Benin, for example, there is virtually no break between 16th- and 17th-century art forms and those that survive on kings' ancestral altars today. The same is true for Christian Ethiopia, where both painted icons and rock-cut churches are still being made. In the cases of Igbo Ukwu and Ile-Ife, recent forms are somewhat different from ancient ones, but the connections between the two eras are nevertheless clear. Some of the more recent versions of these art forms are examined in Chapter 11.

500 BCE

| First sub-Saharan ceramics, fifth century BCE

1 | Nok culture, ca. 500 BCE–200 CE

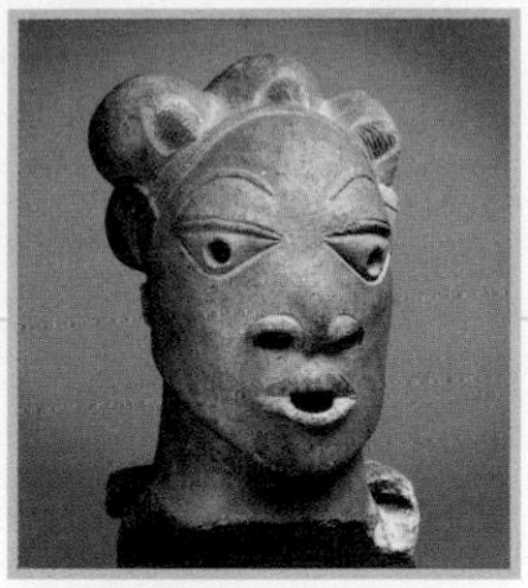

200 CE

| Christianity introduced to Ethiopia, fourth century

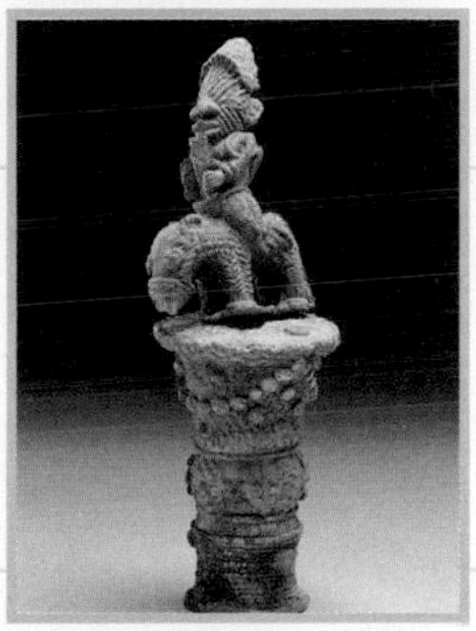

1 Nok head, Nigeria, ca. 500 BCE–200 CE

500

| Islam spreads throughout North Africa, seventh century

800

| First bronze castings, 9th century

2 | Igbo-Ukwu culture, 9th–10th centuries

| Jenne culture, 9th–15th centuries

2 Igbo-Ukwu fly-whisk hilt, Nigeria, 9th to 10th century

1000

| Ile-Ife culture, 11th–12th centuries

| Great Zimbabwe culture, 11th–15th centuries

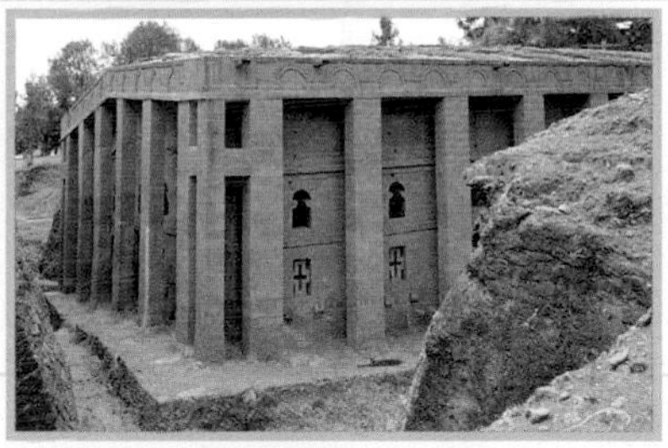

1200

| Benin kingdom, founded 13th century

3

3 Beta Medhane Alem church, Lalibela, Ethiopia, 14th century

1400

| Sapi culture, 15th–16th centuries

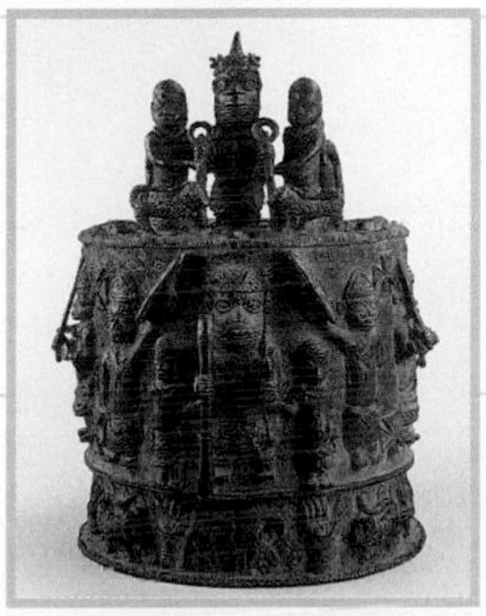

1600

4

1800

4 Altar of the Hand and Arm, Benin, Nigeria, 17th to 18th century

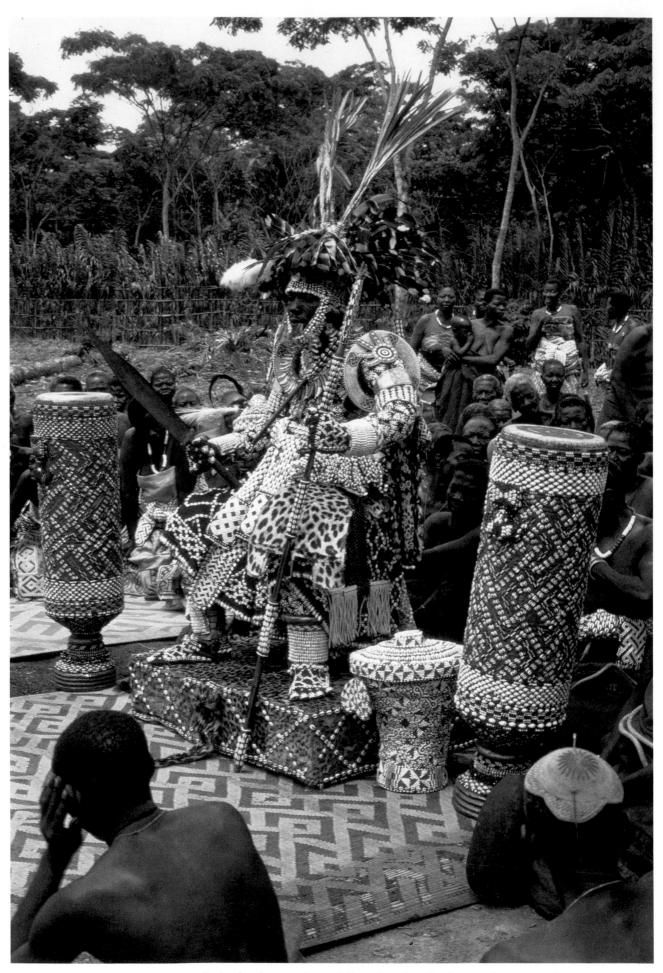

Kuba King Kot a-Mbweeky III during a display for photographer and filmmaker Eliot Elisofon in early 1970, Mushenge, Democratic Republic of Congo.

11

TRADITIONALISM AND INTERNATIONALISM

19TH- AND 20TH-CENTURY AFRICAN ARTS

This chapter surveys the arts of the vast African continent (MAP 11-1) from about 1800 to the present. As in Chapter 10, the organizing principle is chronology. A generation ago African art was often presented as if it had no history, but scholars now recognize that every art form, like every other kind of object or being, has a history. The fact that researchers do not always know the history of African artworks tells more about the people constructing African history than it reveals about the African people who lived it. Our approach to writing the history of African art is to combine information derived from archaeology and field research in Africa (mainly interviews with local people) on the use, function, and meaning of art objects with interpretive strategies devised for the most part by outsiders.

THE 19TH CENTURY

San Art (South Africa)

HISTORICAL ROCK PAINTINGS Rock paintings are among the most ancient arts of Africa (see FIG. 10-1). Yet the tradition also continued well into the historical period. The latest examples were completed as recently as the 19th century, and some of these depict the presence of Europeans. Many examples have been found in South Africa. The one we illustrate (FIG. 11-1), originally about eight feet long but now in fragments, is from near the source of the Mzimkhulu River at Bamboo Mountain and dates to the mid-19th century. Scholars attribute these paintings to the San peoples. San compositions often depict several game animals hunted for food, as well as others, such as the eland (FIG. 11-1, *left*), considered effective in rainmaking and ancestor rituals. By the early to mid-19th century, the increasing development of colonial ranches and the settlements of African agriculturists had greatly impacted the lifestyle and movement patterns of San hunters and gatherers. The San were

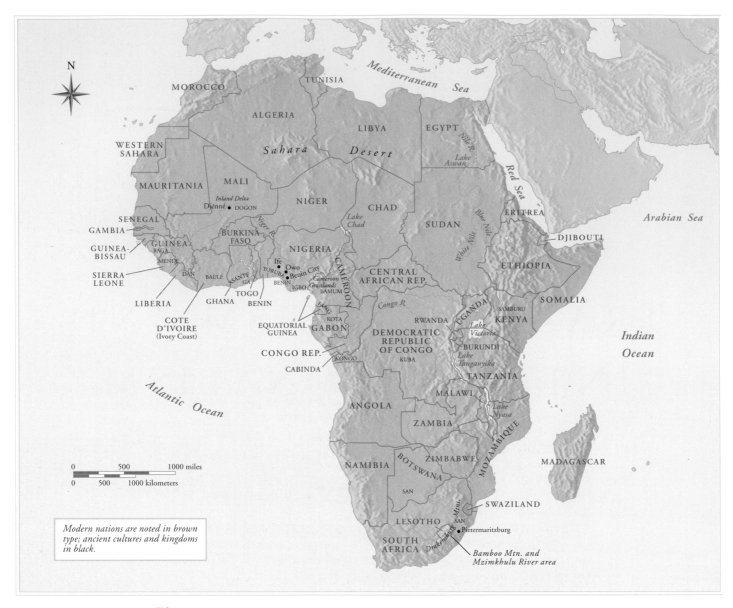

MAP 11-1 Modern Africa.

Modern nations are noted in brown type; ancient cultures and kingdoms in black.

often displaced from their ancestral lands. In some regions, they began to raid local ranches for livestock and horses as an alternate food source. The Bamboo Mountain rock painting appears to have been made after a series of stock raids over a period from about 1838 to 1848. Various South African military and police forces unsuccessfully pursued the San raiders. Poor weather, with frequent rains and fog, added to the difficulty of capturing a people who had lived in the region as hunters and gatherers for many generations and knew its terrain.

On the right side of the composition (not illustrated), two San riders on horses laden with meat drive a large herd of cattle and horses toward a San encampment located left of center and encircled by an outline (FIG. 11-1, *right*). Within the camp are various women and children. To the far left, a single figure (perhaps a diviner or rainmaker) leads an eland toward the encampment (FIG. 11-1, *left*). The similarity of this scene to other rock paintings with spiritual interpretations (a human leading an animal) suggests that this may represent a ritual leader in a trance state. The leader calls on rain—brought by the intervention of the sacred eland— to foil the attempts of the government soldiers and police to locate and punish the San raiders. The close correspondence between the painting's imagery and the actual events of 1838–1848 adds to the

likelihood that this work both indirectly records government action and was designed to facilitate rainmaking.

Fang and "Kota" Art (Cameroon and Gabon)

Although it is often difficult to date African works of art precisely, there are a number of objects without historical references that can still be assigned to the 19th century with some confidence. These include the reliquary guardian figures made by the Fang and several other peoples just south of the equator and the large "power images" of the Kongo peoples who live farther south in the basin of the great Congo (formerly Zaire) River. Both groups of figures are associated with ancestor worship. Across the continent ancestors are venerated for the continuing aid they are believed to provide the living, including help in maintaining the productivity of the earth for bountiful crop production.

ANCESTOR RELIQUARIES In some areas, ancestor veneration takes material form as collections of cranial and other bones gathered in special containers. Among both the Fang of Cameroon and several other peoples (often referred to as "Kota")

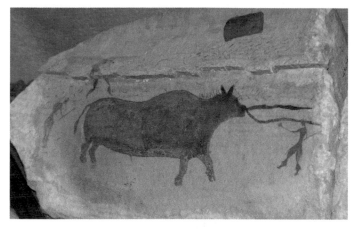

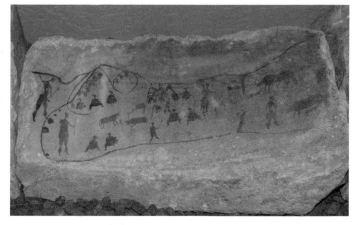

11-1 Stock raid with cattle, horses, encampment, and magical "rain animal," rock painting (two details), San, Bamboo Mountain, South Africa, mid-19th century. Pigments on rock, approx. 8′ long. Natal Museum, Pietermaritzburg.

in neighboring areas, these relic containers were protected by stylized human figures, or in some cases, simply heads. Fang guardian figures, such as the ones we show (FIG. **11-2**), sit on the edge of bark boxes of ancestral bones, insuring that no harm befalls the ancestral spirits. The wood figures are symmetrical, with proportions that greatly emphasize the head, and with a rhythmic buildup of forms that suggests contained power.

The so-called Kota reliquary guardian figures (called *mbulu ngulu*) from Gabon, like the one we illustrate (FIG. **11-3**), have a severely stylized body in the form of an open lozenge below a wooden head covered with strips and sheets of polished copper and brass. The gleaming surfaces are said to have repelled evil. The heads themselves are simplified, with hairstyles flattened out laterally above and beside the face. Geometric ridges, borders, and subdivisions add a kind of textured elegance to the shiny forms. The copper alloy on most of these images was reworked sheet brass (or copper wire) taken from brass basins originating in Europe and traded into this area of equatorial Africa in the 18th and 19th centuries. The lower portion of the image was stuck into a basket or box of ancestral relics.

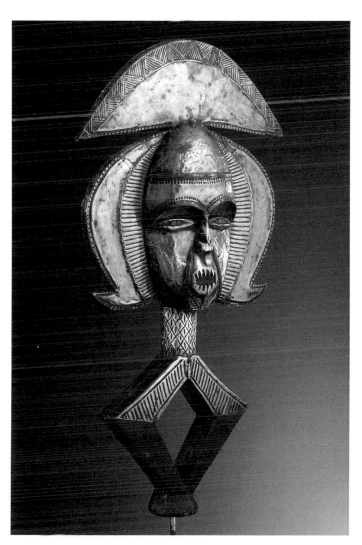

11-2 Reliquary guardian figures on bark boxes, Fang, Cameroon, photographed in 1910. Wood. National Museum of African Art, Smithsonian Institution, Washington, D. C.

11-3 Reliquary guardian figure *(mbulu-ngulu),* "Kota," Gabon, 19th or early 20th century. Wood, copper, iron, and brass, 1′ 9$\frac{1}{16}$″ high. Musée Barbier-Mueller, Geneva.

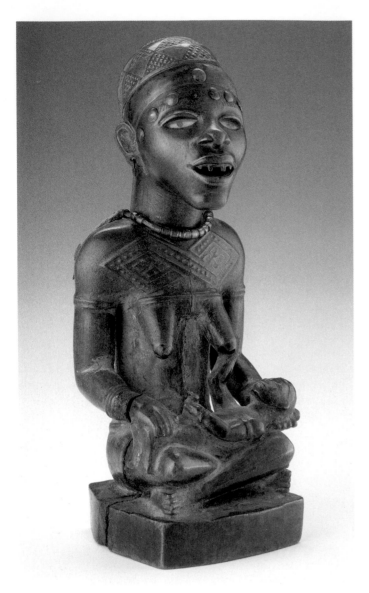

11-4 Mother and child, Kongo, from Mayombe region, Democratic Republic of Congo, 19th or early 20th century. Wood, glass, glass beads, brass tacks, and pigment, $10\frac{1}{8}$″ high. National Museum of African Art, Smithsonian Institution, Washington, D. C.

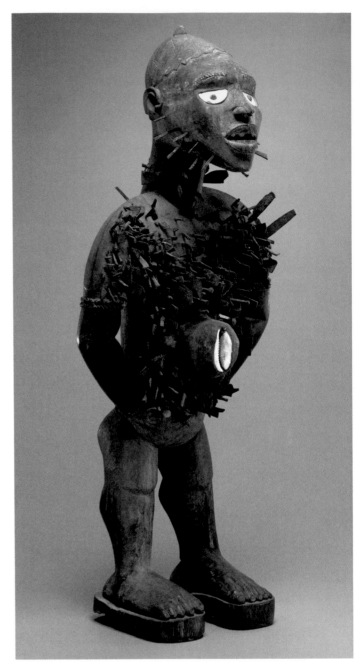

11-5 Nail figure (nkisi n'kondi), Kongo, from Shiloango River area, Democratic Republic of Congo, ca. 1875–1900. Wood, nails, blades, medicinal materials, and cowrie shell, 3′ $10\frac{3}{4}$″ high. Detroit Institute of Arts, Detroit.

Kongo Art (Democratic Republic of Congo)

KONGO POWER IMAGES Ancestral and power images of the Kongo peoples of the lower reaches of the Congo River show varieties of conventionalized naturalism. They served several purposes—commemoration, healing, divination, and social regulation. The woman-and-child carving we illustrate (FIG. 11-4) represents Kongo royalty, indicated by the woman's cap (recalling royal examples of woven banana fiber), chest scarification, and jewelry. The image may commemorate an ancestor or more probably a legendary founding clan mother, a *genetrix*. The Kongo called some of these figures "white chalk," a reference to the medicinal power of white kaolin clay. Diviners owned some of them, and others were used in women's organizations concerned with fertility and the treatment of infertility.

The large, standing male carving (FIG. 11-5), bristling with nails and blades, is a Kongo power figure (nkisi n'kondi) that a trained priest consecrated using precise ritual formulas. Such images embodied spirits believed to heal and give life, or sometimes capable of inflicting harm, disease, or even death. Each figure had its own

specific role, just as it wore particular medicines—here protruding from the abdomen and featuring a large cowrie shell. The Kongo also activated every image differently. Owners appealed to a figure's forces every time they inserted a nail or blade, as if to prod the spirit to do its work. People invoked other spirits by a certain chant, by rubbing them, or by applying special powders. The roles of power figures varied enormously, from curing minor ailments to stimulating crop growth, from punishing thieves to weakening an enemy. Very large Kongo figures, such as this one, had exceptional ascribed powers and aided entire communities. Although benevolent for their owners, the figures stood at the boundary between life and death, and most villagers held them in awe. As is true of the woman-and-child group (FIG. 11-4), this Kongo figure is relatively naturalistic, although the facial features are simplified and the head is magnified in size and thus emphasis. The carvers of both images, though, rendered surfaces as skin over muscled volume.

Dogon Art (Mali)

A STYLIZED COUPLE In contrast to the organic, relatively realistic treatment of the human body in Kongo art is a strongly stylized Dogon carving (FIG. 11-6) of a male and female couple that dates to the 19th century or perhaps earlier. The Dogon live in Mali near the bend of the great Niger River, not far from the inland Niger Delta region where many terracotta images (see FIG. 10-5) have been excavated. This carving of a linked man and woman—probably a shrine or altar, although contextual information is lacking—cogently documents primary gender roles in traditional African society. The man wears a quiver on his back. The woman carries a child on hers. Thus a protective role as hunter or warrior is implied for the man, a nurturing one for the woman. The slightly larger man reaches behind his mate's neck and touches her breast, as if to protect her. His left hand points to his own genitalia. Four stylized figures support the stool upon which they sit. They are probably either spirits or ancestors, but the identity of the larger figures is not known.

The highly conventionalized style of this group makes it a *conceptual* image rather than a *perceptual* one. That is, it is based more on the idea or concept of human forms than on the imitative portrayal of heads, torsos, and limbs as perceived in life. Here, the linked body parts are tubes and columns articulated inorganically. The almost abstract geometry of the overall composition is reinforced by incised rectilinear and diagonal patterns on the surfaces. The sculptor also understood the importance of space, and charged the voids, as well as the sculptural forms, with rhythm and tension. The artist was not at all concerned with naturalism or realism, yet produced a refined and complex image that is very successful as sculpture.

Baule Art (Central Côte d'Ivoire)

BUSH SPIRITS In striking contrast to the Dogon sculptor of the seated man and woman (FIG. 11-6), the artist who created the matched pair of Baule male and female images (FIG. 11-7) consciously perceived many naturalistic aspects of human anatomy,

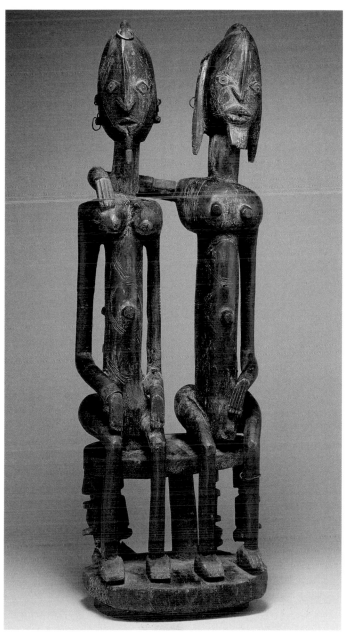

11-6 Seated couple, Dogon, Mali, ca. 1800–1850. Wood, 2′ 4″ high. Metropolitan Museum of Art, New York (gift of Lester Wunderman).

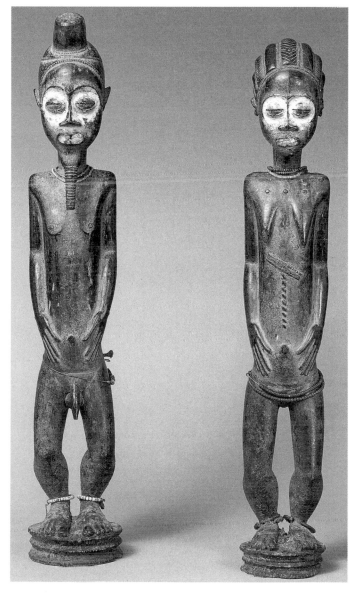

11-7 Male and female figures, probably bush spirits (*asye usu*), Baule, Côte d'Ivoire, late 19th or early 20th century. Wood, beads, and kaolin, man 1′ 9¾″ high, woman 1′ 8⅝″ high. Metropolitan Museum of Art, New York (Michael C. Rockefeller Memorial Collection, gift of Nelson A. Rockefeller).

skillfully translating them into finished sculptural form. At the same time, the sculptor was well aware of creating *waka sran* (people of wood) rather than living beings. Thus, the artist freely exaggerated the length of the figures' necks and the size of their heads and calf muscles, all of which are forms of idealization in Baule culture.

The images probably portray bush spirits (*asye usu*) and were in the possession of a trance diviner, a religious specialist who consulted the spirits symbolized by the figures on behalf of clients either sick or in some way troubled. In Baule thought, bush spirits are actually short, horrible-looking, and sometimes deformed creatures, yet Baule sculptors represent them in the form of beautiful, ideal human beings, because it is said that the spirits would be offended by ugly figures and would refuse to work for the diviner. Among the Baule, as among many West African peoples, bush or wilderness spirits both cause difficulties in life and, if properly addressed and placated, may solve problems or cure sickness. In dance and trance performances—with wooden figures and other objects displayed nearby—the diviner is able to divine or understand the will of his or her unseen spirits, as well as their needs or prophecies, which he or she passes on to clients. When not set up outdoors for a performance, the figures and other objects are stored in the diviner's house or shrine, where more private consultations take place.

The 20th Century

Benin Art (Nigeria)

A ROYAL ANCESTOR SHRINE Some of the most important art produced in Africa during the past century comes from areas with strong earlier artistic traditions. The kingdom of Benin is a prime example. In Chapter 10, we examined a 16th-century Benin ivory mask (see FIG. 10-10) and a 17th- or 18th-century copper alloy altar (see FIG. 10-11). A 20th-century Benin composite shrine to the heads of royal ancestors (FIG. **11-8**) is, according to oral history, similar to centuries-earlier versions. The shrine is in the king's palace today. With a base of sacred riverbank clay, it is an assemblage of varied materials, objects, and symbols: a central copper-alloy altarpiece depicting a sacred king flanked by members of his entourage, plus copper-alloy heads, each fitted on top with an ivory tusk carved in relief. There are also wood staffs and metal bells. The heads represent both the kings themselves and, through the durability of their material, the enduring nature of kingship. These heads were once polished. Their glistening surfaces, seen as red and signaling danger, were believed to repel evil forces that might adversely affect the shrine and thus the king and kingdom. Elephant-tusk relief carvings atop the heads commemorate important events and personages in Benin history. Their bleached white color signifies purity and goodness (probably of royal ancestors), and the tusks themselves represent the vast physical power of elephants, which, like leopards, are metaphors for leaders. The carved wood rattle-staffs standing at the back refer to generations of dynastic ancestors by their bamboolike, segmented forms. The staffs also function musically, as do the several pyramidal copper-alloy bells, to call royal ancestral spirits to rituals performed at the altar.

The Benin king's actual head stands for wisdom, good judgment, and divine guidance for the kingdom. Those qualities are multiplied in the ancestral altar with its several heads. By means of animal sacrifices at this site, the living king annually purifies his own "head" (and being) by invoking the collective strength of his ancestors. Thus the varied objects, symbols, colors, and materials comprising this shrine contribute both visually and ritually to the imaging of royal power, as well as to its history, renewal, and perpetuation. The composition of the shrine, like that of the altar at its center and the altar discussed earlier (see FIG. 10-11), is hierarchical. At the center of all Benin hierarchies stands the king (see FIG. Intro-1).

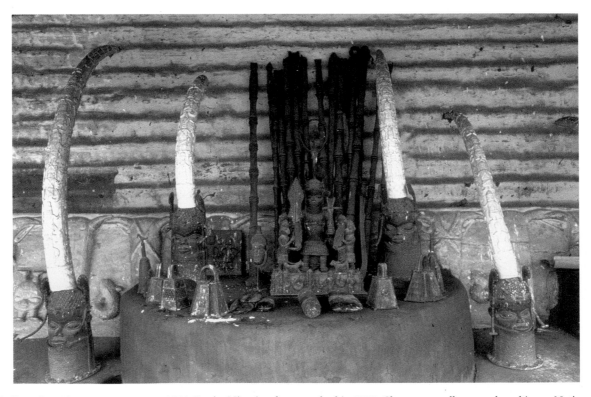

11-8 Altar dedicated to Oba Ovonramwer, ca. 1914, Benin, Nigeria, photographed in 1970. Clay, copper alloy, wood, and ivory. National Museum of African Art, Smithsonian Institution, Washington, D. C.

African Artists and Apprentices

The many styles illustrated in this chapter can often be identified as to place, people, and time. Individual artists also have distinctive styles that enable viewers to recognize their work, and sometimes whether a given work was created early or late in the artist's career. Although African art has often been considered anonymous—because early researchers rarely asked for artists' names—many individual hands or styles can be recognized even when an artist's name has not been recorded. During the past century, however, art historians and anthropologists have been systematically noting the names and life histories of specific individual artists, many of whom are well known regionally. Two 20th-century artists who were renowned, even from one kingdom to another, are Osei Bonsu, who was based in the Asante capital, Kumasi, and the Yoruba sculptor called Olowe of Ise because he came from the town of Ise. Both artists were master carvers, producing sculptures for kings and commoners alike.

Like other great artists in other places and times, both Bonsu (FIGS. 11-10 and 11-11) and Olowe (FIG. 11-12) had apprentices to assist them for several years while learning their trade. Although there are various kinds of apprenticeship in Africa, novices typically lived with their masters and were household servants as well as assistant carvers. They helped fell trees, carry logs, and rough out basic shapes that the master later transformed into finished work. African sculptors typically worked on commission. Sometimes, as in Bonsu's case, patrons traveled to the home of the artist. But other times, even Bonsu moved to the home of a patron for weeks or months while the commission was being completed. Masters, and in some instances also apprentices, were housed and fed in the patron's compound. Olowe, for example, traveled around the Ekiti region of Yorubaland, living with different kings for many months at a time while he carved doors, veranda posts (FIG. 11-12), and other works for royal families.

Akan and Asante Art (Ghana)

FEMALE SCULPTORS Another 20th-century art form that recalls similar works documented in earlier times is the Akan terracotta commemorative head, one of which is just being completed by a woman artist in FIG. **11-9.** Pieter de Marees, a Dutch visitor to Ghana in 1602, described a comparable object and explained its connection to Akan burials:

> Upon the grave they set all kinds of meat and drinke, that they may eat some thing. . . . All his stuffe, as Armes and Clothes are buried with him, and all his gentlemen that served him, have every one of them their Pictures made of Clay, and fairely painted, which are set and placed orderly round about his grave, one by the other.[1]

The woman sculptor has modeled a portrait of a deceased king or court member, just as her predecessors did in the early 17th century and perhaps earlier.

OSEI BONSU The conventionalized, flattened clay head is an Akan style trait that is also found in wood sculpture carved by

---

[1] Pieter de Marees, *A Description and Historical Declaration of the Golden Kingdom of Guinea* (1604), translated by Samuel Purchas. Quoted in Herbert M. Cole and Doran H. Ross, *The Arts of Ghana* (Los Angeles: Museum of Cultural History, 1977, 119.

11-9 Woman sculptor finishing an ancestral portrait, 1965, Akan, Ghana. Terracotta.

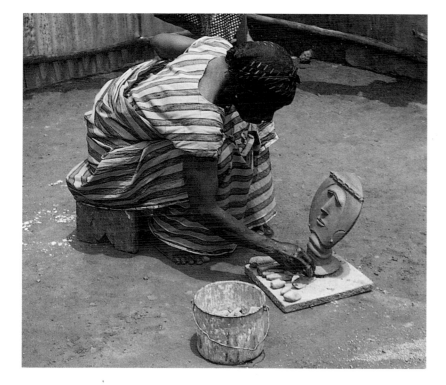

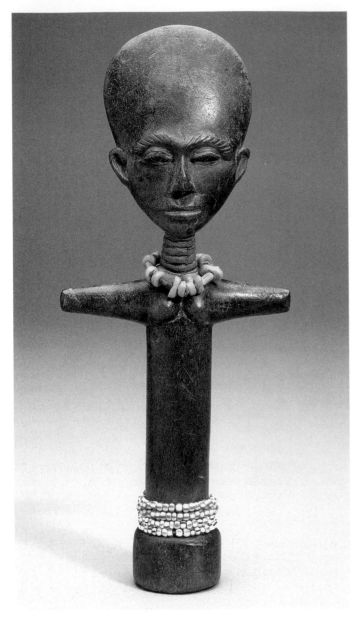

11-10 OSEI BONSU, *akua'ba*, Asante, Ghana, ca. 1935. Wood, beads, and pigment, $10\frac{1}{4}''$ high. Private collection.

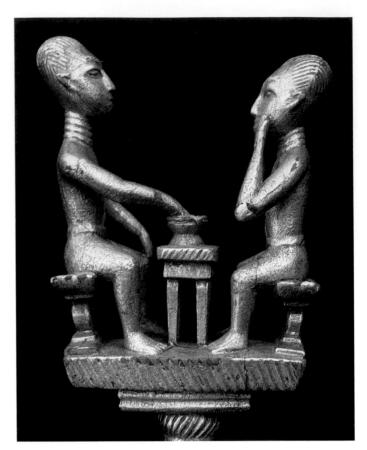

11-11 OSEI BONSU, "linguist's staff" of two men sitting at a table of food, Asante, Ghana, mid-20th century. Wood and gold leaf, section shown approx. 10″ high. Collection of the Paramount Chief of Offinso, Asante. 🔘

Asante men—for example, in an image of a young girl (FIG. **11-10**), or *akua'ba* (Akua's child), by OSEI BONSU (1900–1976; see "African Artists and Apprentices," above). Many Akan peoples considered long, slightly flattened foreheads to be emblems of beauty, and mothers actually gently molded their children's cranial bones to reflect this value. The simplified wood akua'ba sculptures were consecrated at a shrine, then carried by a young woman hoping to conceive. Once pregnant, the woman continued to carry the figure to ensure the safe delivery of a healthy and handsome child— among these matrilineal people, preferably a girl. Many thousands of such wood figures have been carved over the past several centuries, each one different from the next, yet each one showing stylistic traits associated with one or another Akan subgroup, or even a specific artist. Osei Bonsu's personal style—a more naturalistic rendering of the face, and crosshatched eyebrows—is easily recognized by those familiar with the many regional and personal styles seen in Akan sculpture.

Bonsu also carved the gold-covered wood sculpture that depicts two men sitting at a table of food (FIG. **11-11**). This object,

commonly called a "linguist's staff" because its carrier often speaks for a king or chief, has a related proverb: "Food is for its rightful owner, not for the one who happens to be hungry." Food is a metaphor for the office held by the king or chief, which he rightfully holds. The "hungry" man lusts for the office. The linguist, who is an important counselor and adviser to the king, might carry this staff to a meeting at which a rival is contesting the king's title to the stool (his throne, the office). Many hundreds of Akan sculptures have proverbs or other sayings associated with them, so there is a rich verbal tradition relating to the visual arts of these peoples.

Yoruba Art (Nigeria)

OLOWE OF ISE A tall veranda post (FIG. **11-12**) is typical of the style of OLOWE OF ISE (ca. 1873–1938). To achieve greater height, Olowe stacked his weapon-carrying equestrian warrior on top of a platform supported on the heads and upraised arms of four figures, two men and two women. The figures themselves are attenuated, with long necks and enlarged heads. The latter trait is common among most Yoruba sculptors, whereas elongation is an Olowe characteristic, along with finely textured detail, seen in the warrior's tunic. This post was carved in the early decades of the 20th century, a time when Europeans had already become a colonial presence among Yoruba peoples. Olowe subtly records this presence in the billed cap of one of the male supporting figures. The overall design of this house post, more complex and with more open space than most posts by other carvers, signals Olowe's virtuosity.

Costumes and Masquerades

The arts in Africa exist in greatly varied human situations, and knowledge of these contexts is essential for understanding the artworks. In Africa, art (even sculptures and paintings now displayed in museums) is nearly always an active agent in the lives of the continent's peoples. African art also encompasses clothing and masks made of perishable materials. Throughout history, African costumes have been laden with meaning and have projected messages that all members of the society could read. We reproduce a photograph (FIG. 11-13) taken in 1970 of a sacred Kuba king. The king, Kot a-Mbweeky III (r. 1969–present), is seated in state before his court, bedecked in a dazzling multimedia costume with many symbolic elements. The king commissioned the costume he wears and now has become art himself. Eagle feathers, leopard skin, cowrie shells, imported beads, raffia, and other materials combine to overload and expand the image of the man, making him larger than life, and most certainly a work of art. He is a collage, an assemblage. He holds not one but two weapons. Can one doubt his military might, his wealth, dignity, and grandeur in the eyes of his people? The man, with his regalia, embodies the office of sacred kingship. He is a superior being actually and figuratively, raised upon a dais, flanked by ornate drums, with a treasure basket of sacred relics by his foot. The geometric patterns on the king's costume and nearby objects, and the abundance and redundancy of rich materials, epitomize the opulent style of Kuba court arts.

MASQUERADES The art of *masquerade* has long been a quintessential African expressive form, loaded with meaning and cultural importance. This is so today, but was more critically true in

11-12 OLOWE OF ISE, veranda post carved for the chief of Akure, Yoruba, Nigeria, ca. 1900–1938. Wood and pigment, approx. 14′ 6″ high. Denver Art Museum, Denver.

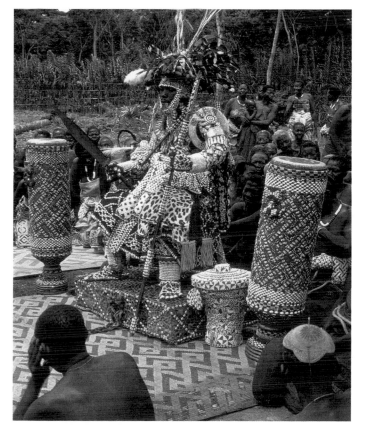

11-13 Kuba King Kot a-Mbweeky III during a display for photographer and filmmaker Eliot Elisofon in early 1970, Mushenge, Democratic Republic of Congo.

colonial times and earlier, when African masking societies boasted extensive regulatory and judicial powers. Such governmental functions were particularly forceful in stateless societies, such as those of the Senufo and Mende, where masks sometimes became so influential they had their own priests and served as power sources or as oracles. Societies empowered maskers to levy fines and to apprehend witches (usually defined as socially destructive people) and criminals, and to judge and punish them. Normally, however — especially today — masks are less threatening and more secular and educational, as well as diversions from the humdrum of daily life. Masked dancers usually embody either ancestors, seen as briefly returning to the human realm, or various nature spirits called upon for their special powers.

The mask, a costume ensemble's focal point, combines with held objects, music, and dance gestures to invoke a specific named character, almost always considered a spirit. A few masked spirits appear by themselves, but more often several characters come out together or in turn. Maskers enact a very broad range of human, animal, and fantastic, otherworldly behavior that is usually both stimulating and didactic. Masquerades, in fact, vary in function or effect along a continuum from weak spirit power and strong entertainment value to those rarely seen but possessing vast executive powers backed by powerful shrines. Most operate between these extremes, crystallizing varieties of human and animal behavior — caricatured, ordinary, comic, bizarre, serious, or threatening. Such actions inform and affect audience members because they are staged dramatically and framed within a performance normally held only occasionally. It is the purpose of most masquerades to move people, to affect them, to effect change.

Thus, masks and masquerades are mediators — between men and women, youths and elders, initiated and uninitiated, powers of nature and those of human agency, and even life and death. For many groups in West and Central Africa, masking plays (or once played) an active role in the socialization process, especially for men, who control most masks. Maskers carry boys away from their mothers to bush initiation camps, put them through ordeals and schooling, and welcome them back to society as men months or even years later. A second major role is in aiding the transformation of important deceased persons into productive ancestors who, in their new roles, can bring benefits to the living community. Because most masking cultures are agricultural, it is not surprising that masquerades are invoked to increase the productivity of the fields, to stimulate the growth of crops, and later to celebrate the harvest.

SENUFO MASKING Senufo men dance many masks, mostly in the context of Poro, the main association for socialization and initiation, a protracted process that takes nearly 20 years for men to complete. Maskers also perform at funerals and other public spectacles. The most recurrent Senufo mask has a small face with fine features, several extensions, and varied motifs — a hornbill bird in our example (FIG. 11-14) — rising from the forehead. These feminine characters, danced only by men, wear knitted body suits or trade-cloth costumes to indicate their beauty and their ties with the order and civilization of the village. Their dances too are feminine. They may be called "pretty young girl," "beautiful lady," or "wife" and some are considered the wives of the heavy, terrorizing masculine masks that appear before or after them.

Large Senufo masks (for example, FIG. 11-15) are composite creatures, combining characteristics of antelope, crocodile, warthog, hyena, and human: sweeping horns, a head, and an open-jawed snout with sharp teeth. Such masks incarnate both

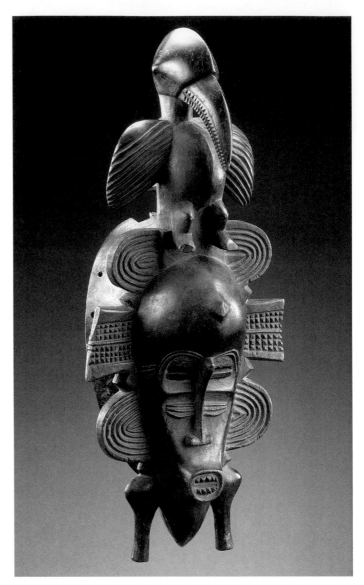

11-14 "Beautiful Lady" dance mask, Senufo, Côte d'Ivoire, late 20th century. Wood, approx. 1' $\frac{1}{2}$" high. Musée Barbier-Mueller, Geneva.

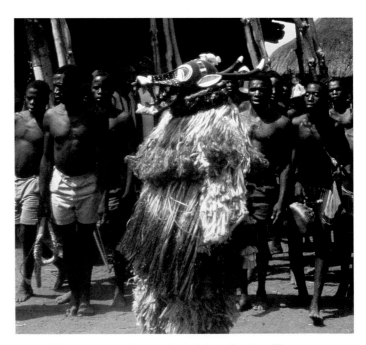

11-15 Gbon masquerader at a funeral, Senufo, Côte d'Ivoire, photographed by Anita Glaze in 1986.

ancestors and bush powers that combat witchcraft and sorcery, malevolent spirits, and the wandering dead. They are protectors who fight evil with their aggressively powerful forms and their medicines. There is a close relationship between function and form, namely the mask as weapon.

At funerals Senufo maskers attend the corpse and help expel the deceased from the village. This is the deceased individual's final transition, a rite of passage parallel to that undergone by all men during their years of Poro socialization, when masks are also employed. When an important person dies, the convergence of several masking groups, as well as the music, dancing, costuming, and feasting of many people, constitute a festive and complex work of art that transcends any one mask or character.

DOGON MASQUERADES In the inland Niger Delta region, elaborate cyclical Dogon masquerades dramatize creation legends. These stories say that women were the first ancestors to imitate spirit maskers and thus the first human masqueraders. Men later took over the masks, forever barring women from direct involvement with masking processes. A mask called Satimbe (FIG. 11-16), which seems to represent all women, commemorates this legend. In ceremonies called Dama, held every several years to honor the lives of people who have died since the last Dama, Satimbe is among the dozens of different masked spirit characters that escort dead souls away from the village. The deceased are sent off to the land of the dead where, as ancestors, they will be enjoined to benefit their living descendants and stimulate agricultural productivity.

WOMEN AS MASK DANCERS Although men own and perform most masks in Africa, women control and dance them in several adjacent cultures of the western Guinea Coast, such as the Mende of Sierra Leone (see "Mende Women as Maskers," page 208). The glistening black surface of the Mende mask we show (FIG. 11-17) evokes female ancestral spirits newly emergent from their underwater homes (also symbolized by the turtle on top). The mask and its parts refer to ideals of female beauty, morality, and behavior. A high broad forehead signifies wisdom and success. Neck ridges—signs of beauty, good health, and prosperity—also symbolize a moth chrysalis, the transformative stage in the insect's life, between worm and flying creature, that is parallel to a young woman's initiation. Intricately woven or plaited hair is

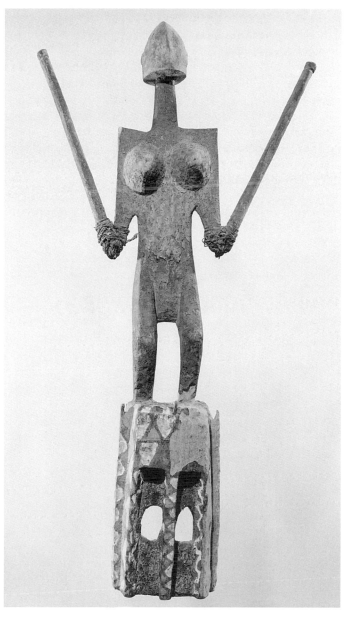

11-16 Satimbe mask, Dogon, Mali, early 20th century. Wood. Private collection.

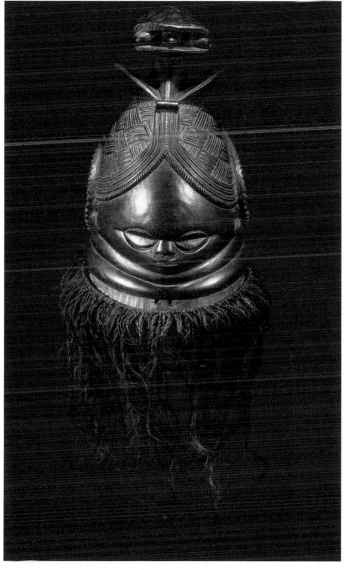

11-17 Female mask, Mende, Sierra Leone, 20th century. Wood and pigment, 1′ 2½″ high. Fowler Museum of Cultural History, University of California, Los Angeles (gift of the Wellcome Trust).

Mende Women as Maskers

The Mende and neighboring peoples of Sierra Leone and Liberia are unique in Africa in that women actually wear masks (FIG. 11-17) and costumes that conceal them totally from the audience attending their performance. The Sande society of the Mende is the women's counterpart to the men's Poro society. These associations control the initiation, education, and acculturation of female and male youth, respectively. Women leaders who dance these masks serve as priestesses and judges during the three years the women's society controls the ritual calendar (alternating with the men's society in this role), thus serving the community as a whole. Women maskers, also initiators, teachers, and mentors, help girl novices with their transformation into educated and marriageable women. Sande women associate their Sowie masks with water spirits and the color black, which the society, in turn, connects with human skin color and

the civilized world. The women wear these helmet masks on top of their heads as headdresses, with black raffia and cloth costumes to hide the wearers' identity during public performances. Elaborate coiffures, shiny black color, dainty triangular-shaped faces with slit eyes, rolls around the neck, and actual and carved versions of amulets and various emblems on the top commonly characterize Sowie masks. These symbolize the adult women's roles as wives, mothers, providers for the family, and keepers of medicines for use within the Sande association and the society at large.

Sande members commission the masks from male carvers, with the carver and patron together determining the type of mask needed for a particular societal purpose. The Mende often keep, repair, and reuse masks for many decades, thereby preserving them as models for subsequent generations of carvers.

the essence of harmony and order found in ideal households. A small closed mouth and downcast eyes indicate the silent, serious demeanor expected of recent initiates. These sorts of masks are worn by leaders and teachers in initiation rites, as well as by leaders and priestesses of the women's society.

KUBA SPIRITS AND ANCESTORS At the court of Kuba kings, three masks, known as Mwashamboy, Bwoom, and Ngady Amwaash, represent legendary royal ancestors. Mwashamboy (FIG. **11-18**) symbolizes the founding ancestor, Woot, and embodies the king's supernatural and political powers. The other mask in the photograph, Bwoom, with its bulging forehead, is said to represent a legendary dwarf or pygmy who signifies the

indigenous peoples on whom kingship was imposed. Bwoom also vies with Mwashamboy for the attention of the beautiful female ancestor, Ngady Amwaash, who symbolizes the first female and all women (FIG. 11-19). On her cheeks are striped tears from the pain of childbirth, and those shed by Ngady herself because to procreate, she must commit incest with her father, Woot. These three characters reenact creation stories while rehearsing various forms of archetypal behaviors that instruct young men during initiation and reinforce basic Kuba societal values. The masks and their costumes, with elaborate beads, feathers, animal pelts, cowrie shells, cut-pile cloth, and ornamental trappings, as well as geometric patterning, echo the sumptuousness of the Kuba king himself (FIG. 11-13) and the precepts of Kuba style.

11-18 Mwashamboy (kneeling) and Bwoom (standing) maskers in a royal ceremony among the Kuba, Democratic Republic of Congo, late 20th century.

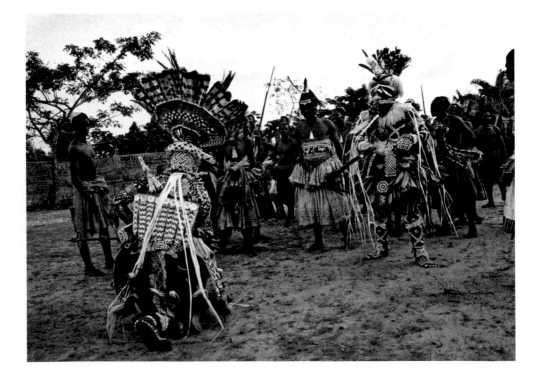

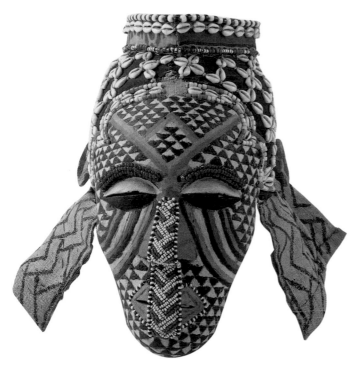

11-19 Ngady Amwaash mask, Kuba, Democratic Republic of Congo, late 19th or early 20th century. Peabody Museum, Harvard University, Cambridge. 💿

These examples of masks and masquerades, from among the thousands on the continent, exemplify the exceptionally diverse and important values and meanings characterizing this art form. Since African nations gained independence, masks that once had powerful roles in social control have become at least partially secularized. Yet masking remains viable and socially relevant in several parts of the continent in the early 21st century.

The past 50 to 100 years have witnessed many changes in the forms, functions, and meanings of African arts. Many shrines have closed down because of conversions to Islam or Christianity. Colonial governments, followed by those of modern independent nations, have contributed to the erosion of leadership arts even though regalia and court ceremonial attire can still be seen in festivals that continue to be value-laden events.

FESTIVAL ARTS IN GHANA Annual festivals in contemporary Ghana, which under British colonial rule was called the Gold Coast, still feature sumptuous royal arts such as gold-leafed wooden sculptures and cast-gold jewelry as well as rich textile arts (FIG. **11-20**). Staffs, swords, stools, and umbrella tops are some of the forms seen, along with rich costuming. The gold-leafed elephant stool represents the dynastic ancestors whose living counterpart, the reigning king, is seated higher up the dais under the double umbrella. Here the visual arts combine with music, dance, and gesture in lavishly orchestrated performances with many purposes. Chiefs and kings are purified as allegiances and loyalties are reaffirmed, the gods and ancestors are honored and thanked (with sacrificial food), first fruits are eaten, deaths of the past year are mourned, and altogether, the community is renewed. This revitalization begins the new year with both the solemnity of ritual and the spectacle of many converging art forms.

IGBO RENEWAL HOUSES Among the Igbo just north of the Niger River delta, powerful nature gods demand about every 50 years that a community build an *mbari house*. The Igbo construct these houses from mud as sacrifices to major deities, often Ala, goddess of the earth. The houses are elaborate unified artistic complexes that incorporate numerous unfired clay sculptures and paintings—occasionally more than a hundred in a single mbari

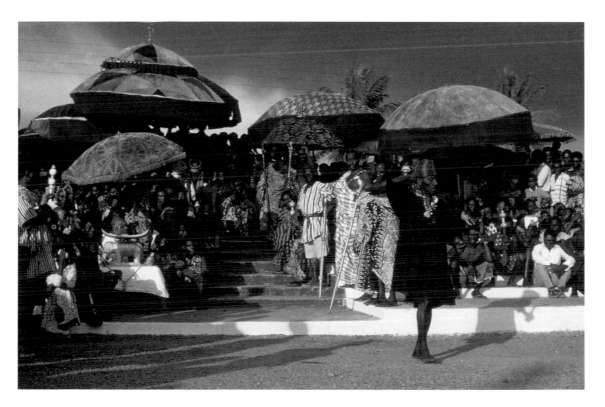

11-20 Akan festival showing gold-leafed wooden stool, royal umbrellas, and court officials seated in state, Akuropon, Ghana, photographed by Herbert Cole in 1972. 💿

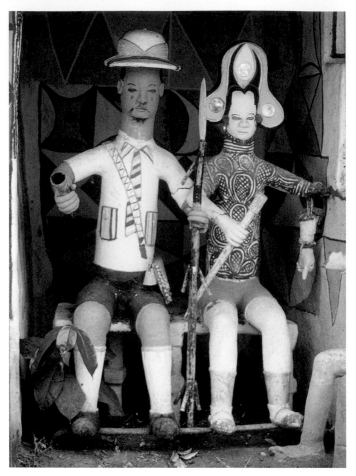

11-21 The thunder god Amadioha and his wife, painted clay sculptures in an *mbari,* Igbo, Umugote Orishaeze, Nigeria, photographed in 1966.

viewed as positive by the men who control the ritual and art. They allow themselves modern things but want their women to remain traditional. The artist enlarged and extended both figures' torsos, necks, and heads to express their aloofness, dignity, and power. More informally posed figures and groups appear on the other sides of the house, including beautiful, amusing, or frightening figures of animals, humans, and spirits taken from mythology, history, dreams, and everyday life—a kaleidoscope of subjects and meanings.

The mbari construction process, veiled in secrecy behind a fence, is a stylized world-renewal ritual. After the ritual opening, the completed monument shows off that world, the cosmos renewed. Ceremonies for unveiling the house to public view indicate that the god accepted the sacrificial offering (of the mbari) and, for a time at least, will be benevolent. An mbari house never undergoes repair. Instead, it is allowed to disintegrate and return to its source, the earth. The Igbo today rarely make mbari complexes for ritual purposes. Two recent ones, sponsored by the Nigerian government essentially as museums—secular variations on the earlier sacred theme—were constructed of cement. In this way the arts of the past have been preserved to educate future generations.

BODY ADORNMENT People in many rural areas of eastern Africa continue to embellish their own bodies, not only for occasional ceremonies, but every day. Samburu men and women in northern Kenya, shown in FIG. **11-22** at a spontaneous dance, each have distinct styles of personal decoration (see "Gender Roles in African Art Production," page 211). Men, particularly warriors who are not yet married, expend hours creating elaborate hairstyles for one another. They paint their bodies with red ocher, and wear bracelets, necklaces, and other bands of beaded jewelry young women make for them. For themselves, women make more lavish constellations of beaded collars, which they mass around their necks. As if to help separate the genders, women shave their heads and adorn them with beaded headbands. Personal decoration begins in childhood, increasing to become lavish and highly self-conscious in young adulthood, and diminishing as people get older. Much of it is coded to reveal information—age, marital or initiation status, parentage of a warrior son—that can be read by those who know the codes. Dress ensembles have evolved over

house. Our illustration (FIG. **11-21**) shows the thunder god Amadioha and his wife in an mbari house at Umugote Orishaeze. The god wears modern clothing, whereas his consort appears with traditional body paint and a fancy hairstyle. These differing modes of dress relate to Igbo concepts of modernity and tradition, both

11-22 Samburu men and women dancing, northern Kenya, photographed by Herbert Cole in 1973.

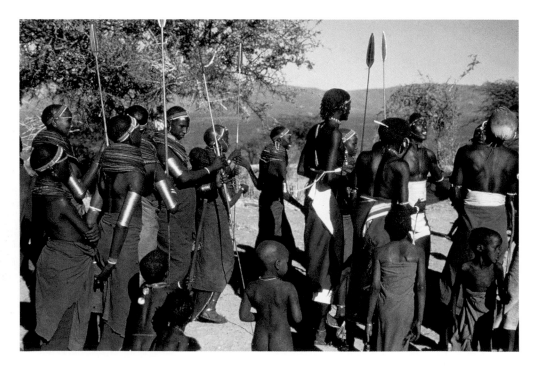

Gender Roles in African Art Production

Until the past decade or two, art production in Africa has been quite rigidly gender specific. Men have been, and largely still are, iron smiths and gold and copper-alloy casters. Men were architects, builders, and carvers of both wood and ivory. Women were, and for the most part remain, wall and body painters, calabash decorators, potters, and often clay sculptors (FIG. 11-9), although men make clay figures in some areas. Both men and women work with beads and weave baskets and textiles, men executing narrow strips (later sewn together) on horizontal looms and women working wider pieces of cloth on vertical looms.

Much African art, however, is collaborative. Men may build a clay wall, for example, but women will normally be called in to decorate it. Igbo mbari houses (FIG. 11-21) are truly collaborative despite the fact that their figures are modeled by professional male artists. Festivals, invoking virtually all the arts, are also collaborative. Masquerades are largely the province of men, yet in some cases women are asked to contribute costume elements such as skirts, wrappers, and scarves. And even though women dance masks among the Mende and related peoples, the masks themselves have always been carved by men.

Until recently in most regions, Africans did not greatly emphasize artists' individuality, even when personal styles were clearly recognizable. This does not mean art is anonymous or that artists are not honored locally. Many artists, like Osei Bonsu (FIGS. 11-10 and 11-11) and Olowe of Ise (FIG. 11-12), were highly appreciated in their own time as they are today. Still, Africans have tended not to exalt artistic individuality as much as Westerners have. All that has been changing over the past few decades, however. Increasingly, even artists in villages want to be recognized for their skills and rewarded for the works they create.

In late colonial and especially in postcolonial times, earlier gender distinctions in art production have been breaking down. Women, as well as men, now weave kente cloth, and a number of women are now sculptors in wood, metal, stone, and composite materials. Men are making pottery, once the exclusive prerogative of women. Both women and men make international art forms in urban and university settings, although male artists are more numerous. One well-known Nigerian woman artist, Sokari Douglas Camp, produces welded metal sculptures, sometimes of masqueraders. Douglas Camp is thus doubly unusual. She might find it difficult to do this work in her traditional home in the Niger River delta, but as she lives and works in London, she encounters no adverse response. In the future there will undoubtedly be a further breaking down of restrictive barriers and greater mobility for artists.

time. Different colors and sizes of beads became available, plastics and aluminum were introduced, and specific fashions have changed, but the overall concept of fine personal adornment— that is, dress raised to the level of art —remains much the same today as it was centuries ago.

MAMY WATA Around 1900 in the Niger River delta there appeared a color lithograph of a light-skinned, straight-haired woman controlling large snakes. This print, seen on the wall in FIG. **11-23**, was imported from Europe in great numbers and seems to have stimulated the growth of the Mamy Wata ("mother of water") cult as a vehicle for the assimilation and expression of contemporary spiritual values grafted onto traditional ones. Snakes, for example, figure as messengers of many African deities. Mamy Wata came from across the sea, as white people did, bringing riches as well as problems. She is charismatic and beautiful, yet she offers help to those in need, at the price of becoming her devotee. Her priests and priestesses consult her as an oracle. Her special province is modern life—passing exams, for example, or finding enough money to buy a moped or a new suit. She appears in peoples' dreams as an exotic temptress offering glamorous products, often imports of the sort she likes herself.

Mamy Wata's shrines (FIG. 11-23) usually feature one or more brightly colored paintings or sculptures of the snake-entwined woman, the original lithograph, powders, soaps, perfumes, glittery jewelry, dolls, candles, medicines, and a mirror. The mirror is present both because the goddess is vain, and because it serves as a symbolic membrane, an illusory water surface, a kind of "Alice's looking glass" within which wondrous things can happen to those who give Mamy Wata the presents and sacrifices she demands. She can bring wealth or poverty, insanity or health, children or barrenness, depending on how she is treated. One becomes a devotee of Mamy

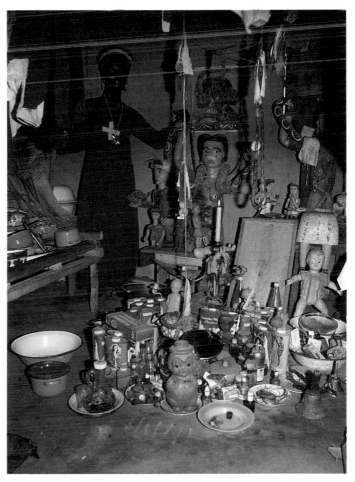

11-23 Mamy Wata shrine with priestess, Igbo, near Owerri town, Nigeria, photographed by Henry J. Drewal in 1978.

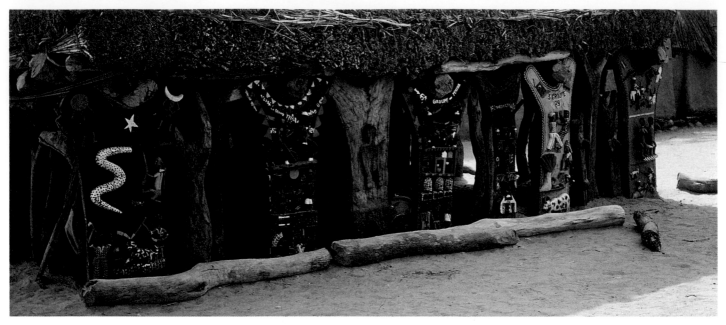

11-24 *Togu na* ("men's house of words"), Dogon, Mali, photographed in 1989. Wood and pigment.

Wata when one dreams of her or has problems that a diviner feels she may be able to help with. Today there are many thousands of Mamy Wata shrines and worshipers across the breadth of West Africa. As in other shrines, the presence of art heightens the mystique and helps to focus the attention of disciples.

DOGON HOUSES OF WORDS Traditionalism and modernism are united in contemporary Dogon *togu na,* or "men's house of words." The togu na is so called because men's deliberations vital to community welfare take place under its sheltering roof. It is considered the "head" and the most important part of the community, which the Dogon characterize with human attributes. The men's houses were built over time. Earlier posts, such as the central one in the togu na we illustrate (FIG. **11-24**), show schematic renderings of legendary female ancestors, similar to stylized ancestral couples (FIG. 11-6) or masked figures (FIG. 11-16). Recent replacement posts feature narrative and topical scenes of varied subjects, such as horsemen or hunters or women preparing food, a lot of descriptive detail, bright polychrome painting in enamels, and even some writing. Unlike earlier traditional sculptors, the contemporary artists who made these posts want to be recognized for their work. Their names are known, and they are eager to sell their work (other than these posts) to tourists.

GA CASKETS Today's African artists also tend to use new forms, techniques, and materials within older functional categories. Carved wooden caskets, created by KANE KWEI (1924–1991) and his sons of the Ga people in urban coastal Ghana, exemplify this type of art. Beginning around 1970, Kwei created figurative coffins intended to reflect the deceased's life, occupation, or major accomplishments. On commission he made such diverse shapes as a cow, a whale, and a bird; various local food crops, such as onions and cocoa pods; airplanes; a Mercedes Benz; and a modern villa. These coffins were not carved, but rather pieced together using nails and glue. The artists are carpenters rather than woodcarvers. Kwei also created coffins in traditional leaders' forms, such as an eagle, an elephant, a leopard, and a stool. The coffin illustrated here (FIG. **11-25**), a hen with chicks, was created for a respected woman with a huge family. Kwei died in 1991, but his sons and former apprentices continue his legacy. Their own commissions—a tiger, a crab, a lobster, a Mercedes, and a fishing canoe—accompanied his coffin from the church to the cemetery.

A CONGOLESE INTERNATIONALIST TRIGO PIULA (b. ca. 1950), a contemporary painter of the international school (trained in Western artistic techniques and styles) from the Democratic Republic of Congo, creates works that fuse Western and Congolese images and objects in a pictorial blend that provides social commentary on present-day Congolese culture. *Ta Tele Gabon* (FIG. **11-26**) depicts a group of Congolese citizens staring transfixed at colorful pictures of life beyond Africa displayed on 14 television screens. The TV images include references to travel to exotic places (such as Paris with the Eiffel Tower), sports events, love, the earth seen from a satellite, and Western worldly goods. A traditional Kongo power figure associated with warfare and divination stands at the composition's center as a visual mediator between the anonymous foreground viewers and the multiple TV images. In traditional Kongo contexts (FIG. 11-5), this figure's feather headdress associates it with supernatural and magical powers from the sky, such as lightning and storms. In Piula's rendition, the headdress perhaps refers to the power of airborne televised pictures. In the stomach area, where Kongo power figures often have glass in front of a medicine packet, Piula painted a television screen showing a second power figure, as if to double the figure's power. The artist shows most of the television viewers with a small, white image of a foreign object—car, shoe, heart (signifying love), bottle, or knife and fork—on the backs of their heads.

One meaning of this picture appears to be that television messages have deadened Congolese peoples' minds to anything but modern thoughts or commodities. The power figure stands squarely on brown earth. Two speaker cabinets set against the back wall beneath the TV screens are wired to the figure, which in the past could inflict harm. In traditional Kongo thinking and color symbolism, the color white and earth tones are associated with spirits and the land of the dead. Perhaps Piula suggests that like earlier power figures, the contemporary world's new television-induced consumerism is poisoning the minds and souls of Congolese people as if by magic or sorcery.

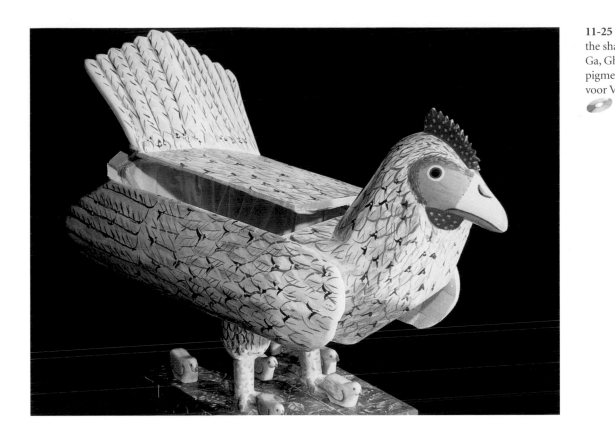

11-25 KANE KWEI, coffin in the shape of a hen with chicks, Ga, Ghana, 1989. Wood and pigment, 7′ 6½′ long. Museum voor Volkenkunde, Rotterdam.

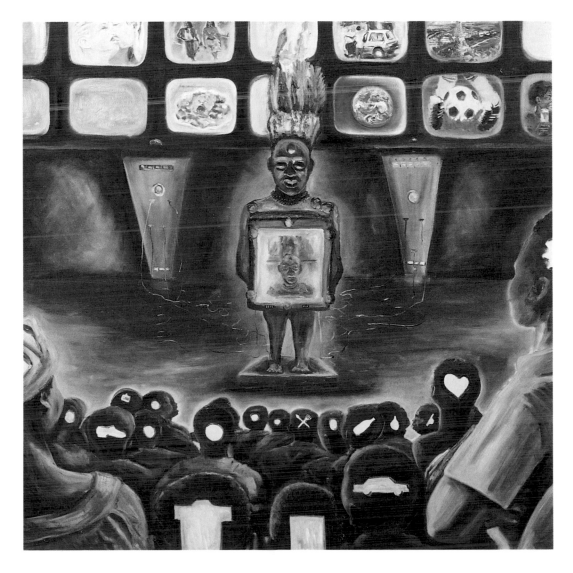

11-26 TRIGO PIULA, *Ta Tele Gabon,* Democratic Republic of Congo, 1988. Oil on canvas, 3′ 3⅜″ × 3′ 4⅜″. National Museum of African Art, Smithsonian Institution, Washington, D. C.

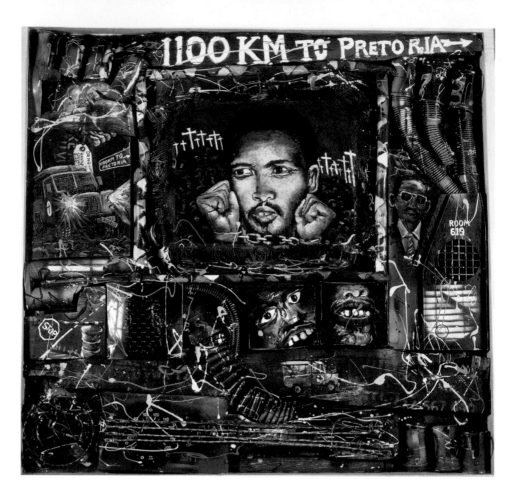

11-27 WILLIE BESTER, *Homage to Steve Biko*, South Africa, 1992. Mixed media, 3′ 7⅚″ × 3′ 7⅚″. Collection of the artist.

ART AND SOCIAL PROTEST Many contemporary African art forms are formally vibrant, as well as concerned with social and political issues. Art in South Africa, for example, first helped protest against *apartheid* (government-sponsored racial separation), then celebrated its demise and the subsequent democratically elected government under the first president, Nelson Mandela. The contemporary artist WILLIE BESTER, in his 1992 *Homage to Steve Biko* (FIG. **11-27**), was among the critics of the apartheid system. Biko, a gentle and heroic leader of the Black Liberation Movement, was killed by white authorities while in detention. The two white doctors in charge of him were exonerated at Biko's inquest, setting off protests around the world. Bester packs his layered picture with references to death and injustice. Biko's portrait, at the center, is near another of the police minister, Kruger, who had him transported 1100 miles to Pretoria in the yellow Land Rover ambulance seen left of center and again beneath Biko's portrait. Bester shows Biko with his chained fists raised in the recurrent protest gesture. This portrait memorializes both Biko and the many others—indicated by the white graveyard crosses above a blue sea of skulls beside Biko's head. The crosses stand out against a red background that recalls the inferno of burned townships. The stop sign (lower left) seems to mean "stop Kruger," or perhaps "stop apartheid." Biko's death is referenced also by the tagged foot, as if in a morgue, above the ambulance (to the left). The red crosses on this vehicle's door and on Kruger's reflective dark glasses repeat, with sad irony, the graveyard crosses.

Blood red and ambulance yellow are in fact unifying colors dripped or painted on many parts of the work. Writing and numbers, found fragments and signs, both stenciled and painted, also appear throughout the composition. Numbers refer to dehumanized life under apartheid. Found objects—wire, sticks, cardboard, sheet metal, cans, and other discards—from which fragile,

impermanent township dwellings are created, remind viewers of the degraded, impoverished lives of most South African people of color. The oilcan guitar (bottom center), another recurrent Bester symbol, refers both to the social harmony and joy provided by music and to the control imposed by apartheid policies. The whole composition is richly textured and dense in its collage combinations of objects, photographs, signs, symbols, and painting. *Homage to Steve Biko* is a radical and powerful critique of an oppressive sociopolitical system, and it exemplifies the extent to which art can be invoked in the political process.

CONCLUSION

African art has always changed and developed in response to the continent's evolving history, both before and after the arrival of Europeans in Africa. During the past two centuries, the encroachments of Christianity, Islam, Western education, market economies, and other colonial imports have led to increasing secularization in all the arts of Africa. Many figures and masks earlier commissioned for shrines or as incarnations of ancestors or spirits are now made mostly for sale to outsiders, essentially as tourist arts. Dogon masks are regularly danced briefly for tourists, after which some of the masks are sold. In towns and cities, painted murals and cement sculptures appear frequently, often making implicit comments about modern life. Nonetheless, despite the growing importance of urbanism (pre-European in a few areas), most African people still live in rural communities. Traditional values, although under pressure, hold considerable force in villages especially, and some people adhere to spiritual beliefs that uphold traditional art forms. African art remains as varied as the vast continent itself and continues to change.

1800

▌ ACTIVE CHRISTIAN MISSIONIZING, 19TH CENTURY

1

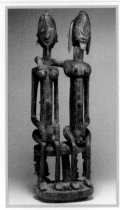

1 Seated couple, Dogon,
Mali, ca. 1800-1850

1850

▌ BERLIN CONFERENCE DIVIDING CONTINENT
AMONG COLONIAL POWERS, 1884-1885

▌ EUROPEAN COUNTRIES COLONIZE MOST OF AFRICA, CA. 1885–1924

▌ BRITISH PUNITIVE EXPEDITION SACKS BENIN, 1897

2

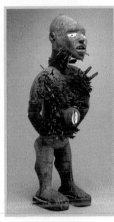

1900

▌ FIRST WORLD WAR, 1914-1918

▌ SECOND WORLD WAR, 1939-1945

2 Nail figure, Kongo,
Democratic Republic
of Congo, ca.
1875–1900

3

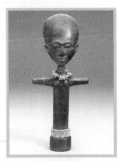

1950

▌ MOST AFRICAN COUNTRIES ACHIEVE INDEPENDENCE, BEGINNING CA. 1960

3 Osei Bonsu, *akua'ba*,
Asante, Ghana, ca. 1935

4

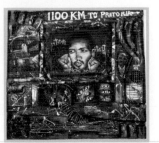

2000

4 Willie Bester, *Homage to Steve
Biko*, South Africa, 1992

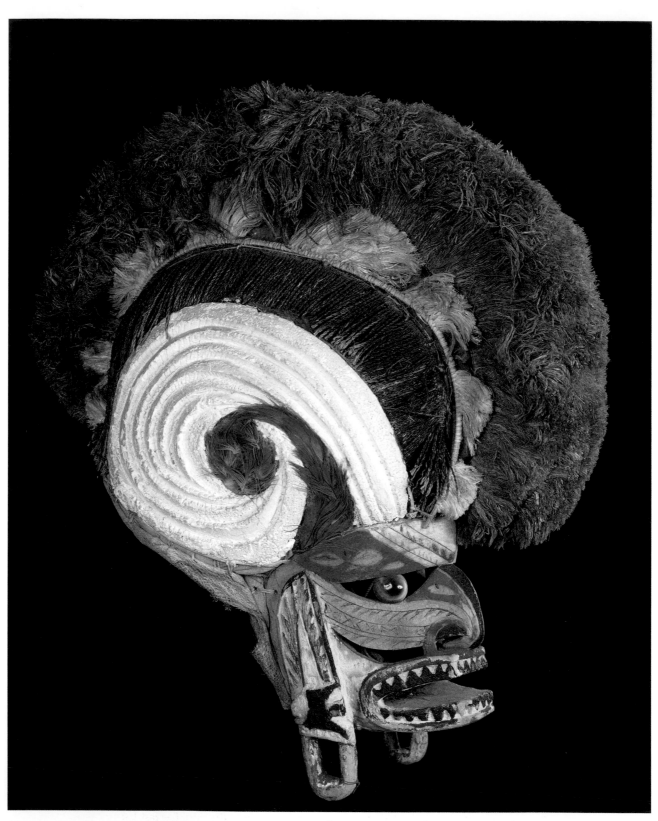

Tatanua mask, from New Ireland. Wood, shell, lime, and fiber, 1′ 5¾″ high. Otago Museum, Otago.

12

THE FLOURISHING
OF ISLAND CULTURES

THE ART OF OCEANIA

Although the term *South Pacific* may well call to mind images of balmy tropical islands, the Pacific Ocean actually encompasses a truly diverse range of habitats and cultures. Environments range from the arid deserts of the Australian outback to the tropical rainforests of inland New Guinea and the coral atolls of the Marshall Islands. Oceanic cultures are not only geographically varied but also politically, linguistically, culturally, and artistically diverse.

WAVES ACROSS THE PACIFIC Oceania (MAP **12-1**) consists of more than 25,000 islands (less than 1,500 inhabitable), including the island continent of Australia. Although documentary evidence does not exist for Oceanic cultures until the arrival of seafaring Europeans in the early 16th century, archaeologists have determined that the islands have been inhabited for tens of thousands of years. Their research has revealed that different parts of the Pacific were populated during distinct migratory waves. The first group arrived in the Pacific during the last Ice Age, approximately 40,000 years ago, when a large continental shelf extended from Southeast Asia and allowed human access to Australia and New Guinea. After the end of the Ice Age, descendants of these first settlers dispersed to other islands. The most recent migratory wave to areas of Micronesia and Polynesia involved people of Asian ancestry. This migration probably took place sometime after 3000 BCE. Knowledge of this movement into Micronesia and western Polynesia is based in part on a type of pottery (known as Lapita) that is common to much of this area. Named after a site on New Caledonia in Melanesia, Lapita pottery (ceramic vessels elaborately decorated with incised, geometric designs) has been found in a geographical region stretching from the straits between New Guinea and New Britain in the west, to Tonga and Samoa in the east. The last Pacific islands colonized were those of Polynesia. Its most far-flung islands—Hawaii, New Zealand, and Rapa Nui (Easter Island)—were inhabited by about 500–1000 CE.

Because of the expansive chronological span of these migrations, Pacific cultures vary widely. For example, the Aboriginal peoples of Australia speak a language unrelated to those of New Guinea, whose diverse languages fall into a family often referred

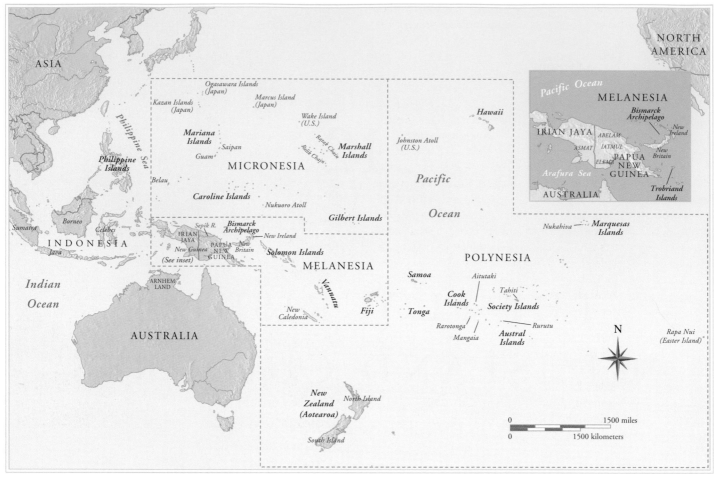

MAP 12-1 Oceania.

to as Papuan. In contrast, most of the rest of the Pacific islanders speak languages derived from the Austronesian language family.

A HISTORY OF COLONIALISM These island groups came to Western attention as a result of the extensive exploration and colonization that began in the 16th century and reached its peak in the 19th century. Virtually all of the major Western cultures established a presence in the Pacific, including Great Britain, France, Spain, Holland, Germany, and the United States. This colonial presence was problematic for many indigenous peoples. Indeed, much of 20th-century Oceanic history has revolved around struggles for independence from colonial powers. Yet such contact also facilitated an exchange of ideas, and Oceanic practices and art influenced the Western world.

PACIFIC REGIONS In 1831, the French explorer Jules Sébastien César Dumont d'Urville proposed the division of the Pacific into major regions based on general geographical, racial, and linguistic distinctions. Despite its limitations, his division of Oceania into the areas of Melanesia ("black islands"), Micronesia ("small islands"), and Polynesia ("many islands") continues to be used today. Melanesia includes the islands of New Guinea, New Ireland, New Britain, New Caledonia, the Admiralty Islands, and the Solomon Islands, along with other smaller island groups. Micronesia consists primarily of the Caroline Islands, the Mariana Islands, the Gilbert Islands, and the Marshall Islands in the western Pacific. Polynesia covers much of the eastern Pacific and

consists of a triangular area defined by the Hawaiian Islands in the north, Rapa Nui (Easter Island) in the east, and New Zealand in the southwest.

THE EVOLUTION OF OCEANIC ART This chapter focuses on Oceanic art from the European discovery of the islands in the 16th century until the present. Some of the objects presented may not seem to conform to traditional Western definitions of art. But although these objects may appear primarily functional, their aesthetic components are no less important, accounting for their discussion in this chapter as art. The ongoing efforts of archaeologists, linguists, anthropologists, ethnologists, and art historians continue to shed light on the development of the arts of Oceania. Knowledge of early Oceanic art and the history of the Pacific islands in general is unfortunately far from complete. Traditionally, the transmission of information from one generation to the next in Pacific societies was largely verbal, rather than written, and this emphasis on oral history has left little archival documentation. It is known, however, that the art and material culture of the islands of Oceania, like those of other cultures worldwide, have constantly evolved. Largely as a result of colonial and missionary intervention in the 18th through 20th centuries, many Oceanic cultures abandoned traditional practices, and production of many of the art forms illustrated in this chapter ceased. In recent years, some Pacific artists have returned to traditional forms for inspiration and have worked to revive and reinterpret traditional indigenous practices and art forms. Today's thriving tourist trade has also contributed to a resurgence of traditional art production.

MELANESIA

DIVERSE ECOSYSTEMS Because of its sheer size, New Guinea dominates Melanesia. This 309,000-square-mile island consists today of parts of two countries — Irian Jaya, a province of nearby Indonesia, on the island's western end, and Papua New Guinea on the eastern end. New Guinea's inhabitants together speak nearly 800 different languages, almost one quarter of the world's known languages. Among the Melanesian cultures discussed in this chapter, the Iatmul, Abelam, Asmat, and Elema peoples of New Guinea all speak Papuan-derived languages and are believed to descend from the early settlers who came to the island in the remote past. In contrast, the people of New Ireland, off the northeast coast of New Guinea, and the Trobriand Islanders, off the southeastern tip of New Guinea, are Austronesian speakers and were probably descendants of a later wave of Pacific migrants.

POWER, PRIVILEGE, AND ART Typical Melanesian societies are fairly democratic and relatively unstratified. What political power exists is vested in groups of elder men and, in some areas, elder women. The elders handle the people's affairs in a communal fashion. Within some of these groups power is accrued by persons of local distinction, known as "Big Men." Such individuals are renowned for their political, economic, and, historically, warrior skills. Because power and position in Melanesia can be earned (within limits), many cultural practices (such as rituals and cults) revolve around the acquisition of knowledge that allows advancement in society. To represent and acknowledge this advancement in rank, Melanesian societies mount elaborate festivals, construct communal meetinghouses, and produce art objects. These cultural products serve to reinforce the social order and maintain social stability. Given the wide diversity in environments and languages, it should come as no surprise that there are hundreds of art styles found on New Guinea alone, only a few of which will be presented here.

The Iatmul (Papua New Guinea)

A SYMBOLIC FEMALE ANCESTOR Prime examples of the social importance and symbolism of Melanesian architecture are the massive saddle-shaped men's ceremonial houses built by the Iatmul people. The Iatmul live along the middle Sepik River in Papua New Guinea in communities based on kinship. Villages include extended families as well as different clans. In terms of both function and form, the men's house reveals the primacy of the kinship network. The meetinghouse reinforces kinship links by serving as the locale for initiation of local youths for advancement in rank, for men's discussions of community issues, and for ceremonies linked to the Iatmul's ancestors. Because advancement in Iatmul society is limited to men, women and uninitiated boys are denied access to the house. In this manner, access to knowledge (and therefore to power) is controlled. Given its important political and cultural role, this house is appropriately monumental, physically dominating Iatmul villages and dwarfing family houses.

Traditionally, the house (FIG. **12-1**) symbolizes the protective mantle of the ancestors and represents an enormous female ancestor. The Iatmul house and its female ancestral figures symbolize a

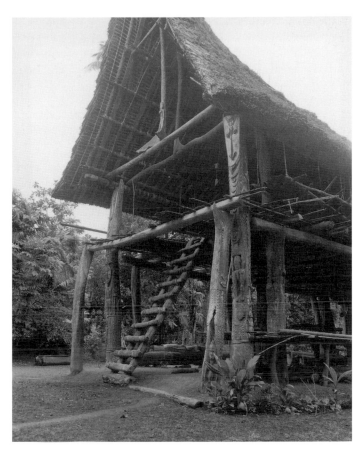

12-1 Exposed interior of ceremonial men's house, Iatmul, Papua New Guinea, photographed in 1953–1954.

reenacted death and rebirth when a clan member enters and exits the second story of the house. The gable ends of such houses are usually covered (though they are exposed in our illustration) and include a giant female gable mask (not visible in the illustration), making the ancestral symbolism visible. The absence of this covering and mask in our example is due to the house's incomplete state. When it was reconstructed after sustaining damage during World War II, it was never finished. Although this hampers our visualization of the exterior, it does expose interior carvings normally hidden from view. The Iatmul placed carved images of clan ancestors on the five central ridge-support posts and on the twelve roof-support posts on both sides of the house. (One central post and two roof-support posts are fully visible in our photograph.) They topped each roof-support post with large faces representing mythical spirits of the clans. At the top of the two raised spires at each end, birds symbolizing the war spirit of the village men sit above carvings of head-hunting victims (on occasion, male ancestors). Iatmul men's houses are the most lavishly decorated of such structures in New Guinea.

The house's interior reflects the social demographic of the village and is subdivided into parts for each clan. This particular meetinghouse has three parts — a front, middle, and end — representing the three major clans who built the house. These parts are further subdivided into additional subclan areas, which also have support posts carved with images of mythical male and female ancestors. Beneath the house, each clan keeps large carved slit-gongs to serve as both instruments of communication (for sending drum messages within and between villages) and the voices of ancestral spirits. Above the two ladders leading to the second level, the Iatmul placed figurative carvings on horizontal crossbeams (see the carving in the open gable space in FIG. 12-1).

These figures symbolize female clan ancestors in a birthing position. The Iatmul also keep various types of portable art in their ceremonial houses. These include ancestors' skulls overmodeled with clay in a likeness of the deceased, ceremonial chairs, sacred flutes, hooks for hanging sacred items and food, and several types of masks.

The Abelam (Papua New Guinea)

A COMPLEX YAM CULT   That Oceanic art relates not only to fundamental spiritual beliefs but also to basic subsistence is highlighted by the yam masks produced by the Abelam people, agriculturists living in the hilly regions north of the Sepik River. The Abelam's principal cultivar is the yam. Such has been the case throughout recent Abelam history and continues to the present day. Relatively isolated, the Abelam received only sporadic visits from foreigners until the 1930s, so little is known about early Abelam history. Because of the importance of yams to the survival of Abelam society, those who can grow the largest yams are endowed with power and prestige. Indeed, the Abelam developed

a complex yam cult, which involves a series of rites and activities intended to promote the growth of yams. Special plantations are devoted to yam cultivation. Only initiated men who observe strict rules of conduct, including sexual abstinence, can work these fields. The Abelam believe that ancestors aid in the growth of yams, and they hold ceremonies to honor these ancestors. Special long yams (distinct from the short yams cultivated for consumption) are placed on display during these festivities, and the largest of the yams are named after important ancestors. Yam masks are an integral part of the ceremonies. These cane or wood frame masks (FIG. 12-2) are usually painted red, white, yellow, and black. Further, the Abelam incorporate sculpted faces, cassowary feathers, and shell ornaments into the yam masks. The Abelam use the same designs to decorate their bodies for dances, revealing how closely they identify with their principal food source.

The Asmat (Irian Jaya)

THE ART OF WARFARE   In contrast with the Abelam, with their relatively peaceful agricultural pursuits, the Asmat face a much harsher life. Living along the coast of southwestern New Guinea, the Asmat eke out their existence by hunting and gathering the varied flora and fauna found in the mangrove swamps, rivers, and tropical forests where they live. Because resources are limited, each Asmat community is in constant competition for these resources. Historically, the Asmat extended this competitive spirit beyond food and materials to energy and power as well. To increase one's personal energy or spiritual power, one had to take it forcibly from someone else. As a result, warfare and head-hunting became central to Asmat culture and art. The Asmat did not believe that any death was natural. It could only be the result of a direct assault (head-hunting or warfare) or sorcery, and it diminished ancestral power. Thus, to restore a balance of spirit power, an enemy's head had to be taken to avenge a death and to add to one's communal spirit power. Head-hunting was common in the 1930s when Europeans established an administrative and missionary presence among the Asmat. As a result of European efforts, head-hunting was effectively abandoned by the 1960s.

AVENGING A DEATH   When they still practiced head-hunting, the Asmat erected *bisj* poles (FIG. 12-3) that served as a pledge to avenge a relative's death. Such poles were constructed when a man could command the support of enough men to undertake a head-hunting raid. Carved from the trunk of the mangrove tree, bisj poles included superimposed figures of individuals who had died. At the top, extending flangelike from the bisj pole, was one of the tree's buttress roots carved into an openwork pattern. All of the decorative elements on the pole were related to head-hunting and foretold a successful raid. The many animals that appeared on bisj poles (and in Asmat art in general) are symbols of head-hunting. The Asmat see the human body as a tree—the feet as the roots, the arms as the branches, and the head as the fruit. Thus any fruit-eating animal (such as the black king cockatoo, the hornbill, or the flying fox) is symbolic of the headhunter and appeared frequently on bisj poles. Asmat art also often includes representations of the praying mantis. The Asmat consider the female praying mantis's practice of beheading her mate after copulation and then eating him as another form of head-hunting. The curvilinear or spiral patterns that filled the pierced openwork at the top of the pole can be related to the characteristic curved tail of the cuscus (a fruit-eating mammal) or the tusk of a boar (related to hunting and virility). Once carved, bisj poles were placed on a

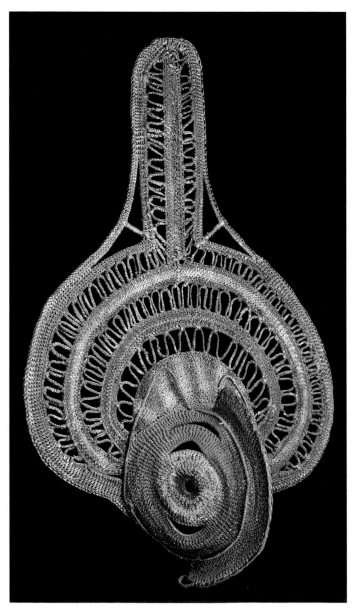

12-2 Yam mask, Abelam, Maprik district, Papua New Guinea, 1′ 6$\frac{9}{10}$″ high.

rack near the men's house, in public view. After the success of the head-hunting expedition, the bisj poles were discarded and allowed to rot, having served their purpose.

The Elema (Papua New Guinea)

VISITING WATER SPIRITS Central to the culture of the Elema people of Orokolo Bay in the Papuan Gulf was Hevehe, an elaborate cycle of ceremonial activities. Conceptualized as the mythical visitation of the water spirits *(ma-hevehe),* the Hevehe cycle involved the production and presentation of large, ornate masks (also called *hevehe).* The Elema last practiced Hevehe in the 1950s. Primarily organized by the male elders of the village, the cycle was a communal undertaking, and normally took from 10 to 20 years to complete. The duration of the Hevehe and the resources and human labor required reveal the role of Hevehe as a social glue — it reinforced cultural and economic relations and maintained the social structure in which elder male authority dominated.

Throughout the cycle, the Elema held ceremonies to initiate male youths into higher ranks. These ceremonies involved the exchange of wealth (such as pigs and shell ornaments), thereby

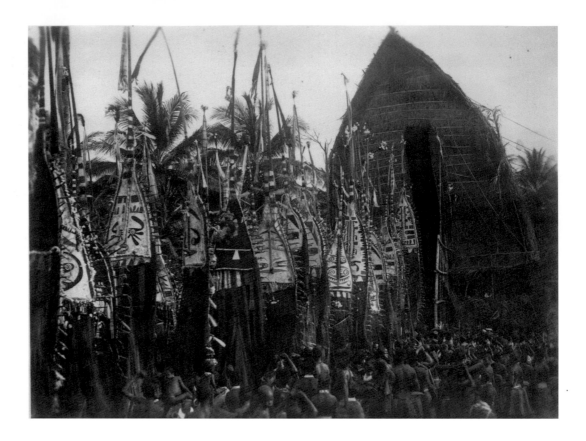

12-4 *Hevehe* masks retreating into the men's house *(eravo)*, Elema, Orokolo Bay, Papua New Guinea.

serving an economic purpose as well. The cycle culminated in the display of the finished hevehe masks. Each mask was constructed of painted barkcloth (see pages 226–227) wrapped around a cane-and-wood frame that fit over the wearer's body. A hevehe mask was normally 9 to 10 feet in height, although extensions often raised the height to as much as 25 feet. Because of its size and intricate design, a hevehe mask required great skill to construct, and only trained men would participate in mask-making. Designs were specific to particular clans and were passed down by elder men from memory. Each mask represented a female sea spirit, but the overall decoration of the mask often incorporated designs from local flora and fauna as well.

The final stage of the cycle focused on the dramatic appearance of the masks from the *eravo* (men's house; FIG. **12-4**). After a procession, men wearing the hevehe mingled with relatives. Upon conclusion of related dancing (often lasting about one month), the masks were ritually killed and then dumped in piles and burned. This destruction allowed the sea spirits to return to their mythic domain and provided a pretext for commencing the cycle again.

The Trobriand Islands (Papua New Guinea)

TRADING PLACES The various rituals of Oceanic cultures discussed thus far often involve exchanges that cement social relationships and reinforce or stimulate the economy. Further, these rituals usually have a spiritual dimension. All of these aspects apply to the practices of the Trobriand Islanders, who live off the coast of the southeastern corner of New Guinea (part of Papua New Guinea). The Trobriand Islanders are well known for *kula*—an exchange of white conus-shell arm ornaments for red chama-shell necklaces. Kula, possibly originating some 500 years ago, came to Western attention through the extensive documentation of anthropologist Bronislaw Malinowski (1884–1942),

published in 1920 and 1922. Kula exchanges can be complex, and there is great competition for valuable shell ornaments (determined by aesthetic appeal and exchange history). Because of the isolation imposed by their island existence, the Trobriand Islanders had to undertake potentially dangerous voyages to participate in kula trading. Appropriately, the Trobrianders lavish a great deal of effort on decorating their large canoes, which are elaborately carved and include ornate prows and splashboards (FIG. **12-5**). These prows and splashboards are carved by artists who have acquired both the necessary carving skill and the knowledge of the symbolism of the kula images. Human, bird, and serpent motifs, as references to sea spirits, ancestors, and totemic animals, appear on prows. These motifs are highly stylized, making specific identification difficult. The curvilinear, intertwined designs are fluidly presented. This intricate style is characteristic of Trobriand art. To ensure a successful kula expedition, the Trobrianders invoked spells when attaching these prows to the canoes. In recent years, Trobrianders have adapted kula to modern circumstances. By the 1970s, they largely abandoned canoes for motorboats, and the exchanges now facilitate contemporary business and political networking.

New Ireland (Papua New Guinea)

HONORING THE DEAD Mortuary rites and memorial festivals are a central concern of the Austronesian-speaking peoples who live in the northern section of the island of New Ireland in Papua New Guinea. The term *malanggan* refers to both the festivals held in honor of the deceased and the carvings and objects produced for these festivals. Malanggan practices have enjoyed longevity. One of the first references to malanggan appears in an 1883 publication, and these rituals continue to be practiced today. Malanggan rites are critical in facilitating the transition of the soul from the world of the

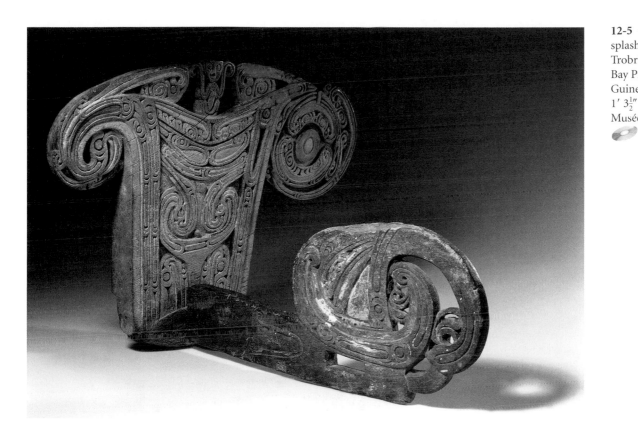

12-5 Canoe prow and splashboard, from Trobriand Islands, Milne Bay Province, Papua New Guinea. Wood and paint, 1′ 3½″ high, 1′ 11″ long. Musée de l'Homme, Paris.

living to the realm of the dead. Because of the ultimate destination of the soul, these rituals are part of an ancestor cult. In addition to the religious function of malanggan, the extended ceremonies also promote social solidarity and stimulate the economy (as a result of the resources necessary to mount impressive festivities). To educate the younger generation about these practices, malanggan also includes the initiation of young men.

Among the many malanggan carvings produced—masks, figures, poles, friezes, and ornaments—are *tatanua* masks (FIG. **12-6**). Although some masks are simply displayed, most of them are worn by dancers. Tatanua represent the spirits of specific deceased people and are constructed of soft wood, vegetable fiber, and rattan. The crested hair, made of fiber, duplicates a hairstyle formerly common among the men. Sea snail opercula (the operculum is the plate that closes the shell when the animal is retracted) are embedded as eyes. Traditionally, the masks are painted black, white, yellow, and red—colors the people of New Ireland associate with warfare, magic spells, and violence. Rather than being destroyed after the conclusion of the many ceremonies, tatanua are stored for future use.

MICRONESIA

THE ART OF SEAFARING CULTURES The Austronesian-speaking cultures of Micronesia tend to be more socially stratified than those found in New Guinea and other Melanesian areas. Such cultures are frequently organized around chieftainships with craft and ritual specializations, and their religions include named deities as well as honored ancestors. Life in virtually all Micronesian cultures centers around seafaring activities—fishing, trading, and long-distance travel in large oceangoing vessels. For this reason, much of their artistic imagery relates to the sea. Micronesian arts include carved canoes, charms, and images of spirits used to protect travelers at sea and for fishing and fertility magic. Micronesian artists also tend to simplify and to abstract geometrically the natural forms of animals, humans, and plants. This characteristic often differentiates Micronesian art from the arts of Melanesia, Polynesia, and Australia.

12-6 *Tatanua* mask, from New Ireland. Wood, shell, lime, and fiber, 1′ 5¾″ high. Otago Museum, Otago.

Belau (Caroline Islands)

HOUSES THAT TELL STORIES On Belau (formerly Palau) in the Caroline Islands, the islanders put much effort into creating and maintaining elaborately painted men's ceremonial clubhouses called *bai*. These bai (FIG. **12-7**) have steep overhanging roofs decorated with geometric patterns along the roof boards. Belau artists carve the gable in low relief and paint it with narrative scenes, as well as various abstracted forms of the shell money used traditionally on Belau as currency. These decorated storyboards illustrate important historical events and myths related to the clan who built the bai. In the illustration, the rooster images along the base of the house symbolize the rising sun, while the multiple frontal human faces carved and painted above the entrance and on the vertical elements above the rooster images represent a deity called Blellek. He warns women to stay away from the ocean and the *bai* or he will molest them. In so doing, the god serves as a social control mechanism within Belau society.

Artists also carve and paint the crossbeams on the inside of the house with similar narratives recounting clan histories and myths. The shell-like abstract patterns found on the exterior roof beams and lower sections of the house all refer to the shell-money wealth of the clan and its chief. While the Iatmul make their ceremonial houses, discussed earlier (FIG. 12-1), by elaborate tying, lashing, and weaving of different-size posts, trees, saplings, and grasses, the Belau people make the main structure of the bai entirely of worked, fitted, joined, and pegged wooden elements, which allows them to assemble it easily.

A PROTECTIVE FEMALE FIGURE Although the bai was the domain of men, women figured prominently in the imagery that covered it. This reality reveals the important symbolic and social positions that women held in this culture (see "The Many Roles of Women in Oceania," page 225). A common element surmounting the main bai entrance was a simple, symmetrical wooden sculpture (on occasion, a painting) of a splayed female figure, known as Dilukai (FIGS. 12-7 and **12-8**). Serving as a symbol of both protection and fertility, the Dilukai was also a moralistic reminder to women to be chaste. According to legend, Dilukai's brother, Bagei, was embarrassed by his sister's promiscuity and carved her image on the bai to shame her. The Dilukai figure demonstrates the ability of an image to control a group (here, women) while at the same time celebrating women's power.

12-7 Men's ceremonial house *(bai)*, from Belau (Palau), Republic of Belau. Staatliche Museen zu Berlin, Stiftung Preussischer Kulturbesitz, Ethnologisches Museum, Berlin.

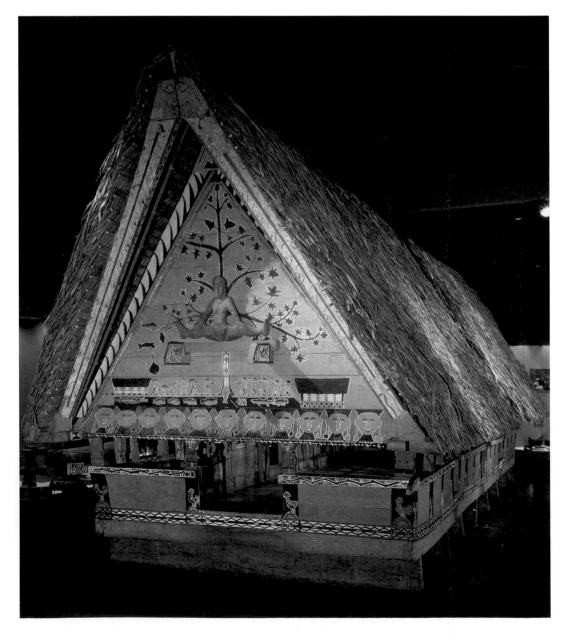

The Many Roles of Women in Oceania

Given the prominence of men's houses and the importance of male initiation in so many Oceanic societies, one might conclude that women are peripheral members of these cultures. Much of the extant material culture—ancestor masks, shields, clubs—seems to corroborate this. In reality, however, women play crucial roles in most Pacific cultures, although those roles may be less ostentatious or public than those of men. In addition to their significant contributions through exchange and ritual activities to the maintenance and perpetuation of the social network upon which the stability of village life depends, women are important producers of art.

For the most part, women's artistic production was historically restricted to forms such as barkcloth, weaving, and pottery. Throughout much of Polynesia, women produced barkcloth (see page 226), which was often dyed and stenciled, and sometimes even perfumed. Women in the Trobriand Islands continue to make brilliantly dyed skirts of shredded banana fiber that not only are aesthetically beautiful but also serve as a form of wealth and are presented symbolically during mortuary rituals. In some cultures in New Guinea, potters were primarily female.

In general, women were largely proscribed from working in hard materials (such as wood, stone, bone, or ivory) or using specialized tools. Further, in most Oceanic cultures, women were rarely allowed to produce images that had religious or spiritual powers or that conferred status on their users. Scholars investigating the role of the artist in Oceania have concluded that these restrictions were due to the perceived difference in innate power. Because women have the natural power to create and control life, male-dominated societies developed elaborate ritual practices that served to counteract this female power. By excluding women from participating in these rituals and denying them access to knowledge about specific practices, men derived a political authority that could be perpetuated. It is important to note,

however, that even in rituals or activities restricted to men, women often participate. For example, in the now-defunct Hevehe ceremonial cycle in Papua New Guinea (see pages 221–222), women helped to construct the hevehe masks, but feigned ignorance about these sacred objects, knowledge of which was limited to initiated men.

Pacific cultures often acknowledged women's innate power in the depictions of women in Oceanic art. For example, the splayed Dilukai female sculpture (FIG. 12-8) that appears regularly on Palauan bai (men's houses) celebrates women's procreative powers. Yet it simultaneously reinforces male authority by moralistically reminding women to limit their sexual activity. The Dilukai figure also confers protection upon visitors to the bai, another symbolic acknowledgment of female power. Similar concepts underlie the design of the Iatmul men's house (FIG. 12-1). Conceived as a giant female ancestor, the men's house incorporates women's natural power into the conceptualization of what is normally the most important architectural structure of an Iatmul village. In addition, the Iatmul associate entrance and departure from the men's house with death and rebirth, thereby reinforcing the primacy of fertility and the perception of the men's house as representing a woman's body.

Women were active participants in all aspects of Oceanic life, and their contributions in various arenas, such as art, are often overlooked. The general perception of Oceania as male dominated is due in part to the fact that the objects collected by visitors to the Pacific in earlier centuries tended to be those that suggest aggressive, warring societies. That the majority of these Western travelers (and collectors) were men and therefore had contact predominantly with men no doubt accounts for this pattern of collecting. Recent scholarship has done a great deal to rectify this misperception, thereby revealing the richness of social, artistic, and political activity in the Pacific.

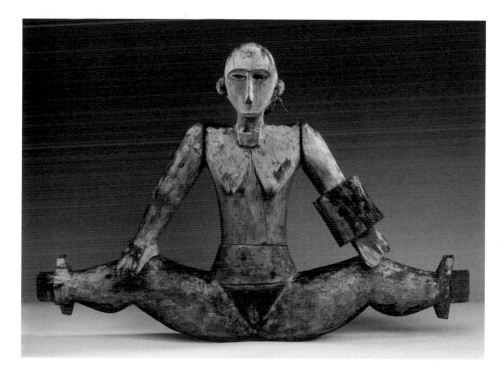

12-8 Dilukai, from Belau (Palau). Wood, pigment, and fiber, 1′ 11⅝″ high. Linden Museum, Stuttgart.

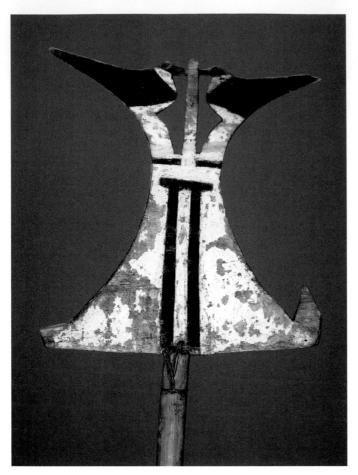

12-9 Canoe prow ornament, from Chuuk, Caroline Islands. Wood and paint. British Museum, London.

Polynesian societies possess elaborate political organizations headed by chiefs and ritual specialists. By the 1800s, some Polynesian cultures (Hawaii and the Society Islands, for example) evolved into kingdoms. Because of this social hierarchy, much of Polynesian art is made for high-ranking persons of noble or high religious background and serves to reinforce their power and prestige. These objects, like their chiefly owners, are often invested with *mana,* or spiritual power.

BEATEN CLOTH Despite the prominence of art for high-ranking individuals, art in Polynesia is not solely the purview of rulers. For example, women throughout Polynesia traditionally produced decorated barkcloth using the inner bark of the paper mulberry tree *(Broussonetia papyrifera).* The finished product goes by various names in Polynesia, including *ahu* (Tahiti), *autea* (Cook Islands), *aute* (New Zealand), *kapa* (Hawaii), *hiapo* (Marquesas Islands), *siapo* (Samoa), and *masi* (Fiji). During the 19th century, when the production of barkcloth reached its zenith, *tapa* became a widely used reference word for such Polynesian barkcloth and still is today. Although tapa was utilized extensively for clothing and bedding, its uses extended beyond mere functionality. For example, in some Polynesian cultures, such as that of Tonga, large sheets (FIG. **12-10**) were (and still are) produced for exchange. Barkcloth can also have a spiritual dimension and can serve to confer sanctity upon the object wrapped. Appropriately, the bodies of high-ranking deceased chiefs were traditionally wrapped in barkcloth.

The use and decoration of tapa have varied over the years. In the 19th century, tapa used for everyday clothing was normally unadorned, whereas tapa used for ceremonial or ritual purposes was dyed, painted, stenciled, and sometimes even perfumed. The designs applied to the tapa differed depending upon the particular island group producing it and the function of the cloth. The production process was complex and time-consuming (see "The Production of Barkcloth," page 227). Indeed, some Oceanic cultures, such as those of Tahiti and Hawaii, constructed buildings specifically for the beating stage in the production of barkcloth.

The production of tapa reached its peak in the early 19th century, partly as a result of the interest expressed by visiting Westerners, such as whalers and missionaries. By the late 19th century, the use of tapa for cloth had been abandoned throughout much of eastern Polynesia, although its use in rituals (for example, as a wrap for corpses of deceased chiefs or as a marker of tabooed sites) continued. Even today, tapa exchanges are still an integral part of funerals and marriage ceremonies, and there is a considerable tourist market for tapa as well.

Rarotonga (Cook Islands)

Even though the Polynesians were skillful navigators, various island groups remained isolated from one another for centuries by the vast distances they would have had to cover in open outriggers. This allowed distinct regional styles to develop within a recognizable general Polynesian style. For example, deity images with multiple figures attached to their bodies surfaced in the material culture of Rarotonga and Mangaia in the Cook Islands and Rurutu in the Austral Islands. These carvings probably represented clan and district ancestors, revered for their protective and procreative powers. All such images refer ultimately to the creator deities the Polynesians revere for their central role in human fertility.

SEAFARING PROTECTION Given the importance of seafaring and long-distance ocean travel in Micronesia, canoe building acquired a prominent position in Micronesian art and culture. This canoe prow ornament (FIG. **12-9**), from Chuuk in the Caroline Islands, was carved by a master canoe builder from a single plank of wood. Fastened to a large, paddled war canoe, a prow ornament such as this was intended to provide protection on arduous or long voyages. Appropriately, the prow ornament design, while seemingly abstract, actually represents two symmetrically placed sea swallows—creatures capable of navigating long distances. The form may also represent a stylized human figure. That these canoe prow ornaments were not permanently attached to the canoe was a matter of function. When approaching another vessel, these ornaments were lowered to signal peaceful intentions, and they were removed from the canoe when not in use.

POLYNESIA

OF CHIEFS AND KINGS Polynesia was one of the last areas in the world that humans colonized. It was not settled until about the end of the first millennium BCE in the west and the first millennium CE in the south. Its inhabitants brought complex sociopolitical and religious institutions with them. Whereas Melanesian societies are fairly egalitarian and advancement in rank is possible, Polynesian societies typically are highly stratified, with power determined by heredity. Indeed, rulers often trace their genealogies directly to the gods of creation. Most

The Production of Barkcloth

Tongan barkcloth provides an instructive example of the labor-intensive process of tapa production. At the time of early contact between Europeans and Polynesians in the late 18th and early 19th centuries, ranking women in Tonga (western Polynesia) made decorated barkcloth *(ngatu)*. Today, women's organizations called *kautaha* produce it. The kautaha may have the honorary patronage of ranking women. In Tonga, men plant the paper mulberry tree and harvest it in two to three years. They cut the trees into about 10-foot lengths and allow them to dry for several days. Then the women strip off the outer bark and soak the inner bark in water to prepare it for further processing. They place these soaked inner bark strips over a wooden anvil and repeatedly strike them with a wooden beater until they spread out and flatten. Folding and layering the strips while beating them, a felting process, results in a wider piece of ngatu than the original strips. Afterward, the beaten barkcloth dries and bleaches in the sun.

The next stage of ngatu production involves the placement of the thin, beaten sheets over semicircular boards. The women then fasten embroidered design tablets *(kupesi)* of low-relief leaf, coconut leaf midribs, and string patterns to the boards. They transfer the patterns on the design tablets to the outer barkcloth by rubbing. Then the women fill in the lines and patterns by painting, covering the large white spaces with painted figures. The Tongans use brown, red, and black pigments derived from various types of bark, clay, fruits, and soot to create the colored patterns on ngatu. Sheets, rolls, and strips of ngatu are made for use on special occasions, such as weddings, funerals, and ceremonial presentations for ranking persons.

A traditionally patterned ngatu (FIG. 12-10) made in 1967 for the coronation of King Tupou IV of Tonga clearly shows the richness of pattern, subtlety of theme, and variation of geometric forms that characterize Tongan royal barkcloths. One of the women barkcloth specialists—MELE SITANI, who made this presentation piece—kneels in the middle of the ngatu covered in triangular patterns known as *manulua*. This pattern is made from the intersection of three or four triangular points. Manulua means "two birds," and the design gives the illusion of two birds flying together. The motif symbolizes chiefly status derived from both parents.

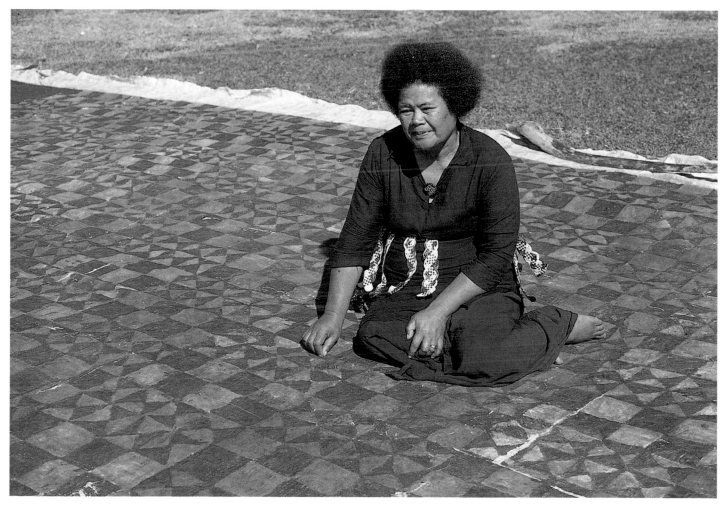

12-10 MELE SITANI, decorated barkcloth *(ngatu)* with two-bird *(manulua)* designs, Tonga, 1967.

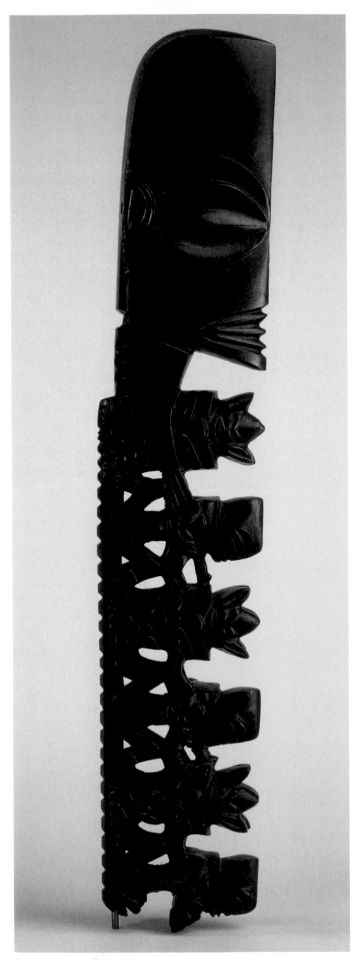

A GOD IN BARKCLOTH The central Polynesian island residents of Rarotonga used various types of carved deity figures well into the early decades of the 19th century, when Christians converted the islanders and destroyed their deities as part of the conversion process. These included carved wooden fishermen's gods, large naturalistic deity images, and at least three types of staff gods (also called district gods), some more than 20 feet long. One of the best-preserved examples (FIG. 12-11) is close to 4 feet high and consists of a long piece of wood, carved at both the top and bottom (not visible in illustration). The long central section is wrapped with decorated barkcloth. The carving on the top depicts a figure with smaller alternating female and male figures projecting from the front of his body. The exact meanings of the primary and secondary figures are unknown and forever lost due to the abrupt conversion to Christianity and the near total destruction of Rarotongan religious imagery in the early 19th century. Some scholars have suggested that the protruding figures were intended to represent familial descent and genealogy. Alternatively, the procreative symbolism and multiple small figures found on this staff god may represent a generative deity creating minor deities from his own body, a trait found frequently in central Polynesian art and religion.

Marquesas Islands

ORNAMENTAL PROTECTION Although Marquesan chiefs trace their right to rule genealogically, the political system before European contact allowed for the acquisition of power by force. As a result, warfare was widespread through the late 19th century. Among the items produced by Marquesan artists were ornaments (FIG. 12-12) that often adorned the hair of warriors. The hollow, cylindrical bone or ivory ornaments (*ivi p'o*) functioned as protective amulets and were worn until the death of a kinsman was avenged. The ornaments are in the form of *tiki*—three-dimensional carvings of exalted, deified ancestor figures. The style of the tiki—large, rounded eyes and wide mouths—is typically Marquesan.

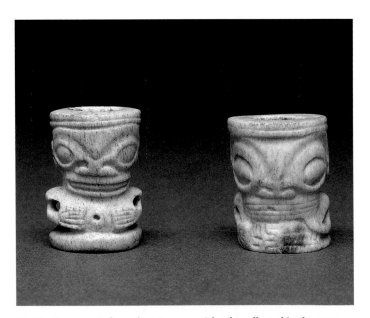

12-11 Head of a staff god, from Rarotonga, Cook Islands, Polynesia, late 18th–early 19th century. Wood. Robert and Lisa Sainsbury Collection, University of East Anglia, Norwich.

12-12 Ornaments from the Marquesas Islands, collected in the 1870s. Bone, 1½″ high × 1″ wide *(left)*, 1⅖″ high × 1″ wide *(right)*. University of Pennsylvania Museum of Archaeology and Anthropology, Philadelphia.

More Than Skin Deep
Tattoo in Polynesia

Throughout Oceanic cultures, the body was a particularly important site for the representation of cultural and personal identity. In addition to the wearing of clothing and ornaments, this representation most often took the form of tattoo. Although tattooing was common among Micronesian cultures, it has become more closely associated with Polynesia due to the extensiveness of the practice there. Indeed, the English term *tattoo* is Polynesian in origin, related to the Tahitian, Samoan, and Tongan word *tatau* or *tatu*. In New Zealand, where tattooing was especially pervasive, the markings were called *moko*.

Within Polynesian cultures, tattoo reached its zenith in the highly stratified societies—New Zealand, the Marquesas Islands, Tahiti, Tonga, Samoa, and Hawaii. Both sexes were tattooed. In general, men were more extensively tattooed than women, and the location of tattoos on the body differed. For instance, in New Zealand, the face and buttocks were the primary areas of male tattoo, whereas tattoos appeared on the lips and chin of women.

Historically, tattooing served a variety of functions in Polynesia. It indicated status. The quantity and quality of tattoos were often linked to rank. In the Marquesas Islands, for example, men of high status were completely tattooed. Further, certain patterns could be applied only to ranking individuals. However, the acquisition of tattoos was not restricted to the chiefly class. Commoners had tattoos, generally on a less extensive scale than higher-ranking individuals. And some people were tattooed for undesirable reasons. For identification purposes, slaves were tattooed on their foreheads in Hawaii and on their backs in New Zealand. There are also accounts of defeated warriors being tattooed. In some Polynesian societies, tattoos identified clan or familial connections. Tattoos could also serve a protective function by in essence wrapping the body in a spiritual armor. And on occasion, tattoos marked significant events such as military victories or rites of passage. In Hawaii, for example, the tongue was sometimes tattooed as a sign of grief. In this instance, the pain endured by the tattooed person was a sign of respect and commemoration for a deceased individual. Of course, decoration was a prominent reason for tattoo.

Throughout much of Polynesia, tattoos were applied by priests who were specially trained in the art form. The importance of tattooing in these Oceanic societies was further indicated by the fact that this practice was accompanied by rituals, chants, or ceremonies and often took place in a structure dedicated to tattooing.

The general technique for tattooing involved the introduction of black, carbon-based pigment under the skin with the use of a bird-bone tattooing comb or chisel and a mallet. In New Zealand, where moko developed to an extremely sophisticated level, a distinctive technique emerged for tattooing the face. In a manner similar to Maori wood carving, a serrated chisel created a groove in the skin. A pigment was then introduced into this groove, thereby producing a colored line.

Polynesian tattoo designs were predominantly geometric, and affinities with other forms of Polynesian art are clearly evident. For example, the curvilinear patterns that predominate in Maori facial moko are reminiscent of the patterns found on *poupou*, decorated wall panels in Maori meetinghouses (FIG. 12-16). Depending on their specific purpose, many tattoos could be "read" or deciphered. For facial tattoos, the Maori generally divided the face into four major, symmetrical zones: the left and right forehead down to the eyes, the left lower face, and the right lower face. The right-hand side conveyed information on the father's rank, tribal affiliations, and social position, whereas the left-hand side provided matrilineal information. Smaller secondary facial zones provided information about the tattooed individual's profession and position in society. The schematic drawing of the moko of Te Pehi Kupe (see FIG. Intro-5) is an example of Maori facial tattoo. Te Pehi Kupe was the paramount chief of the Ngato Toa tribe in the early 19th century and died in 1830. His lineage is indicated by the upward and downward *koru* (unrolled spirals) in the middle of his forehead, which connote his descent from two paramount tribes. The small design in the center of his forehead documents the extent of his domain—north, south, east, and west. The five double koru in front of his left ear indicate that the supreme chief (the highest rank in Maori society) was part of his matrilineal line. The designs on his lower jaw and the anchor-shaped koru nearby reveal that Te Pehi Kupe was not only a master carver, but descended from master carvers as well.

The viability of tattooing was severely impacted by the arrival of Europeans, particularly missionaries, who worked to eradicate the practice. This, in conjunction with changing social systems, led to the abandonment of tattooing in Polynesia by the later 19th century.

FACE-TO-FACE Another important art form for Marquesan warriors during the 19th century was tattoo, which, like the hair ornaments, protected the individual, serving in essence as a form of spiritual armor. Body decoration in general is among the most pervasive art forms found throughout Oceania. Polynesians developed the painful but prestigious art of tattoo more fully than many other Oceanic peoples (see "More Than Skin Deep: Tattoo in Polynesia," above), although tattooing was also common in Micronesia. In Polynesia, with its hierarchical social structure, nobles and warriors in particular accumulated various tattoo patterns over the years to increase their status, mana, and personal beauty. Largely as a result of missionary pressure in the 19th century, tattooing virtually disappeared in many Oceanic societies. In some cultures, tattooing has been revived as an expression of cultural pride.

An early-19th-century engraving (FIG. **12-13**) provides an example of a Marquesan warrior from Nukahiva Island covered with elaborate tattoo patterns. The warrior holds a large wooden war club over his right shoulder and carries a decorated water gourd in his left hand. The various tattoo patterns marking his entire body seem to subdivide his body parts into zones on both sides of a line down the center. Some tattoos accentuate joint areas, whereas others separate muscle masses into horizontal and vertical geometric shapes. The warrior also covered his face, hands, and feet with tattoos.

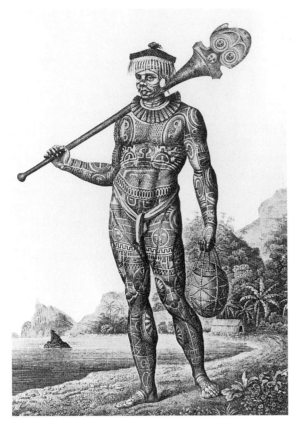

12-13 Tattooed warrior with war club, Nukahiva, Marquesas Islands, 19th century. Engraving.

Hawaii

The Hawaiians developed the most highly stratified social structure in the Pacific. By 1795, the chief Kamehameha unified the major islands of the Hawaiian archipelago and ascended to the pinnacle of power as King Kamehameha I. This kingdom did not endure. As a result of Western contact (with navigators, whalers, and missionaries), Hawaii soon came under American control. The U.S. government annexed Hawaii as a territory in 1898 and eventually conferred statehood on the island group in 1959.

CLOAKED IN MAJESTY Because perpetuation of the social structure was crucial to social stability, most of the material culture produced (before American control) in Hawaii was intended to visualize and reinforce the hierarchy. Chiefly regalia was a prominent part of artistic production. For example, elegant feather cloaks (*'ahu 'ula*) such as this early 19th-century example (FIG. 12-14) were created for chiefly men of high rank. Every aspect of the 'ahu'ula reflected the status of its wearer. The materials were exceedingly precious, particularly the red and yellow feathers from the *'i 'iwi, 'apapane, 'o 'o,* and *mamo* birds. Some of these birds yielded only six or seven suitable feathers, and given that a full-length cloak could require up to 500,000 feathers, the resources and labor required to produce a cloak were extraordinary. The cloak also linked its owner to the gods. The sennit (plaited fiber or cord) base to which the feathers were attached was associated throughout Polynesia with deities. Not only did these cloaks confer the protection of the gods on their wearers, their dense fiber base and feather matting also provided physical protection. Our example originally belonged to King Kamehameha III, who gave it to Commodore Lawrence Kearny of the U.S. frigate *Constellation* in 1843 in gratitude for the Commodore's assistance during a temporary occupation of Hawaii.

A DEFIANT WAR GOD The gods were a pervasive presence in Hawaiian society and were part of every person's life, regardless of status. Chiefs in particular invoked them regularly and publicized their own genealogical links to the gods to reinforce their right to rule. One of the more prominent Hawaiian gods was Kuka'ilimoku, the war god. As chiefs in the prekingdom years struggled to maintain and expand their control, warfare was endemic, hence Kuka'il-imoku's importance. Indeed, Kuka'ilimoku served as Kamehameha I's special tutelary deity, and the Kuka'ilimoku sculpture we

12-14 Feather cloak (*'ahu'ula*), from Hawaii, early 19th century. Red *'i'iwi*, yellow *'o'o*, and black feathers, *olona* cordage and netting, 4' 8⅓" × 8'. Bishop Pauahi Museum, Honolulu.

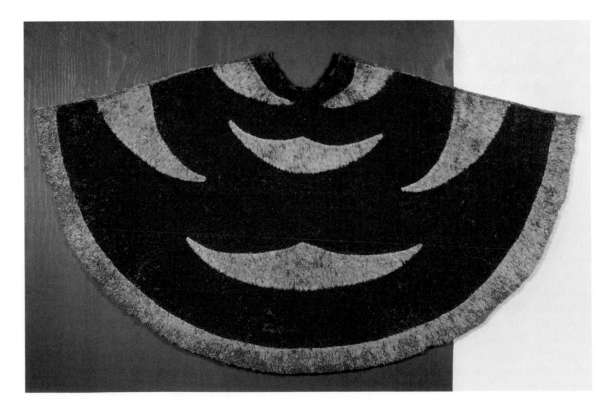

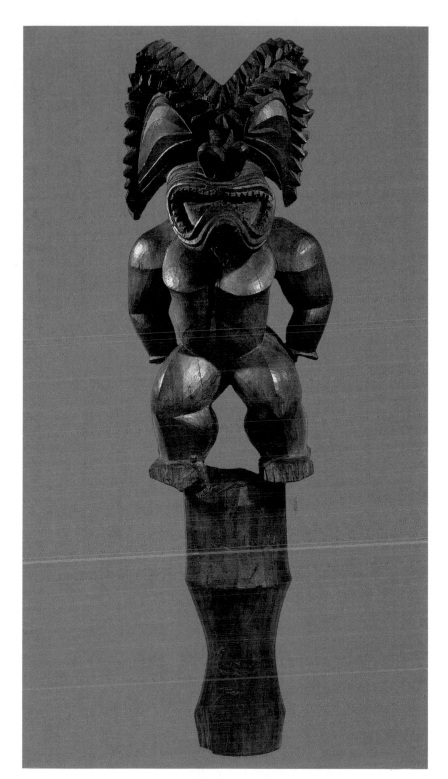

12-15 Kukaʻilimoku (war god), temple image, from Hawaii. Wood, 2′ 5¾″ high (figure only). British Museum, London.

illustrate (FIG. **12-15**) was placed in a *heiau* (temple) on the island of Hawaii, where Kamehameha I originally ruled before expanding his authority to the entire Hawaiian chain. This late-18th- or early-19th-century Hawaiian wooden temple image, more than four feet tall, confronts its audience with a ferocious expression. This war god's head dominates, comprising nearly a third of his entire body. His enlarged, angled eyes and wide-open figure-eight-shaped mouth, with its rows of teeth, convey aggression and defiance. His muscular body appears to stand slightly flexed, as if ready to act. The artist realized this Hawaiian war god's overall athleticism through the full-volumed, faceted treatment of his arms, legs, and the pectoral area of the chest. In addition to sculptures of deities such as this, Hawaiians placed smaller versions of lesser deities and ancestral images in the heiau. Differing styles surface in the various islands of the Hawaiian chain, but the sculptured figures share a tendency toward athleticism and expressive defiance.

The Maori (New Zealand)

SURROUNDED BY ANCESTORS The Maori of New Zealand (Aotearoa) share many cultural practices with other Polynesian societies. As in other cultures, ancestors and lineage play an important role in New Zealand. The Maori meetinghouse demonstrates the primacy of ancestral connections. The Maori conceptualize the entire building as the body of an ancestor—the central beam across the roof is the spine, the rafters are ribs, and the barge boards (the angled boards that outline the house

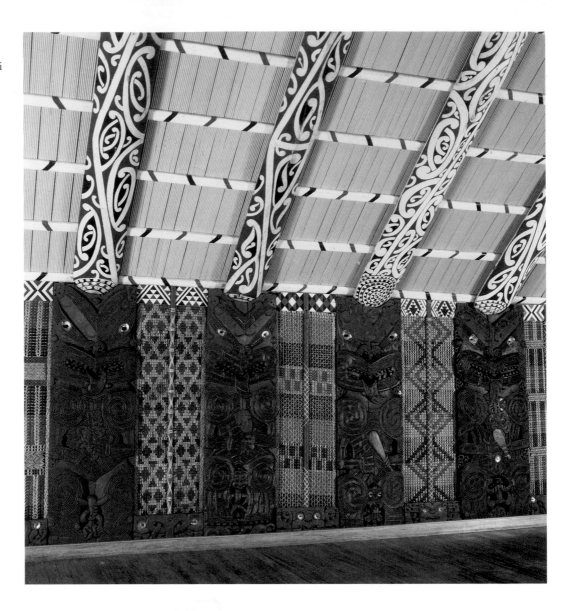

gables) in front represent arms. On the inside of the meetinghouse (FIG. **12-16**), ancestors constitute a very potent presence through their appearance on *poupou* (the relief panels along the walls). These panels depict specific ancestors and are often carved in a style that has come to characterize Maori art. Each ancestor appears frontally with hands across the stomach. Elaborate curvilinear patterns cover the entire poupou and may represent tattoos. Virtually every surface of the meetinghouse is decorated. The spaces between the poupou are filled with *tukutuku* (stitched lattice panels). Above, intricate painted shapes cover the rafters. In the center of the meetinghouse stand *pou tokomanawa*, sculptures of ancestors that support the building's ridgepoles (not visible in our illustration). The composite presence of all of these ancestral images and the energy of the persistent patterning creates a charged space in which collective action can be taken.

Rapa Nui (Easter Island)

SILENT STONE SENTINELS Much of the Oceanic art discussed in this chapter is biodegradable, designed for short-term use, and/or small in scale. The *moai*—stone sculptures (FIG. **12-17**) found on the island of Rapa Nui (Easter Island)—provide

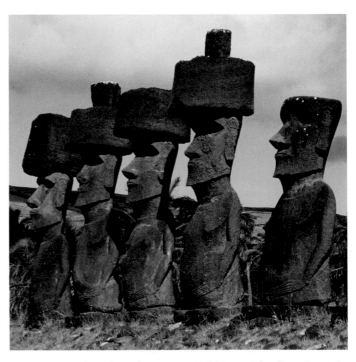

12-17 Statues *(moai)*, Anakena, Rapa Nui (Easter Island), 10th–12th century. Stone. 💿

a contrast. Other Polynesian cultures produced large-scale, permanent artworks. The moai, however, are among the best known. These monumental sculptures, some soaring to heights of up to 40 feet, stand as silent sentinels on stone platforms *(ahu)*. These platforms marked burial sites or were used for religious ceremonies. Most of the moai consist of huge, blocky figures with fairly planar facial features—large, staring eyes, strong jaws, straight noses with carefully articulated nostrils, and elongated earlobes. A number of the moai have *pukao*—small red scoria cylinders that serve as a sort of topknot or hat—placed on their heads.

Although debate continues, many scholars believe that these moai depict ancestral chiefs. These commemorative images were commissioned by lineage heads or their sons. These statues, however, are not portraits in the Western sense. Rather, they are sacred objects due to their ability to accommodate spirits or gods. Moai thus mediate between chiefs and gods, and between the natural and cosmic worlds.

Archaeological surveys have documented close to 900 moai, most of which were quarried at one volcanic site on Rapa Nui. Accordingly, most of the moai are carved of soft volcanic tuff. Red scoria, basalt, and trachyte were used for a small number of the sculptures. After quarrying, the statues were dragged to the particular ahu site, and positioned vertically. Given the extraordinary size of these monoliths, their production and placement serve as testaments to the achievements of Rapa Nui culture. Each statue weighs up to 100 tons. According to one scholar, it would have taken 30 men one year to carve a moai, 90 men two months to move it from the quarry, and 90 men three months to position it vertically on the platform.

AUSTRALIA

Over the past 40,000 years, the Aboriginal peoples of Australia spread out over the entire continent and adapted to a variety of ecological conditions, ranging from those of tropical and subtropical areas in the north to desert regions in the continent's interior and more temperate locales in the south. European explorers reaching the region in the late 18th and early 19th centuries found that the Aborigines had a special relationship with the land they lived on, developed primarily by hunting and gathering. Because of this deep-rooted connection with the environment, the Aboriginal way of thinking and their perception of the world center on a concept known as the Dreamings, ancestral beings whose spirits pervade the present. All Aborigines identify certain Dreamings as totemic ancestors, and those who share the same Dreamings are socially linked. The spiritual domain that the Dreamings occupy is known as Dreamtime, which is both a physical space within which the ancestral beings moved in creating the landscape and a psychic space that provides Aborigines with cultural, religious, and moral direction. Because of the importance of Dreamings to all aspects of Aboriginal life, art in Australia symbolically links Aborigines with these ancestral spirits. Mythological narratives are prominent among the Aborigines. They recite creation myths in concert with songs and dances, and many art forms—body painting, carved figures, sacred objects, decorated stones, and rock and bark painting—serve as essential props in these dramatic re-creations. Unlike the large-scale, permanent art found in Rapa Nui, most Aboriginal art is relatively small and portable. As hunters and gatherers in difficult terrain, most Aborigines were nomadic, rendering monumental art impractical.

Aboriginal Art (Arnhem Land)

IMAGES OF DREAMINGS Bark painting became a mainstay of Aboriginal art. Bark was widely available, as well as portable and lightweight. Dreamings, mythic narratives (often tracing the movement of various ancestral spirits through the landscape), and sacred places were common subjects for paintings. Ancestral spirits were pervasive in the lives of the Aborigines, and these paintings served to give visual form to that presence. Traditionally, an Aborigine could only depict a Dreaming with which he was connected. Thus, Aboriginal designs are "owned" by specific lineages, clans, or regional groups. A bark painting from 1913 (FIG. **12-18**) depicts a Dreaming known as Auuenau and comes from an area called Arnhem Land in northern Australia. The elongated figure is

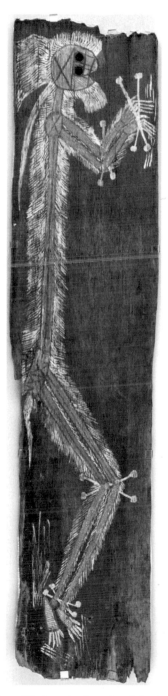

12-18 Auuenau, from Western Arnhem Land, Australia, 1913. Ochre on bark, 4′ 10$\frac{2}{3}$″ × 1′ 1″. South Australian Museum, Adelaide.

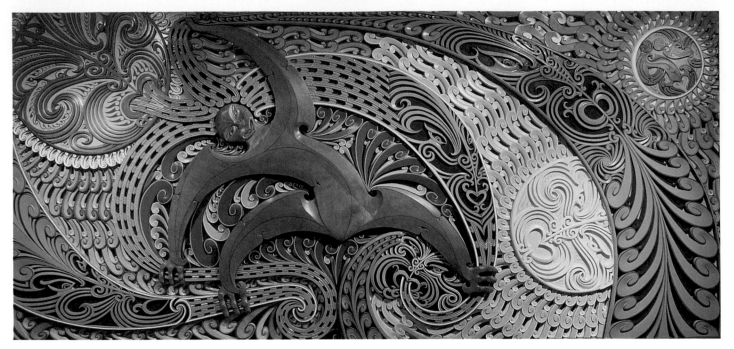

12-19 Cliff Whiting (Te Whanau-A-Apanui), *Tawhiri-Matea (God of the Winds)*, Maori, 1984. Oil on wood and fiberboard, approx. 6′ 4⅜″ × 11′ 10¾″. Collection of the Meteorological Service of New Zealand, Wellington.

represented in a style referred to as "X-ray," which is used to depict both animal and human forms. In this style, the artist simultaneously depicts the subject's interior (internal organs) and exterior. The painting possesses a fluid and dynamic quality, with the X-ray-like figure clearly defined against a solid background.

OCEANIC ART TODAY

Many of the traditional native arts of Oceania, particularly in Polynesia's central and peripheral islands, are not now practiced, for they no longer have critical roles in ensuring cultural continuity and survival, or they were forcibly suppressed by Westerners, especially missionaries. Yet, in many places, with the stimulus of cosmopolitan contacts in a shrinking world, these arts have been revitalized and flourish energetically. New, confident cultural awareness has led native artists to assert their inherited values with pride and to express them in a resurgence of traditional arts, such as weaving, painting, tattooing, and carving.

MAORI CULTURAL RENEWAL One example that represents the many cases of cultural renewal in native Oceanic art is the vigorously productive school of New Zealand artists who draw on their Maori heritage for formal and iconographic inspiration. The historic Maori woodcarving craft (FIG. 12-16) brilliantly reemerges in what the artist CLIFF WHITING (TE WHANAU-A-APANUI) calls a "carved mural" (FIG. **12-19**). Whiting's *Tawhiri-Matea (God of the Winds)* is a masterpiece of woodcrafting designed for the very modern environment of an exhibition gallery. The artist suggested the wind turbulence with the restless curvature of the main motif and its myriad of serrated edges. The 1984 mural depicts events in the Maori creation myth. The central figure, Tawhiri-Matea, god of the winds, wrestles to control *te whanau puhi,* the children of the four winds, seen as

blue spiral forms. Ra, the sun, energizes the scene from the top left, complemented by Marama, the moon, in the opposite corner. The top right image refers to the primal separation of Ranginui, the Sky Father, and Papatuanuku, the Earth Mother. Spiral koru motifs symbolizing growth and energy flow through the composition. Blue waves and green fronds around Tawhiri suggest his brothers Tangaroa and Tane, gods of the sea and forest.

The artist is securely at home with the native tradition of form and technique, as well as with the worldwide aesthetic of modernist design. Out of the seamless fabric made by uniting both, he feels something new can develop that loses nothing of the power of the old. Whiting champions not only the renewal of Maori cultural life and its continuity in art but also the education of the young in the values that made that culture great—values they are asked to perpetuate. The salvation of their native identity will depend on their success in making the Maori culture once again their own.

CONCLUSION

Since the initial population of the Pacific islands tens of thousands of years ago, flourishing cultures have emerged in the areas known as Melanesia, Polynesia, and Micronesia, and on the continent of Australia. Because of the wide chronological span during which the Pacific was populated and the diverse environments of the different island groups, Oceanic cultures vary greatly. The art produced by Pacific islanders ranges from large architectural structures and permanent sculptures to performances and temporary body art. Extensive Euroamerican colonization throughout the Pacific between the 18th and 20th centuries resulted in the abandonment of numerous traditional practices. In recent years, many Pacific artists have revived indigenous art forms, creating new artistic products that combine the old with the contemporary.

1800

I Captain James Cook and other European explorers (re)discover Polynesia, late 18th century

I Kamehameha I unifies Hawaiian Islands and becomes king, 1795

1 I Overthrow of kapu system (traditional Hawaiian religious system), 1819

I Treaty of Waitangi (New Zealand/Aotearoa), 1840

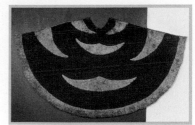

1 'Ahu'ula (feather cloak), Hawaii, early 19th century

1850

2 I Christianity spreads throughout Polynesia by mid-1850s

I European colonization of most of Oceania complete, 1880s–1920

I Overthrow of Hawaiian monarchy, 1893

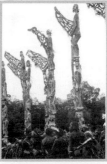

2 Tattooed Marquesan warrior with war club, engraving, 19th century

1900

I Reign of Queen Salote Tupou III of Tonga, 1918–1965

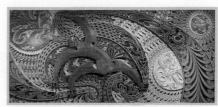

1950

I U.S. statehood conferred on Hawaii, 1959

I Independence for most Oceanic peoples, 1960s–1970s

3 Bisj poles, New Guinea, early–mid-20th century

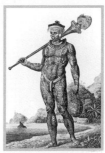

4 Cliff Whiting (Te Whanau-A-Apanui), *Tawhiri-Matea (God of the Winds)*, 1984

2000

GLOSSARY

PRONUNCIATION KEY

ŭ **a**but, kitten   a **co**t, c**a**rt   ā **ba**ke   ă **ba**ck   au **ou**t   ch **chi**n
e **le**ss   ē **ea**sy   g **gi**ft   ĭ **tri**p   ī **li**fe   j **jo**ke   ḵ **ki**ck
ⁿ French vi**n**   ng si**ng**   o fl**a**w   ō b**oa**t   ö bi(**r**)d   oi c**oi**n
u f**oo**t   ū l**oo**t   ü f**ew**   y **yo**yo   zh vi**s**ion

NOTE. The stress mark (′) goes before the stressed syllable (be-′for).

abacus—(ă-ba-′kŭs) The uppermost portion of the *capital* of a *column*.

abrasion—The rubbing or grinding of stone or another material to produce a smooth surface.

additive light—The sum of all the wavelengths composing the visible spectrum; natural light, or sunlight.

additive sculpture—A kind of sculpture technique in which materials (for example, clay) are built up or "added" to create form.

adobe—(a-′dō-bē) The clay used to make a kind of sun-dried mud brick of the same name; a building made of such brick.

ahu—(′ă-hū) A stone platform on which *moai* were placed. Ahu marked burial sites or were used for ceremonial purposes.

'ahu 'ula—(′ă-hū ′ū-lŭ) A Hawaiian feather cloak.

aisle—The portion of a columnar hall flanking the *nave* and separated from it by a row of *columns* or *piers*.

akua'ba (Akua's child)—(a-′kū-a ba) An Akan (Ghana) image of a young girl.

amalaka—(a-mu-′la-ka) In Hindu temple design, the large flat disk with ribbed edges surmounting the beehive-shaped tower.

ambulatory—(′ăm-byŭ-lŭ-to-rē) A covered walkway, outdoors or indoors; especially the passageway around the *apse* and the choir of a church. In Buddhist architecture, the passageway leading around the *stupa* in a *chaitya hall*.

amulet—(′ăm-yŭ-lŭt) An object worn to ward off evil or to aid the wearer.

apse—(ăps) A recess, usually semicircular, in the wall of a Roman basilica or at the east end of a church.

apsidal—Rounded; *apse* shaped.

arabesque—(ă-rŭ-′besk) "Arab-like." A flowing, intricate pattern derived from stylized organic motifs, usually floral; generally, an Islamic decorative motif.

arcade—A series of *arches* supported by *piers* or *columns*.

arch—A curved structural member that spans an opening and is generally composed of wedge-shaped blocks that transmit the downward pressure laterally.

arcuated—*Arch* shaped.

arhat—(′ar-hat) A Buddhist holy person who has achieved enlightenment and *nirvana* by suppression of all desire for earthly things.

armature—(′ar-mŭ-chŭr) In sculpture, the framework for a clay form.

asceticism—Self-discipline and self-denial.

ashlar masonry—Carefully cut and regularly shaped blocks of stone used in construction, fitted together without mortar.

atlantid—(ăt-′lăn tid) A male figure that functions as a supporting *column*.

atlatl—(′ăt(-ŭ)-lăt(-ŭ)l) Spear-thrower, the typical weapon of the Toltecs of ancient Mexico.

atmospheric perspective—See *perspective*.

attribute—A unique characteristic that identifies a figure.

attribution—Assignment of a work to a maker or makers.

avatar—A manifestation of a deity incarnated in some visible form in which the deity performs a sacred function on earth. In Hinduism, an incarnation of a god.

backstrap loom—A simple Andean loom featuring a belt or backstrap encircling the waist of the seated weaver.

bai—(ba c) An elaborately painted men's ceremonial house on Belau (formerly Palau) in the Caroline Islands of Micronesia.

barays—The large reservoirs laid out around Cambodian *wats* that served as means of transportation as well as irrigation. The reservoirs were connected by a network of canals.

barrel vault—See *vault*.

bas-relief—(′ba rŭ-′lē f) See *relief*.

bay—The area between the *columns* or *piers* in the *nave* or *aisles* of a church or any other columnar structure.

beam—Horizontal wooden plank in Chinese buildings.

bhakti—(′bŭk-tē) In Buddhist thought, the adoration of a personalized deity *(bodhisattva)* as a means of achieving unity with it; love felt by the devotee for the deity. In Hinduism, the devout, selfless direction of all tasks and activities of life to the service of one god.

bi—(bē) In ancient China, jade disks carved as ritual objects for burial with the dead. They were often decorated with piercework carving extending entirely through the object.

bisj pole—(bĭ zh) An elaborately carved pole constructed from the trunk of the mangrove tree. The Asmat people of southwestern New Guinea created bisj poles to indicate their intent to avenge a relative's death.

blind arcade—An *arcade* having no actual openings, applied as decoration to a wall surface.

bodhisattva—(bod-hē-sat-va) In Buddhist thought, one of the host of divinities provided to the Buddha to help him save humanity. A potential Buddha.

brocade—The weaving together of threads of different colors.

broken- or flung-ink style—In Japanese art, a loose and rapidly executed painting style in which the ink seems to have been applied by flinging or splashing it onto the paper.

Buddha triad—Central Buddha flanked on each side by a *bodhisattva*.

caliph(s)—(′kā-lef or ′kal-ŭf) *Muslim* rulers, regarded as successors of Muhammad.

calligraphy—Greek, "beautiful writing." Handwriting or penmanship, especially elegant writing as a decorative art.

capital—The uppermost member of a *column*, serving as a transition from the *shaft* to the *lintel*.

casting—Pouring a fluid substance such as bronze into a *mold*.

celadon—(sel-ŭ-dan) A Chinese-Korean pottery *glaze*, fired in an oxygen-deprived kiln to a characteristic gray-green or pale blue color.

cella—(′se-lŭ) The chamber at the center of an ancient temple.

celt—(selt) In Olmec Mexico, an ax-shaped form made of polished jade; generally, a prehistoric metal or stone implement shaped like a chisel or ax head.

central plan—See *plan*.

chaitya hall—(tshī-′tyŭ *hall*) An Indian rock-cut temple hall having a votive *stupa* at one end.

chakra—(′cha-kra) The Buddha's wheel, set in motion at Sarnath.

chakravartin—(cha-kra-′var-tĭ n) In India, the ideal king, the Universal Lord who ruled through goodness.

Chan—See *Zen*.

character—In the Chinese language, a sign that records meaning rather than a sound, as for example, English letters do.

chatra—(′cha-tra) See *yasti*.

chiaroscuro—(kē-ă-rō-′skū-rō) In drawing or painting, the treatment and use of light and dark, especially the gradations of light that produce the effect of *modeling*.

chigi—(chē-gē) The crosspiece at the gables of Japanese shrine architecture.

circumambulation—In Buddhist worship, walking around the *stupa* in a clockwise direction.

cire perdue—(sēr per-′dū) See *lost-wax process.*

codex (pl. **codices**)—(′kō-deks/′kō-dŭ-sēz) Separate pages bound together at one side; the predecessor of the modern book. The codex superseded the scroll. In *Mesoamerica,* a painted and inscribed book on long sheets of bark paper or deerskin coated with fine white plaster and folded into accordion-like pleats.

colonnade—A series or row of *columns,* usually spanned by *lintels.*

colonnette—A thin *column.*

colophon—(′ka-lŭ-fan) An inscription, usually on the last page, giving information about a book's manufacture. In Chinese painting, written texts on attached pieces of paper or silk.

column—A vertical, weight-carrying architectural member, circular in cross-*section* and consisting of a base (sometimes omitted), a *shaft,* and a *capital.*

composition—The way in which an artist organizes *forms* in an artwork, either by placing shapes on a flat surface or arranging forms in space.

congregational mosque—A large *mosque* designed to accommodate a community's entire population for the Friday noonday prayer. Also called the Friday mosque or the great mosque.

connoisseur—(ka-nŭ-sŭr) An expert in assigning artworks to one artist rather than another.

corbel—(′kor-bŭl) A projecting wall member used as a support for some element in the superstructure.

cornice—In architecture, a framing or crowning projection or *molding.*

cross-section—See *section.*

cross vault—See *vault.*

cuerda seca—(′kwer-dŭ ′sā-kŭ) A type of polychrome tilework used in decorating Islamic buildings.

cutaway—An architectural drawing that combines an exterior view with an interior view of part of a building.

darshan—(′dar-shan) In Hindu worship, seeing images of the divinity and being seen by the divinity.

deceptive cadence—In a horizontal scroll, the "false ending," which arrests the viewer's gaze by appearing to be the end of a narrative sequence, but which actually sets the stage for a culminating figure or scene.

dharma—(′dar-mŭ) In Buddhism, moral law based on the Buddha's teaching.

dome—A hemispheric *vault;* theoretically, an *arch* rotated on its vertical axis.

dotaku—(do-ta-kū) Ancient Japanese bronze ceremonial bells, usually featuring raised decoration.

Dravida—Southern style of Hindu temple.

drum—One of the stacked cylindrical stones that form a *column.*

earthenware—Pottery made of clay that is fired at low temperatures and is slightly porous.

eaves—The lower part of a roof that overhangs the wall.

effigy mounds—Ceremonial mounds built in the shape of animals or birds by native North American peoples.

elevation—In architecture, a head-on view of an external or internal wall, showing its features and often other elements that would be visible beyond or before the wall.

embroidery—The technique of sewing threads onto a finished ground to form contrasting designs.

enamel—A decorative coating, usually colored, fused onto the surface of metal, glass, or ceramics.

engaged column—A half-round *column* attached to a wall.

engraving—The process of *incising* a design in hard material, often a metal plate (usually copper); also, the *print* or impression made from such a plate.

eravo—(ŭ-′ra-vō) A men's meeting house constructed by the Elema people in New Guinea.

facade—(fŭ-′sad) Usually, the front of a building; also, the other sides when they are emphasized architecturally.

finial—A crowning ornament.

foreshortening—The use of *perspective* to represent in art the apparent visual contraction of an object that extends back in space at an angle to the perpendicular plane of sight.

form—In art, an object's shape and structure, either in two dimensions (for example, a figure painted on a surface) or in three dimensions (such as a statue).

formal analysis—The visual analysis of artistic form.

freestanding sculpture—See *sculpture in the round.*

fresco—(′fres-kō) Painting on lime plaster, either dry (dry fresco or fresco secco) or wet (true or buon fresco). In the latter method, the pigments are mixed with water and become chemically bound to the freshly laid lime plaster. Also, a painting executed in either method.

Friday mosque—See *congregational mosque.*

frieze—(frēz) A sculptured or painted band in a building.

garbha griha—(′garb-ha ′grē-ha) Hindi, "womb chamber." In Hindu temples, the *cella,* the holy inner sanctum, for the cult image or symbol.

genetrix—A legendary founding clan mother.

genre—(′zhaⁿ-rŭ) A style or category of art; also, a kind of painting that realistically depicts scenes from everyday life.

glaze—A vitreous coating applied to pottery to seal and decorate the surface; it may be colored, transparent, or opaque, and glossy or *matte.*

gopuras—(′gō-pū-rŭz) The massive, ornamented entrance gateway towers of South Indian temple compounds.

gorget—(′gor-jŭt) A neck pendant.

groin—The edge formed by the intersection of two *vaults.*

groin vault—See *vault.*

guang—(gwŭng) In ancient China, covered vessels, often in animal forms, holding wine, water, grain, or meat for sacrificial rites.

handscroll—In Asian art, a horizontal painted scroll that is unrolled to the left and often used to present illustrated religious texts or *landscapes.*

haniwa—(ha-nē-wa) Sculpted fired pottery cylinders, modeled in human, animal, or other forms and placed around early (archaic) Japanese burial mounds.

harmika—(har-′mē-ka) In Buddhist architecture, a stone fence or railing that encloses an area surmounting the dome of a *stupa* that represents one of the Buddhist heavens; from the center arises the *yasti.*

heiau—(hī-yau) A Hawaiian temple structure.

Hevehe—(he-ve-he) An elaborate cycle of ceremonial activities performed by the Elema people of the Papuan Gulf region of New Guinea. Also the large, ornate masks that were produced for and presented during these ceremonies.

hierarchy of scale—An artistic convention in which greater size indicates greater importance.

hieroglyphic—(hī-rō-′glif-ik) A system of writing using symbols or pictures.

high relief—See *relief.*

Hijra—(′hĭj-rŭ) The flight of Muhammad from Mecca to Medina in 622, the year from which Islam dates its beginnings.

hiragana—(hē-ra-ga-na) A sound-based writing system developed in Japan from Chinese characters; it came to be the primary script for Japanese court poetry.

hypostyle hall—(′hī-pŭ-stīl *hall*) A hall with a roof supported by *columns.*

iconography—(ī-kŭn-′a-grŭ-fē) Greek, the "writing of images." The term refers both to the content, or subject, of an artwork and to the study of content in art. It also includes the study of the symbolic, often religious, meaning of objects, persons, or events depicted in works of art.

ikegobo—(ē-kā-gō-bō) A Benin royal shrine.

illusionistic—The depiction of the three-dimensional spatial world on a two-dimensional surface.

imam—(i-′mam or i-′măm) In Islam, the leader of collective worship.

incise—(in-′sīz) To cut into a surface with a sharp instrument; also, a method of decoration, especially on metal and pottery.

inscriptions—Texts written on the same surface as the picture (as in Chinese paintings) or *incised* in stone (as in ancient art). See also *colophon.*

iron-wire lines—In ancient Chinese painting, thin brush lines suggesting tensile strength.

iwan—(′ē-wan) In Islamic architecture, a vaulted rectangular recess opening onto a courtyard.

jataka—(′jă-tă-kă) Tales of the past lives of the Buddha. See also *sutra.*

jomon—(jo-mon) Japanese, "cord markings." A type of Japanese decorative technique characterized by ropelike markings.

Kaaba—('ka-ba) Arabic, "cube." A small cubical building in Mecca, the *Muslim* world's symbolic center.

kami—(ka-mĭ) Shinto deities or spirits, believed in Japan to exist in nature (mountains, waterfalls) and in charismatic people.

karma—('ka-mŭ) In Vedic religions, the ethical consequences of a person's life, which determine his or her fate.

katsina—(kŭ-'chē-nŭ) An art form of Native Americans of the Southwest, the katsina doll represents benevolent supernatural spirits (katsinas) living in mountains and water sources.

kiva—('kē-vŭ) A large circular underground structure that is the spiritual and ceremonial center of Pueblo Indian life.

kondo—(kon-do) Japanese, "golden hall." In a Japanese Buddhist temple complex, the building housing the main sculptural icons.

Koran—(ko-'ran) Islam's sacred book, composed of *surahs* (chapters) divided into verses.

koru—('ka-rū) An unrolled spiral design used by the Maori in their tattoos.

Kufic—('kū-fŭk) An early form of Arabic script, characterized by angularity, with the uprights forming almost right angles with the baseline.

kula—('kū-lŭ) An exchange of white conus-shell arm ornaments and red chama-shell necklaces that takes place among the Trobriand Islanders. These exchanges serve to stimulate the economy and cement social relationships.

lacquer—('lăk-ŭr) A varnishlike substance made from the sap of the Asiatic sumac, used to decorate wood and other organic materials. Often colored with mineral pigments, lacquer cures to great hardness and has a lustrous surface.

lakshana(s)—(laksh-'ha-na) Distinguishing marks of the Buddha. They include the *urna* and *ushnisha.*

lalitasana—(la-'lē-ta-sa-na) In Buddhist iconography, the body pose with one leg folded and the other hanging down, indicating relaxation.

landscape—A picture showing natural scenery, without narrative content.

Lapita pottery—('lă-pĭ-tŭ) Ceramic vessels elaborately decorated with incised, geometric designs. Found in a geographical region roughly bounded by New Guinea in the west and Tonga and Samoa in the east.

lateral section—See *section.*

linear perspective—See *perspective.*

linga—('lin-ga) In Hindu art, the depiction of Shiva as a phallus or cosmic *pillar.*

lintel—('lin-tŭl) A beam used to span an opening.

literati—(lĭ-tŭ-'ra-tē) In China, talented amateur painters and scholars from the landed gentry.

local color—An object's actual color in white light.

logogram—('la-gŭ-gram) One of the thousands of characters in the Chinese writing system, corresponding to one meaningful language unit. See also *pictograph.*

longitudinal plan—See *plan.*

longitudinal section—See *section.*

lost-wax process (cire perdue)—A bronze-casting method in which a figure is modeled in wax and covered with clay; the whole is fired, melting away the wax and hardening the clay, which then becomes a mold for molten metal.

low relief—See *relief.*

madrasa—(mŭ-'dra-sŭ) An Islamic theological college adjoining and often containing a *mosque.*

maebyong—(mī-byŭng) A Korean vase similar to the Chinese *meiping.*

ma-hevehe—(ma-he-ve-hŭ) Mythical water spirits; the Elema people of New Guinea believed that these spirits visited their villages.

malanggan—(ma-lang-gan) Both the festivals held in honor of the deceased in New Ireland (Papua New Guinea) and the carvings and objects produced for these festivals.

mandala—(man-'da-la) Sacred diagram of the universe; Japanese, mandara.

mandara—See *mandala.*

mandapa—(man-'da-pa) *Pillared* hall of a Hindu temple.

mandorla—(măn-'dor-lŭ) An almond-shaped *nimbus* surrounding the figure of Christ or other sacred figure.

manulua—(ma-nu-lu-a) Tongan, "two birds." A Tongan design motif that symbolizes chiefly status derived from both parents.

maqsura—(mak-'sū-ra) In some *mosques,* a screened area in front of the *mihrab* reserved for a ruler.

masquerade—Among some African groups, a ritualized drama performed by several masked dancers, embodying ancestors or nature spirits.

matte (also **mat**)—(măt) In painting, pottery, and photography, a dull finish.

mausoleum—(mo-sō-'lē-ŭm) A monumental tomb. The name derives from the mid-fourth century BCE tomb of Mausolos at Halikarnassos, one of the Seven Wonders of the ancient world.

mbari house—(ŭm-'ba-rĭ) An Igbo renewal house, constructed from mud every 50 years as a sacrifice to a major deity, often Ala, goddess of the earth.

meiping—(mā-ping) A Chinese vase of a high-shouldered shape; the *sgrafitto* technique was used in decorating such vases.

Mesoamerica—The region that comprises Mexico, Guatemala, Belize, Honduras, and the Pacific coast of El Salvador.

metate—(mŭ-'ta-tā) A ceremonial grinding stone, perhaps used as a throne in northern South America and various Central American regions.

Mexica—The name used by a group of initially migratory invaders from northern Mexico to identify themselves. Settling on an island in Lake Texcoco in central Mexico, they are known today as the Aztecs.

mihrab—(mi-'rab) A semicircular niche set into the *qibla* wall of a *mosque.*

minaret—('min-ŭ-ret) A distinctive feature of *mosque* architecture, a tower from which the faithful are called to worship.

minbar—('min-bar) In a *mosque,* the pulpit on which the *imam* stands.

miniatures—Small individual paintings intended by Indian painters to be held in the hand and viewed by one or two individuals at one time.

mithuna—Male and female couple embracing or engaged in sexual intercourse.

moai—(mō-ī) A large, blocky figural stone sculpture found on Rapa Nui (Easter Island).

modeling—The shaping or fashioning of three-dimensional forms in a soft material, such as clay; also, the gradations of light and shade reflected from the surfaces of matter in space, or the illusion of such gradations in a drawing, painting, or print.

module—A basic unit of which the dimensions of the major parts of a work are multiples. The principle is used in sculpture and other art forms, but it is most often employed in architecture, where the module may be the dimensions of an important part of a building, such as the diameter of a *column.*

moko—The form of tattooing practiced by the Maori of New Zealand (Aotearoa).

moksha—See *nirvana.*

mold—A hollow form for shaping a fluid substance.

molding—In architecture, a continuous, narrow surface (projecting or recessed, plain or ornamented) designed to break up a surface, to accent, or to decorate.

monolith—A *column* shaft that is all in one piece.

mortise-and-tenon system—('mor-tŭs-and-'ten-ŭn) See *tenon.*

mosaic—(mō-'zā-ŭk) Patterns or pictures made by embedding small pieces *(tesserae)* of stone or glass in cement on surfaces such as walls and floors; also, the technique of making such works.

mosaic tilework—An Islamic decorative technique in which large ceramic panels are fired, cut into smaller pieces, and set in plaster.

mosque—(mask) The Islamic building for collective worship. From the Arabic word *masjid,* meaning a "place for bowing down."

mudra—('mŭ-drŭ, *or* 'mŭ-drŭ) In Buddhist and Hindu iconography, a stylized and symbolic hand gesture.

Muhaqqaq—(mŭ-ha-'kak) A cursive style of Islamic *calligraphy.*

muqarnas—(mŭ-'kar-nas) Stucco decorations of Islamic buildings in which stalactite-like forms break a structure's solidity.

mural—A wall painting.

Muslim—A believer in Islam.

Nagara—Northern style of Hindu temple.

naturalism—The close observation of the natural world and the depiction in art of a perceptual reality.

nave—The central area of a hypostyle *mosque* or of a church, demarcated from *aisles* by *piers* or *columns*.

ngatu—((n)ga-tu) *Tapa* made by women in Tonga.

nihonga—(nē-hong-ga) A 19th-century Japanese painting style that incorporated some Western techniques in basically Japanese-style painting, as opposed to *yoga* (Western painting).

nimbus—A halo or aureole appearing around the head of a holy figure to signify divinity.

nirvana—In Buddhism and Hinduism, a blissful state brought about by absorption of the individual soul or consciousness into the supreme spirit. Also called moksha.

nishiki-e—(ni-shi-ki-e) Japanese, "brocade pictures." Japanese polychrome woodblock prints valued for their sumptuous colors.

nkisi n'kondi—((n)kē-sē (n)kan-dē) A power figure carved by the Kongo people of the Democratic Republic of Congo. Such images embodied spirits believed to heal and give life or capable of inflicting harm or death.

oil paint—Pigment mixed with oil. Oil paint dries slowly, allowing the painter to lay down the color in superimposed translucent layers. See *glaze*.

overglaze—In *porcelain* decoration, the technique of applying mineral colors over the *glaze* after the work has been fired. The overglaze colors, or *enamels*, fuse to the glazed surface in a second firing at a much lower temperature than the main firing. See also *underglaze*.

pagoda—(pŭ-'gō-dŭ) A Chinese tower, usually associated with a Buddhist temple, having a multiplicity of winged *eaves*; thought to be derived from the Indian *stupa*.

palette—A thin board with a thumb hole at one end on which an artist lays and mixes colors; any surface so used. Also, the colors or kinds of colors characteristically used by an artist.

parinirvana—(pă-ri-nōr-'va-nŭ) Image of the reclining Buddha, often viewed as representing his death.

pediment—In classical architecture, the triangular space (gable) at the end of a building, formed by the ends of the sloping roof above the *colonnade;* also, an ornamental feature having this shape.

personification—An abstract idea represented in bodily form.

pictograph—('pik-tō-grăf) A picture, usually stylized, that represents an idea; also, writing using such means; also painting on rock. See also *hieroglyphic*.

pier—A vertical, freestanding masonry support.

pillar—Usually a weight-carrying member, such as a *pier* or a *column;* sometimes an isolated, freestanding structure used for commemorative purposes.

plan—The horizontal arrangement of the parts of a building or of the buildings and streets of a city or town, or a drawing or diagram showing such an arrangement. In an axial plan, the parts of a building are organized longitudinally, or along a given axis; in a central plan, the parts of the structure are of equal or almost equal dimensions around the center.

plane—A flat or two-dimensional surface.

plinth—The square slab at the base of a *column.*

porcelain—('por-sŭ-lŭn) Extremely fine, hard, white ceramic. Unlike stoneware, porcelain is made from a fine white clay called kaolin mixed with ground petuntse, a type of feldspar. True porcelain is translucent and rings when struck.

portico—('por-tŭ-kō) A roofed *colonnade;* also an entrance porch.

pou tokomanawa—('po-ŭ 'to-ko-ma-na-wa) A sculpture of an ancestor that supports a ridge pole of a Maori meetinghouse.

pouncing—The method of transferring a sketch onto paper by tracing, using thin, transparent gazelle skin placed on top of the sketch, pricking the contours of the design with a pin, placing the skin on paper, and forcing black pigment through the holes.

poupou—('po-ŭ-po-ŭ) A decorated wall panel in a Maori meetinghouse.

prasada—(pra-'sa-dŭ) In Hindu worship, food that becomes sacred by first being given to a god.

pre-Columbian (adj.)—The cultures that flourished in the Western Hemisphere before the arrival of Christopher Columbus and the beginning of European contact and conquest.

print—An artwork on paper, usually produced in multiple impressions.

provenance—('prō-vŭ-naⁿs) Origin or source; findspot.

pueblo—('pwe-blō) A communal multistoried dwelling made of stone or *adobe* brick by the Native Americans of the Southwest; with cap. also used to refer to various groups that occupied such dwellings.

pukao—('pu-ka-ō) A small red scoria cylinder that appears as a hat on *moai*.

qibla—('kē-blŭ) The direction (toward Mecca) *Muslims* face when praying.

quipu—('kē-pū) Andean record-keeping device made of fibers in which numerous knotted strings hung from a main cord were used to record, by position and color, numbers and categories of things.

radiocarbon dating—Method of measuring the decay rate of carbon isotopes in organic matter to provide dates for organic materials such as wood and fiber.

rafter—Sloping wooden planks in roofs of Chinese buildings.

ratha—('rat-ha) Small, freestanding Hindu temple carved from a huge boulder.

relics—The body parts, clothing, or objects associated with a holy figure, such as the Buddha or Christ or a Christian *saint.*

relief—In sculpture, figures projecting from a background of which they are part. The degree of relief is designated high or low *(bas).*

reliquary—('rel-ŭ-kwe-rē) A container for keeping *relics.*

revetment—(rŭ-'vet-mŭnt) In architecture, a wall covering or facing.

rib—A relatively slender, molded masonry *arch* that projects from a surface.

ridgepole—The beam running the length of a building below the peak of the gabled roof.

roof comb—The elaborately sculpted vertical projection surmounting a Maya temple-pyramid.

rotunda—(rō-'tŭnd-ŭ) The circular area under a *dome;* also a domed round building.

roundel—A circular painting or relief sculpture, also called a *tondo.*

sabi—('sa-bĭ) The value found in the old and weathered, suggesting the tranquility reached in old age.

samsara—(sŭm-'sa-rŭ) In Hindu belief, the rebirth of the soul into a succession of lives.

samurai—('sam-ŭ-rī) Medieval Japanese warriors.

sarcophagus (pl. **sarcophagi**)—(sar-'kof-ŭ-gŭs/sar-'kof-ŭ-gī) Latin, "consumer of flesh." A coffin, usually of stone.

saz—(săz) An Ottoman Turkish design of sinuous curved leaves and blossoms.

scarification—('scar-ŭ-fŭ-cā-zhŭn) Decorative markings made with scars on the human body.

school—A chronological and stylistic classification of works of art with a stipulation of place.

sculpture in the round—Freestanding figures, carved or modeled in three dimensions.

section—In architecture, a diagram or representation of a part of a structure or building along an imaginary plane that passes through it vertically. Drawings showing a theoretical slice, or cross-section, across a structure's width are lateral sections. Those cutting through a building's length are longitudinal sections. See also *elevation* and *cutaway.*

sgrafitto—(skraf-'fē-tō) A Chinese ceramic technique in which the design is *incised* through a colored *slip.*

shakti—('shak-tē) In Hinduism, the female power of the deity Devi (or Goddess), which animates the matter of the cosmos.

shikara—The beehive-shaped tower of a Hindu temple.

shogun—('shō-gŭn) In 14th- through 19th-century Japan, a military governor who managed the country on behalf of a figurehead emperor.

slip—A mixture of fine clay and water used in ceramic decoration.

spectrum—The full range of visible wavelengths of light.

squinch—(skwinch) An architectural device used as a transition from a square to a polygonal or circular base for a *dome.* It may be composed of *lintels, corbels,* or *arches.*

stained glass—Colored glass used for windows from the late Middle Ages on.

stele—('stē-lē) A carved stone slab used to mark graves or to commemorate historical events.

still life—A picture depicting an arrangement of objects.

stoneware—Pottery fired at high temperatures to produce a stonelike hardness and density.

strut—Vertical wooden support in Chinese buildings.

stupa—(ˈstū-pŭ) A large, mound-shaped Buddhist shrine.

subtractive light—The light reflected from painting pigments and objects.

subtractive sculpture—A kind of sculpture technique in which materials are taken away from the original mass; carving.

sultan—A *Muslim* ruler.

Sunnah—(ˈsu-nŭ) Collection of the Prophet Muhammad's moral sayings and descriptions of his deeds.

superimposition—The nesting of earlier structures within later ones, a common *Mesoamerican* building trait.

surahs—(ˈsu-rŭs) Chapters of the *Koran*, divided into verses.

sutra—(ˈsū-trŭ) In Buddhism, an account of a sermon by or a dialogue involving the Buddha. A scriptural account of the Buddha. See also *jataka*.

symbol—In art, an image that stands for another image or encapsulates an idea.

tapa—(ta-pa) Barkcloth made particularly in Polynesia. Tapa is often dyed, painted, stenciled, and sometimes perfumed.

tapestry—A weaving technique in which the *weft* threads are packed densely over the *warp* threads so that the designs are woven directly into the fabric.

tarashikomi—(ta-ra-shi-ko-mē) In Japanese art, a painting technique involving the dropping of ink and pigments onto surfaces still wet with previously applied ink and pigments.

tatami—(ta-ta-mē) The traditional woven straw mat used for floor covering in Japanese architecture.

technique—The processes that artists employ to create *form*, as well as the distinctive, personal ways in which they handle their materials and tools.

tenon—(ˈte-nŭn) A projection on the end of a piece of wood that is inserted into a corresponding hole (mortise) in another piece of wood to form a joint.

tenoned—Attached by stone pegs.

terracotta—(te-rŭ-ˈko-tŭ) Hard-baked clay, used for sculpture and as a building material. It may be *glazed* or painted.

tesserae—(ˈtes-ŭ-rē) Greek, "cubes." Tiny stones or pieces of glass cut to the desired shape and size to form a *mosaic*.

texture—The quality of a surface (rough, smooth, hard, soft, shiny, dull) as revealed by light. In represented texture, a painter depicts an object as having a certain texture even though the paint is the actual texture.

thermoluminescence—(ˈthör-mō-lū-mŭ-ˈne-sŭns) A method of dating amounts of radiation found within the clay of ceramic or sculptural forms, as well as in the clay cores from metal castings.

tiki—A Marquesan three-dimensional carving of an exalted, deified ancestor figure.

togu na—(tō-gū na) "House of words." The Dogon (Mali) men's house, where deliberations vital to community welfare take place.

tokonoma—(to-ko-no-ma) A shallow alcove in a Japanese room, which is used for decoration, such as a painting or stylized flower arrangement.

tondo—(ˈton-dō) A circular painting or *relief* sculpture, or any artwork with a circular frame. See *roundel*.

torana—(ˈto-ra-na) Gateway in the stone fence around a *stupa*, located at the cardinal points of the compass.

trefoil—(ˈtrē-foil) A cloverlike ornament or symbol with stylized leaves in groups of three.

trident—A three-pronged pitchfork.

tukutuku—(ˈtu-ku-tu-ku) A stitched lattice panel found in a Maori meetinghouse.

tumulus (pl. **tumuli**)—(ˈtu-myū-lus/ˈtū-myū-li) Earthen burial mound.

ukiyo-e—(ū-kē-yo-ā) Japanese, "pictures of the floating world." A style of Japanese *genre* painting that influenced 19th-century Western art.

underglaze—In *porcelain* decoration, the technique of applying of mineral colors to the surface before the main firing, followed by an application of clear *glaze*. See also *overglaze*.

urna—(ˈŭr-nŭ) A whorl of hair, represented as a dot, between the brows; one of the *lakshanas* of the Buddha.

ushnisha—(ūsh-ˈnesh-ha) A knot of hair on the top of the head; one of the *lakshanas* of the Buddha.

vault—A masonry roof or ceiling constructed on the *arch* principle. A barrel or tunnel vault, semicylindrical in cross-*section*, is in effect a deep arch or an uninterrupted series of arches, one behind the other, over an oblong space. A groin or cross vault is formed at the point at which two barrel vaults intersect at right angles.

Veda—(ˈvā-dŭ) Sanskrit, "knowledge." An early South Asian compilation of religious learning.

vihara—(vē-ˈha-ra) A Buddhist monastery, often cut into a hill.

vimana—(vĭ-ˈma-na) A pyramidal tower over the *garbha griha* of a Hindu temple of the southern, or *Dravida*, style.

votive offering—A gift of gratitude to a deity.

wabi—(wa-bē) A 16th-century Japanese art style characterized by refined rusticity and an appreciation of simplicity and austerity.

waka sran—(wa-ka sran) "People of wood." Baule (Côte d'Ivoire) wooden figural sculptures.

warp—The vertical threads of a loom or cloth.

wat—(wat) A Buddhist monastery in Cambodia.

weft—The horizontal threads of a loom or cloth.

woodblock—See *woodcut*.

woodcut—A wooden block (woodblock) on the surface of which those parts not intended to print are cut away to a slight depth, leaving the design raised; also, the printed impression made with such a block.

yaksha/yakshi—(ˈyak-shŭ/ˈyak-shē) Lesser local male and female Buddhist and Hindu divinities. Yakshis are goddesses associated with fertility and vegetation. Yakshas, the male equivalent of yakshis, are often represented as corpulent, powerful males.

yamato-e—(ya-ma-tō-ā) Also known as native-style painting, a purely Japanese style that often involved colorful, decorative representations of Japanese narratives or *landscapes*.

yang—In Chinese cosmology, the principle of active masculine energy, which permeates the universe in varying proportions with yin, the principle of passive feminine energy.

yasti—(ˈyas-tē) In Buddhist architecture, the mast or pole that arises from the dome of the *stupa* and its *harmika* and symbolizes the axis of the universe; it is adorned with a series of chatras (stone disks).

yin—See *yang*.

yoga—See *nihonga*.

Zen—A Japanese Buddhist sect and its doctrine, emphasizing enlightenment through intuition and introspection rather than the study of scripture. In Chinese, Chan.

BIBLIOGRAPHY

This list of books is intended to be comprehensive enough to satisfy the reading interests of the beginning art history student and general reader, as well as those of more advanced readers who wish to become acquainted with fields other than their own. The resources listed range from works that are valuable primarily for their reproductions to those that are scholarly surveys of schools and periods. No entries for periodical articles are included.

GENERAL STUDIES

Arntzen, Etta, and Robert Rainwater. *Guide to the Literature of Art History.* Chicago: American Library Association, 1981.

Chadwick, Whitney. *Women, Art, and Society.* New York: Thames & Hudson, 1990.

Cheetham, Mark A., Michael Ann Holly, and Keith Moxey, eds. *The Subjects of Art History: Historical Objects in Contemporary Perspective.* New York: Cambridge University Press, 1998.

Chilvers, Ian, and Harold Osborne, eds. *The Oxford Dictionary of Art.* Rev. ed. New York: Oxford University Press, 1997.

Encyclopedia of World Art. 15 vols. New York: Publisher's Guild, 1959–1968. Supplementary vols. 16, 1983; 17, 1987.

Fleming, John, Hugh Honour, and Nikolaus Pevsner. *Penguin Dictionary of Architecture.* 4th ed. New York: Penguin, 1991.

Frazier, Nancy. *The Penguin Concise Dictionary of Art History.* New York: Penguin, 2000.

Haggar, Reginald G. *A Dictionary of Art Terms: Architecture, Sculpture, Painting, and the Graphic Arts.* Poole: New Orchard Editions, 1984.

Hall, James. *Dictionary of Subjects and Symbols in Art.* 2nd rev. ed. London: J. Murray, 1979.

Kultermann, Udo. *The History of Art History.* New York: Abaris, 1993.

Lucie-Smith, Edward. *The Thames & Hudson Dictionary of Art Terms.* London: Thames & Hudson, 1984.

Murray, Peter, and Linda Murray. *A Dictionary of Art and Artists.* 5th ed. New York: Penguin, 1988.

Nelson, Robert S., and Richard Shiff, eds. *Critical Terms for Art History.* Chicago: University of Chicago Press, 1996.

Penny, Nicholas. *The Materials of Sculpture.* New Haven: Yale University Press, 1993.

Pierce, James Smith. *From Abacus to Zeus: A Handbook of Art History.* 7th ed. Upper Saddle River, N.J.: Pearson Prentice Hall, 1998.

Roth, Leland M. *Understanding Architecture: Its Elements, History, and Meaning.* New York: Harper & Row, 1993.

Stangos, Nikos. *The Thames & Hudson Dictionary of Art and Artists.* Rev. ed. New York: Thames & Hudson, 1994.

Turner, Jane, ed. *The Dictionary of Art.* 34 vols. New York: Grove Dictionaries, 1996.

CHAPTER 1
PATHS TO ENLIGHTENMENT:
THE ART OF SOUTH AND SOUTHEAST ASIA
BEFORE 1200

Asher, Frederick M. *The Art of Eastern India, 300–800.* Minneapolis: University of Minnesota Press, 1980.

Blurton, T. Richard. *Hindu Art.* Cambridge, Mass.: Harvard University Press, 1993.

Chaturachinda, Gwyneth, Sunanda Krishnamurty, and Pauline W. Tabtiang. *Dictionary of South and Southeast Asian Art.* Chiang Mai, Thailand: Silkworm Books, 2000.

Chihara, Daigoro. *Hindu-Buddhist Architecture in Southeast Asia.* Leiden: E. J. Brill, 1996.

Craven, Roy C. *Indian Art: A Concise History.* Rev. ed. London: Thames & Hudson, 1997.

Dehejia, Vidya. *Early Buddhist Rock Temples.* Ithaca, N.Y.: Cornell University Press, 1972.

———. *Indian Art.* London: Phaidon, 1997.

Desai, Vishakha N., and Darielle Mason. *Gods, Guardians, and Lovers: Temple Sculptures from North India A.D. 700–1200.* New York: Asia Society Galleries, 1993.

Encyclopedia of Indian Temple Architecture. 8 vols. New Delhi: American Institute of Indian Studies. Philadelphia: University of Pennsylvania Press, 1983–1996.

Fisher, Robert E. *Buddhist Art and Architecture.* New York: Thames & Hudson, 1993.

Frederic, Louis. *Borobudur.* New York: Abbeville Press, 1996.

Gopinatha Rao, T. A. *Elements of Hindu Iconography.* 2nd ed. 4 vols. New York: Paragon, 1968.

Gray, Basil, ed. *The Arts of India.* Ithaca, N.Y.: Cornell University Press, 1981.

Harle, James C. *The Art and Architecture of the Indian Subcontinent.* 2nd ed. New Haven: Yale University Press, 1994.

Huntington, Susan L., and John C. Huntington. *The Art of Ancient India: Buddhist, Hindu, Jain.* New York: Weatherhill, 1985.

Jacques, Claude, and Michael Freeman. *Angkor: Cities and Temples.* Bangkok: River Books, 1997.

Jessup, Helen Ibbitson, and Thierry Zephir, eds. *Sculpture of Angkor and Ancient Cambodia: Millennium of Glory.* Washington, D.C.: National Gallery of Art, 1997.

McIntosh, Jane R. *A Peaceful Realm: The Rise and Fall of the Indus Civilization.* Boulder, Colo.: Westview Press, 2002.

Michell, George. *Hindu Art and Architecture.* New York: Thames & Hudson, 2000.

———. *The Hindu Temple: An Introduction to Its Meaning and Forms.* Chicago: University of Chicago Press, 1988.

Mitter, Partha. *Indian Art.* New York: Oxford University Press, 2001.

Rawson, Phillip. *The Art of Southeast Asia.* New York: Thames & Hudson, 1990.

Srinivasan, Doris Meth. *Many Heads, Arms and Eyes: Origin, Meaning and Form of Multiplicity in Indian Art.* Leiden: E. J. Brill, 1997.

Stierlin, Henri. *Hindu India from Khajuraho to the Temple City of Madurai.* Cologne: Taschen, 1998.

Williams, Joanna G. *The Art of Gupta India: Empire and Province.* Princeton, N.J.: Princeton University Press, 1982.

CHAPTER 2
SULTANS, KINGS, EMPERORS, AND COLONISTS:
THE ART OF SOUTH AND SOUTHEAST ASIA
AFTER 1200

Asher, Catherine B. *Architecture of Mughal India.* New York: Cambridge University Press, 1992.

Beach, Milo Cleveland. *Mughal and Rajput Painting.* Cambridge: Cambridge University Press, 1992.

Blurton, T. Richard. *Hindu Art.* Cambridge, Mass: Harvard University Press, 1993.

Chaturachinda, Gwyneth, Sunanda Krishnamurty, and Pauline W. Tabtiang. *Dictionary of South and Southeast Asian Art.* Chiang Mai: Silkworm Books, 2000.

Craven, Roy C. *Indian Art: A Concise History.* Rev. ed. London: Thames & Hudson, 1997.

Dallapiccola, Anna Libera, ed. *Vijayanagara: City and Empire.* 2 vols. Stuttgart: Steiner, 1985.

Dehejia, Vidya. *Indian Art.* London: Phaidon, 1997.

Encyclopedia of Indian Temple Architecture. 8 vols. New Delhi: American Institute of Indian Studies, and Philadelphia: University of Pennsylvania Press, 1983–1996.

Girard-Geslan, Maud, ed. *Art of Southeast Asia.* New York: Abrams, 1998.

Harle, James C. *The Art and Architecture of the Indian Subcontinent.* 2nd ed. New Haven: Yale University Press, 1994.

Huntington, Susan L., and John C. Huntington. *The Art of Ancient India: Buddhist, Hindu, Jain.* New York: Weatherhill, 1985.

Michell, George. *Architecture and Art of Southern India: Vijayanagara and the Successor States, 1350–1750.* Cambridge: Cambridge University Press, 1995.

———. *Hindu Art and Architecture.* New York: Thames & Hudson, 2000.

———. *The Hindu Temple: An Introduction to Its Meaning and Forms.* Chicago: University of Chicago Press, 1988.

Mitter, Partha. *Indian Art.* New York: Oxford University Press, 2001.

Narula, Karen Schur. *Voyage of the Emerald Buddha.* Kuala Lumpur: Oxford University Press, 1994.

Pal, Pratapaditya, ed. *Master Artists of the Imperial Mughal Court.* Mumbai: Marg, 1991.

Rawson, Phillip. *The Art of Southeast Asia.* New York: Thames & Hudson, 1990.

Stadtner, Donald M. *The Art of Burma: New Studies.* Mumbai: Marg, 1999.

Stevenson, John, and John Guy, eds. *Vietnamese Ceramics: A Separate Tradition.* Chicago: Art Media Resources, 1997.

Stierlin, Henri. *Hindu India from Khajuraho to the Temple City of Madurai.* Cologne: Taschen, 1998.

Welch, Stuart Cary. *Imperial Mughal Painting.* New York: Braziller, 1978.

———. *India: Art and Culture 1300–1900.* New York: Metropolitan Museum of Art, 1985.

CHAPTER 3
THE SILK ROAD AND BEYOND:
THE ART OF EARLY CHINA AND KOREA

Bush, Susan, and Shio-yen Shih. *Early Chinese Texts on Painting.* Cambridge, Mass.: Harvard University Press, 1985.

Cahill, James. *Chinese Painting.* New York: Rizzoli, 1960.

———. *The Painter's Practice: How Artists Lived and Worked in Traditional China.* New York: Columbia University Press, 1994.

Clunas, Craig. *Art in China.* New York: Oxford University Press, 1997.

Fahr-Becker, Gabriele, ed. *The Art of East Asia.* Cologne: Könemann, 1999.

Fisher, Robert E. *Buddhist Art and Architecture.* New York: Thames & Hudson, 1993.

Fong, Wen C. *Beyond Representation: Chinese Painting and Calligraphy, 8th–14th Century.* New Haven: Yale University Press, 1992.

———. *The Great Bronze Age of China: An Exhibition from the People's Republic of China.* New York: Metropolitan Museum of Art, 1980.

Fong, Wen C., and James C. Y. Watt. *Preserving the Past: Treasures from the National Palace Museum, Taipei.* New York: Metropolitan Museum of Art, 1996.

Li, Chu-tsing, ed. *Artists and Patrons: Some Social and Economic Aspects of Chinese Painting.* Lawrence: Kress Department of Art History, in cooperation with Indiana University Press, 1989.

Little, Stephen, and Shawn Eichman. *Taoism and the Arts of China.* Chicago: Art Institute of Chicago, 2000.

Portal, Jane. *Korea: Art and Archaeology.* New York: Thames & Hudson, 2000.

Powers, Martin J. *Art and Political Expression in Early China.* New Haven: Yale University Press, 1991.

Rawson, Jessica. *Ancient China: Art and Archaeology.* New York: Harper & Row, 1980.

———, ed. *The British Museum Book of Chinese Art.* New York: Thames & Hudson, 1992.

Sickman, Laurence, and Alexander C. Soper. *The Art and Architecture of China.* 3rd ed. New Haven: Yale University Press, 1968.

Silbergeld, Jerome. *Chinese Painting Style: Media, Methods, and Principles of Form.* Seattle and London: University of Washington Press, 1982.

Steinhardt, Nancy S., ed. *Chinese Architecture.* New Haven: Yale University Press, 2002.

Sullivan, Michael. *The Arts of China.* 4th ed. Berkeley: University of California Press, 1999.

———. *The Birth of Landscape Painting.* Berkeley: University of California Press, 1962.

Thorp, Robert L. *Son of Heaven: Imperial Arts of China.* Seattle: Son of Heaven Press, 1988.

Thorp, Robert L., and Richard Ellis Vinograd. *Chinese Art and Culture.* New York: Abrams, 2001.

Vainker, S. J. *Chinese Pottery and Porcelain: From Prehistory to the Present.* New York: Braziller, 1991.

Watson, William. *The Arts of China to AD 900.* New Haven: Yale University Press, 1995.

———. *The Arts of China 900–1620.* New Haven: Yale University Press, 2000.

Weidner, Marsha, ed. *Flowering in the Shadows: Women in the History of Chinese and Japanese Painting.* Honolulu: University of Hawaii Press, 1990.

Whitfield, Roger, and Anne Farrer. *Caves of the Thousand Buddhas: Chinese Art of the Silk Route.* New York: Braziller, 1990.

Wu, Hung. *Monumentality in Early Chinese Art.* Stanford, Calif.: Stanford University Press, 1996.

———. *The Wu Liang Shrine: The Ideology of Early Chinese Pictorial Art.* Stanford, Calif.: Stanford University Press, 1989.

Xin, Yang, Nie Chongzheng, Lang Shaojun, Richard M. Barnhart, James Cahill, and Hung Wu. *Three Thousand Years of Chinese Painting.* New Haven: Yale University Press, 1997.

CHAPTER 4
FROM THE MONGOLS TO THE MODERN: THE ART OF LATER CHINA AND KOREA

Andrews, Julia Frances, and Kuiyi Shen. *A Century in Crisis: Modernity and Tradition in the Art of Twentieth-Century China.* New York: Guggenheim Museum, 1998.

Barnhart, Richard M. *Painters of the Great Ming: The Imperial Court and the Zhe School.* Dallas: Dallas Museum of Art, 1993.

Cahill, James. *Chinese Painting.* New York: Rizzoli, 1960.

———. *The Painter's Practice: How Artists Lived and Worked in Traditional China.* New York: Columbia University Press, 1994.

Clunas, Craig. *Art in China.* New York: Oxford University Press, 1997.

Fahr-Becker, Gabriele, ed. *The Art of East Asia.* Cologne: Könemann, 1999.

Fisher, Robert E. *Buddhist Art and Architecture.* New York: Thames & Hudson, 1993.

Fong, Wen C., and James C. Y. Watt. *Preserving the Past: Treasures from the National Palace Museum, Taipei.* New York: Metropolitan Museum of Art, 1996.

Laing, Ellen Johnston. *The Winking Owl: Art in the People's Republic of China.* Berkeley: University of California Press, 1989.

Lee, Sherman E., and Wai-Kam Ho. *Chinese Art under the Mongols: The Yuan Dynasty (1279–1368).* Cleveland: Cleveland Museum of Art, 1969.

Li, Chu-tsing, ed. *Artists and Patrons: Some Social and Economic Aspects of Chinese Painting.* Lawrence: Kress Department of Art History in cooperation with Indiana University Press, 1989.

Nakata, Yujiro, ed. *Chinese Calligraphy.* New York: Weatherhill, 1983.

Portal, Jane. *Korea: Art and Archaeology.* New York: Thames & Hudson, 2000.

Rawson, Jessica, ed. *The British Museum Book of Chinese Art.* New York: Thames & Hudson, 1992.

Silbergeld, Jerome. *Chinese Painting Style: Media, Methods, and Principles of Form.* Seattle: University of Washington Press, 1982.

Steinhardt, Nancy S., ed. *Chinese Architecture.* New Haven: Yale University Press, 2002.

Sullivan, Michael. *Art and Artists of Twentieth-Century China.* Berkeley: University of California Press, 1996.

———. *The Arts of China.* 4th ed. Berkeley: University of California Press, 1999.

Thorp, Robert L. *Son of Heaven: Imperial Arts of China.* Seattle: Son of Heaven Press, 1988.

Thorp, Robert L., and Richard Ellis Vinograd. *Chinese Art and Culture.* New York: Abrams, 2001.

Vainker, S. J. *Chinese Pottery and Porcelain: From Prehistory to the Present.* London: Braziller, 1991.

Watson, William. *The Arts of China 900–1260.* New Haven: Yale University Press, 2000.

Weidner, Marsha, ed. *Flowering in the Shadows: Women in the History of Chinese and Japanese Painting.* Honolulu: University of Hawaii Press, 1990.

———. *Views from Jade Terrace: Chinese Women Artists 1300–1912.* Indianapolis: Indianapolis Museum of Art, 1988.

Xin, Yang, Nie Chongzheng, Lang Shaojun, Richard M. Barnhart, James Cahill, and Wu Hung. *Three Thousand Years of Chinese Painting.* New Haven: Yale University Press, 1997.

CHAPTER 5
SHRINES, STATUES, AND SCROLLS: THE ART OF EARLY JAPAN

Aikens, C. Melvin, and Takayama Higuchi. *Prehistory of Japan.* New York: Academic Press, 1982.

Coaldrake, William H. *Architecture and Authority in Japan.* London: Routledge, 1996.

Elisseeff, Danielle, and Vadime Elisseeff. *Art of Japan.* Translated by I. Mark Paris. New York: Abrams, 1985.

Ienaga, Saburo. *Painting in the Yamato Style.* Translated by John M. Shields. New York: Weatherhill, 1973.

Kidder, J. Edward, Jr. *The Art of Japan.* New York: Park Lane, 1985.

Kurata, Bunsaku. *Horyu-ji: Temple of the Exalted Law.* Translated by W. Chie Ishibashi. New York: Japan Society, 1981.

Mason, Penelope. *History of Japanese Art.* New York: Abrams, 1993.

Nishi, Kazuo, and Kazuo Hozumi. *What Is Japanese Architecture?* Translated by H. Mack Horton. New York: Kodansha International, 1985.

Nishikawa, Kyotaro, and Emily Sano. *The Great Age of Japanese Buddhist Sculpture A.D. 600–1300.* Fort Worth, Tex.: Kimbell Art Museum, 1982.

Noma, Seiroku. *The Arts of Japan.* Translated and adapted by John Rosenfield and Glenn T. Webb. Tokyo: Kodansha International, 1966.

Okudaira, Hideo. *Narrative Picture Scrolls.* Adapted by Elizabeth ten Grotenhuis. New York: Weatherhill, 1973.

Pearson, Richard J. *Ancient Japan.* New York: Braziller, 1992.

Pearson, Richard J., Gina Lee Barnes, and Karl L. Hutterer, eds. *Windows on the Japanese Past.* Ann Arbor: Center for Japanese Studies, University of Michigan, 1986.

Rosenfield, John M. *Japanese Art of the Heian Period, 794–1185.* New York: Asia Society, 1967.

Rosenfield, John M., and Elizabeth ten Grotenhuis. *Journey of the Three Jewels.* New York: Asia Society, 1979.

Rosenfield, John M., and Shujiro Shimada. *Traditions of Japanese Art: Selections from the Kimiko and John Powers Collection.* Cambridge, Mass.: Fogg Art Museum, 1970.

Shimizu, Yoshiaki, ed. *The Shaping of Daimyo Culture 1185–1868.* Washington, D.C.: National Gallery of Art, 1988.

Stanley-Baker, Joan. *Japanese Art.* New York: Thames & Hudson, 1984.

Suzuki, Kakichi. *Early Buddhist Architecture in Japan.* Translated and adapted by Mary Neighbor Parent and Nancy Shatzman Steinhardt. New York: Kodansha International, 1980.

Swann, Peter C. *Concise History of Japanese Art.* New York: Kodansha International, 1979.

Weidner, Marsha, ed. *Flowering in the Shadows: Women in the History of Chinese and Japanese Painting.* Honolulu: University of Hawaii Press, 1990.

CHAPTER 6
FROM THE SHOGUNS TO THE PRESENT: THE ART OF LATER JAPAN

Addiss, Stephen. *The Art of Zen.* New York: Abrams, 1989.

Akiyama, Terukazu. *Japanese Painting.* Geneva: Skira; New York: Rizzoli, 1977.

Baekeland, Frederick. *Imperial Japan: The Art of the Meiji Era (1868–1912).* Ithaca, N.Y.: Herbert F. Johnson Museum of Art, 1980.

Brown, Kendall. *The Politics of Reclusion: Painting and Power in Muromachi Japan.* Honolulu: University of Hawaii Press, 1997.

Cahill, James. *Scholar Painters of Japan.* New York: Asia Society, 1972.

Coaldrake, William H. *Architecture and Authority in Japan.* London: Routledge, 1996.

Drexler, Arthur. *The Architecture of Japan.* New York: Museum of Modern Art, 1966.

Fontein, Jan, and Money L. Hickman. *Zen Painting and Calligraphy.* Greenwich, Conn.: New York Graphic Society, 1970.

Guth, Christine. *Art of Edo Japan: The Artist and the City, 1615–1868.* New York: Abrams, 1996.

Hickman, Money L., John T. Carpenter, Bruce A. Coats, Christine Guth, Andrew J. Pekarik, John M.

Rosenfield, and Nicole C. Rousmaniere. *Japan's Golden Age: Momoyama*. New Haven: Yale University Press, 1996.

Kawakita, Michiaki. *Modern Currents in Japanese Art*. Translated by Charles E. Terry. New York: Weatherhill, 1974.

Kidder, J. Edward, Jr. *The Art of Japan*. New York: Park Lane, 1985.

Lane, Richard. *Images from the Floating World: The Japanese Print*. New York: Dorset, 1978.

Mason, Penelope. *History of Japanese Art*. New York: Abrams, 1993.

Meech-Pekarik, Julia. *The World of the Meiji Print: Impressions of a New Civilization*. New York: Weatherhill, 1986.

Munroe, Alexandra. *Japanese Art after 1945: Scream against the Sky*. New York: Abrams, 1994.

Nishi, Kazuo, and Kazuo Hozumi. *What Is Japanese Architecture?* Translated by H. Mack Horton. New York: Kodansha International, 1985.

Rosenfield, John M., and Elizabeth ten Grotenhuis. *Journey of the Three Jewels*. New York: Asia Society, 1979.

Sanford, James H., William R. LaFleur, and Masatoshi Nagatomi. *Flowing Traces: Buddhism in the Literary and Visual Arts of Japan*. Princeton, N.J.: Princeton University Press, 1992.

Shimizu, Yoshiaki, ed. Japan: *The Shaping of Daimyo Culture, 1185–1868*. Washington, D.C.: National Gallery of Art, 1988.

Singer, Robert T. Edo: *Art in Japan 1615–1868*. Washington, D.C.: National Gallery of Art, 1998.

Stewart, David B. *The Making of a Modern Japanese Architecture, 1868 to the Present*. New York: Kodansha International, 1988.

Watson, William, ed. *The Great Japan Exhibition: Art of the Edo Period, 1600–1868*. London: Royal Academy of Arts, 1981.

Weidner, Marsha, ed. *Flowering in the Shadows: Women in the History of Chinese and Japanese Painting*. Honolulu: University of Hawaii Press, 1990.

CHAPTER 7
IN PRAISE OF ALLAH:
THE ART OF THE ISLAMIC WORLD

Atil, Esin. *The Age of Sultan Suleyman the Magnificent*. Washington, D.C.: National Gallery of Art, 1987.

Baker, Patricia L. *Islamic Textiles*. London: British Museum, 1995.

Blair, Sheila S., and Jonathan Bloom. *The Art and Architecture of Islam 1250–1800*. New Haven: Yale University Press, 1994.

Bloom, Jonathan, and Sheila S. Blair. *Islamic Arts*. London: Phaidon, 1997.

Brend, Barbara. *Islamic Art*. Cambridge, Mass.: Harvard University Press, 1991.

Canby, Sheila. *Persian Painting*. London: British Museum, 1993.

Creswell, Keppel A. C. *A Short Account of Early Muslim Architecture*. Rev. ed. by James W. Allan. Aldershot: Scolar, 1989.

Dodds, Jerrilynn D., ed. *Al-Andalus: The Art of Islamic Spain*. New York: Metropolitan Museum of Art, 1992.

Ettinghausen, Richard. *From Byzantium to Sassanian Iran and the Islamic World*. Leiden: E. J. Brill, 1972.

Ettinghausen, Richard, Oleg Grabar, and Marilyn Jenkins-Madina. *The Art and Architecture of Islam, 650–1250*. Rev. ed. New Haven: Yale University Press, 2001.

Ferrier, Ronald W., ed. *The Arts of Persia*. New Haven: Yale University Press, 1989.

Frishman, Martin, and Hasan-Uddin Khan. *The Mosque: History, Architectural Development and Regional Diversity*. New York: Thames & Hudson, 1994.

Goodwin, Godfrey. *A History of Ottoman Architecture*. 2nd ed. New York: Thames & Hudson, 1987.

Grabar, Oleg. *The Alhambra*. Cambridge, Mass.: Harvard University Press, 1978.

———. *The Formation of Islamic Art*. Rev. ed. New Haven: Yale University Press, 1987.

Grube, Ernst J. *Architecture of the Islamic World: Its History and Social Meaning*. 2nd ed. New York: Thames & Hudson, 1984.

Hattstein, Markus, and Peter Delius, eds. *Islam: Art and Architecture*. Cologne: Könemann, 2000.

Hillenbrand, Robert. *Islamic Architecture: Form, Function, Meaning*. Edinburgh: Edinburgh University Press, 1994.

———. *Islamic Art and Architecture*. New York: Thames & Hudson, 1999.

Irwin, Robert. *Islamic Art in Context: Art, Architecture, and the Literary World*. New York: Abrams, 1997.

Lings, Martin. *The Qur'anic Art of Calligraphy and Illumination*. London: World of Islam Festival Trust, 1976.

Michell, George, ed. *Architecture of the Islamic World*. New York: Thames & Hudson, 1978.

Porter, Venetia. *Islamic Tiles*. London: British Museum, 1995.

Robinson, Frank. *Atlas of the Islamic World*. Oxford: Equinox, 1982.

Schimmel, Annemarie. *Calligraphy and Islamic Culture*. New York: New York University Press, 1984.

Stierlin, Henri. *Islam I: Early Architecture from Baghdad to Cordoba*. Cologne: Taschen, 1996.

———. *Islamic Art and Architecture from Isfahan to the Taj Mahal*. New York: Thames & Hudson, 2002.

Ward, Rachel M. *Islamic Metalwork*. New York: Thames & Hudson, 1993.

Welch, Anthony. *Calligraphy in the Arts of the Islamic World*. Austin: University of Texas Press, 1979.

CHAPTER 8
FROM ALASKA TO THE ANDES:
NATIVE ARTS OF THE AMERICAS BEFORE 1300

Alva, Walter, and Christopher Donnan. *Royal Tombs of Sipán*. Los Angeles: Fowler Museum of Cultural History, 1993.

Benson, Elizabeth P., and Beatriz de la Fuente, eds. *Olmec Art of Ancient Mexico*. Washington, D.C.: National Gallery of Art, 1996.

Berlo, Janet Catherine, ed. *Art, Ideology, and the City of Teotihuacan*. Washington, D.C.: Dumbarton Oaks, 1992.

Berlo, Janet Catherine, and Ruth B. Phillips. *Native North American Art*. New York: Oxford University Press, 1998.

Berrin, Kathleen, ed. *The Spirit of Ancient Peru: Treasures from the Museo Arqueologico Rafael Larco Herrera*. San Francisco: The Fine Arts Museums of San Francisco, 1997.

Berrin, Kathleen, and Esther Pasztory, eds. *Teotihuacan: Art from the City of the Gods*. San Francisco: Thames & Hudson/The Fine Arts Museums of San Francisco, 1993.

Boone, Elizabeth, ed. *Andean Art at Dumbarton Oaks*. 2 vols. Washington, D.C.: Dumbarton Oaks, 1996.

Brody, J. J., and Rina Swentzell. *To Touch the Past: The Painted Pottery of the Mimbres People*. New York: Hudson Hills, 1996.

Brose, David. *Ancient Art of the American Woodland Indians*. New York: Abrams, 1985.

Bruhns, Karen O. *Ancient South America*. New York: Cambridge University Press, 1994.

Burger, Richard. *Chavín and the Origins of Andean Civilization*. New York: Thames & Hudson, 1992.

Carrasco, David. *The Oxford Encyclopedia of Mesoamerican Cultures: The Civilizations of Mexico and Central America*. New York, Oxford University Press, 2001.

Clark, John E., and Mary E. Pye, eds. *Olmec Art and Archaeology in Mesoamerica*. Washington, D.C.: National Gallery of Art, 2000.

Coe, Michael D. *Mexico*. 4th ed. New York: Thames & Hudson, 1994.

———. *The Maya*. 6th ed. New York: Thames & Hudson, 1999.

Coe, Michael D., and Justin Kerr. *The Art of the Maya Scribe*. New York: Abrams, 1998.

Cordell, Linda S. *Ancient Pueblo Peoples*. Washington, D.C.: Smithsonian Institution Press, 1994.

Donnan, Christopher. *Ceramics of Ancient Peru*. Los Angeles: Fowler Museum of Cultural History, 1992.

Fagan, Brian. *Ancient North America: The Archaeology of a Continent*. 2nd ed. New York: Thames & Hudson, 1995.

Fash, William. *Scribes, Warriors, and Kings: The City of Copan and the Ancient Maya*. New York: Thames & Hudson, 1991.

Feest, Christian F. *Native Arts of North America*. 2nd ed. New York: Thames & Hudson, 1992.

Fitzhugh, William W., and Aron Crowell, eds. *Crossroads of Continents: Cultures of Siberia and Alaska*. Washington, D.C.: Smithsonian Institution Press, 1988.

Grube, Nikolai, ed. *Maya: Divine Kings of the Rain Forest*. Cologne: Könemann, 2000.

Hadingham, Evan. *Lines to the Mountain Gods: Nazca and the Mysteries of Peru*. Norman: University of Oklahoma Press, 1988.

Jones, Julie, ed. *The Art of Pre-Columbian Gold: The Jan Mitchell Collection*. New York: Metropolitan Museum of Art, 1985.

Kolata, Alan. *The Tiwanaku: Portrait of an Andean Civilization*. Cambridge: Blackwell, 1993.

Kubler, George. *The Art and Architecture of Ancient America: The Mexican, Maya, and Andean Peoples*. 3rd ed. New Haven: Yale University Press, 1992.

Mathews, Zena, and Aldona Jonaitis, eds. *Native North American Art History*. Palo Alto, Calif.: Peek Publications, 1982.

Miller, Mary Ellen. *The Art of Mesoamerica, from Olmec to Aztec*. 2nd ed. New York: Thames & Hudson, 1996.

———. *Maya Art and Architecture*. New York: Thames & Hudson, 1999.

Miller, Mary Ellen, and Karl Taube. *The Gods and Symbols of Ancient Mexico and the Maya: An Illustrated Dictionary of Mesoamerican Religion*. New York: Thames & Hudson, 1993.

Morris, Craig, and Adriana von Hagen. *The Inka Empire and Its Andean Origins*. New York: Abbeville, 1993.

Nabokov, Peter, and Robert Easton. *Native American Architecture*. New York: Oxford University Press, 1989.

O'Connor, Mallory M. *Lost Cities of the Ancient Southeast*. Gainesville: University Press of Florida, 1995.

Olmecs. Special edition of *Arqueología Mexicana*. Mexico City: Editorial Raíces, 1998.

Pang, Hilda. *Pre-Columbian Art: Investigations and Insights*. Norman: University of Oklahoma Press, 1992.

Pasztory, Esther. *Pre-Columbian Art*. New York: Cambridge University Press, 1998.

Paul, Anne. *Paracas Ritual Attire: Symbols of Authority in Ancient Peru*. Norman: University of Oklahoma Press, 1990.

Penney, David, and George C. Longfish. *Native American Art*. Hong Kong: Hugh Lauter Levin and Associates, 1994.

Schele, Linda, and Peter Mathews. *The Code of Kings: The Language of Seven Sacred Maya Temples and Tombs*. New York: Scribner, 1998.

Schele, Linda, and Mary E. Miller. *The Blood of Kings: Dynasty and Ritual in Maya Art*. Fort Worth, Tex.: Kimbell Art Museum, 1986.

Schmidt, Peter, Mercedes de la Garza, and Enrique Nalda, eds. *Maya*. New York: Rizzoli, 1998.

Stone-Miller, Rebecca. *Art of the Andes from Chavín to Inca*. New York: Thames & Hudson, 1996.

———, ed. *To Weave for the Sun: Andean Textiles in the Museum of Fine Arts, Boston*. Boston: Museum of Fine Arts, 1992.

Townsend, Richard F., ed. *Ancient West Mexico*. Chicago: Art Institute of Chicago, 1998.

———. *Art from Sacred Landscapes*. Chicago: Art Institute of Chicago, 1992.

Von Hagen, Adriana, and Craig Morris. *The Cities of the Ancient Andes*. New York: Thames & Hudson, 1998.

Wardwell, Allen. *Ancient Eskimo Ivories of the Bering Strait*. New York: Rizzoli, 1986.

Weaver, Muriel Porter. *The Aztecs, Mayas, and Their Predecessors*. 3rd ed. San Diego, Calif.: Academic Press, 1993.

Whiteford, Andrew H., Stewart Peckham, and Kate Peck Kent. *I Am Here: Two Thousand Years of Southwest Indian Arts and Crafts*. Santa Fe: Museum of New Mexico Press, 1989.

CHAPTER 9
BEFORE AND AFTER THE CONQUISTADORS: NATIVE ARTS OF THE AMERICAS AFTER 1300

Anderson, Richard, and Karen L. Field, eds. *Art in Small-Scale Societies: Contemporary Readings*. Upper Saddle River, N.J.: Prentice Hall, 1993.

Berlo, Janet Catherine, ed. *Plains Indian Drawings 1865–1935*. New York: Abrams, 1996.

Berlo, Janet Catherine, and Ruth B. Phillips. *Native North American Art*. New York: Oxford University Press, 1998.

Berlo, Janet Catherine, and Lee Anne Wilson, eds. *Arts of Africa, Oceania, and the Americas: Selected Readings*. Upper Saddle River, N.J.: Prentice Hall, 1993.

Boone, Elizabeth. *The Aztec World*. Washington, D.C.: Smithsonian Institution Press, 1994.

———, ed. *Andean Art at Dumbarton Oaks*. 2 vols. Washington, D.C.: Dumbarton Oaks, 1996.

Bruhns, Karen O. *Ancient South America*. New York: Cambridge University Press, 1994.

Coe, Michael D. *The Maya*. 6th ed. New York: Thames & Hudson, 1999.

———. *Mexico*. 4th ed. New York: Thames & Hudson, 1994.

Coe, Michael D., and Justin Kerr. *The Art of the Maya Scribe*. New York: Abrams, 1998.

Diaz, Gisele, and Alan Rodgers. *The Codex Borgia*. New York: Dover, 1993.

Donnan, Christopher. *Ceramics of Ancient Peru*. Los Angeles: Fowler Museum of Cultural History, 1992.

Feest, Christian F. *Native Arts of North America*. 2nd ed. New York: Thames & Hudson, 1992.

Fienup-Riordan, Ann. *The Living Tradition of Yup`ik Masks*. Seattle: University of Washington Press, 1996.

Fitzhugh, William W., and Aron Crowell, eds. *Crossroads of Continents: Cultures of Siberia and Alaska*. Washington, D.C.: Smithsonian Institution Press, 1988.

Gasparini, Graziano, and Luise Margolies. *Inca Architecture*. Bloomington: Indiana University Press, 1980.

Hill, Tom, and Richard W. Hill Sr., eds. *Creation's Journey: Native American Identity and Belief*. Washington, D.C.: Smithsonian Institution Press, 1994.

Jonaitis, Aldona. *From the Land of the Totem Poles: The Northwest Coast Indian Art Collection at the American Museum of Natural History*. Seattle: University of Washington Press, 1988.

Kubler, George. *The Art and Architecture of Ancient America: The Mexican, Maya, and Andean Peoples*. 3rd ed. New Haven: Yale University Press, 1992.

Malpass, Michael A. *Daily Life in the Inca Empire*. Westport, Conn.: Greenwood Press, 1996.

Mathews, Zena, and Aldona Jonaitis, eds. *Native North American Art History*. Palo Alto, Calif.: Peek Publications, 1982.

Matos, Eduardo M. *The Great Temple of the Aztecs: Treasures of Tenochtitlan*. New York: Thames & Hudson, 1988.

Maurer, Evan M. *Visions of the People: A Pictorial History of Plains Indian Life*. Seattle: University of Washington Press, 1992.

Miller, Mary E. *The Art of Mesoamerica, from Olmec to Aztec*. 2nd ed. New York: Thames & Hudson, 1996.

Miller, Mary E., and Karl Taube. *The Gods and Symbols of Ancient Mexico and the Maya: An Illustrated Dictionary of Mesoamerican Religion*. New York: Thames & Hudson, 1993.

Morris, Craig, and Adriana von Hagen. *The Inka Empire and its Andean Origins*. New York: Abbeville, 1993.

Nabokov, Peter, and Robert Easton. *Native American Architecture*. New York: Oxford University Press, 1989.

Pasztory, Esther. *Aztec Art*. New York: Abrams, 1983.

———. *Pre-Columbian Art*. New York: Cambridge University Press, 1998.

Penney, David. *Art of the American Indian Frontier*. Seattle: University of Washington Press, 1992.

Penney, David, and George C. Longfish. *Native American Art*. Hong Kong: Hugh Lauter Levin & Associates, 1994.

Peterson, Susan. *The Living Tradition of Maria Martinez*. Tokyo: Kodansha International, 1977.

Phillips, Ruth B. *Trading Identities: The Souvenir in Native North American Art*. Seattle: University of Washington Press, 1998.

Plazas, Clemencia, Ana Maria Falchetti, and Armand J. Labbé. *Tribute to the Gods: Treasures of the Museo del Oro*. Santa Ana, Calif.: Bowers Museum of Cultural Art, 1992.

Samuel, Cheryl. *The Chilkat Dancing Blanket*. Norman: University of Oklahoma Press, 1982.

Schaafsma, Polly, ed. *Kachinas in the Pueblo World*. Albuquerque: University of New Mexico Press, 1994.

Stewart, Hilary. *Looking at Totem Poles*. Seattle: University of Washington Press, 1993.

Townsend, Richard F., ed. *Art from Sacred Landscapes*. Chicago: Art Institute of Chicago, 1992.

Wardwell, Allen. *Tangible Visions: Northwest Coast Indian Shamanism and Its Art*. New York: Monacelli Press, 1996.

Washburn, Dorothy. *Living in Balance: The Universe of the Hopi, Zuni, Navajo, and Apache*. Philadelphia: University Museum, 1995.

Weaver, Muriel Porter. *The Aztecs, Mayas, and Their Predecessors*. 3rd ed. San Diego: Academic Press, 1993.

Whiteford, Andrew H., Stewart Peckham, and Kate Peck Kent. *I Am Here: Two Thousand Years of Southwest Indian Arts and Crafts*. Santa Fe: Museum of New Mexico Press, 1989.

Wright, Robin K. *Northern Haida Master Carvers*. Seattle: University of Washington Press, 2001.

Wyman, Leland C. *Southwest Indian Drypainting*. Albuquerque: University of New Mexico Press, 1983.

CHAPTER 10
SOUTH FROM THE SAHARA: EARLY AFRICAN ART

Bassani, Ezio, and William Fagg. *Africa and the Renaissance: Art in Ivory*. New York: Center for African Art, 1988.

Ben-Amos, Paula. *The Art of Benin*. New York: Thames & Hudson, 1980.

Blier, Suzanne P. *Royal Arts of Africa: The Majesty of Form*. New York: Abrams, 1998.

Bourgeois, Jean-Louis, and Carollee Pelos. *Spectacular Vernacular: The Adobe Tradition*. New York: Aperture, 1989.

Campbell, Alec, and David Coulson. *African Rock Art: Paintings and Engravings on Stone*. New York: Abrams, 2001.

Connah, Graham. *African Civilizations*. 2nd ed. Cambridge: Cambridge University Press, 2001.

Dark, Philip J. C. *An Introduction to Benin Art and Technology*. Oxford: Clarendon Press, 1973.

Dewey, William J. *Legacies of Stone: Zimbabwe Past and Present*. Tervuren: Royal Museum for Central Africa, 1997.

Drewal, Henry J., John Pemberton, and Rowland Abiodun. *Yoruba: Nine Centuries of African Art and Thought*. New York: Center for African Art, in association with Abrams, 1989.

Eyo, Ekpo, and Frank Willett. *Treasures of Ancient Nigeria*. New York: Knopf, 1980.

Ezra, Kate. *Royal Art of Benin: The Perls Collection in the Metropolitan Museum of Art*. New York: Metropolitan Museum of Art, 1992.

Fagg, Bernard. *Nok Terracottas*. Lagos: Ethnographica, 1977.

Garlake, Peter. *Early Art and Architecture of Africa*. Oxford: Oxford University Press, 2002.

———. *Great Zimbabwe*. London: Thames & Hudson, 1973.

Huffman, Thomas N. *Snakes and Crocodiles: Power and Symbolism in Ancient Zimbabwe*. Johannesburg: Witwatersrand University Press, 1996.

Lajoux, Jean-Dominique. *The Rock Paintings of Tassili*. Cleveland: World Publishing, 1963.

Phillips, Tom, ed. *Africa, the Art of a Continent*. New York: Prestel, 1995.

Phillipson, D. W. *African Archaeology*. 2nd ed. New York: Cambridge University Press, 1993.

———. *Ancient Ethiopia: Aksum, Its Antecedents and Successors*. London: British Museum Press, 1998.

Prussin, Labelle. *Hatumere: Islamic Design in West Africa*. Berkeley and Los Angeles: University of California Press, 1986.

Schädler, Karl-Ferdinand. *Earth and Ore: 2500 Years of African Art in Terra-Cotta and Metal*. Munich: Panterra Verlag, 1997.

Shaw, Thurstan. *Nigeria: Its Archaeology and Early History*. London: Thames & Hudson, 1978.

———. *Unearthing Igbo-Ukwu: Archaeological Discoveries in Eastern Nigeria*. New York: Oxford University Press, 1977.

Vallées du Niger. Paris: Editions de la Réunion des Musées Nationaux, 1993.

Willett, Frank. *Ife in the History of West African Sculpture*. New York: McGraw-Hill, 1967.

CHAPTER 11
TRADITIONALISM AND INTERNATIONALISM: 19TH- AND 20TH-CENTURY AFRICAN ARTS

Abiodun, Roland, Henry J. Drewal, and John Pemberton III, eds. *The Yoruba Artist: New Theoretical Perspectives on African Arts*. Washington, D.C.: Smithsonian Institution Press, 1994.

Blier, Suzanne P. *The Royal Arts of Africa.* New York: Abrams, 1998.

Cole, Herbert M. *Icons: Ideals and Power in the Art of Africa.* Washington, D.C.: National Museum of African Art, Smithsonian Institution, 1989.

———. *Mbari: Art and Life among the Owerri Igbo.* Bloomington: Indiana University Press, 1982.

———, ed. *I Am Not Myself: The Art of African Masquerade.* Los Angeles: UCLA Fowler Museum of Cultural History, 1985.

Cole, Herbert M., and Chike C. Aniakor. *Igbo Art: Community and Cosmos.* Los Angeles: UCLA Fowler Museum of Cultural History, 1984.

Cole, Herbert M., and Doran H. Ross. *The Arts of Ghana.* Los Angeles: UCLA Fowler Museum of Cultural History, 1977.

Cornet, Joseph. *Art Royal Kuba.* Milan: Edizioni Sipiel, 1982.

Enwezor, Okwui, ed. *The Short Century: Independence and Liberation Movements in Africa, 1945–1994.* Munich: Prestel, 2001.

Ezra, Kate. *The Art of the Dogon: Selections from the Lester Wunderman Collection.* New York: Metropolitan Museum of Art, 1988.

Fischer, Eberhard, and Hans Himmelheber. *The Arts of the Dan in West Africa.* Translated by Anne Biddle. Zurich: Museum Rietberg, 1984.

Fraser, Douglas F., and Herbert M. Cole, eds. *African Art and Leadership.* Madison: University of Wisconsin Press, 1972.

Geary, Christraud M. *Things of the Palace: A Catalogue of the Bamum Palace Museum in Foumban (Cameroon).* Weisbaden: Franz Steiner Verlag, 1983.

Glaze, Anita J. *Art and Death in a Senufo Village.* Bloomington: Indiana University Press, 1981.

In/sight: African Photographers, 1940 to the Present. New York: Guggenheim Museum, 1996.

Kasfir, Sidney L. *Contemporary African Art.* London: Thames & Hudson, 1999.

———. *West African Masks and Cultural Systems.* Tervuren: Musée Royal de l'Afrique Centrale, 1988.

Kennedy, Jean. *New Currents, Ancient Rivers: Contemporary African Artists in a Generation of Change.* Washington, D.C.: Smithsonian Institution Press, 1992.

Magnin, Andre, with Jacques Soulillou. *Contemporary Art of Africa.* New York: Abrams, 1996.

McGaffey, Wyatt, and Michael Harris. *Astonishment and Power (Kongo Art).* Washington, D.C.: Smithsonian Institution Press, 1993.

Nooter, Mary H. *Secrecy: African Art That Conceals and Reveals.* New York: Museum for African Art, 1993.

Oguibe, Olu, and Okwui Enwezor, eds. *Reading the Contemporary: African Art from Theory to the Marketplace.* London: Institute of International Visual Arts, 1999.

Perrois, Louis. *Ancestral Art of Gabon from the Collections of the Barbier-Mueller Museum.* Translated by Francine Farr. Geneva: Musée Barbier-Mueller, 1985.

Phillips, Ruth B. *Representing Women: Sande Masquerades of the Mende of Sierra Leone.* Los Angeles: UCLA Fowler Museum of Cultural History, 1995.

Roy, Christopher D. *Art and Life in Africa: Selections from the Stanley Collection.* Iowa City: University of Iowa Museum of Art, 1992.

Sieber, Roy, and Roslyn A. Walker. *African Art in the Cycle of Life.* Washington, D.C.: Smithsonian Institution Press, 1987.

Thompson, Robert F., and Joseph Cornet. *The Four Moments of the Sun: Kongo Art in Two Worlds.* Washington, D.C.: National Gallery of Art, 1981.

Vansina, Jan. *The Children of Woot: A History of the Kuba Peoples.* Madison: University of Wisconsin Press, 1978.

Vinnicombe, Patricia. *People of the Eland: Rock Paintings of the Drakensberg Bushmen as a Reflection of Their Life and Thought.* Pietermaritzburg: University of Natal Press, 1976.

Vogel, Susan M. *Baule: African Art, Western Eyes.* New Haven: Yale University Press, 1997.

———, ed. *Africa Explores: Twentieth-Century African Art.* New York: Te Neues, 1990.

———, ed. *Art/Artifact: African Art in Anthropology Collections.* New York: Te Neues, 1988.

———, ed. *For Spirits and Kings: African Art from the Tishman Collection.* New York: Metropolitan Museum of Art, 1981.

Walker, Roslyn A. *Olowe of Ise: A Yoruba Sculptor to Kings.* Washington, D.C.: National Museum of African Art, 1998.

CHAPTER 12
THE FLOURISHING OF ISLAND CULTURES:
THE ART OF OCEANIA

Barrow, Terence. *The Art of Tahiti and the Neighboring Society, Austral and Cook Islands.* London: Thames & Hudson, 1979.

Berndt, Ronald M., ed. *Australian Aboriginal Art.* New York: Macmillan, 1964.

Corbin, George A. *Native Arts of North America, Africa, and the South Pacific: An Introduction.* New York: HarperCollins, 1988.

Cox, J. Halley, and William H. Davenport. *Hawaiian Sculpture.* Rev. ed. Honolulu: University of Hawaii Press, 1988.

D'Alleva, Anne. *Arts of the Pacific Islands.* New York: Abrams, 1998.

Feldman, Jerome, and Donald H. Rubinstein. *The Art of Micronesia.* Honolulu: University of Hawaii Art Gallery, 1986.

Greub, Suzanne, ed. *Authority and Ornament: Art of the Sepik River, Papua New Guinea.* Basel: Tribal Art Centre, 1985.

Guiart, Jean. *Arts of the South Pacific.* New York: Golden Press, 1963.

Hanson, Allan, and Louise Hanson, eds. *Art and Identity in Oceania.* Honolulu: University of Hawaii Press, 1990.

Kaeppler, Adrienne L., Christian Kaufmann, and Douglas Newton. *Oceanic Art.* New York: Abrams, 1997.

Kooijman, Simon. *Tapa in Polynesia.* Honolulu: Bishop Museum Press, 1972.

Lincoln, Louise, ed. *Assemblage of Spirits: Idea and Image in New Ireland.* New York: Braziller in association with the Minneapolis Institute of Arts, 1987.

Mead, Sidney Moko, ed. *Te Maori: Maori Art from New Zealand Collections.* New York: Abrams in association with the American Federation of Arts, 1984.

Morphy, Howard. *Aboriginal Art.* London: Phaidon Press, 1998.

Rockefeller, Michael C. *The Asmat of New Guinea: The Journal of Michael Clark Rockefeller.* Greenwich, Conn.: New York Graphic Society, 1967.

Schneebaum, Tobias. *Embodied Spirits: Ritual Carvings of the Asmat.* Salem, Mass.: Peabody Museum of Salem, 1990.

Simons, S. C., and H. Stevenson, eds. *Luk Luk Gen! Contemporary Art from Papua New Guinea.* Townsville: Perc Tucker Regional Gallery, 1990.

Smidt, Dirk, ed. *Asmat Art: Woodcarvings of Southwest New Guinea.* New York: Braziller in association with Rijksmuseum voor Volkenkunde, Leiden, 1993.

Starzecka, Dorota, ed. *Maori Art and Culture.* Chicago: Art Media Resources, 1996.

Sutton, Peter, ed. *Dreamings: The Art of Aboriginal Australia.* New York: Braziller in association with the Asia Society Galleries, 1988.

Thomas, Nicholas. *Oceanic Art.* London: Thames & Hudson, 1995.

CREDITS

The authors and publisher are grateful to the proprietors and custodians of various works of art for photographs of these works and permission to reproduce them in this book. Sources not included in the captions are listed here.

KEY TO ABBREVIATIONS

AL   Alinari/Art Resource, NY
A.A.M.   Asian Art Museum of San Francisco, The Avery Brundage Collection
Canali   Canali Photobank, Italy
Gir   Giraudon/Art Resource, NY
Hir   Hirmer Fotoarchiv, Munich
Lessing   Erich Lessing/Art Resource, NY
M.M.A.   The Metropolitan Museum of Art
R.M.N.   Réunion des Musées Nationaux/Art Resource, NY
Saskia   Saskia Ltd Cultural Documentation
Scala   Scala/Art Resource, NY

NOTE: *All references in the following credits are to figure numbers unless otherwise indicated.*

Introduction–Photograph © 1983 M.M.A.: CO, 1; © National Gallery, London: 2; MOA Art Museum, Shizuoka-ken, Japan: 3; Joachim Blauel/Arthothek: 4

Chapter 1–Diego Lezama Orezzoli/Corbis: 1; John C. Huntington: 2, 12; SCP57227 Steatite Pasupati seal, Mohenjodaro, 2300-1750 bce, National Museum of India, New Delhi, India/Bridgeman Art Library: 3; Benoy K. Behl: 4; Edifice/Corbis: 5; Robert Harding Picture Library: 7, 20; © ephotocorp.com: 8a, 11; © The Trustees of The National Museums of Scotland: 9; Freer Gallery of Art, Smithsonian Institution, Washington, D.C.: Purchase, F1949.9: 10; Lindsay Hebberd/Corbis: 13; Douglas Dickins FRPS: 14, 21; Borromeo/Art Resource, NY: 15; Alison Wright/Corbis: 17; ACSAA Slide #3101 ©AAUM: 18; ACSAA Slide #3103 ©AAUM: 19; Robert L. Brown: 22a, 23, 24; Stephanie Colasanti/Corbis: 25; Charles & Josette Lenars/Corbis: 26; Luca I. Tettoni/Corbis: 27, 31; Paul John Miller/Stockphoto: 29

Chapter 2-Sheldan Collins/Corbis: 1; Geoffrey Taunton, Cordaiy Photo Library Ltd./Corbis: 2; Victoria & Albert Museum, London/Art Resource, NY: 3; Freer Gallery of Art, Smithsonian Institution, Washington, D.C., Purchase, F1942.15: opener, 4; Henry Stierlin: 5; Spectrum Colour Library: 8; The Brooklyn Museum of Art, 87.234.6: 9; Robert L. Brown: 10; Luca Tettoni Photography: 11; Alain Mahuzier: 12; Benoy K. Behl: 14.

Chapter 3–Cultural Relics Publishing House, Beijing: 1, 3, 12, 13, 19; A.A.M., B60B1032. Used by permission: 2; The Nelson-Atkins Museum of Art, Kansas City, Missouri (Purchase: Nelson Trust) 33-81. Photo: E. G. Schempf: 4; © Imaginechina: 5; The Nelson-Atkins Museum of Art, Kansas City, Missouri (Purchase: Nelson Trust) 33-521. Photo: Robert Newcombe: 8; A.A.M., B60B1034. Used by permission: 9; Heritage Images/British Museum: 10; R.M.N.: 11; Photograph © 2003 Museum of Fine Art, Boston. Attributed to: Yan Liben, died in 673. The Thirteen Emperors. Chinese, Tang dynasty, Second half of the 7th century (with later replacement). Object Place: China. Handscroll; ink and color on silk. 51.3 × 531cm (20 3/16 × 209 1/16 in.) Museum of Fine Art, Boston. Denman Waldo Ross Collection. 31.643" (Photograph © 2003 Museum of Fine Art, Boston): 15; Victoria & Albert Museum, London/Art Resource, NY: 17; Collection of the National Palace Museum, Taiwan, Republic of China: 18, 23; A.A.M., B60B161. Used by permission: 20; Liu Liqun/Corbis: 21; Photograph © 2003 Museum of Fine Art,. Zhou Jichang, Chinese, second half of 12th century. Lohans Bestowing Alms on Suffering Human Beings. Chinese, Southern Song Dynasty, about 1178. Object Place: China. Ink and color on silk. 111.5 × 53.1cm (43 7/8 × 20 7/8 in.) Museum of Fine Arts, Boston. General Funds. 95.4" (Photograph © 2003 Museum of Fine Art, Boston): 24; Tokyo National Museum. Image TNM Image Archives. Source: http://TnmArchives.jp: 25; Archivo Iconografico, S.A./Corbis: 27

Chapter 4-Collection of the National Palace Museum, Taiwan, Republic of China: 1, 2, 3, 10; Percival David Foundation of Chinese Art, B614: 4; photos12.com, Panorama Stock: 5; Laurence G. Liu: 6, 7; Victoria & Albert Museum, London/Art Resource, NY: 8; Cultural Relics Publishing House, Beijing: 9, 14; Dong Qichang, Chinese, 1555–1636, Ming Dynasty. The Quingbian Mountains. Hanging scroll, ink on paper, 224.5 x 67.2 cm. © The Cleveland Museum of Art, 2003. Leonard C Hanna, Jr., Bequest, 1980: 10, 11; Honolulu Academy of Arts, gift of Mr. Robert Allerton, 1957 (2306.1): 12; John Taylor Photography: 13; Percival David Foundation of Chinese Art, A821: 15; Audrey R. Topping: 16; Copyright © Elvehjem Museum of Art, University of Wisconsin-Madison. Artist Xu Bing: 17; Photo copyright © Korea National Tourism Organisation: 18; Heritage Images/British Museum: 20

Chapter 5–Tokyo National Museum. Image TNM Image Archives. Source: http://TnmArchives.jp: 1, 2, 11; Tomb of Emperor Nintoku. (Nintoku-ryo Tumulus) Sakai, Osaka Prefecture: 3; Jingu Administration Office: 5; Sakamoto Photo Research Laboratory/Corbis: 6, 12, 15; Archivo Iconografico, S.A./Corbis: 7; D.Carrasco/jonarnold.com: 10; The Gotoh Museum, Tokyo: 13; Photograph © 2003 Museum of Fine Art, Boston. Artist Unknown, Japanese. Night Attack on the Sanjo Palace, from the Illustrated Scrolls of the Events of the Heiji Era (Heiji monogatari emaki). Japanese, Kamakura period, second half of the 13th century. Object Place: Japan. Handscroll, ink and color on paper. 41.3 × 699.7 cm (16 1/4 × 275 1/2 in.) Museum of Fine Arts, Boston. Fenollosa-Weld Collection. 11.4000" (Photograph © 2003 Museum of Fine Art, Boston): 16

Chapter 6-Patricia Graham: 1; Tokyo National Museum. Image TNM Image Archives. Source: http://TnmArchives.jp: 2, 3, 5, 9; Sakamoto Photo Research Laboratory/Corbis: 4; © The Hatakeyama Memorial Museum of Fine Art: 6; TRIP photographic library, photographer: F. Good/Art Directors: 7; Photo courtesy of The Art Institute of Chicago 1925.2043. All rights reserved: 11; Photograph © 2003 Museum of Fine Art, Boston, "Katsushika Hokusai," Japanese, 1760–1849. In the Hollow of a Wave off the Coast at Kanagawa. Japanese, Edo Period, about 1830–1831. Object Place: Japan. Woodblock print; ink and color on paper. 25.2 x 37.3 cm (9 15/16 x 14 11/16 in.) Museum of Fine Arts, Boston. William Sturgis Bigelow Collection: 12; Tokyo National University of Fine Arts and Music, 13; Copyright © Shokodo Co., Ltd.: 14; Tokyo Tourist Office, 15; Association de la Jeune Sculpture 1987/2: 17.

Chapter 7–Yoram Lehmann, Jerusalem: 1; Lessing: 2; photo Henri Stierlin: 3, 9, 18, 20, 22, 23, 24; Photo Archives Skira, Geneva, Switzerland: 4; adapted from Stierlin, p. 74: 5; Bildarchiv Preussischer Kulturbesitz/Art Resource, NY: 6; © Yann Arthus-Bertrand/Corbis: 7; © E. Simanor/Robert Harding Picture Library: 10; www.bednorz-photo.de: 11, 12; Adam Woolfitt/Robert Harding Picture Library: 13; © Musée Lorrain, Nancy/photo G. Mangin: 14; The State Hermitage Museum: 15; Reproduced by kind permission of the Trustees of the Chester Beatty Library, Dublin: 16; C. Rennie/Robert Harding Picture Library: 17; Photographer: Daniel McGrath: 26; Collection Prince Sadruddin Aga Khan: 27; Topkapi Palace Museum: 28; R.M.N.: 29

Chapter 8–Danny Lehman/Corbis: 1; Werner Forman/Art Resource, NY: 2; Los Angeles County Museum of Art, The Proctor Stafford Collection, purchased with funds provided by Mr and Mrs Allan C Balch: 3; Yann Arthus-Bertrand/Corbis: 4; Gianni Dagli Orti/Corbis: 5; © Philip Baird www.anthroarcheart.org: 7, 8, 14, 17, 21; Enzo and Paolo Ragazzini/Corbis: 9; National Museum of Anthropology, Mexico City: 10; Peabody Museum, Harvard University, Cambridge: 11; Heritage Images/The British Museum: 12; Dumbarton Oaks, Pre-Columbian Collection, Washington, DC/© Justin Kerr: 13; Jonathan Blair/Corbis: 15; M.M.A., Jan Mitchell & Sons Collection, Gift of Jan Mitchell, 1991 (1991.419.31): Photo-graph by Jan Mitchell, 1991. Photograph © 1984 M.M.A.: 16; Instituto Nacional de Cultura, Lima: 18; Photograph © 2003 Museum of Fine Arts, Boston: 19; The Art Institute of Chicago: 20, 30; Museo Arqueologico Rafael Larco Herrera, Lima: 22; Bruning Archaeological Museum, Lambayeque: 23; Hubert Stadler/Corbis: 24; National Museum of Archaeology, Anthropology and History of Peru, Lima: 25; American Museum of Natural History, NY: 26; Ohio Historical Society: 27; Superstock, Inc.: 28; Courtesy, National Museum of the American Indian, Smithsonian Institution T150853, Photo by David Heald: 29; Tom Bean/Corbis: 31

Chapter 9–Biblioteca Apostolica Vaticana, Rome: 1; adapted from an image by Ned Seidler/National Geographic Society: 2; Gianni Dagli Orti/Corbis: 3, 4; photo courtesy the Library, American Museum of Natural History: 5; Michael Freeman/Corbis: 6; Museum of New Mexico, Santa Fe: 7; Arizona State Museum, University of Arizona, photographer W. McLennan: 8; National Museum of Women in the Arts: 9; American Museum of Natural History, New York: 10, 11; Museum of Anthropology at the University of British Columbia/photo W. McLennan: 12; courtesy the Southwest Museum, Los Angeles, photo # Ct.37/Larry Reynolds, photographer: 13; M.M.A., The Michael C. Rockefeller Memorial Collection, gift of Nelson A. Rockefeller, 1961 (1978.412.76). Photographed © M.M.A.: 14; Joslyn Art Museum: 15; Mr. and Mrs. Charles Diker Collection: 16

Chapter 10–Jean-Dominique Lajoux: 1; Photograph © 1980 Dirk Bakker: 2, 4, 6; IZIKO Museums of Cape Town: 3; National Museum of American Art: 5; Great Zimbabwe Site Museum, Great Zimbabwe: 8; Roger Woods/Corbis: 9; M.M.A., The Michael C Rockefeller Memorial Collection, Gift of Nelson A Rockefeller, 1972 (1978.412.323). Photograph © 1995 M.M.A.: 10; Heritage Images/British Museum: 11; Museo Nazionale Preistorico e Etnografico Luigi Pigorini, Rome: 12

Chapter 11-Natal Museum, Pietermaritzburg: 1; National Museum of African Art, Smithsonian Institution, Washington, D.C.: 2, 4, 26; copyright abm-Archives Barbier-Mueller, photographer Roger Asselberghs: 3; Detroit Institute of Arts: 5; M.M.A., gift of Lester Wunderman, 1977 (1977.394.15), photograph © 1993 M.M.A.: 6; M.M.A., The Michael C. Rockefeller Memorial Collection, gift of Nelson A. Rockefeller, 1969 (1978.412.390,.391), photograph © 1999 M.M.A.: 7; National Museum of African Art Smithsonian Institution/Eliot Elisofon Photographic Archives: 8, 13; photo Roy Sieber, 1964: 9; Private Collection: 10; Skip Cole: 11; Denver Art Museum, Denver: 12; © abm-Archives Barbier-Mueller, photographer Pierre-Alain Ferrazzini: 14; © Anita Glaze: 15; Fowler Museum of Cultural History, University of California, Los Angeles, gift of the Wellcome Trust: 17; Edizioni Sipiel/Joseph Cornet: 18; Peabody Museum, Harvard University, Cambridge: 19; © Herbert M Cole: 20, 21, 22; photo: Henry J. Drewal: 23; photo: Philip Ravenhill: 24; Museum voor Volkenkunde, Rotterdam: 25; © Willie Bester: 26

Chapter 12- courtesy of Library Services, American Museum of Natural History: 1; © abm-archives barbier mueller, photographer Wolfgang Pulfer: 2; Tobias Schneebaum: 3; South Australian Museum Archives: 4; D. Destable/Collection Musee de l'homme, Paris: 5; Copyright Otago Museum, Dunedin, New Zealand, D45.179: 6; Staatliche Museen zu Berlin Preussischer Kulturbesitz, Ethnologisches Museum, photo by Dietrich Graf: 7; Linden Museum, Stuttgart: 8; Heritage Images/British Museum: 9, 15; Adrienne Kaeppler: 10; Robert and Lisa Sainsbury Collection, University of East Anglia, Norwich, photo by James Austin: 11; University of Pennsylvania Museum/T4-3195: 12; Ann Ronan Picture Library, 13; Bishop Museum, Honolulu, Hawaii: 14; copyright Otago Museum, Dunedin, New Zealand: 16; Lessing: 17; Reproduced courtesy of Museum Victoria: 18; Meteorological Service of New Zealand Ltd. Collection, Wellington: 19

INDEX

Boldface names refer to artists. Pages in italics refer to illustrations